Cengage CourseMate

> You have **FREE** access to CourseMate for your text, where you can utilize helpful resources such as flashcards, videos, quizzes, study questions, an interactive eBook and more. Follow the steps below to register your code and start CourseMate now.

1. Go to www.cengagebrain.com and click on "Sign Up" in the top right corner.

CENGAGE brain

Find your Textbook or Materials

Enter ISBN Book Title, Author   search   **Find**

Welcome

Log In   Sign Up   My Cart(0)

username

....

Remember Me   log in

2. Complete the information to create your account, and then go to "My Home" in the top right corner.

Discover CengageBrain   Hi Erin

CENGAGE brain

Find your Textbook or Materials

Enter ISBN Book Title, Author   **Find**

My Home   Log Out   My Cart(0)

3. Enter your unique CourseMate code (located in the card packaged with your textbook) into the box on the right and click "Register"

My Home   My Orders   My Account   My Rentals

My Home

My Courses & Materials

There is currently no content in your dashboard.

Register another Access Code or Aplia Course Key

Register

Your Access Code should be similar to PP8XLP3XD528HC   What's this?
Aplia Course Key example: ABCD-23M4-EFGH

Find Product with Free Access

4. Click "Open" next to CourseMate under My Courses and Materials

5. Click on "Enter Your Course Key" to enroll in your professor's course.

Your Course Key:

You are now ready to use CourseMate! All of your resources will be on the left side of the screen under each chapter. Any book-level resources will appear below the list of resources for each chapter.

ART 2C - Art History: The Baroque through Impressionism

Custom Edition for De Anza and Foothill

14th Edition

Fred S. Kleiner

CENGAGE
Learning·

Australia • Brazil • Japan • Korea • Mexico • Singapore • Spain • United Kingdom • United States

CENGAGE
Learning·

ART 2C - Art History: The Baroque through Impressionism: Custom Edition for De Anza and Foothill, 14th Edition

ART 2C - Art History: The Baroque through Impressionism, Custom Edition for De Anza and Foothill, 14th Edition
Kleiner

© 2012 Cengage Learning. All rights reserved.

Executive Editors:
Maureen Staudt
Michael Stranz

Senior Project Development Manager:
Linda deStefano

Marketing Specialist:
Courtney Sheldon

Senior Production/Manufacturing Manager:
Donna M. Brown

PreMedia Manager:
Joel Brennecke

Sr. Rights Acquisition Account Manager:
Todd Osborne

Cover Image:
Getty Images*

*Unless otherwise noted, all cover images used by Custom Solutions, a part of Cengage Learning, have been supplied courtesy of Getty Images with the exception of the Earthview cover image, which has been supplied by the National Aeronautics and Space Administration (NASA).

This book contains select works from existing Cengage Learning
was produced by Cengage Learning Custom Solutions for colleg
those adopting and/or contributing to this work are responsible
content accuracy, continuity and completeness.

Compilation © 2012 Cengage Learning
ISBN-13: 978-1-285-00842-4

ISBN-10: 1-285-00842-1

Cengage Learning
5191 Natorp Boulevard
Mason, Ohio 45040
USA
Cengage Learning is a leading provider of customized learning sol
office locations around the globe, including Singapore, the United
Australia, Mexico, Brazil, and Japan. Locate your local office at:
international.cengage.com/region.

Cengage Learning products are represented in Canada by Nelson
For your lifelong learning solutions, visit **www.cengage.com/cu**
Visit our corporate website at **www.cengage.com.**

Printed in the United States of America

Custom Brief Contents – Volume 2C

PREFACE

THE GARDNER LEGACY IN THE 21ST CENTURY

I take great pleasure in introducing the extensively revised and expanded 14th edition of *Gardner's Art through the Ages: A Global History*, which, like the enhanced 13th edition, is a hybrid art history textbook—the first, and still the only, introductory survey of the history of art of its kind. This innovative new kind of "Gardner" retains all of the best features of traditional books on paper while harnessing 21st-century technology to increase by 25% the number of works examined—without increasing the size or weight of the book itself and at very low additional cost to students compared to a larger book.

When Helen Gardner published the first edition of *Art through the Ages* in 1926, she could not have imagined that more than 85 years later instructors all over the world would still be using her textbook in their classrooms. Indeed, if she were alive today, she would not recognize the book that, even in its traditional form, long ago became—and remains—the most widely read introduction to the history of art and architecture in the English language. During the past half-century, successive authors have constantly reinvented Helen Gardner's groundbreaking global survey, always keeping it fresh and current, and setting an ever-higher standard with each new edition. I am deeply gratified that both professors and students seem to agree that the 13th edition, released in 2008, lived up to that venerable tradition, for they made it the number-one choice for art history survey courses. I hope they will find the 14th edition of this best-selling book exceeds their high expectations.

In addition to the host of new features (enumerated below) in the book proper, the 14th edition follows the enhanced 13th edition in incorporating an innovative new online component. All new copies of the 14th edition are packaged with an access code to a web site with *bonus essays* and *bonus images* (with zoom capability) of more than 300 additional important paintings, sculptures, buildings, and other art forms of all eras, from prehistory to the present and worldwide. The selection includes virtually all of the works professors have told me they wished had been in the 13th edition, but were not included for lack of space. I am extremely grateful to Cengage Learning/Wadsworth for the considerable investment of time and resources that has made this remarkable hybrid textbook possible.

In contrast to the enhanced 13th edition, the online component is now fully integrated into the 14th edition. Every one of the more than 300 bonus images is cited in the text of the traditional book and a thumbnail image of each work, with abbreviated caption, is inset into the text column where the work is mentioned. The integration extends also to the maps, index, glossary, and chapter summaries, which seamlessly merge the printed and online information. The 14th edition is in every way a unified, comprehensive history of art and architecture, even though the text is divided into paper and digital components.

KEY FEATURES OF THE 14TH EDITION

In this new edition, I have added several important features while retaining the basic format and scope of the previous edition. Once again, the hybrid Gardner boasts roughly 1,700 photographs, plans, and drawings, nearly all in color and reproduced according to the highest standards of clarity and color fidelity, including hundreds of new images, among them a new series of superb photos taken by Jonathan Poore exclusively for *Art through the Ages* during three photographic campaigns in France and Italy in 2009, 2010, and 2011. The online component also includes custom videos made at each site by Sharon Adams Poore. This extraordinary new archive of visual material ranges from ancient Roman ruins in southern France to Romanesque and Gothic churches in France and Tuscany to Le Corbusier's modernist chapel at Ronchamp and the postmodern Pompidou Center and the Louvre Pyramid in Paris. The 14th edition also features the highly acclaimed architectural drawings of John Burge. Together, these exclusive photographs, videos, and drawings provide readers with a visual feast unavailable anywhere else.

The captions accompanying those illustrations contain, as before, a wealth of information, including the name of the artist or architect, if known; the formal title (printed in italics), if assigned, description of the work, or name of the building; the provenance or place of production of the object or location of the building; the date; the material(s) used; the size; and the present location if the work is in a museum or private collection. Scales accompany not only all architectural plans, as is the norm, but also appear next to each photograph of a painting, statue, or other artwork—another unique feature of the Gardner text. The works discussed in the 14th edition of *Art through the Ages* vary enormously in size, from colossal sculptures carved into mountain cliffs and paintings that cover entire walls or ceilings to tiny figurines, coins, and jewelry that one can hold in the hand. Although the captions contain the pertinent dimensions, it is difficult for students who have never seen the paintings or statues in person to translate those dimensions into an appreciation of the real size of the objects. The scales provide an effective and direct way to visualize how big or how small a given artwork is and its relative size compared with other objects in the same chapter and throughout the book.

Also retained in this edition are the Quick-Review Captions introduced in the 13th edition. Students have overwhelmingly reported that they found these brief synopses of the most significant aspects of each artwork or building illustrated invaluable when preparing for examinations. These extended captions accompany not only every image in the printed book but also all the digital images in the online supplement. Another popular tool introduced in the 13th edition to aid students in reviewing and mastering the material reappears in the 14th edition. Each chapter ends with a full-page feature called *The Big Picture,* which sets forth in bullet-point format the most important characteristics of each period or artistic movement discussed in the chapter. Small illustrations of characteristic works accompany the summary of major points. The 14th edition, however, introduces two new features in every chapter: a timeline summarizing the major developments during the era treated (again in bullet-point format for easy review) and a chapter-opening essay on a characteristic painting, sculpture, or building. Called *Framing the Era,* these in-depth essays are accompanied by a general view and four enlarged details of the work discussed.

The 14th edition of *Art through the Ages* is available in several different traditional paper formats—a single hardcover volume; two paperback volumes designed for use in the fall and spring semesters of a yearlong survey course; a six-volume "backpack" set; and an interactive e-book version. Another pedagogical tool not found in any other introductory art history textbook is the *Before 1300* section that appears at the beginning of the second volume of the paperbound version of the book and at the beginning of Book D of the backpack edition. Because many students taking the second half of a survey course will not have access to Volume I or to Books A, B, and C, I have provided a special set of concise primers on architectural terminology and construction methods in the ancient and medieval worlds, and on mythology and religion—information that is essential for understanding the history of art after 1300, both in the West and the East. The subjects of these special boxes are Greco-Roman Temple Design and the Classical Orders; Arches and Vaults; Basilican Churches; Central-Plan Churches; The Gods and Goddesses of Mount Olympus; The Life of Jesus in Art; Buddhism and Buddhist Iconography; and Hinduism and Hindu Iconography.

Boxed essays once again appear throughout the book as well. This popular feature first appeared in the 11th edition of *Art through the Ages,* which in 2001 won both the Texty and McGuffey Prizes of the Text and Academic Authors Association for a college textbook in the humanities and social sciences. In this edition the essays are more closely tied to the main text than ever before. Consistent with that greater integration, almost all boxes now incorporate photographs of important artworks discussed in the text proper that also illustrate the theme treated in the boxed essays. These essays fall under six broad categories:

Architectural Basics boxes provide students with a sound foundation for the understanding of architecture. These discussions are concise explanations, with drawings and diagrams, of the major aspects of design and construction. The information included

is essential to an understanding of architectural technology and terminology. The boxes address questions of how and why various forms developed, the problems architects confronted, and the solutions they used to resolve them. Topics discussed include how the Egyptians built the pyramids; the orders of classical architecture; Roman concrete construction; and the design and terminology of mosques, stupas, and Gothic cathedrals.

Materials and Techniques essays explain the various media artists employed from prehistoric to modern times. Since materials and techniques often influence the character of artworks, these discussions contain essential information on why many monuments appear as they do. Hollow-casting bronze statues; fresco painting; Chinese silk; Andean weaving; Islamic tilework; embroidery and tapestry; engraving, etching, and lithography; and daguerreotype and calotype photography are among the many subjects treated.

Religion and Mythology boxes introduce students to the principal elements of the world's great religions, past and present, and to the representation of religious and mythological themes in painting and sculpture of all periods and places. These discussions of belief systems and iconography give readers a richer understanding of some of the greatest artworks ever created. The topics include the gods and goddesses of Egypt, Mesopotamia, Greece, and Rome; the life of Jesus in art; Buddha and Buddhism; Muhammad and Islam; and Aztec religion.

Art and Society essays treat the historical, social, political, cultural, and religious context of art and architecture. In some instances, specific monuments are the basis for a discussion of broader themes, as when the Hegeso stele serves as the springboard for an exploration of the role of women in ancient Greek society. Another essay discusses how people's evaluation today of artworks can differ from those of the society that produced them by examining the problems created by the contemporary market for undocumented archaeological finds. Other subjects include Egyptian mummification; Etruscan women; Byzantine icons and iconoclasm; artistic training in Renaissance Italy; 19th-century academic salons and independent art exhibitions; the Mesoamerican ball game; Japanese court culture; and art and leadership in Africa.

Written Sources present and discuss key historical documents illuminating important monuments of art and architecture throughout the world. The passages quoted permit voices from the past to speak directly to the reader, providing vivid and unique insights into the creation of artworks in all media. Examples include Bernard of Clairvaux's treatise on sculpture in medieval churches; Giovanni Pietro Bellori's biographies of Annibale Carracci and Caravaggio; Jean François Marmontel's account of 18th-century salon culture; as well as texts that bring the past to life, such as eyewitness accounts of the volcanic eruption that buried Roman Pompeii and of the fire that destroyed Canterbury Cathedral in medieval England.

Finally, in the *Artists on Art* boxes, artists and architects throughout history discuss both their theories and individual works. Examples include Sinan the Great discussing the mosque he designed for Selim II; Leonardo da Vinci and Michelangelo debating the relative merits of painting and sculpture; Artemisia Gentileschi talking about the special problems she confronted as a woman artist; Jacques-Louis David on Neoclassicism; Gustave Courbet on Realism; Henri Matisse on color; Pablo Picasso on Cubism; Diego Rivera on art for the people; and Judy Chicago on her seminal work *The Dinner Party.*

For every new edition of *Art through the Ages,* I also reevaluate the basic organization of the book. In the 14th edition, the unfolding narrative of the history of art in Europe and America is no longer interrupted with "excursions" to Asia, Africa, and Oceania. Those chapters are now grouped together at the end of Volumes I and II and in backpack Books D and F. And the treatment of the art of the later 20th century and the opening decade of the 21st century has been significantly reconfigured. There are now separate chapters on the art and architecture of the period from 1945 to 1980 and from 1980 to the present. Moreover, the second chapter (Chapter 31, "Contemporary Art Worldwide") is no longer confined to Western art but presents the art and architecture of the past three decades as a multifaceted global phenomenon. Furthermore, some chapters now appear in more than one of the paperbound versions of the book in order to provide enhanced flexibility to instructors who divide the global history of art into two or three semester-long courses. Chapter 14—on Italian art from 1200 to 1400—appears in both Volumes I and II and in backpack Books B and D. The Islamic and contemporary art chapters appear in both the Western and non-Western backpack subdivisions of the full global text.

Rounding out the features in the book itself is a greatly expanded Bibliography of books in English with several hundred new entries, including both general works and a chapter-by-chapter list of more focused studies; a Glossary containing definitions of all italicized terms introduced in both the printed and online texts; and, for the first time, a complete museum index listing all illustrated artworks by their present location .

The 14th edition of *Art through the Ages* also features a host of state-of-the-art online resources (enumerated on page xxix).

WRITING AND TEACHING THE HISTORY OF ART

Nonetheless, some things have not changed in this new edition, including the fundamental belief that guided Helen Gardner so many years ago—that the primary goal of an introductory art history textbook should be to foster an appreciation and understanding of historically significant works of art of all kinds from all periods and from all parts of the globe. Because of the longevity and diversity of the history of art, it is tempting to assign responsibility for telling its story to a large team of specialists. The original publisher of *Art through the Ages* took this approach for the first edition prepared after Helen Gardner's death, and it has now become the norm for introductory art history surveys. But students overwhelmingly say the very complexity of the global history of art makes it all the more important for the story to be told with a consistent voice if they are to master so much diverse material. I think Helen Gardner would be pleased to know that *Art through the Ages* once again has a single storyteller—aided in no small part by invaluable advice from well over a hundred reviewers and other consultants whose assistance I gladly acknowledge at the end of this Preface.

I continue to believe that the most effective way to tell the story of art through the ages, especially to anyone studying art history for the first time, is to organize the vast array of artistic monuments according to the civilizations that produced them and to consider each work in roughly chronological order. This approach has not merely stood the test of time. It is the most appropriate way to narrate the *history* of art. The principle underlying my approach to every period of art history is that the enormous variation in the form and meaning of the paintings, sculptures, buildings, and other artworks men and women have produced over the past 30,000 years is largely the result of the constantly changing contexts in which

artists and architects worked. A historically based narrative is therefore best suited for a global history of art because it enables the author to situate each work discussed in its historical, social, economic, religious, and cultural context. That is, after all, what distinguishes art history from art appreciation.

In the 1926 edition of *Art through the Ages,* Helen Gardner discussed Henri Matisse and Pablo Picasso in a chapter entitled "Contemporary Art in Europe and America." Since then many other artists have emerged on the international scene, and the story of art through the ages has grown longer and even more complex. As already noted, that is reflected in the addition of a new chapter at the end of the book on contemporary art in which developments on all continents are treated together for the first time. Perhaps even more important than the new directions artists and architects have taken during the past several decades is that the discipline of art history has also changed markedly—and so too has Helen Gardner's book. The 14th edition fully reflects the latest art historical research emphases while maintaining the traditional strengths that have made previous editions of *Art through the Ages* so popular. While sustaining attention to style, chronology, iconography, and technique, I also ensure that issues of patronage, function, and context loom large in every chapter. I treat artworks not as isolated objects in sterile 21st-century museum settings but with a view toward their purpose and meaning in the society that produced them at the time they were produced. I examine not only the role of the artist or architect in the creation of a work of art or a building, but also the role of the individuals or groups who paid the artists and influenced the shape the monuments took. Further, in this expanded hybrid edition, I devote more space than ever before to the role of women and women artists in societies worldwide over time. In every chapter, I have tried to choose artworks and buildings that reflect the increasingly wide range of interests of scholars today, while not rejecting the traditional list of "great" works or the very notion of a "canon." Indeed, the expanded hybrid nature of the 14th edition has made it possible to illustrate and discuss scores of works not traditionally treated in art history survey texts without reducing the space devoted to canonical works.

CHAPTER-BY-CHAPTER CHANGES IN THE 14TH EDITION

All chapters feature many new photographs, revised maps, revised Big Picture chapter-ending summaries, and changes to the text reflecting new research and discoveries.

Introduction: What is Art History? New painting by Ogata Korin added.

1: Art before History. New Framing the Era essay "The Dawn of Art" and new timeline. Göbekli Tepe added.

2: Mesopotamia and Persia. New Framing the Era essay "The Cradle of Civilization" and new timeline.

3: Egypt under the Pharaohs. New Framing the Era essay "Divine Kingship on the Nile" and new timeline. Hatshepsut's expedition to Punt added.

4: The Prehistoric Aegean. New Framing the Era essay "Greece in the Age of Heroes" and new timeline. Mycenean ivory goddesses added.

5: Ancient Greece. New Framing the Era essay "The Perfect Temple" and new timeline. Euphronios *Death of Sarpedon* and Olympia Apollo added.

6: The Etruscans. New Framing the Era essay "The Rediscovery of Etruscan Art" and new timeline. Tomb of the Augurs added.

7: The Roman Empire. New Framing the Era essay "The Ancient World's Greatest Empire" and new timeline. New box on "Roman Ancestor Portraits" added. Column of Trajan frieze and new portrait of Caracalla added.

8: Late Antiquity. New Framing the Era essay "Romans, Jews, and Christians" and new timeline. Villa Torlonia Jewish catacomb and Mildenhall treasure added.

9: Byzantium. New Framing the Era essay "Church and State United" and new timeline. Revised discussion of iconoclasm and of Byzantine women. New box on "Born to the Purple: Empress Zoe."

10: The Islamic World. New Framing the Era essay "The Rise and Spread of Islam" and new timeline. Muqarnas tilework of Imam Mosque, Isfahan, added.

11: Early Medieval Europe. New Framing the Era essay "Missionaries and the Spread of Christian Art" and new timeline. Detail photos of Book of Kells added.

12: Romanesque Europe. New Framing the Era essay "The Rebirth of Monumental Sculpture" and new timeline. New photos of newly cleaned Autun tympanum and many other French churches. Revised boxes on "Pilgrimage Roads in France and Spain" and "The Veneration of Relics." Reliquary of St. Foy added.

13: Gothic Europe. New Framing the Era essay "The Age of the Great Cathedrals" and new timeline. Extensive new photographic documentation of French churches and portal sculpture. Expanded treatment of German Gothic art and architecture.

14: Late Medieval Italy. New Framing the Era essay "Late Medieval or Proto-Renaissance?" and new timeline. New series of photos of architecture and sculpture in Florence, Orvieto, Pisa, and Siena. Andrea Pisano Baptistery doors added.

15: South and Southeast Asia before 1200. New Framing the Era essay "The Life of the Buddha" and new timeline. New series of photos of Buddhist and Hindu monuments.

16: China and Korea to 1279. New Framing the Era essay "Chinese Silk for the Afterlife" and new timeline. Flying horse of Governor-General Zhang and Korean statuette of bodhisattva Maitreya added.

17: Japan before 1333. New Framing the Era essay "Buddhism Spreads to Japan" and new timeline. Kosho's portrait of the priest Kuya added.

18: Native Arts of the Americas before 1300. New Framing the Era essay "Ancient Cities in a New World" and new timeline. Expanded discussions of Teotihuacán and Chichén Itzá.

19: Africa before 1800. New Framing the Era essay "Sacred Kingship in Benin" and new timeline. Seated statue of a man from Tada added.

20: Late Medieval and Early Renaissance Northern Europe. New Framing the Era essay "The Virgin in a Flemish Home" and new timeline. New section of the *Nuremberg Chronicle* illustrated. Diptych of Martin van Nieuwenhove added.

21: The Renaissance in Quattrocento Italy. New Framing the Era essay "Medici Patronage and Classical Learning" and new timeline. Expanded discussion of Botticelli and Neo-Platonism. Revised boxes on linear and atmospheric perspective and on Cennino Cennini. Tomb of Leonardo Bruni and *Resurrection* by Piero della Francesca added.

22: Renaissance and Mannerism in Cinquecento Italy. New Framing the Era essay "Michelangelo in the Service of Julius II" and new timeline. Michelangelo's late *Pietà* and Parmigianino's self-portrait added. Revised box on "Palma il Giovane and Titian." Series of new photos of Florence, Rome, and Venice.

23: High Renaissance and Mannerism in Northern Europe and Spain. New Framing the Era essay "Earthly Delights in the Netherlands" and new timeline. Dürer's self-portrait and *Melencolia I* and El Greco's *View of Toledo* added.

24: The Baroque in Italy and Spain. New Framing the Era essay "Baroque Art and Spectacle" and new timeline. Bernini's Four Rivers Fountain and Gentileschi's self-portrait added.

25: The Baroque in Northern Europe. New Framing the Era essay "Still-Life Painting in the Dutch Republic" and new timeline. Expanded discussion of Dutch mercantilism. Vermeer's *Woman Holding a Balance* added.

26: Rococo to Neoclassicism: The 18th Century in Europe and America. New Framing the Era essay "Art and Science in the Era of Enlightenment" and new timeline. Expanded discussion of Diderot as art critic. Adelaide Labille-Guiard added.

27: Romanticism, Realism, Photography: Europe & America, 1800 to 1870. New Framing the Era essay "Napoleon at Jaffa" and new timeline. Friedrich's *Wanderer above a Sea of Mist* and Altes Museum, Berlin, added.

28: Impressionism, Post-Impressionism, Symbolism: Europe and America, 1870 to 1900. New Framing the Era essay "Impressions of Modern Life" and new timeline. New discussion of Manet and Monet. Rodin's *Gates of Hell* and James Ensor added.

29: Modernism in Europe and America, 1900 to 1945. New Framing the Era essay "Global War, Anarchy, and Dada" and new timeline. New box on "Walter Gropius and the Bauhaus." Grosz's *Eclipse of the Sun*, de Chirico's *Song of Love*, Arthur Dove, Egon Schiele, Adolf Loos, and Margaret Bourke-White added.

30: Modernism and Postmodernism in Europe and America, 1945 to 1980. Former 1945–Present chapter significantly expanded and divided into two chapters. New Framing the Era essay "Art and Consumer Culture" and new timeline. Arshile Gorky, Lee Krasner, Franz Kline, Robert Motherwell, Joan Mitchell, Bridget Riley, Isamu Noguchi, George Segal, Niki de Saint-Phalle, Lucian Freud, Diane Arbus, Minor White, and Vanna Venturi house added.

31: Contemporary Art Worldwide. Former 1945–Present chapter significantly expanded and divided into two chapters. This chapter also now includes contemporary non-Western art. New Framing the Era essay "Art as Socio-Political Message" and new timeline. Robert Mapplethorpe, Shahzia Sikander, Carrie Mae Weems, Jean-

Michel Basquiat, Kehinde Wiley, Shirin Neshat, Edward Burtynksy, Wu Guanzhong, Emily Kame Kngwarreye, Tara Donovan, Jenny Saville, Marisol, Rachel Whiteread, Andy Goldsworthy, Keith Haring, Andreas Gursky, Zaha Hadid, I.M. Pei, Daniel Libeskind, and green architecture added.

32: South and Southeast Asia, 1200 to 1980. New Framing the Era essay "Painting at the Mughal Imperial Court" and new timeline. Sahifa Banu, Abdul Hasan, and Manohar added.

33: China and Korea, 1279 to 1980. New Framing the Era essay "The Forbidden City" and new timeline. Zhao Mengfu and Ni Zan added.

34: Japan, 1336 to 1980. New Framing the Era essay "Famous Views of Edo" and new timeline. White Heron Castle, Tawaraya Sotatsu, Ando Hiroshige, Kitagawa Utamaro, and Kano Hogai added.

35: Native Arts of the Americas, 1300 to 1980. New Framing the Era essay "The Founding of Tenochtitlán" and new timeline. Expanded discussion of Aztec religion and of the Templo Mayor in Mexico City with recently discovered relief of Tlaltecuhtli. New box on Inka technology. *Codex Mendoza* and Mandan buffalo-hide robe added.

36: Oceania before 1980. New Framing the Era essay "Maori Men's Meetinghouses" and new timeline. *Ambum Stone* and Austral Islands Rurutu added. Expanded discussion of Hawaiian art with new illustrations.

37: Africa, 1800 to 1980. New Framing the Era essay "Kalabari Ijaw Ancestral Screens" and new timeline. Chokwe art and Olowe of Ise's Ikere palace doors added.

Go to the online instructor companion site or PowerLecture for a more detailed list of chapter-by-chapter changes and the Image Transition Guide.

ACKNOWLEDGMENTS

A work as extensive as a global history of art could not be undertaken or completed without the counsel of experts in all areas of world art. As with previous editions, Cengage Learning/Wadsxworth has enlisted more than a hundred art historians to review every chapter of *Art through the Ages* in order to ensure that the text lives up to the Gardner reputation for accuracy as well as readability. I take great pleasure in acknowledging here the important contributions to the 14th edition made by the following : Michael Jay Adamek, Ozarks Technical Community College; Charles M. Adelman, University of Northern Iowa; Christine Zitrides Atiyeh, Kutztown University; Gisele Atterberry, Joliet Junior College; Roann Barris, Radford University; Philip Betancourt, Temple University; Karen Blough, SUNY Plattsburgh; Elena N. Boeck, DePaul University; Betty Ann Brown, California State University Northridge; Alexandra A. Carpino, Northern Arizona University; Anne Walke Cassidy, Carthage College; Harold D. Cole, Baldwin Wallace College; Sarah Cormack, Webster University, Vienna; Jodi Cranston, Boston University; Nancy de Grummond, Florida State University; Kelley Helmstutler Di Dio, University of Vermont; Owen Doonan, California State University Northridge; Marilyn Dunn, Loyola University Chicago; Tom Estlack, Pittsburgh Cultural Trust; Lois Fichner-Rathus, The College of New Jersey; Arne R. Flaten, Coastal Carolina University; Ken Friedman, Swinburne University of Technology; Rosemary Gallick, Northern Virginia Community College; William V. Ganis, Wells College; Marc Gerstein, University of Toledo; Clive F. Getty, Miami University; Michael Grillo, University of Maine; Amanda Hamilton, Northwest Nazarene University; Martina Hesser, Heather Jensen, Brigham Young University; Grossmont College; Mark Johnson, Brigham Young University; Jacqueline E. Jung, Yale University; John F. Kenfield, Rutgers University; Asen Kirin, University of Georgia; Joanne Klein, Boise State University; Yu Bong Ko, Tappan Zee High School; Rob Leith, Buckingham Browne & Nichols School; Adele H. Lewis, Arizona State University; Kate Alexandra Lingley, University of Hawaii–Manoa; Ellen Longsworth, Merrimack College; Matthew Looper, California State University–Chico; Nuria Lledó Tarradell, Universidad Complutense, Madrid; Anne McClanan, Portland State University; Mark Magleby, Brigham Young University; Gina Miceli-Hoffman, Moraine Valley Community College; William Mierse, University of Vermont; Amy Morris, Southeastern Louisiana University; Charles R. Morscheck, Drexel University; Johanna D. Movassat, San Jose State University; Carola Naumer, Truckee Meadows Community College; Irene Nero, Southeastern Louisiana University; Robin O'Bryan, Harrisburg Area Community College; Laurent Odde, Kutztown University of Pennsylvania; E. Suzanne Owens, Lorain County Community College; Catherine Pagani, The University of Alabama; Martha Peacock, Brigham Young University; Mabi Ponce de Leon, Bexley High School; Curtis Runnels, Boston University; Malia E. F. Serrano, Grossmont College; Molly Skjei, Normandale Community College; James Swensen, Brigham Young University; John Szostak, University of Hawaii–Manoa; Fred T. Smith, Kent State University; Thomas F. Strasser, Providence College; Katherine H. Tachau, University of Iowa; Debra Thompson, Glendale Community College; Alice Y. Tseng, Boston University; Carol Ventura, Tennessee Technological University; Marc Vincent, Baldwin Wallace College; Deborah Waite, University of Hawaii–Manoa; Lawrence Waldron, Saint John's University; Victoria Weaver, Millersville University; and Margaret Ann Zaho, University of Central Florida.

I am especially indebted to the following for creating the instructor and student materials for the 14th edition: William J. Allen, Arkansas State University; Ivy Cooper, Southern Illinois University Edwardsville; Patricia D. Cosper, The University of Alabama at Birmingham; Anne McClanan, Portland State University; and Amy M. Morris, Southeastern Louisiana University. I also thank the members of the Wadsworth Media Advisory Board for their input: Frances Altvater, University of Hartford; Roann Barris, Radford University; Bill Christy, Ohio University-Zanesville; Annette Cohen, Great Bay Community College; Jeff Davis, The Art Institute of Pittsburgh–Online Division; Owen Doonan, California State University-Northridge; Arne R. Flaten, Coastal Carolina University; Carol Heft, Muhlenberg College; William Mierse, University of Vermont; Eleanor F. Moseman, Colorado State University; and Malia E. F. Serrano, Grossmont College.

I am also happy to have this opportunity to express my gratitude to the extraordinary group of people at Cengage Learning/ Wadsworth involved with the editing, production, and distribution of *Art through the Ages*. Some of them I have now worked with on various projects for nearly two decades and feel privileged to count among my friends. The success of the Gardner series in all of its various permutations depends in no small part on the expertise and unflagging commitment of these dedicated professionals, especially Clark Baxter, publisher; Sharon Adams Poore, senior development editor (as well as videographer extraordinaire); Lianne Ames, senior content project manager; Mandy Groszko, rights acquisitions specialist; Kimberly Apfelbaum, associate media editor; Robert White, product manager; Ashley Bargende, assistant editor; Elizabeth Newell, editorial assistant; Amy Bither and Jessica Jackson, editorial interns; Cate Rickard Barr, senior art director; Jeanne M. Heston, senior marketing manager, Heather Baxley, senior marketing communications manager, and the incomparable group of local sales representatives who have passed on to me the welcome advice offered by the hundreds of instructors they speak to daily during their visits to college campuses throughout North America.

I am also deeply grateful to the following out-of-house contributors to the 14th edition: the peerless and tireless Joan Keyes, Dovetail Publishing Services; Helen Triller-Yambert, development editor; Ida May Norton, copy editor; Do Mi Stauber and Michael Brackney, indexers; Susan Gall, proofreader; tani hasegawa, designer; Catherine Schnurr, Mary-Lise Nazaire, Lauren McFalls, and Corey Geissler, PreMediaGlobal, photo researchers; Alma Bell, Scott Paul, John Pierce, and Lori Shranko, Thompson Type; Jay and John Crowley, Jay's Publishing Services; Mary Ann Lidrbauch, art manuscript preparer; Kim Meyer, image consulting; and, of course, Jonathan Poore and John Burge, for their superb photos and architectural drawings.

Finally, I owe thanks to my former co-author, Christin J. Mamiya of the University of Nebraska–Lincoln, for her friendship and advice, especially with regard to the expanded contemporary art section of the 14th edition, as well as to my colleagues at Boston University and to the thousands of students and the scores of teaching fellows in my art history courses since I began teaching in 1975. From them I have learned much that has helped determine the form and content of *Art through the Ages* and made it a much better book than it otherwise might have been.

Fred S. Kleiner

FRED S. KLEINER (Ph.D., Columbia University) is the author or co-author of the 10th, 11th, 12th, and 13th editions of *Art through the Ages: A Global History,* as well as the 1st, 2nd, and 3rd editions of *Art through the Ages: A Concise History,* and more than a hundred publications on Greek and Roman art and architecture, including *A History of Roman Art,* also published by Wadsworth, a part of Cengage Learning. He has taught the art history survey course for more than three decades, first at the University of Virginia and, since 1978, at Boston University, where he is currently Professor of Art History and Archaeology and Chair of the Department of History of Art and Architecture. From 1985 to 1998, he was Editor-in-Chief of the *American Journal of Archaeology.* Long acclaimed for his inspiring lectures and dedication to students, Professor Kleiner won Boston University's Metcalf Award for Excellence in Teaching as well as the College Prize for Undergraduate Advising in the Humanities in 2002, and he is a two-time winner of the Distinguished Teaching Prize in the College of Arts and Sciences Honors Program. In 2007, he was elected a Fellow of the Society of Antiquaries of London, and, in 2009, in recognition of lifetime achievement in publication and teaching, a Fellow of the Text and Academic Authors Association.

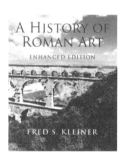

Also by Fred Kleiner: *A History of Roman Art, Enhanced Edition* (Wadsworth/Cengage Learning 2010; ISBN 9780495909873), winner of the 2007 Texty Prize for a new college textbook in the humanities and social sciences. In this authoritative and lavishly illustrated volume, Professor Kleiner traces the development of Roman art and architecture from Romulus's foundation of Rome in the eighth century BCE to the death of Constantine in the fourth century CE, with special chapters devoted to Pompeii and Herculaneum, Ostia, funerary and provincial art and architecture, and the earliest Christian art. The enhanced edition also includes a new introductory chapter on the art and architecture of the Etruscans and of the Greeks of South Italy and Sicily.

RESOURCES

FOR FACULTY

PowerLecture with Digital Image Library

This flashdrive is an all-in-one lecture and class presentation tool that makes it easy to assemble, edit, and present customized lectures for your course using Microsoft® PowerPoint®. The Digital Image Library provides high-resolution images (maps, diagrams, and most of the fine art images from the text, including the over 300 new images) for lecture presentations, either in PowerPoint format, or in individual file formats compatible with other image-viewing software. A zoom feature allows you to magnify selected portions of an image for more detailed display in class, or you can display images side by side for comparison. You can easily add your own images to those from the text. The Google Earth™ application allows you to zoom in on an entire city, as well as key monuments and buildings. There are links to specific figures for every chapter in the book. PowerLecture also includes an Image Transition Guide, an electronic Instructor's Manual and a Test Bank with multiple-choice, matching, short-answer, and essay questions in ExamView® computerized format. The text-specific Microsoft® PowerPoint® slides are created for use with JoinIn™, software for classroom personal response systems (clickers).

WebTutor™ with eBook on WebCT® and Blackboard®

WebTutor™ enables you to assign preformatted, text-specific content that is available as soon as you log on. You can also customize the WebTutor™ environment in any way you choose. Content includes the Interactive ebook, Test Bank, Practice Quizzes, Video Study Tools, and CourseMate™.

To order, contact your Cengage Learning representative.

FOR STUDENTS

CourseMate™ with eBook

Make the most of your study time by accessing everything you need to succeed in one place. Open the interactive eBook, take notes, review image and audio flashcards, watch videos, and take practice quizzes online with CourseMate™. You will find hundreds of zoomable, high-resolution bonus images (represented by thumbnail images in the text) along with discussion of the images, videos created specifically to enhanced your reading comprehension, audio chapter summaries, compare-and-contrast activities, Guide to Studying, and more.

Slide Guides

The Slide Guide is a lecture companion that allows you to take notes alongside thumbnails of the same art images that are shown in class. This handy booklet includes reproductions of the images from the book with full captions, page numbers, and space for note taking. It also includes Google Earth™ exercises for key cities, monuments, and buildings that will take you to these locations to better understand the works you are studying.

To order, go to www.cengagebrain.com

Garden of Earthly Delights is Bosch's most enigmatic painting, but scholars agree it depicts Paradise in the left and central panels and Hell in the right wing. At the left, God as Christ presents Eve to Adam.

In the inky darkness of Bosch's Hell are unidentifiable objects that are imaginative variations on chemical apparatus of the day. Alchemy is a prominent theme of the work.

In the fantastic sunlit landscape that is Bosch's Paradise, scores of nude people in the prime of life blithely cavort. The oversize fruits are fertility symbols, and the scene celebrates procreation.

1 ft.

23-1 Hieronymus Bosch, *Garden of Earthly Delights,* 1505–1510. Oil on wood, center panel 7′ 2⅝″ × 6′ 4¾″, each wing 7′ 2⅝″ × 3′ 2¼″. Museo del Prado, Madrid. ■◀

The horrors of Hell include beastly creatures devouring people, and sinners enduring tortures tailored to their conduct while alive. A glutton vomits eternally. A miser defecates gold coins.

23

HIGH RENAISSANCE AND MANNERISM IN NORTHERN EUROPE AND SPAIN

FRAMING THE ERA

EARTHLY DELIGHTS IN THE NETHERLANDS

The leading Netherlandish painter of the early 16th century was HIERONYMUS BOSCH (ca. 1450–1516), one of the most fascinating and puzzling artists in history. Bosch's most famous painting, the *Garden of Earthly Delights* (FIG. 23-1), is also his most enigmatic, and no interpretation has ever won universal acceptance. Although the work is a monumental triptych, which would suggest a religious function as an altarpiece, *Garden of Earthly Delights* was on display in the palace of Henry III of Nassau, regent of the Netherlands, no later than seven years after its completion. This suggests the triptych was a secular commission, and some scholars have proposed that given the work's central themes of sex and procreation, the painting may commemorate a wedding. Marriage was a familiar theme in Netherlandish painting (FIGS. 20-6 and 20-10). Any similarity to earlier paintings ends there, however. Whereas Jan van Eyck and Petrus Christus grounded their depictions of betrothed couples in 15th-century life and custom, Bosch's image portrays a visionary world of fantasy and intrigue—a painted world without close parallel until the advent of Surrealism more than 400 years later (see Chapter 29).

In the left panel, God (in the form of Christ) presents Eve to Adam in a landscape, presumably the Garden of Eden. Bosch's wildly imaginative setting includes an odd pink fountainlike structure in a body of water and an array of fanciful and unusual animals, including a giraffe, an elephant, and winged fish.

The central panel is a continuation of Paradise, a sunlit landscape filled with nude people, all in the prime of youth, blithely cavorting amid bizarre creatures and unidentifiable objects. The youths play with abandon. Some stand on their hands or turn somersaults. The numerous fruits and birds (fertility symbols) in the scene suggest procreation, and, indeed, many of the figures pair off as couples.

In contrast to the orgiastic overtones of the central panel is the terrifying image of Hell in the right wing, where viewers must search through the inky darkness to find all of the fascinating though repulsive details Bosch recorded. Beastly creatures devour people, while other condemned souls endure tortures tailored to their conduct while alive. A glutton must vomit eternally. A miser defecates gold coins. A spidery monster fondles a promiscuous woman. Scholars have traditionally interpreted Bosch's triptych as a warning of the fate awaiting the sinful, decadent, and immoral, but as a secular work, *Garden of Earthly Delights* may have been intended for a learned audience fascinated by *alchemy*—the study of seemingly magical chemical changes. Details throughout the triptych are based on chemical apparatus of the day, which Bosch knew well because his in-laws were pharmacists.

NORTHERN EUROPE IN THE 16TH CENTURY

The dissolution of the Burgundian Netherlands in 1477 led in the early 16th century to a realignment in the European geopolitical landscape (MAP 23-1). France and the Holy Roman Empire absorbed the former Burgundian territories and increased their power. But by the end of the century, through calculated marriages, military exploits, and ambitious territorial expansion, Spain was the dominant European state. Throughout the Continent, monarchs increasingly used art and architecture to glorify their reigns and to promote a stronger sense of cultural and political unity among their subjects, thereby laying the foundation for today's European nations. Wealthy merchants also cultivated art as a status symbol, as the commissioning and collecting of artworks became less and less the exclusive province of the aristocracy. Some artists,

most notably Albrecht Dürer (FIGS. 23-4 to 23-7), became successful businessmen themselves by selling their works to the public.

These important societal changes occurred against the backdrop of a momentous religious crisis. Concerted attempts to reform Western Christendom led to the Reformation and the establishment of Protestantism (as distinct from Catholicism), which in turn prompted the Catholic Church's response, the Counter-Reformation (see Chapter 22). Ultimately, the Reformation split the Western Church in half and produced a hundred years of civil war between Protestants and Catholics. But the tumultuous religious conflict engulfing 16th-century Europe did not prevent—and may, in fact, have accelerated—the exchange of intellectual and artistic ideas, because artists frequently moved from one area to another in search of religious freedom and lucrative commissions. Catholic Italy and the (mostly) Protestant Holy Roman Empire shared in a lively commerce—economic and cultural—and 16th-century art throughout

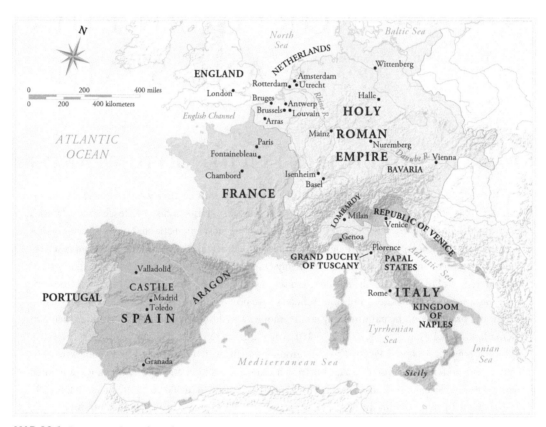

MAP 23-1 Europe in the early 16th century.

HIGH RENAISSANCE AND MANNERISM IN NORTHERN EUROPE AND SPAIN

1500	1530	1560	1600

▌ In Catholic countries, commissions for religious works, such as the *Isenheim Altarpiece,* continue, but, consistent with Reformation values, Protestant patrons prefer secular themes, including portraiture, classical mythology, and the macabre

▌ Albrecht Dürer, master printmaker, becomes the first international art celebrity outside Italy

▌ In France under Henry II (r. 1547–1559), architectural designs are a mix of Italian and Northern Renaissance elements

▌ Netherlandish painters inject moralizing religious messages into seemingly secular genre paintings

▌ Hans Holbein, Caterina van Hemessen, and Levina Teerlinc achieve renown as portrait painters

▌ Pieter Bruegel the Elder, the greatest Netherlandish artist of the mid-16th century, produces masterful landscapes that nonetheless focus on human activities

▌ Greek-born El Greco settles in Toledo and creates paintings that are a uniquely personal mix of Byzantine and Italian Mannerist elements. His hybrid style captured the fervor of Spanish Catholicism

Europe was a major beneficiary of that exchange. Humanism filtered up from Italy and spread throughout northern Europe. Northern humanists, like their southern counterparts, cultivated knowledge of classical cultures and literature, but they focused more on reconciling humanism with Christianity.

Among the most influential of these "Christian humanists" were the Dutch-born Desiderius Erasmus (1466–1536) and the Englishman Thomas More (1478–1535). Erasmus demonstrated his interest in both Italian humanism and religion with his "philosophy of Christ," emphasizing education and scriptural knowledge. Both an ordained priest and avid scholar, Erasmus published his most famous essay, *In Praise of Folly,* in 1509. In this widely read work, he satirized not just the Church but various social classes as well. His ideas were to play an important role in the development of the Reformation, but he consistently declined to join any of the Reformation sects. Equally erudite was Thomas More, who served King Henry VIII (r. 1509–1547). Henry eventually ordered More's execution because of his opposition to England's break with the Catholic Church. In France, François Rabelais (ca. 1494–1553), a former monk who advocated rejecting stagnant religious dogmatism, disseminated the humanist spirit.

The turmoil emerging during the 16th century lasted well into the 17th century and permanently affected the face of Europe. The concerted challenges to established authority and the persistent philosophical inquiry eventually led to the rise of new political systems (for example, the nation-state) and new economic systems (such as capitalism).

HOLY ROMAN EMPIRE

Although at the opening of the 16th century, many in the Holy Roman Empire (MAP 23-1) expressed dissatisfaction with the Church in Rome, Martin Luther had not yet posted the *Ninety-five Theses* that launched the Protestant Reformation. The Catholic clergy in Germany still offered artists important commissions to adorn churches and other religious institutions.

MATTHIAS GRÜNEWALD Matthias Neithardt, known conventionally as MATTHIAS GRÜNEWALD (ca. 1480–1528), worked for the archbishops of Mainz in several capacities, from court painter and decorator to architect, hydraulic engineer, and superintendent of works. Grünewald eventually moved to northern Germany, where he settled at Halle in Saxony. Around 1510, he began work on the *Isenheim Altarpiece* (FIG. 23-2), a complex and fascinating monument reflecting Catholic beliefs and incorporating several references to Catholic doctrines, such as the lamb (symbol of the son of God), whose wound spurts blood into a chalice in the *Crucifixion* scene (FIG. 23-2, *top*) on the exterior of the altarpiece.

Created for the monastic hospital order of Saint Anthony of Isenheim, the *Isenheim Altarpiece* takes the form of a wooden shrine (carved around 1505 by NIKOLAUS HAGENAUER, active 1493–1538) featuring large gilded and polychromed statues of Saints Anthony Abbot, Augustine, and Jerome in the main zone and smaller statues of Christ and the 12 apostles in the predella (FIG. 23-2, *bottom*). To Hagenauer's centerpiece, Grünewald added two pairs of painted moveable wings that open at the center. Hinged at the sides, one pair stands directly behind the other. Grünewald painted the exterior panels of the first pair (visible when the altarpiece is closed,

FIG. 23-2, *top*) between 1510 and 1515: *Crucifixion* in the center, *Saint Sebastian* on the left, *Saint Anthony Abbot* on the right, and *Lamentation* in the predella. When these exterior wings are open, four additional scenes (not illustrated)—*Annunciation, Angelic Concert, Madonna and Child,* and *Resurrection*—appear. Opening this second pair of wings exposes Hagenauer's interior shrine, flanked by Grünewald's panels depicting *Meeting of Saints Anthony and Paul* and *Temptation of Saint Anthony* (FIG. 23-2, *bottom*).

The placement of this altarpiece in the choir of a church adjacent to the monastery's hospital dictated much of the imagery. Saints associated with the plague and other diseases and with miraculous cures, such as Saints Anthony and Sebastian, appear prominently in the *Isenheim Altarpiece*. Grünewald's panels specifically address the themes of dire illness and miraculous healing and accordingly emphasize the suffering of the order's patron saint, Anthony. The painted images served as warnings, encouraging increased devotion from monks and hospital patients. They also functioned therapeutically by offering some hope to the afflicted. Indeed, Saint Anthony's legend emphasized his dual role as vengeful dispenser of justice (by inflicting disease) and benevolent healer.

One of the most memorable scenes is *Temptation of Saint Anthony* (FIG. 23-2, *bottom right*). It is a terrifying image of the five temptations, depicted as an assortment of ghoulish and bestial creatures in a dark landscape, attacking the saint. In the foreground Grünewald painted a grotesque image of a man, whose oozing boils, withered arm, and distended stomach all suggest a horrible disease. Medical experts have connected these symptoms with ergotism (a disease caused by ergot, a fungus that grows especially on rye). Although doctors did not discover the cause of this disease until about 1600, people lived in fear of its recognizable symptoms (convulsions and gangrene). The public referred to this illness as "Saint Anthony's Fire," and it was one of the major diseases treated at the Isenheim hospital. The gangrene often compelled amputation, and scholars have noted that the two moveable halves of the altarpiece's predella (FIG. 23-2, *top*), if slid apart, make it appear as if Christ's legs have been amputated. The same observation applies to the two main exterior panels. Due to the off-center placement of the cross, opening the left panel "severs" one arm from the crucified figure.

Thus, Grünewald carefully selected and presented his altarpiece's iconography to be particularly meaningful for viewers at this hospital. In the interior shrine, the artist balanced the horrors of the disease and the punishments awaiting those who did not repent with scenes such as *Meeting of Saints Anthony and Paul,* depicting the two saints, healthy and aged, conversing peacefully. Even the exterior panels (the closed altarpiece; FIG. 23-2, *top*) convey these same concerns. *Crucifixion* emphasizes Christ's pain and suffering, but the knowledge that this act redeemed humanity tempers the misery. In addition, Saint Anthony appears in the right wing as a devout follower of Christ who, like Christ and for Christ, endured intense suffering for his faith. Saint Anthony's appearance on the exterior thus reinforces the themes Grünewald intertwined throughout this entire work—themes of pain, illness, and death, as well as those of hope, comfort, and salvation. Grünewald also brilliantly used color to enhance the effect of the painted scenes of the altarpiece. He intensified the contrast of horror and hope by playing subtle tones and soft harmonies against shocking dissonances of color.

23-2 Matthias Grünewald, *Isenheim Altarpiece* (closed, *top*; open, *bottom*), from the chapel of the Hospital of Saint Anthony, Isenheim, Germany, ca. 1510–1515. Oil on wood, center panel 9′ 9½″ × 10′ 9″, each wing 8′ 2½″ × 3′ ½″, predella 2′ 5½″ × 11′ 2″. Shrine carved by Nikolaus Hagenauer, ca. 1505. Painted and gilt limewood, 9′ 9½″ × 10′ 9″. Musée d'Unterlinden, Colmar.

Befitting its setting in a monastic hospital, Matthias Grünewald's *Isenheim Altarpiece* includes painted panels depicting suffering and disease but also miraculous healing, hope, and salvation.

HANS BALDUNG GRIEN The son of a prosperous attorney and the brother of a university professor, HANS BALDUNG GRIEN (ca. 1484–1545) chose to pursue painting and printmaking as a profession rather than the law or letters. He settled in Strasbourg, a center of humanistic learning, where he enjoyed a long and successful career. Baldung produced some religious works, although none on the scale of the *Isenheim Altarpiece*. His reputation rested primarily on his exploration of nontraditional subjects, such as witchcraft.

Witches' Sabbath (FIG. 23-3) is a *chiaroscuro woodcut*, a recent German innovation. The technique requires the use of two blocks of wood instead of one. The printmaker carves and inks one block in the usual way in order to produce a traditional black-and-white print (see "Woodcuts, Engravings, and Etchings," Chapter 20, page 556). Then the artist cuts a second block consisting of broad highlights to be inked in grays or colors and printed over the first block's impression. Chiaroscuro woodcuts therefore incorporate some of the qualities of painting and feature tonal subtleties absent in traditional woodcuts.

Witchcraft was a counter-religion in the 15th and 16th centuries involving magical rituals, secret potions, and devil worship. Witches prepared brews they inhaled or rubbed into their skin, sending them into hallucinogenic trances in which they allegedly flew through the night sky on broomsticks or goats. The popes condemned all witches, and Church inquisitors vigorously pursued these demonic heretics and subjected them to torture to wrest confessions from them. Witchcraft fascinated Baldung, and he turned to the subject repeatedly. For him and his contemporaries, witches were evil forces in the world, threats to man—as was Eve herself, whom Baldung also frequently depicted as a temptress responsible for original sin.

In *Witches' Sabbath*, Baldung depicted a night scene in a forest featuring a coven of naked witches. Female nudity and macabre scenes were persistent elements in Baldung's art (compare FIG. 23-3A). These themes were popular with the public, who avidly purchased his relatively inexpensive prints. The coven in this woodcut includes both young seductresses and old hags. They gather around a covered jar from which a fuming concoction escapes into the air. One young witch rides through the night sky on a goat. She sits backward—Baldung's way of suggesting witchcraft is the inversion of the true religion, Christianity.

23-3A BALDUNG GRIEN, *Death and the Maiden*, 1509–1511.

ALBRECHT DÜRER The dominant artist of the early 16th century in the Holy Roman Empire was ALBRECHT DÜRER (1471–1528) of Nuremberg. Dürer was the first artist outside Italy to become an international celebrity. He traveled extensively, visiting and studying in Colmar, Basel, Strasbourg, Venice, Antwerp, and Brussels, among other locales. As a result of these travels, Dürer met many of the leading humanists and artists of his time, including Erasmus of Rotterdam and the Venetian master Giovanni Bellini (FIGS. 22-31A, 22-32, and 22-33). A man of exceptional talents and tremendous energy, Dürer achieved widespread fame in his own time and has enjoyed a lofty reputation ever since.

Fascinated with the classical ideas of the Italian Renaissance, Dürer was among the first Northern Renaissance artists to travel to Italy expressly to study Italian art and its underlying theories at their source. After his first journey in 1494–1495 (the second was in 1505–1506), he incorporated many Italian developments into his art. Art historians have acclaimed Dürer as the first artist north of the Alps to understand fully the basic aims of the Renaissance in Italy. Like Leonardo da Vinci, Dürer wrote theoretical treatises on a variety of subjects, such as perspective, fortification, and the ideal in human proportions. Unlike Leonardo, he both finished and published his writings. Dürer also was the first northern European artist to leave a record of his life and career through his correspondence, a detailed and eminently readable diary, and a series of self-portraits.

SELF-PORTRAITS Dürer's earliest preserved self-portrait—a silverpoint drawing now in the Albertina in Vienna—dates to 1484, when he was only 13, two years before he began his formal education as an apprentice in the workshop of Michel Wolgemut (FIG. 20-21). In 1498, a few years after his first visit to Italy, he painted a likeness of himself in the

23-3 HANS BALDUNG GRIEN, *Witches' Sabbath*, 1510. Chiaroscuro woodcut, 1′ 2⅞″ × 10¼″. British Museum, London.

Baldung's woodcut depicts witches gathered around a cauldron containing a secret potion. One witch flies mounted backward on a goat, suggesting witchcraft is the inversion of Christianity.

1 in.

FALL OF MAN Dürer's fame in his own day, as today, rested more on his achievements as a printmaker than as a painter. Trained as a goldsmith by his father before he took up painting and printmaking, he developed an extraordinary proficiency in handling the burin, the engraving tool. This technical ability, combined with a feeling for the form-creating possibilities of line, enabled him to produce a body of graphic work few artists have rivaled for quality and number. Dürer created numerous book illustrations. He also circulated and sold prints in single sheets, which people of ordinary means could buy, expanding his audience considerably. Aggressively marketing his prints with the aid of an agent, Dürer became a wealthy man from the sale of these works. His wife, who served as his manager, and his mother also sold his prints at markets. Through his graphic works, he exerted strong influence throughout northern Europe and also in Italy. The lawsuit Dürer brought in 1506 against an Italian artist for copying his prints reveals his business acumen. Scholars generally regard this lawsuit as the first in history over artistic copyright.

One of Dürer's early masterpieces, *Fall of Man* (*Adam and Eve*; FIG. 23-5), represents the first distillation of his studies of the Vitruvian theory of human proportions (compare FIG. 22-3A), a theory based on arithmetic ratios. Clearly outlined against the dark

23-4 ALBRECHT DÜRER, *Self-Portrait,* 1500. Oil on wood, 2′ 2¼″ × 1′ 7¼″. Alte Pinakothek, Munich.

Dürer here presents himself as a frontal Christlike figure reminiscent of medieval icons. It is an image of the artist as a divinely inspired genius, a concept inconceivable before the Renaissance.

23-4A DÜRER, *Great Piece of Turf*, 1503.

Italian mode—a seated half-length portrait in three-quarter view in front of a window through which the viewer sees a landscape. The *Self-Portrait* reproduced here (FIG. 23-4), painted just two years later, is markedly different in character. Inscribed with his monogram and the date (*left*) and four lines (*right*) stating the painting depicts him at age 28, the panel portrays the artist in a fur-trimmed coat in a rigid frontal posture against a dark background. Dürer has a short beard and shoulder-length hair, and the portrait intentionally evokes medieval devotional images of Christ. The position of Dürer's right hand resembles but does not duplicate (which would have been blasphemous) Christ's standard gesture of blessing in Byzantine icons (FIG. 9-33). The focus on the hand is also a reference to the artist's hand as a creative instrument. Doubtless deeply affected by the new humanistic view that had emerged in Renaissance Italy of the artist as a divinely inspired genius, Dürer responded by painting himself as a Christlike figure. He also embraced Italian artists' interest in science, as is evident in his botanically accurate 1503 watercolor study *Great Piece of Turf* (FIG. 23-4A).

23-5 ALBRECHT DÜRER, *Fall of Man* (*Adam and Eve*), 1504. Engraving, 9⅞″ × 7⅝″. Museum of Fine Arts, Boston (centennial gift of Landon T. Clay).

Dürer was the first Northern Renaissance artist to achieve international celebrity. *Fall of Man,* with two figures based on ancient statues, reflects his studies of the Vitruvian theory of human proportions.

background of a northern European forest, the two idealized figures of Adam and Eve stand in poses reminiscent of specific classical statues probably known to Dürer through graphic representations. Preceded by numerous geometric drawings in which the artist attempted to systematize sets of ideal human proportions in balanced contrapposto poses, the final print presents Dürer's concept of the "perfect" male and female figures. Yet he tempered this idealization with naturalism, demonstrating his well-honed observational skills in his rendering of the background foliage and animals (compare FIGS. 23-4A and 23-5A). The gnarled bark of the trees and the feathery leaves authenticate the scene, as do the various creatures skulking underfoot. The animals populating the print are symbolic. The choleric cat, the melancholic elk, the sanguine rabbit, and the phlegmatic ox represent humanity's temperaments based on the "four humors," body fluids that were the basis of theories developed by the ancient Greek physician Hippocrates

and practiced in medieval physiology. The tension between cat and mouse in the foreground symbolizes the relation between Adam and Eve at the crucial moment in *Fall of Man.*

MELENCOLIA I Dürer took up the theme of the four humors, specifically melancholy, in one of his most famous engravings, *Melencolia I* (FIG. 23-6), which many scholars regard as a kind of self-portrait of Dürer's artistic psyche as well as a masterful example of the artist's ability to produce a wide range of tonal values and textures. (Erasmus praised Dürer as "the Apelles [the most renowned ancient Greek painter] of black lines,"[1] and the German artist's mastery of all aspects of printmaking is evident also in his woodcuts, for example, FIG. I-9.)

The Italian humanist Marsilio Ficino (1433–1499) had written an influential treatise (*De vita triplici,* 1482–1489) in which he asserted that artists were distinct from the population at large because they were born under the sign of the planet Saturn, named for the ancient Roman god. They shared that deity's melancholic temperament because they had an excess of black bile, one of the four body humors, in their systems. Artists therefore were "saturnine"—eccentric and capable both of inspired artistic frenzy and melancholic depression. Raphael had depicted Michelangelo in the guise of the brooding Heraclitus in his *School of Athens* (FIG. 22-9), and Dürer used a similarly posed female figure for his winged personification of Melancholy in *Melencolia I.* (In 1510, in *De occulta philosophia,* Heinrich Cornelius Agrippa of Nettesheim [1486–1535] identified three levels of melancholy. The first was artistic melancholy, which explains the Roman numeral on the banner carried by the bat—a creature of the dark—in Dürer's engraving.) All around the brooding figure of Melancholy are the tools of the artist and builder (compare FIG. 13-32)—compass, hammer, nails, and saw among them—but they are useless to the frustrated artist while he is suffering from melancholy. Melancholy's face is obscured by shadow, underscoring her state of mind, but Dürer also included a burst of light on the far horizon behind the bat, an optimistic note suggesting artists can overcome their depression and produce works of genius—such as this engraving.

23-6 ALBRECHT DÜRER, *Melencolia I,* 1514. Engraving, $9\frac{3}{8}'' \times 7\frac{1}{2}''$. Victoria & Albert Museum, London.

In this "self-portrait" of his artistic personality, Dürer portrayed Melancholy as a brooding winged woman surrounded by the tools of the artist and builder but incapable of using them.

23-7 ALBRECHT DÜRER, *Four Apostles,* 1526. Oil on wood, each panel 7′ 1″ × 2′ 6″. Alte Pinakothek, Munich. ◼◂

Dürer's support for Lutheranism surfaces in his portraitlike depictions of four saints on two painted panels. Peter, representative of the pope in Rome, plays a secondary role behind John the Evangelist.

FOUR APOSTLES Dürer's major work in the oil medium is *Four Apostles* (FIG. 23-7), a two-panel oil painting he produced without commission and presented to the city fathers of Nuremberg in 1526 to be hung in the city hall. Saints John and Peter appear on the left panel, Mark and Paul on the right. In addition to showcasing Dürer's mastery of the oil technique, of his brilliant use of color and light and shade, and of his ability to imbue the four saints with individual personalities and portraitlike features, *Four Apostles* documents Dürer's support for the German theologian Martin Luther (1483–1546), who sparked the Protestant Reformation. Dürer conveyed his Lutheran sympathies by his positioning of the figures. He relegated Saint Peter (as representative of the pope in Rome) to a secondary role by placing him behind John the Evangelist. John assumed particular prominence for Luther because of the evangelist's focus on Christ's person in his Gospel. In addition, Peter and John both read from the Bible, the single authoritative source of religious truth, according to Luther. Dürer emphasized the Bible's centrality by depicting it open to the passage "In the beginning was the Word, and the Word was with God, and the Word was God" (John 1:1). At the bottom of the panels, Dürer included quotations from the four apostles' books, using Luther's German translation of the New Testament. The excerpts warn against the coming of perilous times and the preaching of false prophets who will distort God's word.

LUTHER AND THE REFORMATION The Protestant Reformation, which came to fruition in the early 16th century, had its roots in long-term, growing dissatisfaction with Catholic Church leadership. The deteriorating relationship between the faithful and the Church of Rome's hierarchy stood as an obstacle for the millions who sought a meaningful religious experience. Particularly damaging was the perception that the Roman popes concerned themselves more with temporal power and material wealth than with the salvation of Church members. The fact that many 15th-century popes and cardinals came from wealthy families, such as the Medici (FIG. 22-10), intensified this perception. It was not only those at the highest levels who seemed to ignore their spiritual duties. Archbishops, bishops, and abbots began to accumulate numerous offices, thereby increasing their revenues but making it more difficult for them to fulfill all of their responsibilities. By 1517, dissatisfaction with the Church had grown so widespread that Luther felt free to challenge papal authority openly by posting in Wittenberg his *Ninety-five Theses,* in which he enumerated his objections to Church practices, especially the sale of indulgences. *Indulgences* were Church-sanctioned remittances (or reductions) of time Catholics had to spend in Purgatory for confessed sins. The increasing frequency of their sale suggested that those who could afford to purchase indulgences were buying their way into Heaven.

Luther's goal was significant reform and clarification of major spiritual issues, but his ideas ultimately led to the splitting of Christendom. According to Luther, the Catholic Church's extensive ecclesiastical structure needed casting out, for it had no basis in scripture. The Bible and nothing else could serve as the foundation for Christianity. Luther declared the pope the Antichrist (for which the pope excommunicated him), called the Church the "whore of Babylon," and denounced ordained priests. He also rejected most of Catholicism's sacraments other than baptism and communion, decrying them as obstacles to salvation (see "Catholic and Protestant Views of Salvation," page 653, and FIG. 23-8). Luther maintained that for Christianity to be restored to its original purity, the Church needed cleansing of all the doctrinal impurities that had collected through the ages. Luther advocated the Bible as the source of all religious truth. The Bible—the sole scriptural authority—was the word of God, which did not exist in the Church's councils, law, and rituals. Luther facilitated the lay public's access to biblical truths by producing the first translation of the Bible in a vernacular language.

ART AND THE REFORMATION In addition to doctrinal differences, Catholics and Protestants took divergent stances on the role of visual imagery in religion. Catholics embraced church decoration as an aid to communicating with God (see "Religious Art in Counter-Reformation Italy," Chapter 22, page 617). In contrast, Protestants believed images of Christ, the Virgin, and saints could lead to idolatry and distracted viewers from focusing on the real reason for their presence in church—to communicate directly with God. Because of this belief, Protestant churches were relatively bare, and the extensive church pictorial programs found especially in Italy but also in northern Europe (FIGS. 20-19, 20-20, and 23-2) were not as prominent in Protestant churches.

The Protestant concern over the role of religious imagery at times escalated to outright *iconoclasm*—the objection to and destruction of religious imagery. In encouraging a more personal relationship with God, Protestant leaders spoke out against much of the religious art being produced. In his 1525 tract *Against the*

Catholic and Protestant Views of Salvation

A central concern of the Protestant reformers was the question of how Christians achieve salvation. Rather than perceive salvation as something for which weak and sinful humans must constantly strive through good deeds performed under the watchful eye of a punitive God, Martin Luther argued that faithful individuals attained redemption solely by God's bestowal of his grace. Therefore, people cannot earn salvation. Further, no ecclesiastical machinery with all its miraculous rites and indulgent forgivenesses could save sinners face-to-face with God. Only absolute faith in Christ could redeem sinners and ensure salvation. Redemption by faith alone, with the guidance of scripture, was the fundamental doctrine of Protestantism.

In *Law and Gospel* (FIG. 23-8), a woodcut dated about a dozen years after Luther set the Reformation in motion with his *Ninety-five Theses,* Lucas Cranach the Elder gave visual expression to the doctrinal differences between Protestantism and Catholicism. Cranach contrasted Catholicism (based on Old Testament law, according to Luther) and Protestantism (based on the Gospel belief in God's grace) in two images separated by a centrally placed tree. On the left half, judgment day has arrived, as represented by Christ's appearance at the top of the scene, hovering amid a cloud halo and accompanied by angels and saints. Christ raises his left hand in the traditional gesture of damnation, and, below, a skeleton drives off a terrified person to burn for eternity in Hell. This person tried to live a good and honorable life, but despite his efforts, he fell short. Moses stands to the side, holding the tablets of the law—the Ten Commandments Catholics follow in their attempt to attain salvation. In contrast to this Catholic reliance on good works and clean living, Protestants emphasized God's grace as the source of redemption. Accordingly, God showers the sinner in the right half of the print with grace, as streams of blood flow from the crucified Christ. At the far left are Adam and Eve, whose original sin necessitated Christ's sacrifice. In the lower right corner of the woodcut, Christ emerges from the tomb and promises salvation to all who believe in him.

23-8 LUCAS CRANACH THE ELDER, *Law and Gospel,* ca. 1530. Woodcut, $10\frac{5}{8}$″ × 1′ $\frac{3}{4}$″. **British Museum, London.**

Lucas Cranach was a close friend of Martin Luther, whose *Ninety-five Theses* launched the Reformation in 1517. This woodcut contrasts Catholic and Protestant views of how to achieve salvation.

1 in.

Heavenly Prophets in the Matter of Images and Sacraments, Martin Luther explained his attitude toward religious imagery:

> I approached the task of destroying images by first tearing them out of the heart through God's Word and making them worthless and despised. . . . For when they are no longer in the heart, they can do no harm when seen with the eyes. . . . I have allowed and not forbidden the outward removal of images. . . . And I say at the outset that according to the law of Moses no other images are forbidden than an image of God which one worships. A crucifix, on the other hand, or any other holy image is not forbidden.[2]

Two influential Protestant theologians based in Switzerland—Ulrich Zwingli (1484–1531) and French-born John Calvin (Jean

Cauvin, 1509–1564)—were more vociferous in cautioning their followers about the potentially dangerous nature of religious imagery. Zwingli and Calvin's condemnation of religious imagery often led to eruptions of iconoclasm. Particularly violent waves of iconoclastic fervor swept Basel, Zurich, Strasbourg, and Wittenberg in the 1520s. In an episode known as the Great Iconoclasm, bands of Calvinists visited Catholic churches in the Netherlands in 1566, shattering stained-glass windows, smashing statues, and destroying paintings and other artworks they perceived as idolatrous. These strong reactions to art not only reflect the religious fervor of the time but also serve as dramatic demonstrations of the power of art—and of how much art mattered.

LUCAS CRANACH THE ELDER The artist most closely associated with the Protestant Reformation and with Martin Luther in particular was LUCAS CRANACH THE ELDER (1472–1553). Cranach and Luther were godfathers to each other's children, and many scholars have dubbed Cranach "the painter of the Reformation." Cranach was also an accomplished graphic artist who used the new, inexpensive medium of prints on paper to promote Lutheran ideology (FIG. 23-8). Cranach's work encompasses a wide range of themes, however. For example, for aristocratic Saxon patrons he produced a large number of paintings of classical myths featuring female nudes in suggestive poses. One classical theme he depicted several times was *Judgment of Paris,* of which the small panel (FIG. 23-9) now in Karlsruhe is the best example. Homer records the story, but Cranach's source was probably the second-century CE Roman author Lucian's elaboration of the tale. Mercury chose a handsome young shepherd named Paris to be the judge of a beauty contest among three goddesses—Juno, wife of Jupiter; Minerva, Jupiter's virgin daughter and goddess of wisdom and war; and Venus, the goddess of love (see "The Gods and Goddesses of Mount Olympus," Chapter 5, page 107, or on page xxix in Volume II and Book D). According to Lucian, each goddess attempted to bribe Paris with rich rewards if he chose her. Venus won by offering Paris the most beautiful woman in the world, Helen of Troy, and thus set in motion the epic war between the Greeks and Trojans recounted in Homer's *Iliad.*

Cranach's painting could never be confused with an ancient depiction of the myth. The setting is a German landscape with a Saxon castle in the background, and the seated shepherd is a knight in full armor wearing a fashionable hat. Mercury, an aged man (as he never is in ancient art), also wearing armor, bends over to draw Paris's attention to the three goddesses. They are nude save for their transparent veils, their fine jewelry, and, in the case of Juno, an elegant hat. Loosely based on classical representations of the Three Graces (compare FIG. 21-1)—ancient artists did not depict Juno or Minerva undressed—Cranach's goddesses do not have the proportions (or modesty) of Praxiteles' *Aphro-*

23-9 LUCAS CRANACH THE ELDER, *Judgment of Paris,* 1530. Oil on wood, 1' 1½" × 9½". Staatliche Kunsthalle, Karlsruhe.

For aristocratic German patrons, Cranach painted many classical myths featuring seductive female nudes. In his *Judgment of Paris,* the Greek shepherd is a knight in armor in a Saxon landscape.

1 in.

dite of Knidos (FIG. 5-62). Slender, with small heads and breasts and long legs, they pose seductively before the judge. Venus performs a dance for Paris, but he seems indifferent to all three goddesses. Only the rearing horse appears to be excited by the spectacle—a touch of humor characteristic of Cranach.

ALBRECHT ALTDORFER As elsewhere in 16th-century Europe, some artists in the Holy Roman Empire worked in the employ of rulers, and their work promoted the political agendas of their patrons. In 1529, for example, the duke of Bavaria, Wilhelm IV (r. 1508–1550), commissioned ALBRECHT ALTDORFER (ca. 1480–1538) to paint *Battle of Issus* (FIG. 23-10) at the commencement of his military campaign against the invading Turks. The panel depicts Alexander the Great's defeat of King Darius III of Persia in 333 BCE at a town called Issus on the Pinarus River. Altdorfer announced the subject—which the Greek painter Philoxenos of Eretria (FIG. 5-70) had represented two millennia before—in the Latin inscription suspended in the sky. The parallels between the historical and contemporary conflicts were no doubt significant

23-10 Albrecht Altdorfer, *Battle of Issus,* 1529. Oil on wood, 5′ 2¼″ × 3′ 11¼″. Alte Pinakothek, Munich.

Interweaving history and 16th-century politics, Albrecht Altdorfer painted Alexander the Great's defeat of the Persians for a patron who had just embarked on a military campaign against the Turks.

1 ft.

to the duke. Both involved Western societies engaged in battles against Eastern foes with different values—the Persians in antiquity and the Turks in 1528. Altdorfer reinforced this connection by attiring the figures in 16th-century armor and depicting them engaged in contemporary military alignments.

Battle of Issus also reveals Altdorfer's love of landscape. The battle takes place in an almost cosmological setting. From a bird's-eye view, the clashing armies swarm in the foreground. In the distance, craggy mountain peaks rise next to still bodies of water. Amid swirling clouds, a blazing sun descends. Although the spectacular

topography may appear invented, Altdorfer derived his depiction of the landscape from maps. Specifically, he set the scene in the eastern Mediterranean with a view from Greece to the Nile in Egypt. In addition, Altdorfer may have acquired his information about this battle from the German scholar Johannes Aventinus (1477–1534), whose account of Alexander's victory describes the bloody daylong battle. Appropriately, given Alexander's designation as the "sun god," the sun sets over the victorious Greeks on the right, while a small crescent moon (a symbol of ancient Persia) hovers in the upper left corner over the retreating enemy forces.

In this double portrait, Holbein depicted two humanists with a collection of objects reflective of their worldliness and learning, but he also included an anamorphic skull, a reminder of death.

HANS HOLBEIN Also in the employ of the rich and powerful for much of his career was HANS HOLBEIN THE YOUNGER (ca. 1497–1543), who excelled as a portraitist. Trained by his father, Holbein produced portraits consistent with the northern European tradition of close realism that had emerged in 15th-century Flemish art (see Chapter 20). The surfaces of Holbein's paintings are as lustrous as enamel, and the details are exact and exquisitely drawn. Yet he also incorporated Italian ideas about monumental composition and sculpturesque form.

Holbein began his artistic career in Basel, where he knew Erasmus of Rotterdam. Because of the immediate threat of a religious civil war in Basel, Erasmus suggested Holbein leave for England and gave him a recommendation to Thomas More, chancellor of England under Henry VIII. Holbein quickly obtained important commissions, for example, to paint a double portrait of the French ambassadors to England, Jean de Dinteville and Georges de Selve (FIG. 23-11), and within a few years of his arrival, he became the official painter to the English court, producing numerous portraits of Henry VIII (FIG. 23-11A).

23-11A HOLBEIN THE YOUNGER, *Henry VIII*, 1540.

The French Ambassadors (FIG. 23-11) exhibits Holbein's considerable talents—his strong sense of composition, his subtle linear patterning, his gift for portraiture, his marvelous sensitivity to color, and his faultless technique. The two men, both ardent humanists, stand at opposite ends of a side table covered with an oriental rug and a collection of objects reflective of their worldliness and their interest in learning and the arts. These include mathematical and astronomical models and implements, a lute with a broken string, compasses, a sundial, flutes, globes, and an open hymnbook with Luther's translation of *Veni, Creator Spiritus* and of the Ten Commandments.

Of particular interest is the long gray shape that slashes diagonally across the picture plane and interrupts the stable, balanced, and serene composition. This form is an *anamorphic image*, a distorted image recognizable only when viewed with a special device, such as a cylindrical mirror, or by looking at the painting at an acute angle. In this case, if the viewer stands off to the right, the gray slash becomes a skull. Although scholars disagree on the skull's precise meaning, it certainly refers to death. Artists commonly incorporated skulls into paintings as reminders of mortality. Indeed, Holbein depicted a skull on the metal medallion on Jean de Dinteville's hat. Holbein may have intended the skulls, in conjunction with the crucifix that appears half hidden behind the curtain in the upper left corner, to encourage viewers to ponder death and resurrection.

This painting may also allude to the growing tension between secular and religious authorities. Jean de Dinteville was a titled landowner, Georges de Selve a bishop. The inclusion of Luther's translations next to the lute with the broken string (a symbol of discord) may subtly refer to this religious strife. In any case, *The French Ambassadors* is a painting of supreme artistic achievement. Holbein rendered the still-life objects with the same meticulous care as he did the men themselves, the woven design of the deep emerald curtain behind them, and the floor tiles, drawn in perfect perspective.

FRANCE

As *The French Ambassadors* illustrates, France in the early 16th century continued its efforts to secure widespread recognition as a political power and cultural force. The French kings were major patrons of art and architecture.

FRANCIS I Under the rule of Francis I (r. 1515–1547), the French established a firm foothold in Milan and its environs. Francis waged a campaign (known as the Habsburg-Valois Wars) against Charles V (the Spanish king and Holy Roman emperor; r. 1516–1558), which occupied him from 1521 to 1544. These wars involved disputed territories—southern France, the Netherlands, the Rhineland, northern Spain, and Italy—and reflect France's central role in the shifting geopolitical landscape.

The French king also took a strong position in the religious controversies of his day. By the mid-16th century, the split between Catholics and Protestants had become so pronounced that subjects often felt compelled either to accept the religion of their sovereign or emigrate to a territory where the sovereign's religion corresponded with their own. France was predominantly Catholic, and in 1534, Francis declared Protestantism illegal. The state persecuted its Protestants, the Huguenots, a Calvinist sect, and drove them underground. (Calvin fled from France to Switzerland two years later.) The Huguenots' commitment to Protestant Calvinism eventually led to one of the bloodiest religious massacres in European history when the Huguenots and Catholics clashed in Paris in August 1572. The violence quickly spread throughout France with the support of many nobles, which presented a serious threat to the king's authority.

In art as well as politics and religion, Francis I was a dominant figure. To elevate his country's cultural profile, he invited several esteemed Italian artists to his court, Leonardo da Vinci among them (see Chapter 22). Under Francis, the Church, the primary patron of art and architecture in medieval France, yielded that position to the French monarchy.

JEAN CLOUET As the rulers of antiquity had done, Francis commissioned portraits of himself to assert his authority. The finest is the portrait (FIG. 23-12) JEAN CLOUET (ca. 1485–1541) painted about a decade after Francis became king. It portrays the French monarch as a worldly ruler magnificently bedecked in silks and brocades, wearing a gold chain with a medallion of the Order of Saint Michael, a French order Louis XI founded in 1469. Legend has it that Francis (known as the "merry monarch") was a great lover and the hero of hundreds of "gallant" deeds. Appropriately, he appears suave and confident, with his hand resting on the pommel of a dagger. Despite the careful detail, the portrait also exhibits an elegantly formalized quality, the result of Clouet's suppression of modeling, which flattens features, seen particularly in Francis's neck. The disproportion between the king's small head and his broad body, swathed in heavy layers of fabric, adds to the formalized nature.

Francis and his court favored art that was at once elegant, erotic, and unorthodox. Appropriately, Mannerism appealed to them most, and Francis thus brought Benvenuto Cellini (FIGS. 22-52 and 22-52A) to France with the promise of a lucrative retainer. He put two prominent Florentine Mannerists—Rosso Fiorentino and Francesco Primaticcio—in charge of decorating the new royal palace at Fontainebleau.

CHÂTEAU DE CHAMBORD Francis I also indulged his passion for building by commissioning several large *châteaux,* among them the Château de Chambord (FIG. 23-13). Reflecting more peaceful times, these châteaux, developed from medieval castles, served as country houses for royalty, who usually built them near forests for use as hunting lodges. Many, including Chambord, still featured protective surrounding moats, however. Construction of the Château de Chambord began in 1519, but Francis I never saw its

23-12 JEAN CLOUET, *Francis I,* ca. 1525–1530. Tempera and oil on wood, 3′ 2″ × 2′ 5″. Musée du Louvre, Paris.

Clouet's portrait of Francis I in elegant garb reveals the artist's attention to detail but also the flattening of features and disproportion between head and body, giving the painting a formalized quality.

completion. Chambord's plan, originally drawn by a pupil of Giuliano da Sangallo (FIGS. 22-26 and 22-27), includes a central square block with four corridors, in the shape of a cross, and a broad central staircase that gives access to groups of rooms—ancestors of the modern suite of rooms or apartments. At each of the four corners, a

23-13 Château de Chambord (looking northwest), Chambord, France, begun 1519. ◼◀

French Renaissance châteaux, which developed from medieval castles, served as country houses for royalty. King Francis I's Château de Chambord reflects Italian palazzo design, but it has a Gothic roof.

23-14 PIERRE LESCOT, west wing of the Cour Carré (Square Court, looking west) of the Louvre, Paris, France, begun 1546. ◼◀

Lescot's design for the Louvre palace reflects the Italian Renaissance classicism of Bramante, but the decreasing height of the stories, large windows, and steep roof are northern European features.

round tower punctuates the square plan. From the exterior, Chambord presents a carefully contrived horizontal accent on three levels, with continuous moldings separating its floors. Windows align precisely, one exactly over another. The Italian Renaissance palazzo served as the model for this matching of horizontal and vertical features, but above the third level the structure's lines break chaotically into a jumble of high dormers, chimneys, and lanterns that recall soaring, ragged Gothic silhouettes on the skyline.

LOUVRE, PARIS Chambord, despite its Italian elements, is essentially a French building. During the reign of Francis's successor, Henry II (r. 1547–1559), however, translations of Italian architectural treatises appeared, and Italian architects themselves came to work in France. Moreover, the French turned to Italy for study and travel. These exchanges caused a more extensive revolution in style than had transpired earlier, although certain French elements derived from the Gothic tradition persisted. This incorporation of Italian architectural ideas characterizes the redesigned Louvre in Paris, originally a medieval palace and fortress (FIG. 20-16). Since Charles V's renovation of the Louvre in the mid-14th century, the castle had fallen into a state of disrepair. Francis I initiated the project to update and expand the royal palace, but died before the work was well under way. His architect, PIERRE LESCOT (1510–1578), continued under Henry II and produced the classical style most closely associated with 16th-century French architecture.

Lescot and his associates were familiar with the architectural style of Bramante and his school. In the west wing of the Cour Carré (Square Court; FIG. 23-14) of the Louvre, each of the stories forms a complete order, and the cornices project enough to furnish a strong horizontal accent. The arcading on the ground story reflects the ancient Roman use of arches and produces more shadow than in the upper stories due to its recessed placement, thereby strengthening the design's visual base. On the second story, the pilasters rising from bases and the alternating curved and angular pediments supported by consoles have direct antecedents in several High Renaissance palaces (for example, FIG. 22-26). Yet the decreasing height of the stories, the scale of the windows (proportionally much larger

than in Italian Renaissance buildings), and the steep roof are northern European elements. Especially French are the pavilions jutting from the wall. A motif the French long favored—double columns framing a niche—punctuates the pavilions. The richly articulated wall surfaces feature relief sculptures by JEAN GOUJON (ca. 1510–1565), who had previously collaborated with Lescot on the Fountain of the Innocents (FIG. 23-14A) in Paris. Other northern European countries imitated this French classical manner—its double-columned pavilions, tall and wide windows, profuse statuary, and steep roofs—although with local variations. The modified classicism the French produced became the model for building projects north of the Alps through most of the 16th century.

23-14A GOUJON, Fountain of the Innocents, 1547–1549.

THE NETHERLANDS

With the demise of the duchy of Burgundy in 1477 and the division of that territory between France and the Holy Roman Empire, the Netherlands at the beginning of the 16th century consisted of 17 provinces (corresponding to modern Holland, Belgium, and Luxembourg). The Netherlands was among the most commercially advanced and prosperous European countries. Its extensive network of rivers and easy access to the Atlantic Ocean provided a setting conducive to overseas trade, and shipbuilding was one of the most profitable enterprises. The region's commercial center shifted toward the end of the 15th century, partly because of the buildup of silt in the Bruges estuary. Traffic relocated to Antwerp, which became the hub of economic activity in the Netherlands after 1510. As many as 500 ships a day passed through Antwerp's harbor, and large trading companies from England, the Holy Roman Empire, Italy, Portugal, and Spain established themselves in the city.

During the second half of the 16th century, Philip II of Spain (r. 1556–1598) controlled the Netherlands. Philip had inherited the region from his father Charles V, and he sought to force the

23-15 JAN GOSSAERT, *Neptune and Amphitrite*, ca. 1516. Oil on wood, 6′ 2″ × 4′ ¾″. Gemälde-galerie, Staatliche Museen zu Berlin, Berlin.

Dürer's *Fall of Man* (FIG. 23-5) inspired the poses of Gossaert's classical deities, but the architectural setting is probably based on sketches of ancient buildings Gossaert made during his trip to Rome.

who traveled to Italy and became fascinated with classical antiquity and mythology (FIG. 23-15), although he also painted traditional Christian themes (FIG. 23-15A). Giorgio Vasari, the Italian artist and biographer and Gossaert's contemporary, wrote that "Jean Gossart [*sic*] of Mabuse

23-15A GOSSAERT, *Saint Luke Drawing the Virgin*, ca. 1520–1525.

was almost the first who took from Italy into Flanders the true method of making scenes full of nude figures and poetical inventions,"[3] although Gossaert derived much of his classicism from Albrecht Dürer.

Indeed, Dürer's *Fall of Man* (FIG. 23-5) inspired the composition and poses in Gossaert's *Neptune and Amphitrite* (FIG. 23-15). However, in contrast to Dürer's exquisitely small engraving, Gossaert's painting is more than six feet tall and four feet wide. The artist executed the painting with characteristic Netherlandish polish, skillfully drawing and carefully modeling the figures. Gossaert depicted the sea god with his traditional attribute, the trident, and wearing a laurel wreath and an ornate conch shell in place of Dürer's fig leaf. Amphitrite is fleshy and, like Neptune, stands in a contrapposto stance. The architectural frame, which resembles the cella of a classical temple (FIG. 5-46), is an unusual mix of Doric and Ionic elements and *bucrania* (ox skull decorations), a common motif in ancient architectural ornamentation. Gossaert likely based the classical setting on sketches he had made of ancient buildings while in Rome. He had traveled to Italy with Philip, bastard of Burgundy, this painting's patron. A Burgundian admiral (hence the Neptune reference), Philip became a bishop and kept this work in the innermost room of his castle.

entire population to become Catholic. His heavy-handed tactics and repressive measures led in 1579 to revolt and the formation of two federations: the Union of Arras, a Catholic union of southern Netherlandish provinces, which remained under Spanish dominion, and the Union of Utrecht, a Protestant union of northern provinces, which became the Dutch Republic (MAP 25-1).

Large-scale altarpieces and other religious works continued to be commissioned for Catholic churches, but with the rise of Protestantism in the Netherlands, artists increasingly favored secular subjects. Netherlandish art of this period provides a wonderful glimpse into the lives of various strata of society, from nobility to peasantry, capturing their activities, environment, and values.

JAN GOSSAERT As in the Holy Roman Empire and France, developments in Italian Renaissance art interested many Netherlandish artists. JAN GOSSAERT (ca. 1478–1535) was one of those

QUINTEN MASSYS Antwerp's growth and prosperity, along with its wealthy merchants' propensity for collecting and purchasing art, attracted artists to the city. Among them was QUINTEN MASSYS (ca. 1466–1530), who became Antwerp's leading master after 1510. The son of a Louvain blacksmith, Massys demonstrated a willingness to explore the styles and modes of a variety of models, from Jan van Eyck and Rogier van der Weyden to Albrecht Dürer, Hieronymous Bosch, and Leonardo da Vinci. Yet his eclecticism was subtle and discriminating, enriched by an inventiveness that gave a personal stamp to his paintings.

23-16 QUINTEN MASSYS, *Money-Changer and His Wife*, 1514. Oil on wood, 2′ 3¾″ × 2′ 2⅜″. Musée du Louvre, Paris.

Massys's depiction of a secular financial transaction is also a commentary on Netherlandish values. The banker's wife shows more interest in the money-weighing than in her prayer book.

1 ft.

In *Money-Changer and His Wife* (FIG. 23-16), Massys presented a professional man transacting business. He holds scales, checking the weight of coins on the table. The artist's detailed rendering of the figures, setting, and objects suggests a fidelity to observable fact, and provides insight into developing commercial practices. But *Money-Changer and His Wife* is also a commentary on Netherlandish values and mores. The painting highlights the financial transactions that were an increasingly prominent part of 16th-century secular life in the Netherlands and that distracted Christians from their religious duties. The banker's wife, for example, shows more interest in watching her husband weigh money than in reading her prayer book. Massys incorporated into his painting numerous references to the importance of a moral, righteous, and spiritual life, including a carafe with water and a candlestick, traditional religious symbols. The couple ignores them, focusing solely on money. On the right, through a window, an old man talks with another man, a reference to idleness and gossip. The reflected image in the convex mirror on the counter offsets this image of sloth and foolish chatter. There, a man reads what is most likely a Bible or prayer book. Behind him is a church steeple. An inscription on the original frame (now lost) read, "Let the balance be just and the weights equal" (Lev. 19:36), an admonition that applies both to the money-changer's professional conduct and the eventual last judgment. Nonetheless, the couple in this painting has tipped the balance in favor of the pursuit of wealth.

PIETER AERTSEN This tendency to inject reminders about spiritual well-being into paintings of everyday life emerges again in *Butcher's Stall* (FIG. 23-17) by PIETER AERTSEN (ca. 1507–1575), who worked in Antwerp for more than three decades. At first glance, this painting appears to be a descriptive *genre* scene (one from daily

23-17 PIETER AERTSEN, *Butcher's Stall*, 1551. Oil on wood, 4′ ⅜″ × 6′ 5¾″. Uppsala University Art Collection, Uppsala.

Butcher's Stall appears to be a genre painting, but in the background, Joseph leads a donkey carrying Mary and the Christ Child. Aertsen balanced images of gluttony with allusions to salvation.

1 in.

life). On display is an array of meat products—a side of a hog, chickens, sausages, a stuffed intestine, pig's feet, meat pies, a cow's head, a hog's head, and hanging entrails. Also visible are fish, pretzels, cheese, and butter. As did Massys, Aertsen embedded strategically placed religious images in his painting. In the background, Joseph leads a donkey carrying Mary and the Christ Child. The holy family stops to offer alms to a beggar and his son, while the people behind the holy family wend their way toward a church. Furthermore, the crossed fishes on the platter and the pretzels and wine in the rafters on the upper left all refer to "spiritual food" (pretzels were often served as bread during Lent). Aertsen accentuated these allusions to salvation through Christ by contrasting them to their opposite—a life of gluttony, lust, and sloth. He represented this degeneracy with the oyster and mussel shells (which Netherlanders believed possessed aphrodisiacal properties) scattered on the ground on the painting's right side, along with the people seen eating and carousing nearby under the roof. Underscoring the general theme is the placard at the right advertising land for sale—Aertsen's moralistic reference to a recent scandal involving the transfer of land from an Antwerp charitable institution to a land speculator. The sign appears directly above the vignette of the Virgin giving alms to the beggar.

CATERINA VAN HEMESSEN With the accumulation of wealth in the Netherlands, portraits increased in popularity. The self-portrait (FIG. 23-18) by Caterina van Hemessen (1528–1587)

is the first known northern European self-portrait by a woman. Here, she confidently presented herself as an artist who interrupts her work to gaze at the viewer. She holds brushes, a palette, and a *maulstick* (a stick used to steady the hand while painting) in her left hand, and delicately applies pigment to the canvas with her right hand. The artist ensured proper identification (and credit) through the inscription in the painting: "Caterina van Hemessen painted me / 1548 / her age 20." Professional women artists remained unusual in the 16th century in large part because of the difficulty in obtaining formal training (see "The Artist's Profession in Flanders," Chapter 20, page 545). Caterina was typical in having been trained by her father, Jan Sanders van Hemessen (ca. 1500–1556), a well-known painter.

LEVINA TEERLINC Another Netherlandish woman who achieved a successful career as an artist was Levina Teerlinc (1515–1576) of Bruges. She established such a high reputation that Henry VIII and his successors invited her to England to paint miniatures for them. There, she was a formidable rival of some of her male contemporaries at the court, such as Holbein (FIG. 23-11A), and received greater compensation for her work than they did for theirs. Teerlinc's considerable skill is evident in a life-size portrait (FIG. 23-19) attributed to her, which depicts Elizabeth I as a composed, youthful princess. Daughter of Henry VIII and Anne

23-18 CATERINA VAN HEMESSEN, *Self-Portrait,* 1548. Oil on wood, 1′ ¾″ × 9⅞″. Kunstmuseum Basel, Basel. ◼◀

In this first known northern European self-portrait by a woman, Caterina van Hemessen represented herself as a confident artist momentarily interrupting her work to look out at the viewer.

23-19 Attributed to LEVINA TEERLINC, *Elizabeth I as a Princess,* ca. 1559. Oil on wood, 3′ 6¾″ × 2′ 8¼″. Royal Collection, Windsor Castle, Windsor. ◼◀

Teerlinc received greater compensation for her work for the British court than did her male contemporaries. Her considerable skill is evident in this life-size portrait of Elizabeth I as a young princess.

23-20 JOACHIM PATINIR, *Landscape with Saint Jerome*, ca. 1520–1524. Oil on wood, 2′ 5⅛″ × 2′ 11⅞″. Museo del Prado, Madrid. ◼◀

Joachim Patinir, a renowned Netherlandish landscape painter, subordinated the story of Saint Jerome to the depiction of craggy rock formations, verdant rolling fields, and expansive bodies of water.

1 ft.

Boleyn, Elizabeth was probably in her late 20s when she posed for this portrait. Appropriate to her station in life, Elizabeth wears an elegant brocaded gown, extravagant jewelry, and a headdress based on a style her mother popularized.

That van Hemessen and Teerlinc enjoyed such success is a testament to their determination and skill, given the difficulties women faced in a profession dominated by men. Women also played an important role as patrons in 16th-century northern Europe. Politically powerful women such as Margaret of Austria (regent of the Netherlands during the early 16th century; 1480–1530) and Mary of Hungary (queen consort of Hungary; 1505–1558) were avid collectors and patrons, and contributed significantly to the thriving state of the arts. As did other art patrons, these women collected and commissioned art not only for the aesthetic pleasure it provided but also for the status it bestowed on them and the cultural sophistication it represented.

JOACHIM PATINIR In addition to portrait and genre painting, landscape painting flourished in the Netherlands. Particularly well known for his landscapes was JOACHIM PATINIR (d. 1524). In fact, the word *Landschaft* (landscape) first emerged in German literature as a characterization of an artistic category when Dürer described Patinir as a "good landscape painter." In *Landscape with Saint Jerome* (FIG. 23-20), Patinir subordinated the saint, who removes a thorn from a lion's paw in the foreground, to the exotic and detailed landscape. Craggy rock formations, verdant rolling fields, villages with church steeples, expansive bodies of water, and a dramatic sky fill most of the panel. Patinir amplified the sense of distance by masterfully using color to enhance the visual effect of recession and advance.

PIETER BRUEGEL THE ELDER The greatest Netherlandish painter of the mid-16th century was PIETER BRUEGEL THE ELDER (ca. 1528–1569). Influenced by Patinir, Bruegel was also a landscape painter, but in his paintings, no matter how huge a slice of the world he depicted, human activities remain the dominant theme. As did many of his contemporaries, Bruegel traveled to Italy, where he probably spent almost two years, going as far south as Sicily. Unlike other artists, however, Bruegel chose not to incorporate classical elements into his paintings.

Bruegel's *Netherlandish Proverbs* (FIG. 23-21) depicts a Netherlandish village populated by a wide range of people (nobility, peasants, and clerics). From a bird's-eye view, the spectator encounters a mesmerizing array of activities reminiscent of the topsy-turvy scenes of Bosch (FIG. 23-1), but the purpose and meaning of Bruegel's anecdotal details are clear. By illustrating more than a hundred proverbs in this one painting, the artist indulged his Netherlandish audience's obsession with proverbs and passion for detailed and clever imagery. As the viewer scrutinizes the myriad vignettes within the painting, Bruegel's close observation and deep understanding of human nature become apparent. The proverbs depicted include, on the far left, a man in blue gnawing on a pillar ("He bites the column"—an image of hypocrisy). To his right, a man "beats his head against a wall" (an ambitious idiot). On the roof a man "shoots one arrow after the other, but hits nothing" (a shortsighted fool). In the far distance, the "blind lead the blind"—a subject to which Bruegel returned several years later in one of his most famous paintings (not illustrated).

In contrast to Patinir's Saint Jerome, lost in the landscape, the myriad, raucous cast of characters of Bruegel's *Netherlandish Proverbs* fills the panel, so much so the artist almost shut out the sky. *Hunters in the Snow* (FIG. 23-22) and *Fall of Icarus*

23-21 PIETER BRUEGEL THE ELDER, *Netherlandish Proverbs*, 1559. Oil on wood, 3′ 10″ × 5′ 4⅛″. Gemäldegalerie, Staatliche Museen zu Berlin, Berlin. ◼◀

In this painting of a Netherlandish village, Bruegel indulged his audience's obsession with proverbs and passion for clever imagery, and demonstrated his deep understanding of human nature.

1 ft.

23-22 PIETER BRUEGEL THE ELDER, *Hunters in the Snow*, 1565. Oil on wood, 3′ 10⅛″ × 5′ 3¾″. Kunsthistorisches Museum, Vienna.

In *Hunters in the Snow*, one of a series of paintings illustrating different seasons, Bruegel draws the viewer diagonally deep into the landscape by his mastery of line, shape, and composition.

1 ft.

23-22A BRUEGEL THE ELDER, *Fall of Icarus,* ca. 1555–1556.

(FIG. 23-22A) are very different in character and illustrate the dynamic variety of Bruegel's work. *Hunters* is one of a series of six paintings (some scholars think there were originally twelve) illustrating seasonal changes. The series grew out of the tradition of depicting seasons and peasants in Books of Hours (FIGS. 20-15 and 20-16). The painting shows human figures and landscape locked in winter cold, reflect-

ing the particularly severe winter of 1565, when Bruegel produced the work. The weary hunters return with their hounds, women build fires, skaters skim the frozen pond, and the town and its church huddle in their mantle of snow. Bruegel rendered the landscape in an optically accurate manner. It develops smoothly from foreground to background and draws the viewer diagonally into its depths. The painter's consummate skill in using line and shape and his subtlety in tonal harmony make this one of the great landscape paintings in Western art.

The Netherlands   **663**

SPAIN

Spain's ascent to power in Europe began in the mid-15th century with the marriage of Isabella of Castile (1451–1504) and Ferdinand of Aragon (1452–1516) in 1469. By the end of the 16th century, Spain had emerged as the dominant European power. Under the Habsburg rulers Charles V and Philip II, the Spanish Empire controlled a territory greater in extent than any ever known—a large part of Europe, the western Mediterranean, a strip of North Africa, and vast expanses in the New World. Spain acquired many of its New World colonies through aggressive overseas exploration. Among the most notable conquistadors sailing under the Spanish flag were Christopher Columbus (1451–1506), Vasco Nuñez de Balboa (ca. 1475–1517), Ferdinand Magellan (1480–1521), Hernán Cortés (1485–1547), and Francisco Pizarro (ca. 1470–1541). The Habsburg Empire, enriched by New World plunder, supported the most powerful military force in Europe. Spain defended and then promoted the interests of the Catholic Church in its battle against the inroads of the Protestant Reformation. Indeed, Philip II earned the title "Most Catholic King." Spain's crusading spirit, nourished by centuries of war with Islam, engaged body and soul in forming the most Catholic civilization of Europe and the Americas. In the 16th century, for good or for ill, Spain left the mark of its power, religion, language, and culture on two hemispheres.

COLEGIO DE SAN GREGORIO During the 15th century and well into the 16th, a Late Gothic style of architecture, the Plateresque, prevailed in Spain. *Plateresque* derives from the Spanish word *platero* (silversmith), and delicately executed ornamentation resembling metalwork is the defining characteristic of the Plateresque style. The Colegio de San Gregorio (Seminary of Saint Gregory; FIG. 23-23) in the Castilian city of Valladolid handsomely exemplifies the Plateresque manner, which Spanish expansion into the Western Hemisphere also brought to "New Spain" (FIG. 23-23A). Great carved retables, like the German altarpieces that influenced them (FIGS. 20-19, 20-20, and 23-2, *bottom*), appealed to church patrons and architects in Spain, and the portals of Plateresque facades often resemble elegantly carved retables set into an otherwise blank wall. The Plateresque entrance of San Gregorio is a lofty sculptured stone screen bearing no functional relation to the architecture behind it. On the entrance level, lacelike tracery reminiscent of Moorish design hems the flamboyant ogival arches. (Spanish hatred of the Moors did not prevent Spanish architects from adapting Moorish motifs.) A great screen, paneled into sculptured compartments, rises above the tracery. In the center, the branches of a huge pomegranate tree (symbolizing Granada, the Moorish capital of Spain the Habsburgs captured in 1492; see Chapter 10) wreathe the coat of arms of King Ferdinand and Queen Isabella. Cupids play among the tree branches, and, flanking the central panel, niches frame armed pages of the court, heraldic wild men symbolizing aggression, and armored soldiers, attesting to Spain's proud new militancy. In typical Plateresque and Late Gothic fashion, the activity of a thousand intertwined motifs unifies the whole design, which, in sum, creates an exquisitely carved panel greatly expanded in scale from the retables that inspired it.

23-23A Casa de Montejo, Mérida, 1549.

EL ESCORIAL Under Philip II, the Plateresque style gave way to an Italian-derived classicism that also characterized

23-23 Portal, Colegio de San Gregorio, Valladolid, Spain, ca. 1498.

The Plateresque architectural style takes its name from *platero* (Spanish, "silversmith"). At the center of this portal's Late Gothic tracery is the coat of arms of King Ferdinand and Queen Isabella.

16th-century French architecture (FIG. 23-13). The Italian style is on display in the expansive complex called El Escorial (FIG. 23-24), which JUAN BAUTISTA DE TOLEDO (d. 1567) and JUAN DE HERRERA (ca. 1530–1597), principally the latter, constructed for Philip II. In his will, Charles V stipulated that a "dynastic pantheon" be built to house the remains of past and future monarchs of Spain. Philip II, obedient to his father's wishes, chose a site some 30 miles northwest of Madrid in rugged terrain with barren mountains. Here, he built El Escorial, not only a royal mausoleum but also a church, a monastery, and a palace. Legend has it that the gridlike plan for the enormous complex, 625 feet wide and 520 feet deep, symbolized the gridiron on which Saint Lawrence, El Escorial's patron saint, suffered his martyrdom.

The vast structure is in keeping with Philip's austere character, his passionate Catholic religiosity, his proud reverence for his dynasty, and his stern determination to impose his will worldwide. He insisted that in designing El Escorial, the architects focus on simplicity of form, severity in the whole, nobility without arrogance, and majesty without ostentation. The result is a classicism of Doric severity, ultimately derived from Italian architecture and with the grandeur of Saint Peter's (FIGS. 24-3 and 24-4) implicit in the scheme, but unique in European architecture.

23-24 Juan de Herrera and Juan Bautista de Toledo, aerial view (looking southeast) of El Escorial, near Madrid, Spain, 1563–1584.

Conceived by Charles V and built by Philip II, El Escorial is a royal mausoleum, church, monastery, and palace in one. The complex is classical in style with severely plain walls and massive towers.

Only the three entrances, with the dominant central portal framed by superimposed orders and topped by a pediment in the Italian fashion, break the long sweep of the structure's severely plain walls. Massive square towers punctuate the four corners. The stress on the central axis, with its subdued echoes in the two flanking portals, anticipates the three-part organization of later Baroque facades (see Chapter 24). The construction material for the entire complex (including the church)—granite, a difficult stone to work—conveys a feeling of starkness and gravity. The church's massive facade and the austere geometry of the interior complex, with its blocky walls and ponderous arches, produce an effect of overwhelming strength and weight. The entire complex is a monument to the collaboration of a great king and remarkably understanding architects. El Escorial stands as the overpowering architectural expression of Spain's spirit in its heroic epoch and of the character of Philip II, the extraordinary ruler who directed it.

EL GRECO Reflecting the increasingly international character of European art as well as the mobility of artists, the greatest Spanish painter of the era was not a Spaniard. Born on Crete, Domenikos Theotokopoulos, called El Greco (ca. 1547–1614), emigrated to Italy as a young man. In his youth, he absorbed the traditions of Late Byzantine frescoes and mosaics. While still young, El Greco went to Venice, where he worked in Titian's studio, although Tintoretto's paintings seem to have made a stronger impression on him (see Chapter 22). A brief trip to Rome explains the influences of Roman and Florentine Mannerism on his work. By 1577, he had left for Spain to spend the rest of his life in Toledo.

El Greco's art is a strong personal blending of Byzantine and Mannerist elements. The intense emotionalism of his paintings, which naturally appealed to Spanish piety, and a great reliance on and mastery of color bound him to 16th-century Venetian art and to Mannerism. El Greco's art was not strictly Spanish (although it

appealed to certain sectors of that society), for it had no Spanish antecedents and little effect on later Spanish painters. Nevertheless, El Greco's hybrid style captured the fervor of Spanish Catholicism.

Burial of Count Orgaz (FIG. 23-25), painted in 1586 for the church of Santo Tomé in El Greco's adoptive home, Toledo, vividly expressed that fervor. El Greco based the painting on the legend that the count of Orgaz, who had died some three centuries before and who had been a great benefactor of Santo Tomé, was buried in the church by Saints Stephen and Augustine, who miraculously descended from Heaven to lower the count's body into its sepulcher. In the painting, El Greco carefully distinguished the terrestrial and celestial spheres. The brilliant Heaven that opens above irradiates the earthly scene. The painter represented the terrestrial realm with a firm realism, whereas he depicted the celestial, in his quite personal manner, with elongated undulating figures, fluttering draperies, and a visionary swirling cloud. Below, the two saints lovingly lower the count's armor-clad body, the armor and heavy draperies painted with all the rich sensuousness of the Venetian school. A solemn chorus of personages dressed in black fills the background. In the carefully individualized features of these figures (who include El Greco himself in a self-portrait, and his young son, Jorge Manuel, as well as the priest who commissioned the painting and the Spanish king Philip II), El Greco demonstrated he was also a great portraitist.

The upward glances of some of the figures below and the flight of an angel above link the painting's lower and upper spheres. The action of the angel, who carries the count's soul in his arms as Saint John and the Virgin intercede for it before the throne of Christ, reinforces this connection. El Greco's deliberate change in style to distinguish between the two levels of reality gives the viewer an opportunity to see the artist's early and late manners in the same work, one below the other. His relatively sumptuous and realistic presentation of the earthly sphere is still strongly rooted in Venetian art,

1 ft.

23-25 EL GRECO, *Burial of Count Orgaz*, 1586. Oil on canvas, 16′ × 12′. Santo Tomé, Toledo.

El Greco's art is a blend of Byzantine and Italian Mannerist elements. His intense emotional content captured the fervor of Spanish Catholicism, and his dramatic use of light foreshadowed the Baroque style.

but the abstractions and distortions El Greco used to show the immaterial nature of the heavenly realm characterize his later style. His elongated figures existing in undefined spaces, bathed in a cool light of uncertain origin, explain El Greco's usual classification as a Mannerist, but it is difficult to apply that label to him without reservation. Although he used Mannerist formal devices, El Greco's primary concerns were emotion and conveying his religious fervor or arousing that of others. The forcefulness of his paintings is the result of his unique, highly developed expressive style.

VIEW OF TOLEDO El Greco's singular vision is equally evident in one of his latest works, *View of Toledo* (FIG. 23-26), the only pure landscape he ever painted. As does so much of El Greco's work, this painting breaks sharply with tradition. The Greek-born artist depicted the Spanish city from a nearby hilltop and drew attention to the great spire of Toledo's cathedral by leading the viewer's eye along the diagonal line of the bridge crossing the Tajo and continuing with the city's walls. El Greco knew Toledo intimately, and every building is recognizable, although he rearranged some of their positions, moving, for example, the Alcazar palace to the right of the cathedral. Yet he rendered no structure in meticulous detail, as most Renaissance painters would have done, and the color palette is not true to nature but limited to greens and grays. The atmosphere is eerie. Dramatic bursts of light in the stormy sky cast a ghostly pall over the city. The artist applied oil pigment to canvas in broad brushstrokes typical of his late, increasingly abstract painting style, with the result that the buildings and trees do not have sharp contours and almost seem to shake.

Art historians have compared *View of Toledo* to Giorgione da Castelfranco's *Tempest* (FIG. 22-34) and the dramatic lighting to works by Tintoretto (FIG. 22-48), and indeed, El Greco's Venetian training is evident. Still, the closest parallels lie not in the past but in the future—in paintings such as Vincent van Gogh's *Starry Night* (FIG. 28-18) and in 20th-century Expressionism and Surrealism (see Chapter 29). El Greco's art is impossible to classify using conventional labels. Although he had ties to Mannerism and foreshadowed developments of the Baroque era in Spain and Italy—examined in the next chapter—he was a singular artist with a unique vision.

1 ft.

23-26 EL GRECO, *View of Toledo*, ca. 1610. Oil on canvas, 3′ 11¾″ × 3′ 6¾″. Metropolitan Museum of Art, New York (H. O. Havemeyer Collection. Bequest of Mrs. H. O. Havemeyer, 1929).

View of Toledo is the only pure landscape El Greco ever produced. The dark, stormy sky casts a ghostly pall over the city. The painting exemplifies the artist's late, increasingly abstract style.

HIGH RENAISSANCE AND MANNERISM IN NORTHERN EUROPE AND SPAIN

HOLY ROMAN EMPIRE

▌ Widespread dissatisfaction with the Church in Rome led to the Protestant Reformation, splitting Christendom in half. Protestants objected to the sale of indulgences and rejected most of the sacraments of the Catholic Church. They also condemned ostentatious church decoration as a form of idolatry that distracted the faithful from communication with God.

▌ As a result, Protestant churches were relatively bare, but art, especially prints, still played a role in Protestantism. Lucas Cranach the Elder, for example, effectively used visual imagery to contrast Catholic and Protestant views of salvation in his woodcut *Law and Gospel*.

▌ The greatest printmaker of the Holy Roman Empire was Albrecht Dürer, who was also a painter. Dürer was the first artist outside Italy to become an international celebrity. His work ranged from biblical subjects to botanical studies. *Fall of Man* reflects Dürer's studies of the Vitruvian theory of human proportions and of classical statuary. Dürer's engravings rival painting in tonal quality.

▌ Other German artists, such as Albrecht Altdorfer, achieved fame as landscape painters. Hans Holbein was a renowned portraitist who became court painter in England. His *French Ambassadors* portrays two worldly humanists and includes a masterfully rendered anamorphic skull.

Dürer, *Fall of Man*, 1504

Holbein, *The French Ambassadors*, 1533

FRANCE

▌ King Francis I fought against Holy Roman Emperor Charles V and declared Protestantism illegal in France. An admirer of Italian art, he invited several prominent Italian painters and sculptors to work at his court and decorate his palace at Fontainebleau.

▌ French architecture of the 16th century mixes Italian and Northern Renaissance elements, as in Pierre Lescot's design of the renovated Louvre palace and Francis's château at Chambord, which combines classical motifs derived from Italian palazzi with a Gothic roof silhouette.

Clouet, *Francis I*, ca. 1525–1530

THE NETHERLANDS

▌ The Netherlands was one of the most commercially advanced and prosperous countries in 16th-century Europe. Much of Netherlandish art of this period provides a picture of contemporary life and values.

▌ Pieter Aertsen of Antwerp, for example, painted *Butcher's Stall,* which seems to be a straightforward genre scene but includes the holy family offering alms to a beggar in the background, providing a stark contrast between gluttony and religious piety.

▌ Landscapes were the specialty of Joachim Patinir. Pieter Bruegel's repertory also included landscape painting. His *Hunters in the Snow* is one of a series of paintings depicting seasonal changes and the activities associated with them, as in traditional Books of Hours.

▌ Women artists of the period include Caterina van Hemessen, who painted the earliest northern European self-portrait of a woman, and Levina Teerlinc, who produced portraits for the English court.

Bruegel, *Hunters in the Snow,* 1565

SPAIN

▌ At the end of the 16th century, Spain was the dominant power in Europe with an empire greater in extent than any ever known, including vast territories in the New World.

▌ The Spanish Plateresque style of architecture takes its name from *platero* (silversmith) and features delicate ornamentation resembling metalwork.

▌ Under Philip II the Plateresque style gave way to an Italian-derived classicism, seen at its best in El Escorial, a royal mausoleum, monastery, and palace complex near Madrid.

▌ The leading painter of 16th-century Spain was the Greek-born El Greco, who combined Byzantine style, Italian Mannerism, and the religious fervor of Catholic Spain in works such as *Burial of Count Orgaz.*

Colegio de San Gregorio, Valladolid, ca. 1498

As water flows from a travertine grotto supporting an ancient Egyptian obelisk, Bernini's marble personifications of major rivers of four continents twist and gesticulate emphatically.

Crowning the grotto is Pope Innocent X's coat of arms and atop the obelisk is the Pamphili family's dove symbolizing the Holy Spirit and Christianity's triumph in all parts of the then-known world.

Each of the four rivers has an identifying attribute. The Ganges (Asia), easily navigable, holds an oar. The Plata (Americas) has a hoard of coins, signifying the wealth of the New World.

24-1 GIANLORENZO BERNINI, Fountain of the Four Rivers (looking southwest with Sant'Agnese in Agone in the background), Piazza Navona, Rome, Italy, 1648–1651. ◀◼

The Danube (Europe) gazes awestruck at the papal arms, and the Nile (Africa) covers his face—Bernini's acknowledgment that the Nile's source was unknown to Europeans at the time.

THE BAROQUE IN ITALY AND SPAIN

BAROQUE ART AND SPECTACLE

One of the most popular tourist attractions in Rome is the Fountain of the Four Rivers (FIG. 24-1) in Piazza Navona by GIANLORENZO BERNINI (1598–1680). Architect, painter, sculptor, playwright, and stage designer, Bernini was one of the most important and imaginative artists of the Baroque era in Italy and its most characteristic and sustaining spirit. Nonetheless, the fountain's patron, Pope Innocent X (r. 1644–1655), did not want Bernini to win this commission. Bernini had been the favorite sculptor of the Pamphili pope's predecessor, Urban VIII (r. 1623–1644), who spent so extravagantly on art and himself and his family that he nearly bankrupted the Vatican treasury. Innocent emphatically opposed the excesses of the Barberini pope and shunned Bernini, awarding new papal commissions to other sculptors and architects. Bernini was also in disgrace at the time because of his failed attempt to erect bell towers for the new facade (FIG. 24-3) of Saint Peter's. When Innocent announced a competition for a fountain in Piazza Navona (MAP 22-1), site of the Pamphili family's palace and parish church, Sant'Agnese in Agone (FIG. 24-1, *rear*), he pointedly did not invite Bernini to submit a design. However, the renowned sculptor succeeded in having a model of his proposed fountain placed where the pope would see it. When Innocent examined it, he was so captivated he declared the only way anyone could avoid employing Bernini was not to look at his work.

Bernini's bold design, executed in large part by his assistants, called for a sculptured travertine grotto supporting an ancient obelisk Innocent had transferred to Piazza Navona from the circus of the Roman emperor Maxentius (r. 305–312) on the Via Appia. The piazza was once the site of the stadium of Domitian (r. 81–96), a long and narrow arena for athletic contests, which explains the piazza's unusual shape and the church's name (*agone* means "foot race" in Italian). Water rushes from the artificial grotto into a basin filled with marble statues personifying major rivers of four continents—the Danube (Europe), Nile (Africa), Ganges (Asia), and Plata (Americas). The reclining figures twist and gesticulate, consistent with Baroque taste for movement and drama. The Nile covers his face—Bernini's way of acknowledging the Nile's source was unknown at the time. The Rio de la Plata has a hoard of coins, signifying the wealth of the New World. The Ganges, easily navigable, holds an oar. The Danube, awestruck, reaches up to the papal coat of arms. A second reference to Innocent X is the Pamphili dove at the apex of the obelisk, which also symbolizes the Holy Spirit and the triumph of Christianity in all parts of the then-known world. The scenic effect of the cascading water would have been heightened whenever Piazza Navona was flooded for festival pageants. Bernini's fountain epitomizes the Baroque era's love for uniting art and spectacle.

"BAROQUE" ART AND ARCHITECTURE

Art historians traditionally describe 17th-century European art as *Baroque,* but the term is problematic because the period encompasses a broad range of styles and genres. Although its origin is unclear, "Baroque" may have come from the Portuguese word *barroco,* meaning an irregularly shaped pearl. Use of the term can be traced to the late 18th century, when critics disparaged the Baroque period's artistic production, in large part because of perceived deficiencies in comparison with the art of the Italian Renaissance. Over time, this negative connotation faded, but the term stuck. "Baroque" remains useful to describe the distinctive new style that emerged during the early 1600s—a style of complexity and drama seen especially in Italian art of this period. Whereas Renaissance artists reveled in the precise, orderly rationality of classical models, Baroque artists embraced dynamism, theatricality, and elaborate ornamentation, all used to spectacular effect, often on a grandiose scale, as in Bernini's Four Rivers Fountain (FIG. 24-1).

ITALY

Although in the 16th century the Roman Catholic Church launched the Counter-Reformation in response to—and as a challenge to—the Protestant Reformation, the considerable appeal of Protestantism continued to preoccupy the popes throughout the 17th century. The Treaty of Westphalia (see Chapter 25) in 1648 had formally recognized the principle of religious freedom, serving to validate Protestantism (predominantly in the German states). With the Catholic Church as the leading art patron in 17th-century Italy, the aim of much of Italian Baroque art was to restore Roman Catholicism's predominance and centrality. The Council of Trent, one 16th-century Counter-Reformation initiative, firmly resisted Protestant objections to using images in religious worship, insisting on their necessity for teaching the laity (see "Religious Art in Counter-Reformation Italy," Chapter 22, page 617). Baroque art in Italy was therefore often overtly didactic.

Architecture and Sculpture

Italian 17th-century art and architecture, especially in Rome, embodied the renewed energy of the Counter-Reformation and communicated it to the populace. At the end of the 16th century, Pope Sixtus V (r. 1585–1590) had played a key role in the Catholic Church's lengthy campaign to reestablish its preeminence. He

24-2 CARLO MADERNO, facade of Santa Susanna (looking north), Rome, Italy, 1597–1603.

Santa Susanna's facade is one of the earliest manifestations of the Baroque spirit. The rhythm of the columns and pilasters mounts dramatically toward the emphatically stressed vertical axis.

augmented the papal treasury and intended to rebuild Rome as an even more magnificent showcase of Church power. Between 1606 and 1667, several strong and ambitious popes—Paul V, Urban VIII, Innocent X, and Alexander VII—made many of Sixtus V's dreams a reality. Rome still bears the marks of their patronage everywhere.

SANTA SUSANNA The facade (FIG. 24-2) CARLO MADERNO (1556–1629) designed at the turn of the century for the Roman church of Santa Susanna stands as one of the earliest manifestations of the

THE BAROQUE IN ITALY AND SPAIN

1600	1625	1650	1675	1700
▎ Paul V commissions Maderno to complete Saint Peter's	▎ Borromini designs San Carlo alle Quattro Fontane and the Chapel of Saint Ivo in Rome	▎ Bernini designs the colonnaded oval piazza in front of Saint Peter's	▎ Gaulli and Pozzo paint illusionistic ceiling frescoes in Il Gesù and Sant'Ignazio	
▎ Carracci introduces quadro riportato fresco painting in the Palazzo Farnese	▎ Gentileschi, the leading woman artist of the 17th century, achieves international renown	▎ Murillo creates the canonical image of the *Virgin of the Immaculate Conception*	▎ Guarini brings the Baroque architectural style of Rome to Turin	
▎ Caravaggio pioneers tenebrism in Baroque painting	▎ Ribera and Zurburán paint scenes of martyrdom in Catholic Spain	▎ Velázquez paints *Las Meninas*		
▎ Bernini creates *David* and *Apollo and Daphne* for Cardinal Scipione Borghese	▎ Philip IV of Spain appoints Velázquez court painter			

24-3 CARLO MADERNO, east facade of Saint Peter's, Vatican City, Rome, Italy, 1606–1612.

For the facade of Saint Peter's, Maderno elaborated on his design for Santa Susanna (FIG. 24-2), but the two outer bays with bell towers were not part of his plan and detract from the verticality he sought.

Baroque artistic spirit. In its general appearance, Maderno's facade resembles Giacomo della Porta's immensely influential design for Il Gesù (FIG. 22-56), the church of the Jesuits in Rome. But the later facade has a greater verticality that concentrates and dramatizes the major features of its model. The tall central section projects forward from the horizontal lower story, and the scroll buttresses connecting the two levels are narrower and set at a sharper angle. The elimination of an arch framing the pediment over the doorway further enhances the design's vertical thrust. The rhythm of Santa Susanna's vigorously projecting columns and pilasters mounts dramatically toward the emphatically stressed central axis. The recessed niches, which contain statues and create pockets of shadow, heighten the sculptural effect.

MADERNO AND SAINT PETER'S The drama inherent in Santa Susanna's facade appealed to Pope Paul V (r. 1605–1621), who commissioned Maderno in 1606 to complete Saint Peter's in Rome. As the symbolic seat of the papacy, the church Constantine originally built over the first pope's tomb (see Chapter 8) was the very emblem of Western Christendom. In light of Counter-Reformation concerns, the Baroque popes wanted to conclude

the already century-long rebuilding project and reap the prestige embodied in the mammoth new church. In many ways Maderno's facade (FIG. 24-3) is a gigantic expansion of the elements of Santa Susanna's first level. But the compactness and verticality of the smaller church's facade are not as prominent because Saint Peter's enormous breadth counterbalances them. Mitigating circumstances must be taken into consideration when assessing this design, however. Because Maderno had to match the preexisting core of an incomplete building, he did not have the luxury of formulating a totally new concept for Saint Peter's. Moreover, the facade's two outer bays with bell towers were not part of Maderno's original design. Hence, had the facade been constructed according to the architect's initial concept, it would have exhibited greater verticality and visual coherence.

Maderno's plan (MAP **24-1**) also departed from the Renaissance central plans for Saint Peter's designed by Bramante (FIG. 22-22) and, later, by Michelangelo (FIG. 22-24). Paul V asked Maderno to add three nave bays to the earlier nucleus because Church officials had decided the central plan was too closely associated with ancient temples, such as the Pantheon (FIG. 7-49). Further, the spatial organization of the longitudinal basilican plan of the original

The dramatic gesture of embrace Bernini's colonnade makes as worshipers enter Saint Peter's piazza symbolizes the welcome the Catholic Church wished to extend during the Counter-Reformation.

fourth-century church (FIG. 8-9) reinforced the symbolic distinction between clergy and laity and also was much better suited for religious processions. Lengthening the nave, however, pushed the dome farther back from the facade, and all but destroyed the effect Michelangelo had planned—a structure pulled together and dominated by its dome. When viewed at close range, the dome barely emerges above the facade's soaring frontal plane. Seen from farther back (FIG. 24-3), it appears to have no drum. Visitors must move back quite a distance from the front (or fly over the church, FIG. 24-4) to see the dome and drum together. Today, visitors to the Vatican can appreciate the effect Michelangelo intended only by viewing Saint Peter's from the back (FIG. 22-25).

BERNINI AND SAINT PETER'S

Old Saint Peter's had a large forecourt, or *atrium* (FIG. 8-9, *right*), in front of the church proper, and in the mid-17th century, Gianlorenzo Bernini, who had long before established his reputation as a supremely gifted architect and sculptor (see page 669), received the prestigious commission to construct a monumental colonnade-framed *piazza* (plaza; FIG. 24-4) in front of Maderno's facade. Bernini's design had to incorporate two preexisting structures on the site—an obelisk the ancient Romans had brought from Egypt (which Pope Sixtus V had moved to its present location in 1585 as part of his vision of Christian triumph in Rome) and a fountain Maderno constructed in front of the church. Bernini co-opted these features to define the long axis of a vast oval embraced by two colonnades joined to Maderno's facade. Four rows of huge Tuscan columns make up the two colonnades, which terminate in classical temple fronts. The colonnades extend a dramatic gesture of embrace to all who enter the piazza, symbolizing the welcome the Roman Catholic Church gave its members during the Counter-Reformation. Bernini himself referred to his colonnades as the welcoming arms of Saint Peter's.

Beyond their symbolic resonance, the colonnades served visually to counteract the natural perspective and bring the facade closer to the viewer. (Bernini's mastery of perspective in architecture is even more evident in his contemporaneous design for the Scala Regia [FIG. 24-4A] of the Vatican palace, a project he undertook at the request of Pope Alexander VII [r. 1655–1667].) Emphasizing the facade's height in this manner, Bernini subtly and effectively compensated for its extensive width. Thus, a Baroque transformation expanded the compact central designs of Bramante and Michelangelo into a dynamic complex of axially ordered elements that reach out and enclose spaces of vast dimension. By its sheer scale and theatricality, the completed Saint Peter's fulfilled the desire of the Counter–Reformation Church to present an awe-inspiring and authoritative vision of itself.

24-4A BERNINI, Scala Regia, Vatican, 1663–1666.

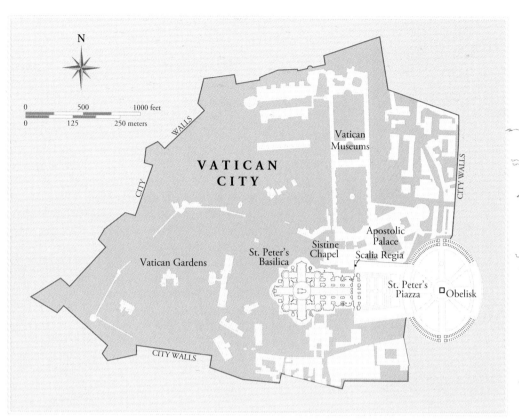

MAP 24-1 Vatican City.

24-5 GIANLORENZO BERNINI, baldacchino (looking west), Saint Peter's, Vatican City, Rome, Italy, 1624–1633.

Bernini's baldacchino serves both functional and symbolic purposes. It marks Saint Peter's tomb and the high altar, and it visually bridges human scale to the lofty vaults and dome above.

BALDACCHINO Prior to being invited to design the piazza in front of Saint Peter's, Bernini had won the commission to erect a gigantic bronze *baldacchino* (FIG. 24-5) under Giacomo della Porta's dome (FIG. 22-25). Completed between 1624 and 1633, the canopylike structure (*baldacco* is Italian for "silk from Baghdad," such as for a cloth canopy) stands almost 100 feet high (the height of an average eight-story building) and serves both functional and symbolic purposes. It marks the high altar and the tomb of Saint Peter, and it visually bridges human scale to the lofty vaults and dome above. Further, for worshipers entering the nave of the huge church, it provides a dramatic, compelling presence at the crossing. Its columns also create a visual frame for the elaborate sculpture representing the throne of Saint Peter (the Cathedra Petri) at the far end of Saint Peter's (FIG. 24-5, *rear*). On a symbolic level, the structure's decorative elements speak to the power of the Catholic Church and of Pope Urban VIII, Partially fluted and wreathed with vines, the baldacchino's four spiral columns are Baroque versions of the comparable columns of the ancient baldacchino over the same spot in Old Saint Peter's, thereby invoking the past to reinforce the primacy of the Roman Catholic Church in the 17th century. At the top of the vine-entwined columns, four colossal angels stand guard at the upper corners of the canopy. Forming the canopy's apex are four serpentine brackets that elevate the orb and the cross. Since the time of Constantine (FIG. 7-81, *right;* compare FIG. 9-2), the orb and the cross had served as symbols of the Church's triumph. The baldacchino also features numerous bees, symbols of Urban VIII's family, the Barberini. The structure effectively gives visual form to the triumph of Christianity and the papal claim to doctrinal supremacy.

The construction of the baldacchino was itself a remarkable feat. Each of the bronze columns consists of five sections cast from wood models using the *lost-wax process* (see "Hollow-Casting Life-Size Bronze Statues," Chapter 5, page 130). Although Bernini did some of the work himself, including cleaning and repairing the wax molds and doing the final cleaning and *chasing* (engraving and embossing) of the bronze casts, he contracted out much of the project to experienced bronze-casters and sculptors. The superstructure is predominantly cast bronze, although some of the sculptural elements are brass or wood. The enormous scale of the baldacchino required a considerable amount of bronze. On Urban VIII's orders, workmen dismantled the portico of the Pantheon (FIG. 7-49) to acquire the bronze for the baldacchino—ideologically appropriate, given the Church's rejection of polytheism.

The concepts of triumph and grandeur permeate every aspect of the 17th-century design of Saint Peter's. Suggesting a great and solemn procession, the main axis of the complex traverses the piazza (marked by the central obelisk) and enters Maderno's nave. It comes to a temporary halt at the altar beneath Bernini's baldacchino, but it continues on toward its climactic destination at another great altar in the apse.

from those earlier masterpieces, however. Michelangelo portrayed David before his encounter with his gigantic adversary, and Donatello and Verrocchio depicted David after his triumph over Goliath. Bernini chose to represent the combat itself and aimed to catch the split-second of maximum action. Bernini's *David,* his muscular legs widely and firmly planted, begins the violent, pivoting motion that will launch the stone from his sling. (A bag full of stones is at David's left hip, suggesting he thought the fight would be tough and long.) Unlike Myron, the fifth-century BCE Greek sculptor who froze his *Discus Thrower* (FIG. 5-39) at a fleeting moment of inaction, Bernini selected the most dramatic of an implied sequence of poses, requiring the viewer to think simultaneously of the continuum and of this tiny fraction of it. The suggested continuum imparts a dynamic quality to the statue. In Bernini's *David,* the energy confined in Michelangelo's figures (FIGS. 22-14 and 22-15) bursts forth. The Baroque statue seems to be moving through time and through space. This kind of sculpture cannot be inscribed in a cylinder or confined in a niche. Its unrestrained action demands space around it. Nor is it self-sufficient in the Renaissance sense, as its pose and attitude direct attention beyond it to the unseen Goliath. Bernini's *David* moves out into the space surrounding it, as do Apollo and Daphne in the marble group (FIG. 24-6A) he carved for the same patron, Cardinal Scipione Borghese (1576–1633). Further, the expression

24-6A BERNINI, *Apollo and Daphne,* 1623–1624.

24-6 GIANLORENZO BERNINI, *David,* 1623. Marble, 5′ 7″ high. Galleria Borghese, Rome. ◼◀

Bernini's sculptures are expansive and theatrical, and the element of time plays an important role in them. His emotion-packed *David* seems to be moving through both time and space.

DAVID Bernini's baldacchino is, like his Four Rivers Fountain (FIG. 24-1), a masterpiece of the sculptor's craft even more than the architect's. In fact, although Bernini achieved an international reputation as an architect, his fame rests primarily on his sculpture. The biographer Filippo Baldinucci (1625–1696) observed: "[T]here was perhaps never anyone who manipulated marble with more facility and boldness. He gave his works a marvelous softness . . . making the marble, so to say, flexible."[1] Bernini's sculpture is expansive and theatrical, and the element of time usually plays an important role in it, as in the pronounced movement of the personified rivers—and the cascading water—in his Piazza Navona fountain.

A sculpture that predates both the Four Rivers Fountain and Saint Peter's baldacchino is Bernini's *David* (FIG. 24-6). The Baroque master surely knew the Renaissance statues of the biblical hero fashioned by Donatello (FIG. 21-12), Verrocchio (FIG. 21-13), and Michelangelo (FIG. 22-13). Bernini's *David* differs fundamentally

24-7 GIANLORENZO BERNINI, *Ecstasy of Saint Teresa,* Cornaro chapel, Santa Maria della Vittoria, Rome, Italy, 1645–1652. Marble, height of group 11′ 6″. ◼◀

The passionate drama of Bernini's depiction of Saint Teresa correlated with the ideas of Ignatius Loyola, who argued that the re-creation of spiritual experience would encourage devotion and piety.

24-8 GIANLORENZO BERNINI, Cornaro chapel, Santa Maria della Vittoria, Rome, Italy, 1645–1652.

In the Cornaro chapel, Bernini, the quintessential Baroque artist, marshaled the full capabilities of architecture, sculpture, and painting to create an intensely emotional experience for worshipers.

conversion occurred after the death of her father, when she fell into a series of trances, saw visions, and heard voices. Feeling a persistent pain, she attributed it to the fire-tipped arrow of divine love an angel had thrust repeatedly into her heart. In her writings, Saint Teresa described this experience as making her swoon in delightful anguish.

In Bernini's hands, the entire Cornaro chapel became a theater for the production of this mystical drama. The niche in which it takes place appears as a shallow *proscenium* (the part of the stage in front of the curtain) crowned with a broken Baroque pediment and ornamented with polychrome marble. On either side of the chapel, sculpted portraits of members of the family of Cardinal Federico Cornaro (1579–1673) watch the heavenly drama unfold from choice balcony seats. Bernini depicted the saint in ecstasy, unmistakably a mingling of spiritual and physical passion, swooning back on a cloud, while the smiling angel aims his arrow. The

of intense concentration on David's face contrasts vividly with the classically placid visages of Donatello's and Verrocchio's versions and is more emotionally charged even than Michelangelo's. The tension in David's face augments the dramatic impact of Bernini's sculpture.

ECSTASY OF SAINT TERESA Another work displaying the motion and emotion that are hallmarks of Italian Baroque art is Bernini's *Ecstasy of Saint Teresa* (FIG. 24-7) in the Cornaro chapel (FIG. 24-8) of the Roman church of Santa Maria della Vittoria. The work exemplifies the Baroque master's refusal to limit his statues to firmly defined spatial settings. For this commission, Bernini marshaled the full capabilities of architecture, sculpture, and painting to charge the entire chapel with palpable tension. In the Cornaro chapel, Bernini drew on the considerable knowledge of the theater he derived from writing plays and producing stage designs. The marble sculpture that serves as the chapel's focus depicts Saint Teresa of Avila (1515–1582), a nun of the Carmelite order and one of the great mystical saints of the Spanish Counter-Reformation. Her

sculptor's supreme technical virtuosity is evident in the visual differentiation in texture among the clouds, rough nun's cloth, gauzy material, smooth flesh, and feathery wings—all carved from the same white marble. Light from a hidden window of yellow glass pours down on golden rays suggesting the radiance of Heaven, whose painted representation covers the vault.

The passionate drama of Bernini's *Ecstasy of Saint Teresa* correlated with the ideas disseminated earlier by Ignatius Loyola (1491–1556), who founded the Jesuit order in 1534 and whom the Catholic Church canonized as Saint Ignatius in 1622. In his book *Spiritual Exercises,* Ignatius argued that the re-creation of spiritual experiences in artworks would do much to increase devotion and piety. Thus, theatricality and sensory impact were useful vehicles for achieving Counter-Reformation goals (see "Religious Art in Counter-Reformation Italy," Chapter 22, page 617). Bernini was a devout Catholic, which undoubtedly contributed to his understanding of those goals. His inventiveness, technical skill, sensitivity to his patrons' needs, and energy made him the quintessential Italian Baroque artist.

Borromini rejected the notion that a church should have a flat frontispiece. He set San Carlo's facade in undulating motion, creating a dynamic counterpoint of concave and convex elements.

SAN CARLO ALLE QUATTRO FONTANE

As gifted as Bernini was as an architect, FRANCESCO BORROMINI (1599–1667) took Italian Baroque architecture to even greater dramatic heights. In the little church of San Carlo alle Quattro Fontane (Saint Charles at the Four Fountains; FIG. 24-9), Borromini went much further than any of his predecessors or contemporaries in emphasizing a building's sculptural qualities. Although Maderno incorporated sculptural elements in his designs for the facades of Santa Susanna (FIG. 24-2) and Saint Peter's (FIG. 24-3), those church fronts still develop along relatively lateral planes. Borromini set his facade in undulating motion, creating a dynamic counterpoint of concave and convex elements on two levels (for example, the sway of the cornices). He enhanced the three-dimensional effect with deeply recessed niches. This facade is not the traditional flat frontispiece that defines a building's outer limits. It is a pulsating, engaging screen inserted between interior and exterior space, designed not to separate but to provide a fluid transition between the two. In fact, San Carlo has not one but two facades, underscoring the functional interrelation of the building and its environment. The second facade, a narrow bay crowned with its own small tower, turns away from the main facade and, following the curve of the street, faces an intersection. Borromini's innovative style had an enormous influence on later Baroque architects throughout Italy. The Palazzo Carignano (FIG. 24-9A) in Turin, for example, designed by GUARINO GUARINI (1624–1683), depends heavily on Borromini's work in Rome.

24-9A GUARINI, Palazzo Carignano, Turin, 1679–1692.

The interior of San Carlo alle Quattro Fontane is not only Borromini's ingenious response to an awkward site but also a provocative variation on the theme of the centrally planned church. In plan (FIG. 24-10), San Carlo is a hybrid of a *Greek cross* (a cross with four arms of equal length) and an oval, with a long axis between entrance and apse. The side walls move in an undulating flow that reverses the facade's motion. Vigorously projecting columns define the space into which they protrude just as much as they accent the walls to which they are attached. Capping this molded interior space is a deeply coffered oval dome (FIG. 24-11) that seems to float on the light entering through windows hidden in its base. Rich variations on the basic theme of the oval—dynamic curves relative to the static circle—create an interior that flows from entrance to altar, unimpeded by the segmentation so characteristic of Renaissance buildings.

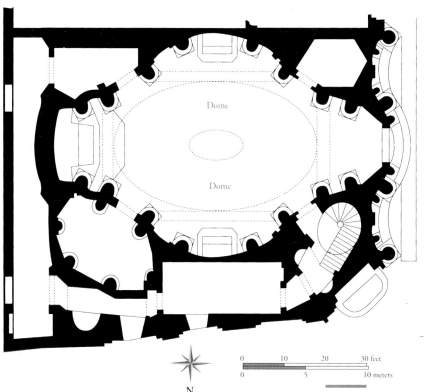

24-10 Francesco Borromini, plan of San Carlo alle Quattro Fontane, Rome, Italy, 1638–1641.

The plan of San Carlo is a hybrid of a Greek cross and an oval. The walls pulsate in a way that reverses the facade's movement. The molded, dramatically lit space flows from entrance to altar.

24-11 Francesco Borromini, San Carlo alle Quattro Fontane (view into dome), Rome, Italy, 1638–1641.

In place of a traditional round dome, Borromini capped the interior of San Carlo with a deeply coffered oval dome that seems to float on the light entering through windows hidden in its base.

24-12 Francesco Borromini, Chapel of Saint Ivo (looking east), College of the Sapienza, Rome, Italy, begun 1642.

In characteristic fashion, Borromini played concave against convex forms on the upper level of the Chapel of Saint Ivo. Pilasters restrain the forces that seem to push the bulging forms outward.

CHAPEL OF SAINT IVO Borromini carried the unification of interior space even further in the Chapel of Saint Ivo (FIG. 24-12) at the east end of the courtyard of the College of the Sapienza (Wisdom) in Rome. In his characteristic manner, Borromini played concave against convex forms on the upper level of the chapel's exterior. The arcaded courtyard, which frames the lower levels of the chapel's facade, had already been constructed when Borromini began work, and he adjusted his design to achieve a harmonious merging of the new and older parts of the college. Above the inward-curving lower two stories of the Saint Ivo chapel rises a convex drumlike structure that supports the dome's lower parts. Clusters of pilasters restrain the forces that seem to push the bulging forms outward. Buttresses above the pilasters curve upward to brace a tall, ornate lantern topped by a spiral that, screwlike, seems to fasten the structure to the sky.

The centralized plan (FIG. 24-13) of the interior of the Saint Ivo chapel is that of a star with rounded points and apses on all sides. Indentations and projections along the angled curving walls create a highly complex plan, with all the elements fully reflected in the interior elevation. From floor to lantern, the wall panels rise in a continuously tapering sweep halted only momentarily by a single horizontal cornice (FIG. 24-14). Thus, the dome is not a separate unit placed on a supporting block, as in Renaissance buildings. It is an organic part that evolves out of and shares the qualities of the supporting walls, and it cannot be separated from them. This carefully designed progression up through the lantern creates a dynamic and cohesive shell that encloses and energetically molds a scalloped fragment of space. Few architects have matched Borromini's ability to translate extremely complicated designs into masterfully unified structures, but some later architects, including Guarini, an accomplished mathematician as well as architect, designed even more complex domes (FIG. 24-14A).

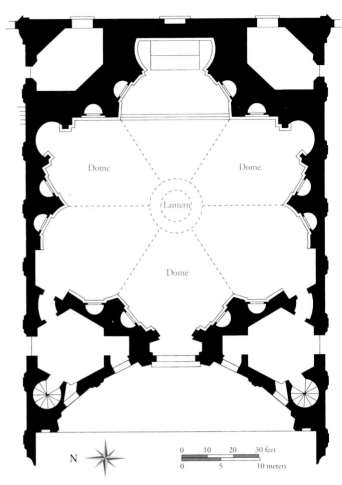

24-13 Francesco Borromini, plan of the Chapel of Saint Ivo, College of the Sapienza, Rome, Italy, begun 1642.

The interior elevation of Borromini's Saint Ivo chapel fully reflects all the elements of its highly complex plan, which is star-shaped with rounded points and apses on all sides.

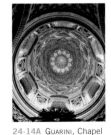

24-14A GUARINI, Chapel of the Holy Shroud, Turin, 1667–1694.

Painting

Although architecture and sculpture provided the most obvious vehicles for manipulating space and creating theatrical effects, painting continued to be an important art form in 17th-century Italy. Among the most noted Italian Baroque painters were Annibale Carracci and Caravaggio, whose styles, although different, were both thoroughly in accord with the period.

Unlike Renaissance domes, Borromini's Baroque dome is an organic part that evolves out of and shares the qualities of the supporting walls, and it cannot be separated from them.

cant institution of its kind in the history of Western art. The Carracci established it on the premises that art can be taught—the basis of any academic philosophy of art—and that art instruction must include the classical and Renaissance traditions in addition to the study of anatomy and life drawing.

In *Flight into Egypt* (FIG. 24-15), based on the biblical narrative from Matthew 2:13–14, Annibale Carracci created the "ideal" or "classical" landscape, in which nature appears ordered by divine law and human reason. Tranquil hills and fields, quietly gliding streams, serene skies, unruffled foliage, shepherds with their flocks—all the props of the pastoral scene and mood familiar in Venetian Renaissance paintings (FIG. 22-35)—expand to fill the picture space in *Flight into Egypt* and similar paintings. Carracci regularly included screens of trees in the foreground, dark against the sky's even light. In contrast to many Renaissance artists, he did not create the sense of deep space through linear perspective but rather by varying light and shadow

ANNIBALE CARRACCI A native of Bologna, ANNIBALE CARRACCI (1560–1609) received much of his training at an art academy founded there by several members of his family, among them his cousin Ludovico Carracci (1555–1619) and brother Agostino Carracci (1557–1602). The Bolognese academy was the first significant

24-15 ANNIBALE CARRACCI, *Flight into Egypt*, 1603–1604. Oil on canvas, 4′ × 7′ 6″. Galleria Doria Pamphili, Rome.

Carracci's landscapes idealize antiquity and the idyllic life. Here, the pastoral setting takes precedence over the narrative of Mary, the Christ Child, and Saint Joseph wending their way slowly to Egypt.

1 ft.

24-16 ANNIBALE CARRACCI, *Loves of the Gods,* ceiling frescoes in the gallery, Palazzo Farnese (FIG. 22-26), Rome, Italy, 1597–1601. ◼◀

On the shallow curved vault of this gallery in the Palazzo Farnese, Carracci arranged the mythological scenes in a quadro riportato format resembling easel paintings on a wall.

to suggest expansive atmosphere. In *Flight into Egypt,* streams or terraces, carefully placed one above the other and narrowed, zigzag through the terrain, leading the viewer's eyes back to the middle ground. There, many Venetian Renaissance landscape artists depicted walled towns or citadels, towers, temples, monumental tombs, and villas (as Carracci did in *Flight into Egypt*). These constructed environments captured idealized antiquity and the idyllic life. Although the artists often took the subjects for these classically rendered scenes from religious or heroic stories, they favored pastoral landscapes over narratives. Here, Annibale greatly diminished the size of Mary, the Christ Child, and Saint Joseph, who simply become part of the landscape as they wend their way slowly to Egypt after having been ferried across a stream.

LOVES OF THE GODS Carracci's most notable works are his frescoes (FIG. 24-16) in the Palazzo Farnese in Rome. Cardinal Odoardo Farnese (1573–1626), a wealthy descendant of Pope Paul III,

who built the palace (FIG. 22-26) in the 16th century, commissioned Annibale to decorate the ceiling of the palace's gallery to celebrate the wedding of the cardinal's brother. Appropriately, the title of the fresco's iconographic program is *Loves of the Gods*—interpretations of the varieties of earthly and divine love in classical mythology.

Carracci arranged the scenes in a format resembling framed easel paintings on a wall, but in the Farnese gallery the paintings cover a shallow curved vault. The term for this type of simulation of easel painting for ceiling design is *quadro riportato* (transferred framed painting). By adapting the northern European and Venetian tradition of easel painting to the Florentine and Roman fresco tradition, Carracci reoriented the direction of painting in central Italy. He made quadro riportato fashionable for more than a century.

Flanking the framed pictures are polychrome seated nude youths, who turn their heads to gaze at the scenes around them, and

24-17 CARAVAGGIO, *Calling of Saint Matthew*, ca. 1597–1601. Oil on canvas, 11' 1" × 11' 5". Contarelli chapel, San Luigi dei Francesi, Rome. ◼◀

The stark contrast of light and dark was a key feature of Caravaggio's style. Here, Christ, cloaked in mysterious shadow, summons Levi the tax collector (Saint Matthew) to a higher calling.

tanding Atlas figures painted to resemble marble statues. Carracci derived these motifs from the Sistine Chapel ceiling (FIG. 22-17), ut he did not copy Michelangelo's figures. Notably, the chiaro-curo of the Farnese gallery frescoes differs for the pictures and the gures surrounding them. Carracci modeled the figures inside the anels in an even light. In contrast, light from beneath illuminates he outside figures, as if they were tangible three-dimensional be-ings or statues lit by torches in the gallery below. This interest in il-usion, already manifest in the Renaissance, continued in the grand eiling compositions (FIGS. 24-21 to 24-24) of the mature Baroque. n the crown of the vault, the long panel, *Triumph of Bacchus,* is n ingenious mixture of Raphael's drawing style and lighting and itian's more sensuous and animated figures. Carracci succeeded adjusting their authoritative styles to create something of his wn—no easy achievement.

ARAVAGGIO Michelangelo Merisi, known as CARAVAGGIO 573–1610) after his northern Italian birthplace, developed a nique style that had tremendous influence throughout Europe. is outspoken disdain for the classical masters (probably more rhe-rical than real) drew bitter criticism from many painters, one of hom denounced him as the "anti-Christ of painting." Giovanni ietro Bellori (1613–1696), the most influential critic of the age and admirer of Annibale Carracci, believed Caravaggio's refusal to nulate the models of his distinguished predecessors threatened e whole classical tradition of Italian painting that had reached s zenith in Raphael's work (see "Giovanni Pietro Bellori on An-bale Carracci and Caravaggio," page 682). Yet despite this criti-sm and the problems in Caravaggio's troubled life (police records

are an important source of infor-mation about the artist), Caravag-gio received many commissions, both public and private, and numer-ous painters paid him the supreme compliment of borrowing from his innovations. His influence on later artists, as much outside Italy as within, was immense. In his art, Caravaggio injected naturalism into both religion and the classics, reducing them to human dramas played out in the harsh and dingy settings of his time and place. The unidealized figures he selected from the fields and the streets of Italy, however, were effective precisely because of their familiarity.

CALLING OF SAINT MATTHEW An early Caravaggio masterpiece, *Calling of Saint Matthew* (FIG. 24-17), is one of two large canvases honoring Saint Matthew the artist created for the Conta-relli chapel in San Luigi dei Francesi (Saint Louis of the French) in Rome. Caravaggio received the com-mission for the San Luigi paintings upon the recommendation of Cardinal Del Monte, for whom the artist had recently painted *Musicians* (FIG. 24-17A). The commonplace setting of the painting—a tavern with unadorned walls—is typical of Caravaggio. Into this mundane envi-ronment, cloaked in mysterious shadow and almost unseen, Christ, identifiable

24-17A CARAVAGGIO, *Musicians,* ca. 1595.

initially only by his indistinct halo, enters from the right. With a commanding gesture, he summons Levi, the Roman tax collector, to a higher calling. The astonished Levi—his face highlighted for the viewer by the beam of light emanating from an unspecified source above Christ's head and outside the picture—points to himself in disbelief. Although Christ's extended arm is reminiscent of the Lord's in Michelangelo's *Creation of Adam* (FIG. 22-18), the position of his hand and wrist is similar to Adam's. This reference was highly appropriate, because the Church considered Christ to be the second Adam. Whereas Adam was responsible for the fall of humankind, Christ is the vehicle of its redemption. The conversion of Levi (who became Matthew) brought his salvation.

Giovanni Pietro Bellori on Annibale Carracci and Caravaggio

The written sources to which art historians turn as aids in understanding the art of the past are invaluable, but they reflect the personal preferences and prejudices of the writers. Pliny the Elder, for example, claimed in the first century CE that "art ceased" after the death of Alexander the Great—a remark usually interpreted as expressing his disapproval of Hellenistic art in contrast to Classical art (see Chapter 5).* Giorgio Vasari, the biographer and champion of Italian Renaissance artists, condemned Gothic art as "monstrous and barbarous," and considered medieval art in general a distortion of the noble art of the Greeks and Romans (see Chapter 13).† Giovanni Pietro Bellori, the leading biographer of Baroque artists, similarly recorded his admiration for Renaissance classicism as well as his distaste for Mannerism and realism in his opposing evaluations of Annibale Carracci and Caravaggio.

In the opening lines of his *Vita* (Life) of Carracci, Bellori praised "the divine Raphael . . . [whose art] raised its beauty to the summit, restoring it to the ancient majesty of . . . the Greeks and the Romans" and lamented that soon after, "artists, abandoning the study of nature, corrupted art with the *maniera*, that is to say, with the fantastic idea based on practice and not on imitation." But fortunately, Bellori observed, just "when painting was drawing to its end," Annibale Carracci rescued "the declining and extinguished art."‡

Bellori especially lauded Carracci's Palazzo Farnese frescoes (FIG. 24-16):

> No one could imagine seeing anywhere else a more noble and magnificent style of ornamentation, obtaining supreme excellence in the compartmentalization and in the figures and executed with the grandest manner in the design with the just proportion and the great strength of chiaroscuro. . . . Among modern works they have no comparison.§

In contrast, Bellori characterized Caravaggio as talented and widely imitated but misguided in his rejection of classicism in favor of realism.

[Caravaggio] began to paint according to his own inclinations; not only ignoring but even despising the superb statuary of antiquity and the famous paintings of Raphael, he considered nature to be the only subject fit for his brush. As a result, when he was shown the most famous statues of [the ancient sculptors] Phidias [FIG. 5-46] and Glykon [FIG. 5-66] in order that he might use them as models, his only answer was to point toward a crowd of people, saying that nature had given him an abundance of masters. . . . [W]hen he came upon someone in town who pleased him he made no attempt to improve on the creations of nature."

[Caravaggio] claimed that he imitated his models so closely that he never made a single brushstroke that he called his own, but said rather that it was nature's. Repudiating all other rules, he considered the highest achievement not to be bound to art. For this innovation he was greatly acclaimed, and many talented and educated artists seemed compelled to follow him . . . Nevertheless he lacked *invenzione*, decorum, *disegno,* or any knowledge of the science of painting. The moment the model was taken from him, his hand and his mind became empty. . . . Thus, as Caravaggio suppressed the dignity of art, everybody did as he pleased, and what followed was contempt for beautiful things, the authority of antiquity and Raphael destroyed. . . . Now began the imitation of common and vulgar things, seeking out filth and deformity.††

*Pliny, *Natural History,* 25.52.
† Giorgio Vasari, *Introduzione alle tre arti del disegno* (1550), ch. 3.
‡Giovanni Pietro Bellori, *Le vite de' pittori, scultori e architetti moderni* (Rome, 1672). Translated by Catherine Enggass, *The Lives of Annibale and Agostino Carracci by Giovanni Pietro Bellori* (University Park: Pennsylvania University Press, 1968), 5–6.
§Ibid., 33.
"Translated by Howard Hibbard, *Caravaggio* (New York: Harper & Row, 1983), 362.
††Ibid., 371–372.

CONVERSION OF SAINT PAUL A piercing ray of light illuminating a world of darkness and bearing a spiritual message is also a central feature of *Conversion of Saint Paul* (FIG. 24-18), which Caravaggio painted for the Cerasi chapel in Santa Maria del Popolo. He depicted the saint-to-be at the moment of his conversion, flat on his back with his arms thrown up. In the background, an old groom seems preoccupied with caring for the horse. At first inspection, little here suggests the momentous significance of the unfolding spiritual event. The viewer could be witnessing a mere stable accident, not a man overcome by a great miracle. Although many of his contemporaries criticized Caravaggio for departing from traditional depictions of religious scenes, the eloquence and humanity with which he imbued his paintings impressed many others.

To compel worshipers' interest and involvement in Paul's conversion, Caravaggio employed a variety of ingenious formal devices. Here, as in the slightly later *Entombment* (FIG. 24-18A), he used a perspective and a chiaroscuro intended to bring viewers as close as possible to the scene's space and action, almost as if they

were participants. The low horizon line augments the sense of inclusion. Further, Caravaggio designed *Conversion of Saint Paul* for its specific location on the chapel wall, positioned at the line of sight of an average-height person standing at the chapel entrance. The sharply lit figures emerge from the dark background as if illuminated by the light from the chapel's windows. The lighting resembles that of a stage production and is analogous to the rays in Bernini's *Ecstasy of Saint Teresa* (FIGS. 24-7 and 24-8).

24-18A CARAVAGGIO, *Entombment,* ca. 1603

Caravaggio's figures are still heroic with powerful bodies and clearly delineated contours in the Renaissance tradition, but the stark and dramatic contrast of light and dark, which at first shocked and then fascinated his contemporaries, obscures the more traditional aspects of his style. Art historians call Caravaggio's use of dark settings enveloping their occupants—which profound

24-18 CARAVAGGIO, *Conversion of Saint Paul,* ca. 1601. Oil on canvas, 7′ 6″ × 5′ 9″. Cerasi chapel, Santa Maria del Popolo, Rome.

Caravaggio used perspective, chiaroscuro, and dramatic lighting to bring viewers into this painting's space and action, almost as if they were participants in Saint Paul's conversion to Christianity.

1 ft.

24-19 ARTEMISIA GENTILESCHI, *Judith Slaying Holofernes,* ca. 1614–1620. Oil on canvas, 6′ 6⅓″ × 5′ 4″. Galleria degli Uffizi, Florence. ◼◀

Narratives involving heroic women were a favorite theme of Gentileschi. In *Judith Slaying Holofernes,* the dramatic lighting of the action in the foreground emulates Caravaggio's tenebrism.

influenced European art, especially in Spain and the Netherlands— *tenebrism,* from the Italian word *tenebroso,* or "shadowy" manner. In Caravaggio's work, tenebrism also contributed greatly to the essential meaning of his pictures. In *Conversion of Saint Paul,* the dramatic spotlight shining down upon the fallen Paul is the light of divine revelation converting him to Christianity.

ARTEMISIA GENTILESCHI Caravaggio's combination of naturalism and drama appealed both to patrons and artists, and he had many followers. Among them was the most celebrated woman artist of the era, ARTEMISIA GENTILESCHI (ca. 1593–1653), whose father Orazio (1563–1639), her teacher, was himself strongly influenced by Caravaggio. The daughter's successful career, pursued in Florence, Venice, Naples, and Rome, helped disseminate Caravaggio's style throughout the peninsula.

In *Judith Slaying Holofernes* (FIG. **24-19**), Gentileschi adopted the tenebrism and what might be called the "dark" subject matter Caravaggio favored. Significantly, she chose a narrative involving a heroic woman, a favorite theme of hers. The story, from the book of Judith, relates the delivery of Israel from the Assyrians. Having succumbed to Judith's charms, the Assyrian general Holofernes invited her to his tent for the night. When he fell asleep, Judith cut off his head. In this version of the scene (Gentileschi produced more than one painting of the subject), Judith and her maidservant behead Holofernes. Blood spurts everywhere as the two women

summon all their strength to wield the heavy sword. The tension and strain are palpable. The controlled highlights on the action in the foreground recall Caravaggio's work and heighten the drama here as well.

LA PITTURA During the brief period Orazio Gentileschi was the official painter of the English king Charles I (r. 1625–1649), Artemisia painted perhaps her most unusual work, an allegory of Painting (*La Pittura;* FIG. **24-20**). Most art historians believe the painting, which was in the collection of the king at the time of his execution in 1649, is a self-portrait.

Gentileschi's personified image of Painting as a woman closely follows the prescription for representing *La Pittura* in a widely circulated handbook by Cesare Ripa (d. 1622) called *Iconologia,* published in 1593. Until the 16th century, only Poetry and Music had a fixed iconography. The inclusion of Painting in Ripa's handbook reflects the newly elevated status painters held during the Renaissance. He describes *La Pittura* as a beautiful woman with disheveled hair painting with her brush in one hand and holding her palette in the other. She wears a gold chain with a pendant in the form of a mask, because masks imitate faces and painting is the art of imitation. The chain symbolizes the continuous linkage of master to pupil from generation to generation. Gentileschi incorporated all of these traits into her painting, but instead of representing *La Pittura* as a frontal, emblematic figure, she portrayed her as actively

The Letters of Artemisia Gentileschi

Artemisia Gentileschi (FIG. 24-20) was the most renowned woman painter in Europe during the first half of the 17th century and the first woman ever admitted to membership in Florence's Accademia del Disegno (Academy of Design). As did other women who could not become apprentices in all-male studios (see "The Artist's Profession," Chapter 20, page 545), she learned her craft from her father. Never forgotten in subsequent centuries, Artemisia's modern fame stems from the seminal 1976 exhibition *Women Artists: 1550–1950,** which opened a new chapter in feminist art history.

In addition to scores of paintings created for wealthy patrons, among them the king of England and the grand duke of Tuscany, Gentileschi left behind 28 letters, some of which reveal she believed patrons treated her differently because of her gender. Three 1649 letters written in Naples to Don Antonio Ruffo (1610–1678) in Messina make her feelings explicit.

> I fear that before you saw the painting you must have thought me arrogant and presumptuous. . . . [I]f it were not for Your Most Illustrious Lordship . . . I would not have been induced to give it for one hundred and sixty, because everywhere else I have been I was paid one hundred *scudi* per figure. . . . You think me pitiful, because a woman's name raises doubts until her work is seen.[†]

> I was mortified to hear that you want to deduct one third from the already very low price that I had asked. . . . It must be that in your heart Your Most Illustrious Lordship finds little merit in me.[‡]

> As for my doing a drawing and sending it, [tell the gentleman who wishes to know the price for a painting that] I have made a solemn vow never to send my drawings because people have cheated me. In particular, just today I found myself [in the situation] that, having done a drawing of souls in Purgatory for the Bishop of St. Gata, he, in order to spend less, commissioned another painter to do the painting using my work. If I were a man, I can't imagine it would have turned out this way, because when the concept has been real-

24-20 ARTEMISIA GENTILESCHI, *Self-Portrait as the Allegory of Painting*, ca. 1638–1639. Oil on canvas, 3′ 2⅞″ × 2′ 5⅝″. Royal Collection, Kensington Palace, London. ◼◀

Gentileschi here portrayed herself in the guise of *La Pittura* (Painting) with brush and palette. To paint a self-portrait from the side, Gentileschi had to set up a pair of mirrors to record her features.

ized and defined with lights and darks, and established by means of planes, the rest is a trifle.[§]

*Ann Sutherland Harris and Linda Nochlin, *Women Artists: 1550–1950* (Los Angeles: Los Angeles County Museum of Art, 1976), 118–124.
[†]Letter dated Janary 30, 1649. Translated by Mary D. Garrard, *Artemisia Gentileschi: The Image of the Female Hero in Italian Baroque Art* (Princeton, N.J.: Princeton University Press, 1989), 390.
[‡]Letter dated October 23, 1649. Ibid., 395–396.
[§]Letter dated November 13, 1649. Ibid., 397–398.

engaged in her craft, seen from her left side. The viewer's eye follows the line of her left arm through the curve of her shoulders and right arm to her right hand, the instrument of artistic genius. It is noteworthy that the canvas in this painting is blank. This is not a self-portrait of the artist at work on a specific painting (compare FIGS. 23-18, 25-11, 26-15, and 26-16) but a portrait of Gentileschi as Painting herself.

In almost all Renaissance and Baroque self-portraits, the artist gazes at the viewer. The frontal view not only provides the fullest view of the artist's features, but it is also the easiest to paint because the artist needs only to look in a mirror in order to record his or her features (FIG. 22-43). To create this self-portrait, however, Gentileschi had to set up two mirrors in order to paint her likeness from

an angle, a highly original break from tradition and an assertion of her supreme skill in a field dominated by men (see "The Letters of Artemisia Gentileschi," above).

GUIDO RENI Caravaggio was not the only early-17th-century painter to win a devoted following. GUIDO RENI (1575–1642), known to his many admirers as "the divine Guido," trained in the Bolognese art academy founded by the Carracci family. The influence of Annibale Carracci and Raphael is evident in *Aurora* (FIG. 24-21), a ceiling fresco in the Casino Rospigliosi in Rome. Aurora (Dawn) leads Apollo's chariot, while the Hours dance about it. Guido conceived *Aurora* as a quadro riportato, following the format of the paintings in Annibale's *Loves of the Gods* (FIG. 24-16), and

24-21 GUIDO RENI, *Aurora*, ceiling fresco in the Casino Rospigliosi, Rome, Italy, 1613–1614.

The "divine Guido" conceived *Aurora* as a quadro riportato, reflecting his training in the Bolognese art academy. The scene of Dawn leading Apollo's chariot derives from ancient Roman reliefs.

provided the quadro with a complex and convincing illusionistic frame. The fresco exhibits a fluid motion, soft modeling, and sure composition, although without Raphael's sculpturesque strength. It is an intelligent interpretation of the Renaissance master's style. Consistent with the precepts of the Bolognese academy, the painter also looked to antiquity for models. The ultimate sources for the *Aurora* composition were Roman reliefs (FIG. 7-42) and coins depicting emperors in triumphal chariots accompanied by flying Victories and other personifications.

PIETRO DA CORTONA The experience of looking up at a painting is different from viewing a painting hanging on a wall. The considerable height and the expansive scale of most ceiling frescoes induce a feeling of awe. Patrons who wanted to burnish their public image or control their legacy found monumental ceiling frescoes to be perfect vehicles. In 1633, Pope Urban VIII commissioned a ceiling fresco for the Gran Salone (the main reception hall) of the Palazzo Barberini in Rome. The most important decorative commission of the 1630s, the lucrative assignment went to PIETRO DA CORTONA (1596–1669), a Tuscan architect and painter who had moved to Rome two decades before. The grandiose and spectacular *Triumph of the Barberini* (FIG. **24-22**) overwhelms spectators with

24-22 PIETRO DA CORTONA, *Triumph of the Barberini,* ceiling fresco in the Gran Salone, Palazzo Barberini, Rome, Italy, 1633–1639.

In this dramatic ceiling fresco, Divine Providence appears in a halo of radiant light directing Immortality, holding a crown of stars, to bestow eternal life on the family of Pope Urban VIII.

24-23 Giovanni Battista Gaulli, *Triumph of the Name of Jesus*, ceiling fresco with stucco figures on the nave vault of Il Gesù (FIG. 22-56), Rome, Italy, 1676–1679.

In the nave of Il Gesù, gilded architecture opens up to offer the faithful a glimpse of Heaven. To heighten the illusion, Gaulli painted figures on stucco extensions that project outside the painting's frame.

the glory of the Barberini family (and Urban VIII in particular). The iconographic program for this fresco, designed by the poet Francesco Bracciolini (1566–1645), centered on the accomplishments of the Barberini. Divine Providence appears in a halo of radiant light directing Immortality, holding a crown of stars, to bestow eternal life on the family. The virtues Faith, Hope, and Charity hold aloft a gigantic laurel wreath (also a symbol of immortality), which frames three bees (the Barberini family's symbols, which also appeared in Bernini's baldacchino, FIG. 24-5). Also present are the papal tiara and keys announcing the personal triumphs of Urban VIII.

GIOVANNI BATTISTA GAULLI The dazzling spectacle of ceiling frescoes also proved very effective for commissions illustrating religious themes. Church authorities realized paintings high above the ground offered perfect opportunities to impress on worshipers the glory and power of the Catholic Church. In conjunction with the theatricality of Italian Baroque architecture and sculpture, monumental frescoes on church ceilings contributed to creating transcendent spiritual environments well suited to the needs of the Catholic Church in Counter-Reformation Rome.

Triumph of the Name of Jesus (FIG. **24-23**) in the nave of Il Gesù (FIGS. 22-56 and 22-57) vividly demonstrates the dramatic impact Baroque ceiling frescoes could have. As the mother church of the Jesuit order, Il Gesù played a prominent role in Counter-Reformation efforts. In this immense fresco by Giovanni Battista Gaulli (1639–1709), gilded architecture opens up in the center of the ceiling to offer the faithful a stunning glimpse of Heaven. Gaulli represented Jesus as a barely visible monogram (IHS) in a blinding radiant light floating heavenward. In contrast, sinners experience a violent descent back to Earth. The painter glazed the gilded architecture to suggest shadows, thereby enhancing the scene's illusionistic quality. To further heighten the illusion, Gaulli painted many of the sinners on three-dimensional stucco extensions projecting outside the painting's frame.

FRA ANDREA POZZO Another master of ceiling decoration was Fra Andrea Pozzo (1642–1709), a lay brother of the Jesuit order and a master of perspective, on which he wrote an influential treatise. Pozzo designed and executed the vast ceiling fresco *Glorification of Saint Ignatius* (FIG. **24-24**) for the church of Sant'Ignazio in Rome. Like Il Gesù, Sant'Ignazio was a prominent Counter-Reformation church because of its dedication to the founder of the Jesuit order. The Jesuits played a major role in Catholic education and sent legions of missionaries to the New World and Asia. As

Gaulli did in Il Gesù, Pozzo created the illusion of Heaven opening up above the congregation. To accomplish this, the artist painted an extension of the church's architecture into the vault so the roof seems to be lifted off. As Heaven and Earth commingle, Christ receives Saint Ignatius in the presence of figures personifying the four corners of the world. A disk in the nave floor marks the spot where the viewer should stand to gain the whole perspective illusion. For worshipers looking up from this point, the vision is complete. They find themselves in the presence of the heavenly and spiritual.

The effectiveness of Italian Baroque religious art depended on the drama and theatricality of individual images, as well as on the interaction and fusion of architecture, sculpture, and painting. Sound enhanced this experience. Architects designed churches with acoustical effects in mind, and in an Italian Baroque church filled with music, the power of both image and sound must have been immensely moving. Through simultaneous stimulation of both the senses of sight and hearing, the faithful might well have been transported into a trancelike state that would, indeed, as the great English poet John Milton (1608–1674) eloquently stated in *Il Penseroso* (1631), "bring all Heaven before [their] eyes."[2]

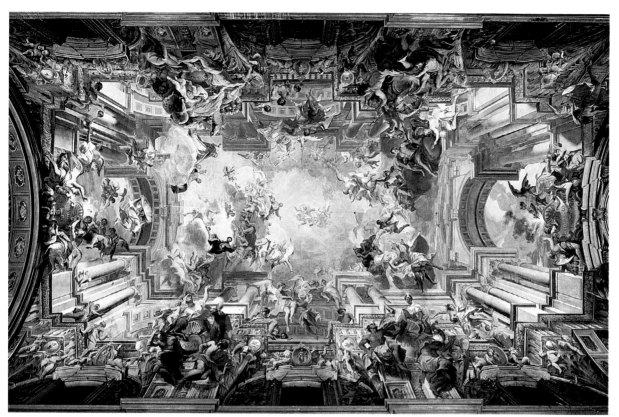

24-24 FRA ANDREA POZZO, *Glorification of Saint Ignatius*, ceiling fresco in the nave of Sant'Ignazio, Rome, Italy, 1691–1694.

By merging real and painted architecture, Pozzo created the illusion the vaulted ceiling of Sant'Ignazio has been lifted off and the nave opens to Heaven above the worshipers' heads.

SPAIN

During the 16th century, Spain had established itself as an international power. The Habsburg kings had built a dynastic state encompassing Portugal, part of Italy, the Netherlands, and extensive areas of the New World (see Chapters 23 and 35). By the beginning of the 17th century, however, the Habsburg Empire was struggling, and although Spain mounted an aggressive effort during the Thirty Years' War (see Chapter 25), by 1660 the imperial age of the Spanish Habsburgs was over. In part, the demise of the Habsburg Empire was due to economic woes. The military campaigns Philip III (r. 1598–1621) and his son Philip IV (r. 1621–1665) waged during the Thirty Years' War were costly and led to higher taxes. The increasing tax burden placed on Spanish subjects in turn incited revolts and civil war in Catalonia and Portugal in the 1640s, further straining an already fragile economy.

Painting

Although the dawn of the Baroque period found the Spanish kings struggling to maintain control of their dwindling empire, both Philip III and Philip IV realized the prestige great artworks brought and the value of visual imagery in communicating to a wide audience. Thus, both of them continued to spend lavishly on art.

JUAN SÁNCHEZ COTÁN One painter who made a major contribution to the development of Spanish art, although he did not receive any royal commissions, was JUAN SÁNCHEZ COTÁN (1560–1627). Born in Orgaz, outside Toledo, Sánchez Cotán moved to Granada and became a Carthusian monk in 1603. Although he painted religious subjects, his greatest works are the *still lifes* (paintings of artfully arranged inanimate objects) he produced before entering monastic life (and never thereafter). Few in number, they nonetheless established still-life painting as an important genre in 17th-century Spain.

Still Life with Game Fowl (FIG. 24-25) is one of Sánchez Cotán's most ambitious compositions, but it conforms to the pattern he adopted for all of his still lifes. A niche or a window—the artist clearly wished the setting to be indeterminate—fills the entire surface of the canvas. At the bottom, fruits and vegetables, including a melon—cut open with a slice removed—rest on a ledge. Above, suspended on strings from a nail or hook outside the frame, are a quince and four game fowl. All are meticulously rendered and

24-25 JUAN SÁNCHEZ COTÁN, *Still Life with Game Fowl*, ca. 1600–1603. Oil on canvas, 2′ 2¾″ × 2′ 10⅞″. Art Institute of Chicago, Chicago (gift of Mr. and Mrs. Leigh B. Block).

Sánchez Cotán established still life as an important genre in Spain. His compositions feature brightly illuminated fruits, vegetables, and birds, hanging or on a ledge, against a dark background.

brightly illuminated, enhancing the viewer's sense of each texture, color, and shape, yet the background is impenetrable shadow. The sharp and unnatural contrast between light and dark imbues the still life with a sense of mystery absent, for example, in Dutch still-life paintings (FIGS. 23-17, 25-1, 25-22, and 25-23). There may, in fact, be a spiritual reference. Sánchez Cotán once described his 11 paintings of fruits, vegetables, and birds as "offerings to the Virgin"—probably a reference to the Virgin as the *fenestra coeli* ("window to Heaven") and the source of spiritual food for the faithful.

BARTOLOMÉ ESTEBAN MURILLO
In the 17th century, Spain maintained its passionate commitment to Catholic orthodoxy, and as in Counter-Reformation Italy, Spanish Ba-

24-25A MURILLO, *Immaculate Conception*, ca. 1661–1670.

roque artists sought ways to move viewers and to encourage greater devotion and piety. BARTOLOMÉ ESTEBAN MURILLO (1617–1682), for example, formulated the canonical image of the *Virgin of the Immaculate Conception* (FIG. 24-25A), in which Mary is a beautiful young woman ascending to Heaven. But scenes of death and martyrdom also had great appeal in Spain. They provided artists with opportunities both to depict extreme emotion and to elicit passionate feelings in viewers. Spain prided itself on its saints—Saint Teresa of Avila (FIG. 24-8) and Saint Ignatius Loyola (FIG. 24-24) were both Spanish-born—and martyrdom scenes surfaced frequently in Spanish Baroque art.

JOSÉ DE RIBERA
As a young man, JOSÉ (JUSEPE) DE RIBERA (ca. 1588–1652) emigrated to Naples and fell under the spell of Caravaggio, whose innovative style he introduced to Spain. Emulating Caravaggio, Ribera made naturalism and compelling drama primary ingredients of his paintings, which often embraced brutal themes, reflecting the harsh times of the Counter-Reformation and the Spanish taste for stories showcasing courage and devotion. Ribera's *Martyrdom of Saint Philip* (FIG. 24-26) is grim and dark in subject and form. Scorning idealization of any kind, Ribera represented Philip's executioners hoisting him into position after tying him to a cross, the instrument of Christ's own martyrdom. The saint's rough, heavy body and swarthy, plebeian features express a kinship between him and his tormentors, who are similar to the types of figures found in Caravaggio's paintings. The patron of this painting is unknown, but it is possible Philip IV commissioned the work, because Saint Philip was the king's patron saint.

FRANCISCO DE ZURBARÁN
Another prominent Spanish painter of dramatic works was FRANCISCO DE ZURBARÁN (1598–1664), whose primary patrons throughout his career were rich Spanish monastic orders. Many of his paintings are quiet and contemplative, appropriate for prayer and devotional purposes. Zurbarán painted *Saint Serapion* (FIG. 24-27) as a devotional image for the funerary chapel of the monastic Order of Mercy in Seville. The saint, who participated in the Third Crusade of 1196, suffered martyrdom while preaching the Gospel to Muslims. According to one account, the monk's captors tied him to a tree and then tortured and decapitated him. The Order of Mercy dedicated itself

24-26 JOSÉ DE RIBERA, *Martyrdom of Saint Philip*, ca. 1639. Oil on canvas, 7′ 8″ × 7′ 8″. Museo del Prado, Madrid.

Martyrdom scenes were popular in Counter-Reformation Spain. Scorning idealization of any kind, Ribera represented Philip's executioners hoisting him into position to die on a cross.

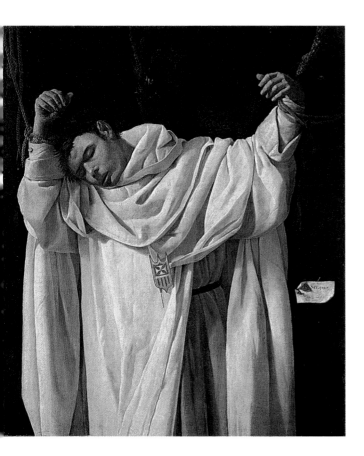

to self-sacrifice, and Serapion's membership in this order amplified the resonance of Zurbarán's painting. In *Saint Serapion*, the monk emerges from a dark background and fills the foreground. The bright light shining on him calls attention to the saint's tragic death and increases the dramatic impact of the image. In the background are two barely visible tree branches. A small note next to the saint identifies him for viewers. The coarse features of the Spanish monk label him as common, no doubt evoking empathy from a wide audience.

DIEGO VELÁZQUEZ The foremost Spanish painter of the Baroque age—and the greatest beneficiary of royal patronage—was Diego Velázquez (1599–1660). An early work, *Water Carrier of Seville* (FIG. **24-28**), painted when Velázquez was only about 20 years old, already reveals his impressive command of the painter's craft. In this genre scene that seems to convey a deeper significance, Velázquez rendered the figures with clarity and dignity, and his careful and convincing depiction of the water jugs in the foreground, complete with droplets of water, adds to the scene's credibility. The plebeian nature of the figures and the contrast of darks and lights again reveal the influence of Caravaggio, whose work Velázquez had studied.

24-28A Velázquez, *Christ on the Cross*, ca. 1631–1632.

As did many other Spanish artists, Velázquez produced religious pictures, for example, *Christ on the Cross* (FIG. **24-28A**), as well as genre scenes, but his renown in his day rested primarily on the works he painted for King Philip IV (see "Velázquez and Philip IV," page 690). After the king appointed Velázquez court painter, the artist largely abandoned both religious and genre subjects in favor of royal portraits (FIG. **24-28B**) and canvases recording historical events.

24-28B Velázquez, *Philip IV*, 1644.

24-28 Diego Velázquez, *Water Carrier of Seville*, ca. 1619. Oil on canvas, 3′ 5½″ × 2′ 7½″. Victoria & Albert Museum, London.

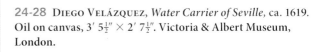

Velázquez and Philip IV

Trained in Seville, Diego Velázquez was quite young when he came to the attention of Philip IV. The painter's immense talent impressed the king, and Philip named him chief court artist and palace chamberlain, a position that also involved overseeing the rapidly growing royal art collection and advising the king on acquisitions and display. Among the works in Philip IV's possession were paintings by Titian, Annibale Carracci, Guido Reni, Albrecht Dürer, and Velázquez's famous Flemish contemporary, Peter Paul Rubens (see Chapter 25).

With the exception of two extended trips to Italy and a few excursions, Velázquez remained in Madrid for the rest of his life. His close relationship with Philip IV and his high office as chamberlain gave him prestige and a rare opportunity to fulfill the promise of his genius. One sign of Velázquez's fertile imagination as well as mastery of the brush is that he was able to create timeless artworks out of routine assignments to commemorate the achievements of his patron, as he did in his record of the Spanish victory over the Dutch in 1625 (*Surrender of Breda*, FIG. 24-29). Velázquez also painted dozens of portraits of Philip IV (FIG. 24-28B) and his family and retinue, including *Las Meninas* (FIG. 24-30), one of the greatest paintings in the history of Western art, a work Philip admired so much he displayed it in his personal office.

24-29 DIEGO VELÁZQUEZ, *Surrender of Breda,* 1634–1635. Oil on canvas, 10′ 1″ × 12′ $\frac{1}{2}$″. Museo del Prado, Madrid.

As Philip IV's court artist, Velázquez produced many history paintings, including fictional representations such as this one depicting the Dutch mayor of Breda surrendering to the Spanish general.

SURRENDER OF BREDA In 1635, Velázquez painted *Surrender of Breda* (FIG. 24-29) as part of an extensive program of decoration for the Hall of Realms in Philip IV's new secondary pleasure palace in Madrid, the Palacio del Buen Retiro. The huge canvas (more than 12 feet long and almost as tall) was one of 10 paintings celebrating recent Spanish military successes around the globe. It commemorates the Spanish victory over the Dutch at Breda in 1625. Among the most troublesome situations for Spain was the conflict in the Netherlands. Determined to escape Spanish control, the northern Netherlands broke from the Habsburg Empire in the late 16th century. Skirmishes continued to flare up along the border between the northern (Dutch) and southern (Spanish) Netherlands, and in 1625 Philip IV sent General Ambrogio di Spínola to Breda to reclaim the town for Spain.

Velázquez depicted the victorious Spanish troops, organized and well armed, on the right side of the painting. In sharp contrast, the defeated Dutch on the left appear bedraggled and disorganized. In the center foreground, the mayor of Breda, Justinus of Nassau, hands the city's keys to the Spanish general—although no encounter of this kind ever occurred. Velázquez's fictional record of the event glorifies not only the strength of the Spanish military but the benevolence of Spínola as well. Velázquez did not portray the Spanish general astride his horse, lording over the vanquished Dutch mayor, but rather painted him standing and magnanimously stopping Justinus from kneeling. Indeed, the terms of surrender were notably lenient, and Spínola allowed the Dutch to retain their arms—which they used to recapture the city in 1637.

LAS MENINAS After an extended visit to Rome from 1648 to 1651, Velázquez returned to Spain. In 1656, he painted his greatest work, *Las Meninas* (*The Maids of Honor;* FIG. **24-30**). The setting is the artist's studio in the palace of the Alcázar, the official royal residence in Madrid. After the death of Prince Baltasar Carlos in 1646, Philip IV ordered part of the prince's chambers converted into a studio for Velázquez. The painter represented himself stand-

24-30 DIEGO VELÁZQUEZ, *Las Meninas* (*The Maids of Honor*), 1656. Oil on canvas, 10′ 5″ × 9′. Museo del Prado, Madrid. ◼◄

Velázquez intended this huge and complex work, with its cunning contrasts of real, mirrored, and picture spaces, to elevate both himself and the profession of painting in the eyes of Philip IV.

In the 17th century, an important new class of patrons emerged in the Dutch Republic—successful merchants who took pride in their material possessions, the fruit of worldwide trade.

Claesz's mastery of the oil medium is evident in details such as the glass ball on the left side of the table, in which the viewer sees the reflected image of the artist painting this still life.

Dutch Baroque still-life paintings are meticulously crafted images that are both scientific in their accurate portrayal of devices such as this timepiece and poetic in their beauty and lyricism.

25-1 PIETER CLAESZ, *Vanitas Still Life,* 1630s. Oil on panel, 1′ 2″ × 1′ 11½″. Germanisches Nationalmuseum, Nuremberg.

THE BAROQUE IN NORTHERN EUROPE

Calvinist morality tempered Dutch citizens' delight in accumulated wealth. In this vanitas still life, the skull and timepiece are *mementi mori,* reminders of life's transience.

STILL-LIFE PAINTING IN THE DUTCH REPUBLIC

In 1648, after decades of continuous border skirmishes with the Spaniards, the northern Netherlands achieved official recognition as the United Provinces of the Netherlands (the Dutch Republic; MAP 25-1). The new independent republic owed its ascendance largely to its success in international trade. Dutch ships laden with goods roamed the world, sailing as far as North and South America, western Africa, China, Japan, and the Pacific islands.

Peter Mundy, a widely traveled Englishman, commented in 1640 on the irony that the Dutch Republic produced almost nothing on its own land yet enjoyed great wealth and could afford rare commodities from around the world:

> For although the land (and that with much labour) is brought only to pasture . . . yet by means of their shipping they are plentifully supplied with what the earth affords for the use of man . . . from any part of the world . . . Europe, Asia, Africa or America . . . with the most precious and rich commodities of those parts.[1]

The prosperous Dutch were justifiably proud of their accomplishments, and the popularity of still-life paintings—particularly images of accumulated goods—reflected this pride. These paintings of worldly possessions marked the emergence of an important new class of art patrons—wealthy merchants—who had tastes distinctly different from those of the leading patrons elsewhere in Baroque Europe, namely royalty and the Catholic Church. Dutch still lifes, which were well suited to the Protestant ethic rejecting most religious art, are among the finest ever painted. They are meticulously crafted images both scientific in their optical accuracy and poetic in their beauty and lyricism.

One of the best Dutch paintings of this genre is *Vanitas Still Life* (FIG. 25-1) by Pieter Claesz (1597–1660), in which the painter presented the material possessions of a prosperous household strewn across a tabletop or dresser. The ever-present morality and humility central to the Calvinist faith tempered Dutch pride in worldly goods, however. Thus, although Claesz fostered the appreciation and enjoyment of the beauty and value of the objects he depicted, he also reminded the viewer of life's transience by incorporating references to death. Art historians call works of this type *vanitas* (vanity) paintings, and each feature a *memento mori* (reminder of death). In *Vanitas Still Life,* references to mortality include the skull, timepiece, tipped glass, and cracked walnut. All suggest the passage of time or something or someone that was here but now is gone. Claesz emphasized this element of time (and demonstrated his technical virtuosity) by including a self-portrait reflected in the glass ball on the left side of the table. He appears to be painting this still life. But in an apparent challenge to the message of inevitable mortality that vanitas paintings convey, the portrait serves to immortalize the artist.

25-2 PETER PAUL RUBENS, *Elevation of the Cross,* from Saint Walburga, Antwerp, 1610. Oil on wood, center panel 15′ 1$\frac{7}{8}$″ × 11′ 1$\frac{1}{2}$″, each wing 15′ 1$\frac{7}{8}$″ × 4′ 11″. Antwerp Cathedral, Antwerp.

In this triptych, Rubens explored foreshortened anatomy and violent action. The whole composition seethes with a power that comes from heroic exertion. The tension is emotional as well as physical.

not only in Christ's face but also in the features of his followers. Bright highlights and areas of deep shadow inspired by Caravaggio's tenebrism, hallmarks of Rubens's work at this stage of his career, enhance the drama.

25-2A RUBENS, *Garden of Love,* 1630–1632.

Although Rubens later developed a much subtler coloristic style in paintings such as *Garden of Love* (FIG. 25-2A), the human body in action, draped or undraped, male or female, remained the focus of his art. This interest, combined with his voracious intellect, led Rubens to copy the works of classical antiquity and of the Italian masters. During his last two years in Rome (1606 to 1608), Rubens made many black-chalk drawings of great artworks, including figures in Michelangelo's Sistine Chapel frescoes (FIG. 22-17) and the ancient marble group (FIG. 5-89) of Laocoön and his two sons. In a Latin treatise he wrote titled *De imitatione statuarum* (*On the Imitation of Statues*), Rubens stated: "I am convinced that in order to achieve the highest perfection one needs a full understanding of the [ancient] statues, indeed a complete absorption in them; but one must make judicious use of them and before all avoid the effect of stone."[2]

MARIE DE' MEDICI Rubens's interaction with royalty and aristocracy provided him with an understanding of the ostentation and spectacle of Baroque (particularly Italian) art that appealed to the wealthy and privileged. Rubens, the born courtier, reveled in the pomp and majesty of royalty. Likewise, those in power embraced the lavish spectacle that served the Catholic Church so well in Italy. The magnificence and splendor of Baroque imagery reinforced the authority and right to rule of the highborn. Among Rubens's royal patrons was Marie de' Medici, a member of the famous Florentine house and widow of Henry IV (r. 1589–1610), the first Bourbon king of France. She commissioned Rubens to paint a series of huge canvases memorializing and glorifying her career. Between 1622 and 1626, Rubens, working with amazing creative energy, produced with the aid of his many assistants 21 historical-allegorical pictures designed to hang in the queen's new palace, the Luxembourg, in Paris.

In *Arrival of Marie de' Medici at Marseilles* (FIG. 25-3), a 13-foot-tall tableau, Marie disembarks at that southern French port after her sea voyage from Italy. An allegorical personification of France, draped in a cloak decorated with the *fleur-de-lis* (the floral symbol of French royalty; compare FIG. 25-24), welcomes her. The sea and sky rejoice at the queen's safe arrival. Neptune

25-3 Peter Paul
Rubens, *Arrival of
Marie de' Medici at
Marseilles*, 1622–1625.
Oil on canvas,
12' 11½" × 9' 7". Musée
du Louvre, Paris.

Rubens painted 21 large
canvases glorifying Marie
de' Medici's career. In
this historical-allegorical
picture of robust figures
in an opulent setting,
the sea and sky rejoice
at the queen's arrival in
France.

1 ft.

and the Nereids (daughters of the sea god Nereus) salute her, and
the winged and trumpeting personified Fame swoops overhead.
Conspicuous in the galley's opulently carved stern-castle, under
the Medici coat of arms, stands the imperious commander of the
vessel, the only immobile figure in the composition. In black and
silver, this figure makes a sharp accent amid the swirling tonal-
ty of ivory, gold, and red. Rubens enriched the surfaces with a
decorative splendor that pulls the whole composition together. The
audacious vigor that customarily enlivens the painter's figures,
beginning with the monumental, twisting sea creatures, vibrates
through the entire design.

CONSEQUENCES OF WAR Rubens's diplomatic missions
gave him great insight into European politics, and he never ceased

Rubens on *Consequences of War*

In the ancient and medieval worlds, artists rarely wrote commentaries on the works they produced. (The Greek sculptor Polykleitos is a notable exception; see "Polykleitos's Prescription for the Perfect Statue," Chapter 5, page 132.) Beginning with the Renaissance, however, the increased celebrity artists enjoyed and the ready availability of paper encouraged artists to record their intentions in letters to friends and patrons.

In March 1638, Peter Paul Rubens wrote a letter to Justus Sustermans (1597–1681), court painter of Grand Duke Ferdinando II de' Medici of Tuscany, explaining his *Consequences of War* (FIG. 25-4) and his attitude toward the European military conflicts of his day.

> The principal figure is Mars, who has left the open temple of Janus (which in time of peace, according to Roman custom, remained closed) and rushes forth with shield and blood-stained sword, threatening the people with great disaster. He pays little heed to Venus, his mistress, who, accompanied by Amors and Cupids, strives with caresses and embraces to hold him. From the other side, Mars is dragged forward by the Fury Alekto, with a torch in her hand. Near by are monsters personifying Pestilence and Famine, those inseparable partners of War. On the ground, turning her back, lies a woman with a broken lute, representing Harmony, which is incompatible with the discord of War. There is also a mother with her child in her arms, indicating that fecundity, procreation and charity are thwarted by War, which corrupts and destroys everything. In addition, one sees an architect thrown on his back, with his instruments in his hand, to show that which in time of peace is constructed for the use and ornamentation of the City, is hurled to the ground by the force of arms and falls to ruin. I believe, if I remember rightly, that you will find on the ground, under the feet of Mars a book and a drawing on paper, to imply that he treads underfoot all the arts and letters. There ought also to be a bundle of darts or arrows, with the band which held them together undone; these when bound form the symbol of Concord. Beside them is the caduceus and an olive branch, attribute of Peace; these are also cast aside. That grief-stricken woman clothed in black, with torn veil, robbed of all her jewels and other ornaments, is the unfortunate Europe who, for so many years now, has suffered plunder, outrage, and misery, which are so injurious to everyone that it is unnecessary to go into detail. Europe's attribute is the globe, borne by a small angel or genius, and surmounted by the cross, to symbolize the Christian world.*

*Translated by Kristin Lohse Belkin, *Rubens* (London: Phaidon, 1998), 288–289.

1 ft.

25-4 PETER PAUL RUBENS, *Consequences of War*, 1638–1639. Oil on canvas, 6′ 9″ × 11′ 3⅞″. Palazzo Pitti, Florence.

Since the Renaissance, artists have left behind many letters shedding light on their lives and work. In a 1638 letter, Rubens explained the meaning of each figure in this allegorical painting.

to promote peace. Throughout most of his career, however, war was constant. When commissioned in 1638 to produce a painting (FIG. 25-4) for Ferdinando II de' Medici, the grand duke of Tuscany (r. 1621–1670), Rubens took the opportunity to express his attitude toward the Thirty Years' War (see "Rubens on *Consequences of War*," above). The fluid articulation of human forms in this work and the energy emanating from the chaotic scene are hallmarks of Rubens's mature style.

ANTHONY VAN DYCK Most of the leading painters of the next generation in Flanders were at one time Rubens's assistants. The master's most famous pupil was ANTHONY VAN DYCK (1599–1641). Early on, the younger man, unwilling to be over-shadowed by Rubens's undisputed stature, left his native Antwerp for Genoa and then London, where he became court portrait-ist to Charles I. Although Van Dyck created dramatic compositions of high quality, his specialty became the portrait. He developed a courtly manner of great elegance that influenced many artists throughout Europe and resounded in English portrait painting well into the 19th century.

In one of his finest works, *Charles I Dismounted* (FIG. **25-5**), the ill-fated English king stands in a landscape with the Thames River in the background. An equerry and a page attend him. The portrait is a stylish image of relaxed authority, as if the king is out for a casual ride in his park, but no one can mistake the regal poise and the air of absolute authority that Charles's Parliament resented and was soon to rise against. Here, the king turns his back on his attendants as he surveys his domain. Van Dyck's placement of the monarch is exceedingly artful. He stands off center but balances the composition with a single keen glance at the viewer. Van Dyck even managed to portray Charles I, who was of short stature, in a position to look down on the observer.

CLARA PEETERS Some Flemish 17th-century artists specialized in still-life painting, as did Sánchez Cotán (FIG. 24-25) in Spain. A pioneer of this genre was CLARA PEETERS (1594–ca. 1657), a native of Antwerp who spent time in Holland and laid the groundwork for Pieter Claesz (FIG. 25-1) and other Dutch masters of still-life painting, including Willem Kalf (FIG. 25-22) and Rachel Ruysch (FIG. 25-23). Peeters won renown for her depictions

25-5 ANTHONY VAN DYCK, *Charles I Dismounted*, ca. 1635. Oil on canvas, 8′ 11″ × 6′ 11½″. Musée du Louvre, Paris.

Van Dyck specialized in court portraiture. In this painting, he depicted the absolutist monarch Charles I at a sharp angle so the king, a short man, appears to be looking down at the viewer.

1 ft.

of food and flowers together, and for still lifes featuring bread and fruit, known as *breakfast pieces*. In *Still Life with Flowers, Goblet, Dried Fruit, and Pretzels* (FIG. **25-6**), Peeters's considerable skills are on full display. One of a series of four paintings, each of which depicts a typical early-17th-century meal, this breakfast piece reveals Peeters's virtuosity in depicting a wide variety of objects convincingly, from the smooth, reflective surfaces of the glass and silver goblets to the soft petals of the blooms in the vase. Peeters often painted the objects in her still lifes against a dark background, thereby negating any sense of deep space (compare FIG. 24-25). In this breakfast piece, she enhanced the sense of depth in the foreground by placing the leaves of the flower on the stone ledge as though they were encroaching into the viewer's space.

25-6 CLARA PEETERS, *Still Life with Flowers, Goblet, Dried Fruit, and Pretzels*, 1611. Oil on panel, 1′ 7¾″ × 2′ 1¼″. Museo del Prado, Madrid. ◼◀

Clara Peeters was a pioneer of still-life painting. Although a Flemish artist, she spent time in Holland and laid the groundwork for many Dutch artists (FIGS. 25-1, 25-22, and 25-23).

DUTCH REPUBLIC

With the founding of the Bank of Amsterdam in 1609, Amsterdam emerged as the financial center of the Continent. In the 17th century, the city had the highest per capita income in Europe. The Dutch economy also benefited enormously from the country's expertise on the open seas, which facilitated establishing far-flung colonies. By 1650, Dutch trade routes extended to North America, South America, the west coast of Africa, China, Japan, Southeast Asia, and much of the Pacific. Due to this prosperity and in the absence of an absolute ruler, political power increasingly passed into the hands of an urban patrician class of merchants and manufacturers, especially in cities such as Amsterdam, Haarlem, and Delft. All of these bustling cities were located in Holland (the largest of the seven United Provinces), which explains why historians informally use the name "Holland" to refer to the entire country.

Ter Brugghen, van Honthorst, Hals, Leyster

Religious differences were a major consideration during the northern Netherlands' insistent quest for independence during the 16th and early 17th centuries. Whereas Spain and the southern Netherlands were Catholic, the people of the northern Netherlands were predominantly Protestant. The prevailing Calvinism demanded a puritanical rejection of art in churches, and thus artists produced relatively little religious art in the Dutch Republic at this time (especially compared with the volume of commissions created in the wake of the Counter-Reformation in areas dominated by Catholicism; see Chapter 24).

HENDRICK TER BRUGGHEN Some artists in the Dutch Republic did produce religious art, however. HENDRICK TER BRUGGHEN (1588–1629) of Utrecht, for example, painted *Calling of Saint Matthew* (FIG. 25-7) in 1621 after returning from a trip to Italy, selecting as his subject a theme Caravaggio had painted (FIG. 24-17) for the church of San Luigi dei Francesi in Rome. The moment of the narrative chosen and the naturalistic depiction of the figures echo Caravaggio's work. But although ter Brugghen was an admirer of the Italian master, he dispensed with Caravaggio's stark contrasts of dark and light and instead presented the viewer with a more colorful palette of soft tints. Further, the Dutch painter compressed the figures into a small but well-lit space, creating an intimate effect compared with Caravaggio's more spacious setting.

MERCANTILIST PATRONAGE Given the absence of an authoritative ruler and the Calvinist concern for the potential misuse of religious art, commissions from royalty or the Catholic Church, prominent in the art of other countries, were uncommon in the United Provinces. With the new prosperity, however, an expanding class of merchants with different tastes emerged as art patrons. In contrast to Italian, Spanish, and Flemish Baroque art, 17th-century Dutch art centered on genre scenes, landscapes, portraits of middle-class men and women, and still lifes, all of which appealed to the newly prosperous Dutch merchants (see "Still-Life Painting in the Dutch Republic," page 695, and "Middle-Class Patronage and the Art Market in the Dutch Republic," page 703).

GERRIT VAN HONTHORST Typical of 17th-century Dutch genre scenes is *Supper Party* (FIG. 25-8) by GERRIT VAN HONTHORST (1590–1656). In this painting, van Honthorst presented an informal gathering of unidealized figures. While a musician serenades the group, his companions delight in watching a young woman feeding a piece of chicken to a man whose hands are both occupied—one holds a jug and the other a glass. Van Honthorst spent several years in Italy, and while there he carefully studied Caravaggio's work, as did fellow Utrecht painter Hendrick ter Brugghen. The Italian artist's influence surfaces in the mundane tavern setting and the nocturnal lighting of *Supper Party*. Fascinated by nighttime effects, van Honthorst frequently placed a hidden light source in his pictures and used it as a pretext to work with dramatic and starkly contrasting dark and light effects. Seemingly lighthearted genre scenes were popular in Baroque Holland, but Dutch viewers could also interpret them moralistically. For example, *Supper Party* can be read as a warning against the sins of gluttony (represented by the man on the right) and lust (the woman feeding the glutton is, in all likelihood, a prostitute with her aged procuress at her side). Or perhaps the painting represents the loose companions of the Prodigal Son (Luke 15:13)—panderers and prostitutes drinking, singing, strumming, and laughing. Strict Dutch Calvinists no doubt approved of such interpretations. Others simply took delight in the immediacy of the scenes and skill of artists such as van Honthorst.

25-7 HENDRICK TER BRUGGHEN, *Calling of Saint Matthew*, 1621. Oil on canvas, 3′ 4″ × 4′ 6″. Centraal Museum, Utrecht.

Although middle-class patrons in the Protestant Dutch Republic preferred genre scenes, still lifes, and portraits, some artists, including Hendrick ter Brugghen, also painted religious scenes.

Middle-Class Patronage and the Art Market in the Dutch Republic

Throughout history, the wealthy have been the most avid art collectors. Indeed, the money necessary to commission major artworks from leading artists can be considerable. During the 17th century in the Dutch Republic, however, the prosperity a large proportion of the population enjoyed significantly expanded the range of art patrons. As a result, one distinguishing hallmark of Dutch art production during the Baroque period was how it catered to the tastes of a middle-class audience, broadly defined. An aristocracy and an upper class of ship owners, rich businesspeople, high-ranking officers, and directors of large companies still existed, and these groups continued to be major patrons of the arts. But with the expansion of the Dutch economy, traders, craftspeople, bureaucrats, and soldiers also commissioned and collected art.

Although steeped in the morality and propriety central to the Calvinist ethic, members of the Dutch middle class sought ways to announce their success and newly acquired status. House furnishings, paintings, tapestries, and porcelain were among the items they collected and displayed in their homes. The Calvinist disdain for excessive ostentation, however, led Dutch collectors to favor small, low-key works—portraits of bourgeois men and women (FIGS. 25-9, 25-10, 25-12, and 25-13), still lifes (FIGS. 25-1, 25-22, and 25-23), genre scenes (FIGS. 25-8, 25-19, and 25-21), and landscapes (FIGS. 25-17, 25-18, 25-18A, and 25-18B). This focus contrasted with the Italian Baroque penchant for large-scale, dazzling ceiling frescoes and opulent room decoration (see Chapter 24). Indeed, the stylistic, as opposed to the chronological, designation "Baroque" is ill suited to these 17th-century northern European artworks.

It is risky to generalize about the spending and collecting habits of the Dutch middle class, but probate records, contracts, and archived inventories reveal some interesting facts. These records suggest an individual earning between 1,500 and 3,000 guilders a year could live quite comfortably. A house could be purchased for 1,000 guilders. Another 1,000 guilders could buy all the necessary furnishings for a middle-class home, including a significant amount of art, particularly paintings. Although there was, of course, considerable variation in prices, many artworks were very affordable. Prints, for example, were extremely cheap because of the high number of copies artists produced of each picture. Paintings of interior and genre scenes were relatively inexpensive in 17th-century Holland, perhaps costing one or two guilders each. Small landscapes fetched between three and four guilders. Commissioned portraits were the most costly. The size of the work and quality of the frame, as well as the reputation of the artist, were other factors in determining the price of a painting, regardless of the subject.

With the exception of portraits, Dutch artists produced most of their paintings for an anonymous market, hoping to appeal to a wide audience. To ensure success, artists in the United Provinces adapted to the changed conditions of art production and sales. They marketed their paintings in many ways, selling their works directly to buyers who visited their studios and through art dealers, exhibitions, fairs, auctions, and even lotteries. Because of the uncertainty of these sales mechanisms (as opposed to the certainty of an ironclad contract for a commission from a church or king), artists became more responsive to market demands. Specialization became common among Dutch artists. For example, painters might limit their practice to portraits, still lifes, or landscapes—the most popular genres among middle-class patrons.

Artists did not always sell their paintings. Frequently they used their work to pay off loans or debts. Tavern debts, in particular, could be settled with paintings, which may explain why many art dealers (such as Jan Vermeer and his father before him) were also innkeepers. This connection between art dealing and other businesses eventually solidified, and innkeepers, for example, often would have art exhibitions in their taverns hoping to make a sale. The institutions of today's open art market—dealers, galleries, auctions, and estate sales—owe their establishment to the emergence in the 17th century of a prosperous middle class in the Dutch Republic.

25-8 GERRIT VAN HONTHORST, *Supper Party,* 1620. Oil on canvas, 4′ 8″ × 7′. Galleria degli Uffizi, Florence.

Genre scenes were popular subjects among middle-class Dutch patrons. Gerrit van Honthorst's *Supper Party* may also have served as a Calvinist warning against the sins of gluttony and lust.

FRANS HALS Many Dutch artists excelled in portraiture in response to popular demand. FRANS HALS (ca. 1581–1666), the leading painter in Haarlem, was one of those who made portraits his specialty. Portrait artists traditionally relied heavily on convention—for example, specific poses, settings, attire, and furnishings—to convey a sense of the sitter. Because the subject was usually someone of status or note, such as a pope, king, duchess, or wealthy banker, the artist's goal was to produce an image appropriate to the subject's station in life. With the increasing number of Dutch middle-class patrons, portrait painting became more challenging. The Calvinists shunned ostentation, instead wearing subdued and dark clothing with little variation or decoration, and the traditional conventions became inappropriate and thus unusable. Despite these difficulties, or perhaps because of them, Hals produced lively portraits that seem far more relaxed than traditional formulaic portraiture. He injected an engaging spontaneity into his images and conveyed the individuality of his sitters as well. His manner of execution intensified the casualness, immediacy, and intimacy in his paintings. Because the touch of Hals's brush was as light and fleeting as the moment he captured the pose, the figure, the highlights on clothing, and the facial expression all seem instantaneously created.

ARCHERS OF SAINT HADRIAN Hals's most ambitious portraits reflect the widespread popularity in the Dutch Republic of vast canvases commemorating the participation of Dutch burghers in civic organizations. These commissions presented greater difficulties to the painter than requests to depict a single sitter. Hals rose to the challenge and achieved great success with this new portrait genre. His *Archers of Saint Hadrian* (FIG. 25-9) is typical in that the subject is one of the many Dutch civic militia groups that claimed credit for liberating the Dutch Republic from Spain. As other companies did, the Archers met on their saint's feast day in dress uniform for a grand banquet. The celebrations sometimes lasted an entire week, prompting an ordinance limiting them to three or four days. These events often included sitting for a group portrait.

In *Archers of Saint Hadrian,* Hals attacked the problem of how to represent each militia member satisfactorily yet retain action and variety in the composition. Whereas earlier group portraits in the Netherlands were rather ordered and regimented images, Hals sought to enliven the depictions. In his portrait of the Saint Hadrian militiamen, each member is both part of the troop and an individual with a distinct physiognomy. The sitters' movements and moods vary markedly. Some engage the viewer directly. Others look away or at a companion. Some are stern, others animated. Each archer is equally visible and clearly recognizable. The uniformity of attire—black military dress, white ruffs, and sashes—did not deter Hals from injecting spontaneity into the work. Indeed, he used those elements to create a lively rhythm extending throughout the composition and energizing the portrait. The impromptu effect—the preservation of every detail and fleeting facial expression—is, of course, the result of careful planning. Yet Hals's vivacious brush appears to have moved instinctively, directed by a plan in his mind but not traceable in any preparatory scheme on the canvas.

25-9 FRANS HALS, *Archers of Saint Hadrian,* ca. 1633. Oil on canvas, 6′ 9″ × 11′. Frans Halsmuseum, Haarlem. ◼◀

In this brilliant composition, Hals succeeded in solving the problem of portraying each individual in a group portrait while retaining action and variety in the painting as a whole.

WOMEN REGENTS OF HAARLEM Hals also produced group portraits of Calvinist women engaged in charitable work. The finest is *The Women Regents of the Old Men's Home at Haarlem* (FIG. 25-10). Although Dutch women had primary responsibility for the welfare of the family and the orderly operation of the home, they also populated the labor force in the cities. Among the more prominent roles educated Dutch women played in public life were as regents of orphanages, hospitals, old age homes, and prisons. In Hals's portrait, the Haarlem regents sit quietly in a manner becoming of devout Calvinists. Unlike the more relaxed, seemingly informal character of his other group portraits, a stern, puritanical, and composed sensibility suffuses Hals's portrayal of these regents. The women—all carefully distinguished as individuals—gaze out from the painting with expressions ranging from dour disinterest to kindly concern. The somber and virtually *monochromatic* (one-color) palette, punctuated only by the white accents of the clothing, contributes to the painting's restraint. Both the coloration and the mood of Hals's portrait are appropriate for this commission. Portraying the Haarlem regents called for a very different kind of portrait from those Hals made of men at festive militia banquets.

JUDITH LEYSTER Some of Hals's students developed thriving careers of their own as portraitists. One was JUDITH LEYSTER (1609–1660), whose *Self-Portrait* (FIG. 25-11) reveals the strong training she received. It is detailed, precise, and accurate but also imbued with the spontaneity found in her master's works. In her portrait, Leyster succeeded at communicating a great deal about herself. She depicted herself as an artist, seated in front of a painting on an easel. The palette in her left hand and brush in her right announce the painting as her creation. She thus invites the viewer to evaluate her skill, which both the fiddler on the canvas and the image of herself demonstrate as considerable. Although she produced a wide range of paintings, including still lifes and floral pieces, her specialty was genre scenes such as the comic image seen on the easel. Leyster's quick smile and relaxed pose as she stops her work to meet the viewer's gaze reveal her self-assurance. Although presenting herself as an artist, Leyster did not paint herself wearing the traditional artist's smock, as her more famous contemporary Rembrandt did in his 1659–1660 self-portrait (FIG. 25-15). Her elegant attire distinguishes her socially as a member of a well-to-do family, another important aspect of Leyster's identity.

Rembrandt

REMBRANDT VAN RIJN (1606–1669), Hals's younger contemporary and the leading Dutch painter of his time, was an undisputed genius—an artist of great versatility, a master of light and shadow, and a unique interpreter of the Protestant conception of scripture. Born in Leiden, he moved to Amsterdam around 1631, where he could attract a more extensive clientele than possible in his native city. Rembrandt had trained as a history painter in Leiden, but in Amsterdam he immediately entered the lucrative market for portraiture and soon became renowned for that genre.

ANATOMY LESSON OF DR. TULP In a painting he completed shortly after he arrived in Amsterdam, *Anatomy Lesson of Dr. Tulp* (FIG. **25-12**), Rembrandt deviated even further from the traditional staid group portrait than had Hals. Despite Hals's determination to enliven his portraits, he still evenly spread his subjects across the canvas. In contrast, Rembrandt chose to portray the members of the surgeons' guild (who commissioned this group portrait) clustered on the painting's left side. In the foreground appears the corpse Dr. Tulp, a noted physician, is in the act of dissecting. Rembrandt diagonally placed and foreshortened the corpse, activating the space by disrupting the strict horizontal, planar orientation typical of traditional portraiture. He depicted each of the "students" specifically, and although they wear virtually identical attire, their poses and facial expressions suggest the varying degrees of intensity with which they watch Dr. Tulp's demonstration—or ignore it. One, at the apex of Rembrandt's triangular composition of bodies, gazes at the viewer instead of at the operating table. Another directs his attention to the open book (an anatomy manual) at the cadaver's feet. Rembrandt produced this painting when he was 26 and just beginning his career. His innovative approach to group portraiture is therefore all the more remarkable.

NIGHT WATCH Rembrandt amplified the complexity and energy of the group portrait in *The Company of Captain Frans Banning Cocq* (FIG. **25-13**), better known as *Night Watch*. This more commonly used title is a misnomer, however. The painting is not of a nocturnal scene. Rembrandt used light in a masterful way, and dramatic lighting certainly enhances the image. Still, the painting's darkness (which explains the commonly used title) is the result of the varnish the artist used, which darkened considerably over time. It was not the painter's intention to portray his subjects moving about at night.

This painting was one of many civic-guard group portraits Dutch artists produced during this period.

From the limited information available about the commission, it appears the two officers, Captain Frans Banning Cocq and Lieutenant Willem van Ruytenburch, along with 16 members of their militia, contributed to Rembrandt's fee. (Despite the prominence of the girl just to the left of center, scholars have yet to ascertain her identity.) *Night Watch* was one of six paintings by different artists commissioned by various groups around 1640 for the assembly and banquet hall of Amsterdam's new Musketeers Hall, the largest and most prestigious interior space in the city. Unfortunately, in 1715, when city officials moved Rembrandt's painting to Amsterdam's town hall, they trimmed it on all sides, leaving an incomplete record of the artist's resolution of the challenge of portraying this group.

Even in its truncated form, *The Company of Captain Frans Banning Cocq* succeeds in capturing the excitement and frenetic activity of men preparing for a parade. Comparing this militia group portrait with Hals's *Archers of Saint Hadrian* (FIG. 25-9) reveals Rembrandt's inventiveness in enlivening what was, by then, becoming a conventional format for Dutch group portraits. Rather than present assembled men posed in orderly fashion, the younger artist chose to portray the company members rushing about in the act of organizing themselves, thereby animating the image considerably. At the same time, he managed to record the three most important stages of using a musket—loading, firing, and readying the weapon for reloading—details that must have pleased his patrons.

RETURN OF THE PRODIGAL SON The Calvinist injunction against religious art did not prevent Rembrandt from making a series of religious paintings and prints. In the Dutch Republic, paintings depicting biblical themes were not objects of devotion, but they still brought great prestige, and Rembrandt and other artists vied to demonstrate their ability to narrate holy scripture in dramatic new ways. One of Rembrandt's earliest biblical paintings, *Blinding of Samson* (FIG. 24-13A), reveals the young artist's debt to Rubens and Caravaggio. His mature works, however, differ markedly from the

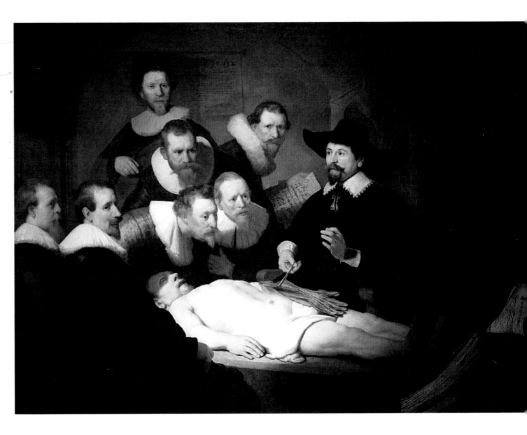

25-13 REMBRANDT VAN RIJN, *The Company of Captain Frans Banning Cocq* (*Night Watch*), 1642. Oil on canvas, 11′ 11″ × 14′ 4″ (trimmed from original size). Rijksmuseum, Amsterdam.

Rembrandt's dramatic use of light contributes to the animation of this militia group portrait in which the artist showed the company members rushing to organize themselves for a parade.

1 ft.

25-13A REMBRANDT, *Blinding of Samson*, 1636.

religious art of Baroque Italy and Flanders. Rembrandt had a special interest in probing the states of the human soul. The spiritual stillness of his later religious paintings is that of inward-turning contemplation, far from the choirs and trumpets and the heavenly tumult of Bernini (FIG. 24-7) or Pozzo (FIG. 24-24).

The Dutch artist's psychological insight and his profound sympathy for human affliction produced, at the end of his life, one of the most moving pictures in all religious art, *Return of the Prodigal Son* (FIG. 25-14). In this biblical parable, the younger of two sons leaves his home and squanders his wealth on a life of sin. When he becomes poor and hungry and sees the error of his ways, he returns home. In Rembrandt's painting, the forgiving father tenderly embraces his lost son, who crouches before him in weeping contrition, while three figures, immersed to varying degrees in the soft shadows, note the lesson of mercy. The light, everywhere mingled with shadow, directs the viewer's attention by illuminating the father and son and largely veiling the witnesses. Its focus is the beautiful, spiritual face of the old man. Secondarily, the light touches the contrasting stern face of the foremost witness. The painting demonstrates the degree to which Rembrandt developed a personal style completely in tune with the simple eloquence of the biblical passage.

25-14 REMBRANDT VAN RIJN, *Return of the Prodigal Son*, ca. 1665. Oil on canvas, 8′ 8″ × 6′ 9″. Hermitage Museum, Saint Petersburg.

The spiritual stillness of Rembrandt's religious paintings is that of inward-turning contemplation, in vivid contrast to the heavenly tumult of Italian Baroque Counter-Reformation works.

1 ft.

25-15 REMBRANDT VAN RIJN, *Self-Portrait,* ca. 1659–1660. Oil on canvas, 3′ 8¾″ × 3′ 1″. Kenwood House, London (Iveagh Bequest). ◼◀

In this late self-portrait, Rembrandt's interest in revealing the soul is evident in the attention given to his expressive face. The controlled use of light and the nonspecific setting contribute to this focus.

GRADATIONS OF LIGHT From the few paintings by Rembrandt discussed thus far, it should be clear the artist's use of light is among the hallmarks of his style. Rembrandt's pictorial method involved refining light and shade into finer and finer nuances until they blended with one another. Earlier painters' use of abrupt lights and darks gave way, in the work of artists such as Rembrandt and Velázquez (FIGS. 24-28 to 24-30), to gradation. Although these later artists sacrificed some of the dramatic effects of sharp chiaroscuro, a greater fidelity to appearances more than offsets those sacrifices. In fact, the recording of light in small gradations is closer to reality because the eye perceives light and dark not as static but as always subtly changing.

In general, Renaissance artists represented forms and faces in a flat, neutral modeling light (even Leonardo's shading is of a standard kind). They represented the *idea* of light, rather than showed how humans perceive light. Artists such as Rembrandt discovered gradations of light and dark as well as degrees of differences in pose, in the movements of facial features, and in psychic states. They arrived at these differences optically, not conceptually or in terms of some ideal. Rembrandt found that by manipulating the direction, intensity, and distance of light and shadow, and by varying the surface texture with tactile brushstrokes, he could render subtle nuances of character and mood, both in individuals and whole scenes. He discovered for the modern world that variation of light and shade, subtly modulated, can be read as emotional differences. In the visible world, light, dark, and the wide spectrum of values

between the two are charged with meanings and feelings that sometimes are independent of the shapes and figures they modify. The theater and the photographic arts have used these discoveries to great dramatic effect.

SELF-PORTRAITS Rembrandt carried over the spiritual quality of his religious works into his later portraits (FIGS. **25-15** and **25-15A**) by the same means—what could be called the "psychology of light." Light and dark are not in conflict in his portraits. They are reconciled, merging softly and subtly to produce the visual equivalent of quietness. Their prevailing mood is one of tranquil meditation, of philosophical resignation, of musing recollection—indeed, a whole cluster of emotional tones heard only in silence.

25-15A REMBRANDT, *Self-Portrait,* 1658.

In his self-portrait now in Kenwood House (FIG. 25-15), the light source outside the upper left of the painting bathes the painter's face in soft highlights, leaving the lower part of his body in shadow. The artist depicted himself as possessing dignity and strength, and the portrait serves as a summary of the many stylistic and professional concerns that occupied him throughout his career. Rembrandt's distinctive use of light is evident, as is the assertive brushwork suggesting his confidence and self-assurance. He presented himself as a working artist holding his brushes, palette, and maulstick (compare FIG. 23-18) and wearing his studio garb—a smock and painter's turban. The circles on the wall behind him (the subject of much scholarly debate) may allude to a legendary sign of artistic virtuosity—the ability to draw a perfect circle freehand. Rembrandt's abiding interest in revealing the human soul emerges here in his careful focus on his expressive visage. His controlled use of light and the nonspecific setting contribute to this focus. Further, X-rays of the painting have revealed that Rembrandt originally depicted himself in the act of painting. His final resolution, with the viewer's attention drawn to his face, produced a portrait not just of the artist but of the man as well. Indeed, Rembrandt's nearly 70 self-portraits in various media have no parallel in sheer quantity. They reflect the artist's deeply personal connection to his craft.

ETCHINGS Rembrandt's virtuosity also extended to the graphic media, especially etching (see "Woodcuts, Engravings, and Etchings," Chapter 20, page 556). Many printmakers adopted etching after its perfection early in the 17th century, because the technique afforded greater freedom than engraving in drawing the design. The etcher covers a copper plate with a layer of wax or varnish, and then incises the design into this surface with a pointed tool, exposing the metal below but not cutting into its surface. Next, the artist immerses the plate in acid, which etches, or eats away, the exposed parts of the metal, acting in the same way the burin does in engraving. The medium's softness gives etchers greater carving freedom than woodcutters and engravers have working directly in more resistant wood and metal. If Rembrandt had never painted, he still would be renowned, as he principally was in his lifetime, for his prints. Prints were a major source of income for Rembrandt, as they were for Albrecht Dürer (see Chapter 23), and he often reworked the plates so they could be used to produce a new issue or edition. This constant reworking was unusual within the context of 17th-century printmaking practices.

1 in.

25-16 REMBRANDT VAN RIJN, *Christ with the Sick around Him, Receiving the Children* (*Hundred-Guilder Print*), ca. 1649. Etching, 11″ × 1′ 3¼″. Pierpont Morgan Library, New York.

Rembrandt's mastery of the newly perfected medium of etching is evident in his expert use of light and dark to draw attention to Christ as he preaches compassionately to the blind and lame.

HUNDRED-GUILDER PRINT One of Rembrandt's most celebrated etchings is *Christ with the Sick around Him, Receiving the Children* (FIG. 25-16). Indeed, the title by which this work has been known since the early 18th century, *Hundred-Guilder Print,* refers to the high sale price it brought during Rembrandt's lifetime. (As noted, a comfortable house could be purchased for 1,000 guilders.) *Christ with the Sick* demonstrates the artist's mastery of all aspects of the printmaker's craft, for Rembrandt used both engraving and etching to depict the figures and the setting. As in his other religious works, Rembrandt suffused this print with a deep and abiding piety, presenting the viewer not the celestial triumph of the Catholic Church but the humanity and humility of Jesus. Christ appears in the center preaching compassionately to, and simultaneously blessing, the blind, the lame, and the young, who are spread throughout the composition in a dazzling array of standing, kneeling, and lying positions. Also present is a young man in elegant garments with his head in his hand, lamenting Christ's insistence that the wealthy need to give their possessions to the poor in order to gain entrance to Heaven. The tonal range of the print is remarkable. At the right, the figures near the city gate are in deep shadow. At the left, the figures, some rendered almost exclusively in outline, are in bright light—not the light of day but the illumination radiating from Christ himself. A second, unseen source of light comes from the right and casts the shadow of the praying man's arms and head onto Christ's tunic. Technically and in terms of its humanity, *Hundred-Guilder Print* is Rembrandt's supreme achievement as a printmaker.

Cuyp and Ruisdael

Due to topography and politics, the Dutch had a unique relationship to the land, one that differed from attitudes of people living in other European countries. After gaining independence from Spain, the Dutch undertook an extensive reclamation project lasting almost a century. Dikes and drainage systems cropped up across the countryside. Because of the effort expended on these endeavors, the Dutch developed a distinctly direct relationship to the land. The reclamation also affected Dutch social and economic life. The marshy and swampy nature of much of the terrain made it less desirable for large-scale exploitation, so the extensive feudal landowning system elsewhere in Europe never developed in the United Provinces. Most Dutch families owned and worked their own farms, cultivating a feeling of closeness to the land. Consequently, landscape scenes abound in 17th-century Dutch art.

25-17 AELBERT CUYP, *Distant View of Dordrecht, with a Milkmaid and Four Cows, and Other Figures (The "Large Dort")*, late 1640s. Oil on canvas, 5′ 1″ × 6′ 4⅞″. National Gallery, London.

Unlike idealized Italian Renaissance landscapes, Cuyp's painting portrays a particular locale. The cows, shepherds, and milkmaid refer to the Dutch Republic's important dairy industry.

AELBERT CUYP One Dutch artist who established his reputation as a specialist in landscape painting was AELBERT CUYP (ca. 1620–1691). His works were the products of careful observation and a deep respect for and understanding of Dutch topography. *Distant View of Dordrecht, with a Milkmaid and Four Cows, and Other Figures* (FIG. **25-17**) reveals Cuyp's substantial skills. Unlike the idealized classical landscapes in many Italian Renaissance paintings, this landscape is particularized. The church in the background, for example, is a faithful representation of the Grote Kerk in Dordrecht. The dairy cows, shepherds, and milkmaid in the foreground refer to a cornerstone of Dutch agriculture—the demand for dairy products such as butter and cheese, which increased with the development of urban centers. The credibility of this and similar paintings rests on Cuyp's pristine rendering of each detail.

JACOB VAN RUISDAEL Depicting the Dutch landscape with precision and sensitivity was also a specialty of JACOB VAN RUISDAEL (ca. 1628–1682). In *View of Haarlem from the Dunes at Overveen* (FIG. **25-18**), Ruisdael provided an overarching view of this major Dutch city. The specificity of the artist's image—the Saint Bavo church in the background, the numerous windmills that refer to the land reclamation efforts, and the figures in the foreground stretching linen to be bleached (a major industry in Haarlem)—reflects the pride Dutch painters took in recording their homeland and the activities of their fellow citizens. Nonetheless, in this painting the inhabitants and dwellings are so minuscule they blend into the land itself, unlike the figures in Cuyp's view of Dordrecht. Moreover, the horizon line is low, so the sky fills almost three-quarters of the picture space, and the sun illuminates the landscape only in patches, where

it has broken through the clouds above. In *View of Haarlem*, Ruisdael not only captured the appearance of a specific locale but also succeeded in imbuing the work with a quiet serenity that is almost spiritual. Less typical of his work, but also one of the great landscape paintings of the 17th century, is Ruisdael's allegorical *Jewish Cemetery* (FIG. **25-18A**).

25-18A RUISDAEL, *Jewish Cemetery*, ca. 1655–1660.

25-18 JACOB VAN RUISDAEL, *View of Haarlem from the Dunes at Overveen*, ca. 1670. Oil on canvas, 1′ 10″ × 2′ 1″. Mauritshuis, The Hague.

In this painting, Ruisdael succeeded in capturing a specific, realistic view of Haarlem, its windmills, and Saint Bavo church, but he also imbued the landscape with a quiet serenity approaching the spiritual.

Vermeer

Although he also painted landscapes, such as *View of Delft* (FIG. 25-18B), JAN VERMEER (1632–1675) made his reputation as a painter of interior scenes, another popular subject among middle-class patrons. These paintings offer the viewer glimpses into the private lives of prosperous, responsible, and cultured citizens of the United Provinces. Despite his fame as a painter today, Vermeer derived much of his income from his work as an innkeeper and art dealer in Delft (see "Middle-Class Patronage and the Art Market," page 703), and he completed no more than 35 paintings that can be definitively attributed to him. He began his career as a painter of biblical and historical themes but soon abandoned those traditional subjects in favor of domestic scenes. Flemish artists of the 15th century also had painted domestic interiors, but sacred personages often occupied those scenes (for example, FIG. 20-1). In contrast, Vermeer and his contemporaries composed neat, quietly opulent interiors of Dutch middle-class dwellings with men, women, and children engaging in household tasks or at leisure. Women are the primary occupants of Vermeer's homes, and his paintings are highly idealized depictions of the social values of Dutch burghers.

WOMAN HOLDING A BALANCE In one of Vermeer's finest canvases, *Woman Holding a Balance* (FIG. 25-19), a beautiful young woman wearing a veil and a fur-trimmed jacket stands in a room in her home. Light coming from a window illuminates the scene, as in many of the artist's paintings. The woman stands before a table on which are spread her most precious possessions—pearl necklaces, gold chains, and gold coins, which reflect the sunlight that also shines on the woman's face and the fingers of her right hand. In fact, the perspective orthogonals direct the viewer's attention neither to the woman's head nor to her treasures but to the hand in which she holds a balance for weighing gold. The scales, however, are empty—in perfect balance, the way Ignatius of Loyola advised Catholics (Vermeer was a Catholic convert in the Protestant Dutch Republic) to lead a temperate, self-aware life and to balance one's sins with virtuous behavior. The mirror on the wall may refer to self-knowledge, but it may also symbolize, as do the pearls and gold, the sin of vanity. Bolstering that interpretation is the large framed *Last Judgment* painting on the back wall in which Christ, weigher of souls, appears in a golden aureole directly above the young woman's head. Therefore, this serene domestic scene is pregnant with hidden meaning. The woman holds the scales in balance and contemplates the kind of life (one free from the temptations of worldly riches) she must lead in order to be judged favorably on judgment day.

Vermeer, like Rembrandt, was a master of pictorial light and used it with immense virtuosity. He could render space so convincingly through his depiction of light that in his works the picture surface functions as an invisible glass pane through which the viewer looks into the constructed illusion. Art historians believe Vermeer used as tools both mirrors and the *camera obscura,* an ancestor of the modern camera based on passing light through a tiny pinhole or lens to project an image on a screen or the wall of a room. (In later versions, artists projected the image on a ground-glass wall of a box whose opposite wall contained the pinhole or lens.) Vermeer did not simply copy the camera's image, however. Instead, the camera obscura and the mirrors helped him obtain results he reworked compositionally, placing his figures and the furniture of a room in a beautiful stability of quadrilateral shapes. Vermeer's compositions evoke a matchless classical serenity. Enhancing this quality are colors so true to the optical facts and so subtly modulated they suggest Vermeer was far ahead of his time in color science. For example, Vermeer realized shadows are not colorless and dark, adjoining colors affect each other, and light is composed of colors. Thus, he painted reflections off of surfaces in colors modified by others nearby. Some scholars have suggested Vermeer also perceived the phenomenon modern photographers call "circles of confusion," which appear on out-of-focus negatives. Vermeer could have seen them in images projected by the camera obscura's primitive lenses. He approximated these effects with light dabs that, in close view, give the impression of an image slightly "out of focus." When the observer draws back a step, however, as if adjusting the lens, the color spots cohere, giving an astonishingly accurate illusion of the third dimension.

25-19 JAN VERMEER, *Woman Holding a Balance,* ca. 1664. Oil on canvas, $1' 3\frac{5}{8}'' \times 1' 2''$. National Gallery of Art, Washington, D.C. (Widener Collection).

Vermeer's woman holding empty scales in perfect balance, ignoring pearls and gold on the table, is probably an allegory of the temperate life. On the wall behind her is a *Last Judgment* painting.

Dutch painters often specialized in domestic scenes, but Vermeer's mother-in-law described this work as the "Art of Painting." Vermeer's tribute to his craft includes a model holding Clio's attributes.

THE ART OF PAINTING Vermeer's stylistic precision and commitment to his profession are evident in *Allegory of the Art of Painting* (FIG. **25-20**). The artist himself appears in the painting, with his back to the viewer and dressed in "historical" clothing (reminiscent of Burgundian attire). He is hard at work on a painting of the model standing before him wearing a laurel wreath and holding a trumpet and book, traditional attributes of Clio, the muse of history. The map of the provinces (an increasingly common wall adornment in Dutch homes) on the back wall serves as yet another reference to history. As

25-20A VERMEER, *The Letter*, 1666.

in *Woman Holding a Balance* and *The Letter* (FIG. **25-20A**), another of Vermeer's domestic scenes, the viewer is outside the space of the action, looking in through the drawn curtain, which also separates the artist in his studio from the rest of the house. Some art historians have suggested the light radiating from an unseen window on the left, illuminating both the model and the canvas being painted, alludes to the light of artistic inspiration. Accordingly, many scholars have interpreted this painting as an allegory—a reference to painting inspired by history. Vermeer's mother-in-law confirmed this allegorical reading in 1677 while seeking to retain the painting after the artist's death, when 26 of his works were scheduled to be sold to pay his widow's debts. She listed the painting in her written claim as "the piece . . . wherein the Art of Painting is portrayed."[3]

Steen

Whereas Vermeer's paintings reveal the charm and beauty of Dutch domesticity, the works of JAN STEEN (ca. 1625–1679) provide a counterpoint. In *Feast of Saint Nicholas* (FIG. **25-21**), instead of depicting a tidy, calm Dutch household, Steen opted for a scene of chaos and disruption. Saint Nicholas has just visited this residence, and the children are in an uproar as they search their shoes for the

25-21 JAN STEEN, *Feast of Saint Nicholas*, ca. 1660–1665. Oil on canvas, 2′ 8¼″ × 2′ 3¾″. Rijksmuseum, Amsterdam.

Steen's lively scene of Dutch children discovering their Christmas gifts may also have an allegorical dimension. *Feast of Saint Nicholas* probably alludes to selfishness, pettiness, and jealousy.

Christmas gifts he has left. Some children are delighted. The little girl in the center clutches her gifts, clearly unwilling to share with the other children despite her mother's pleas. Others are disappointed. The boy on the left is in tears because he received only a birch rod. An appropriately festive atmosphere reigns, which contrasts sharply with the decorum prevailing in Vermeer's works. As do the paintings of other Dutch artists, Steen's lively scenes often take on an allegorical dimension and moralistic tone. Steen frequently used children's activities as satirical comments on foolish adult behavior. *Feast of Saint Nicholas* is not his only allusion to selfishness, pettiness, and jealousy.

Kalf and Ruysch

As already discussed (see "Still-Life Painting in the Dutch Republic," page 695), Dutch patrons had a keen interest in still lifes. In addition to Peter Claesz (FIG. 25-1), the leading Dutch still-life painters included Willem Kalf and Rachel Ruysch.

WILLEM KALF As Dutch prosperity increased, precious objects and luxury items made their way into still-life paintings. *Still Life with a Late Ming Ginger Jar* (FIG. 25-22) by WILLEM KALF (1619–1693) reflects the wealth Dutch citizens had accrued and the painter's exquisite skills, both technical and aesthetic. Kalf highlighted the breadth of Dutch maritime trade through his depiction of the Indian floral carpet and the Chinese jar used to store ginger (a luxury item). He delighted in recording the lustrous sheen of fabric and the light glinting off reflective surfaces. As is evident in this image, Kalf's works present an array of ornamental objects, such as the Venetian and Dutch glassware and the silver dish. The inclusion of the watch, Mediterranean peach, and peeled lemon suggests this work, like Claesz's *Vanitas Still Life* (FIG. 25-1), is also a vanitas painting, consistent with Calvinist values.

RACHEL RUYSCH As living objects that soon die, flowers, particularly cut blossoms, appeared frequently in vanitas paintings. However, floral painting as a distinct genre also flourished in the Dutch Republic. One of the leading practitioners of this art was RACHEL RUYSCH (1663–1750), who from 1708 to 1716 served as court painter to the elector Palatine (the ruler of the Palatinate, a former division of Bavaria) in Düsseldorf, Germany. Ruysch's father was a professor of botany and anatomy, which may account for her interest in and knowledge of plants and insects. She acquired an international reputation for her lush paintings, such as *Flower Still Life* (FIG. 25-23). In this canvas, the lavish floral arrangement is so full, many of the blossoms seem to be spilling out of the vase. Ruysch's careful arrangement of the painting's elements is evident in her composing the flowers to create a diagonal running from the lower left to the upper right corner of the canvas, offsetting the opposing diagonal of the table edge.

25-22 WILLEM KALF, *Still Life with a Late Ming Ginger Jar*, 1669. Oil on canvas, 2′ 6″ × 2′ 1¾″. Indianapolis Museum of Art, Indianapolis (gift in commemoration of the 60th anniversary of the Art Association of Indianapolis, in memory of Daniel W. and Elizabeth C. Marmon).

The opulent objects, especially the Indian carpet and Chinese jar, attest to the prosperous Dutch maritime trade. Kalf's inclusion of a watch suggests this painting may be a vanitas still life.

1 ft.

25-23 RACHEL RUYSCH, *Flower Still Life*, after 1700. Oil on canvas, 2′ 5¾″ × 1′ 11⅞″. Toledo Museum of Art, Toledo (purchased with funds from the Libbey Endowment, gift of Edward Drummond Libbey). ◼◀

Flower paintings were very popular in the Dutch Republic. Ruysch achieved international renown for her lush paintings of floral arrangements, noted also for their careful compositions.

FRANCE

In France, monarchical authority had been increasing for centuries, culminating in the reign of Louis XIV (r. 1661–1715), who sought to determine the direction of French society and culture. Although its economy was not as expansive as the Dutch Republic's, France became Europe's largest and most powerful nation in the 17th century. Against this backdrop, the arts flourished.

Louis XIV

The preeminent French art patron of the 17th century was King Louis XIV himself. Determined to consolidate and expand his power, Louis was a master of political strategy and propaganda. He established a carefully crafted and nuanced relationship with the nobility, granting them sufficient benefits to keep them pacified but simultaneously maintaining rigorous control to avoid insurrection or rebellion. He also ensured subservience by anchoring his rule in *divine right* (belief in a king's absolute power as God's will), rendering Louis's authority incontestable. So convinced was Louis of his importance and centrality to the French kingdom that he eagerly adopted the title "le Roi Soleil" ("the Sun King"). Like the sun, Louis XIV was the center of the universe.

The Sun King's desire for control extended to all realms of French life, including art. Louis and his principal adviser, Jean-Baptiste Colbert (1619–1683), strove to organize art and architecture in the service of the state. They understood well the power of art as propaganda and the value of visual imagery for cultivating a public persona, and they spared no pains to raise great symbols and monuments to the king's absolute power. Louis and Colbert sought to regularize taste and establish the classical style as the preferred French manner. The founding of the Royal Academy of Painting and Sculpture in 1648 served to advance this goal.

PORTRAITURE Louis XIV maintained a workshop of artists, each with a specialization—for example, faces, fabric, architecture, landscapes, armor, or fur. Thus, many of the king's portraits were a group effort, but the finest is the work of one artist. *Louis XIV*

25-24 HYACINTHE RIGAUD, *Louis XIV*, 1701. Oil on canvas, 9′ 2″ × 6′ 3″. Musée du Louvre, Paris. ◼◀

In this portrait set against a stately backdrop, Rigaud portrayed the 5′ 4″ Sun King wearing red high-heeled shoes and with his ermine-lined coronation robes thrown over his left shoulder.

25-25 CLAUDE PERRAULT, LOUIS LE VAU, and CHARLES LE BRUN, east facade of the Louvre (looking southwest), Paris, France, 1667–1670. ◼◀

The design of the Louvre's east facade is a brilliant synthesis of French and Italian classical elements, including a central pavilion resembling an ancient temple front with a pediment.

(FIG. 25-24) by Hyacinthe Rigaud (1659–1743) successfully conveys the image of an absolute monarch. The king, age 63 when Rigaud painted this work, stands with his left hand on his hip and gazes directly at the viewer. His elegant ermine-lined fleur-de-lis coronation robes (compare FIG. 25-3) hang loosely from his left shoulder, suggesting an air of haughtiness. Louis also draws his garment back to expose his legs. (The king was a ballet dancer in his youth and was proud of his well-toned legs.) The portrait's majesty derives in large part from the composition. The Sun King is the unmistakable focal point of the image, and Rigaud placed him so he seems to look down on the viewer. (Louis XIV was only five feet four inches tall—a fact that drove him to invent the red-heeled shoes he wears in the portrait.) The carefully detailed environment in which the king stands also contributes to the painting's stateliness and grandiosity. Indeed, when the king was not present, Rigaud's portrait, which hung over the throne, served in his place, and courtiers knew never to turn their backs on the painting.

THE LOUVRE The first great architectural project Louis XIV and his adviser Colbert undertook was the closing of the east side of the Louvre's Cour Carré (FIG. 23-14), left incomplete by Pierre Lescot in the 16th century. The king summoned Gianlorenzo Bernini (see Chapter 24) from Rome to submit plans, but Bernini envisioned an Italian palace on a monumental scale, which would have involved the demolition of all previous work. His plan rejected, Bernini indignantly returned to Rome. Louis then turned to three

French architects—Claude Perrault (1613–1688), Louis Le Vau (1612–1670), and Charles Le Brun (1619–1690)—for the Louvre's east facade (FIG. 25-25). The design is a brilliant synthesis of French and Italian classical elements, culminating in a new and definitive formula. The facade has a central and two corner projecting columnar pavilions resting on a stately podium. The central pavilion is in the form of a classical temple front. To either side is a giant colonnade of paired columns, resembling the columned flanks of a temple folded out like wings. The designers favored an even roofline, balustraded and broken only by the central pediment, over the traditional French pyramidal roof of the Louvre's west wing (FIG. 23-14). The emphatically horizontal sweep of the 17th-century facade brushed aside all memory of Gothic verticality. The stately proportions and monumentality of the Baroque design were both an expression of the new official French taste and a symbol of centrally organized authority.

VERSAILLES PALACE Work on the Louvre barely had begun when Louis XIV decided to convert a royal hunting lodge at Versailles, south of Paris, into a great palace. He assembled a veritable army of architects, decorators, sculptors, painters, and landscape designers under the general management of Charles Le Brun. In their hands, the conversion of a simple lodge into the palace of Versailles (FIG. 25-26) became the greatest architectural project of the age—a defining statement of French Baroque style and an undeniable symbol of Louis XIV's power and ambition.

25-26 Jules Hardouin-Mansart, Charles Le Brun, and André Le Nôtre, aerial view of the palace and gardens (looking northwest), Versailles, France, begun 1669.

Louis XIV ordered his architects to convert a royal hunting lodge at Versailles into a gigantic palace and park with a satellite city whose three radial avenues intersect in the king's bedroom.

25-27 JULES HARDOUIN-MANSART and CHARLES LE BRUN, Galerie des Glaces (Hall of Mirrors), palace of Versailles, Versailles, France, ca. 1680.

This hall overlooks the Versailles park from the second floor of Louis XIV's palace. Hundreds of mirrors illusionistically extend the room's width and once reflected gilded and jeweled furnishings.

Planned on a gigantic scale, the project called not only for a large palace flanking a vast park but also for the construction of a satellite city to house court and government officials, military and guard detachments, courtiers, and servants (undoubtedly to keep them all under the king's close supervision). Le Brun laid out this town to the east of the palace along three radial avenues that converge on the palace. Their axes, in a symbolic assertion of the ruler's absolute power over his domains, intersected in the king's spacious bedroom, which served as an official audience chamber. The palace itself, more than a quarter mile long, is perpendicular to the dominant east-west axis running through the associated city and park.

Every detail of the extremely rich decoration of the palace's interior received careful attention. The architects and decorators designed everything from wall paintings to doorknobs in order to reinforce the splendor of Versailles and to exhibit the very finest sense of artisanship. Of the literally hundreds of rooms within the palace, the most famous is the Galerie des Glaces, or Hall of Mirrors (FIG. 25-27), designed by JULES HARDOUIN-MANSART (1646–1708) and Le Brun. This hall overlooks the park from the second floor and extends along most of the width of the central block. Although deprived of its original sumptuous furniture, which included gold and silver chairs and bejeweled trees, the Galerie des Glaces retains much of its splendor today. Hundreds of mirrors, set into the wall opposite the windows, alleviate the hall's tunnel-like quality and illusionistically extend the width of the room. The mirror, that ultimate source of illusion, was a favorite element of Baroque interior design. Here, it also enhanced the dazzling extravagance of the great festivals Louis XIV was so fond of hosting.

VERSAILLES PARK The enormous palace might appear unbearably ostentatious were it not for its extraordinary setting in a vast park, which makes the palace seem almost an adjunct. From the Galerie des Glaces, the king and his guests could enjoy a sweeping vista down the park's tree-lined central axis and across terraces, lawns, pools, and lakes toward the horizon. The park of Versailles, designed by ANDRÉ LE NÔTRE (1613–1700), must rank among the world's greatest artworks in both size and concept. Here, the French architect transformed an entire forest into a park. Although its geometric plan may appear stiff and formal, the park in fact offers an almost unlimited assortment of vistas, as Le Nôtre used not only the multiplicity of natural forms but also the terrain's slightly rolling contours with stunning effectiveness.

The formal gardens near the palace provide a rational transition from the frozen architectural forms to the natural living ones. Here, the elegant shapes of trimmed shrubs and hedges define the tightly designed geometric units. Each unit is different from its neighbor and has a focal point in the form of a sculptured group, a pavilion, a reflecting pool, or perhaps a fountain. Farther away from the palace, the design loosens as trees, in shadowy masses, screen or frame views of open countryside. Le Nôtre carefully composed all vistas for maximum effect. Light and shadow, formal and informal, dense growth and open meadows—all play against one another in unending combinations and variations. No photograph or series of photographs can reveal the design's full richness. The park unfolds itself only to those walking through it. In this respect, it is a temporal artwork. Its aspects change with the time of day, the seasons, and the relative position of the observer.

GROTTO OF THETIS For the Grotto of Thetis above a dramatic waterfall in the gardens of Versailles, FRANÇOIS GIRARDON (1628–1715) designed *Apollo Attended by the Nymphs* (FIG. **25-28**). Both stately and graceful, the nymphs have a compelling charm as they minister to the god Apollo at the end of the day. (The three nymphs in the background are the work of THOMAS REGNAUDIN [1622–1706].) Girardon's close study of Greco-Roman sculpture heavily influenced his design of the figures, and the figure compositions of the most renowned French painter of the era, Nicholas Poussin (FIG. 25-31), inspired their arrangement. Since Apollo was often equated with the sun god (see "The Gods and Goddesses of Mount Olympus," Chapter 5, page 107, or page xxix in Volume II and Book D), the group refers obliquely to Louis XIV as the Roi Soleil. This doubtless helped to assure the work's success at court. Girardon's classical style and mythological symbolism well suited France's glorification of royal majesty.

ROYAL CHAPEL In 1698, Hardouin-Mansart received the commission to add a Royal Chapel to the Versailles palace complex. The chapel's interior (FIG. **25-29**) is essentially rectangular, but because its apse is as high as the nave, the fluid central space takes on a curved Baroque quality. However, the light entering through the large clerestory windows lacks the directed dramatic effect of the Italian Baroque, instead illuminating the interior's precisely chiseled details brightly and evenly. Pier-supported arcades carry a majestic row of Corinthian columns defining the royal gallery. The royal pew is at the rear, accessible directly from the king's apartments. Amid the restrained decoration, only the illusionistic ceiling paintings, added in 1708 and 1709 by ANTOINE COYPEL (1661–1722), suggest the drama and complexity of Italian Baroque art.

As a symbol of absolute power, Versailles has no equal. It also expresses, in the most monumental terms of its age, the rationalistic creed—based on scientific advances, such as the physics of Sir Isaac

25-30 JULES HARDOUIN-MANSART, Église du Dôme (looking north), Church of the Invalides, Paris, France, 1676–1706. ◼◀

Hardouin-Mansart's church marries the Italian and French architectural styles. The grouping of the orders is similar to the Italian Baroque manner but without the dramatic play of curved surfaces.

established for the disabled soldiers of his many wars. Two firmly separated levels, the upper one capped by a pediment, compose the frontispiece. The grouping of the orders and of the bays they frame is not unlike that in Italian Baroque architecture but without the dramatic play of curved surfaces characteristic of many 17th-century Italian churches, for example, Borromini's San Carlo (FIG. 24-9) in Rome. The compact facade is low and narrow in relation to the vast drum and dome, seeming to serve simply as a base for them. The overpowering dome, conspicuous on the Parisian skyline, is itself expressive of the Baroque love for dramatic magnitude, as is the way its designer aimed for theatrical effects of light and space. The dome consists of three shells, the lowest cut off so a visitor to the interior looks up through it to the one above, which is filled with light from hidden windows in the third, outermost dome. CHARLES DE LA FOSSE (1636–1716) painted the second dome in 1705 with an Italian-inspired representation of the heavens opening up to receive Saint Louis, patron of France (see "Louis IX, the Saintly King," Chapter 13, page 385).

Poussin

Louis XIV's embrace of classicism enticed many French artists to study Rome's ancient and Renaissance monuments. But even before the Sun King ascended to the throne in 1661, NICOLAS POUSSIN (1594–1665) of Normandy had spent most of his life in Rome, where he produced grandly severe paintings modeled on those of Titian and Raphael. He also carefully formulated a theoretical explanation of his method and was ultimately responsible for establishing classical painting as an important ingredient of 17th-century French art (see "Poussin's Notes for a Treatise on Painting," page 719). His classical style presents a striking contrast to the contemporaneous Baroque style of his Italian counterparts in Rome (see Chapter 24), underscoring the multifaceted character of the art of 17th-century Europe.

ET IN ARCADIA EGO Poussin's *Et in Arcadia Ego* (*Even in Arcadia, I* [am present]; FIG. 25-31) exemplifies the "grand manner" of painting the artist advocated. It features a lofty subject rooted in the classical world and figures based on antique statuary. Rather than depicting dynamic movement and intense emotions, as his Italian contemporaries in Rome did, Poussin emulated the rational order and stability of Raphael's paintings. Dominating the foreground are three shepherds living in the idyllic land of Arcadia. They study an inscription on a tomb as a statuesque female figure quietly places her hand on the shoulder of one of them. She may be the spirit of death, reminding these mortals, as does the inscription that death is found even in Arcadia, supposedly a spot of paradisiacal bliss. The countless draped female statues surviving in Italy from Roman times supplied the models for this figure, and the posture of the youth with one foot resting on a boulder derives from Greco-Roman statues of Neptune, the sea god, leaning on his trident. The classically compact and balanced grouping of the figures, the even light, and the thoughtful and reserved mood complement Poussin's classical figure types.

Newton (1642–1727) and the mathematical philosophy of René Descartes (1596–1650)—that all knowledge must be systematic and all science must be the consequence of the intellect imposed on matter. The majestic and rational design of Versailles proudly proclaims the mastery of human intelligence (and the mastery of Louis XIV) over the disorderliness of nature.

ÉGLISE DU DÔME, PARIS Another of Hardouin-Mansart's masterworks, the Église du Dôme (FIG. 25-30), or Church of the Invalides, in Paris, also marries the Italian Baroque and French classical architectural styles. An intricately composed domed square of great scale, the church adjoins the veterans hospital Louis XIV

Poussin's Notes for a Treatise on Painting

As the leading proponent of classical painting in 17th-century Rome, Nicolas Poussin outlined the principles of classicism in notes for an intended treatise on painting, left incomplete at his death. In those notes, Poussin described the essential ingredients necessary to produce a beautiful painting in "the grand manner":

The grand manner consists of four things: subject-matter or theme, thought, structure, and style. The first thing that, as the foundation of all others, is required, is that the subject-matter shall be grand, as are battles, heroic actions, and divine things. But assuming that the subject on which the painter is laboring is grand, his next consideration is to keep away from minutiae . . . [and paint only] things magnificent and grand . . . Those who elect mean subjects take refuge in them because of the weakness of their talents.*

The idea of beauty does not descend into matter unless this is prepared as carefully as possible. This preparation consists of three things: arrangement, measure, and aspect or form. Arrangement means the relative position of the parts; measure refers to their size; and form consists of lines and colors. Arrangement and relative position of the parts and making every limb of the body hold its natural place are not sufficient unless measure is added, which gives to each limb its correct size, proportionate to that of the whole body [compare "Polykleitos's Prescription for the Perfect Statue," Chapter 5, page 132], and unless form joins in, so that the lines will be drawn with grace and with a harmonious juxtaposition of light and shadow.†

Poussin applied these principles in paintings such as *Et in Arcadia Ego* (FIG. 25-31), a work peopled with perfectly proportioned statuesque figures attired in antique garb.

*Translated by Robert Goldwater and Marco Treves, eds., *Artists on Art*, 3d ed. (New York: Pantheon Books, 1958), 155.
†Ibid., 156.

25-31 NICOLAS POUSSIN, *Et in Arcadia Ego*, ca. 1655. Oil on canvas, 2′ 10″ × 4′. Musée du Louvre, Paris.

1 ft.

Poussin was the leading proponent of classicism in 17th-century Rome. His "grand manner" paintings are models of "arrangement and measure" and incorporate figures inspired by ancient statuary.

25-32 NICOLAS POUSSIN, *Landscape with Saint John on Patmos*, 1640. Oil on canvas, 3' 3½" × 4' 5⅝". Art Institute of Chicago, Chicago (A. A. Munger Collection). ◼◀

Poussin placed Saint John in a classical landscape amid broken columns, an obelisk, and a ruined temple, suggesting the decay of great civilizations and the coming of the new Christian era.

SAINT JOHN ON PATMOS In *Et in Arcadia Ego*, monumental figures dominate the landscape setting, but the natural world looms large in many of Poussin's paintings. *Landscape with Saint John on Patmos* (FIG. 25-32) is one of a pair of canvases Poussin painted for Gian Maria Roscioli (d. 1644), secretary to Pope Urban VIII. The second landscape represents Saint Matthew, reclining in right profile, who faced Saint John when the two canvases, now in different museums on different continents, hung side by side in Rome. An eagle stands behind John, just as an angel, Matthew's attribute, stands beside him. John, near the end of his life on the Greek island of Patmos, composed the book of Revelation, his account of the end of the world and the second coming of Christ, a prophetic

25-32A POUSSIN, *Burial of Phocion*, 1648.

vision of violent destruction and the last judgment. Poussin's setting, however, is a serene classical landscape beneath a sunny sky. (He created a similar setting in *Burial of Phocion* [FIG. 25-32A], which he painted later in the decade.) Saint John reclines in the foreground, posed like a Greco-Roman river god, amid shattered columns and a pedestal for a statue that disappeared long ago. In the middle ground, two oak trees frame the ruins of a classical temple and an Egyptian obelisk, many of which the Romans brought to their capital from the Nile and the popes reused in their building projects, for example, in the piazza in front of Saint Peter's (FIG. 24-4) and in Bernini's Fountain of the Four Rivers (FIG. 24-1). The decaying buildings suggest the decline of great empires—to be replaced by Christianity in a new era. In the distance are hills, sky, and clouds, all of which Poussin represented with pristine clarity, ignoring the rules of atmospheric perspective. His landscapes are not portraits of specific places, as are the Dutch landscapes of Ruisdael (FIG. 25-18) and Vermeer (FIG. 25-18B). Rather, they are imaginary settings constructed according to classical rules of design. Poussin's clouds, for example, echo the contours of his hills.

Claude Lorrain

Claude Gellée, called CLAUDE LORRAIN (1600–1682) after his birthplace in the duchy of Lorraine, rivaled Poussin in fame. Claude modulated in a softer style Poussin's disciplined rational art, with its sophisticated revelation of the geometry of landscape. Unlike the figures in Poussin's pictures, those in Claude's landscapes tell no dramatic story, point out no moral, praise no hero, and celebrate no saint. Indeed, the figures in Claude's paintings often appear to be added as mere excuses for the radiant landscape itself. For the French artist, painting involved essentially one theme—the beauty of a broad sky suffused with the golden light of dawn or sunset glowing through a hazy atmosphere and reflecting brilliantly off rippling water.

In *Landscape with Cattle and Peasants* (FIG. 25-33), the figures in the right foreground chat in animated fashion. In the left foreground, cattle relax contentedly. In the middle ground, cattle amble slowly away. The well-defined foreground, distinct middle ground, and dim background recede in serene orderliness, until all form dissolves in a luminous mist. Atmospheric and linear perspective reinforce each other to turn a vista into a typical Claudian vision, an ideal classical world bathed in sunlight in infinite space (compare FIG. I-12).

Claude's formalizing of nature with balanced groups of architectural masses, screens of trees, and sheets of water followed the great tradition of classical landscape. It began with the backgrounds of Venetian paintings (FIGS. 22-33 to 22-35) and continued in the art of Annibale Carracci (FIG. 24-15) and Poussin (FIGS. 25-32 and 25-32A). Yet Claude, like the Dutch painters, studied the light and the atmospheric nuances of nature, making a unique contribution. He recorded carefully in hundreds of sketches the look of the Roman countryside, its gentle terrain accented by stone-pines, cypresses, and poplars and by the ever-present ruins of ancient aqueducts, tombs, and towers. He made these the fundamental elements of his compositions. Travelers could understand the picturesque beauties of the outskirts of Rome in Claude's landscapes.

25-33 CLAUDE LORRAIN, *Landscape with Cattle and Peasants,* 1629. Oil on canvas, 3′ 6″ × 4′ 10½″. Philadelphia Museum of Art, Philadelphia (George W. Elkins Collection).

Claude used atmospheric and linear perspective to transform the rustic Roman countryside filled with peasants and animals into an ideal classical landscape bathed in sunlight in infinite space.

1 ft.

reveren
of any
their f
Tl
charac
this by
drama
volum
sical a
elemer
spiritu

Claude achieved his marvelous effects of light by painstakingly placing tiny value gradations, which imitated, though on a very small scale, the range of values of outdoor light and shade. Avoiding the problem of high-noon sunlight overhead, Claude preferred, and convincingly represented, the sun's rays as they gradually illuminated the morning sky or, with their dying glow, set the pensive mood of evening. Thus, he matched the moods of nature with those of human subjects. Claude's infusion of nature with human feeling and his recomposition of nature in a calm equilibrium greatly appealed to many landscape painters of the 18th and early 19th centuries.

Le Nain, Callot, La Tour

Although classicism was an important element of French art during the 17th and early 18th centuries, not all artists embraced the "grand manner."

LOUIS LE NAIN The works of LOUIS LE NAIN (ca. 1593–1648) have more in common with contemporaneous Dutch art than Renaissance or ancient art. Nevertheless, subjects that in Dutch painting were opportunities for boisterous good humor (FIG. 25-21), Le Nain treated with somber stillness. *Family of Country People* (FIG. **25-34**) reflects the thinking of 17th-century French social theorists who celebrated the natural virtue of peasants who worked the soil. Le Nain's painting expresses the grave dignity of one peasant family made stoic and resigned by hardship. These drab country folk surely had little reason for merriment. The peasant's lot, never easy, was miserable during the Thirty Years' War.

25-34 LOUIS LE NAIN, *Family of Country People,* ca. 1640. Oil on canvas, 3′ 8″ × 5′ 2″. Musée du Louvre, Paris.

Le Nain's painting expresses the grave dignity of a peasant family made stoic by hardship. It reflects 17th-century French social theory, which celebrated the natural virtue of those who worked the soil.

25-38 Sir Christopher Wren, west facade of Saint Paul's Cathedral, London, England, 1675–1710.

Wren's cathedral replaced an old Gothic church. The facade design owes much to Palladio (FIG. 22-30) and Borromini (FIG. 24-12). The great dome recalls Saint Peter's in Rome (FIGS. 22-25 and 24-4).

Jones superimposed two orders, using columns in the center and pilasters near the ends. The balustraded roofline, uninterrupted in its horizontal sweep, antedates the Louvre's east facade (FIG. 25-25) by more than 40 years. Palladio would have recognized and approved all of the design elements, but the building as a whole is not a copy of his work. Although relying on the revered Italian's architectural vocabulary and syntax, Jones retained his independence as a designer. For two centuries his influence in English architecture was almost as authoritative as Palladio's.

CHRISTOPHER WREN London's majestic Saint Paul's Cathedral (FIG. 25-38) is the work of England's most renowned architect, CHRISTOPHER WREN (1632–1723). A mathematical genius and skilled engineer whose work won Isaac Newton's praise, Wren became professor of astronomy in London at age 25. Mathematics led to architecture, and Charles II (r. 1649–1685) asked Wren to prepare a plan for restoring the old Gothic church of Saint Paul. Wren proposed to remodel the building based on Roman structures. Within a few months, the Great Fire of London, which destroyed the old structure and many churches in the city in 1666, gave Wren his opportunity. Although Jones's work strongly influenced him, Wren also traveled in France, where the splendid palaces and state buildings being created in and around Paris at the time of the com-

petition for the Louvre design must have impressed him. Wren also closely studied prints illustrating Baroque architecture in Italy. In Saint Paul's, he harmonized Palladian, French, and Italian Baroque features.

In view of its size, the cathedral was built with remarkable speed—in little more than 30 years—and Wren lived to see it completed. The building's form underwent constant refinement during construction, and Wren did not determine the final appearance of the towers until after 1700. In the splendid skyline composition, two foreground towers act effectively as foils to the great dome. Wren must have known similar schemes Italian architects had devised for Saint Peter's (FIG. 24-4) in Rome to solve the problem of the relationship between the facade and dome. Certainly, the influence of Borromini (FIG. 24-12) is evident in the upper levels and lanterns of the towers. The lower levels owe a debt to Palladio (FIG. 22-30), and the superposed paired columnar porticos recall the Louvre's east facade (FIG. 25-25). Wren's skillful eclecticism brought all these foreign features into a monumental unity.

Wren designed many other London churches after the Great Fire. Even today, Wren's towers and domes punctuate the skyline of London. Saint Paul's dome is the tallest of all. Wren's legacy was significant and long-lasting, both in England and in colonial America (see Chapter 26).

THE BAROQUE IN NORTHERN EUROPE

FLANDERS

- In the 17th century, Flanders remained Catholic and under Spanish control. Flemish Baroque art is more closely tied to the Baroque art of Italy than is the art of much of the rest of northern Europe.

- The leading Flemish painter of this era was Peter Paul Rubens, whose work and influence were international in scope. A diplomat as well as an artist, he counted kings and queens among his patrons and friends. His paintings exhibit Baroque splendor in color and ornament, and feature robust and foreshortened figures in swirling motion.

Rubens, *Consequences of War*, 1638–1639

DUTCH REPUBLIC

- The Dutch Republic received official recognition of its independence from Spain in the Treaty of Westphalia of 1648. Worldwide trade and banking brought prosperity to its predominantly Protestant citizenry, which largely rejected church art in favor of private commissions of portraits, genre scenes, landscapes, and still lifes.

- Frans Hals produced innovative portraits of middle-class patrons in which a lively informality replaced the formulaic patterns of traditional portraiture. Aelbert Cuyp and Jacob van Ruisdael specialized in landscapes depicting specific places, not idealized Renaissance settings. Peter Claesz, Willem Kalf, and others painted vanitas still lifes featuring meticulous depictions of worldly goods amid reminders of death.

- Rembrandt van Rijn, the greatest Dutch artist of the age, treated a broad range of subjects, including religious themes and portraits. His oil paintings are notable for their dramatic impact and subtle gradations of light and shade as well as the artist's ability to convey human emotions. Rembrandt was also a master printmaker renowned for his etchings.

- Jan Vermeer specialized in painting the occupants of serene, comfortable Dutch homes. His convincing representation of interior spaces depended in part on his employment of the camera obscura. Vermeer was also a master of light and color and understood shadows are not colorless.

Rembrandt, *Hundred-Guilder Print*, ca. 1649

Vermeer, *Woman Holding a Balance*, ca. 1664

FRANCE AND ENGLAND

- The major art patron in 17th-century France was the Sun King, the absolutist monarch Louis XIV, who expanded the Louvre and built a gigantic palace-and-garden complex at Versailles featuring sumptuous furnishings and sweeping vistas. Among the architects Louis employed were Charles Le Brun and Jules Hardouin-Mansart, who succeeded in marrying Italian Baroque and French classical styles.

- The leading French proponent of classical painting was Nicolas Poussin, who spent most of his life in Rome and championed the "grand manner" of painting. This style called for heroic or divine subjects and classical compositions with figures often modeled on ancient statues.

- Claude Lorraine, whose fame rivaled Poussin's, specialized in classical landscapes rendered in linear and atmospheric perspective. His compositions often incorporated ancient ruins.

- In 17th-century England, architecture was the most important art form. Two architects who achieved international fame were Inigo Jones and Christopher Wren, who harmonized the architectural principles of Andrea Palladio with the Italian Baroque and French classical styles.

Poussin, *Et in Arcadia Ego*, ca. 1655

Wren, Saint Paul's, London, 1675–1710

Joseph Wright of Derby specialized in dramatically lit paintings celebrating the scientific advances of the Enlightenment era. Here, a man listening to a learned lecture takes careful notes.

At the center of Wright's canvas, a scholar demonstrates an orrery, a mechanical model of the solar system in which each planet revolves around the sun at the correct relative velocity.

Awestruck children crowd close to the orbs representing the planets within the arcing bands symbolizing their orbits. Light from a lamp creates shadows, heightening the drama of the scene.

26-1 JOSEPH WRIGHT OF DERBY, *A Philosopher Giving a Lecture at the Orrery*, ca. 1763–1765. Oil on canvas, 4′ 10″ × 6′ 8″. Derby Museums and Art Gallery, Derby.

The wonders of scientific knowledge mesmerize everyone in Wright's painting, adults as well as children. At the right, two gentlemen pay rapt attention to the demonstration.

ROCOCO TO NEOCLASSICISM: THE 18TH CENTURY IN EUROPE AND AMERICA

ART AND SCIENCE IN THE ERA OF ENLIGHTENMENT

The dawn of the *Enlightenment* in the 18th century brought a new way of thinking critically about the world and about humankind, independently of religion, myth, or tradition. Enlightenment thinkers rejected unfounded beliefs in favor of empirical evidence and promoted the questioning of all assertions. Thus, the Enlightenment encouraged and stimulated the habit and application of mind known as the "scientific method" and fostered technological invention. The scientific advances of the Enlightenment era affected the lives of everyone, and most people enthusiastically responded to wonders of the Industrial Revolution such as the steam engine, which gave birth to the modern manufacturing economy and the prospect of a seemingly limitless supply of goods and services.

The fascination science had for ordinary people as well as for the learned is the subject of *A Philosopher Giving a Lecture at the Orrery* (FIG. 26-1) by the English painter JOSEPH WRIGHT OF DERBY (1734–1797). Wright studied painting near Birmingham (MAP 27-2), the center of the Industrial Revolution, and specialized in dramatically lit scenes showcasing modern scientific instruments and experiments. In this painting, a scholar demonstrates a mechanical model of the solar system called an *orrery,* in which each planet (represented by a metal orb) revolves around the sun (a lamp) at the correct relative velocity. Light from the lamp pours forth from in front of the boy silhouetted in the foreground to create shadows that heighten the drama of the scene. Awestruck children crowd close to the tiny orbs representing the planets within the arcing bands symbolizing their orbits. An earnest listener makes notes, while the lone woman seated at the left and the two gentlemen at the right pay rapt attention. Scientific knowledge mesmerizes everyone in Wright's painting. The artist visually reinforced the fascination with the orrery by composing his image in a circular fashion, echoing the device's orbital design. The postures and gazes of all the participants and observers focus attention on the cosmic model. Wright scrupulously and accurately rendered every detail of the figures, the mechanisms of the orrery, and even the books and curtain in the shadowy background.

Wright's choice of subjects and realism in depicting them appealed to the great industrialists of his day, including Josiah Wedgwood (1730–1795), who pioneered many techniques of mass-produced pottery, and Sir Richard Arkwright (1732–1792), whose spinning frame revolutionized the textile industry. Both men often purchased paintings by Wright featuring scientific advances. To them, the Derby artist's elevation of the theories and inventions of the Industrial Revolution to the plane of history painting was exciting and appropriately in tune with the new era of Enlightenment.

A CENTURY OF REVOLUTIONS

In 1700, Louis XIV still ruled France as the Sun King (see Chapter 25), presiding over his realm and French culture from his palatial residence at Versailles (FIG. 25-26). The French king's palace inspired the construction of many other grandiose homes on the Continent and across the English Channel during the early 18th century, including Blenheim Palace (FIG. **26-1A**), which SIR JOHN VANBRUGH (1664–1726) and NICHOLAS HAWKSMOOR (1661–1736) designed for the duke of Marlborough. By 1800, however, revolutions had overthrown the monarchy in France and achieved independence for the British colonies in America (MAP **26-1**). The 18th century also gave birth to a revolution of a different kind—the Industrial Revolution, which began in England and soon transformed the economies of continental Europe and North America and eventually the world.

26-1A VANBRUGH and HAWKSMOOR, Blenheim Palace, 1705–1725.

Against this backdrop of revolutionary change, social as well as political, economic, and technological, came major transformations in the arts. Compare, for example, Antoine Watteau's *Pilgrimage to Cythera* (FIG. 26-7), painted 1717–1719, which unfolds in a lush landscape and celebrates the romantic dalliances of the moneyed elite, with Jacques-Louis David's 1784 *Oath of the Horatii* (FIG. 26-25), set in an austere Doric hall and glorifying the civic virtue and heroism of an ancient Roman family. The two works have little in common other than both are French oil paintings. In the 18th century, shifts in style and subject matter were both rapid and significant.

ROCOCO

The death of Louis XIV in 1715 brought many changes in French high society. The elite quickly abandoned the court of Versailles for the pleasures of town life. Although French citizens still owed allegiance to a monarch, the early 18th century brought a resurgence of aristocratic social, political, and economic power. Members of the nobility not only exercised their traditional privileges (for example, exemption from certain taxes and from forced labor on public works) but also sought to expand their power. In the cultural realm, aristocrats reestablished their predominance as art patrons.

MAP 26-1   The United States in 1800.

The *hôtels* (townhouses) of Paris soon became the centers of a new, softer style called *Rococo*. Associated with the regency (1715–1723) following the death of Louis XIV and with the reign of Louis XV (r. 1723–1774), the Rococo style in art and architecture was the perfect expression of the lighthearted elegance the wealthy cultivated in their opulent homes (see "Femmes Savants and Salon Culture," page 729).

ROCOCO TO NEOCLASSICISM:
THE 18TH CENTURY IN EUROPE AND AMERICA

1700	1725	1750	1775	1800

- The Rococo style becomes the rage in the opulent townhouses of Paris
- Watteau creates a new painting genre—the *fête galante*

- Neumann adapts the intimate Rococo domestic style to ecclesiastical architecture
- Chardin rejects the frivolity of Rococo painting in favor of "natural" art
- Canaletto paints views of Venice as souvenirs of the Grand Tour of Italy

- The Enlightenment admiration for Greece and Rome prompts a Neoclassical revival in architecture
- During the Industrial Revolution, Wright celebrates scientific advances in dramatically lit paintings
- First use of iron in bridge construction at Coalbrookdale, England

- Reynolds achieves renown for Grand Manner portraits
- Vigée-Lebrun and Labille-Guiard gain admission to the French Royal Academy of Painting and Sculpture
- David becomes the painter-ideologist of the French Revolution
- Jefferson promotes Neoclassicism as the official architectural style of the new American republic

Femmes Savants and Salon Culture

The feminine look of the Rococo style suggests the taste and social initiative of women, and to a large extent, women dominated the cultural sphere during the Rococo age. In the 18th century, aristocratic women—including Madame de Pompadour (1721–1764), mistress of Louis XV of France; Maria Theresa (1717–1780), archduchess of Austria and queen of Hungary and Bohemia; and Empresses Elizabeth (r. 1741–1762) and Catherine the Great (r. 1762–1796) of Russia—held some of the most influential positions in Europe. Female taste also was a defining factor in numerous smaller courts as well as in the private sphere.

In the early 1700s, Paris was the social capital of Europe, and the Rococo salon (FIG. 26-2) was the center of Parisian society. Wealthy, ambitious, and clever society hostesses competed to attract the most famous and accomplished people to their salons. The medium of social intercourse was conversation spiced with wit, repartee as quick and deft as a fencing match. Artifice reigned supreme, and participants considered enthusiasm or sincerity in bad taste.

The women who hosted these salons, whether in Paris or elsewhere in Europe (FIG. 26-3), referred to themselves as *femmes savants*—learned women. Chief among them was Julie de Lespinasse (1732–1776), one of the most articulate, urbane, and intelligent French women of the time. She held daily salons from five o'clock until nine in the evening. The memoirs of Jean François Marmontel (1723–1799), published in 1827, documented the liveliness of these gatherings and the remarkable nature of this hostess.

26-2 GERMAIN BOFFRAND, Salon de la Princesse, with paintings by CHARLES-JOSEPH NATOIRE and sculptures by JEAN-BAPTISTE LEMOYNE, Hôtel de Soubise, Paris, France, 1737–1740.

Rococo rooms such as this one, featuring sinuous curves, gilded moldings and mirrors, small sculptures and paintings, and floral ornamentation, were the center of Parisian social and intellectual life.

> The circle was formed of persons who were not bound together. She [Julie de Lespinasse] had taken them here and there in society, but so well assorted were they that once [in her salon] they fell into harmony like the strings of an instrument touched by an able hand. Following out that comparison, I may say that she played the instrument with an art that came of genius; she seemed to know what tone each string would yield before she touched it; I mean to say that our minds and our natures were so well known to her that in order to bring them into play she had but to say a word. Nowhere was conversation more lively, more brilliant, or better regulated than at her house. It was a rare phenomenon indeed, the degree of tempered, equable heat which she knew so well how to maintain, sometimes by moderating it, sometimes by quickening it. The continual activity of her soul was communicated to our souls, but measurably; her imagination was the mainspring, her reason the regulator. Remark that the brains she stirred at will were neither feeble nor frivolous. . . . Her talent for casting out a thought and giving it for discussion to men of that class, her own talent in discussing it with precision, sometimes with eloquence, her talent for bringing forward new ideas and varying the topic—always with the facility and ease of a fairy . . . these talents, I say, were not those of an ordinary woman. It was not with the follies of fashion and vanity that daily, during four hours of conversation, without languor and without vacuum, she knew how to make herself interesting to a wide circle of strong minds.*

*Jean François Marmontel, *Memoirs of Marmontel* (1827), translated by Brigit Patmore (London: Routledge, 1930), 270.

Architecture

Rococo appeared in France in about 1700, primarily as a style of interior design. The French Rococo exterior was most often simple, or even plain, but Rococo exuberance took over the interior. The term derived from the French word *rocaille* (pebble), but it referred especially to the small stones and shells used to decorate grotto interiors. Shells or forms resembling shells were the principal motifs in Rococo ornamentation.

SALON DE LA PRINCESSE A typical French Rococo room is the Salon de la Princesse (FIG. 26-2) in the Hôtel de Soubise in Paris, designed by GERMAIN BOFFRAND (1667–1754) in collaboration with the painter JOSEPH NATOIRE (1700–1777) and the sculptor JEAN-BAPTISTE LEMOYNE (1704–1778). Parisian salons such as this one were the center of Rococo social life. They usurped the role Louis XIV's Versailles palace (FIG. 25-26) played in the 17th century, when the Sun King set the tone for French culture. In the

26-3 François de Cuvilliés, Hall of Mirrors, the Amalienburg, Nymphenburg Palace park, Munich, Germany, early 18th century.

Designed by a French architect, this circular hall in a German lodge displays the Rococo architectural style at its zenith, dazzling the eye with the organic interplay of mirrors, crystal, and stucco relief.

early 18th century, the centralized and grandiose palace-based culture of Baroque France gave way to a much more intimate and decentralized culture based in private homes. The new architectural style mirrored this social and cultural shift. A comparison between the Salon de la Princesse and the Galerie des Glaces (FIG. 25-27) at Versailles reveals how Boffrand softened the strong architectural lines and panels of the earlier style into flexible, sinuous curves luxuriantly multiplied in mirror reflections. The walls melt into the vault. Irregular painted shapes, surmounted by sculpture and separated by the ubiquitous rocaille shells, replace the hall's cornices. Painting, architecture, and sculpture combine to form a single ensemble. The profusion of curving tendrils and sprays of foliage blend with the shell forms to give an effect of freely growing nature, suggesting the designer permanently bedecked the Rococo room for a festival.

French Rococo interiors were lively total works of art. Exquisitely wrought furniture, enchanting small sculptures, ornamented mirror frames, delightful ceramics and silver, small paintings, and decorative *tapestries* complemented the architecture, relief sculptures, and mural paintings. Unfortunately, the Salon de la Princesse has lost most of the moveable furnishings that once contributed so much to its total ambience. Visitors can imagine, however,

how this and similar Rococo rooms—with their alternating gilded moldings, vivacious relief sculptures, and daintily colored ornamentation of flowers and garlands—must have harmonized with the chamber music played in them, with the elaborate costumes of satin and brocade, and with the equally elegant etiquette and sparkling wit of the people who graced them.

AMALIENBURG The French Rococo style quickly spread beyond Paris. The Amalienburg, a small lodge the French architect FRANÇOIS DE CUVILLIÉS (1695–1768) built in the park of the Nymphenburg Palace in Munich, is a prime example of Germany's adoption of the Parisian style. The most spectacular room in the lodge is the circular Hall of Mirrors (FIG. **26-3**), a silver-and-blue ensemble of architecture, stucco relief, silvered bronze mirrors, and crystal. The hall dazzles the eye with myriad scintillating motifs, forms, and figurations and showcases the full ornamental repertoire of the Rococo style at its zenith. Silvery light, reflected and amplified by windows and mirrors, bathes the room and creates shapes and contours that weave rhythmically around the upper walls and the ceiling coves. Everything seems organic, growing, and in motion, an ultimate refinement of illusion the architect, artists, and artisans created with virtuoso flourishes.

26-4 BALTHASAR NEUMANN, interior of the pilgrimage church of Vierzehnheiligen (looking east), near Staffelstein, Germany, 1743–1772.

Neumann adapted the intimate Rococo style to ecclesiastical architecture. Vierzehnheiligen's interior is light and delicate in contrast to the dynamic energy of Italian Baroque church designs.

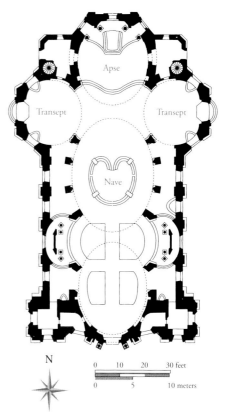

26-5 BALTHASAR NEUMANN, plan of the pilgrimage church of Vierzehnheiligen, near Staffelstein, Germany, 1743–1772.

Vierzehnheiligen's plan features undulating lines and a dynamic composition of tangent ovals and circles. It is even more complex than Borromini's influential church plans (FIGS. 24-10 and 24-13).

26-3A FISCHER VON ERLACH, Karlskirche, Vienna, 1716–1737.

VIERZEHNHEILIGEN Rococo style was not exclusively a domestic phenomenon, however. Although in the early 18th century, some architects, such as JOHANN BERNHARD FISCHER VON ERLACH (1656–1723), continued to design churches incorporating Baroque and classical elements—for example, Karlskirche (FIG. 26-3A) in Vienna—others eagerly adopted the Rococo style for ecclesiastical architecture. One of the most splendid examples is the pilgrimage church of Vierzehnheiligen (Fourteen Saints; FIGS. 26-4 and 26-5) near Staffelstein (MAP 25-1), which the German architect BALTHASAR NEUMANN (1687–1753) began as construction was about to be concluded on the grandiose palace (FIG. 26-5A) he had designed in 1719 for the prince-bishops of Würzburg. The interior (FIG. 26-4) of Neumann's church exhibits a vivacious play of architectural fantasy that retains the dynamic energy of Italian Baroque architecture (see Chapter 24) but not its drama. Numerous large windows in the richly decorated walls of Vierzehnheiligen flood the interior with an even, bright, and cheerful light. The feeling is one of lightness and delicacy.

Vierzehnheiligen's plan (FIG. 26-5) reveals the influence of Francesco Borromini (FIGS. 24-10 and 24-13), as does the contemporaneous Wieskirche (Church of the Meadow; FIG. 26-5B) by DOMINIKUS ZIMMERMANN (1685–1766). The Staffelstein plan, however, is even more complex than the plans for Borromini's churches in Rome. Neumann, perhaps deliberately, banished all straight lines. The composition, made up of tangent ovals and circles, achieves a quite different interior effect within the essential outlines of a traditional rectilinear basilican church with a nave, transept, and apse. Undulating space is in continuous motion, creating unlimited vistas bewildering in their variety and surprise effects. The structure's features pulse, flow, and commingle as if they were ceaselessly in the process of being molded. The design's fluidity of line, the floating and hovering surfaces, the interwoven spaces, and the dematerialized masses combine to suggest a "frozen" counterpart to the intricacy of voices in a Baroque fugue by Johann Sebastian Bach (1685–1750). The church is a brilliant ensemble of architecture, painting, sculpture, and music that dissolves the boundaries among the arts.

26-5A NEUMANN, Kaisersaal, Würzburg, 1719–1744.

26-5B ZIMMERMANN, Wieskirche, Füssen, 1745–1754.

Painting and Sculpture

The unification of diverse artistic media that characterizes the Rococo style did not preclude the rise to prominence of painters of independent works. Chief among them were Antoine Watteau, François Boucher, and Jean-Honoré Fragonard in France.

ANTOINE WATTEAU The painter whom scholars most closely associate with French Rococo is ANTOINE WATTEAU (1684–1721). The sharp differences between the Rococo and Baroque ages in France quickly become evident by contrasting Watteau's *L'Indifférent* (*The Indifferent One;* FIG. 26-6) with Rigaud's portrait of Louis XIV (FIG. 25-24). Rigaud portrayed pompous majesty in supreme glory, as if the French monarch were reviewing throngs of bowing courtiers at Versailles. Watteau's painting is more delicate and lighter in both color and tone. The artist presented a languid, gliding dancer whose stilted minuet might constitute a parody of the monarch's solemnity if the paintings were hung together. (The contrast in scale would be equally stark: The portrait of Louis XIV is almost 10 feet tall. Watteau's dancer is 10 inches tall.) In Rigaud's portrait, stout architecture, bannerlike curtains, flowing ermine, and fleur-de-lis exalt the king. In Watteau's painting, the dancer moves in a rainbow shimmer of color, emerging onto the stage of the intimate comic opera to the silken sounds of strings. As in architecture, this contrast of paintings also highlights the shift in artistic patronage from one era to the next.

26-6 ANTOINE WATTEAU, *L'Indifférent,* ca. 1716. Oil on canvas, 10″ × 7″. Musée du Louvre, Paris. ◼◀

This small Rococo painting of a dancer exhibits lightness and delicacy in both color and tone. It differs significantly from Rigaud's majestic portrait (FIG. 25-24) of the pompous Louis XIV.

1 ft.

26-7 ANTOINE WATTEAU, *Pilgrimage to Cythera,* 1717. Oil on canvas, 4′ 3″ × 6′ 4½″. Musée du Louvre, Paris. ◼◀

Watteau's *fête galante* paintings depict the outdoor amusements of French upper-class society. The haze of color, subtly modeled shapes, gliding motion, and air of suave gentility match Rococo taste.

Whereas royal patronage, particularly on the part of Louis XIV, dominated the French Baroque period, Rococo was the culture of a wider aristocracy in which private patrons dictated taste.

PILGRIMAGE TO CYTHERA Watteau was largely responsible for creating a specific type of Rococo painting, called a *fête galante* (amorous festival) painting. These paintings depicted the outdoor entertainment or amusements of French high society. The premier example of a fête galante painting is Watteau's masterpiece (painted in two versions), *Pilgrimage to Cythera* (FIG. 26-7). The painting was the artist's entry for admission to the French Royal Academy of Painting and Sculpture (see "Academic Salons," Chapter 28, page 802). In 1717 the fête galante was not an acceptable category for submission, but rather than reject Watteau's candidacy, the academy created a new category to accommodate his entry. At the turn of the 18th century, two competing doctrines sharply divided the membership of the French academy. Many members followed Nicolas Poussin in teaching that form was the most important element in painting, whereas "colors in painting are as allurements for persuading the eyes."[1] Colors were additions for effect and not really essential. The other group took Rubens as its model and proclaimed the natural supremacy of color and the coloristic style as the artist's proper guide. Depending on which doctrine they supported, academy members were either *Poussinistes* or *Rubénistes*. Watteau was Flemish and Rubens's coloristic style heavily influenced his work. With Watteau in their ranks, the Rubénistes carried the day, establishing Rococo painting as the preferred style of the early 18th century.

Watteau's *Pilgrimage to Cythera* (FIG. 26-7) presents luxuriously costumed lovers who have made a "pilgrimage" to Cythera, the island of eternal youth and love, sacred to Aphrodite. (Some art historians think the lovers are returning from Cythera rather than having just arrived. Watteau provided few clues to settle the question definitively.) The elegant figures move gracefully from the protective shade of a woodland park, filled with amorous cupids and voluptuous statuary. Watteau's figural poses blend elegance and sweetness. He composed his generally quite small paintings from albums of drawings in which he sought to capture slow movement from difficult and unusual angles, searching for the smoothest, most poised, and most refined attitudes. As he experimented with nuances of posture and movement, Watteau also strove for the most exquisite shades of color difference, defining in a single stroke the shimmer of silk at a bent knee or the iridescence that touches a glossy surface as it emerges from shadow. The haze of color, the subtly modeled shapes, the gliding motion, and the air of suave gentility appealed greatly to Watteau's wealthy patrons, whom, as he was dying from tuberculosis, he still depicted as carefree and at leisure in his most unusual painting, *Signboard of Gersaint* (FIG. 26-7A).

26-7A WATTEAU, *Signboard of Gersaint*, 1721.

FRANÇOIS BOUCHER After Watteau's death at age 36 brought his brilliant career to a premature end, FRANÇOIS BOUCHER (1703–1770) rose to the dominant position in French painting, in large part because he was Madame de Pompadour's favorite artist. Although Boucher was an excellent portraitist,

his success rested primarily on his graceful canvases depicting Arcadian shepherds, nymphs, and goddesses cavorting in shady glens engulfed in pink and sky-blue light. *Cupid a Captive* (FIG. 26-8) presents a rosy pyramid of infant and female flesh set off against a cool, leafy background, with fluttering draperies both hiding and revealing the nudity of the figures. Boucher used the full range of Italian

1 ft.

26-8 FRANÇOIS BOUCHER, *Cupid a Captive*, 1754. Oil on canvas, 5′ 6″ × 2′ 10″. Wallace Collection, London. ◼◀

Boucher was Madame de Pompadour's favorite artist. In this Rococo tableau, he painted a pyramid of rosy infant and female flesh and fluttering draperies set off against a cool, leafy background.

and French Baroque devices—the dynamic play of crisscrossing diagonals, curvilinear forms, and slanting recessions—to create his masterly composition. But he dissected powerful Baroque curves into a multiplicity of decorative flourishes, dissipating Baroque drama into sensual playfulness. Lively and lighthearted, Boucher's artful Rococo fantasies became mirrors for his affluent French patrons to behold the ornamental reflections of their cherished pastimes.

JEAN-HONORÉ FRAGONARD Boucher's greatest student, JEAN-HONORÉ FRAGONARD (1732–1806), was a first-rate colorist whose decorative skill almost surpassed his master's. An example of his manner can stand as characteristic not only of his work but also of the later Rococo in general. In *The Swing* (FIG. 26-9), a young gentleman has convinced an unsuspecting old bishop to swing the young man's pretty sweetheart higher and higher, while her lover (and the work's patron), in the lower left corner, stretches out to admire her ardently from a strategic position on the ground. The young lady flirtatiously and boldly kicks off her shoe toward the little statue of Cupid. The infant love god holds his finger to his lips. The landscape emulates Watteau's—a luxuriant perfumed bower in

1 ft.

26-9 JEAN-HONORÉ FRAGONARD, *The Swing*, 1766. Oil on canvas, 2′ 8⅝″ × 2′ 2″. Wallace Collection, London. ◼◀

Fragonard's *Swing* epitomizes Rococo style. Pastel colors and soft light complement a scene in which a young lady flirtatiously kicks off her shoe at a statue of Cupid while her lover watches.

26-10 GIAMBATTISTA TIEPOLO, *Apotheosis of the Pisani Family,* ceiling painting in the Villa Pisani, Stra, Italy, 1761–1762. Fresco, 77′ 1″ × 44′ 3″.

A master of illusionistic ceiling painting in the Baroque tradition, Tiepolo adopted the bright and cheerful colors and weightless figures of Rococo easel paintings for huge frescoes.

⊥ 1 in.

26-11 CLODION, *Nymph and Satyr Carousing,* ca. 1780–1790. Terracotta, 1′ 11¼″ high. Metropolitan Museum of Art, New York (bequest of Benjamin Altman, 1913).

The erotic playfulness of Boucher and Fragonard is evident in Clodion's tabletop terracotta sculptures representing sensuous fantasies often involving satyrs and nymphs, the followers of Bacchus.

a park that very much resembles a stage scene for comic opera. The glowing pastel colors and soft light convey, almost by themselves, the theme's sensuality.

GIAMBATTISTA TIEPOLO *The Swing* is less than 3 feet in height and Watteau's *L'Indifférent* (FIG. 26-6), as already noted, barely 10 inches tall. But the intimate Rococo style could also be adapted for paintings of huge size, as the work of GIAMBATTISTA TIEPOLO (1696–1770) demonstrates. A Venetian, Tiepolo worked for patrons in Austria, Germany, and Spain, as well as in Italy. He was a master of illusionistic ceiling decoration in the Baroque tradition, but favored the bright, cheerful colors and relaxed compositions of Rococo easel paintings. In *Apotheosis of the Pisani Family* (FIG. 26-10), a ceiling fresco in the Villa Pisani at Stra in northern Italy (MAP 25-1), Tiepolo depicted seemingly weightless figures fluttering through vast sunlit skies and fleecy clouds, their forms casting dark accents against the brilliant light of high noon. The painter elevated Pisani family members to the rank of gods in a heavenly scene recalling the ceiling paintings of Pozzo (FIG. 24-24). But while retaining 17th-century illusionism in his works, Tiepolo softened the rhetoric and created pictorial schemes of great elegance and grace, unsurpassed for their sheer effectiveness as decor.

CLODION Rococo was nonetheless a style best suited for small-scale works projecting a mood of sensual intimacy. Claude Michel, called CLODION (1738–1814), specialized in small, lively sculptures representing sensuous Rococo fantasies. Clodion lived and worked in Rome for several years after winning a cherished Prix de Rome (Rome Prize) from the French royal academy to study art and paint or sculpt in the eternal city. Clodion's work incorporates echoes of Italian Mannerist sculpture. His small group, *Nymph and Satyr Carousing* (FIG. 26-11), depicts two followers of Bacchus, the Roman god of wine. The sensuous nymph who rushes to pour wine from a cup into the open mouth of a semihuman goat-legged satyr is reminiscent of the nude female figures of Benvenuto Cellini (FIGS. 22-52 and 22-52A), who worked at Fontainebleau for Francis I, and of Giovanni da Bologna (FIG. 22-53), a French Mannerist sculptor who moved to Italy. The erotic playfulness of Boucher and Fragonard is also evident in Clodion's 2-foot-tall terracotta group destined for display on a marble tabletop in an elegant Rococo salon.

THE ENLIGHTENMENT

The aristocratic culture celebrated in Rococo art did not go unchallenged during the 18th century. Indeed, the feudal system that served as the foundation of social and economic life in Europe dissolved, and the rigid social hierarchies that provided the basis for Rococo art and patronage relaxed. By the end of the 18th century, revolutions had erupted in France and America. A major factor in these political, social, and economic changes was the Enlightenment.

Philosophy and Science

Enlightenment thinkers championed an approach to the acquisition of knowledge based on empirical observation and scientific experimentation (see "Art and Science in the Era of Enlightenment," page 727). Enlightenment-era science had roots in the work of René Descartes (1596–1650), Blaise Pascal (1623–1662), Isaac Newton (1642–1727), and Gottfried Wilhelm von Leibnitz (1646–1716) in the 17th century. England and France were the principal centers of the Enlightenment, though its dictums influenced the thinking of intellectuals throughout Europe and in the American colonies. Benjamin Franklin (1706–1790), Thomas Jefferson (1743–1826), and other American notables embraced its principles.

NEWTON AND LOCKE Of particular importance for Enlightenment thought was the work of Isaac Newton and John Locke (1632–1704) in England. In his scientific studies, Newton insisted on empirical proof of his theories and encouraged others to avoid metaphysics and the supernatural—realms that extended beyond the natural physical world. This emphasis on both tangible data and concrete experience became a cornerstone of Enlightenment thought. In addition, Newton's experiments revealed rationality in the physical world, and Enlightenment thinkers transferred that concept to the sociopolitical world by promoting a rationally organized society. Locke, whose works acquired the status of Enlightenment gospel, developed these ideas further. According to Locke's "doctrine of empiricism," knowledge comes through sensory perception of the material world. From these perceptions alone people form ideas. Locke asserted human beings are born good, not cursed by original sin. The laws of nature grant them the natural rights of life, liberty, and property as well as the right to freedom of conscience. Government is by contract, and its purpose is to protect these rights. If and when government abuses these rights, the citizenry has the further natural right of revolution. Locke's ideas empowered people to take control of their own destinies.

PHILOSOPHES The work of Newton and Locke also inspired many French intellectuals, or *philosophes*. These thinkers conceived of individuals and societies at large as parts of physical nature. They shared the conviction the ills of humanity could be remedied by applying reason and common sense to human problems. They criticized the powers of church and state as irrational limits placed on political and intellectual freedom. They believed by accumulating and propagating knowledge, humanity could advance by degrees to a happier state than it had ever known. This conviction matured into the "doctrine of progress" and its corollary doctrine, the "perfectibility of humankind." Previous societies, for the most part, perceived the future as inevitable—the cycle of life and death. They believed religious beliefs determined fate. The notion of progress—the systematic and planned improvement of society—first developed during the 18th century and continues to influence 21st-century thought.

DIDEROT Animated by their belief in human progress and perfectibility, the philosophes took on the task of gathering knowledge and making it accessible to all who could read. Their program was, in effect, the democratization of knowledge. Denis Diderot (1713–1784) greatly influenced the Enlightenment's rationalistic and materialistic thinking. He became editor of the pioneering *Encyclopédie*, a compilation of articles written by more than a hundred contributors, including all the leading philosophes. The *Encyclopédie* was truly comprehensive (its formal title was *Systematic Dictionary of the Sciences, Arts, and Crafts*) and included all available knowledge—historical, scientific, and technical as well as religious and moral—and political theory. The first volume appeared in 1751 and the last of the 35 volumes of text and illustrations in 1780. Other Enlightenment authors produced different compilations of knowledge. Diderot's contemporary, Georges-Louis Leclerc (1707–1788), Comte de Buffon, undertook a kind of encyclopedia of the natural sciences. His *Natural History*, a monumental work of 44 volumes, was especially valuable for its zoological study. Buffon's contemporary, the Swedish botanist Carolus Linnaeus (1707–1778) established a system of plant classification.

The political, economic, and social consequences of this increase in knowledge and the doctrine of progress were explosive. It is no coincidence the French Revolution, the American Revolution, and the Industrial Revolution in England all occurred during this period. These upheavals precipitated yet other major changes, including the growth of cities and of an urban working class, and the expansion of colonialism as the demand for cheap labor and raw materials increased. This enthusiasm for growth gave birth to the doctrine of Manifest Destiny—the ideological justification for continued territorial expansion. Thus, the Age of Enlightenment ushered in a new way of thinking and affected historical developments worldwide.

VOLTAIRE François Marie Arouet, better known as Voltaire (1694–1778), was the most representative figure—almost the personification—of the Enlightenment spirit. Voltaire was instrumental in introducing Newton and Locke to the French intelligentsia. He hated, and attacked through his writings, the arbitrary despotic rule of kings, the selfish privileges of the nobility and the church, religious intolerance, and, above all, the injustice of the French *ancien regime* (the "old order"). In his numerous books and pamphlets, which the authorities regularly condemned and burned, he protested against government persecution of the freedoms of thought and religion. Voltaire believed humankind could never be happy until an enlightened society removed the traditional obstructions to the progress of the human mind. His personal and public involvement in the struggle against established political and religious authority gave authenticity to his ideas. Voltaire persuaded a whole generation that fundamental changes were necessary, paving the way for a revolution in France he never intended and probably would never have approved. Voltaire did not believe "all men are created equal," the credo of Jean-Jacques Rousseau, Thomas Jefferson, and the American Declaration of Independence.

INDUSTRIAL REVOLUTION The Enlightenment emphasis on scientific investigation and technological invention opened up new possibilities for human understanding of the world and for control of its material forces. Research into the phenomena of electricity and combustion, along with the discovery of oxygen and the power of steam, had enormous consequences. Steam power as an adjunct to, or replacement for, human labor initiated a new era in world history, beginning with the Industrial Revolution in England. These and other technological advances—admiringly recorded in the paintings of Joseph Wright of Derby (FIGS. 26-1 and 26-11A)—epitomized the Enlightenment notion of progress and gave birth to the Industrial Revolution. Most scholars mark the dawn of that technological revolution in the 1740s with the invention of steam engines in England for industrial produc-

26-11A WRIGHT OF DERBY, *Experiment on a Bird*, 1768.

tion. By 1850, England could boast the world's first manufacturing economy. Within a century, the harnessed power of steam, coal, oil, iron, steel, and electricity working in concert transformed Europe. These scientific and technological advances also affected the arts, particularly through the invention of photography (see Chapter 27) and the use of new materials for constructing buildings.

COALBROOKDALE BRIDGE

The first use of iron in bridge design was in the cast-iron bridge (FIG. 26-12) built over the Severn River, near Coalbrookdale in England (MAP 30-1), where ABRAHAM DARBY III (1750–1789), one of the bridge's two designers, ran his family's cast-iron business. The Darby family had spearheaded the evolution of the iron industry in England, and they vigorously supported the investigation of new uses for the material. The fabrication of cast-iron rails and bridge elements inspired Darby to work with architect THOMAS F. PRITCHARD (1723–1777) in designing the Coalbrookdale Bridge. The cast-iron armature supporting the roadbed springs from stone pier to stone pier until it leaps the final 100 feet across the Severn River gorge. The style of the graceful center arc echoes the grand arches of Roman aqueducts (FIG. 7-33). At the same time, the exposed structure of the bridge's cast-iron parts prefigured the skeletal use of iron and steel in the 19th century, when exposed structural armatures became expressive factors in the design of buildings such as the Crystal Palace (FIG. 27-47) in England and the Eiffel Tower (FIG. 28-38) in France.

ROUSSEAU The second key figure of the French Enlightenment, who was also instrumental in preparing the way ideologically for the French Revolution, was Jean-Jacques Rousseau (1712–1778). Voltaire believed the salvation of humanity lay in the advancement of science and the rational improvement of society. In contrast, Rousseau argued the arts, sciences, society, and civilization in general had corrupted "natural man"—people in their primitive state. He was convinced humanity's only salvation lay in a return to something like "the ignorance, innocence and happiness" of its original condition. According to Rousseau, human capacity for feeling, sensibility, and emotions came before reason: "To exist is to feel; our feeling is undoubtedly earlier than our intelligence, and we had feelings before we had ideas." Nature alone must be the guide: "All our natural inclinations are right." Fundamental to Rousseau's thinking was the notion "Man by nature is good . . . he is depraved and perverted by society." He rejected the idea of progress, insisting "Our minds have been corrupted in proportion as the arts and sciences have improved."[2] Rousseau's elevation of feelings above reason as the most primitive—and hence the most "natural"—of human expressions led him to exalt as the ideal the peasant's simple life, with its honest and unsullied emotions.

26-12 ABRAHAM DARBY III and THOMAS F. PRITCHARD, iron bridge (looking northwest), Coalbrookdale, England, 1776–1779.
The first use of iron in bridge design was in this bridge over the Severn River. The Industrial Revolution brought engineering advances and new materials that revolutionized architectural construction.

Diderot on Chardin and Boucher

Denis Diderot was a pioneer in the field of art criticism as well as in the encyclopedic compilation of human knowledge. Between 1759 and 1781, he contributed reviews of the biennial Salon of the French Royal Academy of Painting and Sculpture (see "Academic Salons," Chapter 28, page 802) to the Parisian journal *Correspondence littéraire*. In his review of the 1763 Salon, Diderot had the following praise for Chardin's still lifes and for naturalism in painting.

26-13 JEAN-BAPTISTE-SIMÉON CHARDIN, *Saying Grace*, 1740. Oil on canvas, 1′ 7″ × 1′ 3″. Musée du Louvre, Paris.

Chardin embraced naturalism and celebrated the simple goodness of ordinary people, especially mothers and children, who lived in a world far from the frivolous Rococo salons of Paris.

There are many small pictures by Chardin at the Salon, almost all of them depicting fruit with the accoutrements for a meal. This is nature itself. The objects stand out from the canvas and they are so real that my eyes are fooled by them. . . . In order to look at other people's paintings, I feel as though I need different eyes; but to look at Chardin's, I need only keep the ones nature gave me and use them properly. If I had painting in mind as a career for my child, I'd buy this one [and have him copy it]. . . . Yet nature itself may be no more difficult to copy. . . . O Chardin, it's not white, red or black pigment that you grind on your palette but rather the very substance of objects; it's real air and light that you take onto the tip of your brush and transfer onto the canvas. . . . It's magic, one can't understand how it's done: thick layers of colour, applied one on top of the other, each one filtering through from underneath to create the effect. . . . Close up, everything blurs, goes flat and disappears. From a distance, everything comes back to life and reappears.*

Diderot could write scathing reviews as well as lavish praise on the leading artists of his day. He admired Chardin (FIG. 26-13) because his work was the antithesis of the Rococo manner in painting, which Diderot deplored. Here, for example, is what Diderot had to say about François Boucher (FIG. 26-8), who also exhibited in the Salon of 1763, and his younger protégés emulating his Rococo style:

What a misuse of talent! How much time gone to waste! You could have had twice the effect for half the effort. . . . When one writes, does one have to write everything? And when one paints, does one have to paint everything? . . . This man is the ruination of all young apprentice painters. Barely able to handle a brush and hold a palette, they torture themselves stringing together infantile garlands, painting chubby crimson bottoms, and hurl themselves headlong into all kinds of follies which cannot be redeemed by originality, fire, tenderness nor by any magic in their models. For they lack all of these.†

*Translated by Kate Tunstall, in Charles Harrison, Paul Wood, and Jason Gaiger, eds., *Art in Theory 1648–1815: An Anthology of Changing Ideas* (Oxford: Blackwell, 2000), 604.
†Ibid., 603–604.

"NATURAL" ART

Rousseau's views, popular and widely read, were largely responsible for the turning away from the Rococo sensibility in the arts and the formation of a taste for the "natural," as opposed to the artificial and frivolous.

CHARDIN Reflecting Rousseau's values, JEAN-BAPTISTE-SIMÉON CHARDIN (1699–1779) painted quiet scenes of domestic life, which offered the opportunity to praise the simple goodness of ordinary people, especially mothers and young children, who in spirit, occupation, and environment lived far from corrupt society. In *Saying Grace* (FIG. 26-13), Chardin ushers the viewer into a modest room where a mother and her two daughters are about to dine. The mood of quiet attention is at one with the hushed lighting and mellow color and with the closely studied still-life accessories whose worn surfaces tell their own humble domestic history. The viewer witnesses a moment of social instruction, when mother and older sister supervise the younger sister in the simple, pious ritual of giving thanks to God before a meal. The simplicity of the composition reinforces the subdued charm of this scene, with the three figures highlighted against the dark background. Chardin was the poet of the commonplace and the master of its nuances. A gentle sentiment

26-14 JEAN-BAPTISTE GREUZE, *Village Bride*, 1761. Oil on canvas, 3′ × 3′ 10½″. Musée du Louvre, Paris.

Greuze was a master of sentimental narrative, which appealed to a new audience that admired "natural" virtue. Here, in an unadorned room, a father blesses his daughter and her husband-to-be.

prevails in all his pictures, an emotion not contrived and artificial but born of the painter's honesty, insight, and sympathy. Chardin's paintings had wide appeal, even in unexpected places. Louis XV, the royal personification of the Rococo in his life and tastes, once owned *Saying Grace*. The painter was also a favorite of Diderot, the leading art critic of the day as well as the editor of the *Encyclopédie* (see "Diderot on Chardin and Boucher," page 738).

JEAN-BAPTISTE GREUZE The sentimental narrative in art became the specialty of French artist JEAN-BAPTISTE GREUZE (1725–1805), whose most popular work, *Village Bride* (FIG. 26-14), sums up the characteristics of the genre. The setting is an unadorned room in a rustic dwelling. In a notary's presence, the elderly father has passed his daughter's dowry to her youthful husband-to-be and blesses the pair, who gently take each other's arms. The old mother tearfully gives her daughter's arm a farewell caress, while the youngest sister melts in tears on the shoulder of the demure bride. An envious older sister broods behind her father's chair. Rosy-faced, healthy children play around the scene. The picture's story is simple—the happy climax of a rural romance. The picture's moral is just as clear—happiness is the reward of "natural" virtue.

Greuze produced this work at a time when the audience for art was expanding. The strict social hierarchy that provided the foundation for Rococo art and patronage gave way to a bourgeois economic and social system. The newly important bourgeois class embraced art, and paintings such as *Village Bride* particularly appealed to ordinary hard-working people. They carefully analyzed each gesture and each nuance of sentiment and reacted with tumultuous enthusiasm. At the 1761 Salon of the Royal Academy, Greuze's picture received enormous attention. Diderot, who reviewed the exhibition for *Correspondence littéraire*, reported it was difficult to get near the canvas because of the throngs of admirers.

ÉLISABETH-LOUISE VIGÉE-LEBRUN Another manifestation of the "naturalistic" impulse in 18th-century French art was the emergence of a new mode of portraiture exemplified by *Self-Portrait* (FIG. 26-15) by ÉLISABETH-LOUISE VIGÉE-LEBRUN (1755–1842). The painter looks directly at viewers and pauses in her work to return their gaze. Although her mood is lighthearted and her costume's details echo the serpentine curve Rococo artists and wealthy patrons loved, nothing about Vigée-Lebrun's pose or her mood speaks of Rococo frivolity. Hers is the self-confident stance of a woman whose art has won her an independent role in society. She

6-15 ÉLISABETH-LOUISE VIGÉE-LEBRUN, *Self-Portrait*, 1790. Oil on canvas, 8′ 4″ × 6′ 9″. Galleria degli Uffizi, Florence.

igée-Lebrun was one of the few women admitted to the Royal Academy Painting and Sculpture. In this self-portrait, she depicted herself onfidently painting the likeness of Queen Marie Antoinette.

portrayed herself in a close-up, intimate view at work on one of the many portraits (for example, FIG. 26-15A) she painted of her most important patron, Queen Marie Antoinette (1755–1793). Like many of her contemporaries, Vigée-Lebrun lived a life of extraordinary personal and economic independence, working for the nobility throughout Europe. She was famous for the force and grace of her portraits, especially those of highborn ladies and royalty. She was successful during the age of the late monarchy in France and was one of the few women admitted to the Royal Academy of Painting and Sculpture. After the French Revolution, however, the academy rescinded her membership, because women were no longer welcome, but she enjoyed continued success owing to her talent, wit, and ability to forge connections with those in power in the postrevolutionary period.

ADÉLAÏDE LABILLE-GUIARD Six years older than Vigée-Lebrun, ADÉLAÏDE LABILLE-GUIARD (1749–1803) was the second-most important woman painter in Paris at the end of the 18th century, but she never achieved the renown enjoyed by her younger rival. She trained with François-Élie Vincent (1708–1790) and later with his son François-André Vincent (1746–1816), whom she married after her divorce from her first husband, Louis-Nicolas Guiard, a clerk. Like Vigée-Lebrun, Labille-Guiard boasted royal patronage but not of the same order. She became the official painter of the "mesdames"—the aunts of King Louis XVI—in 1787, four years after she was admitted to the royal painting academy on the same day as Vigée-Lebrun. The two painters captured the remaining two of four memberships reserved for women, a quota Labille-Guiard worked hard to lift after gaining admission. The two artists took opposite sides during the French Revolution, and Labille-Guiard painted portraits of some of the uprising's leaders, including one of the few known portraits of Maximilien Robespierre (1758–1794), the most prominent figure calling for the death of King Louis XVI.

A comparison between Labille-Guiard's *Self-Portrait with Two Pupils* (FIG. 26-16) and Vigée-Lebrun's *Self-Portrait* (FIG. 26-15) underscores the two women's different self-images. The younger painter presented herself at work on a portrait of her most important patron, Marie Antoinette. The subject of the canvas Labille-Guiard is painting is unknown. Her self-portrait focuses instead on her role as a teacher. She had as many as nine women in her studio at one time. Here, two apprentices—dressed more simply than their elegantly clad instructor—cluster behind her, one intently studying the painting in progress, the other, as Labille-Guiard, gazing at the viewer. The three figures form a classical pyramidal composition, echoed by the easel. In the V formed by the two triangles is a portrait bust of the artist's father. Appropriately for this early feminist, her muse is a man, a reversal of the traditional gender roles.

WILLIAM HOGARTH Across the Channel, a truly English style of painting emerged with WILLIAM HOGARTH (1697–1764), who satirized the lifestyle of the newly prosperous middle class with comic zest. Traditionally, the British imported painters from the Continent—Holbein, Rubens, and Van Dyck among them. Hogarth waged a lively campaign throughout his career against the English feeling of dependence on, and inferiority to, these artists. Although Hogarth would have been the last to admit it, his own painting owed much to the work of his contemporaries in France, the Rococo

26-16 ADÉLAÏDE LABILLE-GUIARD, *Self-Portrait with Two Pupils*, 1785. Oil on canvas, 6′ 11″ × 4′ 11½″. Metropolitan Museum of Art, New York (gift of Julia A. Berwind, 1953).

In contrast to Vigée-Lebrun (FIG. 26-15), Labille-Guiard, her older contemporary, depicted herself as a teacher. Her father's bust portrait serves as her muse in a reversal of traditional gender roles.

artists. Yet his subject matter, frequently moral in tone, was distinctively English. This was the great age of English satirical writing, and Hogarth—who admired that literary genre and included Henry Fielding (1701–1754), the author of *Tom Jones*, among his closest friends—clearly saw himself as translating satire into the visual arts.

Hogarth's favorite device was to make a series of narrative paintings and prints, in a sequence similar to chapters in a book or scenes in a play, following a character or group of characters in their encounters with some social evil. *Breakfast Scene* (FIG. 26-17) from *Marriage à la Mode*, is one in a sequence of six paintings satirizing the marital immoralities of the moneyed classes in England. In it, the marriage of a young viscount is just beginning to founder. The husband and wife are tired after a long night spent in separate pursuits. While the wife stayed at home for an evening of cards and music-making, her young husband had been away from the house for a night of suspicious business. He thrusts his hands deep into the empty money-pockets of his breeches, while his wife's small dog sniffs inquiringly at a woman's lacy cap protruding from his coat pocket. A steward, his hands full of unpaid bills, raises his eyes in despair at the actions of his noble master and mistress. The house is palatial, but Hogarth filled it with witty clues to the dubious taste of

Hogarth won fame for his paintings and prints satirizing English life with comic zest. This is one of a series of six paintings in which he chronicled the marital immoralities of the moneyed class.

its occupants. For example, the row of pious religious paintings on the upper wall of the distant room concludes with a curtained canvas undoubtedly depicting an erotic subject. According to the custom of the day, ladies could not view this discretely hidden painting, but at the pull of a cord, the master and his male guests could enjoy a tableau of cavorting figures. In *Breakfast Scene,* as in all his work, Hogarth proceeded as a novelist might, elaborating on his subject with carefully chosen detail, the discovery of which heightens the comedy.

Hogarth designed the marriage series to be published as a set of engravings. The prints of this and his other moral narratives were so popular that unscrupulous entrepreneurs produced unauthorized versions almost as fast as the artist created his originals. The popularity of these prints speaks not only to the appeal of their subjects but also to the democratization of knowledge and culture the Enlightenment fostered and to the exploitation of new printing technologies that opened the way for a more affordable and widely disseminated visual culture.

THOMAS GAINSBOROUGH

A contrasting blend of "naturalistic" representation and Rococo setting is found in *Mrs. Richard Brinsley Sheridan* (FIG. 26-18), a characteristic portrait by British painter THOMAS GAINSBOROUGH (1727–1788). Gainsborough presented Mrs. Sheridan as a lovely, informally dressed woman seated in a rustic landscape faintly reminiscent of Watteau (FIG. 26-7) in its soft-hued light and feathery brushwork. Gainsborough's goal was to match the natural, unspoiled

26-18 THOMAS GAINSBOROUGH, *Mrs. Richard Brinsley Sheridan,* 1787. Oil on canvas, 7′ 2⅝″ × 5′ ⅝″. National Gallery of Art, Washington, D.C. (Andrew W. Mellon Collection).

In this life-size portrait, Gainsborough sought to match Mrs. Sheridan's natural beauty with that of the landscape. The rustic setting, soft-hued light, and feathery brushwork recall Rococo painting.

1 ft.

beauty of the landscape with that of his sitter. Mrs. Sheridan's dark brown hair blows freely in the slight wind, and her clear "English complexion" and air of ingenuous sweetness contrast sharply with the pert sophistication of the subjects of Continental Rococo portraits. Gainsborough planned to give the picture a more pastoral air by adding several sheep, but he did not live long enough to complete the canvas. Even without the sheep, the painting clearly expresses Gainsborough's deep interest in the landscape setting. Although he won greater fame in his time for his portraits, he had begun as a landscape painter and always preferred painting scenes of nature to depicting individual likenesses.

JOSHUA REYNOLDS Morality of a more heroic tone than found in the work of Greuze, yet in harmony with "naturalness," included the virtues of honor, valor, and love of country. The Enlightenment concept of "nobility," especially in the view of Rousseau, referred to character, not to aristocratic birth. As the century progressed and people felt the tremors of coming revolutions, the virtues of courage and resolution, patriotism, and self-sacrifice assumed greater importance. Having risen from humble origins, the modern military hero, not the decadent aristocrat, brought the excitement of war into the company of the "natural" emotions.

Sir Joshua Reynolds (1723–1792) specialized in what became known as *Grand Manner portraiture* and often painted likenesses of key participants in the great events of the latter part of the 18th century. Although clearly depicting specific individuals, Grand Manner portraits elevated the sitters by conveying refinement and elegance. Painters communicated a person's grace and class through certain standardized conventions, such as the large scale of the figure relative to the canvas, the controlled pose, the landscape setting, and the low horizon line.

Reynolds painted *Lord Heathfield* (FIG. **26-19**) in 1787. The sitter was a perfect subject for a Grand Manner portrait—a burly, ruddy English officer, the commandant of the fortress at Gibraltar. Heathfield had doggedly defended the British stronghold against the Spanish and French, and later received the honorary title Baron Heathfield of Gibraltar. Here, he holds the huge key to the fortress, the symbol of his victory. He stands in front of a curtain of dark smoke rising from the battleground, flanked by one cannon pointing ineffectively downward and another whose tilted barrel indicates it lies uselessly on its back. Reynolds portrayed the features of the general's heavy, honest face and his uniform with unidealized realism. But Lord Heathfield's posture and the setting dramatically suggest the heroic themes of battle, courage, and patriotism.

BENJAMIN WEST Some American artists also became well known in England. Benjamin West (1738–1820), born in Pennsylvania on what was then the colonial frontier (MAP 26-1), traveled to Europe early in life to study art and then went to England, where he met with almost immediate success. A cofounder of the Royal Academy of Arts, West succeeded Reynolds as its president. He became official painter to George III (r. 1760–1801) and retained that position even during the strained period of the American Revolution.

In *Death of General Wolfe* (FIG. **26-20**), West depicted the mortally wounded young English commander just after his defeat of the French in the decisive battle of Quebec in 1759, which gave Canada to Great Britain. Because his subject was a recent event, West clothed his characters in contemporary costumes (although the military uniforms are not completely accurate in all details). However, West blended this realism of detail with the grand tradition of history painting by arranging his figures in a complex and

26-19 Sir Joshua Reynolds, *Lord Heathfield*, 1787. Oil on canvas, 4′ 8″ × 3′ 9″. National Gallery, London.

In this Grand Manner portrait, Reynolds depicted the English commander who defended Gibraltar. As is typical for this genre, Heathfield stands in a dramatic pose and his figure takes up most of the canvas.

theatrically ordered composition. His modern hero dies among grieving officers on the field of victorious battle in a way that suggests the death of a saint. (The composition, in fact, derives from paintings of the lamentation over the dead Christ.) West wanted to present this hero's death in the service of the state as a martyrdom charged with religious emotions. His innovative and highly effective combination of the conventions of traditional heroic painting with a look of modern realism influenced history painting well into the 19th century.

JOHN SINGLETON COPLEY American artist John Singleton Copley (1738–1815) matured as a painter in the Massachusetts Bay Colony. Like West, Copley later emigrated to England where he absorbed the fashionable English portrait style. But unlike Grand Manner portraiture, Copley's *Paul Revere* (FIG. **26-21**) painted before the artist left Boston, conveys a sense of directness and faithfulness to visual fact that marked the taste for honesty and plainness noted by many late-18th- and 19th-century visitors to America. When Copley painted his portrait, Revere was not yet the familiar hero of the American Revolution. In the picture, he is working at his profession of silversmithing. The setting is plain, the lighting clear and revealing. Revere sits in his shirtsleeves, bent over a teapot in progress. He pauses and turns his head to look the observer straight in the eyes. The painter treated the reflections in the polished wood of the tabletop with as much care as he did Revere's

26-20 BENJAMIN WEST, *Death of General Wolfe*, 1771. Oil on canvas, 4' 11½" × 7'. National Gallery of Canada, Ottawa (gift of the Duke of Westminster, 1918).

West's great innovation was to blend contemporary subject matter and costumes with the grand tradition of history painting. Here, the painter likened General Wolfe's death to that of a martyred saint.

figure, his tools, and the teapot resting on its leather graver's pillow. Copley gave special prominence to Revere's eyes by reflecting intense reddish light onto the darkened side of his face and hands. The informality and the sense of the moment link this painting to contemporaneous English and Continental portraits. But the spare style and the emphasis on the sitter's down-to-earth character differentiate this American work from its European counterparts.

THE GRAND TOUR The 18th-century public also sought "naturalness" in artists' depictions of landscapes. Documentation of specific places became popular, in part due to growing travel opportunities and expanding colonialism. These depictions of geographic settings also served the needs of the many scientific expeditions mounted during the century and satisfied the desires of genteel tourists for mementos of their journeys. By this time, a Grand Tour of the major sites of Europe was an essential part of every well-bred person's education (see "The Grand Tour and Veduta Painting," page 744). Those who embarked on a tour of the Continent wished to return with souvenirs to help them remember their experiences and impress those at home with the wonders

26-21 JOHN SINGLETON COPLEY, *Paul Revere*, ca. 1768–1770. Oil on canvas, 2' 11⅛" × 2' 4". Museum of Fine Arts, Boston (gift of Joseph W., William B., and Edward H. R. Revere).

In contrast to Grand Manner portraiture, Copley's *Paul Revere* emphasizes his subject's down-to-earth character, differentiating this American work from its European counterparts.

"Natural" Art **743**

The Grand Tour and Veduta Painting

Although travel throughout Europe was commonplace in the 18th century, Italy became an especially popular destination. This "pilgrimage" of aristocrats, the wealthy, politicians, and diplomats from France, England, Germany, Flanders, Sweden, the United States, Russia, Poland, and Hungary came to be known as the Grand Tour. Italy's allure fueled the revival of classicism, and the popularity of Neoclassical art drove the fascination with Italy. One British observer noted: "All our religion, all our arts, almost all that sets us above savages, has come from the shores of the Mediterranean."*

The Grand Tour was not simply leisure travel. The education available in Italy to the inquisitive mind made such a tour an indispensable experience for anyone who wished to make a mark in society. The Enlightenment had made knowledge of ancient Rome and Greece imperative, and a steady stream of Europeans and Americans traveled to Italy in the late 18th and early 19th centuries. These tourists aimed to increase their knowledge of literature, the visual arts, architecture, theater, music, history, customs, and folklore. Given this extensive agenda, it is not surprising a Grand Tour could take a number of years to complete. Most travelers moved from location to location, following an established itinerary.

The British were the most avid travelers, and they conceived the initial "tour code," including required itineraries to important destinations. Although they designated Rome early on as the primary destination in Italy, visitors traveled as far north as Venice and as far south as Naples. Eventually, Paestum, Sicily, Florence, Siena, Pisa, Genoa, Milan, Bologna, and Parma (MAP 25-1) all appeared in guidebooks and in paintings. Joseph Wright of Derby (FIGS. 26-1 and 26-11A) and Joseph Mallord William Turner (FIG. 27-22) were among the many British artists to undertake a Grand Tour.

Many visitors to Italy returned home from their Grand Tour with a painting by Antonio Canaletto, the leading painter of scenic views (*vedute*) of Venice. It must have been very cheering on a gray winter afternoon in England to look up and see a sunny, panoramic view such as that in Canaletto's *Riva degli Schiavoni, Venice* (FIG. 26-22), with its cloud-studded sky, picturesque water traffic, and well-known Venetian landmarks painted in scrupulous perspective and minute detail. (The Doge's Palace [FIG. 14-21] is at the left in *Riva degli Schiavoni*.) Canaletto usually made drawings "on

26-22 ANTONIO CANALETTO, *Riva degli Schiavoni, Venice,* ca. 1735–1740. Oil on canvas, 1' 6½" × 2' ⅞". Toledo Museum of Art, Toledo.

Canaletto was the leading painter of Venetian *vedute,* which were treasured souvenirs for 18th-century travelers visiting Italy on a Grand Tour. He used a camera obscura for his on-site drawings.

location" to take back to his studio and use as sources for paintings. To help make the on-site drawings true to life, he often used a camera obscura, as Vermeer (FIGS. 25-19 to 25-20A) did before him. These instruments were darkened chambers (some of them virtually portable closets) with optical lenses fitted into a hole in one wall through which light entered to project an inverted image of the subject onto the chamber's opposite wall. The artist could trace the main details from this image for later reworking and refinement. The camera obscura enabled artists to create convincing representations incorporating the variable focus of objects at different distances. Canaletto's paintings give the impression of capturing every detail, with no "editing." In fact, he presented each site according to Renaissance perspective conventions and exercised great selectivity about which details to include and which to omit to make a coherent and engagingly attractive veduta.

*Cesare de Seta, "Grand Tour: The Lure of Italy in the Eighteenth Century," in Andrew Wilton and Ilaria Bignamini, eds., *Grand Tour: The Lure of Italy in the Eighteenth Century* (London: Tate Gallery, 1996), 13.

they had seen. The English were especially eager collectors of travel pictures. Venetian artists in particular found it profitable to produce paintings of the most characteristic *vedute* (scenic views) of their city to sell to British visitors. Chief among those artists was

ANTONIO CANALETTO (1697–1768), whose works, for example *Riva degli Schiavoni, Venice (Bank of the Slaves, Venice;* FIG. **26-22**) English tourists avidly acquired as evidence of their visit to Italy' magical city of water.

The Excavations of Herculaneum and Pompeii

Among the developments stimulating the European fascination with classical antiquity was the initiation of systematic excavations at two ancient Roman cities on the Bay of Naples—Herculaneum and Pompeii—in 1738 and 1748, respectively. The violent eruption of Mount Vesuvius in August 79 CE had buried both cities under volcanic ash and lava (see "An Eyewitness Account of the Eruption of Mount Vesuvius," Chapter 7, page 188), protecting the sites for hundreds of years from looters and the ravages of nature. Consequently, the 18th-century excavations yielded an unprecedented number of well-preserved paintings, sculptures, vases, and other household objects, and provided rich evidence for reconstructing Roman art and life. As a result, European ideas about and interest in ancient Rome expanded tremendously, and collectors eagerly acquired as many of the newly discovered antiquities as they could. One of the most avid collectors was Sir William Hamilton (1731–1803), British consul in Naples from 1764 to 1800, who purchased numerous painted vases and other ancient objects and then sold them to the British Museum in 1772. The finds at Pompeii and Herculaneum, therefore, quickly became available to a wide public.

"Pompeian" style soon became all the rage in England, as is evident, for example, in Robert Adam's Etruscan Room (FIG. 26-23) at Osterley Park House, which was inspired by the frescoes of the Third and early Fourth Styles of Roman mural painting (FIGS. 7-21 and 7-22). Adam took decorative motifs (medallions, urns, vine scrolls, sphinxes, and tripods) from Roman art and arranged them sparsely within broad, neutral spaces and slender margins, as in his elegant, linear ancient models. This new Neoclassical style almost entirely displaced the curvilinear Rococo (FIGS. 26-2 and 26-3) in the homes of the wealthy after midcentury. Adam was also an archaeologist, and he had explored and written accounts of the ruins of Diocletian's palace (FIG. 7-74) at Split. Kedleston House in Derbyshire, Adelphi Terrace in London, and a great many other structures he designed show how the Split palace influenced his work.

The archaeological finds from Herculaneum and Pompeii also affected garden and landscape design, fashion, and tableware.

26-23 ROBERT ADAM, Etruscan Room, Osterley Park House, Middlesex, England, begun 1761. Reconstructed in the Victoria & Albert Museum, London.

Inspired by archaeological discoveries at Herculaneum and Pompeii in the mid-18th century, Adam incorporated decorative motifs from Roman mural painting into his Etruscan Room at Osterley Park.

Clothing based on classical garb became popular, and Emma, Lady Hamilton (1761–1815), Sir William's wife, often gave lavish parties dressed in delicate Greek-style drapery. Neoclassical taste also determined the pottery designs of John Flaxman (1755–1826) and Josiah Wedgwood. Wedgwood established his reputation in the 1760s with his creamware inspired by ancient art. He eventually produced vases based on what were then thought to be Etruscan designs (they were, in fact, imported Greek vases deposited in Etruscan tombs) and expanded his business by producing small busts of classical figures as well as cameos and medallions adorned with copies of antique reliefs and statues.

NEOCLASSICISM

One of the defining characteristics of the late 18th century was a renewed admiration for classical antiquity, which the Grand Tour was instrumental in fueling. This interest gave rise to the artistic movement known as *Neoclassicism*, which incorporated the subjects and styles of ancient art. Painting, sculpture, and architecture, however, were only the most prominent manifestations of Neoclassicism. Fascination with Greek and Roman culture was widespread and extended to the public culture of fashion and home decor. The Enlightenment's emphasis on rationality in part explains this classical focus, because the geometric harmony of classical art and architecture embodied Enlightenment ideals. In addition, classical cultures represented the pinnacle of civilized society. Greece and

Rome served as models of enlightened political organization. With their traditions of liberty, civic virtue, morality, and sacrifice, these cultures were ideal models during a period of great political upheaval. Given these traditional associations, it is not coincidental that Neoclassicism was particularly appealing during the French and American revolutions.

Further whetting the public appetite for classicism were the excavations near Naples of Herculaneum and Pompeii, which the volcanic eruption of Mount Vesuvius had buried (see "The Excavations of Herculaneum and Pompeii," above). Soon, murals based on the paintings unearthed in the excavations began to appear in European townhouses, such as the Etruscan Room (FIG. 26-23) by ROBERT ADAM (1728–1792) in Osterley Park House in Middlesex, begun 1761.

26-24 ANGELICA KAUFFMANN, *Cornelia Presenting Her Children as Her Treasures,* or *Mother of the Gracchi,* ca. 1785. Oil on canvas, 3′ 4″ × 4′ 2″. Virginia Museum of Fine Arts, Richmond (Adolph D. and Wilkins C. Williams Fund).

Kauffmann's painting of a virtuous Roman mother who presented her children to a visitor as her jewels exemplifies the Enlightenment fascination with classical antiquity and with classical art.

WINCKELMANN The enthusiasm for classical antiquity also permeated much of the scholarship of the time. In the late 18th century, the ancient world increasingly became the focus of academic research. A visit to Rome inspired Edward Gibbon (1737–1794) to begin his monumental *Decline and Fall of the Roman Empire,* which appeared between 1776 and 1788. Earlier, in 1755, Johann Joachim Winckelmann (1717–1768), widely recognized as the first modern art historian, published *Reflections on the Imitation of Greek Works in Painting and Sculpture,* in which the German scholar unequivocally designated Greek art as the most perfect to come from human hands. For Winckelmann, classical art was far superior to the "natural" art of his day.

> Good taste, which is becoming more prevalent throughout the world, had its origins under the skies of Greece. . . . The only way for us to become great . . . is to imitate the ancients. . . . In the masterpieces of Greek art, connoisseurs and imitators find not only nature at its most beautiful but also something beyond nature, namely certain ideal forms of its beauty. . . . A person enlightened enough to penetrate the innermost secrets of art will find beauties hitherto seldom revealed when he compares the total structure of Greek figures with most modern ones, especially those modelled more on nature than on Greek taste.[3]

In his later *History of Ancient Art* (1764), Winckelmann carefully described major works of classical art and positioned each one within a huge inventory organized by subject matter, style, and period. Before Winckelmann, art historians had focused on biography, as did Giorgio Vasari and Giovanni Pietro Bellori in the 16th and 17th centuries (see "Giovanni Pietro Bellori on Annibale Carracci and Caravaggio," Chapter 24, page 682). Winckelmann thus initiated one modern art historical method thoroughly in accord with Enlightenment ideas of ordering knowledge—a system of description and classification that provided a pioneering model for the understanding of stylistic evolution. Winckelmann's familiarity with classical art derived predominantly (as was the norm) from Roman works and Roman copies of Greek art in Italy. Yet Winckelmann was instrumental in bringing to scholarly attention the differences between Greek and Roman art. Thus, he paved the way for more thorough study of the distinct characteristics of the art and architecture of these two cultures.

Painting

Winckelmann's influence extended beyond the world of scholarship. He also was instrumental in promoting Neoclassicism as a major stylistic movement in late-18th-century painting. He was, for example, the scholar who advised his countryman ANTON RAPHAEL MENGS (1728–1779) on classical iconography when Mengs painted *Parnassus* (FIG. 26-23A), the fresco many art historians regard as the first Neoclassical painting.

26-23A MENGS, *Parnassus,* 1761.

ANGELICA KAUFFMANN Another pioneer of Neoclassical painting was ANGELICA KAUFFMANN (1741–1807). Born in Switzerland and trained in Italy, Kauffmann spent many of her productive years in England. A student of Reynolds (FIG. 26-19), she was a founding member of the British Royal Academy of Arts and enjoyed an enviable reputation. Her *Cornelia Presenting Her Children as Her Treasures,* or *Mother of the Gracchi* (FIG. 26-24), is an *exemplum virtutis* (example or model of virtue) drawn from Greek and Roman history and literature. The moralizing pictures of Greuze (FIG. 26-14) and Hogarth (FIG. 26-17) already had marked a change in taste, but Kauffmann replaced the modern setting and characters of their works. She clothed her actors in ancient Roman garb and posed them in statuesque attitudes within Roman interiors. The theme of *Mother of the Gracchi* is the virtue of Cornelia, mother of the future political leaders Tiberius and Gaius Gracchus, who, in the second century BCE, attempted to reform the Roman Republic. Cornelia reveals her character in this scene, which takes place after a visitor had shown off her fine jewelry and then haughtily insisted Cornelia show hers. Instead of taking out her own precious adornments, Cornelia brought her sons forward, presenting them as her jewels. The architectural setting is severely Roman, with no

David on Greek Style and Public Art

Jacques-Louis David was the leading Neo-classical painter in France at the end of the 18th century. He championed a return to Greek style and the painting of inspiring heroic and patriotic subjects. In 1796 he made the following statement to his pupils:

> I want to work in a pure Greek style. I feed my eyes on antique statues, I even have the intention of imitating some of them. The Greeks had no scruples about copying a composition, a gesture, a type that had already been accepted and used. They put all their attention and all their art on perfecting an idea that had been already conceived. They thought, and they were right, that in the arts the way in which an idea is rendered, and the manner in which it is expressed, is much more important than the idea itself. To give a body and a perfect form to one's thought, this—and only this—is to be an artist.*

David also strongly believed paintings depicting noble events in ancient history, such as his *Oath of the Horatii* (FIG. 26-25), would serve to instill patriotism and civic virtue in the public at large in postrevolutionary France. In November 1793 he wrote:

> [The arts] should help to spread the progress of the human spirit, and to propagate and transmit to posterity the striking examples of the efforts of a tremendous people who, guided by reason and philosophy, are bringing back to earth the reign of liberty, equality, and law. The arts must therefore contribute forcefully to the education of the public. . . . The arts are the imitation of nature in her most beautiful and perfect form. . . .

26-25 Jacques-Louis David, *Oath of the Horatii*, 1784. Oil on canvas, 10′ 10″ × 13′ 11″. Musée du Louvre, Paris. ◼◀

David was the Neoclassical painter-ideologist of the French Revolution. This huge canvas celebrating ancient Roman patriotism and sacrifice features statuesque figures and classical architecture.

> [T]hose marks of heroism and civic virtue offered the eyes of the people [will] electrify the soul, and plant the seeds of glory and devotion to the fatherland.†

*Translated by Robert Goldwater and Marco Treves, eds., *Artists on Art*, 3d ed. (New York: Pantheon Books, 1958), 206.
†Ibid., 205.

Rococo motif in evidence, and the composition and drawing have the simplicity and firmness of low-relief carving, qualities shared with Mengs's *Parnassus* (FIG. 26-23A).

JACQUES-LOUIS DAVID The Enlightenment idea of a participatory and knowledgeable citizenry lay behind the revolt against the French monarchy in 1789, but the immediate causes of the French Revolution were France's economic crisis and the clash between the Third Estate (bourgeoisie, peasantry, and urban and rural workers) and the First and Second Estates (the clergy and nobility, respectively). They fought over the issue of representation in the legislative body, the Estates-General, which had been convened to discuss taxation as a possible solution to the economic problem. However, the ensuing revolution revealed the instability of the monarchy and of French society's traditional structure and resulted in a succession of republics and empires as France struggled to find a way to adjust to these fundamental changes.

Jacques-Louis David (1748–1825) became the Neoclassical painter-ideologist of the French Revolution. A distant relative of François Boucher (FIG. 26-8), he followed the Rococo painter's style until a period of study in Rome won the younger man over to the classical art tradition. David favored academic teachings about using the art of the ancients and of the great Renaissance masters as models. He, as Winckelmann, rebelled against Rococo style as an "artificial taste" and exalted the "perfect form" of Greek art (see "David on Greek Style and Public Art," above).

OATH OF THE HORATII David concurred with the Enlightenment belief that the subject of an artwork should have a moral. Paintings representing noble deeds in the past could inspire virtue in the present. A milestone painting in the Neoclassical master's career, *Oath of the Horatii* (FIG. 26-25), depicts a story from pre-Republican Rome, the heroic phase of Roman history. The topic was not too obscure for David's audience. Pierre Corneille (1606–1684) had retold this story of conflict between love and patriotism, first recounted by the ancient Roman historian Livy, in a play performed in Paris several years earlier. According to the story, the leaders of the warring cities of Rome and Alba decided to resolve their conflicts in a series of encounters waged by three representatives from each side. The Romans chose as their champions the three Horatius brothers, who had to face the three sons of the Curatius family from Alba. A sister of the Horatii, Camilla, was the bride-to-be of one of the Curatius sons, and the wife of the youngest Horatius was the sister of the Curatii. David's painting shows the Horatii as they swear on their swords, held high by their father, to win or die for Rome, oblivious to the anguish and sorrow of the Horatii women.

Oath of the Horatii is a paragon of the Neoclassical style. Not only does the subject matter deal with a narrative of patriotism and sacrifice excerpted from Roman history, but the painter also employed formal devices to present the image with force and clarity. The action unfolds in a shallow space much like a stage setting, defined by a severely simple architectural framework. David deployed his statuesque and carefully modeled figures across the space, close to the foreground, in a manner reminiscent of ancient relief sculpture. The rigid, angular, and virile forms of the men on the left effectively contrast with the soft curvilinear shapes of the distraught women on the right. This juxtaposition visually pits virtues the Enlightenment leaders ascribed to men (such as courage, patriotism, and unwavering loyalty to a cause) against the emotions of love, sorrow, and despair the women in the painting express. The French viewing audience perceived such emotionalism as characteristic of the female nature. The message was clear and of a type readily identifiable to the prerevolutionary French public. The picture created a sensation at its first exhibition in Paris in 1785. Although David had painted it under royal patronage and did not intend the painting as a revolutionary statement, *Oath of the Horatii* aroused his audience to patriotic zeal. The Neoclassical style soon became the semiofficial voice of the French Revolution.

DEATH OF MARAT When the revolution broke out in 1789, David threw in his lot with the Jacobins, the radical and militant revolutionary faction. He accepted the role of de facto minister of propaganda, organizing political pageants and ceremonies requiring floats, costumes, and sculptural props. David believed art could play an important role in educating the public and that dramatic paintings emphasizing patriotism and civic virtue would prove effective as rallying calls. However, rather than continuing to create artworks focused on scenes from antiquity, David began to portray scenes from the French Revolution itself.

In 1793, David painted *Death of Marat* (FIG. 26-26), which he wanted not only to serve as a record of an important event in the struggle to overthrow the monarchy but also to provide inspiration and encouragement to the revolutionary forces. The painting commemorates the assassination that year of Jean-Paul Marat (1743–1793), an influential writer who was David's friend. The artist depicted the martyred revolutionary in his bathtub after Charlotte Corday (1768–1793), a member of a rival political faction, stabbed him to death. (Marat suffered from a painful skin disease and required frequent medicinal baths.) David presented the scene with directness and clarity. The cold neutral space above Marat's figure slumped in the tub produces a chilling oppressiveness. The painter vividly placed all narrative details in the foreground—the knife, the wound, the blood, the letter with which Corday gained entrance—to sharpen the sense of pain and outrage. David masterfully composed the painting to present Marat as a tragic martyr who died

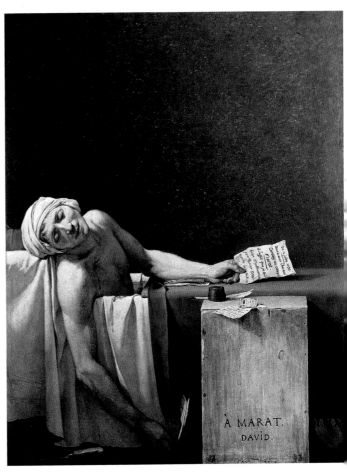

26-26 JACQUES-LOUIS DAVID, *Death of Marat*, 1793. Oil on canvas, 5′ 5″ × 4′ 2½″. Musées Royaux des Beaux-Arts de Belgique, Brussels. ◼◄

David depicted the revolutionary Marat as a tragic martyr, stabbed to death in his bath. Although the painting displays severe Neoclassical spareness, its convincing realism conveys pain and outrage.

in the service of the revolution. He based Marat's figure on Christ in Michelangelo's *Pietà* (FIG. 22-12) in Saint Peter's in Rome. The reference to Christ's martyrdom made the painting a kind of "altarpiece" for the new civic "religion," inspiring the French people with the saintly dedication of their slain leader.

Architecture and Sculpture

Architects in the Enlightenment era also formed a deep admiration for the Greco-Roman past. Fairly early in the 18th century, they began to turn away from the theatricality and ostentation of Baroque design, still evident in grandiose structures such as Blenheim Palace (FIG. 26-1A) in England and Karlskirche (FIG. 26-3A) in Austria, as well as from the delicate flourishes of Rococo salons (FIGS. 26-2 and 26-3), palaces (FIG. 26-5A), and churches (FIGS. 26-4 and 26-5B). The style they instead embraced offered a more streamlined antique look.

PANTHÉON The Parisian church of Sainte-Geneviève, now the Panthéon (FIG. 26-27), by JACQUES-GERMAIN SOUFFLOT (1713–1780) stands as testament to the revived interest in classical architecture. The Roman ruins at Baalbek in Lebanon, especially the titanic colonnade of the temple of Jupiter, provided much of the inspiration for Soufflot's design. The columns, reproduced with studied archaeological precision, stand out from walls that are severely blank, except for a repeated garland motif near the top. The colonnaded dome, a Neoclassical version of the domes of Saint

26-27 JACQUES-GERMAIN SOUFFLOT, Panthéon (Sainte-Geneviève; looking northeast), Paris, France, 1755–1792.

Soufflot's Panthéon is a testament to the Enlightenment admiration for Greece and Rome. It combines a portico based on an ancient Roman temple with a colonnaded dome and a Greek-cross plan.

cal systems ranging from Athenian democracy to Roman imperial rule. Thus, parliamentary England joined revolutionary France in embracing Neoclassicism. In England, Neoclassicism's appeal also was due to its clarity and simplicity. These characteristics provided a stark contrast to the complexity and opulence of Baroque art, then associated with the flamboyant rule of absolute monarchy. In English architecture, the preference for a simple and rational style derived indirectly from the authority of the ancient Roman architect Vitruvius through Andrea Palladio (FIGS. 22-28 to 22-31) in the 16th century and Inigo Jones (FIG. 25-37) in the 17th.

RICHARD BOYLE (1695–1753), earl of Burlington, strongly restated Jones's Palladian doctrine in the new Neoclassical idiom in Chiswick House (FIG. 26-28), which he built on London's outskirts with the help of WILLIAM KENT (ca. 1686–1748). Paving the way for this shift in style was, among other things, the publication of Colin Campbell's *Vitruvius Britannicus* (1715), three volumes of engravings of ancient buildings, prefaced by a denunciation of Italian Baroque and high praise for Palladio and Jones. Chiswick House is a free variation on the theme of Palladio's Villa Rotonda (FIG. 22-28). The exterior design provided a clear alternative to the colorful splendor of Versailles (FIG. 25-26). In its simple symmetry, unadorned planes, right angles, and precise proportions, Chiswick looks very classical and rational. But the Palladian-style villa's setting within informal gardens, where a charming irregularity of layout and freely growing uncropped foliage dominate the scene, mitigates the classical severity and rationality. Just as the owners of English villas cultivated irregularity in the landscaping surrounding their homes, they sometimes preferred interiors ornamented in a style more closely related to Rococo decoration. At Chiswick, the interior design creates a luxurious Baroque foil to the stern symmetry of the exterior and the plan.

Peter's (FIG. 22-25) in Rome, the Église du Dôme (FIG. 25-30) in Paris, and Saint Paul's (FIG. 25-38) in London, rises above a Greek-cross plan. Both the dome and the vaults rest on an interior grid of splendid freestanding Corinthian columns, as if the portico's colonnade continued within. Although the whole effect, inside and out, is Roman, the structural principles employed were essentially Gothic. Soufflot was one of the first 18th-century builders to apply the logical engineering of Gothic cathedrals (see "The Gothic Cathedral," Chapter 13, page 373) to modern buildings. With few exceptions, however, such as Strawberry Hill (FIG. 26-27A), owned and largely designed by HORACE WALPOLE (1717–1797), the revival of interest in the Gothic architectural style did not take hold until the following century (see Chapter 27 and FIGS. 27-43 and 27-43A).

CHISWICK HOUSE The appeal of classical architecture extended well beyond French borders. The popularity of Greek and Roman cultures was due not only to their association with morality, rationality, and integrity but also to their connection to politi-

Palladian classicism prevailed in English architecture until about 1760, when it began to evolve into Neoclassicism. Playing a pivotal role in the shift from a dependence on Renaissance examples to ancient models was the publication in 1762 of the first volume of *Antiquities of Athens*

26-28 RICHARD BOYLE and WILLIAM KENT, Chiswick House (looking northwest), near London, England, begun 1725.

For this English villa, Boyle and Kent emulated the simple symmetry and unadorned planes of the Palladian architectural style. Chiswick House is a free variation on the Villa Rotonda (FIG. 22-28).

26-28A STUART, Doric Portico, Hagley Park, 1758.

by two British painters and architects, JAMES STUART (1713–1788) and Nicholas Revett (1720–1804). Indeed, the purest expression of Greek-inspired architecture in 18th-century England was Stuart's design for the Doric portico (FIG. 26-28A) at Hagley Park.

STOURHEAD PARK English architects also made a significant contribution to the history of architecture by developing the *picturesque garden* in the 18th century, a garden designed in accord with the Enlightenment taste for the "natural." This approach to landscape architecture was in strong opposition to the formality and symmetry of Continental gardens such as those of the palace at Versailles (FIG. 25-26), which epitomized the imposition of rational order on untamed nature. Despite their "unordered" appearance, English gardens were carefully planned and often made allusions to classical antiquity, satisfying the demands of their patrons to surround themselves with mementos of the Grand Tour (see "The Grand Tour," page 744) they undertook in their youth.

An early masterpiece of this genre is the park at Stourhead (FIG. 26-29), designed by HENRY FLITCROFT (1697–1769) in collaboration with the property's owner, HENRY HOARE (1705–1785), the son of a wealthy banker. Hoare's country estate in Wiltshire overlooked a lush valley in which Flitcroft created an irregularly shaped artificial lake by damming up the Stour River. Around it, he placed a winding path leading to and from a grotto adorned with statues of a river god and a nymph. The twisting road and the grotto conjured for Hoare the voyage of Aeneas and the entrance to the Underworld in Virgil's *Aeneid*, required reading (in the original Latin) for any properly educated British gentleman. Flitcroft also placed around Hoare's version of Lake Avernus a bridge with five arches modeled on Andrea Palladio's bridge at Vicenza and pavilions that are free variations on famous classical buildings, including the Temple of Venus (FIG. 7-72) at Baalbek and the Pantheon (FIG. 7-49) in Rome.

Flitcroft sited all the structures strategically to create vistas resembling those in the paintings of Claude Lorrain (FIG. 25-33), beloved by those who had completed a Grand Tour. In fact, the view reproduced here of Flitcroft's Pantheon beyond the Palladian bridge on the far side of the lake at Stourhead specifically emulates Claude's 1672 *Landscape with Aeneas at Delos* in the National Gallery in London, in turn inspired by the *Aeneid*. Still, consistent with the eclectic tastes of 18th-century patrons, Hoare's park also contains Chinese bridges, a Turkish tent, and a Gothic tower.

THOMAS JEFFERSON Because the appeal of Neoclassicism was due in part to the values with which it was associated—morality, idealism, patriotism, and civic virtue—it is not surprising that in the new American republic (MAP 26-1), THOMAS JEFFERSON (1743–1826) spearheaded a movement to adopt Neoclassicism as the national architectural style. Jefferson—economist, educational theorist, gifted amateur architect, as well as stateman—admired Palladio immensely and read carefully the Italian architect's *Four Books of Architecture*. Later, while minister to France, he studied 18th-century French classical architecture and city planning and visited the Maison Carrée (FIG. 7-32), an ancient Roman temple at Nîmes. After his European sojourn, Jefferson completely remodeled Monticello (FIG. 26-30), his home near Charlottesville, Virginia, which he originally had designed in a different style. The final version of Monticello is somewhat reminiscent of Palladio's Villa Rotonda (FIG. 22-28) and of Chiswick House (FIG. 26-28), but its materials are the local wood and brick used in Virginia.

UNIVERSITY OF VIRGINIA Jefferson's Neoclassicism was an extension of the Enlightenment belief in the perfectibility of human beings and in the power of art to help achieve that perfection. When he became president, he selected Benjamin Latrobe (1764–1820) to build the U.S. Capitol in Washington, D.C., specifying that Latrobe use a Roman style. Jefferson's choice in part reflected his admiration for the beauty of the Roman buildings he had seen in Europe and in part his association of those buildings

26-29 HENRY FLITCROFT and HENRY HOARE, the park at Stourhead, England, 1743–1765.

Flitcroft's design for Hoare's Wiltshire estate included a replica of the Pantheon overlooking an artificial lake and a grotto alluding to Aeneas's journey to the Underworld from Lake Avernus.

26-30 THOMAS JEFFERSON, Monticello, Charlottesville, Virginia, 1770–1806. ◼◀

Jefferson led the movement to adopt Neoclassicism as the architectural style of the United States. Although built of local materials, his Palladian Virginia home recalls Chiswick House (FIG. 26-28).

with an idealized Roman republican government and, through that, with the democracy of ancient Greece.

In his own designs for public buildings, Jefferson also looked to Rome for models. He modeled the State Capitol in Richmond, Virginia, on the Maison Carrée (FIG. 7-32). For the University of Virginia, which he founded, Jefferson turned to the Pantheon (FIG. 7-49). The Rotunda (FIG. **26-31**) is the centerpiece of Jefferson's "academical village" in Charlottesville. It sits on an elevated platform at one end of a grassy quadrangle ("the Lawn"), framed by Neoclassical pavilions and colonnades—just as temples in Roman forums (FIGS. 7-12 and 7-44) stood at one short end of a colonnaded square. Each of the ten pavilions (five on each side) resembles a small classical temple. No two are exactly alike. Jefferson ex-

perimented with variations of all the different classical orders in his pavilions. He had thoroughly absorbed the principles of classical architecture and clearly delighted in borrowing motifs from major buildings. Jefferson was no mere copyist, however. His designs were highly original—and, in turn, frequently emulated.

JEAN-ANTOINE HOUDON Neoclassicism also became the preferred style for public sculpture in the new American republic. When members of the Virginia legislature wanted to erect a life-size marble statue of Virginia-born George Washington (1732–1799), they awarded the commission to the leading French Neoclassical sculptor of the late 18th century, JEAN-ANTOINE HOUDON (1741–1828). Houdon had already carved a bust portrait of Benjamin Franklin

26-31 THOMAS JEFFERSON, Rotunda and Lawn (looking north), University of Virginia, Charlottesville, Virginia, 1819–1826.

Modeled on the Pantheon (FIG. 7-49), Jefferson's Rotunda sits like a temple in a Roman forum on an elevated platform overlooking the colonnaded Lawn of the University of Virginia.

26-32 JEAN-ANTOINE HOUDON, *George Washington*, 1788–1792. Marble, 6′ 2″ high. State Capitol, Richmond.

Houdon portrayed Washington in contemporary garb, but he incorporated the Roman *fasces* and Cincinnatus's plow in the statue, because Washington similarly had returned to his farm after his war service.

26-33 HORATIO GREENOUGH, *George Washington*, 1840. Marble, 11′ 4″ high. Smithsonian American Art Museum, Washington, D.C.

In this posthumous portrait, Greenough likened Washington to a god by depicting him seminude and enthroned in the manner of Phidias's Olympian statue of Zeus, king of the Greek gods.

(1706–1790) when he was America's ambassador to France. His portrait of Washington (FIG. **26-32**) is the sculptural equivalent of a painted Grand Manner portrait (FIG. 26-19). But although Washington wears 18th-century garb, the statue makes overt reference to the Roman Republic. The "column" on which Washington leans is a bundle of rods with an ax attached—the ancient Roman *fasces*, an emblem of authority (used much later as the emblem of Mussolini's Fascist—the term derives from "fasces"—government in 20th-century Italy). The 13 rods symbolize the 13 original states. The plow behind Washington alludes to Cincinnatus, a patrician of the early Roman Republic who was elected dictator during a time of war and resigned his position as soon as victory had been achieved in order to return to his farm. Washington wears the badge of the Society of the Cincinnati (visible beneath the bottom of his waistcoat), an association founded in 1783 for officers in the revolutionary army who had resumed their peacetime roles. Tellingly, Washington no longer holds his sword in Houdon's statue.

HORATIO GREENOUGH After his death, Washington gradually took on almost godlike stature as the "father of his country." In 1840 the U.S. Congress commissioned American sculptor HORATIO GREENOUGH (1805–1852) to create a statue (FIG. **26-33**) of the country's first president for the Capitol. Greenough used Houdon's portrait as his model for the head, but he portrayed Washington as seminude and enthroned, as Phidias depicted Zeus in the famous lost statue he made for the god's temple at Olympia in ancient Greece. The colossal statue—Washington is more than 11 feet tall, seated—epitomizes the Neoclassical style, but it did not win favor with either the Congress that commissioned it or the public. Although no one ever threw Greenough's statue into the Potomac River, as one congressman suggested, the legislators never placed it in its intended site beneath the Capitol dome. In fact, by 1840 the Neoclassical style itself was no longer in vogue. The leading artists of Europe and America had embraced a new style, Romanticism, examined in the next chapter.

ROCOCO TO NEOCLASSICISM:
THE 18TH CENTURY IN EUROPE AND AMERICA

ROCOCO

▌ In the early 18th century, the centralized and grandiose palace-based culture of Baroque France gave way to the much more intimate Rococo culture based in the townhouses of Paris. There, aristocrats and intellectuals gathered for witty conversation in salons featuring delicate colors, sinuous lines, gilded mirrors, elegant furniture, and small paintings and sculptures.

▌ The leading Rococo painter was Antoine Watteau, whose usually small canvases feature light colors and elegant figures in ornate costumes moving gracefully through lush landscapes. His *fête galante* paintings depict the outdoor amusements of French high society.

▌ Watteau's successors included François Boucher and Jean-Honoré Fragonard, who carried on the Rococo style late into the 18th century. In Italy, Giambattista Tiepolo adapted the Rococo manner to huge ceiling frescoes in the Baroque tradition.

Boffrand, Salon de la Princesse, Paris 1737–1740

THE ENLIGHTENMENT

▌ By the end of the 18th century, revolutions had overthrown the monarchy in France and achieved independence for the British colonies in America. A major factor was the Enlightenment, a new way of thinking critically about the world independently of religion and tradition.

▌ The Enlightenment promoted scientific questioning of all assertions and embraced the doctrine of progress, epitomized by the Industrial Revolution, which began in England in the 1740s. The paintings of Joseph Wright of Derby celebrated the scientific inventions of the Enlightenment era.

Wright, *A Lecture at the Orrery,* ca. 1763–1765

▌ The Enlightenment also made knowledge of ancient Rome imperative for the cultured elite, and Europeans and Americans in large numbers undertook a Grand Tour of Italy. Among the most popular souvenirs of the Grand Tour were Antonio Canaletto's *vedute* of Venice rendered in precise Renaissance perspective with the aid of a camera obscura.

▌ Rejecting the idea of progress, Rousseau, one of the leading French *philosophes,* argued for a return to natural values and exalted the simple, honest life of peasants. His ideas had a profound impact on artists such as Jean-Baptiste-Siméon Chardin and Jean-Baptiste Greuze, who painted sentimental narratives about rural families.

Canaletto, *Riva degli Schiavoni, Venice,* ca. 1735–1740

▌ The taste for naturalism also led to the popularity of portrait paintings with landscape backgrounds, a specialty of Thomas Gainsborough, and to a reawakening of interest in realism. Benjamin West represented the protagonists in his history paintings wearing contemporary costumes.

NEOCLASSICISM

▌ The Enlightenment revival of interest in Greece and Rome, which spurred systematic excavations at Herculaneum and Pompeii, also gave rise in the late 18th century to the artistic movement known as Neoclassicism, which incorporated the subjects and styles of ancient art.

▌ One pioneer of the new style was Angelica Kauffmann, who often chose subjects drawn from Roman history for her paintings. Jacques-Louis David, who exalted classical art as "the imitation of nature in her most beautiful and perfect form," also favored ancient Roman themes. Painted on the eve of the French Revolution, *Oath of the Horatii,* set in a severe classical hall, served as an example of patriotism and sacrifice.

Kauffmann, *Mother of the Gracchi,* ca. 1785

▌ Architects also eagerly embraced the Neoclassical style. Ancient Roman and Italian Renaissance structures inspired Jacques-Germain Soufflot's Panthéon in Paris and Richard Boyle's Chiswick House near London. A Greek temple in Athens was the model for James Stuart's Doric portico in Worcestershire.

▌ In the United States, Thomas Jefferson adopted the Neoclassical style in his designs for Monticello and the University of Virginia. He championed Neoclassicism as the official architectural style of the new American republic because it represented for him idealism, patriotism, and civic virtue.

Soufflot, Panthéon, Paris, 1755–1792

In the shadows of the left side of the huge canvas are dying and dead Arabs, including a seated man in despair. Gros based the figure on one of the damned in Michelangelo's *Last Judgment* (FIG. 22-19).

Foreshadowing Romanticism, Gros carefully recorded the exotic people, costumes, and architecture of Jaffa, including the distinctive Islamic striped horseshoe arches of the mosque-hospital.

Napoleon, fearless among the plague-stricken, reaches out to touch one man's sores. Gros portrayed the French general as Christlike, implying he possessed miraculous power to heal the sick.

27-1 Antoine-Jean Gros, *Napoleon at the Plague House at Jaffa*, 1804. Oil on canvas, 17′ 5″ × 23′ 7″. Musée du Louvre, Paris.

Among the dying whom Napoleon has come to comfort is a kneeling nude man with left arm extended. His posture recalls that of the dead Christ in Michelangelo's emotional *Pietà* (FIG. 22-20).

ROMANTICISM, REALISM, PHOTOGRAPHY: EUROPE AND AMERICA, 1800 TO 1870

NAPOLEON AT JAFFA

In the opening decade of the 19th century, many of the leading French artists produced major artworks glorifying the most powerful man in Europe at the time—Napoleon Bonaparte (1769–1821), since 1799 First Consul of the French Republic and from 1804 to 1815, Emperor of the French. One of those artists was ANTOINE-JEAN GROS (1771–1835), a pupil of Jacques-Louis David (FIGS. 26-25 and 26-26), Napoleon's favorite painter. Gros, like David, produced several paintings that contributed to Napoleon's growing mythic status. In *Napoleon at the Plague House at Jaffa* (FIG. 27-1), the artist, at Napoleon's request, recorded an incident during an outbreak of the bubonic plague in the course of the general's Syrian campaign of 1799. This fearsome disease struck Muslim and French forces alike, and to quell the growing panic and hysteria, on March 11, 1799, Napoleon himself visited the mosque at Jaffa that had been converted into a hospital for those who had contracted the dreaded disease. Gros depicted Napoleon's staff officers covering their noses against the stench of the place, whereas Napoleon, amid the dead and dying, is fearless and in control. He comforts those still alive, who are clearly awed by his presence and authority. Indeed, by depicting the French leader having removed his glove to touch the sores of a plague victim, Gros implied Napoleon possessed the miraculous power to heal. The composition recalls scenes of the doubting Thomas touching Christ's wound. Here, however, Napoleon is not Saint Thomas but a Christlike figure tending to the sick, as in Rembrandt's *Hundred-Guilder Print* (FIG. 25-16), which Gros certainly knew. The French painter also based the despairing seated figure at the lower left on the comparable figure (one of the damned) in Michelangelo's *Last Judgment* (FIG. 22-19). The kneeling nude man with extended arm at the right recalls the dead Christ in Michelangelo's late *Pietà* (FIG. 22-20).

The action in *Napoleon at the Plague House in Jaffa* unfolds against the exotic backdrop of the horseshoe arches and Moorish arcades of the mosque-hospital's courtyard (compare FIG. 10-9). On the left are Muslim doctors distributing bread and ministering to plague-stricken Arabs in the shadows. On the right, in radiant light, are Napoleon and his soldiers in their splendid tailored uniforms. David had used this polarized compositional scheme and an arcaded backdrop to great effect in his *Oath of the Horatii* (FIG. 26-25), and Gros emulated these features in this painting. However, the younger artist's fascination with the exoticism of the Muslim world, as is evident in his attention to the details of architecture and costume, represented a departure from Neoclassicism. This, along with Gros's emphasis on death, suffering, and an emotional rendering of the scene, presaged core elements of the artistic movement that would soon displace Neoclassicism—Romanticism.

ART UNDER NAPOLEON

The revolution of 1789 initiated a new era in France, but the overthrow of the monarchy also opened the door for Napoleon Bonaparte to exploit the resulting disarray and establish a different kind of monarchy with himself at its head. In 1799, after serving in various French army commands and leading major campaigns in Italy and Egypt, Napoleon became First Consul of the French Republic, a title with clear and intentional links to the ancient Roman Republic (see Chapter 7). During the next 15 years, the ambitious general gained control of almost all of continental Europe in name or through alliances (MAP 27-1). In May 1804, for example, he became king of Italy. Later that year, the pope journeyed to Paris for Napoleon's coronation as Emperor of the French (FIG. 27-2). In 1812, however, Napoleon launched a disastrous invasion of Russia that ended in retreat, and in 1815 he suffered a devastating defeat at the hands of the British at Waterloo in present-day Belgium. Forced to abdicate the imperial throne, Napoleon went into exile on the island of Saint Helena in the South Atlantic, where he died six years later.

After Napoleon's death, the political geography of Europe changed dramatically (MAP 27-2, page 758), but in many ways the more significant changes during the first half of the 19th century

MAP 27-1 The Napoleonic Empire in 1815.

ROMANTICISM, REALISM, PHOTOGRAPHY: EUROPE AND AMERICA, 1800 TO 1870

1800	1815	1840	1870

- Napoleon appoints David as First Painter of the Empire and brings Canova from Rome to Paris
- Vignon designs La Madeleine, Napoleon's Neoclassical "temple of glory"
- Gros, Girodet, and Ingres form a bridge between Neoclassicism and Romanticism

- Romanticism is the leading art movement in Europe. Delacroix and other painters favor exotic and fantastic subjects featuring unleashed emotion, vibrant color, and bold brushstrokes
- Friedrich, Turner, Cole, and other Romantic artists specialize in painting transcendental landscapes
- Gothic style enjoys a revival in architecture
- Daguerre and Talbot invent photography

- Courbet exhibits his work in the Pavilion of Realism. He and other Realist painters in Europe and America insist people and events of their own time are the only valid subjects for art
- Manet's paintings get a hostile reception because of their shocking subject matter and nonillusionistic style
- Paxton pioneers prefabricated glass-and-iron construction in the Crystal Palace
- Technological advances enable artists to make on-the-spot photographs of the Civil War

were technological and economic. The Industrial Revolution caused a population boom in European cities, and railroads spread to many parts of the Continent, facilitating the transportation of both goods and people. Transformation also occurred in the art world. The century opened with Neoclassicism still supreme, but by 1870 Romanticism and Realism in turn had captured the imagination of artists and public alike. New construction techniques had a major impact on architectural design, and the invention of photography revolutionized picturemaking of all kinds.

27-1A DAVID, *Napoleon Crossing Saint-Bernard*, 1800–1801.

DAVID AND NAPOLEON At the fall of the French revolutionary Maximilien Robespierre and his party in 1794, Jacques-Louis David, who had aligned himself personally and through his work with the revolutionary forces, barely escaped with his life. He stood trial and went to prison. After his release in 1795, he worked hard to resurrect his career. When Napoleon approached David in 1804 and offered him the position of First Painter of the Empire, David seized the opportunity. The artist, who had earlier painted a series of portraits of the emperor on horseback crossing the Alps (FIG. 27-1A), exemplified Neoclassicism, the artistic style Napoleon favored because he aspired to rule an empire that might one day rival ancient Rome's. The French emperor consequently embraced all links with the classical past as symbolic sources of authority.

CORONATION OF NAPOLEON The new emperor was well aware of the power of art for constructing a public image and of David's ability to produce inspiring patriotic images. The most grandiose work First Painter David produced for his new imperial patron was *Coronation of Napoleon* (FIG. 27-2), an immense (20 by 32 feet) canvas documenting the pomp and pageantry of the crowning ceremony of December 1804. To a large extent, David adhered to historical fact in depicting Napoleon's coronation, duly recording, for example, the appearance of the interior of Paris's Notre Dame Cathedral as the emperor's architects Charles Percier (1764–1838) and Pierre-François-Léonard Fontaine (1762–1853) had decorated it for the occasion. David also faithfully portrayed those in attendance: Napoleon; his wife Josephine (1763–1814), who kneels to receive her crown; Pope Pius VII (r. 1800–1823), seated behind Napoleon; Joseph (1768–1814) and Louis (1778–1846) Bonaparte; Napoleon's ministers; the retinues of the emperor and empress; a representative group of the clergy; and David himself, seated among the rows of spectators in the balconies. Preliminary studies and drawings reveal, however, that, at Napoleon's request, David made changes to his initially accurate record of the event. For example, the emperor insisted the painter depict the pope with his hand raised in blessing. Further, Napoleon's mother, who had refused to attend the coronation, appears prominently in the center background.

Given the number of figures and details David had to incorporate in his painting, it is remarkable he was able to impose upon the lavish pageant the structured composition central to the Neoclassical style. As in his *Oath of the Horatii* (FIG. 26-25), David presented

27-2 JACQUES-LOUIS DAVID, *Coronation of Napoleon,* 1805–1808. Oil on canvas, 20′ 4$\frac{1}{2}$″ × 32′ 1$\frac{3}{4}$″. Musée du Louvre, Paris.

As First Painter of the Empire, David recorded Napoleon at his December 1804 coronation crowning his wife with the pope as witness, thus underscoring the authority of the state over the church.

MAP 27-2 Europe around 1850.

the action as if on a theater stage—which in this instance was literally the case, even if the stage Percier and Fontaine constructed was inside a church. In addition, as he did in his arrangement of the men and women in *Oath of the Horatii,* David conceptually divided the painting to highlight polarities. The pope, prelates, and priests representing the Catholic Church appear on the right. The members of Napoleon's imperial court are on the left. The relationship between church and state was one of this period's most contentious issues. Napoleon's decision to crown himself, rather than to allow the pope to perform the coronation, as was traditional, reflected Napoleon's concern about the church-state power relationship. For the painting commemorating the occasion, the emperor insisted David depict the moment when, having already crowned himself,

27-2A INGRES, *Napoleon on His Imperial Throne,* 1806.

Napoleon placed a crown on his wife's head, further underscoring his authority. Thus, although this painting appears at first to be a detailed, objective record of a historical event, it is, in fact, a carefully crafted tableau designed to present Napoleon in the way he wished to be seen. In that respect, as well as stylistically, David was emulating the artists in the employ of the ancient Roman emperors (see Chapter 7), as did his pupil, JEAN-AUGUSTE-DOMINIQUE INGRES (1780–1867) in a contemporaneous portrait (FIG. 27-2A) of Napoleon enthroned.

LA MADELEINE Napoleon also embraced Neoclassical architecture as an ideal vehicle for expressing his imperial authority. For example, the emperor resumed construction of the church of La Madeleine (FIG. 27-3) in Paris, which had been interrupted in 1790. However, he converted the building into a "temple of glory" for France's imperial armies. (The structure reverted again to a church after Napoleon's defeat and long before its completion in 1842.) Designed by PIERRE VIGNON (1763–1828), the grandiose Napoleonic temple includes a high podium and broad flight of stairs leading to a deep porch in the front. These architectural features, coupled with the Corinthian columns, recall Roman temples in France, such as the Maison Carrée (FIG. 7-32) at Nîmes, making La Madeleine a symbolic link between the Napoleonic and Roman empires. Curiously, the building's classical shell surrounds an interior covered by a sequence of three domes, a feature found in Byzantine and Romanesque churches. Vignon in essence clothed a traditional church in the costume of imperial Rome.

ANTONIO CANOVA Neoclassical sculpture also was in vogue under Napoleon. His favorite sculptor was ANTONIO CANOVA (1757–1822), who somewhat reluctantly left a successful career in Italy to settle in Paris and serve the emperor. Once in France, Canova became Napoleon's admirer and made numerous portraits, all in the Neoclassical style, of the emperor and his family. The most remarkable is the marble portrait (FIG. 27-4) of Napoleon's sister, Pauline Borghese (1780–1825), as Venus. Initially, Canova, who had gained renown for his sculptures of classical gods and heroes—for

Napoleon constructed La Madeleine as a "temple of glory" for his armies. Based on ancient temples (FIG. 7-32) in France, Vignon's Neoclassical design linked the Napoleonic and Roman empires.

The French public never got to admire Canova's portrait, however. Napoleon had arranged the marriage of his sister to an heir of the noble Roman Borghese family. Once Pauline was in Rome, her behavior was less than dignified, and the public gossiped extensively about her affairs. Pauline's insistence on being represented as the goddess of love reflected her self-perception. Because of his wife's questionable reputation, Prince Camillo Borghese (1775–1832), the work's official patron, kept the sculpture sequestered in the Villa Borghese in Rome (where it still is). Borghese allowed relatively few people to see the portrait. Still, knowledge of the existence of the sculpture was widespread and increased the notoriety of both artist and subject.

27-4A CANOVA, Cupid and Psyche, 1787–1793.

example, *Cupid and Psyche* (FIG. 27-4A)—had suggested depicting Borghese as Diana, goddess of the hunt. Pauline, however, demanded she be portrayed as Venus, the goddess of love. Thus she appears, reclining on a divan and gracefully holding the golden apple, the symbol of the goddess's triumph in the judgment of Paris. Canova clearly based his work on Greek statuary—the sensuous pose and seminude body recall Hellenistic works such as *Venus de Milo* (FIG. 5-83)—and the reclining figure has parallels on Roman sarcophagus lids (FIG. 7-61; compare FIG. 6-5).

DAVID'S STUDENTS Given David's stature as an artist in Napoleonic France, along with the popularity of Neoclassicism, it is not surprising the First Painter attracted numerous students and developed an active and flourishing teaching studio (see "David on Greek Style," Chapter 26, page 747). He gave practical instruction to and deeply influenced many important artists of the period. So strong was David's commitment to classicism that he encouraged all his students to learn Latin, the better to immerse themselves in and understand classical culture. David even initially demanded his pupils select their subjects from Plutarch, the ancient author of *Lives of the Noble Greeks and Romans* and a principal source of Neoclassical subject matter. Due to this thorough classical foundation, David's students all produced work that at its core retains Neoclassical elements. Yet David was far from authoritarian in his teaching, and he encouraged his students to find their own artistic identities. The work of his three most famous students—Gros (FIG. 27-1), Ingres (FIGS. 27-2A, 27-6, and 27-7), and Girodet-Trioson (FIGS. 27-5 and 27-5A)—represents a departure from the structured confines of Neoclassicism. David's pupils laid the foundation for the Romantic movement (see page 762) by exploring the realm of the exotic and the erotic, and often by turning to fictional narratives for the subjects of their paintings, as the Romantic artists would also do.

27-4 ANTONIO CANOVA, *Pauline Borghese as Venus*, 1808. Marble, 6′ 7″ long. Galleria Borghese, Rome.

Canova was Napoleon's favorite sculptor. Here, the artist depicted the emperor's sister—at her request—as the nude Roman goddess of love in a marble statue inspired by classical models.

Girodet's depiction of Native American
lovers in the Louisiana wilderness
appealed to the French public's
fascination with what it perceived
as the passion and primitivism of
the New World.

GIRODET-TRIOSON *Burial of Atala* (FIG. **27-5**) by ANNE-LOUIS GIRODET-TRIOSON (1767–1824) is an important bridge between Neoclassicism and Romanticism. Girodet based the painting on *The Genius of Christianity,* a novel by François René de Chateaubriand (1768–1848). The section of the novel dealing with Atala appeared as an excerpt a year before the publication of the entire book in 1802. Both the excerpt and the novel were enormously successful, and as a result, Atala became almost a cult figure. The exoticism and eroticism integral to the narrative accounted in large part for the public's interest in *The Genius of Christianity.* Set in Louisiana, Chateaubriand's work focuses on two young Native Americans, Atala and Chactas. The two, from different tribes, fall in love and run away together through the wilderness. Erotic passion permeates the story, and Atala, sworn to lifelong virginity, finally commits suicide rather than break her oath. Girodet's painting depicts this tragedy. Atala's grief-stricken lover, Chactas, buries the heroine in the shadow of a cross. Assisting in the burial is a cloaked priest, whose presence is appropriate given Chateaubriand's emphasis on the revival of Christianity (and the Christianization of the New World) in his novel. Like Gros's depiction of the exotic Muslim world of Jaffa (FIG. 27-1), Girodet's representation of American Indian lovers in the Louisiana wilderness appealed to the public's fascination (whetted by the Louisiana Purchase in 1803) with what it perceived as the passion and primitivism of Native American life in the New World. *Burial of Atala* speaks here to emotions, rather than inviting philosophical meditation or revealing some grand order of nature and form. Unlike David's appeal in *Oath of the Horatii* (FIG. 26-25) to feelings that inspire public action, the appeal here is to the viewer's private world of fantasy and emotion. But Girodet-Trioson also occasionally addressed contemporary themes in his work, as he did in his portrait (FIG. **27-5A**) of Jean-Baptiste Belley, a French legislator and former slave.

27-5A GIRODET-TRIOSON,
Jean-Baptiste Belley, 1797.

INGRES David's greatest pupil, J.-A.-D. Ingres (FIG. 27-2A), arrived at David's studio in the late 1790s after Girodet-Trioson had left to establish an independent career. Ingres's study there was to be short-lived, however, as he soon broke with David on matters of style. Ingres adopted what he believed to be a truer and purer Greek style than David's Neoclassical manner. The younger artist employed flat, linear forms approximating those found in Greek vase painting (see Chapter 5), and often placed the main figures in the foreground of his composition, emulating classical low-relief sculpture.

APOTHEOSIS OF HOMER Ingres exhibited his huge composition *Apotheosis of Homer* (FIG. **27-6**) at the Salon of 1827 (see "Academic Salons," Chapter 28, page 802). The painting presented in a single statement the doctrines of ideal form and of Neoclassical taste, and generations of academic painters remained loyal to that style. Winged Victory (or Fame) crowns the epic poet Homer, who sits like a god on a throne before an Ionic temple. At Homer's feet are two statuesque women, personifications of the *Iliad* and the *Odyssey,* the offspring of his imagination. Symmetrically grouped about him is a company of the "sovereign geniuses"—as Ingres called them—who expressed humanity's highest ideals in philosophy, poetry, music, and art. To Homer's left are the Greek poet Anacreon with his lyre, Phidias with his sculptor's hammer, the philosophers Plato and Socrates, and other ancient worthies of different eras. They gather together in the painter's world of suspended time as Raphael united them in *School of Athens* (FIG. 22-9), which was the inspiration for *Apotheosis of Homer.* To the far right in Ingres's assembly of literary and artistic giants are the Roman poets Horace and Vergil, and two Italians: Dante, and, conspicuously, Raphael. Among the forward group on the painting's left side are Poussin (pointing) and Shakespeare (half concealed). At the right are French writers Jean Baptiste Racine, Molière, Voltaire, and François de Salignac de la Mothe Fénelon. Ingres had planned a much larger and more inclusive group, but he never completed the project.

27-6 **Jean-Auguste-Dominique Ingres**, *Apotheosis of Homer*, 1827. Oil on canvas, 12′ 8″ × 16′ 10¾″. Musée du Louvre, Paris. ◼◀

Inspired by *School of Athens* (FIG. 22-9) by Raphael, Ingres's favorite painter, this monumental canvas is a Neoclassical celebration of Homer and other ancient worthies, Dante, and select French authors.

languid pose, small head and elongated limbs, and the generally cool color scheme reveal the painter's debt to Parmigianino (FIG. 22-44) and the Italian Mannerists. However, by converting the figure to an *odalisque* (woman in a Turkish harem), Ingres, unlike Canova, made a strong concession to the burgeoning Romantic taste for the exotic.

This rather strange mixture of artistic allegiances—the combination of precise classical form and Romantic themes—prompted

GRANDE ODALISQUE Despite his commitment to ideal form and careful compositional structure, Ingres also produced works that, like those of Gros and Girodet, his contemporaries saw as departures from Neoclassicism. The most famous is *Grande Odalisque* (FIG. 27-7). The subject—the reclining nude female figure—followed the grand tradition of antiquity and the Renaissance (FIGS. 22-16 and 22-39) in sculpture as well as painting, as did Canova's *Pauline Borghese as Venus* (FIG. 27-4). *Grande Odalisque* again shows Ingres's admiration for Raphael in his borrowing of that master's type of female head (FIGS. 22-7 and 22-8). The figure's

confusion, and when Ingres first exhibited *Grande Odalisque* in 1814, the painting drew acid criticism. Critics initially saw Ingres as a rebel in terms of both the form and content of his works. They did not cease their attacks until the mid-1820s, when a greater enemy of David's Neoclassical style, Eugène Delacroix, appeared on the scene. Then critics suddenly perceived that Ingres's art, despite its innovations and deviations, still contained crucial elements adhering to the Neoclassical taste for the ideal. In fact, Ingres soon became the leader of the academic forces in their battle against the "barbarism" of Delacroix, Théodore Géricault, and the Romantic movement.

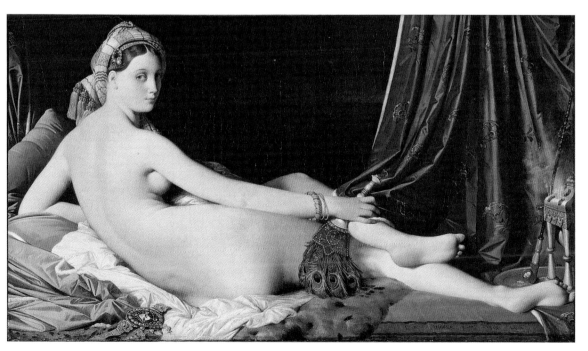

27-7 **Jean-Auguste-Dominique Ingres**, *Grande Odalisque*, 1814. Oil on canvas, 2′ 11⅞″ × 5′ 4″. Musée du Louvre, Paris. ◼◀

The reclining female nude was a Greco-Roman subject, but Ingres converted his Neoclassical figure into an odalisque in a Turkish harem, consistent with the new Romantic taste for the exotic.

ROMANTICISM

Whereas Neoclassicism's rationality reinforced Enlightenment thought (see Chapter 26), particularly Voltaire's views, Rousseau's ideas contributed to the rise of *Romanticism*. Rousseau's exclamation "Man is born free, but is everywhere in chains!"—the opening line of his *Social Contract* (1762)—summarizes a fundamental Romantic premise. Romanticism emerged from a desire for freedom—not only political freedom but also freedom of thought, of feeling, of action, of worship, of speech, and of taste. Romantics asserted freedom was the right and property of all. They believed the path to freedom was through imagination rather than reason and functioned through feeling rather than through thinking.

The allure of the Romantic spirit grew dramatically during the late 18th century, when the term originated among German literary critics. Their aim was to distinguish peculiarly "modern" traits from the Neoclassical traits that already had displaced Baroque and Rococo design elements. Consequently, some scholars refer to Romanticism as a phenomenon that began around 1750 and ended about 1850, but most use the term more narrowly to denote a movement that flourished from about 1800 to 1840, between Neoclassicism and Realism.

Roots of Romanticism

The transition from Neoclassicism to Romanticism represented a shift in emphasis from reason to feeling, from calculation to intuition, and from objective nature to subjective emotion. Among Romanticism's manifestations were the interests in the medieval period and in the sublime. For people living in the 18th century, the Middle Ages were the "dark ages," a time of barbarism, superstition, dark mystery, and miracle. The Romantic imagination stretched its perception of the Middle Ages into all the worlds of fantasy open to it, including the ghoulish, the infernal, the terrible, the nightmarish, the grotesque, the sadistic, and all the imagery that comes from the chamber of horrors when reason sleeps. Related to the imaginative sensibility was the period's notion of the sublime. Among the individuals most involved in studying the sublime was the British politician and philosopher Edmund Burke (1729–1797). In *A Philosophical Enquiry into the Origins of Our Ideas of the Sublime and Beautiful* (1757), Burke articulated his definition of the sublime—feelings of awe mixed with terror. Burke observed that pain or fear evoked the most intense human emotions and that these emotions could also be thrilling. Thus, raging rivers and great storms at sea could be sublime to their viewers.

Accompanying this taste for the sublime was the taste for the fantastic, the occult, and the macabre—for the adventures of the soul voyaging into the dangerous reaches of the imagination.

HENRY FUSELI The concept of the nightmare is the subject of a 1781 painting (FIG. **27-8**) by HENRY FUSELI (1741–1825). Swiss by birth, Fuseli settled in England and eventually became a member of the Royal Academy and an instructor there. Largely self-taught, he contrived a distinctive manner to express the fantasies of his vivid imagination. Fuseli specialized in night moods of horror and in dark fantasies—in the demonic, in the macabre, and often in the sadistic. In *The Nightmare,* a beautiful young woman lies asleep, draped across the bed with her limp arm dangling over the side. An *incubus,* a demon believed in medieval times to prey, often sexually, on sleeping women, squats ominously on her body. In the background, a ghostly horse with flaming eyes bursts into the scene from beyond the curtain. Despite the temptation to see the painting's title as a pun because of this horse, the word *nightmare* in fact derives from "night" and "Mara." Mara was a spirit in Scandinavian mythology who tormented and suffocated sleepers. Fuseli was among the first to attempt to depict the dark terrain of the human subconscious that became fertile ground for later artists to harvest.

WILLIAM BLAKE In their images of the sublime and the terrible, Romantic artists often combined something of Baroque dynamism with naturalistic details in their quest for grippingly moving visions. These elements became the mainstay of Romantic art and contrasted with the more intellectual, rational Neoclassical themes and compositions. The two were not mutually exclusive, however. Gros, Girodet-Trioson, and Ingres effectively integrated elements of Neoclassicism with Romanticism. So, too, did the visionary English poet, painter, and engraver WILLIAM BLAKE (1757–1827). Blake greatly admired ancient Greek art because it exemplified for him the mathematical and thus the eternal, and his work often incorporated classical references. Yet Blake did not align himself with prominent Enlightenment figures. Like many other Romantic

27-8 HENRY FUSELI, *The Nightmare,* 1781. Oil on canvas, 3′ 3¾″ × 4′ 1½″. Detroit Institute of the Arts (Founders Society purchase with funds from Mr. and Mrs. Bert L. Smokler and Mr. and Mrs. Lawrence A. Fleishman).

The transition from Neoclassicism to Romanticism marked a shift in emphasis from reason to feeling. Fuseli was among the first painters to depict the dark terrain of the human subconscious.

of his Michelangelesque physique keeps him firmly planted on his heavenly perch. In this image Blake merged ideal classical anatomy with the inner dark dreams of Romanticism.

Spain and France

From its roots in the work of Fuseli, Blake, and other late-18th-century artists, Romanticism gradually displaced Neoclassicism as the dominant painting style of the first half of the 19th century. Romantic artists, including Francisco Goya in Spain and Théodore Géricault and Eugène Delacroix in France, reveled in exploring the exotic, erotic, and fantastic.

FRANCISCO GOYA Although Francisco José de Goya y Lucientes (1746–1828) was David's contemporary, their work has little in common. Goya, however, did not arrive at his general dismissal of Neoclassicism without considerable thought about the Enlightenment and the Neoclassical penchant for rationality and order. In *The Sleep of Reason Produces Monsters* (FIG. **27-10**), an

27-9 William Blake, *Ancient of Days,* frontispiece of *Europe: A Prophecy,* 1794. Metal relief etching, hand colored, $9\frac{1}{2}'' \times 6\frac{3}{4}''$. Pierpont Morgan Library, New York.

Although art historians classify Blake as a Romantic artist, he incorporated classical references in his works. Here, ideal classical anatomy merges with the inner dark dreams of Romanticism.

artists, he also found the art of the Middle Ages appealing. Blake derived the inspiration for many of his paintings and poems from his dreams. The importance he attached to these nocturnal experiences led him to believe the rationalist search for material explanations of the world stifled the spiritual side of human nature. He also believed the stringent rules of behavior that orthodox religions imposed killed the individual creative impulse.

Blake's vision of the Almighty in *Ancient of Days* (FIG. **27-9**) combines his ideas and interests in a highly individual way. For Blake, this figure united the concept of the Creator with that of wisdom as a part of God. He chose *Ancient of Days* as the frontispiece for his book *Europe: A Prophecy,* and juxtaposed it with a quotation ("When he set a compass upon the face of the deep") from Proverbs 8:27. The speaker is Wisdom, who tells the reader how she was with the Lord through all the time of the creation (Prov. 8:22–23, 27–30). Energy fills Blake's composition. The Almighty leans forward from a fiery orb, peering toward earth and unleashing power through his outstretched left arm into twin rays of light. These emerge between his spread fingers like an architect's measuring instrument—a conception of creation with precedents in Gothic manuscript painting (FIG. 13-32). Here, however, a mighty wind surges through the Creator's thick hair and beard. Only the strength

1 in.

27-10 Francisco Goya, *The Sleep of Reason Produces Monsters,* from *Los Caprichos,* ca. 1798. Etching and aquatint, $8\frac{1}{2}'' \times 5\frac{7}{8}''$. Metropolitan Museum of Art, New York (gift of M. Knoedler & Co., 1918).

In this print, Goya depicted himself asleep while threatening creatures converge on him, revealing his commitment to the Romantic spirit—the unleashing of imagination, emotions, and nightmares.

etching from a series titled *Los Caprichos* (*The Caprices*), Goya depicted himself asleep, slumped onto a desk, while threatening creatures converge on him. Seemingly poised to attack the artist are owls (symbols of folly) and bats (symbols of ignorance). The viewer might read this as a portrayal of what emerges when reason is suppressed and, therefore, as advocating Enlightenment ideals. However, the print also can be interpreted as Goya's commitment to the creative process and the Romantic spirit—the unleashing of imagination, emotions, and even nightmares.

27-10A GOYA, *Family of Charles IV*, 1800.

THIRD OF MAY, 1808 Much of Goya's multifaceted work deals not with Romantic fantasies but with contemporary events. In 1786, he became an official artist in the court of Charles IV (r. 1788–1808) and produced portraits of the king and his family (FIG. **27-10A**). Dissatisfaction with the king's rule increased dramatically during Goya's tenure at the court, and the Spanish people eventually threw their support behind the king's son, Ferdinand VII, in the hope he would initiate reform. To overthrow his father and mother, Queen Maria Luisa (1751–1819), Ferdinand enlisted the aid of Napoleon Bonaparte, who possessed uncontested authority and military expertise at that time. Napoleon had designs on the Spanish throne and thus readily agreed to send French troops to Spain. Not surprisingly, as soon as he ousted Charles IV, Napoleon revealed his plan to rule Spain himself by installing his brother Joseph Bonaparte (r. 1808–1813) on the Spanish throne.

The Spanish people, finally recognizing the French as invaders, sought a way to expel the foreign troops. On May 2, 1808, Spaniards attacked Napoleon's soldiers in a chaotic and violent clash. In retaliation and as a show of force, the French responded the next day by rounding up and executing Spanish citizens. This tragic event is the subject of Goya's most famous painting, *Third of*

May, 1808 (FIG. **27-11**), commissioned in 1814 by Ferdinand VII (r. 1813–1833), who had reclaimed the throne after the ouster of the French. In emotional fashion, Goya depicted the anonymous murderous wall of Napoleonic soldiers ruthlessly executing the unarmed and terrified Spanish peasants. The artist encouraged empathy for the Spaniards by portraying horrified expressions and anguish on their faces, endowing them with a humanity lacking in the French firing squad. Moreover, the peasant about to be shot throws his arms out in a cruciform gesture reminiscent of Christ's position on the cross. Goya enhanced the emotional drama of the massacre by using stark darks and lights and by extending the time frame depicted. Although Goya captured the specific moment when one man is about to be executed, he also recorded the bloody bodies of others lying dead on the ground. Still others have been herded together to be shot in a few moments.

SATURN Over time, Goya became increasingly disillusioned and pessimistic, and his declining health further contributed to this state of mind. Among Goya's later works are the "Black Paintings," frescoes he painted on the walls of his farmhouse in Quinta del Sordo, outside Madrid. Because Goya created these works solely on his terms and for his private viewing, they provide great insight into the artist's outlook, which is terrifying and disturbing. *Saturn Devouring One of His Children* (FIG. **27-12**) depicts the raw carnage and violence of Saturn (the Greek god Kronos; see "The Gods and Goddesses of Mount Olympus," Chapter 5, page 107, or page xxix in Volume II and Book D), wild-eyed and monstrous, as he consumes one of his offspring. Because of the similarity of Kronos and *khronos* (the Greek word for "time"), Saturn has come to be associated with time. This has led some to interpret Goya's painting as an expression of the artist's despair over the passage of time. Despite the simplicity of the image, it conveys a wildness, boldness, and brutality that evokes an elemental response from all viewers. Goya's work, rooted both in personal and national history, presents darkly emotional images well in keeping with Romanticism.

27-11 FRANCISCO GOYA, *Third of May, 1808*, 1814–1815. Oil on canvas, 8′ 9″ × 13′ 4″. Museo del Prado, Madrid. ■◀

Goya encouraged empathy for the massacred Spanish peasants by portraying horrified expressions on their faces, endowing them with a humanity lacking in the French firing squad.

27-12 Francisco Goya, *Saturn Devouring One of His Children*, 1819–1823. Fresco, later detached and mounted on canvas, 4' $9\frac{1}{8}$" × 2' $8\frac{5}{8}$". Museo del Prado, Madrid.

This disturbing fresco in Goya's farmhouse uses a mythological tale to express the aging artist's despair over the passage of time. Saturn's Greek name *Kronos* is similar to the Greek word for "time."

THÉODORE GÉRICAULT In France, one of the artists most closely associated with the Romantic movement was Théodore Géricault (1791–1824), who studied with an admirer of David, Pierre-Narcisse Guérin (1774–1833). Although Géricault retained an interest in the heroic and the epic and completed rigorous training in classical drawing, he chafed at the rigidity of the Neoclassical style, instead producing works that captivate viewers with their drama, visual complexity, and emotional force.

RAFT OF THE MEDUSA Géricault's most ambitious project was a gigantic canvas (approximately 16 by 23 feet) titled *Raft of the Medusa* (FIG. 27-13), exhibited in the Salon of 1819, seven years after he burst onto the Parisian art scene with *Charging Chasseur* (FIG. 27-13A). In both works, Géricault abandoned the idealism of Neoclassicism and embraced the theatricality of Romanticism. The subject of *Raft of the Medusa* is the 1816 shipwreck off the African coast of the French frigate *Medusa,* which ran aground on a reef due to the incompetence of the captain, a political appointee. In an attempt to sur-

27-13A Géricault, *Charging Chasseur,* 1812.

vive, 150 passengers built a makeshift raft from pieces of the disintegrating ship. The raft drifted for 12 days, and the number still alive dwindled to 15. Finally, a ship spotted the raft and rescued the emaciated survivors. This horrendous event was political dynamite once it became public knowledge.

In *Raft of the Medusa,* which took Géricault eight months to complete, the artist sought to capture the horror, chaos, and emotion of the tragedy yet invoke the grandeur and impact of Neoclassical history painting.

27-13 Théodore Géricault, *Raft of the Medusa*, 1818–1819. Oil on canvas, 16' 1" × 23' 6". Musée du Louvre, Paris. ◼◀

In this gigantic history painting, Géricault rejected Neoclassical compositional principles and, in the Romantic spirit, presented a jumble of writhing bodies in every attitude of suffering, despair, and death.

Géricault went to great lengths to ensure the accuracy of his representation. He visited hospitals and morgues to examine corpses, interviewed the survivors, and had a model of the raft constructed in his studio. In the painting, the few despairing survivors summon what little strength they have left to flag down the passing ship far on the horizon. The subdued palette and prominent shadows lend an ominous pall to the scene. Géricault departed from the straightforward organization of Neoclassical compositions and instead presented a jumble of writhing bodies. He arranged the survivors and several corpses in a powerful X-shaped composition, and piled one body on another in every attitude of suffering, despair, and death (recalling the plague-stricken figures in Gros's *Napoleon at the Plague House at Jaffa*, FIG. 27-1). One light-filled diagonal axis stretches from bodies at the lower left up to the black man raised on his comrades' shoulders and waving a piece of cloth toward the horizon. The cross axis descends from the dark, billowing sail at the upper left to the shadowed upper torso of the body trailing in the open sea. Géricault's decision to place the raft at a diagonal so that a corner juts outward further draws viewers into the tragic scene. Indeed, it seems as though some of the corpses are sliding off the raft into the viewing space.

Raft of the Medusa is also the artist's commentary on the practice of slavery. Géricault was a member of an abolitionist group that sought ways to end the slave trade in the colonies, the cause promoted in the French legislature by Jean-Baptiste Belley (FIG. 27-5A). Given Géricault's antipathy to slavery, it is appropriate he placed Jean Charles, a black soldier who was one of the few survivors, at the top of the pyramidal heap of bodies.

1 ft.

27-14 THÉODORE GÉRICAULT, *Insane Woman*, 1822–1823. Oil on canvas, 2′ 4″ × 1′ 9″. Musée des Beaux-Arts, Lyons.

The insane and the influence of aberrant states of mind on the appearance of the human face fascinated Géricault and other Romantic artists, who rebelled against Enlightenment rationality.

INSANE WOMAN Mental aberration and irrational states of mind could not fail to interest the rebels against Enlightenment rationality. Géricault, like Goya, examined the influence of mental states on the human face and believed, as many of his contemporaries did, that a face accurately revealed character, especially at the moment of death (FIG. 27-11) and in madness (FIG. 27-12). Géricault made many studies of the inmates of hospitals and institutions for the criminally insane, and he studied the severed heads of guillotine victims. Scientific and artistic curiosity often accompanied the morbidity of the Romantic interest in derangement and death.

Insane Woman (FIG. **27-14**) is one of several of Géricault's portraits of the insane possessing a peculiar hypnotic power. The woman looks away from the viewer, her mouth tense and her eyes red-rimmed with suffering. The portrait presents the psychic facts with astonishing authenticity and breaks sharply with traditional portraiture in which the sitter's visage is idealized, the expression placid, and the setting designed to communicate the elevated stature of the person portrayed.

EUGÈNE DELACROIX Art historians often present the history of painting during the first half of the 19th century as a contest between two major artists—Ingres, the Neoclassical draftsman, and EUGÈNE DELACROIX (1798–1863; FIG. 27-50), the Romantic colorist. Their dialogue recalls the quarrel between the Poussinistes and the Rubénistes at the end of the 17th century and the beginning of the 18th (see Chapter 26). The Poussinistes were conservative defenders of academism who insisted that drawing was superior to color, whereas the Rubénistes proclaimed the importance of color over line (line quality being more intellectual and thus more restrictive than color). Delacroix's works were products of his view that the artist's powers of imagination would in turn capture and inflame the viewer's imagination. Literature of imaginative power served Delacroix (and many of his contemporaries) as a useful source of subject matter (see "The Romantic Spirit in Art, Music, and Literature," page 767). Théophile Gautier (1811–1872), the prominent Romantic critic and novelist, recalled:

> In those days painting and poetry fraternized. The artists read the poets, and the poets visited the artists. We found Shakespeare, Dante, Goethe, Lord Byron and Walter Scott in the studio as well as in the study. There were as many splashes of color as there were blots of ink in the margins of those beautiful books which we endlessly perused. Imagination, already excited, was further fired by reading those foreign works, so rich in color, so free and powerful in fantasy.[1]

DEATH OF SARDANAPALUS Delacroix's 1827 *Death of Sardanapalus* (FIG. **27-15**) is perhaps the grandest Romantic pictorial drama ever painted. Although inspired by the 1821 narrative poem *Sardanapalus* by Lord Byron (1788–1824), the painting does not illustrate that text faithfully. Delacroix depicted the last hour of the Assyrian king Ashurbanipal (r. 668–627 BCE; FIG. 2-23), whom the Greeks called Sardanapalus. The king has just received news of his armies' defeat and the enemies' entry into his city. The setting Delacroix painted is much more tempestuous and crowded than Byron described, and orgiastic destruction has replaced the sacrificial suicide of the poem. Sardanapalus reclines on his funeral pyre, soon to be set alight, and gloomily watches the destruction of all of his most precious possessions—his women, slaves, horses, and treasure. The king's favorite concubine throws herself on the bed, determined to go up in flames with her master. The Assyrian ruler presides like a genius of evil over the tragic scene. Most conspicuous

The Romantic Spirit in Art, Music, and Literature

The appeal of Romanticism, with its emphasis on freedom and feeling, extended well beyond the realm of the visual arts. The imagination and vision that characterized Romantic paintings and sculptures were equally moving and riveting in musical or written form. In European music, literature, and poetry, the Romantic spirit was a dominant presence during the late 18th and early 19th centuries. Composers and authors alike rejected classicism's structured order in favor of the emotive and expressive. In music, the compositions of Franz Schubert (1797–1828), Franz Liszt (1811–1886), Frédéric Chopin (1810–1849), and Johannes Brahms (1833–1897) emphasized the melodic or lyrical. For these composers, music had the power to express the unspeakable and to communicate the subtlest and most powerful human emotions.

In literature, Romantic poets such as John Keats (1795–1821), William Wordsworth (1770–1850), and Samuel Taylor Coleridge (1772–1834) published volumes of poetry manifesting the Romantic interest in lyrical drama. *Ozymandias,* by Percy Bysshe Shelley (1792–1822), transported readers to faraway, exotic locales. The setting of Lord Byron's *Sardanapalus* is the ancient Assyrian Empire (see Chapter 2). Byron's poem conjures images of eroticism and fury unleashed—images Eugène Delacroix made concrete in his painting *Death of Sardanapalus* (FIG. 27-15). One of the best examples of the Romantic spirit is the engrossing novel *Frankenstein,* written in 1818 by Shelley's wife, Mary Wollstonecraft Shelley (1797–1851). This fantastic tale of a monstrous creature run amok remains popular to the present day. As was true of many Romantic artworks, the novel not only embraced emotionalism but also rejected the rationalism underlying Enlightenment thought. Dr. Frankenstein's monster was a product of science, and the novel is an indictment of the tenacious belief in science that Voltaire and other Enlightenment thinkers promoted. *Frankenstein* served as a cautionary tale of the havoc that could result from unrestrained scientific experimentation and from the arrogance of scientists.

27-15 EUGÈNE DELACROIX, *Death of Sardanapalus,* 1827. Oil on canvas, 12′ 1½″ × 16′ 2⅞″. Musée du Louvre, Paris. ◼◀

Inspired by Byron's 1821 poem, Delacroix painted the Romantic spectacle of an Assyrian king on his funeral pyre. The richly colored and emotionally charged canvas is filled with exotic figures.

are the tortured and dying bodies of the harem women. In the foreground, a muscular slave plunges his knife into the neck of one woman. Delacroix filled this awful spectacle of suffering and death with the most daringly difficult and tortuous poses, and chose the richest intensities of hue. With its exotic and erotic overtones, *Death of Sardanapalus* tapped into the Romantic fantasies of 19th-century viewers.

Although *Death of Sardanapalus* is a seventh-century BCE drama, Delacroix, as Géricault, also turned to current events, particularly tragic or sensational ones, for his subject matter. For example, he produced several images based on the Greek War for Independence (1821–1829), including a huge canvas painted while the war was in progress recording the Turkish massacre of the Greeks of Chios (FIG. 27-15A). The French perception of the Greeks locked in a brutal struggle for freedom from the cruel and exotic Ottoman Turks generated great interest in Romantic circles.

27-15A DELACROIX, *Massacre at Chios,* 1822–1824.

27-16 EUGÈNE DELACROIX, *Liberty Leading the People*, 1830. Oil on canvas, 8′ 6″ × 10′ 8″. Musée du Louvre, Paris. ◼◀

In a balanced mix of history and poetic allegory, Delacroix captured the passion and energy of the 1830 revolution in this painting of Liberty leading the Parisian uprising against Charles X.

Delacroix's color Theory

LIBERTY LEADING THE PEOPLE Closer to home, Delacroix captured the passion and energy of the 1830 revolution in *Liberty Leading the People* (FIG. **27-16**). Based on the Parisian uprising against Charles X (r. 1824–1830) at the end of July 1830, it depicts the allegorical personification of Liberty defiantly thrusting forth the republic's tricolor banner as she urges the masses to fight on. The scarlet Phrygian cap (the symbol of a freed slave in antiquity) she wears reinforces the urgency of this struggle. Arrayed around Liberty are bold Parisian types—the street boy brandishing his pistols, the menacing worker with a cutlass, and the intellectual dandy in a top hat brandishing a musket. As in Géricault's *Raft of the Medusa* (FIG. 27-13), dead bodies are all around. In the background, the towers of Notre-Dame (FIG. 13-11) rise through the smoke and haze. The painter's inclusion of this recognizable Parisian landmark announces the specificity of locale and event, balancing contemporary historical fact with poetic allegory.

27-17A DELACROIX, *Women of Algiers*, 1834.

TIGER HUNT An enormously influential event in Delacroix's life that affected his art in both subject and form was his visit to North Africa in 1832 (see "Delacroix in Morocco," page 769). Things he saw there shocked his imagination with fresh impressions that lasted throughout his life and resulted in paintings such as *Tiger Hunt* (FIG. **27-17**), which he completed more than two decades after his trip. Among the canvases he painted immediately upon his return is *Women of Algiers* (FIG. **27-17A**), which captivated the public when exhibited in the 1834 Salon. Delacroix's African experience further heightened his already considerable awareness of the expressive power of color and light. What Delacroix knew about color he passed on to later painters of the 19th century, particularly the Impressionists (see Chapter 28). He observed that pure colors are as rare in nature as lines and that color appears only in an infinitely varied scale of different tones, shadings, and reflections, which he tried to re-create in his paintings. He recorded his observations in his journal, which became for later painters and scholars a veritable handbook of pre-Impressionist color theory. Although Delacroix anticipated the later development of Impressionist color science, that art-science had to await the discoveries by Michel Eugène Chevreul (1786–1889) and Hermann von Helmholtz (1821–1894) of the laws of light decomposition and the properties of complementary colors. Only then could the problems of color perception and juxtaposition in painting be properly formulated (see "19th Century Color Theory," Chapter 28, page 813). Nevertheless, Delacroix's observations were significant, and he advised other artists not to fuse their brushstrokes, as those strokes would appear to fuse naturally from a distance.

No other painter of the time explored the domain of Romantic subject and mood as thoroughly and definitively as Delacroix. His technique was impetuous, improvisational, and instinctive, rather than deliberate, studious, and cold. It epitomized Romantic colorist painting, catching the impression quickly and developing it in the execution process. His contemporaries commented on how furiously Delacroix worked once he had an idea, keeping the whole painting progressing at once. The fury of his attack matched the fury of his imagination and his subjects.

Delacroix in Morocco

Romantic painters often depicted exotic faraway places they had never seen, but Eugène Delacroix journeyed to Morocco in 1832 and discovered in the sun-drenched landscape—and in the hardy and colorful Moroccans dressed in robes reminiscent of the Roman toga—new insights into a culture built on proud virtues. He found in North Africa a culture more classical than anything European Neoclassicism could conceive. In a letter to his friend Fréderic Villot dated February 29, 1832, he wrote:

> This place is made for painters. . . . [B]eauty abounds here; not the over-praised beauty of fashionable paintings. The heroes of David and Co. with their rose-pink limbs would cut a sorry figure beside these children of the sun, who moreover wear the dress of classical antiquity with a nobler air, I dare assert.*

In a second letter, written June 4, 1832, he reported to Auguste Jal:

> You have seen Algiers and you can imagine what the natives of these regions are like. Here there is something even simpler and more primitive; there is less of the Turkish alloy; I have Romans and Greeks on my doorstep: it makes me laugh heartily at David's Greeks, apart, of course, from his sublime skill as a painter. I know now what they were really like; . . . If painting schools persist in [depicting classical subjects], I am convinced, and you will agree with me, that they would gain far more from being shipped off as cabin boys on the first boat bound for the Barbary coast than from spending any more time wearing out the classical soil of Rome. Rome is no longer to be found in Rome.†

The gallantry, valor, and fierce love of liberty of the Moroccans made them, in Delacroix's eyes, unspoiled heroes uncontaminated by European decadence. The Moroccan voyage reinforced Delacroix's Romantic conviction that beauty exists in the fierceness of nature, natural processes, and natural beings, especially animals. After he experienced Morocco, more and more of Delacroix's subjects involved combats between beasts or between beasts and men. He painted snarling tangles of lions and tigers, battles between horses, and clashes of Muslims with great cats in swirling hunting scenes using compositions reminiscent of those of Rubens (FIG. I-14), as in his 1854 painting *Tiger Hunt* (FIG. 27-17), which clearly speaks to the Romantic interest in faraway lands and exotic cultures.

*Translated by Jean Stewart, in Charles Harrison, Paul Wood, and Jason Gaiger, eds., *Art in Theory 1815–1900: An Anthology of Changing Ideas* (Oxford: Blackwell, 1998), 87.
†Ibid., 88.

27-17 EUGÈNE DELACROIX, *Tiger Hunt*, 1854. Oil on canvas, 2′ 5″ × 3′. Musée d'Orsay, Paris.

Delacroix's 1832 trip to Morocco inspired *Tiger Hunt* and had a lasting impact on his art. His paintings of men battling ferocious beasts are consistent with the Romantic interest in exotic places.

FRANÇOIS RUDE The Romantic spirit pervaded all media during the early 19th century. As did the painters of the period, many sculptors produced work incorporating both Neoclassical and Romantic elements. The colossal limestone group *Departure of the Volunteers of 1792* (FIG. 27-18), also called *La Marseillaise*, is one example. The relief, the work of FRANÇOIS RUDE (1784–1855), decorates one of the gigantic piers of the Arc de Triomphe in Paris. This French landmark was an 1806 Napoleonic commission designed by Jean François Thérèse Chalgrin (1739–1811) on the model of the triumphal arches of ancient Rome (FIGS. 7-40, 7-44B, and 7-75). Work on the arch stopped after Napoleon's defeat but resumed in 1833. Three years later, workmen inserted Rude's group (and three similar ones by other sculptors) into the completed arch. The sculpture depicts the volunteers of 1792 departing to defend France's borders against the foreign enemies of the revolution. The Roman goddess of war, Bellona (who here personifies liberty as well as the "Marseillaise," the revolutionary hymn that is now France's national anthem), soars above patriots of all ages, exhorting them forward with her thundering battle cry. The figures recall David's classically armored (FIG. 26-25) or nude heroes, as do the rhetorical gestures of the wide-flung arms and the striding poses. Yet the violence of motion, the jagged contours, and the densely packed, overlapping

masses relate more closely to the compositional method of dramatic Romanticism, as found in the canvases of Géricault (FIG. 27-13) and Delacroix (FIG. 27-16). Indeed, the allegorical figure in *La Marseillaise* is the spiritual sister of Delacroix's Liberty. Rude's stone figure shares the same Phrygian cap, the badge of liberty, with Delacroix's earlier painted figure, but Rude's soldiers wear classical costumes or are heroically nude, whereas those in Delacroix's painting appear in modern Parisian dress. Both works are allegorical, but one looks to the past and the other to the present.

Landscape Painting

Landscape painting came into its own in the 19th century as a fully independent and respected genre. Briefly eclipsed at the century's beginning by the taste for ideal form, which favored figural composition and history, landscape painting flourished as leading painters adopted the genre as their specialty. Increasing tourism, which came courtesy of improved and expanded railway systems both in Europe (MAP 27-2) and America, contributed to the popularity of landscape painting.

The notion of the picturesque became particularly resonant in the Romantic era. Already in the 18th century, artists had regarded the pleasurable, aesthetic mood that natural landscape inspired as making the landscape itself "picturesque"—that is, worthy of being painted. Rather than simply describe nature, Romantic poets and artists often used nature as allegory. In this manner, artists commented on spiritual, moral, historical, or philosophical issues. Landscape painting was a particularly effective vehicle for such commentary.

In the early 19th century, most northern European (especially German) landscape painting to some degree expressed the Romantic view (first extolled by Rousseau) of nature as a "being" that included the totality of existence in organic unity and harmony. In nature—"the living garment of God," as German poet and dramatist Johann Wolfgang von Goethe (1749–1832) called it—artists found an ideal subject to express the Romantic theme of the soul unified with the natural world. As all nature was mysteriously permeated by "being," landscape artists had the task of interpreting the signs, symbols, and emblems of universal spirit disguised within visible material things. Artists no longer merely beheld a landscape but participated in its spirit, becoming translators of nature's transcendent meanings.

CASPAR DAVID FRIEDRICH Among the first northern European artists to depict the Romantic transcendental landscape was CASPAR DAVID FRIEDRICH (1774–1840). For Friedrich, landscapes were temples, and his paintings were altarpieces. The reverential mood of his works demands from the viewer the silence appropriate to sacred places filled with a divine presence. *Abbey in the Oak Forest* (FIG. 27-19) serves as a solemn requiem. Under a winter sky, through the leafless oaks of a snow-covered cemetery, a funeral procession bears a coffin into the ruins of a Gothic church Friedrich based on the remains of Eldana Abbey in Greifswald. The emblems of death are everywhere—the season's desolation, the leaning crosses and tombstones, the black of mourning the grieving wear, the skeletal trees, and the destruction time has wrought on the church. The painting is a kind of meditation on human mortality. As Friedrich himself remarked: "Why, it has often occurred to me to ask myself do I so frequently choose death, transience, and the grave as subject for my paintings? One must submit oneself many times to death in order some day to attain life everlasting."[2] The artist's sharp-focused rendering of details demonstrates his keen perception of everything in the physical environment relevant to his message. Friedrich's work

10 ft.

27-18 FRANÇOIS RUDE, *Departure of the Volunteers of 1792* (*La Marseillaise*), Arc de Triomphe, Paris, France, 1833–1836. Limestone, 41′ 8″ high. ◼◂

This historical-allegorical sculpture features the Roman war goddess Bellona, but the violent motion, jagged contours, and densely packed masses typify Romantic painting compositions.

27-19 CASPAR DAVID FRIEDRICH, *Abbey in the Oak Forest*, 1810. Oil on canvas, $4' \times 5' 8\frac{1}{2}''$. Nationalgalerie, Staatliche Museen zu Berlin, Berlin. ◼◄

Friedrich was a master of the Romantic transcendental landscape. The reverential mood of this winter scene with a ruined Gothic church and cemetery demands the silence appropriate to sacred places.

balances inner and outer experience. "The artist," he wrote, "should not only paint what he sees before him, but also what he sees within him. If he does not see anything within him, he should give up painting what he sees before him."[3] Although Friedrich's works may not have the theatrical energy of the paintings of Géricault or Delacroix, a resonant and deep emotion pervades them.

WANDERER ABOVE A SEA OF MIST In *Abbey in the Oak Forest* and many of Friedrich's landscapes, the human figure plays an insignificant role. Indeed, in many instances the human actors are difficult even to discern. But in other paintings, one or more figures seen from behind gazing at the natural vista dominate the canvas. In *Wanderer above a Sea of Mist* (FIG. **27-20**), probably Friedrich's most famous painting, a solitary man dressed in German attire suggestive of a bygone era stands on a rocky promontory and leans on his cane. He surveys a vast panorama of clouds, mountains, and thick mist. Because Friedrich chose a point of view on the level of the man's head, the viewer has the sensation of hovering in space behind him—an impossible position that enhances the aura of mystery the scene conveys. Scholars dispute whether Friedrich intended the viewer to identify with the man seen from behind or if he wanted the viewer to contemplate the man gazing at the misty landscape. In either case, the painter communicated an almost religious awe at the beauty and vastness of the natural world. *Wanderer above a Sea of Mist* perfectly expresses the Romantic notion of the sublime in nature.

JOHN CONSTABLE In England, one of the most momentous developments in Western history—the Industrial Revolution—had a profound impact on the evolution of Romantic landscape painting. Although discussion of the Industrial Revolution invariably focuses on technological advances, factory development, and growth of urban centers (see Chapter 26), industrialization had no less pronounced an effect on the countryside and the land itself. The detrimental economic effect the Industrial Revolution had

1 ft.

27-20 CASPAR DAVID FRIEDRICH, *Wanderer above a Sea of Mist*, 1817–1818. Oil on canvas, $3' 1\frac{3}{4}'' \times 2' 5\frac{3}{8}''$. Hamburger Kunsthalle, Hamburg.

Friedrich's painting of a solitary man on a rocky promontory gazing at a vast panorama of clouds, mountains, and thick mist perfectly expresses the Romantic notion of the sublime in nature.

27-21 John Constable, *The Haywain*, 1821. Oil on canvas, 4′ 3¼″ × 6′ 1″. National Gallery, London.

The Haywain is a nostalgic view of the disappearing English countryside during the Industrial Revolution. Constable had a special gift for capturing the texture that climate and weather give to landscape.

on prices for agrarian products produced significant unrest in the English countryside. In particular, increasing numbers of displaced farmers could no longer afford to farm their small land plots.

John Constable (1776–1837) addressed this agrarian crisis in his landscape paintings. He made countless studies from nature for each of his canvases, which helped him produce in his paintings the convincing sense of reality that won so much praise from his contemporaries. In his quest for the authentic landscape, Constable studied it as a meteorologist (which he was by avocation). His special gift was for capturing the texture that climate and weather, which delicately veil what is seen, give to landscape. Constable's use of tiny dabs of local color, stippled with white, created a sparkling shimmer of light and hue across the canvas surface—the vibration itself suggestive of movement and process.

The Haywain (FIG. **27-21**) is representative of Constable's art and reveals much about his outlook. A small cottage sits on the left of this placid, picturesque scene of the countryside, and in the center foreground, a man leads a horse and wagon across the stream. Billowy clouds float lazily across the sky. The muted greens and golds and the delicacy of Constable's brushstrokes complement the scene's tranquility. The artist portrayed the oneness with nature the Romantic poets sought. The relaxed figures are not observers but participants in the landscape's "being."

In terms of content, *The Haywain* is significant for precisely what it does not show—the civil unrest of the agrarian working class and the resulting outbreaks of violence and arson. The people populating Constable's landscapes blend into the scenes and are at one with nature. Rarely does the viewer see workers engaged in tedious labor. Indeed, this painting has a nostalgic, wistful air to it, and reflects Constable's memories of a disappearing rural pastoralism. The artist's father was a rural landowner of considerable wealth, and many of the scenes Constable painted (*The Haywain* included) depict his family's property near East Bergholt in Suffolk, East Anglia. This nostalgia, presented in such naturalistic terms, renders Constable's works Romantic in tone. That the painter felt a kindred spirit with the Romantic artists is revealed by his comment, "Painting is but another word for feeling."[4]

J.M.W. TURNER Constable's contemporary in the English school of landscape painting, Joseph Mallord William Turner (1775–1851), produced work that also responded to encroaching industrialization. However, whereas Constable's paintings are serene and precisely painted, Turner's feature turbulent swirls of frothy pigment. The passion and energy of Turner's works reveal the Romantic sensibility that was the foundation for his art and also clearly illustrate Edmund Burke's concept of the sublime—awe mixed with terror.

Among Turner's most notable works is *The Slave Ship* (FIG. **27-22**). Its subject is a 1783 incident reported in a widely read book titled *The History of the Abolition of the Slave Trade*, by Thomas Clarkson. Because the book had just been reprinted in 1839, Clarkson's account probably prompted Turner's choice of subject for this 1840 painting. The incident involved the captain of a slave ship who, on realizing his insurance company would reimburse him only for slaves lost at sea but not for those who died en route, ordered the sick and dying slaves thrown overboard. Appropriately, the painting's full title is *The Slave Ship* (*Slavers Throwing Overboard the Dead and Dying, Typhoon Coming On*). Turner's frenzied emotional depiction of this act matches its barbaric nature. The artist transformed the sun into an incandescent comet amid flying scarlet clouds. The slave ship moves into the distance, leaving in its wake a turbulent sea choked with the bodies of slaves sinking to their deaths. The relative scale of the minuscule human forms compared with the vast sea and overarching sky reinforces the sense of the sublime, especially the immense power of nature over humans. Almost lost in the boiling colors are the event's particulars, but on close inspection, the viewer can discern the iron shackles and manacles around the wrists and ankles of the drowning slaves, cruelly denying them any chance of saving themselves.

A key ingredient of Turner's highly personal style is the emotive power of pure color. The haziness of the painter's forms and the indistinctness of his compositions intensify the colors and energetic brushstrokes. Turner's innovation in works such as *The Slave Ship* was to release color from any defining outlines so as to express both the forces of nature and the painter's emotional response to them. In his paintings, the reality of color is at one with the reality of feeling. Turner's methods had an incalculable effect on the later

27-22 JOSEPH MALLORD WILLIAM TURNER, *The Slave Ship* (*Slavers Throwing Overboard the Dead and Dying, Typhoon Coming On*), 1840. Oil on canvas, 2′ 11¼″ × 4′. Museum of Fine Arts, Boston (Henry Lillie Pierce Fund).

The essence of Turner's innovative style is the emotive power of color. He released color from any defining outlines to express both the forces of nature and the painter's emotional response to them.

ongoing exploration of the individual's and the country's relationship to the land. American landscape painters frequently focused on identifying qualities that made America unique. One American painter of English birth, THOMAS COLE (1801–1848), often referred to as the leader of the Hudson River School, articulated this idea:

development of painting. His discovery of the aesthetic and emotive power of pure color and his pushing of the medium's fluidity to a point where the paint itself is almost the subject were important steps toward 20th-century abstract art, which dispensed with shape and form altogether (see Chapter 30).

THOMAS COLE In America, landscape painting was the specialty of a group of artists known as the Hudson River School, so named because its members drew their subjects primarily from the uncultivated regions of New York's Hudson River Valley, although many of these painters depicted scenes from across the country. As did the early-19th-century landscape painters in Germany and England, the artists of the Hudson River School not only presented Romantic panoramic landscape views but also participated in the

Whether he [an American] beholds the Hudson mingling waters with the Atlantic—explores the central wilds of this vast continent, or stands on the margin of the distant Oregon, he is still in the midst of American scenery—it is his own land; its beauty, its magnificence, its sublimity—all are his; and how undeserving of such a birthright, if he can turn towards it an unobserving eye, an unaffected heart![5]

Another issue that surfaced frequently in Hudson River School paintings was the moral question of America's direction as a civilization. Cole addressed this question in *The Oxbow* (*View from Mount Holyoke, Northampton, Massachusetts, after a Thunderstorm*; FIG. **27-23**). A splendid scene opens before the viewer, dominated by the lazy oxbow-shaped turning of the Connecticut River. Cole divided the composition in two, with the dark, stormy wilderness on the left and the more developed civilization on the right. The minuscule artist in the bottom center of the painting (wearing a top hat), dwarfed by the landscape's scale, turns to the viewer as if to ask for input in deciding the country's future course. Cole's depictions of expansive wilderness incorporated reflections and moods romantically appealing to the public.

27-23 THOMAS COLE, *The Oxbow* (*View from Mount Holyoke, Northampton, Massachusetts, after a Thunderstorm*), 1836. Oil on canvas, 4′ 3½″ × 6′ 4″. Metropolitan Museum of Art, New York (gift of Mrs. Russell Sage, 1908). ■◀

Cole divided his canvas into dark wilderness on the left and sunlit civilization on the right. The minuscule painter at the bottom center seems to be asking for advice about America's future course.

27-24 ALBERT BIERSTADT, *Among the Sierra Nevada Mountains, California,* 1868. Oil on canvas, 6′ × 10′. National Museum of American Art, Smithsonian Institution, Washington, D.C.

Bierstadt's panoramic landscape presents the breathtaking natural beauty of the American West, reinforcing the 19th-century doctrine of Manifest Destiny, which justified America's western expansion.

ALBERT BIERSTADT Other Hudson River artists used the landscape genre as an allegorical vehicle to address moral and spiritual concerns. ALBERT BIERSTADT (1830–1902) traveled west in 1858 and produced many paintings depicting the Rocky Mountains, Yosemite Valley, and other dramatic locales. These works, such as *Among the Sierra Nevada Mountains, California* (FIG. 27-24), present breathtaking scenery and natural beauty. This panoramic view (the painting is 10 feet wide) is awe-inspiring. Deer and waterfowl appear at the edge of a placid lake, and steep and rugged mountains soar skyward on the left and in the distance. A stand of trees, uncultivated and wild, frames the lake on the right. To underscore the almost transcendental nature of this scene, Bierstadt depicted the sun's rays breaking through the clouds overhead, which suggests a heavenly consecration of the land. That Bierstadt's focus was the American West is not insignificant. By calling national attention to the splendor and uniqueness of the regions beyond the Rocky Mountains, Bierstadt's paintings reinforced the idea of Manifest Destiny. This popular 19th-century doctrine held that westward expansion across the continent was the logical destiny of the United States. As John L. O'Sullivan (1813–1895) expounded in the earliest known use of the term in 1845, "Our manifest destiny [is] to overspread the continent allotted by Providence for the free development of our yearly multiplying millions."[6] Paintings of the scenic splendor of the West helped to mute growing concerns over the realities of conquest, the displacement of Native Americans, and the exploitation of the environment. It should come as no surprise that among those most eager to purchase Bierstadt's work were mail-service magnates and railroad builders—entrepreneurs and financiers involved in westward expansion.

27-25 FREDERIC EDWIN CHURCH, *Twilight in the Wilderness,* 1860s. Oil on canvas, 3′ 4″ × 5′ 4″. Cleveland Museum of Art, Cleveland (Mr. and Mrs. William H. Marlatt Fund).

Church's paintings eloquently express the Romantic notion of the sublime. Painted during the Civil War, this wilderness landscape presents an idealistic view of America free of conflict.

FREDERIC CHURCH Another painter usually associated with the Hudson River School was FREDERIC EDWIN CHURCH (1826–1900), but his interest in landscape scenes extended beyond America. He traveled widely—to South America, Mexico, Europe, the Middle East, Newfoundland, and Labrador. Church's paintings are firmly in the idiom of the Romantic sublime, yet they also reveal contradictions and conflicts in the constructed mythology of American providence and character. *Twilight in the Wilderness* (FIG. 27-25) presents a panoramic view of the sun setting over the majestic landscape. Beyond Church's precise depiction of the magnificent spectacle of nature, the painting, like Constable's *Haywain* (FIG. 27-21), is remarkable for what it does not depict. As did Constable, Church and the other Hudson River School painters worked in a time of great upheaval. *Twilight in the Wilderness* dates to the 1860s, when the Civil War was tearing apart the no-longer-united states. Yet this painting does not display evidence of turbulence or discord. Indeed, it does not include even a single figure. By constructing such an idealistic and comforting view, Church contributed to the national mythology of righteousness and divine providence—a mythology that had become increasingly difficult to maintain in the face of conflict.

Landscape painting was immensely popular in the late 18th and early 19th centuries, in large part because it provided viewers with breathtaking and sublime spectacles of nature. Artists also could allegorize nature, and it was rare for a landscape painting not to touch on spiritual, moral, historical, or philosophical issues. Landscape painting became the perfect vehicle for artists (and the viewing public) to "naturalize" conditions, rendering debate about contentious issues moot and eliminating any hint of conflict.

REALISM

Advances in industrial technology during the early 19th century reinforced Enlightenment faith in the connection between science and progress. Both intellectuals and the general public increasingly embraced *empiricism* and *positivism.* To empiricists, the basis of knowledge is observation and direct experience. Positivists

ascribed to the philosophical model developed by Auguste Comte (1798–1857), who believed scientific laws governed the environment and human activity and could be revealed through careful recording and analysis of observable data. Comte's followers promoted science as the mind's highest achievement and advocated a purely empirical approach to nature and society.

France

Realism was a movement that developed in France around midcentury against this backdrop of an increasing emphasis on science. Consistent with the philosophical tenets of the empiricists and positivists, Realist artists argued that only the contemporary world—what people can see—was "real." Accordingly, Realists focused their attention on the people and events of their own time and disapproved of historical and fictional subjects on the grounds they were neither visible nor present and therefore were not real.

GUSTAVE COURBET The leading figure of the Realist movement in 19th-century art was GUSTAVE COURBET (1819–1877). In fact, even though he shunned labels, Courbet used the term *Realism* when exhibiting his own works (see "Courbet on Realism," page 776). The Realists' sincerity about scrutinizing their environment led them to paint subjects artists had traditionally deemed unworthy of depiction—the mundane and trivial, working-class laborers and peasants, and so forth. Moreover, by depicting these subjects on a scale and with an earnestness and seriousness previously reserved for historical, mythological, and religious painting, Realist artists sought to establish parity between contemporary subject matter and the traditional themes of "high art."

THE STONE BREAKERS An early work that exemplifies Courbet's championing of everyday life as the only valid subject for the modern artist is *The Stone Breakers* (FIG. 27-26), in which the Realist painter presented a glimpse into the life of rural menial laborers. Courbet represented in a straightforward manner two men—one about 70, the other quite young—in the act of breaking stones, traditionally the lot of the lowest members of French society. By juxtaposing youth and age, Courbet suggested those born

27-26 GUSTAVE COURBET, *The Stone Breakers,* 1849. Oil on canvas, 5′ 3″ × 8′ 6″. Formerly Gemäldegalerie, Dresden (destroyed in 1945).

Courbet was the leading figure in the Realist movement. Using a palette of dirty browns and grays, he conveyed the dreary and dismal nature of menial labor in mid-19th-century France.

Courbet on Realism

The academic jury selecting work for the 1855 Salon (part of the Exposition Universelle in Paris that year) rejected two of Courbet's paintings, declaring his subjects and figures were too coarse (so much so as to be plainly "socialistic") and too large. Typical of Courbet's work are *The Stone Breakers* (FIG. 27-26), which depicts menial laborers, and *Burial at Ornans* (FIG. 27-27), which represents the funeral of an ordinary man and is nearly 22 feet long. In response to the jury's decision, Courbet withdrew all of his works, including those that had been accepted, and set up his own exhibition outside the grounds, calling it the Pavilion of Realism. This was in itself a bold action. Courbet was the first artist ever known to have staged a private exhibition of his own work. His pavilion and the statement he issued to explain the paintings shown there amounted to the Realist movement's manifesto. Although Courbet maintained he founded no school and was of no school, he did, as the name of his pavilion suggests, accept the term *Realism* as descriptive of his art.

The statement Courbet distributed at his pavilion reads in part:

> The title of "realist" has been imposed upon me . . . Titles have never given a just idea of things; were it otherwise, the work would be superfluous. . . . I have studied the art of the moderns, avoiding any preconceived system and without prejudice. I have no more wanted to imitate the former than to copy the latter; nor have I thought of achieving the idle aim of "art for art's sake." No! I have simply wanted to draw from a thorough knowledge of tradition the reasoned and free sense of my own individuality. . . . To be able to translate the customs, ideas, and appearances of my time as I see them—in a word, to create a living art—this has been my aim.[*]

Six years later, on Christmas Day, 1861, Courbet wrote an open letter, published a few days later in the *Courier du dimanche,* addressed to prospective students. In the letter, the painter reflected on the nature of his art.

> [An artist must apply] his personal faculties to the ideas and the events of the times in which he lives. . . . [A]rt in painting should consist only of the representation of things that are visible and tangible to the artist. Every age should be represented only by its own artists, that is to say, by the artists who have lived in it. I also maintain that painting is an essentially concrete art form and can consist only of the representation of both real and existing things. . . . An abstract object, not visible, nonexistent, is not within the domain of painting.[†]

Courbet's most famous statement, however, is his blunt dismissal of academic painting, in which he concisely summed up the core principle of Realist painting:

> I have never seen an angel. Show me an angel, and I'll paint one.[‡]

[*]Translated by Robert Goldwater and Marco Treves, eds., *Artists on Art from the XIV to the XX Century* (New York: Pantheon), 295.
[†]Translated by Petra ten-Doesschate Chu, *Letters of Gustave Courbet* (Chicago: University of Chicago Press, 1992), 203–204.
[‡]Quoted by Vincent van Gogh in a July 1885 letter to his brother Theo, in Ronald de Leeuw, *The Letters of Vincent van Gogh* (New York: Penguin, 1996), 302.

27-27 GUSTAVE COURBET, *Burial at Ornans,* 1849. Oil on canvas, 10′ 3½″ × 21′ 9½″. Musée d'Orsay, Paris.

Although as monumental in scale as a traditional history painting, *Burial at Ornans* horrified critics because of the ordinary nature of the subject and Courbet's starkly antiheroic composition.

to poverty remain poor their entire lives. The artist neither roman-
ticized nor idealized the men's work but depicted their thankless
toil with directness and accuracy. Courbet's palette of dirty browns
and grays further conveys the dreary and dismal nature of the task,
and the angular positioning of the older stone breaker's limbs suggests a mechanical monotony.

Courbet's interest in the working poor as subject matter had
a special resonance for his mid-19th-century French audience. In
1848, laborers rebelled against the bourgeois leaders of the newly
formed Second Republic and against the rest of the nation, de-
manding better working conditions and a redistribution of property. The army quelled the uprising in three days, but not without
long-lasting trauma and significant loss of life. The 1848 revolution
raised the issue of labor as a national concern. Courbet's depiction
of stone breakers in 1849 was thus timely and populist.

BURIAL AT ORNANS Many art historians regard Courbet's
Burial at Ornans (FIG. **27-27**) as his masterpiece. The huge (10 by
22 feet) canvas depicts a funeral set in a bleak provincial landscape
outside the artist's home town. Attending the funeral are the types
of ordinary people Honoré de Balzac (1799–1850) and Gustave
Flaubert (1821–1880) presented in their novels. While an officious
clergyman reads the Office of the Dead, those attending cluster
around the excavated gravesite, their faces registering all degrees
of response to the ceremony. Although the painting has the monumental scale of a traditional history painting, the subject's ordinari-
ness and the starkly antiheroic composition horrified critics. Arranged in a wavering line extending across the enormous breadth
of the canvas are three groups—the somberly clad women at the
back right, a semicircle of similarly clad men by the open grave,
and assorted churchmen at the left. This wall of figures blocks any
view into deep space. The faces are portraits. Some of the models
were Courbet's sisters (three of the women in the front row, toward
the right) and friends. Behind and above the figures are bands of
overcast sky and barren cliffs. The dark pit of the grave opens into
the viewer's space in the center foreground. Despite the unposed
look of the figures, Courbet controlled the composition in a masterful way by his sparing use of bright color. In place of the heroic,
the sublime, and the dramatic, Courbet aggressively presented
the viewer with the mundane realities of daily life and death. In
1857, Jules-François-Félix Husson Champfleury (1821–1889), one of
the first critics to recognize and appreciate Courbet's work, wrote
of *Burial at Ornans*, "[I]t represents a small-town funeral and yet
reproduces the funerals of *all* small towns."[7] Unlike the theatricality of Romanticism, Realism captured the ordinary rhythms of
daily life.

Of great importance for the later history of art, Realism also
involved a reconsideration of the painter's primary goals and departed from the established emphasis on illusionism. Accordingly,
Realists called attention to painting as a pictorial construction
by the ways they applied pigment or manipulated composition.
Courbet's intentionally simple and direct methods of expression
in composition and technique seemed unbearably crude to many
of his more traditional contemporaries, who called him a primitive. Although his bold, somber palette was essentially traditional,
Courbet often used the *palette knife* for quickly placing and uni-
fying large daubs of paint, producing a roughly wrought surface.
His example inspired the young artists who worked for him (and
later Impressionists such as Claude Monet and Auguste Renoir; see
Chapter 28), but the public accused him of carelessness and critics
wrote of his "brutalities."

JEAN-FRANÇOIS MILLET As did Courbet, JEAN-FRANÇOIS
MILLET (1814–1878) found his subjects in the people and occupa-
tions of the everyday world. Millet was one of a group of French
painters of country life who, to be close to their rural subjects,
settled near the village of Barbizon in the forest of Fontainebleau.
This Barbizon School specialized in detailed pictures of forest and
countryside. Millet, their most prominent member, was of peasant
stock and identified with the hard lot of the country poor. In *The
Gleaners* (FIG. **27-28**), he depicted three impoverished women—
members of the lowest level of peasant society—performing the
backbreaking task of gleaning. Land-
owning nobles traditionally permitted peasants to glean, or collect, the
wheat scraps left in the field after
the harvest. Millet characteristically
placed his monumental figures in the
foreground, against a broad sky. Although the field stretches back to a
rim of haystacks, cottages, trees, distant workers, and a flat horizon, the
gleaners quietly doing their tedious
and time-consuming work dominate
the canvas.

27-28 JEAN-FRANÇOIS MILLET,
The Gleaners, 1857. Oil on canvas,
2′ 9″ × 3′ 8″. Musée d'Orsay, Paris.

Millet and the Barbizon School painters
specialized in depictions of French
country life. Here, Millet portrayed three
impoverished women gathering the scraps
left in the field after a harvest.

Lithography

In 1798, the German printmaker Alois Senefelder (1771–1834) created the first prints using stone instead of metal plates or wooden blocks. In contrast to earlier printing techniques (see "Woodcuts, Engravings, and Etchings," Chapter 20, page 556), in which the artist applied ink either to a raised or incised surface, in *lithography* (Greek, "stone writing") the printing and nonprinting areas of the plate are on the same plane.

The chemical phenomenon fundamental to lithography is the repellence of oil and water. The lithographer uses a greasy, oil-based crayon to draw directly on a stone plate and then wipes water onto the stone, which clings only to the areas the drawing does not cover.

Next, the artist rolls oil-based ink onto the stone, which adheres to the drawing but is repelled by the water. When the artist presses the stone against paper, only the inked areas—the drawing—transfer to the paper. Color lithography requires multiple plates, one for each color, and the printmaker must take special care to make sure each impression lines up perfectly with the previous one so that each color prints in its proper place.

One of the earliest masters of this new printmaking process was Honoré Daumier, whose politically biting lithographs (FIG. 27-29) published in a widely read French journal reached an audience of unprecedented size.

27-29 HONORÉ DAUMIER, *Rue Transnonain*, 1834. Lithograph, 1′ × 1′ 5½″. Philadelphia Museum of Art, Philadelphia (bequest of Fiske and Marie Kimball).

Daumier used the recent invention of lithography to reach a wide audience for his social criticism and political protest. This print records the horrific 1834 massacre in a workers' housing block.

Although Millet's paintings evoke a sentimentality absent from Courbet's, the French public still reacted to his work with disdain and suspicion. In the aftermath of the 1848 revolution, Millet's investiture of the poor with solemn grandeur did not meet with approval from the prosperous classes. In particular, middle-class landowners resisted granting gleaning rights, and thus Millet's relatively dignified depiction of gleaning antagonized them. The middle class also linked the poor with the dangerous, newly defined working class, which was finding outspoken champions in men such as Karl Marx (1818–1883), Friedrich Engels (1820–1895), and the novelists Émile Zola (1840–1902) and Charles Dickens (1812–1870). Socialism was a growing movement, and both its views on property and its call for social justice, even economic equality, threatened and frightened the bourgeoisie. Millet's sympathetic portrayal of the poor seemed to much of the public to be a political manifesto.

HONORÉ DAUMIER Because people widely recognized the power of art to serve political ends, the political and social agitation accompanying the violent revolutions in France and the rest of Europe in the later 18th and early 19th centuries prompted the French people to suspect artists of subversive intention. A person could be jailed for too bold a statement in the press, in literature, in art—even in music and drama. Realist artist HONORÉ DAUMIER (1808–1879) was a defender of the urban working classes, and in his art he boldly confronted authority with social criticism and political protest. In response, the authorities imprisoned the artist. A painter, sculptor, and, like Dürer, Rembrandt, and Goya, one of history's great printmakers, Daumier produced lithographs (see "Lithography," above) that enabled him to create an unprecedented number of prints, thereby reaching an exceptionally large and broad audience. In addition to producing individual prints for sale

27-30 HONORÉ DAUMIER, *Third-Class Carriage,* ca. 1862. Oil on canvas, 2′ 1¾″ × 2′ 11½″. Metropolitan Museum of Art, New York (H. O. Havemeyer Collection, bequest of Mrs. H. O. Havemeyer, 1929).

Daumier frequently depicted the plight of the disinherited masses of 19th-century industrialization. Here, he portrayed the anonymous poor cramped together in a grimy third-class railway carriage.

Daumier also contributed satirical lithographs to the widely read, liberal French Republican journal *Caricature,* further increasing the number of people exposed to his work. In *Caricature,* Daumier mercilessly lampooned the foibles and misbehavior of politicians, lawyers, doctors, and the rich bourgeoisie in general.

RUE TRANSNONAIN Daumier's lithograph *Rue Transnonain* (FIG. 27-29) depicts an atrocity having the same shocking impact as Goya's *Third of May, 1808* (FIG. 27-11). The title refers to a street in Paris where an unknown sniper killed a civil guard, part of a government force trying to repress a worker demonstration. Because the fatal shot had come from a workers' housing block, the remaining guards immediately stormed the building and massacred all of its inhabitants. With Goya's power, Daumier created a view of the slaughter from a sharp angle of vision. But unlike Goya, he depicted not the dramatic moment of execution but the terrible, quiet aftermath. The limp bodies of the workers—and of a child crushed beneath his father's corpse—lie amid violent disorder. The print's power lies in its factualness. Daumier's pictorial manner is rough and spontaneous, and that approach to representation, which is a central characteristic of Realist art, accounts in large measure for its remarkable force.

THIRD-CLASS CARRIAGE For his paintings, Daumier chose the same kind of subjects and representational manner as in his graphic work, especially after the 1848 revolution. His unfinished *Third-Class Carriage* (FIG. 27-30) provides a glimpse into the cramped and grimy railway cars of the 1860s. The riders are poor and can afford only third-class tickets. First- and second-class carriages had closed compartments, but third-class passengers had to cram together on hard benches stretching from one end of their carriage to the other. The disinherited masses of 19th-century industrialization were Daumier's indignant concern. He depicted them in the unposed attitudes and unplanned arrangements of the millions thronging the modern cities—anonymous, insignificant, dumbly patient with a lot they could not change. Daumier saw people as they ordinarily appeared, their faces vague, impersonal, and blank—unprepared for any observers. He tried to achieve the real by isolating a random collection of the unrehearsed details of human existence from the continuum of ordinary life. Daumier's vision anticipated the spontaneity and candor of scenes captured with the camera by the end of the century.

ROSA BONHEUR The most celebrated woman artist of the 19th century was MARIE-ROSALIE (ROSA) BONHEUR (1822–1899). The winner of the gold medal at the Salon of 1848, Bonheur became in 1894 the first woman officer in the French Legion of Honor. As was typical for women since the Renaissance (see "The Artist's Profession," Chapter 20, page 545), Bonheur received her artistic training from her father, Oscar-Raymond Bonheur (1796–1849), who was a proponent of *Saint-Simonianism,* an early-19th-century utopian socialist movement that championed the education and enfranchisement of women. As a result of her father's influence, Bonheur launched her career believing that as a woman and an artist, she had a special role to play in creating a new and perfect society. A Realist passion for accuracy in painting drove Bonheur, but she resisted depicting the problematic social and political themes seen in the work of Courbet, Millet, Daumier, and other Realists. Rather, she turned to the animal world—not, however, to the exotic wild animals that so fascinated Delacroix (FIG. 27-17), but to animals common in the French countryside, especially horses, but also rabbits, cows, and sheep. She went to great lengths to observe the anatomy of living horses at the great Parisian horse fair and spent long hours studying the anatomy of carcasses in the Paris slaughterhouses.

27-31 ROSA BONHEUR, *The Horse Fair*, 1853–1855. Oil on canvas, 8′ ¼″ × 16′ 7½″. Metropolitan Museum of Art, New York (gift of Cornelius Vanderbilt, 1887).

Bonheur was the most celebrated woman artist of the 19th century. A Realist, she went to great lengths to record accurately the anatomy of living horses, even studying carcasses in slaughterhouses.

For *The Horse Fair* (FIG. 27-31), Bonheur's best-known work, the artist chose a panoramic composition similar to that in Courbet's *Burial at Ornans* (FIG. 27-27). She filled her broad canvas with the sturdy farm Percherons and their grooms seen on parade at the annual Parisian horse sale. Some horses, not quite broken, rear up. Others plod or trot, guided on foot or ridden by their keepers. Bonheur recorded the Percherons' uneven line of march, their thunderous pounding, and their seemingly overwhelming power based on her close observation of living animals, even though she acknowledged some inspiration from the Parthenon frieze (FIG. 5-50, *top*). The dramatic lighting, loose brushwork, and rolling sky also reveal her admiration of Géricault's style (FIGS. 27-13 and 27-13A). The equine drama in *The Horse Fair* captivated viewers, who eagerly bought engraved reproductions of Bonheur's painting, making it one of the most popular artworks of the century.

ÉDOUARD MANET As pivotal a figure in 19th-century European art as Gustave Courbet was the painter ÉDOUARD MANET (1832–1883). Like Courbet, Manet was influential in articulating Realist principles, but the younger artist also played an important role in the development of Impressionism in the 1870s (see Chapter 28). Manet's *Le Déjeuner sur l'Herbe* (*Luncheon on the Grass*; FIG. 27-32), widely recognized only later as a seminal work in the history of art, depicts two clothed men and one nude and one clothed woman at a picnic. Consistent with Realist principles, Manet based all four figures on real people. The seated nude is Victorine Meurend (Manet's favorite model at the time), and the gentlemen are his brother Eugène (with cane) and probably the sculptor Ferdinand Leenhof, although scholars have suggested other identifications. The two men wear fashionable Parisian attire of the 1860s. The nude woman is a distressingly unidealized figure who also seems disturbingly unabashed and at ease, gazing directly at the viewer without shame or flirtatiousness.

This audacious painting outraged the French public. Rather than a traditional pastoral scene, for example, Titian's *Pastoral Symphony* (FIG. 22-35), populated by anonymous idealized figures in an idyllic setting, *Le Déjeuner* featured ordinary men and promiscuous women in a Parisian park. One hostile critic, no doubt voicing public opinion, said: "A commonplace woman of the demimonde, as naked as can be, shamelessly lolls between two dandies dressed to the teeth. These latter look like schoolboys on a holiday, perpetrating an outrage to play the man. . . . This is a young man's practical joke—a shameful, open sore."[8] Manet surely anticipated criticism of his painting, but shocking the public was not his primary aim. His goal was more complex and far more ambitious. With *Le Déjeuner,* he sought to reassess the nature of painting. The work contains sophisticated references and allusions to many artistic genres—history painting, portraiture, pastoral scenes, nudes, and even religious scenes. *Le Déjeuner* is Manet's impressive synthesis and critique of the entire history of painting.

The negative response to Manet's painting on the part of public and critics alike extended beyond subject matter. The painter's manner of presenting his figures also elicited severe criticism. He rendered the men and women in soft focus and broadly painted the landscape, including the pool in which the second woman bathes. The loose manner of painting contrasts with the clear forms of the harshly lit foreground trio and of the pile of discarded female clothes and picnic foods at the lower left. The lighting creates strong contrasts between dark and highlighted areas. In the main figures, many values are summed up in one or two lights or darks. The effect is both to flatten the forms and set them off sharply from the setting. Form, rather than a matter of line, is only a function of paint and light. Manet aimed to move away from illusionism toward an open acknowledgment of painting's properties, such as the flatness of the painting surface, which would become a core principle of many later 19th-century painters as well as their successors

27-32 ÉDOUARD MANET, *Le Déjeuner sur l'Herbe (Luncheon on the Grass)*, 1863. Oil on canvas, 7′ × 8′ 8″. Musée d'Orsay, Paris.

Manet shocked his contemporaries with both his subject matter and manner of painting. Moving away from illusionism, he used colors to flatten form and to draw attention to the painting surface.

to the present day. The mid-19th-century French public, however, saw only a crude sketch lacking the customary finish of paintings exhibited in the Paris Salon. The style of the painting, coupled with the unorthodox subject matter, made *Le Déjeuner sur l'Herbe* one of the most controversial artworks ever created.

OLYMPIA Even more scandalous to the French viewing public, however, was Manet's *Olympia* (FIG. **27-33**), painted the same year. Manet's subject was a young white prostitute (Olympia was a common "professional" name for prostitutes in 19th-century France). She reclines on a bed that extends across the full width of

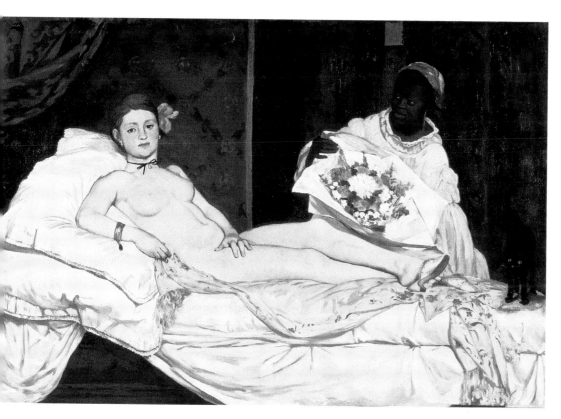

27-33 ÉDOUARD MANET, *Olympia*, 1863. Oil on canvas, 4′ 3″ × 6′ 2$\frac{1}{4}$″. Musée d'Orsay, Paris. ◼◀

Manet's painting of a nude prostitute and her black maid carrying a bouquet from a client scandalized the public. Critics also faulted his rough brushstrokes and abruptly shifting tonalities.

Realism **781**

the painting (and beyond) and is nude except for a thin black ribbon tied around her neck, a bracelet on her arm, an orchid in her hair, and fashionable slippers on her feet. Like the seated nude in *Le Déjeuner,* Olympia meets the viewer's eye with a look of cool indifference. The only other figure in the painting is a black maid, who presents Olympia a bouquet of flowers from a client.

Olympia horrified public and critics alike. Although images of prostitutes were not unheard of during this period, the shamelessness of Olympia and her look verging on defiance shocked viewers. The depiction of a black woman was also not new to painting, but the French public perceived Manet's inclusion of both a black maid and a nude prostitute as evoking moral depravity, inferiority, and animalistic sexuality. The contrast of the black servant with the fair-skinned courtesan also conjured racial divisions. One critic described Olympia as "a courtesan with dirty hands and wrinkled feet . . . her body has the livid tint of a cadaver displayed in the morgue; her outlines are drawn in charcoal and her greenish, bloodshot eyes appear to be provoking the public, protected all the while by a hideous Negress."[9] From this statement, it is clear viewers were responding not solely to the subject matter but to Manet's artistic style as well. The painter's brushstrokes are much rougher and the shifts in tonality are far more abrupt than those found in traditional academic painting. This departure from accepted practice exacerbated the audacity of the subject matter. *Olympia*—indeed, all of Manet's work—represented a radical departure from the academic style then in favor, as exemplified by the work of ADOLPHE-WILLIAM BOUGUEREAU (1825–1905; FIG. 27-33A), an artist largely forgotten today, although he was a towering figure in the French art world during the second half of the 19th century.

27-33A BOUGUEREAU, *Nymphs and a Satyr,* 1873.

Germany and the United States

Although French artists took the lead in promoting the depiction of the realities of modern life as the only valid goal for artists, the Realist movement was neither exclusively French nor confined to Europe.

WILHELM LEIBL In Germany, WILHELM LEIBL (1844–1900) shared French Realists' commitment to representing the contemporary world and real people in his paintings. *Three Women in a Village Church* (FIG. 27-34) is typical of Leibl's work, which focused on country life. The painting records a sacred moment—the moment of prayer—in the life of three women of different generations. Dressed in rustic costume, their Sunday-church best, they quietly pursue their devotions, their prayer books held in large hands roughened by work. Their manners and their dress reflect their unaffected nature, untouched by the refinements of urban life. Leibl highlighted their natural virtues: simplicity, honesty, steadfastness, patience. He spent three years working on this image of peasants in their village church, often under impossible conditions of lighting and temperature. Despite the meticulous application of paint and sharpness of focus, the picture is a moving expression of the artist's compassionate view of his subjects, a reading of character without sentimentality.

WINSLOW HOMER Realism received an especially warm welcome in the United States. One of the leading American Realist painters was WINSLOW HOMER (1836–1910) of Boston. Homer

27-34 WILHELM LEIBL, *Three Women in a Village Church,* 1878–1882. Oil on canvas, 2′ 5″ × 2′ 1″. Hamburger, Kunsthalle, Hamburg.

French Realism spread quickly to Germany, where Leibl painted this moving depiction of simple peasant women of different generations holding their prayer books in hands roughened by work.

experienced at first hand the most momentous event of his era—the Civil War. In 1860, he joined the Union campaign as an artist reporter for *Harper's Weekly.* At the end of the war, he painted *Veteran in a New Field* (FIG. 27-35). Although it is relatively simple and direct, Homer's painting is a significant commentary on the effect and aftermath of America's catastrophic national conflict. At the center of the canvas is a man with his back to the viewer, harvesting wheat. Homer identified him as a veteran by including his uniform and canteen carelessly thrown on the ground in the lower right corner. The man's current occupation, however, is as a farmer, and he has cast aside his former role as a soldier. The veteran's involvement in meaningful and productive work implies a smooth transition from war to peace. This postwar transition to work and the fate of disbanded soldiers were national concerns. Echoing the sentiment behind Houdon's portrayal of George Washington as the new Cincinnatus (FIG. 26-32), the *New York Weekly Tribune* commented "Rome took her great man from the plow, and made him a dictator—we must now take our soldiers from the camp and make them farmers."[10] America's ability to effect a smooth transition was seen as evidence of its national strength. "The peaceful and harmonious

Veteran in a New Field also comments symbolically about death. By the 1860s, farmers used cradled scythes to harvest wheat. For this detail, however, Homer rejected realism in favor of symbolism. The former soldier's tool is a single-bladed scythe. The artist thus transformed the man who lived through the Civil War into a symbol of Death—the Grim Reaper himself. In addition to being a tribute to the successful transition to peace, *Veteran in a New Field* is an elegy to the thousands of soldiers who did not return from the war. It may also be a lamentation on the recent assassination of President Abraham Lincoln.

disbanding of the armies in the summer of 1865," poet Walt Whitman (1819–1892) wrote, was one of the "immortal proofs of democracy, unequall'd in all the history of the past."[11] Homer's painting thus reinforced the perception of the country's greatness.

THOMAS EAKINS Even more resolutely a Realist than Homer was Philadelphia-born THOMAS EAKINS (1844–1916), whose work reflects his keen appetite for recording the realities of the human experience. Eakins studied both painting and medical anatomy in Philadelphia before undertaking further study under French artist Jean-Léon Gérôme (1824–1904). Eakins aimed to paint things as he saw them rather than as the public might wish them portrayed. This attitude was very much in tune with 19th-century American taste, combining an admiration for accurate depiction with a hunger for truth.

The too-brutal Realism of Eakins's early masterpiece, *The Gross Clinic* (FIG. **27-36**), prompted the art jury to reject it for the Philadelphia exhibition celebrating the American independence centennial in 1876. The painting portrays the renowned surgeon Dr. Samuel Gross in the operating amphitheater of the Jefferson Medical College in Philadelphia, where the painting hung for 130 years until its sale in 2006 to raise funds for the college. Eakins's decision to depict

an operation in progress reflects the public's increasing faith that scientific and medical advances could enhance—and preserve—lives. Dr. Gross, with bloody fingers and scalpel, lectures about his surgery on a young man's leg. The patient suffered from osteomyelitis, a bone infection. Watching the surgeon, acclaimed for his skill in this particular operation, are several colleagues—all of whom historians have identified—and the patient's mother, who covers her face. Also present is an anesthetist, who holds a cloth over the patient's face. Anesthetics had been introduced in 1846, and their development eliminated a major obstacle to extensive surgery. The painting is an unsparing description of an unfolding event, with a good deal more reality than many viewers could endure. "It is a picture," one critic said, "that even strong men find difficult to look at long, if they can look at it at all."[12]

Consistent with the dominance of empiricism in the latter half of the 19th century, Eakins believed careful observation—and, where relevant, scientific knowledge—were prerequisites for his art, and he created his paintings in a deliberate, methodical way based on firsthand study of his subject. For example, Eakins's focus on anatomical correctness led him to investigate the human form and humans in motion, both with regular photographic apparatuses and with a special camera devised by the French kinesiologist (a person who studies the physiology of body movement) Étienne-Jules Marey (1830–1904). Eakins later collaborated with Eadweard Muybridge (FIG. 27-54) in the photographic study of animal and human action of all types, anticipating the 20th-century invention of the motion picture.

JOHN SINGER SARGENT The expatriate American artist JOHN SINGER SARGENT (1856–1925), born in Florence, Italy, was a younger contemporary of Eakins. Sargent developed a looser, more dashing Realist portrait style, in contrast to Eakins's carefully rendered details. Sargent studied art in Paris before settling in London, where he won renown both as a cultivated and cosmopolitan gentleman and as an accomplished portrait painter. He learned his adept application of paint in thin layers and his effortless achievement of quick and lively illusion from his study of Velázquez, whose masterpiece, *Las Meninas* (FIG. 24-30), may have influenced Sargent's family portrait *The Daughters of Edward Darley Boit* (FIG. **27-37**). The four girls (the children of one of Sargent's close friends) appear in a hall and small drawing room in their Paris home. The informal, eccentric arrangement of their slight figures suggests how much at ease they are within this familiar space and with objects such as the monumental Japanese vases, the red screen, and the fringed rug, whose scale subtly emphasizes the children's diminutive stature. Sargent must have known the Boit daughters well. Relaxed and trustful, they gave the artist an opportunity to record a gradation of young innocence. He sensitively captured the naive, wondering openness of the little girl in the foreground, the grave artlessness of the 10-year-old child, and the slightly self-conscious poise of the adolescents. Sargent's casual positioning of the figures and seemingly random choice of the setting communicate a sense of spontaneity. The children seem to be attending momentarily to an adult who has asked them to interrupt their activity. The painting embodies the Realist belief that the artist's business is to record modern people in modern contexts.

HENRY OSSAWA TANNER Typical of the Realist painter's desire to depict the lives of ordinary people engaged in everyday activities is the early work of African American artist HENRY OSSAWA TANNER (1859–1937). Tanner studied art with Eakins before moving to Paris. There he combined Eakins's belief in careful study from nature with a desire to portray with dignity the life of the working people he had been raised among as a minister's son in Pennsylvania. The mood in *The Thankful Poor* (FIG. **27-38**) is one of quiet devotion not far removed from the Realism of Millet (FIG. 27-28) and

27-37 JOHN SINGER SARGENT, *The Daughters of Edward Darley Boit*, 1882. Oil on canvas, 7′ 3$\frac{3}{8}$″ × 7′ 3$\frac{5}{8}$″. Museum of Fine Arts, Boston (gift of Mary Louisa Boit, Florence D. Boit, Jane Hubbard Boit, and Julia Overing Boit, in memory of their father, Edward Darley Boit).

Sargent's casual positioning of the Boit sisters creates a sense of the momentary and spontaneous, consistent with Realist painters' interest in recording modern people in modern contexts.

1 ft.

Leibl (FIG. 27-34). Tanner painted the grandfather, grandchild, and main objects in the room in great detail, whereas everything else dissolves into loose strokes of color and light. Expressive lighting reinforces the painting's reverent spirit, with deep shadows intensifying the man's devout concentration and golden light pouring in the window to illuminate the quiet expression of thanksgiving on the younger face. The deep sense of sanctity expressed here in terms of everyday experience became increasingly important for Tanner. Within a few years of completing *The Thankful Poor,* he began painting biblical subjects grounded in direct study from nature and in the love of Rembrandt that had inspired him from his days as a Philadelphia art student.

EDMONIA LEWIS About 15 years older than Tanner, the sculptor EDMONIA LEWIS (ca. 1845–after 1909), the daughter of a Chippewa mother and African American father, produced work stylistically indebted to Neoclassicism but depicting contemporary Realist themes. *Forever Free* (FIG. **27-39**) is a marble sculpture Lewis carved while living in Rome, surrounded by examples of both classical and Renaissance art. It represents two freed African American slaves. The man stands heroically in a contrapposto stance reminiscent of classical statues. His right hand rests on the shoulder of the kneeling woman, and his left hand holds aloft a broken manacle and chain as literal and symbolic references to his former servitude. Produced four years after President Lincoln's issuance of the Emancipation Proclamation, *Forever Free* (originally titled *The Morning*

27-39 EDMONIA LEWIS, *Forever Free,* 1867. Marble, 3′ 5¼″ high. James A. Porter Gallery of Afro-American Art, Howard University, Washington, D.C.

Lewis was a sculptor whose work owes a stylistic debt to Neoclassicism but depicts contemporary Realist themes. She carved *Forever Free* four years after Lincoln's Emancipation Proclamation.

1 ft.

27-40 JOHN EVERETT MILLAIS, *Ophelia*, 1852. Oil on canvas, 2′ 6″ × 3′ 8″. Tate Gallery, London. ◼◀

Millet was a founder of the Pre-Raphaelite Brotherhood, whose members refused to be limited to the contemporary scenes that strict Realists portrayed. The drowning of Ophelia is a Shakespearean subject.

of Liberty) was widely perceived as an abolitionist statement. However, other factors caution against an overly simplistic reading. For example, scholars have debated the degree to which the sculptor attempted to inject a statement about gender relationships into this statue and whether the kneeling position of the woman is a reference to female subordination in the African American community.

Lewis's accomplishments as a sculptor speak to the increasing access to training available to women in the 19th century. Educated at Oberlin College (the first American college to grant degrees to women), Lewis financed her trip to Rome with the sale of medallions and marble busts. Her success in a field dominated by white male artists is a testament to both her skill and her determination.

Pre-Raphaelite Brotherhood

Realism did not appeal to all artists, of course. In England, a group of painters who called themselves the *Pre-Raphaelite Brotherhood* refused to be limited to the contemporary scenes strict Realists portrayed. These artists chose instead to represent fictional, historical, and fanciful subjects, albeit with a significant degree of convincing illusion.

JOHN EVERETT MILLAIS One of the founders of the Pre-Raphaelite Brotherhood was JOHN EVERETT MILLAIS (1829–1896). So painstakingly careful was Millais in his study of visual facts closely observed from nature that Charles Baudelaire (1821–1867) called him "the poet of meticulous detail." The Pre-Raphaelite Brotherhood, organized in 1848, wished to create fresh and sincere art, free from what its members considered the tired and artificial manner propagated in the academies by the successors of Raphael. Influenced by the critic, artist, and writer John Ruskin (1819–1900), the Pre-Raphaelites shared his distaste for the materialism and ugliness of the contemporary industrializing world. They also expressed appreciation for the spirituality and idealism (as well as the art and artisanship) of past times, especially the Middle Ages and the Early Renaissance.

Millais's *Ophelia* (FIG. 27-40) garnered enthusiastic praise when the painter exhibited it in the Exposition Universelle in Paris in 1855—the exhibition at which Courbet set up his Pavilion of Realism. The subject, from Shakespeare's *Hamlet* (4.7.176–179), is the drowning of Ophelia, who, in her madness, is unaware of her plight:

> Her clothes spread wide,
> And mermaidlike awhile they bore her up—
> Which time she chanted snatches of old tunes,
> As one incapable of her own distress.

To make the pathos of the scene visible, Millais became a faithful and feeling witness of its every detail, reconstructing it with a lyricism worthy of the original poetry. Although the scene is fictitious and therefore one Realist painters would have rejected, Millais worked diligently to present it with unswerving fidelity to visual fact. He painted the background on site at a spot along the Hogsmill River in Surrey. For the figure of Ophelia, Millais had a friend lie in a heated bathtub full of water for hours at a time.

DANTE GABRIEL ROSSETTI Another founder of the Pre-Raphaelite Brotherhood was DANTE GABRIEL ROSSETTI (1828–1882), who established an enviable reputation as both a painter and poet. Like other members of the group, Rossetti focused on literary and biblical themes in his art. He also produced numerous portraits of women that projected an image of ethereal beauty and melded apparent opposites—for example, a Victorian prettiness with sensual allure. His *Beata Beatrix* (FIG. 27-41) is ostensibly a portrait of a literary figure—Beatrice, from Dante's *Vita Nuova*—as she overlooks Florence in a trance after being mystically transported to Heaven. Yet the portrait also had personal resonance for Rossetti. It served as a memorial to his wife, Elizabeth Siddal (the model for Millais's *Ophelia*). Siddal had died shortly before Rossetti began this painting in 1862. In the image, the woman (Siddal-Beatrice) sits in a trancelike state, while a red dove (a messenger of both love

27-41 DANTE GABRIEL ROSSETTI, *Beata Beatrix,* ca. 1863. Oil on canvas, 2′ 10″ × 2′ 2″. Tate Gallery, London.

This painting of a beautiful and sensuous woman is ostensibly a literary portrait of Dante's Beatrice, but the work also served as a memorial to Rossetti's wife, who died of an opium overdose.

and death) deposits a poppy (symbolic of sleep and death) in her hands. Because Siddal died of an opium overdose, the presence of the poppy assumes greater significance.

ARCHITECTURE

At the opening of the 19th century, Napoleon had co-opted the classical style as the official architectural expression of his empire. Neoclassicism was in vogue elsewhere in Europe and in the new American republic too, but other historical styles also enjoyed revivals at the same time architects were exploring the expressive possibilities that new construction technologies had fostered. The buildings constructed during the 19th century are consequently among the most stylistically diverse in history.

ALTES MUSEUM, BERLIN After the fall of Napoleon, who had occupied the Prussian capital of Berlin from 1806 to 1808, a fervent nationalistic spirit emerged in Germany. One manifestation of Prussian nationalism was the decision to build Europe's first public art museum to house the extensive and growing royal collection. The commission went to KARL FRIEDRICH SCHINKEL (1781–1841), who worked in many revival styles during his career, including Romanesque, Gothic, and Italian Renaissance, but who chose the Neoclassical style for what he and Crown Prince Friedrich Wilhelm III (1755–1861) conceived as a "temple of culture."

The Altes (Old) Museum (FIG. 27-42), constructed on an island in the Spree River across from the royal palace in Berlin, is not truly templelike, however. Rather, with its broad facade of 18 Ionic columns on a high podium, it more closely resembles a Greek stoa (FIG. 5-77) than a pediment-capped classical temple. Noteworthy for its perfect proportions, Schinkel's austere design expresses nobility, tradition, and elite culture, now made accessible to the public in a building whose style Europeans associated with the democratic values of ancient Greece and Rome.

27-42 KARL FRIEDRICH SCHINKEL, Altes Museum, Berlin, Germany, 1822–1830.

Schinkel conceived the first public art museum in Europe as a Neoclassical "temple of culture." The Altes Museum's facade of 18 Ionic columns resembles an ancient Greek stoa (FIG. 5-77).

27-43 CHARLES BARRY and AUGUSTUS WELBY NORTHMORE PUGIN, Houses of Parliament, London, England, designed 1835. ◼◀

During the 19th century, architects revived many historical styles, often reflecting nationalistic pride. The Houses of Parliament have an exterior veneer and towers that recall English Late Gothic style.

The Neoclassical facade masks a very practical plan that has no model in classical temples or stoas. A broad central staircase leads into a foyer and then a cubical central block, which projects above the facade's colonnade. The central block houses a sculpture-filled domed rotunda loosely based on the Pantheon (FIGS. 7-50 and 7-51) in Rome. To either side is a courtyard whose windows provide light to the painting galleries all around. Large windows on the side and rear walls of the Altes Museum also illuminate the galleries. The museum was revolutionary in organizing the artworks it contained in chronological order, emphasizing the history of art, as opposed to simply displaying aesthetic treasures (compare FIG. 25-1A).

GOTHIC REVIVAL As 19th-century scholars gathered the documentary materials of European history in encyclopedic enterprises, each nation came to value its past as evidence of the validity of its ambitions and claims to greatness. Intellectuals appreciated the art of the remote past as a product of cultural and national genius. Italy, of course, had its Roman ruins, which had long inspired later architects. A reawakening of interest in Gothic architecture also surfaced at this time, even in France under Napoleon. In 1802, Chateaubriand published his influential *Genius of Christianity*—the source for Girodet-Trioson's *Burial of Atala* (FIG. 27-5)—which defended religion on the grounds of its beauty and mystery rather than on the grounds of truth. Gothic cathedrals, according to Chateaubriand, were translations of the sacred groves of the ancient Gauls into stone and should be cherished as manifestations of France's holy history. One result of this new nationalistic respect for the Gothic style was that Eugène Emmanuel Viollet-le-Duc (1814–1879) received a commission in 1845 to restore the interior of Paris's Notre Dame to its Gothic splendor after removing the Baroque and Napoleonic (FIG. 27-2) alterations.

HOUSES OF PARLIAMENT England also celebrated its medieval heritage with *Neo-Gothic* buildings. In London, when the old Houses of Parliament burned in 1834, the Parliamentary Commission decreed that designs for the new building be either Gothic or Elizabethan. CHARLES BARRY (1795–1860), with the assistance of AUGUSTUS WELBY NORTHMORE PUGIN (1812–1852), submitted

the winning design (FIG. 27-43) in 1835. By this time, architectural style had become a matter of selection from the historical past. Barry had traveled widely in Europe, Greece, Turkey, Egypt, and Palestine, studying the architecture of each place. He preferred the classical Renaissance styles, but he had designed some earlier Neo-Gothic buildings, and Pugin successfully influenced him in the direction of English Late Gothic. Pugin was one of a group of English artists and critics who saw moral purity and spiritual authenticity in the religious architecture of the Middle Ages and revered the careful medieval artisans who built the great cathedrals. The Industrial Revolution was flooding the market with cheaply made and ill-designed commodities. Machine work was replacing handicraft. Many, Pugin included, believed in the necessity of restoring the old artisanship, which they felt embodied honesty as well as quality. Pugin was also the author of the influential *True Principles of Pointed or Christian Architecture* (1841), which RICHARD UPJOHN (1802–1878) consulted for his Neo-Gothic Trinity Church (FIG. 27-43A) in New York City. The design of the Houses of Parliament, however, is not genuinely Gothic, despite its picturesque tower groupings (the Clock Tower, housing Big Ben, at one end, and the Victoria Tower at the other). The building has a formal axial plan and a kind of Palladian regularity beneath its Neo-Gothic detail. Pugin himself said of it, "All Grecian, Sir. Tudor [English Late Gothic] details on a classical body."[13]

27-43A UPJOHN, Trinity Church, New York, 1841–1852.

ROYAL PAVILION Although the Neoclassical and Neo-Gothic styles dominated early-19th-century architecture, exotic new approaches of all manner soon began to appear, due in part to European imperialism and in part to the Romantic spirit permeating all the arts. Great Britain's forays throughout the world, particularly India, had exposed English culture to a broad range of non-Western artistic styles. The Royal Pavilion (FIG. 27-44), designed

27-44 JOHN NASH, Royal Pavilion, Brighton, England, 1815–1818.

British territorial expansion brought a familiarity with many exotic styles. This palatial "Indian Gothic" seaside pavilion is a conglomeration of Islamic domes, minarets, and screens.

by JOHN NASH (1752–1835), exhibits a wide variety of these styles. Nash was an established architect, known for Neoclassical buildings in London, when the prince regent (later King George IV) asked him to design a royal pleasure palace in the seaside resort of Brighton. The architecture of Greece, Egypt, and China influenced the interior décor of the Royal Pavilion, but the fantastic exterior is a conglomeration of Islamic domes, minarets, and screens architectural historians describe as "Indian Gothic." Underlying the exotic facade is a cast-iron skeleton, an early (if hidden) use of this material in noncommercial construction. Nash also put this metal to fanciful use, creating life-size palm-tree columns in cast iron to support the Royal Pavilion's kitchen ceiling. The building, an appropriate enough backdrop for gala throngs pursuing pleasure by the seaside, has served as a prototype for countless playful architectural exaggerations still found in European and American resorts.

PARIS OPÉRA Another style that found favor in 19th-century architecture was the Baroque, because it was well suited to conveying a grandeur worthy of the riches the European elite acquired during this age of expansion. The Paris Opéra (FIG. **27-45**), designed by CHARLES GARNIER (1825–1898), mirrored the opulent lives of these privileged few. The opera house has a festive and spectacularly theatrical Neo-Baroque front and two wings resembling Baroque domed central-plan churches. Inside, intricate arrangements of corridors, vestibules, stairways, balconies, alcoves, entrances, and exits facilitate easy passage throughout the building and provide space for entertainment and socializing at intermissions.

The Baroque grandeur of the layout and of the building's ornamental appointments are characteristic of an architectural style called *Beaux-Arts*, which flourished in the late 19th and early 20th centuries in France. Based on ideas taught at the dominant École des Beaux-Arts (School of Fine Arts) in Paris, the Beaux-Arts style incorporated classical principles (such as symmetry in design, including interior spaces extending radially from a central core or axis) and featured extensive exterior ornamentation. As an example of a Beaux-Arts building, Garnier's Opéra proclaims, through its majesty and lavishness, its function as a gathering place for fashionable audiences in an era of conspicuous wealth. The style was so attractive to the moneyed classes who supported the arts that theaters and opera houses continued to reflect the Paris Opéra's design until World War I transformed society (see Chapter 29).

27-45 CHARLES GARNIER, Opéra (looking north), Paris, France, 1861–1874. ◼◀

For Paris's opera house, Garnier chose a festive and spectacularly theatrical Neo-Baroque facade well suited to a gathering place for fashionable audiences in an age of conspicuous wealth.

SAINTE-GENEVIÈVE LIBRARY

Work on Garnier's opera house began in 1861, but by the middle of the 19th century, many architects had already abandoned sentimental and Romantic designs from the past. Since the 18th century, bridges had been constructed of cast iron (FIG. 26-12) because of its tensile strength and resistance to fire, and steel became available after 1860 as a building material that enabled architects to create new designs involving vast enclosed spaces, as in the great train sheds of railroad stations (FIG. 28-4) and in exposition halls. Most other utilitarian architecture—factories, warehouses, dockyard structures, mills, and the like—long had been built simply and without historical ornamentation.

The Bibliothèque Sainte-Geneviève, built by HENRI LABROUSTE (1801–1875), is an interesting mix of Renaissance revival style and modern cast-iron construction. The library's two-story facade with arched windows recalls Renaissance palazzo designs, but Labrouste exposed the structure's metal skeleton on the interior. The lower story of the building housed the book stacks. The upper floor featured a spacious reading room (FIG. 27-46) consisting essentially of two barrel-vaulted halls, roofed in terracotta and separated by a row of slender cast-iron columns on concrete pedestals. The columns, recognizably Corinthian, support the iron roof arches pierced with intricate vine-scroll ornamentation derived from the Renaissance

27-47 JOSEPH PAXTON, Crystal Palace, London, England, 1850–1851; enlarged and relocated at Sydenham, England, 1852–1854. Detail of a color lithograph by ACHILLE-LOUIS MARTINET, ca. 1862. Private collection.

The tensile strength of iron enabled Paxton to experiment with a new system of glass-and-metal roof construction. Constructed of prefabricated parts, the vast Crystal Palace required only six months to build.

27-46A ROEBLING, Brooklyn Bridge, 1867–1883.

architectural repertoire. Labrouste's design highlights how the peculiar properties of the new structural material aesthetically transformed the shapes of traditional masonry architecture. But it is also clear how reluctant some 19th-century architects were to surrender traditional forms, even when fully aware of new possibilities for design and construction. Architects scoffed at "engineers' architecture" for many years and continued to clothe their steel-and-concrete structures in the Romantic "drapery" of a historical style. For example, the designer of the Brooklyn Bridge (FIG. 27-46A), JOHN AUGUSTUS ROEBLING (1806–1869), combined the latest steel technology with motifs from Gothic and Egyptian architecture.

CRYSTAL PALACE Completely "undraped" construction first became popular in the conservatories (greenhouses) of English country estates. JOSEPH PAXTON (1801–1865) built several of these structures for his patron, the duke of Devonshire. In the largest—300 feet long—he used an experimental system of glass-and-metal roof construction. Encouraged by the success of this system, Paxton submitted a winning glass-and-iron building design in the competition for the hall to house the Great Exhibition of 1851 in London, organized to present "works of industry of all nations." Paxton constructed the exhibition building, the Crystal Palace (FIG. 27-47), with prefabricated parts. This enabled workers to build the vast structure in the then-unheard-of time of six months and to dismantle it quickly at the exhibition's closing to avoid permanent obstruction of the park. The plan borrowed much from Roman and Christian basilicas, with a central flat-roofed "nave" and a barrel-vaulted crossing "transept." The design provided ample interior space to contain displays of huge machines as well as to accommodate decorative touches in the form of large working fountains and giant trees. The public admired the Crystal Palace so much that the workers who dismantled it put up an enlarged version of the glass-and-steel exhibition hall at a new location on the outskirts of London at Sydenham, where it remained until fire destroyed it in 1936. Fortunately, a few old black-and-white photographs and several color lithographs (FIG. 27-47) preserve a record of the Crystal Palace's appearance.

PHOTOGRAPHY

A technological device of immense consequence for the modern experience was invented shortly before the mid-19th century: the camera, with its attendant art of photography. From the time Frenchman LOUIS-JACQUES-MANDÉ DAGUERRE (1789–1851) and Briton William Henry Fox Talbot (1800–1877) announced the first practical photographic processes in 1839, people have celebrated photography's ability to make convincing pictures of people, places, and things. The relative ease of the process, even in its earliest and most primitive form, seemed a dream come true for scientists and artists, who for centuries had grappled with less satisfying methods of capturing accurate images of their subjects. Photography also perfectly suited an age that saw the emergence of Realism as an art movement and a pronounced shift of artistic patronage away from the elite few toward a broader base of support. The growing and increasingly powerful middle class

embraced both the comprehensible images of the new artistic medium and their lower cost.

For the traditional artist, photography suggested new answers to the great debate about what is real and how to represent the real in art. Because photography easily and accurately enabled the reproduction of three-dimensional objects on a two-dimensional surface, the new medium also challenged the place of traditional modes of pictorial representation originating in the Renaissance. Artists as diverse as Delacroix, Ingres, Courbet, and the Impressionist Edgar Degas (see Chapter 28) welcomed photography as a helpful auxiliary to painting. Other artists, however, feared the camera was a mechanism that would displace the painstaking work of skilled painters. From the moment of its invention, photography threatened to expropriate the realistic image, until then the exclusive property of painting. But just as some painters looked to the new medium of photography for answers on how best to render an image in paint, so some photographers looked to painting for suggestions about ways to imbue the photographic image with qualities beyond simple reproduction. Indeed, the first subjects photographers chose to record were traditional painting themes, for example, still lifes and portraits—in part to establish photography as a legitimate artistic medium on a par with painting. A debate immediately began over whether the photograph was an art form or if the camera was merely a scientific instrument. An 1862 court case provided the answer: Photography was an art, and photographs were entitled to copyright protection.

Artists themselves were instrumental in the development of the new photographic technology. The camera obscura was familiar to 18th-century artists. In 1807, the invention of the *camera lucida* (lighted room) replaced the enclosed chamber of the camera obscura. Now the photographer aimed a small prism lens, hung on a stand, downward at an object. The lens projected the image of the object onto a sheet of paper. Artists using either of these devices found the process long and arduous, no matter how accurate the resulting work. All yearned for a more direct way to capture a subject's image. Two very different scientific inventions that accomplished this—the *daguerreotype* and the *calotype* (see "Daguerreotypes, Calotypes, and Wet-Plate Photography," page 792)—appeared almost simultaneously in France and England in 1839.

DAGUERREOTYPES The French government presented the new daguerreotype process at the Academy of Science in Paris on January 7, 1839, with the understanding that its details would be made available to all interested parties without charge (although the inventor received a large annuity in appreciation). Soon, people worldwide began making pictures with the daguerreotype "camera" (a name shortened from camera obscura) in a process almost immediately christened "photography," from the Greek *photos* (light) and *graphos* (writing). From the start, the possibilities of the process as a new art medium intrigued painters. Paul Delaroche (1797–1856), a leading academic painter of the day, wrote in an official report to the French government that anticipated the 1862 legal ruling:

> Daguerre's process completely satisfies all the demands of art, carrying certain essential principles of art to such perfection that it must become a subject of observation and study even to the most accomplished painters. The pictures obtained by this method are as remarkable for the perfection of the details as for the richness and harmony of the general effect. Nature is reproduced in them not only with truth, but also with art.[14]

Daguerreotypes, Calotypes, and Wet-Plate Photography

The earliest photographic processes were the *daguerreotype* (FIGS. 27-48 and 27-49), named after L.J.M. Daguerre, and the *calotype* (FIG. 27-54). Daguerre was an architect and theatrical set painter and designer. This background led Daguerre and a partner to open a popular entertainment called the Diorama. Audiences witnessed performances of "living paintings" created by changing the lighting effects on a "sandwich" composed of a painted backdrop and several layers of painted translucent front curtains. Daguerre used a camera obscura for the Diorama, but he wanted to find a more efficient and effective procedure. Through a mutual acquaintance, he met Joseph Nicéphore Niépce (1765–1833), who in 1826 had successfully made a permanent picture of the cityscape outside his upper-story window by exposing, in a camera obscura, a metal plate covered with a light-sensitive coating. Niépce's process, however, had the significant drawback that it required an eight-hour exposure time. After Niépce died in 1833, Daguerre continued his work, making two important discoveries. Latent development—that is, bringing out the image through treatment in chemical solutions—considerably shortened the length of time needed for exposure. Daguerre also discovered a better way to "fix" the image by chemically stopping the action of light on the photographic plate, which otherwise would continue to darken until the image turned solid black.

The daguerreotype reigned supreme in photography until the 1850s, but the second major photographic invention, the ancestor of the modern negative-print system, eventually replaced it. On January 31, 1839, less than three weeks after Daguerre unveiled his method in Paris, William Henry Fox Talbot presented a paper on his "photogenic drawings" to the Royal Institution in London. As early as 1835, Talbot made "negative" images by placing objects on sensitized paper and exposing the arrangement to light. This created a design of light-colored silhouettes recording the places where opaque or translucent objects had blocked light from darkening the paper's emulsion. In his experiments, Talbot next exposed sensitized papers inside simple cameras and, with a second sheet, created "positive" images. He further improved the process with more light-sensitive chemicals and a chemical development of the negative image. This technique enabled multiple prints. However, in Talbot's process, which he named the calotype (from the Greek word *kalos,* "beautiful"), the photographic images incorporated the texture of the paper. This produced a slightly blurred, grainy effect very different from the crisp detail and wide tonal range available with the daguerreotype. Also discouraging widespread adoption of the calotype were the stiff licensing and equipment fees charged for many years after Talbot patented his new process in 1841.

One of the earliest masters of an improved kind of calotype photography was the multitalented Frenchman known as Nadar (FIGS. 27-50 and 27-51). He used glass negatives and albumen (prepared with egg white) printing paper (FIGS. 27-52 and 27-53), which could record finer detail and a wider range of light and shadow than Talbot's calotype process. The new *wet-plate* technology (so named because the photographic plate was exposed, developed, and fixed while wet) almost at once became the universal way of making negatives until 1880. However, wet-plate photography had drawbacks. The plates had to be prepared and processed on the spot. Working outdoors meant taking along a portable darkroom—a wagon, tent, or box with light-tight sleeves for the photographer's arms.

Refinements of these early processes served photographers well for a century and a half but have been largely supplanted today by digital photography (see Chapter 31).

27-48 LOUIS-JACQUES-MANDÉ DAGUERRE, *Still Life in Studio,* 1837. Daguerreotype, $6\frac{1}{4}'' \times 8\frac{1}{4}''$. Société Française de Photographie, Paris. ◼◀

One of the first plates Daguerre produced after perfecting his new photographic process was this still life, in which he was able to capture amazing detail and finely graduated tones of light and shadow.

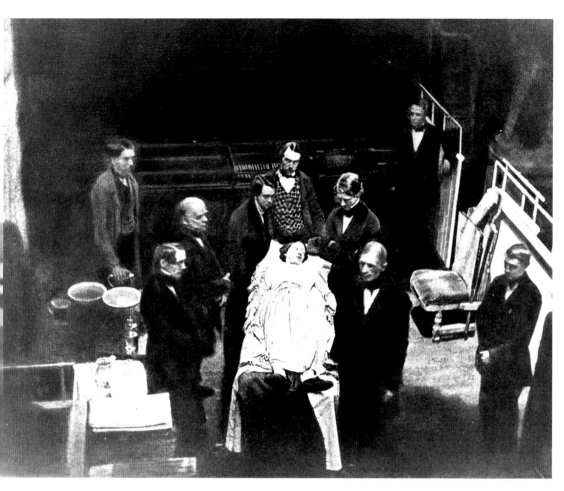

27-49 Josiah Johnson Hawes and Albert Sands Southworth, *Early Operation under Ether, Massachusetts General Hospital*, ca. 1847. Daguerreotype, $6\frac{1}{2}'' \times 8\frac{1}{2}''$. Massachusetts General Hospital Archives and Special Collections, Boston. ◼◀

In this early daguerreotype, which predates Eakins's *The Gross Clinic* (FIG. 27-36) by almost 30 years, Hawes and Southworth demonstrated the documentary power of the new medium of photography.

Unlike photographs people make today, whether printed from traditional film negatives or from computerized digital images, each daguerreotype is a unique work. *Still Life in Studio* (FIG. 27-48) is one of the first successful plates Daguerre produced after perfecting his method. The process captured every detail—the subtle forms, the varied textures, the finely graduated tones of light and shadow—in Daguerre's carefully constructed tableau. The three-dimensional forms of the sculptures, the basket, and the bits of cloth spring into high relief. The inspiration for the composition came from 17th-century Dutch vanitas still lifes, such as those of Pieter Claesz (FIG. 25-1). As did Claesz, Daguerre arranged his objects to reveal their textures and shapes clearly. Unlike a painter, Daguerre could not alter anything within his arrangement to create a stronger image. However, he could suggest a symbolic meaning through his choice of objects. Like the skull and timepiece in Claesz's painting, Daguerre's sculptural and architectural fragments and the framed print of an embrace suggest even art is vanitas and will not endure forever.

HAWES AND SOUTHWORTH In the United States, photographers began to make daguerreotypes within two months of Daguerre's presentation in Paris. Two particularly avid and resourceful advocates of the new medium were JOSIAH JOHNSON HAWES (1808–1901), a painter, and ALBERT SANDS SOUTHWORTH (1811–1894), a pharmacist and teacher. Together, they ran a daguerreotype studio in Boston specializing in portraiture, then popular due to the shortened exposure time required for the process (although it was still long enough to require head braces to help subjects remain motionless while photographers recorded their images).

The partners also took their equipment outside the studio to record places and events of particular interest to them. One resultant image is *Early Operation under Ether, Massachusetts General Hospital* (FIG. 27-49). This daguerreotype, taken from the vantage point of the gallery of a hospital operating room, put the viewer in the position of medical students looking down on a lecture-demonstration typical throughout the 19th century. An image of historical record, this early daguerreotype predates Eakins's *Gross Clinic* (FIG. 27-36) by almost three decades. The focus of attention in *Early Operation* is the white-draped patient surrounded by a circle of darkly clad doctors. The details of the figures and the room's furnishings are in sharp focus, but the slight blurring of several of the figures betrays motion during the exposure. The elevated viewpoint flattens the spatial perspective and emphasizes the relationships of the figures in ways the Impressionists, especially Degas, found intriguing.

NADAR Portraiture was one of the first photography genres to use a technology that improved the calotype. Making portraits was an important economic opportunity for most photographers, as Southworth and Hawes proved, but the greatest of the early portrait photographers was undoubtedly Gaspar-Félix Tournachon. Known simply as NADAR (1820–1910), Tournachon was a French novelist, journalist, enthusiastic balloonist, and caricaturist, who became an early champion of photography. Photographic studies for his caricatures led Nadar to open a portrait studio. So talented was he at capturing the essence of his subjects that the most important people in France, including Delacroix, Daumier, Courbet, and Manet, flocked to his studio to have their portraits made. Nadar said he sought in his work "that instant of understanding that puts you in touch with the model—helps you sum him up,

1 in.

27-50 NADAR, *Eugène Delacroix*, ca. 1855. Modern print, $8\frac{1}{2}'' \times 6\frac{2}{3}''$, from the original negative. Bibliothèque Nationale, Paris.

Nadar was one of the earliest portrait photographers. His prints of the leading artists of the day, such as this one of Delacroix, reveal the sitters' personalities as well as record their features.

NADAR élevant la Photographie à la hauteur de l'Art

27-51 HONORÉ DAUMIER, *Nadar Raising Photography to the Height of Art*, 1862. Lithograph, $10\frac{3}{4}'' \times 8\frac{3}{4}''$. Museum of Fine Arts, Boston.

Daumier's lithograph of Nadar (FIG. 27-50) in a balloon "elevating the art of photography" commemorates a court decision acknowledging photographs as artworks protected by copyright.

guides you to his habits, his ideas, and character and enables you to produce . . . a really convincing and sympathetic likeness, an intimate portrait."[15]

Nadar's *Eugène Delacroix* (FIG. 27-50) shows the painter at the height of his career. In this photograph, the artist appears with remarkable presence. Even in half-length, his gesture and expression create a mood that seems to reveal much about him. Perhaps Delacroix responded to Nadar's famous gift for putting his clients at ease by assuming the pose that best expressed his personality. The new photographic materials made possible the rich range of tones in Nadar's images.

Nadar achieved so much fame for his wet-plate photographic portraits (see "Daguerreotypes, Calotypes, and Wet-Plate Photography," page 792) that he became the subject of a Daumier lithograph (FIG. 27-51) that provides incisive and amusing commentary about the struggle of photography to be recognized as a fine art. Daumier made his print in response to the 1862 court decision acknowledging photographs were indeed artworks. In the lithograph, Nadar energetically takes pictures with his camera as his balloon rises over Parisian rooftops—Daumier's literal representation of the elevation of photography's status the French judge reaffirmed. The image also refers to the fact that Nadar was a staunch advocate of balloon transportation and aerial reconnaissance. He produced the first aerial photographs of Paris in 1858 from his balloon *Le Géant* (The Giant).

JULIA MARGARET CAMERON Among the most famous portrait photographers in 19th-century England was JULIA MARGARET CAMERON (1815–1879), who did not take up photography seriously until the age of 48. Although she produced images of many well-known men of the period, including Charles Darwin, Alfred Tennyson, and Thomas Carlyle, she photographed more women than men, as was true of many women photographers. *Ophelia, Study No. 2* (FIG. 27-52) typifies her portrait style. Cameron often depicted her female subjects as characters in literary or biblical narratives. The slightly blurred focus also became a distinctive feature of her work—the byproduct of photographing with a lens with a short focal length, which allowed only a small area of sharp focus. The blurriness adds an ethereal, dreamlike tone to the photographs, appropriate for Cameron's fictional "characters." Her photograph of Ophelia has a mysterious, fragile quality reminiscent of Pre-Raphaelite paintings (FIG. 27-41) of literary heroines.

TIMOTHY O'SULLIVAN Photographers were quick to realize the documentary power of their new medium. Thus began the story of photography's influence on modern life and of the immense changes it brought to communication and information management. Historical events could be recorded in permanent form on the spot for the first time. The photographs taken of the Crimean War (1856) by Roger Fenton (1819–1869) and of the American Civil War by Mathew B. Brady (1823–1896), ALEXANDER GARDNER (1821–1882),

and Timothy O'Sullivan (1840–1882) remain unsurpassed as incisive accounts of military life, unsparing in their truth to detail and poignant as expressions of human experience.

Of the Civil War photographs, the most moving are the inhumanly objective records of combat deaths. Perhaps the most reproduced of these Civil War photographs is Gardner's print of O'Sullivan's *A Harvest of Death, Gettysburg, Pennsylvania* (FIG. **27-53**). Although viewers could regard this image as simple reportage, it also functions to impress on people the high price of war. Corpses litter the battlefield as far as the eye can see. O'Sullivan presented a scene stretching far to the horizon. As the photograph modulates from the precise clarity of the bodies of Union soldiers in the foreground, boots stolen and pockets picked, to the indistinct corpses in the distance, the suggestion of innumerable other dead soldiers is unavoidable. This "harvest" is far more sobering and depressing than that in Winslow Homer's Civil War painting, *Veteran in a New Field* (FIG. 27-35). Though it was years before photolithography could reproduce photographs such as this in newspapers, photographers exhibited them publicly. They made an impression newsprint engravings never could.

Negative by T. H. O'SULLIVAN.   Entered according to act of Congress, in the year 1865, by A. Gardner, in the Clerk's Office of the District Court of the District of Columbia.   Positive by A. GARDNER, 511 7th St., Washington.

A Harvest of Death, Gettysburg, Pennsylvania.

27-54 EADWEARD MUYBRIDGE, *Horse Galloping,* 1878. Calotype print, 9″ × 12″. George Eastman House, Rochester. ◼◀

Muybridge specialized in photographic studies of the successive stages in human and animal motion—details too quick for the human eye to capture. Modern cinema owes a great deal to his work.

EADWEARD MUYBRIDGE The Realist photographer and scientist EADWEARD MUYBRIDGE (1830–1904) came to the United States from England in the 1850s and settled in San Francisco, where he established a prominent international reputation for his photographs of the western United States. In 1872, the governor of California, Leland Stanford (1824–1893), sought Muybridge's assistance in settling a bet about whether, at any point in a stride, all four feet of a horse galloping at top speed are off the ground. Through his sequential photography, as seen in *Horse Galloping* (FIG. **27-54**), Muybridge proved they were. This experience was the beginning of Muybridge's photographic studies of the successive stages in human and animal motion—details too quick for the human eye to capture. These investigations culminated in 1885 at the University of Pennsylvania with a series of multiple-camera motion studies that recorded separate photographs of progressive moments in a single action. Muybridge's discoveries received extensive publicity through the book *Animal Locomotion* (1887), and his motion photographs earned him a place in the history of science, as well

as art. These sequential motion studies, along with those of Eakins and Marey, influenced many other artists, including their contemporary, the painter and sculptor Edgar Degas (FIG. 28-10), and 20th-century artists such as Marcel Duchamp (FIG. 29-35).

Muybridge presented his work to scientists and general audiences with a device called the *zoopraxiscope,* which he invented to project his sequences of images (mounted on special glass plates) onto a screen. The result was so lifelike one viewer said it "threw upon the screen apparently the living, moving animals. Nothing was wanting but the clatter of hoofs upon the turf."[16] The illusion of motion in Muybridge's photographic exhibits was the result of a physical fact of human eyesight called "persistence of vision." Stated simply, it means the brain retains whatever the eye sees for a fraction of a second after the eye stops seeing it. Thus, viewers saw a rapid succession of different images merging one into the next, producing the illusion of continuous change. This illusion lies at the heart of the motion-picture industry that debuted in the 20th century. Thus, with Muybridge's innovations in photography, yet another new art form was born—the cinema.

ROMANTICISM, REALISM, PHOTOGRAPHY: EUROPE AND AMERICA, 1800 TO 1870

ART UNDER NAPOLEON

▍ As Emperor of the French from 1804 to 1815, Napoleon embraced the Neoclassical style in order to associate his regime with the empire of ancient Rome. Roman temples were the models for La Madeleine in Paris, which Pierre Vignon built as a temple of glory for France's imperial armies.

▍ Napoleon chose Jacques-Louis David as First Painter of the Empire. His favorite sculptor was Antonio Canova, who carved marble Neoclassical portraits of the imperial family, including a reclining image of Napoleon's sister, Pauline Borghese, in the guise of Venus.

▍ The beginning of a break from Neoclassicism can already be seen in the work of some of David's students, including Gros, Girodet-Trioson, and Ingres, all of whom painted some exotic subjects reflecting Romantic taste.

Vignon, La Madeleine, Paris, 1807–1842

ROMANTICISM

▍ The roots of Romanticism are in the 18th century, but usually the term more narrowly denotes the artistic movement that flourished from 1800 to 1840, between Neoclassicism and Realism. Romantic artists gave precedence to feeling and imagination over Enlightenment reason. Romantic painters explored the exotic, erotic, and fantastic in their art.

▍ In Spain, Francisco Goya's *Los Caprichos* series celebrated the unleashing of imagination, emotions, and even nightmares. In France, Eugène Delacroix led the way in depicting Romantic narratives set in faraway places and distant times. Ancient Assyria, for example, is the subject of his colorful *Death of Sardanapalus*.

▍ Romantic painters often chose landscapes as an ideal subject to express the theme of the soul unified with the natural world. Masters of the transcendental landscape include Friedrich in Germany, Constable and Turner in England, and Cole, Bierstadt, and Church in the United States.

Delacroix, *Death of Sardanapalus*, 1827

REALISM

▍ Realism developed as an artistic movement in mid-19th-century France. Its leading proponent was Gustave Courbet, whose paintings of menial laborers and ordinary people exemplify his belief that painters should depict only their own time and place. Honoré Daumier boldly confronted authority with his satirical lithographs commenting on the plight of the urban working classes. Édouard Manet shocked the public with his paintings featuring promiscuous women, and his rough brushstrokes, which emphasized the flatness of the painting surface, paved the way for modern abstract art.

▍ Among the leading American Realists were Winslow Homer, Thomas Eakins, and John Singer Sargent. Eakins's painting of surgery in progress was too brutally realistic for the Philadelphia art jury that rejected it.

Courbet, *The Stone Breakers*, 1849

ARCHITECTURE

▍ Territorial expansion, the Romantic interest in exotic locales and earlier eras, and nationalistic pride led to the revival in the 19th century of older architectural styles, especially the Gothic, exemplified by London's Houses of Parliament.

▍ By the middle of the century, many architects had already abandoned sentimental and Romantic designs from the past in favor of exploring the possibilities of cast-iron construction, as in Henri Labrouste's Saint-Geneviève Library in Paris and Joseph Paxton's Crystal Palace in London.

Barry and Pugin, Houses of Parliament, London, 1835

PHOTOGRAPHY

▍ In 1839, Daguerre in Paris and Talbot in London invented the first practical photographic processes. In 1862, a French court formally recognized photography as an art form subject to copyright protection. Many of the earliest photographers, including Nadar and Cameron, specialized in portrait photography, but others, including Hawes, Southworth, and O'Sullivan in the United States quickly realized the documentary power of the new medium. Muybridge's sequential photos of human and animal motion were the forerunners of the modern cinema.

Daguerre, *Still Life in Studio*, 1837

In summer 1874, Manet recorded Monet painting—*en plein air* directly on canvas without any preliminary sketchpreliminar— in his floating studio on the Seine at Argenteuil, 22 minutes from Paris by train.

With Monet is his wife, Camille Doncieux. Monet, underappreciated as an artist, had recently sold some paintings, enabling the couple to purchase the small boat he equipped with a cabin and easel.

In this painting, Manet adopted not only Monet's Impressionist subject matter but also the younger artist's short brushstrokes and fascination with the reflection of sunlight on water.

28-1 ÉDOUARD MANET, *Claude Monet in His Studio Boat,* 1874. Oil on canvas, 2′ 8″ × 3′ 3¼″. Neue Pinakothek, Munich. ◼◀

In the distance are the factories and smokestacks of Argenteuil. Manet thus recorded the two poles of modern life—the leisure activities of the bourgeosie and the industrialization along the Seine.

IMPRESSIONISM, POST-IMPRESSIONISM, SYMBOLISM: EUROPE AND AMERICA, 1870 TO 1900

IMPRESSIONS OF MODERN LIFE

Impressionism was an art movement born in late-19th-century industrialized, urbanized Paris as a reaction to the sometimes brutal and chaotic transformation of French life, which made the world seem unstable and insubstantial. As the poet and critic Charles Baudelaire (1821–1867) observed in his 1860 essay *The Painter of Modern Life:* "[M]odernity is the transitory, the fugitive, the contingent."[1] Accordingly, Impressionist painters built upon the innovations of the Realists in turning away from traditional mythological and religious themes in favor of daily life, but they sought to convey the elusiveness and impermanence of the subjects they portrayed.

In 1872, the painter CLAUDE MONET (1840–1926), a leading Impressionist, moved to Argenteuil, a prosperous industrial town on the Seine (MAP 28-1) that was also a favorite leisure destination of the city dwellers of Paris—only 22 minutes by train from the Saint-Lazare train station (FIG. 28-4). Situated at a point where the river widened into a deep basin, Argenteuil was an ideal spot for boating of all kinds, from casual rowing to formal regattas. In 1873, after accumulating enough money from recent sales of his paintings, the underappreciated and financially strapped Monet was able to purchase a small boat, which he equipped with a tiny wooden cabin and a striped awning and used as his floating studio.

During the summer of 1874, Édouard Manet (FIGS. 27-32 and 27-33) joined Monet at Argenteuil and painted side-by-side with the younger artist. One day, Manet recorded Monet in his studio boat (FIG. 28-1) at work on *Sailboats on the Seine, Argenteuil,* a painting now in the Fine Arts Museum of San Francisco. Monet, wearing a straw hat, sits at the front of the boat with his easel before him. Camille Doncieux, Monet's wife (compare FIG. 28-2A), is at once the painter's admirer and his muse. In the distance are the factories and smokestacks that represent the opposite pole of life at Argenteuil. In capturing both the leisure activities of the bourgeoisie and the industrialization along the Seine in the 1870s on the same canvas, Manet, like Monet, was fulfilling Baudelaire's definition of "the painter of modern life."

Claude Monet in His Studio Boat is noteworthy as a document of Monet's preference for painting outdoors (*en plein air*)—a radical practice at the time—in order to record his "impression" of the Seine by placing colors directly on a white canvas without any preliminary sketch—also a sharp break from traditional studio techniques. The painting further attests to Monet's influence on his older friend Manet, who here adopted the younger painter's subject matter, short brushstrokes, and fascination with the reflection of light on water.

MARXISM, DARWINISM, MODERNISM

The momentous developments of the early 19th century in Europe—industrialization, urbanization, and increased economic and political interaction worldwide—matured during the latter half of the century. The Industrial Revolution born in England spread so rapidly to the Continent and the United States that historians often refer to the third quarter of the 19th century as the second Industrial Revolution. Whereas the first Industrial Revolution centered on textiles, steam, and iron, the second focused on steel, electricity, chemicals, and oil. The discoveries in these fields provided the foundation for developments in plastics, machinery, building construction, and automobile manufacturing and paved the way for the invention of the radio, electric light, telephone, and electric streetcar.

A significant consequence of industrialization was urbanization. The number and size of Western cities grew dramatically during the latter part of the 19th century, largely due to migration from the countryside. Farmers in large numbers relocated to urban centers because expanded agricultural enterprises squeezed smaller property owners from their land. The widely available work opportunities in the cities, especially in the factories, were also a major factor in this population shift. Improving health and living conditions in the cities further contributed to their explosive growth.

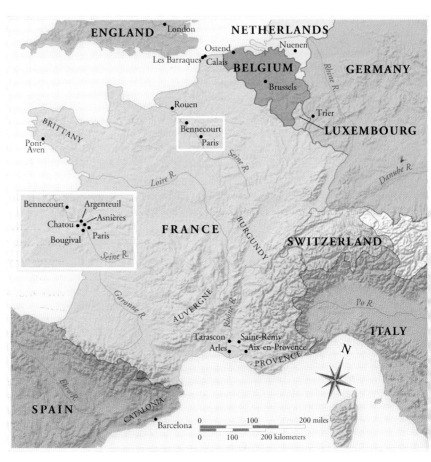

MAP 28-1 France around 1870.

MARXISM AND DARWINISM The rise of the urban working class was fundamental to the ideas of Karl Marx (1818–1883), one of the era's dominant figures. Born in Trier, Germany, Marx received a doctorate in philosophy from the University of Berlin. After moving to Paris, he met fellow German Friedrich Engels (1820–1895), who became his lifelong collaborator. Together they wrote *The Communist Manifesto* (1848), which called for the working class to overthrow the capitalist system. As did other 19th-century empiricists, Marx believed scientific, rational law governed nature and, indeed, all human history. For Marx, economic forces based on class struggle induced historical change. Throughout history, insisted Marx, those who controlled the means of production conflicted with those whose labor they exploited for their own enrichment—a dynamic he called "dialectical materialism." Marx advocated the creation of a socialist state in which the working class seized power and destroyed capitalism. This new political, social, and economic system—Marxism—held great appeal for the oppressed as well as for many intellectuals.

Equally influential was the English naturalist Charles Darwin (1809–1882), whose theory of natural selection did much to increase interest in science. Darwin and his compatriot Alfred Russel Wallace (1823–1913), working independently, proposed a mode for the process of evolution based on mechanistic laws, rather than attributing evolution to random chance or God's plan. They postulated a competitive system in which only the fittest survived. Darwin's controversial ideas, as presented in *On the Origin of Species by Means of Natural Selection* (1859), contradicted the biblical narrative of creation. By challenging traditional religious beliefs, Darwinism contributed to growing secularism.

IMPRESSIONISM, POST-IMPRESSIONISM, SYMBOLISM: EUROPE AND AMERICA, 1870 TO 1900

1870	1880	1890	1900
▌ Claude Monet and the Impressionists mount their first independent exhibition in Paris ▌ Monet, Pierre-Auguste Renoir, Berthe Morisot, and other Impressionists paint landscapes and bourgeois life outdoors ▌ European artists begin to collect Japanese prints ▌ Gustave Moreau explores eroticism and fantasy in Symbolist paintings	▌ Georges Seurat develops pointillism ▌ Vincent van Gogh moves to France and explores the expressive power of color ▌ Auguste Rodin receives the commission for *Gates of Hell* ▌ Alexandre-Gustave Eiffel builds the Eiffel Tower in Paris	▌ Paul Cézanne seeks "to do Poussin over entirely from nature" ▌ The Art Nouveau movement emerges in architecture and the decorative arts ▌ Gustav Klimt's paintings epitomize fin-de-siècle culture in Austria ▌ Louis Sullivan builds steel, glass, and stone skyscrapers in America	

Other theorists and social thinkers, most notably British philosopher Herbert Spencer (1820–1903), applied Darwin's principles to the rapidly changing socioeconomic realm. As in the biological world, they asserted, industrialization's intense competition led to the survival of the most economically fit companies, enterprises, and countries. The social Darwinists provided Western nations with justification for the colonization of peoples and cultures they deemed less advanced. By 1900, the major economic and political powers had divided up much of the world. The French had colonized most of North Africa and Indochina, while the British occupied India, Australia, and large areas of Africa, including Nigeria, Egypt, Sudan, Rhodesia, and the Union of South Africa. The Dutch were a major presence in the Pacific, and the Germans, Portuguese, Spanish, and Italians all established themselves in various areas of Africa.

MODERNISM The combination of extensive technological changes and increased exposure to other cultures, coupled with the rapidity of these changes, led to an acute sense in Western cultures of the world's impermanence. Darwin's ideas of evolution and Marx's emphasis on a continuing sequence of conflicts reinforced this awareness of a constantly shifting reality. These societal changes in turn fostered a new and multifaceted artistic approach that art historians call *modernism*. Modernist artists seek to capture the images and sensibilities of their age, but modernism transcends the simple depiction of the contemporary world—the goal of Realism (see Chapter 27). Modernist artists also critically examine the premises of art itself, as Manet did in his seminal 1863 painting *Le Déjeuner sur l'Herbe* (FIG. 27-32). Modernism thus implies certain concerns about art and aesthetics internal to art production, regardless of whether the artist is portraying modern life. Clement Greenberg (1909–1994), an influential American art critic who wrote about the revolutionary art movements of the decades following World War II (see Chapter 30), explained:

> The essence of Modernism lies . . . in the use of the characteristic methods of a discipline to criticize the discipline itself—not in order to subvert it, but to entrench it more firmly in its area of competence. . . . Realistic, illusionist art had dissembled the medium, using art to conceal art. Modernism used art to call attention to art. The limitations that constitute the medium of painting—the flat surface, the shape of the support, the properties of pigment—were treated by the Old Masters as negative factors that could be acknowledged only implicitly or indirectly. Modernist painting has come to regard these same limitations as positive factors that are to be acknowledged openly.[2]

Although the work of Gustave Courbet and the Realists already expressed this modernist viewpoint, modernism emerged even more forcefully in the late-19th-century movements that art historians call Impressionism, Post-Impressionism, and Symbolism.

IMPRESSIONISM

A hostile critic applied the term *Impressionism* in response to Claude Monet's *Impression: Sunrise* (FIG. 28-2), exhibited in the first Impressionist show in 1874 (see "Academic Salons and Independent Art Exhibitions," page 802). Although the critic intended the label to be derogatory, by the third Impressionist show in 1878, the artists had embraced it and were calling themselves Impressionists.

CLAUDE MONET Artists and critics had used the term *Impressionism* before, but only in relation to sketches. Impression-

ist paintings do incorporate the qualities of sketches—abbreviation, speed, and spontaneity. This is apparent in *Impression: Sunrise* (FIG. 28-2), in which Monet made no attempt to disguise the brushstrokes or blend the pigment to create smooth tonal gradations and an optically accurate scene. This concern with acknowledging the paint and the canvas surface continued the modernist exploration the Realists began. Beyond this connection to the sketch, Impressionism operated at the intersection of what the artists saw and what they felt. In other words, the "impressions" these artists recorded in their paintings were neither purely objective descriptions of the exterior world nor solely subjective responses, but the interaction between the two. They were sensations—the Impressionists' subjective and personal responses to nature.

In sharp contrast to traditional studio artists, Monet painted outdoors, often on the banks of the Seine (FIG. 28-2A) northwest of Paris or in a boat on the river (FIG. 28-1). Painting *en plein air* sharpened Monet's focus on the roles light and color play in capturing an instantaneous representation of atmosphere and climate. Monet carried the

28-2A MONET, *Bank of the Seine, Bennecourt*, 1868.

systematic investigation of light and color further than any other Impressionist, but all of them recognized the importance of carefully observing and understanding how light and color operate. Such thorough study enabled the Impressionists to present images that truly conveyed a sense of the momentary and transitory. Lila Cabot Perry (1848–1933), a student of Monet's late in his career, gave this description of Monet's approach:

> I remember his once saying to me: "When you go out to paint, try to forget what objects you have before you—a tree, a house, a field, or whatever. Merely think, here is a little square of blue, here an oblong of pink, here a streak of yellow, and paint it just as it looks to you, the exact color and shape, until it gives your own naïve impression of the scene before you."[3]

Scientific studies of light and the invention of chemically synthesized pigments increased artists' sensitivity to the multiplicity of colors in nature and gave them new colors for their work. After scrutinizing the effects of light and color on forms, the Impressionists concluded that *local color*—an object's color in white light—becomes modified by the quality of the light shining on it, by reflections from other objects, and by the effects juxtaposed colors produce. Shadows do not appear gray or black, as many earlier painters thought, but seem to be composed of colors modified by reflections or other conditions. If artists use complementary colors (see "19th-Century Color Theory," page 813) side by side over large enough areas, the colors intensify each other, unlike the effect of small quantities of adjoining mixed pigments, which blend into neutral tones. Furthermore, the "mixing" of colors by juxtaposing them on a canvas produces a more intense hue than the same colors mixed on the palette. It is not strictly true the Impressionists used only primary hues, placing them side by side to create secondary colors (blue and yellow, for example, to create green). But they did achieve remarkably brilliant effects with their characteristically short, choppy brushstrokes, which so accurately caught the vibrating quality of light. The fact their canvas surfaces look unintelligible at close range and their forms and objects appear only when the eye fuses the strokes at a certain distance accounts for much of the early adverse criticism leveled at their work. Some critics even accused the Impressionists of firing their paint at the canvas with pistols.

Academic Salons and Independent Art Exhibitions

For both artists and art historians, modernist art stands in marked contrast—indeed in forceful opposition—to academic art, that is, to the art promoted by the established art schools such as the Royal Academy of Painting and Sculpture in France (founded in 1648) and the Royal Academy of Arts in Britain (founded in 1768). These academies provided instruction for art students and sponsored exhibitions, exerting tight control over the art scene. The annual exhibitions, called "Salons" in France, were highly competitive, as was membership in these academies. Subsidized by the government, the French Royal Academy supported a limited range of artistic expression, focusing on traditional subjects and highly polished technique. Because of the challenges modernist art presented to established artistic conventions, the juries for the Salons and other exhibitions often rejected the works more adventurous artists wished to display, thereby preventing the public from viewing any art other than the officially sanctioned forms of expression. When, however, the 1855 jury rejected some of Gustave Courbet's paintings, the artist reacted by setting up his own Pavilion of Realism (see "Courbet on Realism," Chapter 27, page 776). Years later, he wrote:

> [I]t is high time that someone have the courage to be an honest man and that he say that the Academy is a harmful, all-consuming institution, incapable of fulfilling the goal of its so-called mission.*

Growing dissatisfaction with the decisions of the French Academy's jurors prompted Napoleon III (r. 1852–1870) in 1863 to establish the Salon des Refusés (Salon of the Rejected) to show all of the works not accepted for exhibition in the regular Salon. Édouard Manet's *Le Déjeuner sur l'Herbe* (FIG. 27-32) was among them. The public greeted it and the entire exhibition with derision. One reviewer of the rejected works summed up the prevailing attitude:

> This exhibition, at once sad and grotesque, . . . offers abundant proof . . . that the jury always displays an unbelievable leniency. Save for one or two questionable exceptions there is not a painting which deserves the honor of the official galleries . . . There is even something cruel about this exhibition; people laugh as they do at a farce.†

In 1867, after further rejections, Manet, following Courbet, mounted a private exhibition of 50 of his paintings outside the Paris World's Fair. Six years later, Claude Monet (FIG. 28-2) and the other Impressionists formed their own society and began mounting shows of their works in Paris. This action provided the Impressionists much freedom, for they did not have to contend with the Royal Academy's authoritative and confining viewpoint. The Impressionist exhibitions took place at one- or two-year intervals from 1874 until 1886.

Another group of artists unhappy with the official Salon's conservative nature adopted the same renegade idea. In 1884, these artists formed the Société des Artistes Indépendants (Society of Independent Artists) and held annual Salons des Indépendants. Georges Seurat's *A Sunday on La Grande Jatte* (FIG. 28-16) was one of the paintings in the Independents' 1886 salon.

As the art market expanded, venues for the exhibition of art increased. Art circles and societies sponsored private shows in which both amateurs and professionals participated. Dealers became more aggressive in promoting the artists they represented by mounting exhibitions in a variety of spaces, some fairly intimate and small, others large and grandiose. All of these proliferating opportunities for exhibition gave French artists alternatives to the traditional constraints of the Salon and provided fertile breeding ground for the development of radically new art forms and styles.

*Letter to Jules-Antoine Castagnary, October 17, 1868. Translated by Petra ten-Doesschate Chu, *Letters of Gustave Courbet* (Chicago: University of Chicago Press, 1992), 346.
†Maxime du Camp, in *Revue des deux mondes,* 1863, quoted in George Heard Hamilton, *Manet and His Critics* (New Haven: Yale University Press, New Haven, Conn., 1986), 42–43.

28-2 CLAUDE MONET, *Impression: Sunrise,* 1872. Oil on canvas, 1' 7½" × 2' 1½". Musée Marmottan, Paris.

A hostile critic applied the derogatory term *Impressionism* to this painting because of its sketchy quality and undisguised brushstrokes. Monet and his circle embraced the label for their movement.

28-3 Claude Monet, *Rouen Cathedral: The Portal (in Sun)*, 1894. Oil on canvas, 3′ 3¼″ × 2′ 1⅞″. Metropolitan Museum of Art, New York (Theodore M. Davis Collection, bequest of Theodore M. Davis, 1915).

Monet painted a series of views of Rouen Cathedral at different times of day and under various climatic conditions. The real subject of this painting is not the building but the sunlight shining on it.

ROUEN CATHEDRAL Monet's intensive study of the phenomena of light and color is especially evident in several series of paintings he made of the same subject. In one series, he painted more than three dozen views of Rouen Cathedral, northwest of Paris. For each canvas in the series, Monet observed the cathedral from nearly the same viewpoint but at different times of the day or under various climatic conditions. In the painting illustrated here (FIG. **28-3**), Monet depicted the church bathed in bright light. With scientific precision, he carefully recorded the passing of time as seen in the movement of light over identical forms. In fact, the real subject of Monet's painting—as the title *Rouen Cathedral: The Portal (in Sun)* implies—is not the cathedral, which he showed only in part, but the sunlight on the building's main portal. Later critics accused Monet and his companions of destroying form and order for fleeting atmospheric effects, but Monet focused on light and color precisely to reach a greater understanding of the appearance of form.

SAINT-LAZARE Most of the Impressionists painted scenes in and around Paris, the heart of modern life in France. Monet's *Saint-Lazare Train Station* (FIG. **28-4**) depicts a dominant aspect of the contemporary urban scene. The expanding railway network had made travel more convenient, bringing throngs of people into Paris and enabling city dwellers to reach rural areas quickly. In this painting, Monet captured the energy and vitality of Paris's modern transportation hub. The train, emerging from the steam and smoke it emits, rumbles into the station. In the background haze are the tall buildings that were becoming a major component of the Parisian landscape. Monet's agitated paint application contributes to the sense of energy and conveys the atmosphere of urban life.

28-4 Claude Monet, *Saint-Lazare Train Station*, 1877. Oil on canvas, 2′ 5¾″ × 3′ 5″. Musée d'Orsay, Paris. 🎥◀

Impressionist paintings are unintelligible at close range, but the eye fuses the brushstrokes at a distance. The agitated application of paint contributes to the sense of energy in this urban scene.

Impressionism   **803**

Georges Rivière (1855–1943), a critic and friend of some of the Impressionists, saw this painting in the third Impressionist exhibition and recorded the essence of what Monet had tried to achieve:

> Like a fiery steed, stimulated rather than exhausted by the long trek that it has only just finished, [the locomotive] tosses its mane of smoke, which lashes the glass roof of the main hall. . . . We see the vast and manic movements at the station where the ground shakes with every turn of the wheel. The platforms are sticky with soot, and the air is full of that bitter scent exuded by burning coal. As we look at this magnificent picture, we are overcome by the same feelings as if we were really there, and these feelings are perhaps even more powerful, because in the picture the artist has conveyed his own feelings as well.[4]

GUSTAVE CAILLEBOTTE Other Impressionists also represented facets of city life, although not always using Monet's impressionistic brushstrokes. The setting of *Paris: A Rainy Day* (FIG. **28-5**) by GUSTAVE CAILLEBOTTE (1849–1893) is a junction of spacious boulevards resulting from the redesigning of Paris begun in 1852. The city's population had reached close to 1.5 million by midcentury. To accommodate this congregation of humanity—and to facilitate the movement of troops in the event of another revolution—Napoleon III ordered Paris rebuilt. The emperor named Baron Georges Haussmann (1809–1891), a city superintendent, to oversee the entire project. In addition to new water and sewer systems, street lighting, and new residential and commercial buildings, a major component of the new Paris was the creation of the wide, open boulevards seen in Caillebotte's painting. These great avenues, whose construction caused the demolition of thousands of old buildings and streets, transformed medieval Paris into the present-day city, with its superb vistas and wide uninterrupted arteries for the flow of vehicular and pedestrian traffic. Caillebotte chose to focus on these markers of the city's rapid urbanization.

Although Caillebotte did not dissolve his image into the broken color and brushwork characteristic of Impressionism, he did use an informal and asymmetrical composition. The figures seem randomly placed, with the frame cropping them arbitrarily, suggesting the transitory nature of the street scene. Well-dressed Parisians of the leisure class share the viewer's space. Despite the sharp focus of *Paris: A Rainy Day,* the picture captures the artist's "impression" of urban life.

CAMILLE PISSARRO Other Impressionists also found Paris's spacious boulevards and avenues—the product of "Haussmannization"—attractive subjects for paintings. *La Place du Théâtre Français* (FIG. **28-6**) is one of many panoramic scenes of the city CAMILLE PISSARRO (1830–1903) painted. The artist recorded the blurred dark accents against a light ground that constituted his visual sensations of a crowded Parisian square viewed from several stories above street level. The moment Pissarro captured on his canvas is not so much of fugitive light effects as it is of the street life, achieved through a deliberate casualness in the arrangement of figures. To accomplish this sense of spontaneity, Pissarro sometimes used photography to record the places he wished to paint, as did many of his fellow Impressionists. Indeed, the visual parallels between Impressionist paintings and photographs are striking. In *La Place du Théâtre Français,* these parallels include the arbitrary cutting off of figures at the edges of the painting and the curious flattening spatial effect produced by the high viewpoint.

BERTHE MORISOT Many Impressionist paintings depict scenes from resort areas on the seashore or along the Seine River such as Argenteuil (FIG. 28-1), Bennencourt (FIG. 28-2A), Bougival, and Chatou (MAP 28-1). The railway line running to and from Saint-Lazare station connected Argenteuil to Paris, so transportation was not an obstacle. Parisians often would take the train out to these resort areas for a day of sailing, picnicking, and strolling

28-5 GUSTAVE CAILLEBOTTE, *Paris: A Rainy Day,* 1877. Oil on canvas, 6′ 9″ × 9′ 9″. Art Institute of Chicago, Chicago (Worcester Fund).

Although Caillebotte did not use Impressionistic broken brushstrokes, the seemingly randomly placed figures and the arbitrary cropping of the vista suggest the transitory nature of modern life.

along the Seine. BERTHE MORISOT (1841–1895), Édouard Manet's sister-in-law, regularly exhibited with the Impressionists. Most of her paintings focus on domestic subjects, the one realm of Parisian life where society allowed an upper-class woman such as Morisot free access, but she also produced many outdoor scenes, including *Villa at the Seaside* (FIG. 28-7), painted in 1874, and *Summer's Day* (FIG. 28-7A), in 1879. The subject and style of both works correlate well with Impressionist concerns.

The setting of *Villa at the Seaside* is the shaded veranda of a summer hotel at a fashionable seashore resort. A woman elegantly but not ostentatiously dressed sits gazing out across the railing to a sunlit beach. Her child, its discarded toy boat a splash of red, gazes at the passing sails on the placid sea. The mood is of relaxed leisure. Morisot used the open brushwork and the *plein air* lighting characteristic of Impressionism. Sketchy brushstrokes record her quick perceptions. Nowhere did Morisot linger on contours or enclosed details. She presented the scene in a slightly filmy, soft focus conveying a feeling of airiness. The composition also recalls the work of other Impressionists. The figures fall informally into place, as someone who shared their intimate space would perceive them. Morisot was both immensely ambitious and talented, as her ability to catch the pictorial moment demonstrates. She escaped the hostile criticism directed at most of the other Impressionists. People praised her work for its sensibility, grace, and delicacy.

28-7A MORISOT, *Summer's Day*, 1879. ◼◀

28-7 BERTHE MORISOT, *Villa at the Seaside*, 1874. Oil on canvas, 1′ 7¾″ × 2′ ⅛″. Norton Simon Art Foundation, Los Angeles. ◼◀

In this informal view of a woman and child enjoying their leisure time at a fashionable seashore resort, Morisot used swift, sketchy strokes of light colors to convey a feeling of airiness.

Impressionism **805**

Renoir on the Art of Painting

Many 19th-century artists were concerned with the theoretical basis of picturemaking. One of the most cogent statements on this subject is Pierre-Auguste Renoir's concise summary of how he, as an Impressionist, painted pictures and what he hoped to achieve as an artist.

> I arrange my subject as I want it, then I go ahead and paint it, like a child. I want a red to be sonorous, to sound like a bell; if it doesn't turn out that way, I add more reds and other colors until I get it. I am no cleverer than that. I have no rules and no methods; . . . I have no secrets. I look at a nude; there are myriads of tiny tints. I must find the ones that will make the flesh on my canvas live and quiver. . . . [I]f they could explain a picture, it wouldn't be art. Shall I tell you what I think are the two qualities of art? It must be indescribable and it must be inimitable. . . . The work of art must seize upon you, wrap you up in itself, carry you away. It is the means by which the artist conveys his passions. . . . I want people to feel that neither the setting nor the figures are dull and lifeless.*

There is certainly nothing dull or lifeless about *Le Moulin de la Galette* (FIG. 28-8), in which Renoir depicted throngs of people gathered in a popular Parisian dance hall. Some crowd the tables and chatter, while others dance energetically. So lively is the atmosphere the viewer can virtually hear the sounds of music, laughter, and tinkling glasses. The painter dappled the whole scene with sunlight and shade, artfully blurred into the figures to produce precisely the effect of floating and fleeting light the Impressionists so cultivated. Renoir's casual unposed placement of the figures and the suggested continuity of space, spreading in all directions and only accidentally limited by the frame, position the viewer as a participant rather than as an outsider. Whereas classical art sought to express universal and timeless qualities, Impressionism attempted to depict just the opposite—the incidental, momentary, and passing aspects of reality.

*Quoted in Eric Protter, ed., *Painters on Painting* (New York: Grosset & Dunlap, 1971), 145.

28-8 PIERRE-AUGUSTE RENOIR, *Le Moulin de la Galette*, 1876. Oil on canvas, 4′ 3″ × 5′ 8″. Musée d'Orsay, Paris. ◼◀

Renoir's painting of this popular Parisian dance hall is dappled by sunlight and shade, artfully blurred into the figures to produce the effect of floating and fleeting light the Impressionists cultivated.

PIERRE-AUGUSTE RENOIR Ample time for leisure activities was another facet of the new, industrialized Paris, and scenes of dining and dancing, café-concerts, opera, ballet, and other forms of urban recreation became mainstays of Impressionism. Although seemingly unrelated, industrialization facilitated these pursuits. With the advent of set working hours, people's schedules became more regimented, enabling them to plan their favorite pastimes. One Impressionist who turned repeatedly to Parisian nightlife for the subjects of his canvases was PIERRE-AUGUSTE RENOIR (1841–1919), who in 1874 painted *en plein air* alongside Monet and Manet at Argenteuil (FIG. 28-1) and was also one of the most eloquent writers on the aims of Impressionism (see "Renoir on the Art of Painting," above). His *Le Moulin de la Galette* (FIG. 28-8) of 1876 is a superb example of this Impressionist genre.

28-9 ÉDOUARD MANET, *A Bar at the Folies-Bergère,* 1882. Oil on canvas, 3′ 1″ × 4′ 3″. Courtauld Institute of Art Gallery, London. ◼◀

In this painting set in a Parisian café, Manet called attention to the canvas surface by creating spatial inconsistencies, such as the relationship between the barmaid and her apparent reflection in a mirror.

of modeling and perspective are minimal. This painting method further calls attention to the surface by forcing the viewer to scrutinize the work to make sense of the scene. But it is difficult to do so, because visual discrepancies immediately emerge. For example, what initially seems easily recognizable as a mirror behind the barmaid creates confusion throughout the rest of the painting. Is the woman on the right the barmaid's reflection? If both figures are the same person, it is impossible to reconcile the spatial relationship between the barmaid, the mirror, the bar's frontal horizontality, and the barmaid's seemingly displaced reflection. These visual contradictions reveal Manet's insistence on calling attention to the pictorial structure of his painting, in keeping with his modernist interest in examining the basic premises of the medium.

ÉDOUARD MANET The immensely versatile Manet, whose career bridged Realism (FIGS. 27-32 and 27-33) and Impressionism (FIG. 28-1), also depicted Parisian nightlife. One of his later works in the Impressionist mode is *A Bar at the Folies-Bergère* (FIG. 28-9), painted in 1882. The Folies-Bergère was a popular café with music-hall performances, one of the fashionable gathering places for Parisian revelers that many Impressionists frequented. In Manet's painting, a barmaid, centrally placed, looks out from the canvas but seems disinterested or lost in thought, divorced from her patrons as well as from the viewer. Manet blurred and roughly applied the brushstrokes, particularly those in the background, and the effects

EDGAR DEGAS Impressionists also depicted more-formal leisure activities. The fascination EDGAR DEGAS (1834–1917) had with patterns of motion brought him to the Paris Opéra (FIG. 27-45) and its ballet school. There, his keen observational power took in the formalized movements of classical ballet, one of his favorite subjects. In *The Rehearsal* (FIG. 28-10), Degas used several devices to bring the observer into the pictorial space. The frame cuts off the spiral stair, the windows in the background, and the group of figures in the right foreground. The figures are not at the center of a

28-10 EDGAR DEGAS, *The Rehearsal,* 1874. Oil on canvas, 1′ 11″ × 2′ 9″. Glasgow Art Galleries and Museum, Glasgow (Burrell Collection). ◼◀

The arbitrarily cut-off figures of dancers, the patterns of light splotches, and the blurry images reveal Degas's interest in reproducing fleeting moments, as well as his fascination with photography.

Japonisme

Despite Europe's and America's extensive colonization during the 19th century, Japan avoided Western intrusion until 1853–1854, when Commodore Matthew Perry (1794–1858) and American naval forces exacted trading and diplomatic privileges from Japan. From the increased contact, Westerners became familiar with Japanese culture. So intrigued were the French with Japanese art and culture that they coined a specific term—*Japonisme*—to describe the Japanese aesthetic, which, because of both its beauty and exoticism, greatly appealed to the fashionable segment of Parisian society. In 1867 at the Exposition Universelle in Paris, the Japanese pavilion garnered more attention than any other. Soon, Japanese kimonos, fans, lacquer cabinets, tea caddies, folding screens, tea services, and jewelry flooded Paris. Japanese-themed novels and travel books were immensely popular as well. As demand for Japanese merchandise grew in the West, the Japanese began to develop import-export businesses, and the foreign currency flowing into Japan helped to finance much of its industrialization.

Artists in particular were great admirers of Japanese art. Among those the Japanese aesthetic influenced were the Impressionists and Post-Impressionists, especially Édouard Manet, Edgar Degas, Mary Cassatt, James Abbott McNeill Whistler, Henri de Toulouse-Lautrec, Paul Gauguin, and Vincent van Gogh. Indeed, van Gogh collected and copied Japanese prints (FIG. 28-16B; compare FIG. 34-1). For the most part, the Japanese presentation of space in woodblock prints (see "Japanese Woodblock Prints," Chapter 34, page 1016), which were more readily available in the West than any other Asian art form, intrigued these artists. Because of the simplicity of the woodblock printing process, the Japanese prints feature broad areas of flat color with a limited amount of modulation or gradation. This flatness interested modernist painters, who sought ways to call attention to the picture surface. The right side of Degas's *The Tub* (FIG. 28-11), for example, has this two-dimensional quality. Degas, in fact, owned a print by Japanese artist Torii Kiyonaga depicting eight women at a bath in various poses and states of undress. That print inspired Degas's painting. A comparison between Degas's bather and a detail (FIG. 28-12) of a bather from another of Kiyonaga's prints is striking, although Degas did not closely copy any of the Japanese artist's figures. Instead he absorbed the essence of Japanese compositional style and the distinctive angles employed in representing human figures, and he translated them into the Impressionist mode.

The decorative quality of Japanese images also appealed to the artists associated with the Arts and Crafts movement in England. Artists such as William Morris (FIG. 28-34) and Charles Rennie Mackinstosh (FIG. 28-35) found Japanese prints attractive because those artworks intersected nicely with two fundamental Arts and Crafts principles: art should be available to the masses, and functional objects should be artistically designed.

1 in.

28-11 EDGAR DEGAS, *The Tub,* 1886. Pastel, 1' 11½" × 2' 8⅜". Musée d'Orsay, Paris. ◼◄

The Tub reveals the influence of Japanese prints, especially the sharp angles that artists such as Kiyonaga used in representing figures. Degas translated his Japanese model into the Impressionist mode.

28-12 TORII KIYONAGA, detail of *Two Women at the Bath,* ca. 1780. Color woodblock, full print 10½" × 7½"; detail 3¾" × 3½". Musée Guimet, Paris.

classically balanced composition. Instead, Degas arranged them in a seemingly random manner. The prominent diagonals of the wall bases and floorboards lead the viewer's eye into and along the directional lines of the dancers. Finally, as is customary in Degas's ballet pictures, a large, off-center, empty space creates the illusion of a continuous floor connecting the observer with the pictured figures.

The often arbitrarily cut-off figures, the patterns of light splotches, and the blurriness of the images in this and other Degas works indicate the artist's interest in reproducing single moments. They also reveal his fascination with photography. Degas not only studied the photographs of others but regularly used a camera to make preliminary studies for his works, particularly photographing figures in interiors. Japanese woodblock prints (see "Japonisme," page 808) were another inspirational source for paintings such as *The Rehearsal*. The cunning spatial projections in Degas's paintings probably derived in part from Japanese prints, such as those by Suzuki Harunobu (FIG. 34-12). Japanese artists used diverging lines not only to organize the flat shapes of figures but also to direct the viewer's attention into the picture space. The Impressionists, acquainted with these woodblocks as early as the 1860s, greatly admired the spatial organization, familiar and intimate themes, and flat unmodeled color areas of the Japanese prints, and avidly incorporated these features into their own paintings.

THE TUB Although color and light were major components of the Impressionists' quest to capture fleeting sensations, these artists considered other formal elements as well. Degas, for example, became a master of line, so much so his works often differ significantly from those of Monet and Renoir. Degas specialized in studies of figures in rapid and informal action, recording the quick impression of arrested motion, as is evident in *The Rehearsal* (FIG. 28-10). He often employed lines to convey his sense of movement. In *The Tub* (FIG. 28-11), inspired by a Japanese print similar to the one illustrated here (FIG. 28-12) by TORII KIYONAGA (1752–1815), a young woman crouches in a washing tub. Degas outlined the major objects in the painting—the woman, tub, and pitchers—and covered all surfaces with linear hatch marks. He was able to achieve this leaner quality by using *pastels*, his favorite medium. With these dry sticks of powered pigment, Degas drew directly on the paper, as one would with a piece of chalk, thus accounting for the linear basis of his work. Although the applied pastel is subject to smudging, the colors tend to retain their autonomy, so they appear fresh and bright.

The Tub also reveals how Degas's work, like that of the other Impressionists, continued the modernist exploration of the premises of painting by acknowledging the artwork's surface. Although the viewer clearly perceives the woman as a depiction of a three-dimensional form in space, the tabletop or shelf on the right of the image appears severely tilted, so much so it seems to parallel the picture plane. The two pitchers on the table complicate this visual conflict between the table's flatness and the illusion of the bathing woman's three-dimensional volume. The limited foreshortening of the pitchers and their shared edge, in conjunction with the rest of the image, create a visual perplexity for the viewer.

MARY CASSATT In the Salon of 1874, Degas admired a painting by a young American artist, MARY CASSATT (1844–1926), the daughter of a Philadelphia banker. Degas befriended and influenced Cassatt, who exhibited regularly with the Impressionists. She had trained as a painter before moving to Europe to study masterworks in France and Italy. As a woman, she could not easily frequent the cafés with her male artist friends, and she had the responsibility of caring for her aging parents, who had moved to Paris to join her. Because of these restrictions, Cassatt's subjects, like Morisot's (FIG. 28-7), were principally women and children, whom she presented with a combination of objectivity and genuine sentiment. Works such as *The Bath* (FIG. 28-13) show the tender relationship between a mother and child. As in Degas's *The Tub*, the visual solidity of the mother and child contrasts with the flattened patterning of the wallpaper and rug. Cassatt's style in this work owed much to the compositional devices of Degas and of Japanese prints, but the painting's design has an originality and strength all its own.

1 ft.

28-13 MARY CASSATT, *The Bath,* ca. 1892. Oil on canvas, 3′ 3″ × 2′ 2″. Art Institute of Chicago, Chicago (Robert A. Walker Fund). ◼◀

Cassatt's compositions owe much to Degas and Japanese prints, but her subjects differ from those of most Impressionist painters, in part because, as a woman, she could not frequent cafés.

Whistler on "Artistic Arrangements"

Underscoring the insistence by late-19th-century artists, both in Europe and America, that paintings are independent two-dimensional artworks and not windows opening onto the three-dimensional world, American-born James Abbott Mc-Neill Whistler, who produced his most famous works in London, called his paintings "arrangements" or "nocturnes." *Nocturne in Black and Gold* (FIG. 28-14) is a daring painting with gold flecks and splatters representing an exploded firework punctuating the darkness of the night sky. More interested in conveying the atmospheric effects than in providing details of the scene, Whistler emphasized creating a harmonious arrangement of shapes and colors on the rectangle of his canvas, an approach many 20th-century artists adopted. Whistler's works angered many 19th-century viewers, however. The British critic John Ruskin (1819–1900) responded to this painting by writing a scathing review accusing Whistler of "flinging a pot of paint in the public's face" with his style. In reply, Whistler sued Ruskin for libel. During the trial, Ruskin's attorney asked Whistler about the subject of *Nocturne*:

"What is your definition of a Nocturne?"

"It is an arrangement of line, form, and colour first; . . . Among my works are some night pieces; and I have chosen the word Nocturne because it generalizes and amplifies the whole set of them. . . . The nocturne in black and gold is a night piece and represents the fireworks at Cremorne [Gardens in London]."

"Not a view of Cremorne?"

"If it were a view of Cremorne, it would certainly bring about nothing but disappointment on the part of the beholders. It is an artistic arrangement."*

The court transcript notes the spectators in the courtroom laughed at that response, but Whistler won the case. However, his victory had sadly ironic consequences for him. The judge in the case, show-ing where his—and the public's—sympathies lay, awarded the arti[st] only one farthing (less than a penny) in damages and required hi[m] to pay all of the court costs, which ruined him financially.

*Quoted in Charles Harrison, Paul Wood, and Jason Gaiger, *Art in Theory, 1815–1900* (Oxford: Blackwell, 1998), 835–836.

28-14 James Abbott McNeill Whistler, *Nocturne in Black and Gold* (*The Falling Rocket*), ca. 1875. Oil on panel, $1' 11\frac{5}{8}'' \times 1' 6\frac{1}{2}''$. Detroit Institute of Arts, Detroit (gift of Dexter M. Ferry Jr.).

In this painting, Whistler displayed an Impressionist's interest in conveying the atmospheric effects of fireworks at night, but he also emphasized the abstract arrangement of shapes and colors.

JAMES WHISTLER Another American expatriate artist in Europe was James Abbott McNeill Whistler (1834–1903), who spent time in Paris before settling finally in London. He met many of the French Impressionists, and his art, for example, *Nocturne in Black and Gold*, or *The Falling Rocket* (FIG. 28-14), is a unique combination of some of their concerns and his own (see "Whistler on 'Artistic Arrangements,'" above). Whistler shared the Impressionists' interests in the subject of contemporary life and the sensations color produces on the eye. To these influences he added his own desire to create harmonies paralleling tho[se] achieved in music.

Nature contains the elements, in color and form, of all pictures, a[s] the keyboard contains the notes of all music. But the artist is bor[n] to pick, and choose, and group with science, these elements, that the result may be beautiful—as the musician gathers his notes, and forms his chords, until he brings forth from chaos glorious harmony.[5]

POST-IMPRESSIONISM

By 1886 most critics and a large segment of the public accepted the Impressionists as serious artists. Just when their images of contemporary life no longer seemed crude and unfinished, however, some of these painters and a group of younger followers came to feel the Impressionists were neglecting too many of the traditional elements of picturemaking in their attempts to capture momentary sensations of light and color on canvas. In a conversation with the influential art dealer Ambroise Vollard (1866–1939) in about 1883, Renoir commented: "I had wrung impressionism dry, and I finally came to the conclusion that I knew neither how to paint nor how to draw. In a word, impressionism was a blind alley, as far as I was concerned."[6] By the 1880s, some artists were more systematically examining the properties and the expressive qualities of line, pattern, form, and color. Among them were Dutch-born Vincent van Gogh and the French painter Paul Gauguin, who focused their artistic efforts on exploring the expressive capabilities of formal elements, and Georges Seurat and Paul Cézanne, also from France, who were more analytical in orientation. Because their art had its roots in Impressionist precepts and methods, but was not stylistically homogeneous, these artists and others, including Henri de Toulouse-Lautrec, became known as the *Post-Impressionists.*

HENRI DE TOULOUSE-LAUTREC Closest to the Impressionists in many ways was the French artist HENRI DE TOULOUSE-LAUTREC (1864–1901), who deeply admired Degas and shared the Impressionists' interest in capturing the sensibility of modern life. His work, however, has an added satirical edge to it and often borders on caricature. Genetic defects stunted his growth and partially crippled him, leading to his self-exile from the high society his ancient aristocratic name entitled him to enter. He became a denizen of the night world of Paris, consorting with a tawdry population of entertainers, prostitutes, and other social outcasts. He reveled in the energy of the city's music halls, such as the Moulin Rouge (FIG. 28-15) and the Jardin de Paris (FIG. 28-15A), cafés, and bordellos. *At the Moulin Rouge* reveals the influ-

28-15A TOULOUSE-LAUTREC, *Jane Avril,* 1893.

ences of Degas, of Japanese prints, and of photography in the oblique and asymmetrical composition, the spatial diagonals, and the strong line patterns with added dissonant colors. But although Toulouse-Lautrec based everything he painted on firsthand observation and the scenes he captured were already familiar to viewers in the work of the Impressionists, he so emphasized or exaggerated each element that the tone is new. Compare, for instance, the mood of *At the Moulin Rouge* with the relaxed and casual atmosphere of Renoir's *Le Moulin de la Galette* (FIG. 28-8). Toulouse-Lautrec's scene is nightlife, with its glaring artificial light, brassy music, and assortment of corrupt, cruel, and masklike faces. (He included himself in the background—the diminutive man wearing a derby hat accompanying the very tall man, his cousin.) Such distortions by simplification of the figures and faces anticipated Expressionism (see Chapter 29), when artists' use of formal elements—for example, brighter colors and bolder lines than ever before—increased the effect of the images on observers.

28-16 GEORGES SEURAT, *A Sunday on La Grande Jatte*, 1884–1886. Oil on canvas, 6′ 9″ × 10′. Art Institute of Chicago, Chicago (Helen Birch Bartlett Memorial Collection, 1926). ◼◀

Seurat's color system—pointillism—involved dividing colors into their component parts and applying those colors to the canvas in tiny dots. The forms become comprehensible only from a distance.

GEORGES SEURAT The themes GEORGES SEURAT (1859–1891) addressed in his paintings were also Impressionist subjects, but he depicted them in a resolutely intellectual way. He devised a disciplined and painstaking system of painting focused on color analysis. Seurat was less concerned with the recording of immediate color sensations than he was with their careful and systematic organization into a new kind of pictorial order. He disciplined the free and fluent play of color characterizing Impressionism into a calculated arrangement based on scientific color theory. Seurat's system, known as *pointillism* or *divisionism,* involved carefully observing color and separating it into its component parts (see "Pointillism and 19th-Century Color Theory," page 813). The artist then applies these pure component colors to the canvas in tiny dots (points) or daubs. Thus, the shapes, figures, and spaces in the image become comprehensible only from a distance, when the viewer's eyes blend the many pigment dots.

Seurat introduced pointillism to the French public at the eighth and last Impressionist exhibition in 1886, where he displayed *A Sunday on La Grande Jatte* (FIG. **28-16**). The subject of the painting is consistent with Impressionist recreational themes, and Seurat also shared the Impressionists' interest in analyzing light and color. But Seurat's rendition of Parisians at leisure is rigid and remote, unlike the spontaneous representations of Impressionism. Seurat's pointillism instead produced a carefully composed and painted image. By using meticulously calculated values, the painter carved out a deep rectangular space. He played on repeated motifs both to create flat patterns and to suggest spatial depth. Reiterating the profile of the female form, the parasol, and the cylindrical forms of the figures, Seurat placed each in space to set up a rhythmic movement in depth as well as from side to side. Sunshine fills the picture, but the painter did not break the light into transient patches of color. Light, air, people, and landscape are formal elements in an abstract design in which line, color, value, and shape cohere in a precise and tightly controlled organization. Seurat's orchestration of the many forms across the monumental (almost 7 by 10 feet) canvas created rhythmic cadence harmonizing the entire composition.

Seurat once stated: "They see poetry in what I have done. No, apply my method, and that is all there is to it."[7] Despite this claim, Seurat's art is much more than a scientifically based system. *La Grande Jatte* reveals the painter's recognition of the tenuous and shifting social and class relationships at the time. La Grande Jatte (The Big Bowl) is an island in the Seine River near Asnières, one of late-19th-century Paris's rapidly growing industrial suburbs. Seurat's painting captures public life on a Sunday—a congregation of people from various classes, from the sleeveless worker lounging in the left foreground, to the middle-class man and woman seated next to him. Most of the people wear their Sunday best, making class distinctions less obvious.

VINCENT VAN GOGH In marked contrast to Seurat, VINCENT VAN GOGH (1853–1890) explored the capabilities of color

Pointillism and 19th-Century Color Theory

In the 19th century, advances in the sciences contributed to changing theories about color and how people perceive it. Many physicists and chemists immersed themselves in studying optical reception and the behavior of the human eye in response to light of differing wavelengths. They also investigated the psychological dimension of color. These new ideas about color and its perception provided a framework within which artists such as Georges Seurat (FIG. 28-16) worked. Although historians do not know which publications on color Seurat himself read, he no doubt relied on aspects of these evolving theories to develop pointillism.

Discussions of color often focus on *hue* (for example, red, yellow, and blue), but it is important to consider the other facets of color—*saturation* (the hue's brightness or dullness) and *value* (the hue's lightness or darkness). Most artists during the 19th century understood the concepts of *primary colors* (red, yellow, and blue), *secondary colors* (orange, purple, and green), and *complementary colors* (red and green, yellow and purple, blue and orange; see Introduction, page 7).

Chemist Michel-Eugène Chevreul (1786–1889) extended artists' understanding of color dynamics by formulating the law of *simultaneous contrasts* of colors. Chevreul asserted juxtaposed colors affect the eye's reception of each, making the two colors as dissimilar as possible, both in hue and value. For example, placing light green next to dark green has the effect of making the light green look even lighter and the dark green darker. Chevreul further provided an explanation of *successive contrasts*—the phenomenon of colored afterimages. When a person looks intently at a color (green, for example) and then shifts to a white area, the fatigued eye momentarily perceives the complementary color (red).

Charles Blanc (1813–1882), who coined the term *optical mixture* to describe the visual effect of juxtaposed complementary colors, asserted the smaller the areas of adjoining complementary colors, the greater the tendency for the eye to "mix" the colors, so that the viewer perceives a grayish or neutral tint. Seurat used this principle frequently in his paintings.

Also influential for Seurat was the work of physicist Ogden Rood (1831–1902), who published his ideas in *Modern Chromatics, with Applications to Art and Industry* in 1879. Expanding on the ideas of Chevreul and Blanc, Rood constructed an accurate and understandable diagram of contrasting colors. Further (and particularly significant to Seurat), Rood explored representing color gradation. He suggested artists could achieve gradation by placing small

Detail of *A Sunday on La Grande Jatte* (FIG. 28-16).

1 ft.

dots or lines of color side by side, which he observed blended in the eye of the beholder when viewed from a distance.

The color experiments of Seurat and other late-19th-century artists were also part of a larger discourse about human vision and how people see and understand the world. The theories of physicist Ernst Mach (1838–1916) focused on the psychological experience of sensation. He believed humans perceive their environments in isolated units of sensation the brain then recomposes into a comprehensible world. Another scientist, Charles Henry (1859–1926), also pursued research into the psychological dimension of color—how colors affect people, and under what conditions. He went even further to explore the physiological effects of perception. Seurat's work, though characterized by a systematic and scientifically minded approach, also incorporated his concerns about the emotional tone of the images.

nd distorted forms to express his emotions as he confronted nature. The son of a Dutch Protestant pastor, van Gogh believed he had a religious calling and did missionary work in the coal-mining area of Belgium. Repeated professional and personal failures brought him close to despair. Only after he turned to painting did he find a way to communicate his experiences. He completed his first major work, *The Potato Eaters* (FIG. 28-16A), when he was 32 years old. Five years later, considering himself a failure as an artist and an outcast not only from artistic circles but also from society at large, van Gogh fatally shot himself. He sold only one painting during his lifetime. Since his death, however, van Gogh's reputation and the

appreciation of his art have grown dramatically. Subsequent painters, especially the Fauves and German Expressionists (see Chapter 29), built on van Gogh's use of color and the expressiveness of his art. This kind of influence is an important factor in determining artistic significance, and it is no exaggeration to state that today van Gogh is one of the most revered artists in history.

28-16A VAN GOGH, *The Potato Eaters*, 1885.

The Letters of Vincent van Gogh

Throughout his life, Vincent van Gogh wrote letters to his brother Theo van Gogh (1857–1891), a Parisian art dealer, on matters both mundane and philosophical. The letters are precious documents of the vicissitudes of the painter's life and reveal his emotional anguish. In many of the letters, van Gogh also forcefully stated his views about art, including his admiration for Japanese prints (FIG. 28-16B). In one letter, he told Theo: "In both my life and in my painting, I can very well do without God but I cannot, ill as I am, do without something which is greater than I, . . . the power to create."* For van Gogh, the power to create involved the expressive use of color. "Instead of trying to reproduce exactly what I have before my eyes, I use color more arbitrarily so as to express myself forcibly."† Color in painting, he argued, is "not locally true from the point of view of the delusive realist, but color suggesting some emotion of an ardent temperament."‡

Some of van Gogh's letters contain vivid descriptions of his paintings, which are invaluable to art historians in gauging his intentions and judging his success. For example, about *Night Café* (FIG. 28-17), he wrote:

I have tried to express the terrible passions of humanity by means of red and green. The room is blood red and dark yellow with a green billiard table in the middle; there are four citron-yellow lamps with a glow of orange and green. Everywhere there is a clash and contrast of the most disparate reds and greens in the figures

28-17 VINCENT VAN GOGH, *Night Café,* 1888. Oil on canvas, 2′ 4½″ × 3′. Yale University Art Gallery, New Haven (bequest of Stephen Carlton Clark).

In *Night Café,* van Gogh explored ways colors and distorted forms can express emotions. The thickness, shape, and direction of the brushstrokes create a tactile counterpart to the intense colors.

of little sleeping hooligans, in the empty, dreary room, in violet and blue. The blood-red and the yellow-green of the billiard table, for instance, contrast with the soft, tender Louis XV green of the counter, on which there is a pink nosegay. The white coat of the landlord, awake in a corner of that furnace, turns citron-yellow, or pale luminous green.§

*Vincent van Gogh to Theo van Gogh, September 3, 1888, in W. H. Auden, ed., *Van Gogh: A Self-Portrait. Letters Revealing His Life as a Painter* (New York: Dutton, 1963), 319.
†August 11, 1888. Ibid., 313.
‡September 8, 1888. Ibid., 321.
§September 8, 1888. Ibid., 320.

28-16B VAN GOGH, *Flowering Plum Tree,* 1887.

NIGHT CAFÉ Van Gogh moved to Paris in 1886, where he began to collect—and copy (FIG. 28-16B)—Japanese prints. In 1888, he relocated to Arles in southern France, where he painted *Night Café* (FIG. 28-17), one of his most important and innovative canvases. Although the subject is apparently benign, van Gogh invested it with a charged energy. As he stated in a letter to his brother Theo (see "The Letters of Vincent van Gogh," above), he wanted the painting to convey an oppressive atmosphere—"a place where one can ruin oneself, go mad, or commit a crime."8 The proprietor rises like a specter from the edge of the billiard table, which the painter depicted in such a steeply tilted perspective that it threatens to slide out of the painting into the viewer's space. Van Gogh communicated the "madness" of the place by selecting vivid hues whose juxtaposition augmented their intensity. His insistence

on the expressive values of color led him to develop a corresponding expressiveness in his paint application. The thickness, shape, and direction of his brushstrokes created a tactile counterpart to his intense color schemes. He moved the brush vehemently back and forth or at right angles, giving a textilelike effect, or squeezed dots or streaks onto his canvas from his paint tube. This bold, almost slapdash attack enhanced the intensity of his colors.

STARRY NIGHT Similarly illustrative of van Gogh's "expressionist" method is *Starry Night* (FIG. 28-18), which the artist painted in 1889, the year before his death. At this time, van Gogh was living at the asylum of Saint-Paul-de-Mausole in Saint-Rémy, near Arles where he had committed himself. In *Starry Night,* the artist did not represent the sky's appearance. Rather, he communicated his feelings about the electrifying vastness of the universe, filled with whirling and exploding stars, with the earth and humanity huddling beneath it. The church nestled in the center of the village is, perhaps, van

28-18 VINCENT VAN GOGH, *Starry Night*, 1889. Oil on canvas, 2′ 5″ × 3′ ¼″. Museum of Modern Art, New York (acquired through the Lillie P. Bliss Bequest). ◼◀

In this late work, van Gogh painted the vast night sky filled with whirling and exploding stars, the earth huddled beneath it. The painting is an almost abstract pattern of expressive line, shape, and color.

lent brushstrokes, the color suggests a quiet but pervasive depression. A letter van Gogh wrote to his brother on July 16, 1888, reveals his contemplative state of mind:

> Perhaps death is not the hardest thing in a painter's life. . . . [L]ooking at the stars always makes me dream, as simply as I dream over the black dots representing towns and villages on a map. Why, I ask myself, shouldn't the shining dots of the sky be as accessible as the black dots on the map of France? Just as we take the train to get to Tarascon or Rouen, we take death to reach a star.[9]

PAUL GAUGUIN After painting as an amateur, PAUL GAUGUIN (1848–1903) took lessons with Camille Pissarro and then resigned from his prosperous brokerage business in 1883 to devote his time entirely to painting. As van Gogh did, Gauguin rejected objective representation in favor of subjective expression. He also broke with the Impressionists' studies of minutely contrasted hues because he believed color above all must be expressive. For Gauguin, the artist's power to determine the colors in a painting was a central element of creativity. However, whereas van Gogh's heavy, thick brushstrokes were an important component of his expressive style, Gauguin's color areas appear flatter, often visually dissolving into abstract patches or patterns.

Gogh's attempt to express or reconcile his conflicted views about religion. Although the style of *Starry Night* suggests a very personal vision, this work does correspond in many ways to the view available to the painter from the window of his room in Saint-Paul-de-Mausole. The existence of cypress trees and the placement of the constellations have been confirmed as matching the view visible to van Gogh during his stay in the asylum. Still, the artist translated everything he saw into his unique vision. Given van Gogh's determination to "use color . . . to express [him]self forcibly," the dark, deep blue suffusing the entire painting cannot be overlooked. Together with the turbu-

In 1886, attracted by Brittany's unspoiled culture, its ancient Celtic folkways, and the still-medieval Catholic piety of its people, Gauguin moved to Pont-Aven. Although in the 1870s and 1880s, Brittany had been transformed into a profitable market economy, Gauguin still viewed the Bretons as "natural" men and women, perfectly at ease in their unspoiled peasant environment. At Pont-Aven, he painted *Vision after the Sermon* (FIG. **28-19**), also known as *Jacob Wrestling with the Angel,* a work in which he decisively rejected both Realism and Impressionism. The painting shows Breton women, wearing their starched white Sunday caps and black dresses, visualizing the

28-19 PAUL GAUGUIN, *Vision after the Sermon* (*Jacob Wrestling with the Angel*), 1888. Oil on canvas, 2′ 4¾″ × 3′ ½″. National Gallery of Scotland, Edinburgh. ◼◀

Gauguin admired Japanese prints, stained glass, and cloisonné enamels. Their influences are evident in this painting of Breton women, in which firm outlines enclose large areas of unmodulated color.

Gauguin on *Where Do We Come From?*

Paul Gauguin's *Where Do We Come From? What Are We? Where Are We Going?* (FIG. 28-20), painted in Tahiti in 1897, was, in the artist's judgment, his most important work. It can be read as a summary of his artistic methods and of his views on life. The scene is a tropical landscape, populated with native women and children. Despite the setting, most of the canvas surface, other than the figures, consists of broad areas of flat color, which convey a lushness and intensity.

Two of Gauguin's letters to friends contain lengthy discussions of this work and shed important light on the artist's intentions and on the painting's meaning.

> Where are we going? Near to death an old woman. . . . What are we? Day to day existence. . . . Where do we come from? Source. Child. Life begins. . . . Behind a tree two sinister figures, cloaked in garments of sombre colour, introduce, near the tree of knowledge, their note of anguish caused by that very knowledge in contrast to some simple beings in a virgin nature, which might be paradise as conceived by humanity, who give themselves up to the happiness of living.*

> I wanted to kill myself. I went to hide in the mountains, where my corpse would have been eaten up by ants. I didn't have a revolver but I did have arsenic . . . Was the dose too large, or was it the fact of vomiting, which overcame the effects of the poison by getting

rid of it? I know not. . . . . Before I died I wanted to paint a large canvas that I had worked out in my head, and all month long I worked day and night at fever pitch. I can assure you it's nothing like a canvas by Puvis de Chavannes [FIG. 28-23], with studies from nature, then a preparatory cartoon, etc. No, it's all done without a model, feeling my way with the tip of the brush on a piece of sackcloth that is full of knots and rough patches; so it looks terribly unpolished. [Contrary to this assertion, Gauguin did make a detailed preliminary drawing, now in the Louvre, for *Where Do We Come From?* He is here altering the facts in order to establish a persona for himself as an inspired genius who created great works without recourse to traditional studio methods.] People will say it is slipshod, unfinished . . . [but] I do believe that not only is this painting worth more than all the previous ones but also that I will never do a better one or another like it. I put all my energy into it before dying, such painful passion amid terrible circumstances . . . and life burst from it.†

Where Do We Come From? is, therefore, a sobering, pessimistic image of the life cycle's inevitability.

*Letter to Charles Morice, March 1898. Translated by Belinda Thompson, *Gauguin by Himself* (Boston: Little, Brown, 1993), 270–271.
†Letter to Daniel de Monfreid, February 1898. Translated by Thompson, ibid., 257–258.

28-20 PAUL GAUGUIN, *Where Do We Come From? What Are We? Where Are We Going?* 1897. Oil on canvas, 4′ 6¾″ × 12′ 3″. Museum of Fine Arts, Boston (Tompkins Collection).

In search of a place far removed from European materialism, Gauguin moved to Tahiti, where he used native women and tropical colors to present a pessimistic view of the inevitability of the life cycle.

sermon they have just heard in church on Jacob's encounter with the Holy Spirit (Gen. 32:24–30). The women pray devoutly before the apparition, as they would have before the roadside crucifix shrines that were characteristic features of the Breton countryside. Gauguin departed from optical realism and composed the picture elements to focus the viewer's attention on the idea and intensify its message.

The images are not what the Impressionist eye would have seen and replicated but what memory would have recalled and imagination would have modified. Thus the artist twisted the perspective and allotted the space to emphasize the innocent faith of the unquestioning women, and he shrank Jacob and the angel, wrestling in a ring enclosed by a Breton stone fence, to the size of fighting cocks

Wrestling matches were regular features at the entertainment held after high mass, so Gauguin's women are spectators at a contest that was, for them, a familiar part of their culture.

Gauguin did not unify the picture with a horizon perspective, light and shade, or naturalistic use of color. Instead, he abstracted the scene into a pattern. Pure unmodulated color fills flat planes and shapes bounded by firm line: white caps, black dresses, and the red field of combat. The shapes are angular, even harsh. The caps, the sharp fingers and profiles, and the hard contours suggest the austerity of peasant life and ritual. Gauguin admired Japanese prints, stained glass, and *cloisonné* metalwork (FIGS. 11-2 and 11-3). These art forms contributed to his daring experiment to transform traditional painting and Impressionism into abstract, expressive patterns of line, shape, and pure color. His revolutionary method found its first authoritative expression in *Vision after the Sermon.*

WHERE DO WE COME FROM? After a brief period of association with van Gogh in Arles in 1888, Gauguin, in his restless search for provocative subjects and for an economical place to live, settled in Tahiti (MAP 36-1). The South Pacific island attracted Gauguin because he believed it offered him a life far removed from materialistic Europe and an opportunity to reconnect with nature. Upon his arrival, he discovered that Tahiti, under French control since 1842, had been extensively colonized. Disappointed, Gauguin tried to maintain his vision of an untamed paradise by moving to the Tahitian countryside, where he expressed his fascination with primitive life in a series of canvases in which he often based the design, although indirectly, on native motifs. The tropical flora of the island inspired the colors he chose for these paintings—unusual harmonies of lilac, pink, and lemon.

Despite the allure of the South Pacific, Gauguin continued to struggle with life. His health suffered, and his art had a hostile reception. In 1897, worn down by these obstacles, Gauguin decided to take his own life, but not before painting a large canvas titled *Where Do We Come From? What Are We? Where Are We Going?* (FIG. 28-20), which he wrote about in letters to his friends (see "Gauguin on *Where Do We Come From?*" page 816). His attempt to commit suicide in Tahiti was unsuccessful, but Gauguin died a few years later, in 1903, in the Marquesas Islands, his artistic genius still unrecognized.

PAUL CÉZANNE Although a lifelong admirer of Delacroix, PAUL CÉZANNE (1839–1906) allied himself early in his career with the Impressionists, especially Pissarro (FIG. 28-6). He at first accepted their color theories and their faith in subjects chosen from everyday life, but his own studies of the Old Masters in the Louvre persuaded him Impressionism lacked form and structure. Cézanne declared he wanted to "make of Impressionism something solid and durable like the art of the museums."[10]

The basis of Cézanne's art was his unique way of studying nature in works such as *Mont Sainte-Victoire* (FIG. 28-21), one of many views he painted of this mountain near his home in Aix-en-Provence. His aim was not truth in appearance, especially not photographic truth, nor was it the "truth" of Impressionism. Rather, he sought a lasting structure behind the formless and fleeting visual information the eyes absorb. Instead of employing the Impressionists' random approach when he was face-to-face with nature, Cézanne developed a more analytical style. His goal was to order the lines, planes, and colors comprising nature. He constantly and painstakingly checked his painting against the part of the scene—he called it the "motif"—he was studying at the moment. In a March 1904 letter, Cézanne stated his goal as a painter: "[to do] Poussin over entirely from nature . . . in the open air, with color and light, instead of one of those works imagined in a studio, where

28-21 PAUL CÉZANNE, *Mont Sainte-Victoire*, 1902–1904. Oil on canvas, 2′ 3½″ × 2′ 11¼″. Philadelphia Museum of Art, Philadelphia (George W. Elkins Collection). ◼◀

In his landscapes, Cézanne replaced the transitory visual effects of changing atmospheric conditions—the Impressionists' focus—with careful analysis of the lines, planes, and colors of nature.

everything has the brown coloring of feeble daylight without reflections from the sky and sun."[11] He sought to achieve Poussin's effects of distance, depth, structure, and solidity not by using traditional perspective and chiaroscuro but by recording the color patterns he deduced from an optical analysis of nature.

With special care, Cézanne explored the properties of line, plane, and color and their interrelationships. He studied the effect of every kind of linear direction, the capacity of planes to create the sensation of depth, the intrinsic qualities of color, and the power of colors to modify the direction and depth of lines and planes. To create the illusion of three-dimensional form and space, Cézanne focused on carefully selecting colors. He understood the visual properties—hue, saturation, and value—of different colors vary (see "Color Theory," page 813). Cool colors tend to recede, whereas warm ones advance. By applying to the canvas small patches of juxtaposed colors, some advancing and some receding, Cézanne created volume and depth in his works. On occasion, the artist depicted objects chiefly in one hue and achieved convincing solidity by modulating the intensity (or saturation). At other times, he juxtaposed contrasting colors—for example, green, yellow, and red—of similar saturation (usually in the middle range rather than the highest intensity) to compose specific objects, such as fruit or bowls.

In *Mont Sainte-Victoire,* Cézanne replaced the transitory visual effects of changing atmospheric conditions, effects that preoccupied Monet, with a more concentrated, lengthier analysis of the colors in large lighted spaces. The main space stretches out behind and beyond the canvas plane and includes numerous small elements, such as roads, fields, houses, and the viaduct at the far right, each seen from a slightly different viewpoint. Above this shifting, receding perspective rises the largest mass of all, the mountain, with an effect—achieved by equally stressing background and foreground contours—of being simultaneously near and far away. This portrayal approximates the experience a person has when viewing the landscape forms piecemeal. The relative proportions of objects vary rather than being fixed by strict perspective, such as that normally found in a photograph. Cézanne immobilized the shifting colors of Impressionism into an array of clearly defined planes composing the objects and spaces in his scene. Describing his method in a letter to a fellow painter, he wrote:

> [T]reat nature by the cylinder, the sphere, the cone, everything in proper perspective so that each side of an object or a plane is directed towards a central point. Lines parallel to the horizon give breadth . . . Lines perpendicular to this horizon give depth. But nature for us men is more depth than surface, whence the need of introducing into our light vibrations, represented by reds and yellows, a sufficient amount of blue to give the impression of air.[12]

BASKET OF APPLES Still life was another good vehicle for Cézanne's experiments, as he could arrange a limited number of selected objects to provide a well-ordered point of departure. So analytical was Cézanne in preparing, observing, and painting still lifes (in contrast to the Impressionist emphasis on spontaneity) that he had to abandon using real fruit and flowers because they tended to rot. In *Basket of Apples* (FIG. 28-22), the objects have lost something of their individual character as bottles and fruit and have almost become cylinders and spheres. Cézanne captured the solidity of each object by juxtaposing color patches. His interest in the study of volume and solidity is evident from the disjunctures in the painting—the table edges are discontinuous, and various objects seem to be depicted from different vantage points. In his zeal to understand three-dimensionality and to convey the placement of forms relative to the space around them, Cézanne explored his still-life arrangements from different viewpoints. This resulted in paintings that, though conceptually coherent, do not appear optically realistic. Cézanne created what might be called, paradoxically, an architecture of color.

In keeping with the modernist concern with the integrity of the painting surface, Cézanne's methods never allow the viewer to disregard the actual two-dimensionality of the picture plane.

28-22 **PAUL CÉZANNE,** *Basket of Apples,* ca. 1895. Oil on canvas, 2′ $\frac{3}{8}$″ × 2′ 7″. **Art Institute of Chicago, Chicago (Helen Birch Bartlett Memorial Collection, 1926).** ◼◀

Cézanne's still lifes reveal his analytical approach to painting. He captured the solidity of bottles and fruit by juxtaposing color patches, but the resulting abstract shapes are not optically realistic.

28-22A CÉZANNE, *Large Bathers*, 1906.

In this manner, Cézanne achieved a remarkable feat—presenting the viewer with two-dimensional and three-dimensional images simultaneously. His late works, such as his unfinished *The Large Bathers* (FIG. **28-22A**), profoundly influenced the development of Cubism in the early 20th century (see Chapter 29).

SYMBOLISM

The Impressionists and Post-Impressionists believed their emotions and sensations were important elements for interpreting nature, but the depiction of nature remained a primary focus of their efforts. By the end of the 19th century, the representation of nature became completely subjective. Artists no longer sought to imitate nature but created free interpretations of it, concerned solely with expressing their individual spirit. They rejected the optical world as observed in favor of a fantasy world, of forms they conjured in their free imagination, with or without reference to things conventionally seen. Color, line, and shape, divorced from conformity to the optical image, became symbols of personal emotions in response to the world. Deliberately choosing to stand outside of convention and tradition, artists spoke in signs and symbols, as if they were prophets.

Many of the artists following this path adopted an approach to subject and form that associated them with a general European movement called *Symbolism*. Symbolists, whether painters or writers, disdained Realism as trivial. The task of Symbolist artists, both visual and verbal, was not to see things but to see through them to a significance and reality far deeper than what superficial appearance revealed. In this function, as the poet Arthur Rimbaud (1854–1891) insisted, artists became beings of extraordinary insight. (One group of Symbolist painters called itself the *Nabis,* the Hebrew word for

"prophet.") Rimbaud, whose poems had great influence on the artistic community, went so far as to say, in his *Letter from a Seer* (1871), that to achieve the seer's insight, artists must become deranged. In effect, they must systematically unhinge and confuse the everyday faculties of sense and reason, which served only to blur artistic vision. The artists' mystical vision must convert the objects of the commonsense world into symbols of a reality beyond that world and, ultimately, a reality from within the individual. Elements of Symbolism appeared in the works of van Gogh and Gauguin, but their art differed from mainstream Symbolism in their insistence on showing unseen powers as linked to a physical reality, instead of attempting to depict an alternate, wholly interior life.

The extreme subjectivism of the Symbolists led them to cultivate all the resources of fantasy and imagination, no matter how deeply buried or obscure. Moreover, they urged artists to stand against the vulgar materialism and conventional mores of industrial and middle-class society. Above all, the Symbolists wished to purge literature and art of anything utilitarian, to cultivate an exquisite aesthetic sensitivity. The subjects of the Symbolists, conditioned by this reverent attitude toward art and exaggerated aesthetic sensation, became increasingly esoteric and exotic, mysterious, visionary, dreamlike, and fantastic. Perhaps not coincidentally, contemporary with the Symbolists, Sigmund Freud (1856–1939), the founder of psychoanalysis, began the age of psychiatry with his *Interpretation of Dreams* (1900), an introduction to the concept and the world of unconscious experience.

PIERRE PUVIS DE CHAVANNES Although he never formally identified himself with the Symbolists, the French painter PIERRE PUVIS DE CHAVANNES (1824–1898) became the "prophet" of those artists. Puvis rejected Realism and Impressionism and went his own way in the 19th century, serenely unaffected by these movements. He produced an ornamental and reflective art—a dramatic rejection of Realism's noisy everyday world. In *Sacred Grove* (FIG. **28-23**), which may have influenced Seurat's *Grande Jatte*

28-23 PIERRE PUVIS DE CHAVANNES, *Sacred Grove,* 1884. Oil on canvas, 2′ 11½″ × 6′ 10″. Art Institute of Chicago, Chicago (Potter Palmer Collection).

The Symbolists revered Puvis de Chavannes for his rejection of Realism. His statuesque figures in timeless poses inhabit a tranquil landscape, their gestures suggesting a symbolic ritual significance.

(FIG. 28-16), he deployed statuesque figures in a tranquil landscape with a classical shrine. Suspended in timeless poses, the figures' contours are simple and sharp, and their modeling is as shallow as *bas-relief*. The calm and still atmosphere suggests some consecrated place where all movements and gestures have a permanent ritual significance. The stillness and simplicity of the forms, the linear patterns their rhythmic contours create, and the suggestion of their symbolic weight constitute a type of anti-Realism. Puvis garnered support from a wide range of artists. The conservative French Academy and the government applauded his classicism. The Symbolists revered Puvis for his vindication of imagination and his independence from the capitalist world of materialism and the machine.

GUSTAVE MOREAU In keeping with Symbolist tenets, GUSTAVE MOREAU (1826–1898) gravitated toward subjects inspired by dreaming, which was as remote as possible from the everyday world. Moreau presented these subjects sumptuously, and his natural love of sensuous design led him to incorporate gorgeous color, intricate line, and richly detailed shape in all his paintings.

The Apparition (FIG. 28-24), one of two versions of the same subject Moreau submitted to the Salon of 1876, treats a theme that fascinated him and many of his contemporaries—the *femme fatale* (fatal woman), the destructive temptress of men. The seductive heroine here is the biblical Salome (Mark 6:211–28), who danced enticingly before her stepfather, King Herod, and demanded

28-24A MOREAU, *Jupiter and Semele*, ca. 1875.

in return the head of Saint John the Baptist (compare FIG. 21-8). In Moreau's representation of the story, Herod sits in the background, enthroned not in a Middle Eastern palace but in a classical columnar hall resembling a Roman triumphal arch. Salome is in the foreground, scantily clad in a gold- and gem-encrusted costume. She points to an apparition hovering in the air at the level of Herod's head. In a radiant circle of light is the halo-framed head of John the Baptist that Salome desired, dripping with blood but with eyes wide open. The combination of hallucinatory imagery, eroticism, precise drawing, rich color, and opulent setting is the hallmark of Moreau's highly original style (compare FIG. 28-24A). His paintings foreshadow the work of the Surrealists in the next century (see Chapter 29).

ODILON REDON Like Moreau, fellow French Symbolist ODILON REDON (1840–1916) was a visionary. He had been aware of an intense inner world since childhood and later wrote of "imaginary things" haunting him. Redon adapted the Impressionist palette and stippling brushstroke for a very different purpose. In *The Cyclops* (FIG. 28-25), Redon projected a figment of the imagination as if it were visible, coloring it whimsically with a rich profusion of fresh saturated hues that harmonized with the mood he felt fit the subject. The fetal head of the shy, simpering Polyphemus, with its single huge loving eye, rises balloonlike above the sleeping Galatea. The image born of the dreaming world and the color

28-24 GUSTAVE MOREAU, *The Apparition*, 1874–1876. Watercolor on paper, 3′ 5¾″ × 2′ 4⅜″. Musée du Louvre, Paris.

Moreau's painting of Salome, a biblical femme fatale, combines hallucinatory imagery, eroticism, precise drawing, rich color, and an opulent setting—hallmarks of Moreau's Symbolist style.

analyzed and disassociated from the waking world come together here at the artist's will. The contrast with Raphael's representation of the same subject (FIG. 22-11) could hardly be more striking. As Redon himself observed: "All my originality consists . . . in making unreal creatures live humanly by putting, as much as possible, the logic of the visible at the service of the invisible."[13]

HENRI ROUSSEAU The imagination of HENRI ROUSSEAU (1844–1910) engaged a different but equally powerful world of personal fantasy. Gauguin had journeyed to the South Seas in search of primitive innocence. Rousseau was a "primitive" without leaving Paris—a self-taught amateur who turned to painting full-time only after his retirement from service in the French government. Nicknamed "Le Douanier" (The Customs Inspector), he first exhibited in the Salon of 1885 when he was 41. Derided by the critics, Rousseau turned to the Salon des Indépendants in 1886 and thereafter exhibited his works there almost every year until his death. Even in that more liberal venue, Rousseau still received almost universally unfavorable reviews because of his lack of formal training, imperfect perspective, doll-like figures, and settings resembling constructed theater sets more than natural landscapes. Rousseau compensated for his apparent visual, conceptual, and technical naïveté with a natural talent for design and an imagination teeming with exotic images of mysterious tropical landscapes, which are the setting for two of his most famous works, *Sleeping Gypsy* (FIG. 28-26) of 1897 and *The Dream* (FIG. 28-26A), painted 13 years later. In the earlier painting, the recumbent figure occupies a desert

28-26A ROUSSEAU, *The Dream*, 1910.

world, silent and secret, and dreams beneath a pale, perfectly round moon. In the foreground, a lion resembling a stuffed, but somehow menacing, animal doll sniffs at the gypsy. A critical encounter impends—an encounter of the type that recalls the uneasiness of a person's vulnerable subconscious self during sleep—a subject of central importance to Rousseau's contemporary, Sigmund Freud. Rousseau's art of drama and fantasy has its own sophistication and, after the artist's death, influenced the development of Surrealism (see Chapter 29).

JAMES ENSOR Not all Symbolist artists were French. The leading Belgian painter of the late 19th century was JAMES ENSOR (1860–1949), the son of an expatriate Englishman and a Flemish mother, who spent most of his life in the seaside resort village of Ostend, far from the artistic centers of Europe. In 1883 he cofounded Les Vingts (The Twenty), a group of Belgian artists who staged unjuried exhibitions in Brussels modeled on the independent salons of Paris. A fervent nationalist, he left the group when it began to exhibit the work of foreign artists. In fact, Ensor's most monumental

28-25 ODILON REDON, *The Cyclops,* 1898. Oil on canvas, 2′ 1″ × 1′ 8″. Kröller-Müller Foundation, Otterlo.

In *The Cyclops*, the Symbolist painter Odilon Redon projected a figment of the imagination as if it were visible, coloring it whimsically with a rich profusion of hues adapted from the Impressionist palette.

28-26 HENRI ROUSSEAU, *Sleeping Gypsy,* 1897. Oil on canvas, 4′ 3″ × 6′ 7″. Museum of Modern Art, New York (gift of Mrs. Simon Guggenheim).

In *Sleeping Gypsy*, Rousseau depicted a doll-like but menacing lion sniffing at a recumbent dreaming figure in a mysterious landscape. The painting suggests the vulnerable subconscious during sleep.

28-27 JAMES ENSOR, *Christ's Entry into Brussels in 1889*, 1888. Oil on canvas, 8' 3½" × 14' 1½". J. Paul Getty Museum, Los Angeles.

Ensor's gigantic canvas is an indictment of corrupt modern values. Christ enters Brussels on a donkey in 1889, ignored by the dense crowd of soldiers and citizens wearing grotesque, grimacing masks.

work, *Christ's Entry into Brussels in 1889* (FIG. **28-27**), is very likely a critical response to Georges Seurat's *La Grande Jatte* (FIG. 28-16), exhibited by Les Vingt in 1887.

Whereas Seurat's canvas celebrates the leisure activities of contented bourgeois Parisians, Ensor's even larger (14 feet long) painting is a socialist commentary on the decadence and alienation of urban life at the end of the 19th century. The giant canvas is the artist's pessimistic vision of how Christ would be greeted if he entered the Belgian capital in 1889. Christ is a small and insignificant figure on a donkey in the background of the painting, ignored by the dense crowd of soldiers and citizens wearing grotesque masks inspired by the papier-mâché carnival masks Ensor's family sold in their curio shop in Ostend. Some of the people carry banners and signs. One reads "Long Live Jesus, King of Brussels," another "Long Live Socialism." Complementing the ugly, grimacing masked faces of the anonymous crowd, which eloquently express Ensor's condemnation of the corrupt values of modern society, are the discordant combination of reds, blues, and greens and the coarse texture of the thickly applied oil pigment. As an indictment of the immorality of modern life, Ensor's canvas has few equals.

EDVARD MUNCH Also linked in spirit to the Symbolists were the English artist AUBREY BEARDSLEY (1872–1898; FIG. **28-27A**) and the Norwegian EDVARD MUNCH (1863–1944). Munch felt deeply the pain of human life. He believed humans were powerless before the great natural forces of death and love. The emotions associated with them—jealousy, loneliness, fear, desire, despair—became the theme of most of his art. Because Munch's goal was

to describe the conditions of "modern psychic life," as he put it, Realist and Impressionist techniques were inappropriate, focusing as they did on the tangible world. In the spirit of Symbolism, Munch used color, line, and figural distortion for expressive ends. Influenced by Gauguin, Munch produced both paintings and prints whose high emotional charge was a major source of inspiration for the German Expressionists in the early 20th century (see Chapter 29).

28-27A BEARDSLEY, *The Peacock Skirt*, 1894.

Munch's *The Scream* (FIG. **28-28**) exemplifies his style. The image—a man standing on a bridge or jetty in a landscape—comes from the real world, but Munch's treatment of the image departs significantly from visual reality. *The Scream* evokes a visceral, emotional response from the viewer because of the painter's dramatic presentation. The man in the foreground, simplified to almost skeletal form, emits a primal scream. The landscape's sweeping curvilinear lines reiterate the shapes of the man's mouth and head, almost like an echo, as the cry seems to reverberate through the setting. The fiery red and yellow stripes that give the sky an eerie glow also contribute to this work's resonance. Munch wrote a revealing epigraph to accompany the painting: "I stopped and leaned against the balustrade, almost dead with fatigue. Above the blue-black fjord hung the clouds, red as blood and tongues of fire. My friends had left me, and alone, trembling with anguish, I became aware of the vast, infinite cry of nature."[14] Appropriately, the original title of this work was *Despair*.

FIN-DE-SIÈCLE Historians have adopted the term *fin-de-siècle,* which literally means "end of the century," to describe the spirit of dissolution and anxiety that characterized European, and especially Austrian, culture of the late 1800s. This designation is not merely chronological but also refers to a certain sensibility. The increasingly large and prosperous middle classes aspired to the advantages the aristocracy traditionally enjoyed. They too strove to live "the good life," which evolved into a culture of decadence and indulgence. Characteristic of the fin-de-siècle period was an intense preoccupation with sexual drives, powers, and perversions. People at the end of the century also immersed themselves in an exploration of the unconscious. This culture was unrestrained and freewheeling, but the determination to enjoy life masked an anxiety prompted by significant political upheaval and an uncertain future. The country most closely associated with fin-de-siècle culture was Austria.

GUSTAV KLIMT The Viennese artist GUSTAV KLIMT (1863–1918) captured this period's flamboyance in his work but tempered it with unsettling undertones. In *The Kiss* (FIG. 28-29), his best-known work, Klimt depicted a couple locked in an embrace. The setting is ambiguous, an indeterminate place apart from time and space. Moreover, all the viewer sees of the embracing couple is a small segment of each body—and virtually nothing of the man's face. The rest of the canvas dissolves into shimmering, extravagant flat patterning. This patterning has clear ties to Art Nouveau and to the Arts and Crafts movement (discussed later) and also evokes the conflict between two- and three-dimensionality intrinsic to the work of Degas and other modernists. In *The Kiss,* however, those patterns also signify gender contrasts—rectangles for the man's garment, circles for the woman's. Yet the patterning also unites the two lovers into a single formal entity, underscoring their erotic union.

GERTRUDE KÄSEBIER Photography, which during the 19th century most people regarded as the ultimate form of Realism, could also be manipulated by artists to produce effects more akin to painting than to factual records of contemporary life. After the first great breakthroughs (see Chapter 27), which bluntly showed what was before the eye, some photographers began to pursue

entire image slightly. In *Blessed Art Thou among Women*, the soft focus invests the whole scene with an aura of otherworldly peace. The photograph showcases Käsebier's ability to inject a sense of the spiritual and the divine into scenes from everyday life.

SCULPTURE

The three-dimensional art of sculpture could not capture the optical sensations many painters favored in the later 19th century. Its very nature—its tangibility and solidity—suggests permanence. Consequently, the sculptors of this period pursued artistic goals markedly different from those of contemporaneous painters and photographers.

JEAN-BAPTISTE CARPEAUX In France, Jean-Baptiste Carpeaux (1827–1875) combined an interest in Realism with a love of ancient, Renaissance, and Baroque sculpture. He based his group *Ugolino and His Children* (FIG. 28-31) on a passage in Dante's *Inferno* (33.58–75) in which Count Ugolino and his four sons starve to death while shut up in a tower. In Hell, Ugolino relates to Dante how, in a moment of extreme despair, he bit both his hands in grief. His children, thinking he did it because of his hunger, offered him

28-30 GERTRUDE KÄSEBIER, *Blessed Art Thou among Women*, 1899. Platinum print on Japanese tissue, $9\frac{3}{8}'' \times 5\frac{1}{2}''$. Museum of Modern Art, New York (gift of Mrs. Hermine M. Turner).

Symbolist Käsebier injected a sense of the spiritual and the divine into scenes from everyday life. The deliberately soft focus of this photograph invests the scene with an aura of otherworldly peace.

new ways of using the medium as a vehicle of artistic expression. A leading practitioner of what might be called the pictorial style in photography was the American GERTRUDE KÄSEBIER (1852–1934), who took up the camera in 1897 after raising a family and working as a portrait painter. She soon became famous for photographs with Symbolist themes, such as *Blessed Art Thou among Women* (FIG. 28-30). The title repeats the phrase the angel Gabriel used to announce to the Virgin Mary that she will be the mother of Jesus. In the context of Käsebier's photography, the words suggest a parallel between the biblical Mother of God and the modern mother in the image, who both protects and sends forth her daughter. The white setting and the mother's pale gown shimmer in soft focus behind the serious girl, who wears darker tones and whom the photographer captured with sharper focus. Käsebier deliberately combined an out-of-focus background with a sharp or almost-sharp foreground in order to achieve an expressive effect by blurring the

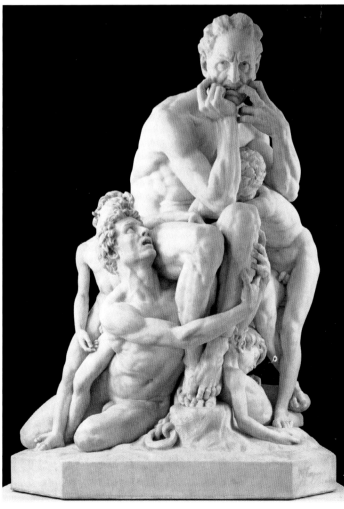

28-31 JEAN-BAPTISTE CARPEAUX, *Ugolino and His Children*, 1865–1867. Marble, 6′ 5″ high. Metropolitan Museum of Art, New York (Josephine Bay Paul and C. Michael Paul Foundation, Inc., and the Charles Ulrich and Josephine Bay Foundation, Inc., gifts, 1967).

As in Dante's *Inferno*, Carpeaux represented Ugolino biting his hands in despair as he and his sons await death by starvation. The twisted forms suggest the self-devouring torment of frustration.

Rodin on Movement in Art and Photography

Photography had a profound effect on 19th-century art, and many artists used photographs as an aid in capturing "reality" on canvas or in stone. Eadweard Muybridge's photographs of a galloping horse (FIG. 27-54), for example, definitively established that at certain times all four hooves of the animal are in the air. But not all artists believed photography was "true to life." The sculptor Auguste Rodin (FIGS. 28-32, 28-32A, and 28-33) was one of the doubters.

I have always sought to give some indication of movement [in my statues]. I have very rarely represented complete repose. I have always endeavoured to express the inner feelings by the mobility of the muscles. . . . The illusion of life is obtained in our art by good modelling and by movement. . . . [M]ovement is the transition from one attitude to another. . . . Have you ever attentively examined instantaneous photographs of walking figures? . . . [Photographs] present the odd appearance of a man suddenly stricken with paralysis and petrified in his pose. . . . If, in fact, in instantaneous photographs, the figures, though taken while moving, seem suddenly fixed in mid-air, it is because, all parts of the body being reproduced exactly at the same twentieth or fortieth of a second, there is no progressive development of movement as there is in art. . . . [I]t is the artist who is truthful and it is photography which lies, for in reality time does not stop.*

* Translated by Robin Fedden, in Elizabeth Gilmore Holt, ed., *From the Classicists to the Impressionists: Art and Architecture in the 19th Century* (New Haven, Conn.: Yale University Press, 1966; reprint 1986), 406–409.

28-32 AUGUSTE RODIN, *Walking Man*, 1905. Bronze, 6′ 11¾″ high. Musée d'Orsay, Paris.

In this study for a statue of Saint John the Baptist, Rodin depicted a headless and armless figure in midstride. *Walking Man* demonstrates Rodin's mastery of anatomy and ability to capture transitory motion.

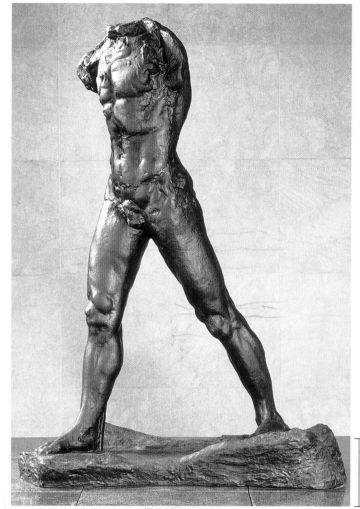

1 ft.

28-31A CARPEAUX, *The Dance*, 1867–1869.

their own flesh as food. In Carpeaux's statuary group, the powerful forms—twisted, intertwined, and densely concentrated—suggest the self-devouring torment of frustration and despair wracking the unfortunate Ugolino. A careful student of Michelangelo's male figures, Carpeaux also said he had the Laocoön group (FIG. 5-89) in mind. Certainly, the storm and stress of *Ugolino and His Children* recall similar characteristics of that ancient work. Regardless of these influences, the sense of vivid reality in the anatomy of Carpeaux's figures shows the artist's interest in study from life. The French public did not share that interest, however, and preferred the idealized bodies of classical sculptures—one of the reasons Carpeaux was forced to remove *The Dance* (FIG. 28-31A) from the facade of the Paris opera house (FIG. 27-45).

AUGUSTE RODIN The leading French sculptor of the later 19th century was AUGUSTE RODIN (1840–1917), who conceived and executed his sculptures with a Realist sensibility. The human body in

motion (see "Rodin on Movement in Art and Photography," above) fascinated Rodin, as it did Eakins and Muybridge (FIG. 27-54) before him. Rodin was also well aware of the Impressionists' innovations. Although color was not a significant factor in Rodin's work, the influence of Impressionism is evident in the artist's abiding concern for the effect of light on sculpted surfaces. When focusing on the human form, he joined his profound knowledge of anatomy and movement with special attention to the body's exterior, saying, "The sculptor must learn to reproduce the surface, which means all that vibrates on the surface, soul, love, passion, life. . . . Sculpture is thus the art of hollows and mounds, not of smoothness, or even polished planes."[15] Primarily a modeler of pliable material rather than a carver of hard wood or stone, Rodin worked his surfaces with fingers sensitive to the subtlest variations of surface, catching the fugitive play of constantly shifting light on the body. In his studio, he often would have a model move around in front of him while he created preliminary versions of his sculptures with coils of clay.

In *Walking Man* (FIG. 28-32), a preliminary study for the sculptor's *Saint John the Baptist Preaching*, Rodin succeeded in representing a fleeting moment in cast bronze. He portrayed a headless and armless figure in midstride at the moment when weight is transferred across the pelvis from the back leg to the front. In addition to capturing the sense of the transitory, Rodin demonstrated his mastery of realistic detail in his meticulous rendition of muscle, bone, and tendon.

GATES OF HELL Rodin also made many nude and draped studies for each of the figures in two of his most ambitious works—the life-size group *Burghers of Calais* (FIG. **28-32A**) and the *Gates of Hell* (FIG. **28-33**), which occupied the sculptor for two decades. After he failed to gain admission to the École des Beaux-Arts, Rodin enrolled in the École Impériale Spéciale de Dessin et Mathématiques, the French school of decorative arts, known as the "Petit École" (Little School) because it was a lesser version of the more prestigious Beaux-Arts academy. Nonetheless, Rodin gained attention for the outstanding realism of some of his early sculptures, and on August 16, 1880, he received a major governmental commission to design a pair of doors for a planned Museum of Decorative Arts in Paris. Rodin worked on the project for 20 years, but the museum was never built (the Musée d'Orsay now occupies the intended site). It was not until after the sculptor's death that others cast his still-unfinished doors in bronze.

28-32A RODIN, *Burghers of Calais*, 1884–1889.

The commission permitted Rodin to choose his own subject. He selected *The Gates of Hell,* based on Dante's *Inferno* and Baudelaire's *Flowers of Evil.* Originally inspired by Lorenzo Ghiberti's *Gates of Paradise* (FIG. 21-9), which he had seen in Florence, Rodin quickly abandoned the idea of a series of framed narrative panels and decided instead to cover each of the doors with a continuous writhing mass of tormented men and women, sinners condemned to Dante's second circle of Hell for their lust. Because of the varying height of the relief and the variegated surfaces, the figures seem to be in flux, moving in and out of an undefined space in a reflection of their psychic turmoil. The dreamlike (or rather, the nightmarish) vision connects Rodin with the Symbolists, and the pessimistic mood exemplifies the fin-de-siècle spirit. The swirling composition and emotionalism recall Eugène Delacroix's *Death of Sardanapalus* (FIG. 27-15) and Michelangelo's *Last Judgment* (FIG. 22-19). But Rodin's work defies easy stylistic classification.

The nearly 200 figures of *The Gates of Hell* spill over onto the jambs and the lintel. Rodin also included freestanding figures, which, cast separately in multiple versions, are among his most famous works. Above the doors, *The Three Shades* is a trio of twisted nude male figures, essentially the same figure with elongated arms in three different positions. The group evokes Jean Baptiste Carpeaux's *Ugolino and His Children* (FIG. 28-31). *The Thinker,* Rodin's famous seated nude man with a powerful body who rests his chin

28-33 AUGUSTE RODIN, *The Gates of Hell,* 1880–1900 (cast in 1917). Bronze, 20′ 10″ × 13′ 1″. Musée Rodin, Paris.

Rodin's most ambitious work, inspired by Dante's *Inferno* and Ghiberti's *Gates of Paradise* (FIG. 21-9), presents nearly 200 tormented sinners in relief below *The Three Shades* and *The Thinker.*

on his clenched right hand, ponders the fate of the tormented souls on the doors below. *The Gates of Hell,* more than 20 feet tall, was Rodin's most ambitious project. It greatly influenced the painters and sculptors of the Expressionist movements of the early 20th century (see Chapter 29).

Rodin's ability to capture the quality of the transitory through his highly textured surfaces while revealing larger themes and deeper, lasting sensibilities is one of the reasons he had a strong influence on 20th-century artists. Because many of his works, such as

28-33A SAINT-GAUDENS, *Adams Memorial*, 1886–1891.

Walking Man, were deliberate fragments, he was also instrumental in creating a taste for the incomplete, an aesthetic many later sculptors embraced enthusiastically.

AUGUSTUS SAINT GAUDENS

Other leading sculptors of the late 19th century pursued more traditional goals, however. In America, for example, AUGUSTUS SAINT-GAUDENS (1848–1907) produced monumental statues expressing the majestic calm of ancient Greek and Roman sculpture, as in his *Adams Memorial* (FIG. 28-33A) in Washington, D.C.

ARCHITECTURE AND DECORATIVE ARTS

The decisive effects of industrialization were impossible to ignore, and although many artists embraced this manifestation of "modern life" or at least explored its effects, other artists, especially those associated with the Arts and Crafts movement in England, decried the impact of rampant industrialism. This movement, which developed during the last decades of the 19th century, was shaped by the ideas of John Ruskin, the critic who skewered Whistler's "arrangements" (see "Whistler," page 810), and the artist William Morris. Both men shared a distrust of machines and industrial capitalism, which they believed alienated workers from their own nature. Accordingly, they advocated an art "made by the people for the people as a joy for the maker and the user."[16] This condemnation of capitalism and support for manual laborers were consistent with the tenets of socialism, and many artists in the Arts and Crafts movement, especially in England, considered themselves socialists and participated in the labor movement.

This democratic, or at least populist, attitude carried over to the art they produced as well. Members of the Arts and Crafts movement dedicated themselves to making functional objects with high aesthetic value for a wide public. They advocated a style based on natural, rather than artificial, forms, which often consisted of repeated designs of floral or geometric patterns. For Ruskin, Morris, and others in the Arts and Crafts movement, high-quality artisanship and honest labor were crucial ingredients of superior works of decorative art.

WILLIAM MORRIS To promote these ideals, WILLIAM MORRIS (1834–1896) formed a decorating firm dedicated to Arts and Crafts principles: Morris, Marshall, Faulkner, and Company, Fine Arts Workmen in Painting, Carving, Furniture, and Metals. His company did a flourishing business producing wallpaper, textiles, furniture, books, rugs, stained glass, tiles, and pottery. In 1867, Morris received the commission to decorate the Green Dining Room (FIG. 28-34) at London's South Kensington Museum (now the Victoria & Albert Museum), the center of public art education and home of decorative art collections. The range of room features—windows, lights, and *wainscoting* (paneling on the lower part of interior walls)—Morris created for this unified, beautiful, and functional environment was all-encompassing. Nothing escaped his eye. Morris's design for this room also reveals the penchant of Arts and Crafts designers for intricate patterning.

28-34 WILLIAM MORRIS, Green Dining Room, South Kensington Museum (now Victoria & Albert Museum), London, England, 1867.

William Morris was a founder of the Arts and Crafts movement. His Green Dining Room exemplifies the group's dedication to creating intricately patterned yet unified and functional environments.

28-35 CHARLES RENNIE MACKINTOSH and MARGARET MACDONALD MACKINTOSH, Ladies' Luncheon Room, Ingram Street Tea Room, Glasgow, Scotland, 1900–1912. Reconstructed (1992–1995) in the Glasgow Art Galleries and Museum, Glasgow.

The Mackintoshes' Ladies' Luncheon Room in Glasgow features functional and exquisitely designed Arts and Crafts decor, including stained-glass windows and pristinely geometric furnishings.

CHARLES RENNIE MACKINTOSH Numerous Arts and Crafts societies in America, England, and Germany carried on this ideal of artisanship. In Scotland, CHARLES RENNIE MACKINTOSH (1868–1929) designed a number of tea rooms, including the Ladies' Luncheon Room (FIG. **28-35**) located in the Ingram Street Tea Room in Glasgow. The room decor is consistent with Morris's vision of a functional, exquisitely designed art. The chairs, stained-glass windows, and large panels of colored gesso with twine, glass beads, thread, mother-of-pearl, and tin leaf—made by MARGARET MACDONALD MACKINTOSH (1864–1933), an artist-designer and Mackintosh's wife, who collaborated with him on many projects—are all pristinely geometric and rhythmical in design.

ART NOUVEAU An important international architectural and design movement that developed out of the ideas the Arts and Crafts movement promoted was *Art Nouveau* (New Art), which took its name from a shop in Paris called L'Art Nouveau. Known by that name in France, Belgium, Holland, England, and the United States, the style had other names in other places: *Jugendstil* in Austria and Germany (after the magazine *Jugend,* "youth"), *Modernismo* in Spain, and *Floreale* in Italy. Proponents of this movement tried to synthesize all the arts in a determined attempt to create art based on natural forms that could be mass-produced for a large audience. The Art Nouveau style adapted the twining plant form to the needs of architecture, painting, sculpture, and all of the decorative arts.

28-36 VICTOR HORTA, staircase in the Van Eetvelde House, Brussels, 1895.

The Art Nouveau movement was an attempt to create art and architecture based on natural forms. Here, every detail conforms to the theme of the twining plant and functions as part of a living whole.

VICTOR HORTA The mature Art Nouveau style of the 1890s is on display in the houses the Belgian architect VICTOR HORTA (1861–1947) designed. A characteristic example is the staircase (FIG. **28-36**) in the Van Eetvelde House, which Horta built in Brussels in 1895, three years after designing the Tassel House (FIG. **28-36A**), his first major commission. Every detail of the Van Eetvelde interior functions as part of a living whole. Furniture, drapery folds, veining in the lavish stone paneling, and the patterning of the door moldings join with real plants to provide graceful counterpoints for the twining-plant theme. Metallic tendrils curl around the railings and posts, delicate metal tracery fills the glass dome, and floral and leaf motifs spread across the fabric panels of the screen. Flower and plant motifs also figure prominently in the immensely popular stained-glass lamps (FIG. **28-36B**) of LOUIS COMFORT TIFFANY (1848–1933).

The Art Nouveau style reflects several influences. In addition to the rich, foliated two-dimensional ornamentation of Arts and Crafts design and that movement's respect for materials, the sinuous whiplash curve of Japanese print designs (FIG. 34-13) inspired Art Nouveau artists. Art Nouveau also borrowed from the expressively patterned styles of van Gogh (FIGS. 28-17 and 28-18), Gauguin (FIGS. 28-19 and 28-20), and their Post-Impressionist and Symbolist contemporaries.

ANTONIO GAUDI Art Nouveau achieved its most personal expression in the work of the Spanish architect ANTONIO GAUDI (1852–1926). Before becoming an architect, Gaudi had trained as an ironworker. As many young artists of his time, he longed to create a style both modern and appropriate to his country. Taking inspiration from Moorish architecture and from the simple architecture of his native Catalonia, Gaudi developed a personal aesthetic. He conceived a building as a whole and molded it almost as a sculptor might shape a figure from clay. Although work on his designs proceeded slowly under the guidance of his intuition and imagination, Gaudi was a master who invented many new structural techniques that facilitated construction of his visions. His Barcelona apartment house, Casa Milá (FIG. **28-37**), is a wondrously free-form mass wrapped around a street corner. Lacy iron railings enliven the swelling curves of the cut-stone facade. Dormer windows peep from the undulating tiled roof, from which fantastically writhing chimneys poke energetically into the air above. The rough surfaces of the stone walls suggest naturally worn rock. The entrance portals look like eroded sea caves, but their design also may reflect the excitement that swept Spain following the 1879 discovery of Paleolithic cave paintings at Altamira (FIG. 1-9). Gaudi felt each of his buildings was symbolically a living thing, and the passionate naturalism of his Casa Milá is the spiritual kin of early-20th-century Expressionist painting and sculpture (see Chapter 29).

28-37 ANTONIO GAUDI, Casa Milá (looking north), Barcelona, Spain, 1907.

Spanish Art Nouveau architect Gaudi conceived this apartment house as if it were a gigantic sculpture to be molded from clay. Twisting chimneys cap the undulating roof and walls.

28-38 Alexandre-Gustave Eiffel, Eiffel Tower (looking southeast), Paris, France, 1889. ◼◀

New materials and technologies and the modernist aesthetic fueled radically new architectural designs in the late 19th century. Eiffel jolted the world with the exposed iron skeleton of his tower.

ALEXANDRE-GUSTAVE EIFFEL In the later 19th century, new technologies and the changing needs of urbanized, industrialized society affected architecture throughout the Western world. Since the 18th century, bridges had been built of cast iron (FIG. 26-12), which enabled engineering advancements in the construction of larger, stronger, and more fire-resistant structures. Steel, available after 1860, made it possible for architects to enclose ever larger spaces, such as those found in railroad stations (FIG. 28-4) and exposition halls. The Realist impulse also encouraged architectural designs that honestly expressed a building's purpose, rather than elaborately disguising its function. The elegant metal-skeleton structures of the French engineer-architect ALEXANDRE-GUSTAVE EIFFEL (1832–1923) were responses to this idea, and they constituted an important contribution to the development of the 20th-century skyscraper. A native of Burgundy, Eiffel trained in Paris before beginning a distinguished career designing exhibition halls, bridges, and the interior armature for France's anniversary gift to the United States—the *Statue of Liberty* by Frédéric Auguste Bartholdi (1834–1904).

Eiffel designed his best-known work, the Eiffel Tower (FIG. 28-38), for an exhibition in Paris in 1889. Originally seen as a symbol of modern Paris and still considered a symbol of 19th-century civilization, the elegant iron tower thrusts its needle shaft 984 feet above the city, making it at the time of its construction (and for some time thereafter) the world's tallest structure. The tower rests on four giant supports connected by gracefully arching open-frame skirts that provide a pleasing mask for the heavy horizontal girders needed to strengthen the legs. Visitors can take two successive elevators to the top, or they can use the internal staircase. Either way, the view of Paris and the Seine from the tower is incomparable, as is the design of the tower itself. The transparency of Eiffel's structure blurs the distinction between interior and exterior to an extent never before achieved or even attempted. This interpenetration of inner and outer space became a hallmark of 20th-century art and architecture. Eiffel's tower and the earlier iron skeletal frames designed by Labrouste (FIG. 27-46) and Paxton (FIG. 27-47) jolted the architectural profession into a realization that modern materials and processes could germinate a completely new style and a radically innovative approach to architectural design.

AMERICAN SKYSCRAPERS The desire for greater speed and economy in building, as well as for a reduction in fire hazards, prompted the use of cast and wrought iron for many building programs, especially commercial ones. Designers in both England and the United States enthusiastically developed cast-iron architecture until a series of disastrous fires in the early 1870s in New York, Boston, and Chicago demonstrated that cast iron by itself was far from impervious to fire. This discovery led to encasing the metal in masonry, combining the first material's strength with the second's fire resistance.

In cities, convenience required closely grouped buildings, and increased property values forced architects literally to raise the roof. Even an attic could command high rentals if the builders installed one of the new elevators, used for the first time in the Equitable Building in New York (1868–1871). Metal, which could support these towering structures, gave birth to the American skyscraper.

28-39 Henry Hobson Richardson, Marshall Field wholesale store, Chicago, 1885–1887 (demolished 1930).

Richardson was a pioneer in designing commercial structures using a cast-iron skeleton encased in fire-resistant masonry. This construction technique enabled the insertion of large windows in the walls.

HENRY HOBSON RICHARDSON One of the pioneers in designing these modern commercial structures was Henry Hobson Richardson (1838–1886), but he also had a profound respect for earlier architectural styles. Because Richardson had a special fondness for the Romanesque architecture of the Auvergne area in France, he frequently used heavy round arches and massive masonry walls. Architectural historians sometimes consider his work to constitute a Romanesque revival related to the Neo-Gothic style (FIGS. 27-43 and 27-43A). This designation does not do credit to the originality and quality of most of the buildings Richardson designed during his brief 18-year practice. Trinity Church in Boston and his smaller public libraries, residences, railroad stations, and courthouses in New England and elsewhere best demonstrate his vivid imagination and the solidity (the sense of enclosure and permanence) so characteristic of his style. However, his most important and influential building was the Marshall Field wholesale store (FIG. 28-39) in Chicago, begun in 1885 and demolished in 1930. This vast building occupied an entire city block. Designed for the most practical of purposes, it nonetheless recalled historical styles without imitating them. The tripartite elevation of a Renaissance palace (FIG. 21-37) or of the Roman aqueduct (FIG. 7-33) near Nîmes, France, may have been close to Richardson's mind. But he used no classical ornamentation, made much of the massive courses of masonry, and, in the strong horizontality of the window-sills and the interrupted courses defining the levels, stressed the long sweep of the building's lines, as well as the edifice's ponderous weight. Although the structural frame still lay behind and in conjunction with the masonry screen, the great glazed arcades opened up the walls of the monumental store. They pointed the way to the modern total penetration of walls and the transformation of them into mere screens or curtains that serve both to echo the underlying structural grid and to protect it from the weather.

LOUIS HENRY SULLIVAN As skyscrapers proliferated, architects refined the visual vocabulary of these buildings. Louis Henry Sullivan (1856–1924), whom many architectural historians call the first truly modern architect, arrived at a synthesis of industrial structure and ornamentation that perfectly expressed the spirit of late-19th-century commerce. To achieve this, he used the latest technological developments to create light-filled, well-ventilated office buildings and adorned both exteriors and interiors with ornate embellishments. Such decoration served to connect commerce and culture, and imbued these white-collar workspaces with a sense of refinement and taste. These characteristics are evident in the Guaranty (Prudential) Building (FIG. 28-40) in Buffalo, built

28-40 Louis Henry Sullivan, Guaranty (Prudential) Building (looking southwest), Buffalo, New York, 1894–1896.

Sullivan drew on the latest technologies to create this light-filled, well-ventilated Buffalo office building. He added ornate surface embellishments to impart a sense of refinement and taste.

Sullivan's slogan was "form follows function." He tailored the design of this steel, glass, and stone Chicago department store to meet the needs of its employees and customers.

28-40A SULLIVAN, Wainwright Building, St. Louis, 1890–1891.

between 1894 and 1896, and in his earlier Wainwright Building (FIG. 28-40A) in St. Louis. The Buffalo skyscraper is steel, sheathed with terracotta. The imposing scale of the building and the regularity of the window placements served as an expression of the large-scale, refined, and orderly office work taking place within. Sullivan tempered the severity of the structure with lively ornamentation, both on the piers and cornice on the exterior of the building and on the stairway balustrades, elevator cages, and ceiling in the interior. The Guaranty Building illustrates Sullivan's famous dictum "form follows function," which became the slogan of many early-20th-century architects. Still, Sullivan did not advocate a rigid and doctrinaire correspondence between exterior and interior design. Rather, he espoused a free and flexible relationship—one his pupil Frank Lloyd Wright (see Chapter 29) later described as similar to that between the hand's bones and tissue.

Sullivan also designed the Carson, Pirie, Scott Building (FIG. 28-41) in Chicago. Built between 1899 and 1904, this department store required broad, open, well-illuminated display spaces. Sullivan again used a minimal structural steel skeleton to achieve this goal. The architect gave over the lowest two levels of the building to an ornament in cast iron (of his invention) made of wildly fantastic motifs. He regarded the display windows as pictures, which merited elaborate frames. As in the Guaranty Building, Sullivan revealed his profound understanding of the maturing consumer economy and tailored the Carson, Pirie, Scott Building to meet the functional and symbolic needs of its users.

Thus, in architecture as well as in the pictorial arts, the late 19th century was a period during which artists challenged traditional modes of expression, often emphatically rejecting the past. Architects and painters as different as Sullivan, Monet, van Gogh, and Cézanne, each in his own way, contributed significantly to the entrenchment of modernism as the new cultural orthodoxy of the early 20th century (see Chapter 29).

IMPRESSIONISM, POST-IMPRESSIONISM, SYMBOLISM: EUROPE AND AMERICA, 1870 TO 1900

IMPRESSIONISM

▌ A hostile critic applied the term *Impressionism* to the paintings of Claude Monet because of their sketchy quality. The Impressionists—Monet, Pierre-Auguste Renoir, Edgar Degas, and others—strove to capture fleeting moments and transient effects of light and climate on canvas. They also focused on recording the contemporary urban scene in Paris, frequently painting bars, dance halls, the ballet, wide boulevards, and railroad stations.

▌ Complementing the Impressionists' sketchy, seemingly spontaneous brushstrokes are the compositions of their paintings. Reflecting the influence of Japanese prints and photography, Impressionist works often have arbitrarily cut-off figures and settings seen at sharply oblique angles.

Renoir, *Le Moulin de la Galette,* 1876

POST-IMPRESSIONISM AND SYMBOLISM

▌ Post-Impressionism is not a unified style. The term refers to the group of late-19th-century artists, including Georges Seurat, Vincent van Gogh, Paul Gauguin, and Paul Cézanne, who followed the Impressionists and took painting in new directions. Seurat refined the Impressionist approach to color and light into pointillism—the disciplined application of pure color in tiny daubs. Van Gogh explored the capabilities of colors and distorted forms to express emotions. Gauguin, an admirer of Japanese prints, moved away from Impressionism in favor of large areas of flat color bounded by firm lines. Cézanne replaced the transitory visual effects of the Impressionists with a rigorous analysis of the lines, planes, and colors that make up landscapes and still lifes.

▌ Gustave Moreau, Odilon Redon, and Henri Rousseau were the leading French Symbolists. They disdained Realism as trivial and sought to depict a reality beyond that of the everyday world, rejecting materialism and celebrating fantasy and imagination. Their subjects were often mysterious, exotic, and sensuous.

van Gogh, *Starry Night,* 1889

Rousseau, *Sleeping Gypsy,* 1897

SCULPTURE

▌ Sculpture cannot capture transitory optical effects or explore the properties of color and line, and late-19th-century sculptors pursued goals different from those of contemporaneous painters.

▌ The leading figure of the era was Auguste Rodin, who explored Realist themes and the representation of movement. His vision of tormented, writhing figures in Hell connects his work with the Symbolists. Rodin also made statues that were deliberate fragments, creating a taste for the incomplete that appealed to many later sculptors.

Rodin, *Gates of Hell,* 1880–1900

ARCHITECTURE AND DECORATIVE ARTS

▌ Not all artists embraced the industrialization transforming daily life during the 19th century. The Arts and Crafts movement in England and the international Art Nouveau style formed in opposition to modern mass production. Both schools advocated natural forms and high-quality craftsmanship.

▌ New technologies and the changing needs of urbanized, industrialized society transformed architecture in the late 19th century. The exposed iron skeleton of the Eiffel Tower jolted architects into realizing how modern materials and processes could revolutionize architectural design. Henry Hobson Richardson and Louis Sullivan were pioneers in designing the first metal, stone, and glass skyscrapers.

Eiffel, Eiffel Tower, Paris, 1889

NOTES

Introduction

1. Quoted in George Heard Hamilton, *Painting and Sculpture in Europe, 1880–1940*, 6th ed. (New Haven, Conn.: Yale University Press, 1993), 345.

2. Quoted in *Josef Albers: Homage to the Square* (New York: Museum of Modern Art, 1964), n.p.

Chapter 2

1. Translated by Françoise Tallon, in Prudence O. Harper et al., *The Royal City of Susa* (New York: Metropolitan Museum of Art, 1991), 132.

Chapter 3

1. The chronology adopted in this chapter is that of John Baines and Jaromír Malék, *Atlas of Ancient Egypt* (Oxford: Oxford University Press, 1980), 36–37. The division of kingdoms is that of, among others, Mark Lehner, *The Complete Pyramids* (New York: Thames & Hudson, 1997), 89, and David P. Silverman, ed., *Ancient Egypt* (New York: Oxford University Press, 1997), 20–39.

2. Translated by James P. Allen, *The Ancient Egyptian Pyramid Texts* (Atlanta, Ga.: Society of Biblical Literature, 2005), 31.

3. Allen, 57.

4. Allen, 56.

Chapter 4

1. Homer, *Iliad*, 2.466–649.

Chapter 5

1. Diodorus Siculus, *Library of History*, 1.91.

2. Pausanias, *Description of Greece*, 5.16.1.

3. Plutarch, *Life of Pericles*, 12.

4. Pliny, *Natural History*, 34.74.

5. Ibid., 36.20.

6. Lucian, *Amores*, 13–14; *Imagines*, 6.

7. Plutarch, *Moralia*, 335A–B. Translated by J. J. Pollitt, *The Art of Ancient Greece: Sources and Documents* (New York: Cambridge University Press, 1990), 99.

8. Pliny, *Natural History*, 35.110.

9. Ibid., 34.88.

Chapter 7

1. Livy, *History of Rome*, 25.40.1–3.

2. Juvenal, *Satires*, 3.225, 232.

Chapter 8

1. Translated by Raymond Davis, *The Book of Pontiffs* (Liverpool: Liverpool University Press, 1989), 18–19.

Chapter 9

1. Paulus Silentiarius, *Descriptio Sanctae Sophiae*, 617–646. Translated by Cyril Mango, *The Art of the Byzantine Empire, 312–1453: Sources and Documents* (reprint of 1972 ed., Toronto: University of Toronto Press, 1986), 85–86.

2. Procopius, *De aedificiis*, 1.1.23ff. Translated by Mango, 74.

3. Paulus Silentiarius, *Descriptio*, 489, 668. Translated by Mango, 83, 86.

4. Translated by Colin Luibheid, *Pseudo-Dionysius: The Complete Works* (New York: Paulist Press, 1987), 68ff.

5. Procopius, 1.1.23ff. Translated by Mango, 75.

6. *Libri Carolini*, 4.2. Translated by Herbert L. Kessler, *Spiritual Seeing: Picturing God's Invisibility in Medieval Art* (Philadelphia: University of Pennsylvania Press, 2000), 119.

7. Nina G. Garsoïan, "Later Byzantium," in John A. Garraty and Peter Gay, eds., *The Columbia History of the World* (New York: Harper & Row, 1972), 453.

8. Garsoïan, 460.

Chapter 11

1. Translated by Françoise Henry, *The Book of Kells* (New York: Alfred A. Knopf, 1974), 165.

2. *Beowulf*, 3162–3164. Translated by Kevin Crossley-Holland (New York: Farrar, Straus & Giroux, 1968), 119.

3. *Beowulf*, 33.

4. Translated by John W. Williams, in *The Art of Medieval Spain A.D. 500–1200* (New York: Metropolitan Museum of Art, 1993), 156.

5. Translated by Adam S. Cohen, *The Uta Codex* (University Park: Pennsylvania University Press, 2000), 11, 41.

Chapter 12

1. Translated by Calvin B. Kendall, *The Allegory of the Church: Romanesque Portals and Their Verse Inscriptions* (Toronto: University of Toronto Press, 1998), 207.

2. Translated by John Williams, *A Spanish Apocalypse: The Morgan Beatus Manuscript* (New York: George Braziller, 1991), 223.

3. Translated by Charles P. Parkhurst Jr., in Elizabeth G. Holt, *A Documentary History of Art* (Princeton, N.J.: Princeton University Press, 2d ed., 1981), 1: 18.

4. Translated by Giovanna De Appolonia, Boston University.

5. Bernard of Clairvaux, *Apologia* 12.28. Translated by Conrad Rudolph, *The "Things of Greater Importance": Bernard of Clairvaux's* Apologia *and the Medieval Attitude toward Art* (Philadelphia: University of Pennsylvania Press, 1990), 281, 283.

6. *Rule of Saint Benedict*, 57.1. Translated by Timothy Fry, *The Rule of St. Benedict* (Collegeville, Minn.: Liturgical Press, 1981), 265.

Chapter 13

1. Giorgio Vasari, "Introduzione alle tre arti del disegno" (1550), ch. 3, in Paul Frankl, *The Gothic: Literary Sources and Interpretation through Eight Centuries* (Princeton, N.J.: Princeton University Press, 1960), 290–291, 859–860.

2. Dante, *Divine Comedy*, Purgatory, 11.81.

3. Translated by Roland Behrendt, *Johannes Trithemius, In Praise of Scribes: De laude scriptorum* (Lawrence, Kansas: Coronado Press, 1974), 71.

4. Frankl, *The Gothic*, 55.

Chapter 20

1. Francisco de Hollanda, *De pintura antigua* (1548), quoted in Robert Klein and Henri Zerner, *Italian Art, 1500–1600: Sources and Documents* (Englewood Cliffs, N.J.: Prentice-Hall, 1966), 33.

Chapter 21

1. Ghiberti, *I commentarii,* II. Quoted in Elizabeth Gilmore Holt, ed., *A Documentary History of Art, I: The Middle Ages and the Renaissance* (Princeton, N.J.: Princeton University Press, 1981), 157–158.

2. Translated by Catherine Enggass, in Howard Saalman, ed., *Antonio Manetti, Life of Brunelleschi* (University Park: Pennsylvania State University Press, 1970), 42.

3. Giorgio Vasari, *Life of Lorenzo Ghiberti.* Translated by Gaston du C. de Vere, ed., *Giorgio Vasari, Lives of the Painters, Sculptors, and Architects* (New York: Knopf, 1996), 1: 304.

4. Ghiberti, *I commentarii,* II. Quoted in Holt, 161.

5. Quoted in H. W. Janson, *The Sculpture of Donatello* (Princeton, N.J.: Princeton University Press, 1965), 154.

6. Vasari, *Life of Masaccio.* Translated by Gaston du C. de Vere, 1: 318.

7. Martial, *Epigrams,* 10.32.

Chapter 22

1. Plato, *Ion,* 534. Translated by Benjamin Jowett, *The Dialogues of Plato,* 4th ed., vol. 1 (Oxford: Clarendon Press, 1953), 107–108.

2. Da Vinci to Ludovico Sforza, ca. 1480–1481. In Elizabeth Gilmore Holt, ed., *A Documentary History of Art* (Princeton: Princeton University Press, 1981), I: 274–275.

3. Quoted in Anthony Blunt, *Artistic Theory in Italy, 1450–1600* (London: Oxford University Press, 1964), 34.

4. Quoted in James M. Saslow, *The Poetry of Michelangelo: An Annotated Translation* (New Haven, Conn.: Yale University Press, 1991), 407.

5. Giorgio Vasari, *Lives of the Painters, Sculptors, and Architects.* Translated by Gaston du C. de Vere (New York: Knopf, 1996), 2: 736.

6. Quoted in A. Richard Turner, *Renaissance Florence: The Invention of a New Art* (New York: Abrams, 1997), 163.

7. Quoted in Bruce Boucher, *Andrea Palladio: The Architect in His Time* (New York: Abbeville Press, 1998), 229.

8. Quoted in Robert J. Clements, *Michelangelo's Theory of Art* (New York: New York University Press, 1961), 320.

Chapter 23

1. Translated by Erwin Panofsky, in Wolfgang Stechow, *Northern Renaissance Art 1400–1600: Sources and Documents* (Evanston, Ill.: Northwestern University Press, 1989), 123.

2. Translated by Bernhard Erling, in Stechow, 129–130.

3. Giorgio Vasari, *Lives of the Painters, Sculptors, and Architects.* Translated by Gaston du C. de Vere (New York: Knopf, 1996), 2: 863.

Chapter 24

1. Filippo Baldinucci, *Vita del Cavaliere Giovanni Lorenzo Bernini* (1681). Translated by Robert Enggass, in Enggass and Jonathan Brown, *Italian and Spanish Art 1600–1750: Sources and Documents* (Evanston, Ill.: Northwestern University Press, 1992), 116.

2. John Milton, *Il Penseroso* (1631, published 1645), 166.

Chapter 25

1. Quoted in Julie Berger Hochstrasser, *Still Life and Trade in the Dutch Golden Age* (New Haven, Conn.: Yale University Press, 2007), 16.

2. Translated by Kristin Lohse Belkin, *Rubens* (London: Phaidon, 1998), 47.

3. Albert Blankert, *Johannes Vermeer van Delft 1632–1675* (Utrecht: Spectrum, 1975), 133, no. 51. Translated by Bob Haak, *The Golden Age: Dutch Painters of the Seventeenth Century* (New York: Abrams, 1984), 450.

Chapter 26

1. Translated by Robert Goldwater and Marco Treves, eds., *Artists on Art,* 3d ed. (New York: Pantheon Books, 1958), 157.

2. Quoted in Thomas A. Bailey, *The American Pageant: A History of the Republic,* 2d ed. (Boston: Heath, 1961), 280.

3. Translated by Elfriede Heyer and Roger C. Norton, in Charles Harrison, Paul Wood, and Jason Gaiger, eds., *Art in Theory 1648–1815: An Anthology of Changing Ideas* (Oxford: Blackwell, 2000), 451–453.

Chapter 27

1. Théophile Gautier, *Histoire de Romantisme* (Paris: Charpentier, 1874), 204.

2. Quoted in Helmut Borsch-Supan, *Caspar David Friedrich* (New York: Braziller, 1974), 7.

3. Translated by Jason Gaiger, in Charles Harrison, Paul Wood, and Jason Gaiger, eds., *Art in Theory 1815–1900: An Anthology of Changing Ideas* (Oxford: Blackwell, 1998), 54.

4. Quoted by Brian Lukacher, in Stephen F. Eisenman, ed., *Nineteenth Century Art: A Critical History* (New York: Thames & Hudson, 2007), 126.

5. Quoted in John W. McCoubrey, *American Art 1700–1960: Sources and Documents* (Upper Saddle River, N.J.: Prentice Hall, 1965), 98.

6. Quoted in Thomas A. Bailey, *The American Pageant: A History of the Republic,* 2d ed. (Boston: Heath, 1961), 280.

7. Quoted in Linda Nochlin, *Realism and Tradition in Art 1848–1900* (Upper Saddle River, N.J.: Prentice Hall, 1966), 42.

8. Quoted in George Heard Hamilton, *Manet and His Critics* (New Haven, Conn.: Yale University Press, 1954), 45.

9. Quoted in Eisenman, ed., *Nineteenth Century Art,* 336.

10. *New York Weekly Tribune,* September 30, 1865.

11. Quoted in Nikolai Cikovsky Jr. and Franklin Kelly, *Winslow Homer* (Washington, D.C.: National Gallery of Art, 1995), 26.

12. Quoted in Lloyd Goodrich, *Thomas Eakins, His Life and Work* (New York: Whitney Museum of American Art, 1933), 51–52.

13. Quoted in Nicholas Pevsner, *An Outline of European Architecture* (Baltimore: Penguin, 1960), 627.

14. Letter from Delaroche to François Arao, quoted in Helmut Gernsheim, *Creative Photography* (New York: Bonanza Books, 1962), 24.

15. Quoted in Naomi Rosenblum, *A World History of Photography,* 4th ed. (New York: Abbeville Press, 2007), 69.

16. Quoted in Kenneth MacGowan, *Behind the Screen* (New York: Delta, 1965), 49.

Chapter 28

1. Quoted in Linda Nochlin, *Realism* (Harmondsworth: Penguin, 1971), 28.

2. Clement Greenberg, "Modernist Painting," *Art and Literature,* no. 4 (Spring 1965): 193–194.

3. Quoted in Linda Nochlin, *Impressionism and Post-Impressionism 1874–1904: Sources and Documents* (Englewood Cliffs, N.J.: Prentice Hall, 1966), 35.

4. Translated by Carola Hicks, in Charles Harrison, Paul Wood, and Jason Gaiger, *Art in Theory 1815–1900* (Oxford: Blackwell, 1998), 595.

5. Quoted in John McCoubrey, *American Art 1700–1960: Sources and Documents* (Englewood Cliffs, N.J.: Prentice Hall, 1965), 184.

6. Quoted in Robert Goldwater and Marco Treves, eds., *Artists on Art, from the XIV to the XX Century* (New York: Pantheon, 1945), 322.

7. Ibid., 375.

8. Vincent van Gogh to Theo van Gogh, September 1888, in J. van Gogh-Bonger and V. W. van Gogh, eds., *The Complete Letters of Vincent van Gogh* (Greenwich, Conn.: New York Graphic Society, 1979), 3: 534.

9. Vincent van Gogh to Theo van Gogh, July 16, 1888, in W. H. Auden, ed., *Van Gogh: A Self-Portrait. Letters Revealing His Life as a Painter* (New York: Dutton, 1963), 299.

10. Quoted in Sam Hunter, John Jacobus, and Daniel Wheeler, *Modern Art,* 3d ed. (Upper Saddle River, N.J.: Prentice Hall, 2004), 28.

11. Cézanne to Émile Bernard, March 1904. Quoted in Goldwater and Treves, *Artists on Art,* 363.

12. Cézanne to Émile Bernard, April 15, 1904. Ibid., 363.

13. Translated by Akane Kawakami, in Harrison, Wood, and Gaiger, *Art in Theory,* 1066.

14. Quoted in George Heard Hamilton, *Painting and Sculpture in Europe 1880–1940,* 6th ed. (New Haven, Conn.: Yale University Press, 1993), 124.

15. Quoted in V. Frisch and J. T. Shipley, *Auguste Rodin* (New York: Stokes, 1939), 203.

16. Quoted in Eileen Boris, *Art and Labor: Ruskin, Morris, and the Craftsman Ideal in America* (Philadelphia: Temple University Press, 1986), 7.

Chapter 29

1. Quoted in John Elderfield, *The "Wild Beasts": Fauvism and Its Affinities* (New York: Museum of Modern Art, 1976), 29.

2. Translated by Charles Harrison and Paul Wood, eds., *Art in Theory 1900–2000: An Anthology of Changing Ideas* (Oxford: Blackwell, 2003), 65.

3. Quoted in Frederick S. Levine, *The Apocalyptic Vision: The Art of Franz Marc as German Expressionism* (New York: Harper & Row, 1979), 57.

4. Quoted in Sam Hunter, John Jacobus, and Daniel Wheeler, *Modern Art,* rev. 3d ed. (Upper Saddle River, N.J.: Prentice Hall, 2004), 121.

5. Quoted in George Heard Hamilton, *Painting and Sculpture in Europe 1880–1940*, 6th ed. (New Haven, Conn.: Yale University Press, 1993), 246.

6. Ibid., 238.

7. Quoted in Edward Fry, ed., *Cubism* (London: Thames & Hudson, 1966), 112–113.

8. Quoted in Françoise Gilot and Carlton Lake, *Life with Picasso* (New York: McGraw-Hill, 1964), 77.

9. Pablo Picasso, "Statement to Simone Téry," in Harrison and Wood, eds., *Art in Theory 1900–2000*, 649.

10. Quoted in Roland Penrose, *Picasso: His Life and Work*, rev. ed. (New York: Harper & Row, 1971), 311.

11. Filippo Tommaso Marinetti, *The Foundation and Manifesto of Futurism* (*Le Figaro*, February 20, 1909). Translated by Joshua C. Taylor, in Herschel B. Chipp, *Theories of Modern Art: A Source Book by Artists and Critics* (Berkeley and Los Angeles: University of California Press, 1968), 284.

12. Ibid., 286.

13. Quoted in Robert Short, *Dada and Surrealism* (London: Octopus Books, 1980), 18.

14. Quoted in Robert Motherwell, ed., *The Dada Painters and Poets: An Anthology*, 2d ed. (Cambridge, Mass.: Belknap Press of Harvard University, 1989).

15. Hans Richter, *Dada: Art and Anti-Art* (London: Thames & Hudson, 1961), 64–65.

16. Ibid., 57.

17. Quoted in Arturo Schwarz, *The Complete Works of Marcel Duchamp* (London: Thames & Hudson, 1965), 466.

18. Translated by Howard Dearstyne, in Robert L. Herbert, *Modern Artists on Art*, 2d ed. (Mineola, N.Y.: Dover, 2000), 117.

19. Ibid., 124.

20. Translated by Herbert Read and Leslie Martin, quoted in Chipp, *Theories of Modern Art*, 325–330.

21. Quoted in Sam Hunter, *American Art of the 20th Century* (New York: Abrams, 1972), 30.

22. Ibid., 37.

23. Charles C. Eldredge, "The Arrival of European Modernism," *Art in America* 61 (July–August 1973): 35.

24. Quoted in Gail Stavitsky, "Reordering Reality: Precisionist Directions in American Art 1915–1941," in *Precisionism in America 1915–1941: Reordering Reality* (New York: Abrams, 1994), 12.

25. Quoted in Karen Tsujimoto, *Images of America: Precisionist Painting and Modern Photography* (Seattle: University of Washington Press, 1982), 70.

26. Dorothy Norman, *Alfred Stieglitz: An American Seer* (Millerton, N.Y.: Aperture, 1973), 9–10.

27. Ibid., 161.

28. Quoted in Vincent Scully Jr., *Frank Lloyd Wright* (New York: Braziller, 1960), 18.

29. Quoted in Edgar Kauffmann, ed., *Frank Lloyd Wright: An American Architect* (New York: Horizon, 1955), 205, 208.

30. Quoted in Matthias Eberle, *World War I and the Weimar Artists: Dix, Grosz, Beckmann, Schlemmer* (New Haven, Conn.: Yale University Press, 1985), 54.

31. Ibid., 22.

32. Ibid., 42.

33. Quoted in William S. Rubin, *Dada, Surrealism, and Their Heritage* (New York: Museum of Modern Art, 1968), 64.

34. Quoted in Hamilton, *Painting and Sculpture in Europe 1880–1940*, 6th ed. (New Haven, Conn.: Yale University Press, 1993), 392.

35. Quoted in Richter, *Dada*, 155.

36. Ibid., 159.

37. Quoted in Rubin, *Dada, Surrealism*, 111.

38. Quoted in Hunter, Jacobus, and Wheeler, *Modern Art*, 179.

39. Quoted in William S. Rubin, *Miró in the Collection of the Museum of Modern Art* (New York: Museum of Modern Art, 1973), 32.

40. Translated by Norbert Guterman, quoted in Chipp, *Theories of Modern Art*, 182–186.

41. Translated by Nicholas Bullock, quoted in Harrison and Wood, *Art in Theory 1900–2000*, 281.

42. Quoted in Kenneth Frampton, *Modern Architecture: A Critical History*, 4th ed. (New York: Thames & Hudson, 2007), 147.

43. Quoted in Michel Seuphor, *Piet Mondrian: Life and Work* (New York: Abrams, 1956), 117.

44. Piet Mondrian, *Plastic Art and Pure Plastic Art* (1937), quoted in Hamilton, *Painting and Sculpture*, 319.

45. Mondrian, *Plastic Art*, quoted in Chipp, *Theories of Modern Art*, 349.

46. Ibid., 350.

47. Quoted in H. H. Arnason and Peter Kalb, *History of Modern Art*, 5th ed. (Upper Saddle River, N.J.: Prentice Hall, 2004), 154.

48. Quoted in Herbert, *Modern Artists on Art*, 173.

49. Ibid., 177.

50. Quoted in Hans L. Jaffé, comp., *De Stijl* (New York: Abrams, 1971), 185–188.

51. Piet Mondrian, *Dialogue on the New Plastic* (1919). Translated by Harry Holzman and Martin S. James, in Harrison and Wood, *Art in Theory 1900–2000*, 285.

52. Quoted in Wayne Craven, *American Art: History and Culture* (Madison, Wis.: Brown & Benchmark, 2003), 403.

53. Quoted in Vivian Endicott Barnett, "Banned German Art: Reception and Institutional Support of Modern German Art in the United States, 1933–45," in Stephanie Barron, *Exiles and Emigrés: The Flight of European Artists from Hitler* (Los Angeles: Los Angeles County Museum of Art, 1997), 283.

54. Quoted in Frances K. Pohl, *Ben Shahn: New Deal Artist in a Cold War Climate, 1947–1954* (Austin: University of Texas Press, 1989), 159.

55. Quoted in Henry Louis Gates Jr., "New Negroes, Migration, and Cultural Exchange," in Elizabeth Hutton Turner, ed., *Jacob Lawrence: The Migration Series* (Washington, D.C.: Phillips Collection, 1993), 20.

56. Wanda M. Corn, *Grant Wood: The Regionalist Vision* (New Haven, Conn.: Yale University Press, 1983), 131.

57. Quoted in Matthew Baigell, *A Concise History of American Painting and Sculpture* (New York: Harper & Row, 1984), 264.

58. Quoted in Milton Meltzer, *Dorothea Lange: A Photographer's Life* (New York: Farrar, Straus, Giroux, 1978), 133, 220.

59. Quoted in Philip Johnson, *Mies van der Rohe*, rev. ed. (New York: Museum of Modern Art, 1954), 200–201.

Chapter 30

1. Dawn Ades and Andrew Forge, *Francis Bacon* (London: Thames & Hudson, 1985), 8; and David Sylvester, *The Brutality of Fact: Interviews with Francis Bacon*, 3d ed. (London: Thames & Hudson, 1987), 182.

2. Clement Greenberg, "Toward a Newer *Laocoon*," *Partisan Review* 7, no. 4 (July–August 1940): 305.

3. Clement Greenberg, "Sculpture in Our Time," *Arts Magazine* 32, no. 9 (June 1956): 22.

4. Marcus Rothko and Adolph Gottlieb, quoted in Edward Alden Jewell, "The Realm of Art: A New Platform and Other Matters: 'Globalism' Pops into View," *New York Times*, June 13, 1943, 9.

5. Reprinted in Harold Rosenberg, *The Tradition of the New* (New York: Horizon, 1959), 25.

6. Quoted in Thomas Hess, *Barnett Newman* (New York: Walker and Company, 1969), 51.

7. Quoted in John P. O'Neill, ed., *Barnett Newman: Selected Writings and Interviews* (New York: Knopf, 1990), 108.

8. Rothko and Gottlieb, "The Realm of Art," 9.

9. Quoted in Selden Rodman, *Conversations with Artists* (New York: Devin-Adair, 1957), 93–94.

10. Clement Greenberg, "Recentness of Sculpture," in Gregory Battcock, ed., *Minimal Art: A Critical Anthology* (New York: Dutton, 1968), 183–184.

11. Louise Nevelson, quoted in John Gordon, *Louise Nevelson* (New York: Praeger, 1967), 12.

12. Quoted in Deborah Wye, *Louise Bourgeois* (New York: Museum of Modern Art, 1982), 22.

13. Ibid., 25.

14. Quoted in Lucy Lippard, *Eva Hesse* (New York: New York University Press, 1976), 165.

15. Ibid., 56.

16. Quoted in Richard Francis, *Jasper Johns* (New York: Abbeville, 1984), 21.

17. Andy Warhol, *The Philosophy of Andy Warhol* (New York: Harcourt Brace Jovanovich, 1975), 100.

18. Quoted in Christine Lindey, *Superrealist Painting and Sculpture* (London: Orbis, 1980), 50.

19. Quoted in Sebastian Smee, *Lucian Freud: Beholding the Animal* (Cologne: Taschen, 2009), 61.

20. Ibid., 7

21. Lindey, *Superrealist Painting*, 130.

22. Quoted in Susanna Torruella Leval, "Recapturing History: The (Un)official Story in Contemporary Latin American Art," *Art Journal* 51, no. 4 (Winter 1992): 74.

23. Ibid.

24. Hannah Wilke, "Visual Prejudice," in *Hannah Wilke: A Retrospective* (Columbia: University of Missouri Press, 1989), 141.

25. Quoted in Mary Jane Jacob, *Magdalena Abakanowicz* (New York: Abbeville, 1982), 94.

26. Peter Blake, *Frank Lloyd Wright* (Harmondsworth: Penguin, 1960), 115.

27. Quoted in Nancy Holt, ed., *The Writings of Robert Smithson* (New York: New York University Press, 1975), 111.

28. Quoted in H. H. Arnason and Peter Kalb, *History of Modern Art*, 5th ed. (Upper Saddle River, N.J.: Prentice Hall, 2004), 489.

29. Quoted in Barbara Haskell, *Blam! The Explosion of Pop, Minimalism, and Performance 1958-1964* (New York: Whitney Museum of American Art), 53.

30. Quoted in Bruce McPherson, ed., *More Than "Meat Joy": Complete Performance Works and Selected Writings* (New Paltz, N.Y.: Documentext, 1979), 52.

31. Quoted in Caroline Tisdall, *Joseph Beuys* (New York: Thames & Hudson, 1979), 6.

32. Quoted in "Joseph Kosuth: Art as Idea as Idea," in Jeanne Siegel, ed., *Artwords: Discourse on the 60s and 70s* (Ann Arbor, Mich.: UMI Research Press, 1985), 221, 225.

33. Quoted in Brenda Richardson, *Bruce Nauman: Neons* (Baltimore: Baltimore Museum of Art, 1982), 20.

Chapter 31

1. Quoted in Arlene Hirschfelder, *Artists and Craftspeople* (New York: Facts on File, 1994), 115.

2. Quoted in Richard Marshall and Robert Mapplethorpe, *50 New York Artists* (San Francisco: Chronicle Books, 1986), 448-449.

3. Quoted in Junichi Shiota, *Kimio Tsuchiya, Sculpture 1984-1988* (Tokyo: Morris Gallery, 1988), 3.

4. Michelle Meagher, "Jenny Saville and a Feminist Aesthetics of Disgust," *Hypatia* 18.4 (Fall/Winter 2003), 23-41.

5. Quoted in Donald Hall, *Corporal Politics* (Cambridge: MIT List Visual Arts Center, 1993), 46.

6. Quoted in "Vietnam Memorial: America Remembers," *National Geographic* 167, no. 5 (May 1985): 557.

7. Quoted in Calvin Tomkins, "The Art World: *Tilted Arc*," *New Yorker*, May 20, 1985, 100.

Chapter 33

1. Translated by Wang Youfen. Quoted by Wen C. Fong, in Ouyang Zhongshi, Wen C. Fong et al., *Chinese Calligraphy* (New Haven, Conn.: Yale University Press, 2008), 26.

Chapter 34

1. Jiro Yoshihara, "Gutai Art Manifesto" (1956), translated by Reiko Tomii, in *Japanese Art after 1945: Scream against the Sky* (Yokohama: Yokohama Museum of Art, 1994), 370.

Chapter 35

1. Diego de Landa, *Yucatan before and after the Conquest,* translated by William Gates (Mineola, N.Y.: Dover, 1978), 13, 82.

2. Bernal Díaz del Castillo, *The Discovery and Conquest of Mexico.* Translated by A. P. Maudslay (New York: Farrar, Straus, Giroux, 1956), 218-219.

GLOSSARY

Note: Text page references are in parentheses. References to bonus image online essays are in blue.

a secco—Italian, "dried." See *fresco*. (603)

abacus—The uppermost portion of the *capital* of a *column*, usually a thin slab. (116)

abbess—See *abbey*. (322)

abbey—A religious community under the direction of an abbot (for monks) or an abbess (for nuns). (322)

abbot—See *abbey*. (322)

abhaya—See *mudra*. (427, 984)

abrasion—The rubbing or grinding of stone or another material to produce a smooth finish. (64)

abstract—Non-representational; forms and colors arranged without reference to the depiction of an object. (5)

Abstract Expressionism—The first major American avant-garde movement, Abstract Expressionism emerged in New York City in the 1940s. The artists produced *abstract* paintings that expressed their state of mind and that they hoped would strike emotional chords in viewers. The movement developed along two lines: *gestural abstraction* and *chromatic abstraction*. (902, 1046)

acropolis—Greek, "high city." In ancient Greece, usually the site of the city's most important temple(s). (117)

action painting—Also called *gestural abstraction*. The kind of *Abstract Expressionism* practiced by Jackson Pollock, in which the emphasis was on the creation process, the artist's gesture in making art. Pollock poured liquid paint in linear webs on his canvases, which he laid out on the floor, thereby physically surrounding himself in the painting during its creation. (905, 1019)

additive light—Natural light, or sunlight, the sum of all the wavelengths of the visible *spectrum*. See also *subtractive light*. (7)

additive sculpture—A kind of sculpture *technique* in which materials (for example, clay) are built up or "added" to create form. (11)

adobe—The clay used to make a kind of sun-dried mud brick of the same name; a building made of such brick. (508, 529)

aerial perspective—See *perspective*. (567)

agora—An open square or space used for public meetings or business in ancient Greek cities. (138)

ahu—A stone platform on which the *moai* of Easter Island stand. Ahu marked burial sites or served ceremonial purposes. (1052)

'ahu 'ula—A Hawaiian feather cloak. (1058)

airbrush—A tool that uses compressed air to spray paint onto a surface. (918)

aisle—The portion of a *basilica* flanking the *nave* and separated from it by a row of *columns* or *piers*. (12, 189, 243)

akua'ba—"Akua's child." A Ghanaian image of a young girl. (1071)

ala (pl. alae)—One of a pair of rectangular recesses at the back of the *atrium* of a Roman house. (190)

album leaf—A painting on a single sheet of paper for a collection stored in an album. (459, 999)

alchemy—The study of seemingly magical changes, especially chemical changes. (645)

altar frontal—A decorative panel on the front of a church altar. (367)

altarpiece—A panel, painted or sculpted, situated above and behind an altar. See also *retable*. (392, 404)

alternate-support system—In church architecture, the use of alternating wall supports in the *nave*, usually *piers* and *columns* or *compound piers* of alternating form. (324)

amalaka—In Hindu temple design, the large flat disk with ribbed edges surmounting the beehive-shaped tower (*shikara*). (439)

Amazonomachy—In Greek mythology, the battle between the Greeks and Amazons. (136)

ambo—A church *pulpit* for biblical readings. (392)

ambulatory—A covered walkway, outdoors (as in a church *cloister*) or indoors; especially the passageway around the *apse* and the *choir* of a church. In Buddhist architecture, the passageway leading around the *stupa* in a *chaitya* hall. (244, 430)

amphiprostyle—A *classical* temple *plan* in which the *columns* are placed across both the front and back but not along the sides. (115)

amphitheater—Greek, "double theater." A Roman building type resembling two Greek theaters put together. The Roman amphitheater featured a continuous elliptical *cavea* around a central *arena*. (189, 401)

amphora—An ancient Greek two-handled jar used for general storage purposes, usually to hold wine or oil. (110)

amulet—An object worn to ward off evil or to aid the wearer. (61)

Analytic Cubism—The first phase of *Cubism*, developed jointly by Pablo Picasso and Georges Braque, in which the artists analyzed form from every possible vantage point to combine the various views into one pictorial whole. (847)

anamorphic image—A distorted image that must be viewed by some special means (such as a mirror) to be recognized. (656)

ancien régime—French, "old order." The term used to describe the political, social, and religious order in France before the Revolution at the end of the 18th century. (736)

antae—The molded projecting ends of the walls forming the *pronaos* or *opisthodomos* of an ancient Greek temple. (115)

ante legem—Latin, "before the law." In Christian thought, the period before Moses received the Ten Commandments. See also *sub lege*. (392)

apadana—The great audience hall in ancient Persian palaces. (51)

apostle—Greek, "messenger." One of the 12 disciples of Jesus. (240)

apotheosis—Elevated to the rank of gods, or the ascent to heaven. (206, 18-10A)

apotropaic—Capable of warding off evil. (118)

apoxyomenos—Greek, "athlete scraping oil from his body." (147)

apse—A recess, usually semicircular, in the wall of a building, commonly found at the east end of a church. (28, 134, 208, 243, 413, 1031)

apsidal—Rounded; *apse*-shaped. (429)

arcade—A series of *arches* supported by *piers* or *columns*. (52, 243, 287, 290, 413, 20-4A)

Arcadian (adj.)—In Renaissance and later art, depictions of an idyllic place of rural peace and simplicity. Derived from Arcadia, an ancient district of the central Peloponnesos in southern Greece. (625)

arch—A curved structural member that spans an opening and is generally composed of wedge-shaped blocks (*voussoirs*) that transmit the downward pressure laterally. See also *thrust*. (48, 12-10A)

Archaic—The artistic style of 600–480 BCE in Greece, characterized in part by the use of the *composite view* for painted and *relief* figures and of Egyptian stances for statues. (111)

Archaic smile—The smile that appears on all *Archaic* Greek statues from about 570 to 480 BCE. The smile is the Archaic sculptor's way of indicating that the person portrayed is alive. (112)

architrave—The *lintel* or lowest division of the *entablature*; also called the epistyle. (116, 640)

archivolt—The continuous molding framing an *arch*. In *Romanesque* and *Gothic* architecture, one of the series of concentric bands framing the *tympanum*. (344)

arcuated—*Arch*-shaped. (48, 175, 206)

arena—In a Roman *amphitheater*, the central area where bloody *gladiatorial* combats and other boisterous events took place. (189)

armature—The crossed, or diagonal, *arches* that form the skeletal framework of a *Gothic rib vault*. In sculpture, the framework for a clay form. (11, 368)

arriccio—In *fresco* painting, the first layer of rough lime plaster applied to the wall. (408)

Art Deco—Descended from *Art Nouveau*, this movement of the 1920s and 1930s sought to upgrade industrial design as a "fine art" and to work new materials into decorative patterns that could be either machined or handcrafted. Characterized by streamlined, elongated, and symmetrical design. (871)

Art Nouveau—French, "new art." A late-19th- and early-20th-century art movement whose proponents tried to synthesize all the arts in an effort to create art based on natural forms that could be mass produced by technologies of the industrial age. The movement had other names in other countries: Jugendstil in Austria and Germany, Modernismo in Spain, and Floreale in Italy. (828)

asceticism—Self-discipline and self-denial. (427)

ashlar masonry—Carefully cut and regularly shaped blocks of stone used in construction, fitted together without mortar. (62, 1031)

assemblage—An artwork constructed from already existing objects. (914)

asye usu—Baule (Côte d'Ivoire) bush spirits. (1069)

atlantid—A male figure that functions as a supporting *column*. See also *caryatid*. (72, 506)

atlatl—Spear-thrower, the typical weapon of the Toltecs of ancient Mexico. (506)

atmospheric perspective—See *perspective*. (194, 567)

atrium—The central reception room of a Roman house that is partly open to the sky. Also the open, *colonnaded* court in front of and attached to a Christian *basilica*. (190, 243, 672)

attic—The uppermost story of a building, *triumphal arch*, or city gate. (201)

attribute—(n.) The distinctive identifying aspect of a person, for example, an object held, an associated animal, or a mark on the body. (v.) To make an *attribution*. (5)

attribution—Assignment of a work to a maker or makers. (6)

augur—A Roman priest who determined the will of the gods from the flight of birds and whose attribute is the *lituus*. (165)

automatism—In painting, the process of yielding oneself to instinctive motions of the hands after establishing a set of conditions (such as size of paper or medium) within which a work is to be created. (875)

avant-garde—French, "advance guard" (in a platoon). Late-19th- and 20th-century artists who emphasized innovation and challenged established convention in their work. Also used as an adjective. (836)

avatar—A manifestation of a deity incarnated in some visible form in which the deity performs a sacred function on earth. In Hinduism, an incarnation of a god. (435, 981)

axial plan—See *plan*. (72)

axis mundi—Latin, "axis of the universe." In South Asia, a tall pillar planted deep in the ground, connecting earth and sky. (15-6A)

backstrap loom—A simple Andean loom featuring a belt or backstrap encircling the waist of the seated weaver. (510)

bai—An elaborately painted men's ceremonial house on Belau (formerly Palau) in the Caroline Islands of Micronesia. (1050)

baldacchino—A canopy on *columns*, frequently built over an altar. The term derives from *baldacco*. (243, 673)

baldacco—Italian, "silk from Baghdad." See *baldacchino*. (673)

baldric—A sashlike belt worn over one shoulder and across the chest to support a sword. (24-28B)

baptism—The Christian bathing ceremony in which an infant or a convert becomes a member of the Christian community. (236)

baptistery—In Christian architecture, the building used for *baptism*, usually situated next to a church. Also, the designated area or hall within a church for baptismal rites. (236)

bar tracery—See *tracery*. (375)

baray—One of the large reservoirs laid out around Cambodian *wats* that served as means of transportation as well as irrigation. A network of canals connected the reservoirs. (444)

barge boards—The angled boards that outline the exterior gables of a Maori meetinghouse. (1043)

Baroque—The traditional blanket designation for European art from 1600 to 1750. The stylistic term *Baroque*, which describes art that features dramatic theatricality and elaborate ornamentation in contrast to the simplicity and orderly rationality of *Renaissance* art, is most appropriately applied to Italian art of this period. The term derives from *barroco*. (670)

barrel vault—See *vault*. (184, 338, 585, 981)

barroco—Portuguese, "irregularly shaped pearl." See *Baroque*. (670)

base—In ancient Greek architecture, the molded projecting lowest part of *Ionic* and *Corinthian* *columns*. (*Doric* columns do not have bases.) (51, 116)

basilica (adj. **basilican**)—In Roman architecture, a public building for legal and other civic proceedings, rectangular in plan with an entrance usually on a long side. In Christian architecture, a church somewhat resembling the Roman basilica, usually entered from one end and with an *apse* at the other. (189, 413, 583)

bas-relief—See *relief*. (12, 820)

batik—An Indonesian fabric-dyeing technique using melted wax to form patterns the dye cannot penetrate. (31-22B)

battlement—A low parapet at the top of a circuit wall in a fortification. (382, 416)

Bauhaus—A *school* of architecture in Germany in the 1920s under the aegis of Walter Gropius, who emphasized the unity of art, architecture, and design. (884)

bay—The space between two columns, or one unit in the *nave arcade* of a church; also, the passageway in an *arcuated* gate. (411, 413, 457)

beam—A horizontal structural member that carries the load of the superstructure of a building; a timber *lintel*. (457)

Beaux-Arts—An architectural *style* of the late 19th and early 20th centuries in France. Based on ideas taught at the École des Beaux-Arts in Paris, the Beaux-Arts style incorporated *classical* principles, such as symmetry in design, and included extensive exterior ornamentation. (789)

begging bowl—The bowl Buddhist monks use to collect alms, either money or food. (486)

belvedere—Italian, "beautiful view." A building or other structure with a view of a *landscape* or seascape. (623)

ben-ben—A pyramidal stone; an emblem of the Egyptian god Re. (57, 61)

benday dots—Named after the newspaper printer Benjamin Day, the benday dot system involves the modulation of *colors* through the placement and size of colored dots. (916)

benedictional—A Christian religious book containing bishops' blessings. (312)

bent-axis plan—A *plan* that incorporates two or more angular changes of direction, characteristic of Sumerian architecture. (33)

bestiary—A collection of illustrations of real and imaginary animals. (343)

bhakti—In Buddhist thought, the adoration of a personalized deity (*bodhisattva*) as a means of achieving unity with it; love felt by the devotee for the deity. In Hinduism, the devout, selfless direction of all tasks and activities of life to the service of one god. (981)

Bharat Mata—Mother India; the female personification of India. (32-10A)

bhumisparsha—See *mudra*. (427)

bi—In ancient China, jade disks carved as ritual objects for burial with the dead. They were often decorated with piercings that extended entirely through the object, as well as with surface carvings. (453, 454)

bichrome—Two-color. (511)

bieri—The wooden *reliquary* guardian figures of the Fang in Gabon and Cameroon. (1064)

bilateral symmetry—Having the same *forms* on either side of a central axis. (64)

bilingual vases—Experimental Greek vases produced for a short time in the late sixth century BCE; one side featured *black-figure* decoration, the other *red-figure*. (121)

Biomorphic Surrealism—See *Surrealism*. (875)

bisj pole—An elaborately carved pole constructed from the trunk of the mangrove tree. The Asmat people of southwestern New Guinea created bisj poles to indicate their intent to avenge a relative's death. (1046)

black-figure painting—In early Greek pottery, the silhouetting of dark figures against a light background of natural, reddish clay, with linear details *incised* through the silhouettes. (111)

blind arcade—An *arcade* having no true openings, applied as decoration to a wall surface. (52, 290)

block statue—In ancient Egyptian sculpture, a cubic stone image with simplified body parts. (74)

bocio—A Fon (Republic of Benin) empowerment figure. (1066)

bodhisattva—In Buddhist thought, a potential Buddha who chooses not to achieve enlightenment in order to help save humanity. (427)

Book of Hours—A Christian religious book for private devotion containing prayers to be read at specified times of the day. (312)

boshan—A Chinese incense burner. (455, 16-6A)

boss—A circular knob. (426)

bottega—An artist's studio-shop. (569)

braccia—Italian, "arm." A unit of measurement; 1 braccia equals 23 inches. (582)

breakfast piece—A *still life* that includes bread and fruit. (701)

breviary—A Christian religious book of selected daily prayers and Psalms. (312, 386, 550)

bucranium (pl. **bucrania**)—Latin, "bovine skull." A common motif in classical architectural ornament. (659, 1-16A)

Buddha triad—A three-figure group with a central Buddha flanked on each side by a *bodhisattva*. (475)

buon fresco—See *fresco*. (408, 603)

burgher—A middle-class citizen. (28-32A)

burin—A pointed tool used for *engraving* or *incising*. (556)

bust—A freestanding sculpture of the head, shoulders, and chest of a person. (12)

buttress—An exterior masonry structure that opposes the lateral *thrust* of an *arch* or a *vault*. A pier buttress is a solid mass of masonry. A flying buttress consists typically of an inclined member carried on an arch or a series of arches and a solid buttress to which it transmits lateral thrust. (184)

byobu—Japanese painted folding screens. (1010)

Byzantine—The art, territory, history, and culture of the Eastern Christian Empire and its capital of Constantinople (ancient Byzantium). (256)

caduceus—In ancient Greek mythology, a magical rod entwined with serpents, the attribute of Hermes (Roman, Mercury), the messenger of the gods. (107, 559)

caldarium—The hot-bath section of a Roman bathing establishment. (220)

caliph(s)—Islamic rulers, regarded as successors of Muhammad. (285)

calligrapher—One who practices *calligraphy*. (294, 466, 997)

calligraphy—Greek, "beautiful writing." Handwriting or penmanship, especially elegant writing as a decorative art. (294, 466, 997)

calotype—From the Greek *kalos*, "beautiful." A photographic process in which a positive image is made by shining light through a negative image onto a sheet of sensitized paper. (791, 792)

came—A lead strip in a *stained-glass* window that joins separate pieces of colored glass. (375)

camera lucida—Latin, "lighted room." A device in which a small lens projects the image of an object downward onto a sheet of paper. (791)

camera obscura—Latin, "dark room." An ancestor of the modern camera in which a tiny pinhole, acting as a lens, projects an image on a screen, the wall of a room, or the ground-glass wall of a box; used by artists in the 17th, 18th, and early 19th centuries as an aid in drawing from nature. (711)

campanile—A bell tower of a church, usually, but not always, freestanding. (350, 416)

canon—A rule, for example, of proportion. The ancient Greeks considered beauty to be a matter of "correct" proportion and sought a canon of proportion, for the human figure and for buildings. The fifth-century BCE sculptor Polykleitos wrote the *Canon*, a treatise incorporating his formula for the perfectly proportioned statue. (10, 66)

canon table—A concordance, or matching, of the corresponding passages of the four *Gospels* as compiled by Eusebius of Caesarea in the fourth century. (312)

canonized—Declared a saint by the Catholic Church. (354, 14-5A)

canopic jar—In ancient Egypt, the container in which the organs of the deceased were placed for later burial with the mummy. (61)

capital—The uppermost member of a *column*, serving as a transition from the *shaft* to the *lintel*. In *classical* architecture, the form of the capital varies with the *order*. (51, 60, 116, 402, 429)

Capitolium—An ancient Roman temple dedicated to the gods Jupiter, Juno, and Minerva. (189)

capriccio—Italian, "originality." One of several terms used in Italian *Renaissance* literature to praise the originality and talent of artists. (604)

caput mundi—Latin, "head (capital) of the world." (180)

cardo—The north-south street in a Roman town, intersecting the *decumanus* at right angles. (189)

Caroline minuscule—The alphabet that *Carolingian* scribes perfected, from which the modern English alphabet was developed. (317)

Carolingian (adj.)—Pertaining to the empire of Charlemagne (Latin, "Carolus Magnus") and his successors. (317)

carpet page—In early medieval manuscripts, a decorative page resembling a textile. (311)

cartography—The art of mapmaking. (13-38B)

cartoon—In painting, a full-size preliminary drawing from which a painting is made. (408, 602)

carving—A *technique* of sculpture in which the artist cuts away material (for example, from a stone block) in order to create a *statue* or a *relief*. (11)

caryatid—A female figure that functions as a supporting *column*. See also *atlantid*. (72, 117)

cassone (pl. **cassoni**)—A carved chest, often painted or gilded, popular in *Renaissance* Italy for the storing of household clothing. (631)

castellum—See *westwork*. (323)

casting—A sculptural *technique* in which the artist pours liquid metal, plaster, clay, or another material into a *mold*. When the material dries, the sculptor removes the cast piece from the mold. (11)

castrum—A Roman military encampment. (207)

catacombs—Subterranean networks of rock-cut galleries and chambers designed as cemeteries for the burial of the dead. (237)

cathedra—Latin, "seat." See *cathedral*. (350)

cathedral—A bishop's church. The word derives from *cathedra*, referring to the bishop's chair. (350, 412)

cavea—Latin, "hollow place or cavity." The seating area in ancient Greek and Roman theaters and *amphitheaters*. (151, 189)

celadon—A Chinese-Korean pottery *glaze*, fired in an oxygen-deprived kiln to a characteristic gray-green or pale blue color. (472)

cella—The chamber at the center of an ancient temple; in a *classical* temple, the room (Greek, *naos*) in which the *cult statue* usually stood. (33, 115, 618)

celt—In Olmec Mexico, an ax-shaped form made of polished jade; generally, a prehistoric metal or stone implement shaped like a chisel or ax head. (494)

cemen—The winglike openwork projection at the top of an Asmat *bisj* pole. (1046)

centaur—In ancient Greek mythology, a creature with the front or top half of a human and the back or bottom half of a horse. (105)

centauromachy—In ancient Greek mythology, the battle between the Greeks and *centaurs*. (120)

central plan—See *plan*. (244, 288, 583)

cestrum—A small spatula used in *encaustic* painting. (218)

chacmool—A *Mesoamerican* statuary type depicting a fallen warrior on his back with a receptacle on his chest for sacrificial offerings. (491, 883)

chaitya hall—A South Asian rock-cut temple hall having a votive *stupa* at one end. (429)

chakra—The Buddha's wheel, set in motion at Sarnath. (423, 429)

chakravartin—In South Asia, the ideal king, the Universal Lord who ruled through goodness. (429, 985)

Chan—See *Zen*. (470, 1007)

chancel arch—The arch separating the chancel (the *apse* or *choir*) or the *transept* from the *nave* of a basilica or church. (228, 243, 413)

chantry—An endowed chapel for the chanting of the mass for the founder of the chapel. (13-42A)

chaplet—A metal pin used in hollow-casting to connect the *investment* with the clay core. (130)

chapter house—The meeting hall in a *monastery*. (585)

characters—In Chinese writing, signs that record spoken words. (450, 997)

chartreuse—A Carthusian *monastery*. (537)

charun—An Etruscan death demon. (176)

chasing—The engraving or embossing of metal. (673)

chasseur—French cavalry officer. (27-13A)

château (pl. **châteaux**)—French, "castle." A luxurious country residence for French royalty, developed from medieval castles. (657)

chatra—See *yasti*. (430)

cherub—A chubby winged child angel. (552)

chiaroscuro—In drawing or painting, the treatment and use of light and dark, especially the gradations of light that produce the effect of *modeling*. (409)

chiaroscuro woodcut—A *woodcut* technique using two blocks of wood instead of one. The printmaker carves and inks one block in the usual way in order to produce a traditional black-and-white print. Then the artist cuts a second block consisting of broad highlights that can be inked in gray or color and printed over the first block's impression. (649)

chigi—Decorative extensions of the *rafters* at each end of the roof of a Japanese shrine. (480)

chimera—A monster of Greek invention with the head and body of a lion and the tail of a serpent. A second head, that of a goat, grows out of one side of the body. (174)

chisel—A tool with a straight blade at one end for cutting and shaping stone or wood. (18)

chiton—A Greek tunic, the essential (and often only) garment of both men and women, the other being the *himation*, or mantle. (115)

choir—The space reserved for the clergy and singers in the church, usually east of the *transept* but, in some instances, extending into the *nave*. (12, 264)

Christ—Savior. (240)

Christogram—The three initial letters (chi-rho-iota, or ☧) of Christ's name in Greek, which came to serve as a monogram for Christ. (230, 264, 307)

chromatic abstraction—A kind of *Abstract Expressionism* that focuses on the emotional resonance of color, as exemplified by the work of Barnett Newman and Mark Rothko. (903)

chronology—In art history, the dating of art objects and buildings. (2)

chryselephantine—Fashioned of gold and ivory. (94)

Cinquecento—Italian, "500," that is, the 1500s or 16th century. (599)

circumambulation—In Buddhist worship, walking around the *stupa* in a clockwise direction, a process intended to bring the worshiper into harmony with the cosmos. (430)

cire perdue—See *lost-wax process*. (130, 507, 673, 983)

cista (pl. **cistae**)—An Etruscan cylindrical container made of sheet bronze with cast handles and feet, often with elaborately engraved bodies, used for women's toiletry articles. (175)

city-state—An independent, self-governing city. (31, 406)

Classical—The art and culture of ancient Greece between 480 and 323 BCE. Lowercase *classical* refers more generally to Greco-Roman art and culture. (402)

clerestory—The *fenestrated* part of a building that rises above the roofs of the other parts. The oldest known clerestories are Egyptian. In Roman *basilicas* and medieval churches, clerestories are the windows that form the *nave*'s uppermost level below the timber ceiling or the *vaults*. (73, 184, 243, 373, 413, 20-4A)

cloison—French, "partition." A cell made of metal wire or a narrow metal strip soldered edge-up to a metal base to hold *enamel*, semiprecious stones, pieces of colored glass, or glass paste fired to resemble sparkling jewels. (310)

cloisonné—A decorative metalwork technique employing *cloisons*; also, decorative brickwork in later Byzantine architecture. (271, 310, 817)

cloister—A *monastery* courtyard, usually with covered walks or *ambulatories* along its sides. (322, 341, 576)

cluster pier—See *compound pier*. (340, 373, 12-4A, 14-12A)

codex (pl. **codices**)—Separate pages of *vellum* or *parchment* bound together at one side; the predecessor of the modern book. The codex superseded the *rotulus*. In *Mesoamerica*, a painted and inscribed book on long sheets of bark paper or deerskin coated with fine white plaster and folded into accordion-like pleats. (249, 1023)

coffer—A sunken panel, often ornamental, in a *vault* or a ceiling. (210)

collage—A composition made by combining on a flat surface various materials, such as newspaper, wallpaper, printed text and illustrations, photographs, and cloth. (8, 835, 850)

colonnade—A series or row of *columns*, usually spanned by *lintels*. (70)

colonnette—A thin *column*. (194, 290)

colophon—An inscription, usually on the last page, giving information about a book's manufacture. In Chinese painting, written texts on attached pieces of paper or silk. (312, 997)

color—The value, or tonality, of a color is the degree of its lightness or darkness. The intensity, or saturation, of a color is its purity, its brightness or dullness. See also *primary colors, secondary colors,* and *complementary colors*. (7, 813)

color-field painting—A variant of *Post-Painterly Abstraction* in which artists sought to reduce painting to its physical essence by pouring diluted paint onto unprimed canvas and letting these pigments soak into the fabric, as exemplified by the work of Helen Frankenthaler and Morris Louis. (908)

colorito—Italian, "colored" or "painted." A term used to describe the application of paint. Characteristic of the work of 16th-century Venetian artists who emphasized the application of paint as an important element of the creative process. Central Italian artists, in contrast, largely emphasized *disegno*—the careful design preparation based on preliminary drawing. (625)

colossal order—An architectural design in which the *columns* or *pilasters* are two or more stories tall. Also called a giant order. (594)

column—A vertical, weight-carrying architectural member, circular in cross-*section* and consisting of a *base* (sometimes omitted), a *shaft*, and a *capital*. (10, 51, 402)

combines—The name American artist Robert Rauschenberg gave to his *assemblages* of painted passages and sculptural elements. (914)

commedia dell'arte—A traditional Italian comic play performed by actors and musicians. (29-19A)

complementary colors—Those pairs of *colors*, such as red and green, that together embrace the entire *spectrum*. The complement of one of the three *primary colors* is a mixture of the other two. (7, 813)

compline—The last prayer of the day in a *Book of Hours*. (550)

compose—See *composition*. (7, 21, 38)

Composite capital—A capital combining *Ionic* volutes and *Corinthian* acanthus leaves, first used by the ancient Romans. (206, 587, 21-36A)

composite view—A convention of representation in which part of a figure is shown in profile and another part of the same figure is shown frontally; also called twisted perspective. (23, 523)

composition—The way in which an artist organizes *forms* in an artwork, either by placing shapes on a flat surface or arranging forms in space. (7, 21, 38)

compound pier—A *pier* with a group, or cluster, of attached *shafts*, or *responds*, especially characteristic of *Gothic* architecture. (340, 373, 12-4A, 14-12A)

Conceptual Art—An American *avant-garde* art movement of the 1960s whose premise was that the "artfulness" of art lay in the artist's idea rather than its final expression. (936)

conceptual representation—The representation of the fundamental distinguishing properties of a person or object, not the way a figure or object appears in space and light at a specific moment. See *composite view*. (35)

concrete—A building material invented by the Romans and consisting of various proportions of lime mortar, volcanic sand, water, and small stones. (184)

condottiere (pl. **condottieri**)—An Italian mercenary general. (560)

confraternity—In Late Antiquity, an association of Christian families pooling funds to purchase property for burial. In late medieval Europe, an organization founded by laypersons who dedicated themselves to strict religious observances. (237, 404)

congregational mosque—A city's main *mosque*, designed to accommodate the entire *Muslim* population for the Friday noonday prayer. Also called the great mosque or Friday mosque. (288, 977)

connoisseur—An expert in *attributing* artworks to one artist rather than another. More generally, an expert on artistic *style*. (6)

Constructivism—An early-20th-century Russian art movement formulated by Naum Gabo, who built up his sculptures piece by piece in space instead of carving or *modeling* them. In this way the sculptor worked with "volume of mass" and "volume of space" as different materials. (860)

consuls—In the Roman Republic, the two chief magistrates. (181)

continuous narration—The depiction of the same figure more than once in the same space at different stages of a story. (7-44A)

contour line—In art, a continuous line defining the outer shape of an object. (7)

contrapposto—The disposition of the human figure in which one part is turned in opposition to another part (usually hips and legs one way, shoulders and chest another), creating a counterpositioning of the body about its central axis. Sometimes called "weight shift" because the weight of the body tends to be thrown to one foot, creating tension on one side and relaxation on the other. (129, 564)

corbel—A projecting wall member used as a support for some element in the superstructure. Also, *courses* of stone or brick in which each course projects beyond the one beneath it. Two such walls, meeting at the topmost course, create a corbeled *arch* or corbeled *vault*. (416, 640)

corbeled arch—An *arch* formed by the piling of stone blocks in horizontal *courses*, cantilevered inward until the blocks meet at a *keystone*. (99)

corbeled vault—A *vault* formed by the piling of stone blocks in horizontal *courses*, cantilevered inward until the two walls meet in an *arch*. (27, 99)

Corinthian capital—A more ornate form than *Doric* or *Ionic*; it consists of a double row of acanthus leaves from which tendrils and flowers grow, wrapped around a bell-shaped *echinus*. Although this *capital* form is often cited as the distinguishing feature of the Corinthian *order*, no such order exists, in strict terms, but only this type of capital used in the *Ionic* order. (151, 402, 587)

cornice—The projecting, crowning member of the *entablature* framing the *pediment*; also, any crowning projection. (116, 586)

corona civica—Latin, "civic crown." A Roman honorary wreath worn on the head. (7)

course—In masonry construction, a horizontal row of stone blocks. (28, 62, 1031)

covenant—In Judaism and Christianity, a binding agreement between God and humans. (561)

crenel—See *crenellation*. (382)

crenellation—Alternating solid merlons and open crenels in the notched tops of walls, as in *battlements*. (382)

crossing—The space in a *cruciform* church formed by the intersection of the *nave* and the *transept*. (246, 323, 14-18A)

cross-hatching—See *hatching*. (555)

cross vault—See *vault*. (184)

crossing square—The area in a church formed by the intersection (*crossing*) of a *nave* and a *transept* of equal width, often used as a standard *module* of interior proportion. (323, 583)

crossing tower—The tower over the *crossing* of a church. (246)

cruciform—Cross-shaped. (246, 583)

Crusades—In medieval Europe, armed pilgrimages aimed at recapturing the Holy Land from the *Muslims*. (346)

crypt—A *vaulted* space under part of a building, wholly or partly underground; in churches, normally the portion under an *apse*. (340)

cubiculum (pl. **cubicula**)—A small cubicle or bedroom that opened onto the *atrium* of a Roman house. Also, a chamber in an Early Christian *catacomb* that served as a mortuary chapel. (190, 237)

Cubism—An early-20th-century art movement that rejected *naturalistic* depictions, preferring *compositions* of shapes and *forms* abstracted from the conventionally perceived world. See also *Analytic Cubism* and *Synthetic Cubism*. (847)

cuerda seca—A type of polychrome tilework used in decorating Islamic buildings. (299)

cuirass—A military leather breastplate. (186)

cult statue—The *statue* of the deity that stood in the *cella* of an ancient temple. (115)

cuneiform—Latin, "wedge-shaped." A system of writing used in ancient Mesopotamia, in which wedge-shaped characters were produced by pressing a *stylus* into a soft clay tablet, which was then baked or otherwise allowed to harden. (33)

cuneus (pl. **cunei**)—In ancient Greek and Roman theaters and *amphitheaters*, the wedge-shaped section of stone benches separated by stairs. (151)

cupola—An exterior architectural feature composed of a *drum* with a shallow cap; a *dome*. (638, 9-32A)

cutaway—An architectural drawing that combines an exterior view with an interior view of part of a building. (12, 605)

Cycladic—The prehistoric art of the Aegean Islands around Delos, excluding Crete. (87)

Cyclopean masonry—A method of stone construction, named after the mythical *Cyclopes*, using massive, irregular blocks without mortar, characteristic of the Bronze Age fortifications of Tiryns and other *Mycenaean* sites. (97)

Cyclops (pl. **Cyclopes**)—A mythical Greek one-eyed giant. (97)

cylinder seal—A cylindrical piece of stone usually about an inch or so in height, decorated with an *incised* design, so that a raised pattern is left when the seal is rolled over soft clay. In the ancient Near East, documents, storage jars, and other important possessions were signed, sealed, and identified in this way. Stamp seals are an earlier, flat form of seal used for similar purposes. (39)

Dada—An early-20th-century art movement prompted by a revulsion against the horror of World War I. Dada embraced political anarchy, the irrational, and the intuitive. A disdain for convention, often enlivened by humor or whimsy, is characteristic of the art the Dadaists produced. (835, 856)

Daedalic—The Greek *Orientalizing* sculptural style of the seventh century BCE named after the legendary artist Daedalus. (111)

daguerreotype—A photograph made by an early method on a plate of chemically treated metal; developed by Louis J. M. Daguerre. (791, 792, 983)

daimyo—Local lords who controlled small regions and owed obeisance to the *shogun* in the Japanese *shogunate* system. (1006)

damnatio memoriae—The Roman decree condemning those who ran afoul of the Senate. Those who suffered damnatio memoriae had their memorials demolished and their names erased from public inscriptions. (206, 219)

darbar—The official audience of a *Mughal* emperor. (32-5A)

darshan—In Hindu worship, seeing images of the divinity and being seen by the divinity. (435)

De Stijl—Dutch, "the style." An early-20th-century art movement (and magazine), founded by Piet Mondrian and Theo van Doesburg, whose members promoted utopian ideals and developed a simplified geometric style. (880)

deconstruction—An analytical strategy developed in the late 20th century according to which all cultural "constructs" (art, architecture, literature) are "texts." People can read these texts in a variety of ways, but they cannot arrive at fixed or uniform meanings. Any interpretation can be valid, and readings differ from time to time, place to place, and person to person. For those employing this approach, deconstruction means destabilizing established meanings and interpretations while encouraging subjectivity and individual differences. (942)

Deconstructivism—An architectural *style* using *deconstruction* as an analytical strategy. Deconstructivist architects attempt to disorient the observer by disrupting the conventional categories of architecture. The haphazard presentation of *volumes, masses, planes*, lighting, and so forth challenges the viewer's assumptions about *form* as it relates to function. (962)

decumanus—The east-west street in a Roman town, intersecting the *cardo* at right angles. (189)

decursio—The ritual circling of a Roman funerary pyre. (215)

Deësis—Greek, "supplication." An image of Christ flanked by the figures of the Virgin Mary and John the Baptist, who intercede on behalf of humankind. (276)

demos—Greek, "the people," from which the word *democracy* is derived. (106)

demotic—Late Egyptian writing. (56)

denarius—The standard Roman silver coin from which the word *penny* ultimately derives. (187)

Der Blaue Reiter—German, "the blue rider." An early-20th-century *German Expressionist* art movement founded by Vassily Kandinsky and Franz Marc. The artists selected the whimsical name because of their mutual interest in the color blue and horses. (841)

dharma—In Buddhism, moral law based on the Buddha's teaching. (423, 15-8A)

dharmachakra—See *mudra*. (427)

dhyana—See *mudra*. (427)

di sotto in sù—Italian, "from below upward." A *perspective* view seen from below. (595, 637)

diagonal rib—See *rib*. (373)

diaphragm arch—A transverse, wall-bearing *arch* that divides a *vault* or a ceiling into compartments, providing a kind of firebreak. (12-27A)

dictator—In the Roman Republic, the supreme magistrate with extraordinary powers, appointed during a crisis for a specified period. Julius Caesar eventually became *dictator perpetuo*, dictator for life. (181, 187)

dictator perpetuo—See *dictator*. (181, 187)

Die Brücke—German, "the bridge." An early-20th-century *German Expressionist* art movement under the leadership of Ernst Ludwig Kirchner. The group thought of itself as the bridge between the old age and the new. (839)

Dilukai—A female figure with splayed legs, a common motif over the entrance to a Belau *bai*, serving as both guardian and fertility symbol. (1052)

dipteral—See *peristyle*. (115)

diptych—A two-paneled painting or *altarpiece*; also, an ancient Roman, Early Christian, or Byzantine hinged writing tablet, often of ivory and carved on the external sides. (251, 540)

disegno—Italian, "drawing" and "design." *Renaissance* artists considered drawing to be the external physical manifestation (*disegno esterno*) of an internal idea of design (*disegno interno*). (604, 625)

disputatio—Latin, "logical argument." The philosophical methodology used in *Scholasticism*. (372)

divine right—The belief in a king's absolute power as God's will. (714)

divisionism—See *pointillism*. (812)

documentary evidence—In art history, the examination of written sources in order to determine the date of an artwork, the circumstances of its creation, or the identity of the artist(s) who made it. (2)

doge—Duke; a ruler of the Republic of Venice, Italy. (274)

dome—A hemispherical *vault*; theoretically, an *arch* rotated on its vertical axis. In *Mycenaean* architecture, domes are beehive-shaped. (99, 184, 977, 14-18A)

domus—A Roman private house. (190)

donor portrait—A portrait of the individual(s) who commissioned (donated) a religious work, for example, an *altarpiece*, as evidence of devotion. (535)

Doric—One of the two systems (or *orders*) invented in ancient Greece for articulating the three units of the elevation of a *classical* building—the platform, the *colonnade*, and the superstructure (*entablature*). The Doric order is characterized by, among other features, *capitals* with funnel-shaped *echinuses*, *columns* without *bases*, and a *frieze* of *triglyphs* and *metopes*. See also *Ionic*. (116, 587, 640)

doryphoros—Greek, "spear bearer." (132)

dotaku—Ancient Japanese bronze ceremonial bells, usually featuring raised decoration. (477)

double monastery—A *monastery* for both monks and nuns. (352)

dressed masonry—Stone blocks shaped to the exact dimensions required, with smooth faces for a perfect fit. (62, 586)

dromos—The passage leading to a *tholos tomb*. (99)

drum—One of the stacked cylindrical stones that form the *shaft* of a *column*. Also, the cylindrical wall that supports a *dome*. (116, 184, 271)

dry painting—See *sand painting*. (1032)

drypoint—An *engraving* in which the design, instead of being cut into the plate with a *burin*, is scratched into the surface with a hard steel "pencil." See also *etching, intaglio*. (556)

duomo—Italian, "cathedral." (417)

earthenware—Pottery made of clay that is fired at low temperatures and is slightly porous. Also, clay figurines and statues produced in the same manner. (451)

earthworks—See *Environmental Art*. (932)

eaves—The lower part of a roof that overhangs the wall. (457)

echinus—The convex element of a *capital* directly below the *abacus*. (116)

écorché—The representation of a nude body as if without skin. (582)

edition—A set of impressions taken from a single print surface. (556)

effigy mounds—Ceremonial mounds built in the shape of animals or birds by native North American peoples. (517)

elevation—In architecture, a head-on view of an external or internal wall, showing its features and often other elements that would be visible beyond or before the wall. (12, 413)

emblema—The central framed figural panel of a *mosaic* floor. (149)

embroidery—The technique of sewing threads onto a finished ground to form contrasting designs. Stem stitching employs short overlapping strands of thread to form jagged lines. Laid-and-couched work creates solid blocks of color. (362, 449, 510)

emir—A Muslim ruler. (293)

empiricism—The search for knowledge based on observation and direct experience. (775)

enamel—A decorative coating, usually colored, fused onto the surface of metal, glass, or ceramics. (301, 992, 28-24A)

encaustic—A painting *technique* in which pigment is mixed with melted wax and applied to the surface while the mixture is hot. (111, 218, 914)

engaged column—A half-round *column* attached to a wall. See also *pilaster*. (60, 290, 340, 588)

engraving—The process of *incising* a design in hard material, often a metal plate (usually copper); also, the *print* or impression made from such a plate. (555, 556)

Enlightenment—The Western philosophy based on empirical evidence that dominated the 18th century. The Enlightenment was a new way of thinking critically about the world and about humankind, independently of religion, myth, or tradition. (727)

en plein air—See *plein air*. (798, 799, 801, 805, 806, 28-2A, 28-7A)

ensi—A Sumerian ruler. (36)

entablature—The part of a building above the *columns* and below the roof. The entablature has three parts: *architrave, frieze,* and *pediment*. (116)

entasis—The convex profile (an apparent swelling) in the *shaft* of a *column*. (118)

Environmental Art—An American art form that emerged in the 1960s. Often using the land itself as their material, Environmental artists construct monuments of great scale and minimal form. Permanent or impermanent, these works transform some section of the environment, calling attention both to the land itself and to the hand of the artist. Sometimes referred to as earthworks. (932)

eravo—A ceremonial men's meetinghouse constructed by the Elema people in New Guinea. (1048)

escutcheon—An emblem bearing a coat of arms. (628)

etching—A kind of *engraving* in which the design is *incised* in a layer of wax or varnish on a metal plate. The parts of the plate left exposed are then etched (slightly eaten away) by the acid in which the plate is immersed after incising. See also *drypoint, intaglio*. (556)

Eucharist—In Christianity, the partaking of the bread and wine, which believers hold to be either Christ himself or symbolic of him. (241, 538)

evangelist—One of the four authors (Matthew, Mark, Luke, John) of the New Testament *Gospels*. (314)

Events—See *Fluxus*. (935)

exedra—Recessed area, usually semicircular. (196, 929)

exemplum virtutis—Latin, "example or model of virtue." (746)

Expressionism (adj. **Expressionist**)—Twentieth-century art that is the result of the artist's unique inner or personal vision and that often has an emotional dimension. Expressionism contrasts with art focused on visually describing the empirical world. (839)

facade—Usually, the front of a building; also, the other sides when they are emphasized architecturally. (52, 412)

faience—A low-fired opaque glasslike silicate. (94)

fan vault—See *vault*. (391)

fantasia—Italian, "imagination." One of several terms used in Italian *Renaissance* literature to praise the originality and talent of artists. (604)

fasces—A bundle of rods with an ax attached, representing an emblem of authority in ancient Rome. (752)

fauces—Latin, "jaws." In a Roman house, the narrow foyer leading to the *atrium*. (190)

Fauves—French, "wild beasts." See *Fauvism*. (836)

Fauvism—An early-20th-century art movement led by Henri Matisse. For the Fauves, *color* became the formal element most responsible for pictorial coherence and the primary conveyor of meaning. (836)

Favrile—A type of leaded stained glass patented by Louis Comfort Tiffany in the late 19th century. (28-36B)

femmages—The name American artist Miriam Schapiro gave to her sewn *collages,* assembled from fabrics, quilts, buttons, sequins, lace trim, and rickrack collected at antique shows and fairs. (922)

femme fatale—French, "fatal woman." A destructive temptress of men. (820)

femme savante—French, "learned woman." The term used to describe the cultured hostesses of *Rococo* salons. (729)

fenestra coeli—Latin, "window to Heaven." (688)

fenestrated—Having windows. (184)

fenestration—The arrangement of the windows of a building. (184)

fête galante—French, "amorous festival." A type of *Rococo* painting depicting the outdoor amusements of French upper class society. (732, 733)

feudalism—The medieval political, social, and economic system held together by the relationship between landholding *liege lords* and the *vassals* who were granted tenure of a portion of their land and in turn swore allegiance to the liege lord. (334, 536)

fibula (pl. **fibulae**)—A decorative pin, usually used to fasten garments. (167, 309)

fin-de-siècle—French, "end of the century." A period in Western cultural history from the end of the 19th century until just before World War I, when decadence and indulgence masked anxiety about an uncertain future. (823)

findspot—Place where an artifact was found; *provenance.* (18)

finial—A crowning ornament. (294, 541, 977)

First Style mural—The earliest style of Roman *mural* painting. Also called the Masonry style, because the aim of the artist was to imitate, using painted *stucco relief,* the appearance of costly marble panels. (191)

Flamboyant—A Late French *Gothic* style of architecture superseding the *Rayonnant* style and named for the flamelike appearance of its pointed bar *tracery.* (381)

flashing—In making *stained-glass* windows, fusing one layer of colored glass to another to produce a greater range of *colors.* (375)

fleur-de-lis—A three-petaled iris flower; the royal flower of France. (376, 388, 698)

Floreale—See *Art Nouveau.* (828)

florin—The denomination of gold coin of *Renaissance* Florence that became an international currency for trade. (417)

flute or **fluting**—Vertical channeling, roughly semicircular in cross-section and used principally on *columns* and *pilasters.* (51, 68, 116, 3-5A)

Fluxus—A group of American, European, and Japanese artists of the 1960s who created *Performance Art.* Their performances, or Events, often focused on single actions, such as turning a light on and off or watching falling snow, and were more theatrical than *Happenings.* (935)

flying buttress—See *buttress.* (12, 372, 373, 20-4A)

folio—A page of a manuscript or book. (248, 249)

fons vitae—Latin, "fountain of life." A symbolic fountain of everlasting life. (538)

foreshortening—The use of *perspective* to represent in art the apparent visual contraction of an object that extends back in space at an angle to the perpendicular plane of sight. (10, 44, 123, 401)

form—In art, an object's shape and structure, either in two dimensions (for example, a figure painted on a surface) or in three dimensions (such as a *statue*). (7)

formal analysis—The visual analysis of artistic *form.* (7)

formalism—Strict adherence to, or dependence on, stylized shapes and methods of *composition.* An emphasis on an artwork's visual elements rather than its subject. (902)

forum—The public square of an ancient Roman city. (189)

Fourth Style mural—In Roman *mural* painting, the Fourth Style marks a return to architectural *illusionism,* but the architectural vistas of the Fourth Style are irrational fantasies. (194)

freedmen, freedwomen—In ancient and medieval society, men and women who had been freed from servitude, as opposed to having been born free. (187)

freestanding sculpture—See *sculpture in the round.* (12, 18)

fresco—Painting on lime plaster, either dry (dry fresco, or fresco secco) or wet (true, or buon, fresco). In the latter method, the pigments are mixed with water and become chemically bound to the freshly laid lime plaster. Also, a painting executed in either method. (408, 409, 502)

fresco secco—See *fresco.* (74, 408, 603)

Friday mosque—See *congregational mosque.* (288)

frieze—The part of the *entablature* between the *architrave* and the *cornice;* also, any sculptured or painted band in a building. See *register.* (31, 116)

frigidarium—The cold-bath section of a Roman bathing establishment. (220)

furta sacra—Latin, "holy theft." (336)

fusuma—Japanese painted sliding-door panels. (1008)

Futurism—An early-20th-century Italian art movement that championed war as a cleansing agent and that celebrated the speed and dynamism of modern technology. (853)

garbha griha—Hindi, "womb chamber." In Hindu temples, the *cella,* the holy inner sanctum often housing the god's image or *symbol.* (439, 977)

genius—Latin, "spirit." In art, the personified spirit of a person or place. (22-52A)

genre—A *style* or category of art; also, a kind of painting that realistically depicts scenes from everyday life. (5, 551, 660)

Geometric—The *style* of Greek art during the ninth and eighth centuries BCE, characterized by *abstract* geometric ornament and schematic figures. (108)

German Expressionism—An early-20th-century regional Expressionist movement. (839)

gesso—Plaster mixed with a binding material, used as the base coat for paintings on wood panels. (545)

gestural abstraction—Also known as *action painting.* A kind of *abstract* painting in which the gesture, or act of painting, is seen as the subject of art. Its most renowned proponent was Jackson Pollock. See also *Abstract Expressionism.* (903)

giant order—See *colossal order.* (594)

gigantomachy—In ancient Greek mythology, the battle between gods and giants. (118, 22-54A)

giornata (pl. **giornate**)—Italian, "day." The section of plaster that a *fresco* painter expects to complete in one session. (408)

gladiator—An ancient Roman professional fighter, usually a slave, who competed in an *amphitheater.* (203)

glaze—A vitreous coating applied to pottery to seal and decorate the surface; it may be colored, transparent, or opaque, and glossy or *matte.* In *oil painting,* a thin, transparent, or semitransparent layer applied over a *color* to alter it slightly. (110, 451, 539, 583, 986, 992)

glazier—A glassworker. (375)

Gobelin tapestry—A *tapestry* produced on a vertical loom using a weaving *technique* in which no *weft* threads extend the full width of the fabric. (29-66B)

gold leaf—Gold beaten into tissue-paper-thin sheets that then can be applied to surfaces. (405)

gopis—South Asian herdswomen. (32-7A)

gopuras—The massive, ornamented entrance gateway towers of southern Indian temple compounds. (981)

gorget—A neck pendant, usually made of shell. (517)

gorgon—In ancient Greek mythology, a hideous female demon with snake hair. Medusa, the most famous gorgon, was capable of turning anyone who gazed at her into stone. (118)

Gospels—The four New Testament books that relate the life and teachings of Jesus. (312)

Gothic—Originally a derogatory term named after the Goths, used to describe the history, culture, and art of western Europe in the 12th to 14th centuries. Typically divided into periods designated Early (1140–1194), High (1194–1300), and Late (1300–1500). (365)

Gothic Revival—See *Neo-Gothic.* (788)

gouache—A painting *medium* consisting of watercolor mixed with gum. (843)

Grand Manner portraiture—A type of 18th-century portrait painting designed to communicate a person's grace and class through certain standardized conventions, such as the large scale of the figure relative to the canvas, the controlled pose, the *landscape* setting, and the low *horizon line.* (742)

granulation—A decorative technique in which tiny metal balls (granules) are fused to a metal surface. (167)

graver—An *engraving* tool. See also *burin.* (556)

great mosque—See *congregational mosque.* (288)

Greek cross—A cross with four arms of equal length. (271, 620, 676)

green architecture—Ecologically friendly architectural design using clean energy to sustain the natural environment. (961)

griffin—An eagle-headed winged lion. (51, 99, 4-9B, 10-5B)

grisaille—A *monochrome* painting done mainly in neutral grays to simulate sculpture. (409, 614, 13-36A, 20-8A)

groin—The edge formed by the intersection of two barrel *vaults.* (184)

groin vault—See *vault.* (184, 340, 350, 982, 14-12A)

ground line—In paintings and *reliefs,* a painted or carved baseline on which figures appear to stand. (20, 31)

guang—An ancient Chinese covered vessel, often in animal form, holding wine, water, grain, or meat for sacrificial rites. (452)

guild—An association of merchants, craftspersons, or scholars in medieval and *Renaissance* Europe. (366, 410)

haboku—In Japanese art, a loose and rapidly executed painting *style* in which the ink seems to have been applied by flinging or splashing it onto the paper. (1008)

Hadith—The words and exemplary deeds of the Prophet Muhammad. (285)

haiku—A 17-syllable Japanese poetic form. (1014)

halberd—A combination spear and battle-ax. (626)

hall church—See *Hallenkirche.* (348)

Hallenkirche—German, "hall church." A church design favored in Germany, but also used elsewhere, in which the *aisles* rise to the same height as the *nave.* (396)

handscroll—In Asian art, a horizontal painted scroll that is unrolled right to left, section by section, and often used to present illustrated religious texts or *landscapes.* (459, 991)

hanging scroll—In Asian art, a vertical scroll hung on a wall with pictures mounted or painted directly on it. (459, 991)

haniwa—Sculpted fired pottery cylinders, modeled in human, animal, or other forms and placed on Japanese *tumuli* of the Kofun period. (478)

Happenings—A term coined by American artist Allan Kaprow in the 1960s to describe loosely structured performances, whose creators were trying to suggest the aesthetic and dynamic qualities of everyday life; as actions, rather than objects, Happenings incorporate the fourth dimension (time). (934)

hard-edge painting—A variant of *Post-Painterly Abstraction* that rigidly excluded all reference to gesture and incorporated smooth knife-edge geometric forms to express the notion that painting should be reduced to its visual components. (907)

harmika—In Buddhist architecture, a stone fence or railing that encloses an area surmounting the *dome* of a *stupa* that represents one of the Buddhist heavens; from the center arises the *yasti.* (430)

harpies—Mythological creatures of the underworld. (22-8A)

haruspex (pl. **haruspices**)—An Etruscan priest who foretells events by studying animal livers. (6-13A)

hatching—A series of closely spaced drawn or *engraved* parallel lines. Cross-hatching employs sets of lines placed at right angles. (555)

head cluster—An abbreviated way of representing a crowd by painting or carving many heads close together, usually with too few bodies for the number of heads. (246)

heiau—A Hawaiian temple. (1057)

Helladic—The prehistoric art of the Greek mainland (*Hellas* in Greek). (87)

Hellas—The ancient name of Greece. (106)

Hellenes (adj. **Hellenic**)—The name the ancient Greeks called themselves as the people of *Hellas.* (106)

Hellenistic—The term given to the art and culture of the roughly three centuries between the death of Alexander the Great in 323 BCE and the death of Queen Cleopatra in 30 BCE, when Egypt became a Roman province. (153)

henge—An arrangement of *megalithic* stones in a circle, often surrounded by a ditch. (28)

heraldic composition—A *composition* that is symmetrical on either side of a central figure. (38)

herm—A bust on a quadrangular *pillar.* (133)

Hevehe—An elaborate cycle of ceremonial activities performed by the Elema people of the Papuan Gulf region of New Guinea. Also, the large, ornate masks produced for and presented during these ceremonies. (1047)

Hiberno-Saxon—An art *style* that flourished in the *monasteries* of the British Isles in the early Middle Ages. Also called Insular. (311)

hierarchy of scale—An artistic convention in which greater size indicates greater importance. (11, 31, 14-16A)

hieroglyphic—A system of writing using *symbols* or pictures. (55, 493)

high relief—See *relief.* (12, 65)

High-Tech—A contemporary architectural *style* calling for buildings that incorporate the latest innovations in engineering and technology and expose the structures' component parts. (961)

Hijra—The flight of Muhammad from Mecca to Medina in 622, the year from which Islam dates its beginnings. (285)

himation—An ancient Greek mantle worn by men and women over the *chiton* and draped in various ways. (115)

Hippodamian plan—A city *plan* devised by Hippodamos of Miletos ca. 466 BCE, in which a strict grid was imposed on a site, regardless of the terrain, so that all streets would meet at right angles. (154)

hiragana—A phonetic cursive script developed in Japan from Chinese *characters;* it came to be the primary script for Japanese court poetry. (484, 17-13B)

historiated—Ornamented with representations, such as plants, animals, or human figures, that have a narrative—as distinct from a purely decorative—function. (342)

hokkyo—Japanese, "bridge of the law." The third-highest rank among Buddhist monks. (34-9A)

hookah—A Moroccan water pipe. (27-17A)

horizon line—See *perspective.* (567)

hôtel—French, "town house." (728)

hubris—Greek, "arrogant pride." (143)

hue—The name of a *color.* See also *primary colors, secondary colors,* and *complementary colors.* (7, 813)

humanism—In the *Renaissance,* an emphasis on education and on expanding knowledge (especially of *classical* antiquity), the exploration of individual potential and a desire to excel, and a commitment to civic responsibility and moral duty. (407)

hydria—An ancient Greek three-handled water pitcher. (145)

hypaethral—A building having no *pediment* or roof, open to the sky. (154)

hypostyle hall—A hall with a roof supported by *columns.* (73, 288, 289)

icon—A portrait or image; especially in Byzantine churches, a panel with a painting of sacred personages that are objects of veneration. In the visual arts, a painting, a piece of sculpture, or even a building regarded as an object of veneration. (268, 269, 405)

iconoclasm—The destruction of religious or sacred images. In Byzantium, the period from 726 to 843 when there was an imperial ban on such images. The destroyers of images were known as iconoclasts. Those who opposed such a ban were known as iconophiles. (257, 269, 543, 652)

iconoclast—See *iconoclasm.* (257, 269, 543, 652)

iconography—Greek, the "writing of images." The term refers both to the content, or subject, of an artwork and to the study of content in art. It also includes the study of the symbolic, often religious, meaning of objects, persons, or events depicted in works of art. (5)

iconophile—See *iconoclasm.* (269)

iconostasis—Greek, "icon stand." In Byzantine churches, a screen or a partition, with doors and many tiers of *icons,* separating the sanctuary from the main body of the church. (279)

ikegobo—A Benin royal shrine. (520, 521)

illuminated manuscript—A luxurious handmade book with painted illustrations and decorations. (249, 405)

illusionism (adj. **illusionistic**)—The representation of the three-dimensional world on a two-dimensional surface in a manner that creates the illusion that the person, object, or place represented is three-dimensional. See also *perspective.* (8)

imagines—In ancient Rome, wax portraits of ancestors. (185, 196, 200)

imam—In Islam, the leader of collective worship. (288)

impasto—A layer of thickly applied pigment. (632, 902)

imperator—Latin, "commander in chief," from which the word *emperor* derives. (197)

impluvium—In a Roman house, the basin located in the *atrium* that collected rainwater. (190)

impost block—The uppermost block of a wall or *pier* beneath the *springing* of an *arch.* (21-31A)

Impressionism—A late-19th-century art movement that sought to capture a fleeting moment, thereby conveying the elusiveness and impermanence of images and conditions. (799)

in antis—In ancient Greek architecture, the area between the *antae.* (115)

incise—To cut into a surface with a sharp instrument; also, a method of decoration, especially on metal and pottery. (556)

incrustation—Wall decoration consisting of bright panels of different *colors*. (202, 355)

incubus—A demon believed in medieval times to prey, often sexually, on sleeping women. (762)

indulgence—A religious pardon for a sin committed. (374, 616, 652)

ingegno—Italian, "innate talent." One of several terms used in Italian *Renaissance* literature to praise the originality and talent of artists. (604)

installation—An artwork that creates an artistic environment in a room or gallery. (950, 30-25B)

insula (pl. **insulae**)—In Roman architecture, a multistory apartment house, usually made of brick-faced *concrete*; also refers to an entire city block. (213)

Insular—See *Hiberno-Saxon*. (311)

intaglio—A graphic technique in which the design is *incised,* or scratched, on a metal plate, either manually (*engraving, drypoint*) or chemically (*etching*). The incised lines of the design take the ink, making this the reverse of the *woodcut* technique. (556)

intensity—See *color*. (7)

interaxial or **intercolumniation**—The distance between the center of the lowest *drum* of a *column* and the center of the next. (135)

intercolumniation—See *interaxial*. (135)

internal evidence—In art history, the examination of what an artwork represents (people, clothing, hairstyles, and so on) in order to determine its date. Also, the examination of the *style* of an artwork to identify the artist who created it. (3)

International style—A *style* of 14th- and 15th-century painting begun by Simone Martini, who adapted the French *Gothic* manner to Sienese art fused with influences from northern Europe. This style appealed to the aristocracy because of its brilliant *color*, lavish costumes, intricate ornamentation, and themes involving splendid processions of knights and ladies. Also, a style of 20th-century architecture associated with Le Corbusier, whose elegance of design came to influence the look of modern office buildings and skyscrapers. (413, 886)

intonaco—In *fresco* painting, the last layer of smooth lime plaster applied to the wall; the painting layer. (408)

invenzione—Italian, "invention." One of several terms used in Italian *Renaissance* literature to praise the originality and talent of artists. (604)

investment—In hollow-casting, the final clay *mold* applied to the exterior of the wax model. (130)

Ionic—One of the two systems (or *orders*) invented in ancient Greece for articulating the three units of the elevation of a *classical* building: the platform, the *colonnade*, and the superstructure (*entablature*). The Ionic order is characterized by, among other features, *volutes, capitals, columns* with *bases*, and an uninterrupted *frieze*. (116, 587)

iron-wire lines—In ancient Chinese painting, thin brush lines suggesting tensile strength. (459, 482)

ivi p'o—Hollow, cylindrical bone or ivory ornaments produced in the Marquesas Islands (Polynesia). (1054)

iwan—In Islamic architecture, a *vaulted* rectangular recess opening onto a courtyard. (52, 288)

iy'oba—Benin queen mother. (532, 19-13A)

jambs—In architecture, the side posts of a doorway. (344)

Japonisme—The French fascination with all things Japanese. Japonisme emerged in the second half of the 19th century. (808)

jataka—Tales of the past lives of the Buddha. See also *sutra*. (430)

joined-wood technique—A Japanese sculptural *technique* in which a statue is assembled from multiple wood blocks, each hollowed out to make the pieces lighter. (17-13A)

jomon—Japanese, "cord markings." A type of Japanese ceramic technique characterized by ropelike markings. (476)

Jugendstil—See *Art Nouveau*. (828)

junzi—Chinese, "superior person" or "gentleman." A person who is a model of Confucian behavior. (463)

ka—In ancient Egypt, the immortal human life force. (57, 61)

Kaaba—Arabic, "cube." A small cubical building in Mecca, the Islamic world's symbolic center. (285)

kami—Shinto deities or spirits, believed in Japan to exist in nature (mountains, waterfalls) and in charismatic people. (479)

karesansui—Japanese dry-landscape gardening. (1006)

karma—In Vedic religions (see *Veda*), the ethical consequences of a person's life, which determine his or her fate. (427)

katsina—An art form of Native Americans of the Southwest, the katsina doll represents benevolent supernatural spirits (katsinas) living in mountains and water sources. (1033)

katsuogi—Wooden logs placed at right angles to the *ridgepole* of a Japanese shrine to hold the thatched roof in place. (480)

kautaha—Women's organizations in Tonga (Polynesia) that produce barkcloth. (1053)

keep—A fortified tower in a castle that served as a place of last refuge. (383)

kente—Brightly colored patterned cloth woven by Asante men on horizontal looms in long narrow strips sewn together to form *toga*-like robes. (1070, 1071, 37-13A)

keystone—See *voussoir*. (175, 344, 640)

khan—An Ottoman lord, or *sultan*. (10-23A)

khipu—Andean record-keeping device consisting of numerous knotted strings hanging from a main cord; the strings signified, by position and *color,* numbers and categories of things. (1030)

king's gallery—The band of *statues* running the full width of the *facade* of a *Gothic cathedral* directly above the *rose window*. (379, 380)

kiva—A square or circular underground structure that is the spiritual and ceremonial center of Pueblo Indian life. (518, 1032)

kline (pl. **klinai**)—A couch or funerary bed. A type of *sarcophagus* with a reclining portrait of the deceased on its lid. (217)

kodo—The lecture hall in a Japanese Buddhist temple complex. (475)

Kogan—The name of a distinctive type of *Shino* water jar. (1012)

kondo—Japanese, "golden hall." The main hall for worship in a Japanese Buddhist temple complex. The kondo contained *statues* of the Buddha and the *bodhisattvas* to whom the temple was dedicated. (475)

Koran—Islam's sacred book, composed of *surahs* (chapters) divided into verses. (285)

kore (pl. **korai**)—Greek, "young woman." An *Archaic* Greek *statue* of a young woman. (111)

koru—An unrolled spiral design used by the Maori of New Zealand in their *tattoos*. (1055)

kouros (pl. **kouroi**)—Greek, "young man." An *Archaic* Greek *statue* of a young man. (112)

krater—An ancient Greek wide-mouthed bowl for mixing wine and water. (102)

Kufic—An early form of Arabic script, characterized by angularity, with the uprights forming almost right angles with the baseline. (294)

kula—An exchange of white conus-shell arm ornaments and red chama-shell necklaces that takes place among the Trobriand Islanders of Papua New Guinea. (1049)

kupesi—Embroidered design tablets used by Tonga (Polynesia) women in the production of barkcloth. (1053)

kylix—An ancient Greek drinking cup with a wide bowl and two horizontal handles. (5-23A)

labrys—Minoan double-ax. (90)

labyrinth—Maze. The English word derives from the mazelike plan of the *Minoan* palace at Knossos. (90)

lacquer—A varnishlike substance made from the sap of the Asiatic sumac tree, used to decorate wood and other organic materials. Often colored with mineral pigments, lacquer cures to great hardness and has a lustrous surface. (453, 995)

laid-and-couched work—See *embroidery*. (362)

lakshana—One of the distinguishing marks of the Buddha. The lakshanas include the *urna* and *ushnisha*. (427)

lalitasana—In Buddhist iconography, the body pose with one leg folded and the other hanging down, indicating relaxation. (460)

lamassu—Assyrian guardian in the form of a man-headed winged bull. (46)

lancet—In *Gothic* architecture, a tall narrow window ending in a *pointed arch*. (370, 373, 890, 14-5A, 27-43A)

landscape—A picture showing natural scenery, without narrative content. (5, 27, 416)

Landschaft—German, "landscape." (662)

lateral section—See *section*. (12)

laudatio—Latin, "essay of praise." (570)

leading—In the manufacture of *stained-glass* windows, the joining of colored glass pieces using lead *cames*. (375)

lectionary—A book containing passages from the *Gospels*, arranged in the sequence that they are to be read during the celebration of religious services, including the *Mass*, throughout the year. (312)

lekythos (pl. **lekythoi**)—A flask containing perfumed oil; lekythoi were often placed in Greek graves as offerings to the deceased. (142)

libation—The pouring of liquid as part of a religious ritual. (36)

liege lord—In *feudalism*, a landowner who grants tenure of a portion of his land to a *vassal*. (334)

line—The extension of a point along a path, made concrete in art by drawing on or chiseling into a *plane*. (7)

linear perspective—See *perspective*. (192, 565, 567)

linga—In Hindu art, the depiction of Shiva as a phallus or cosmic *pillar*. (435)

linguist's staff—In Africa, a staff carried by a person authorized to speak for a king or chief. (1072)

lintel—A horizontal *beam* used to span an opening. (73, 99, 344)

literati—In China, talented amateur painters and scholars from the landed gentry. (956, 991, 31-22A, 33-1A)

lithograph—See *lithography*. (778)

lithography—A printmaking technique in which the artist uses an oil-based crayon to draw directly on a stone plate and then wipes water onto the stone. When ink is rolled onto the plate, it adheres only to the drawing. The *print* produced by this method is a lithograph. (778)

liturgy (adj. **liturgical**)—The official ritual of public worship. (242)

lituus—The curved staff carried by an *augur*. (165)

local color—An object's true *color* in white light. (801)

loculi—Openings in the walls of *catacombs* to receive the dead. (237)

loggia—A gallery with an open *arcade* or a *colonnade* on one or both sides. (576, 14-19A)

lohan—A Buddhist holy person who has achieved enlightenment and *nirvana* by suppression of all desire for earthly things. (468)

longitudinal plan—See *plan*. (243)

longitudinal section—See *section*. (12)

lost-wax (cire perdue) process—A bronze-casting method in which a figure is modeled in wax and covered with clay; the whole is fired, melting away the wax (French, *cire perdue*) and hardening the clay, which then becomes a *mold* for molten metal. (130, 507, 673, 983)

low relief—See *relief*. (12)

lunette—A semicircular area (with the flat side down) in a wall over a door, niche, or window; also, a painting or *relief* with a semicircular frame. (237, 344, 551, 7-54A)

lux nova—Latin, "new light." Abbot Suger's term for the light that enters a *Gothic* church through *stained-glass* windows. (369, 375)

machicolated gallery—A gallery in a defensive tower with holes in the floor to allow stones or hot liquids to be dumped on enemies below. (416)

madrasa—An Islamic theological college adjoining and often containing a *mosque*. (296)

maebyeong—A Korean vase similar to the Chinese *meiping*. (472)

magus (pl. **magi**)—One of the three wise men from the East who presented gifts to the infant Jesus. (240)

ma-hevehe—Mythical Oceanic water spirits. The Elema people of New Guinea believed these spirits visited their villages. (1047)

malanggan—Festivals held in honor of the deceased in New Ireland (Papua New Guinea). Also, the carvings and objects produced for these festivals. (1049)

mana—In Polynesia, spiritual power. (1052)

mandala—Sanskrit term for the sacred diagram of the universe; Japanese, mandara. (430, 439, 483)

mandapa—*Pillared* hall of a Hindu temple. (439)

mandara—See *mandala*. (430, 439, 483)

mandorla—An almond-shaped *nimbus* surrounding the figure of Christ or other sacred figure. In Buddhist Japan, a lotus-petal-shaped nimbus. (267, 460)

maniera—Italian, "style" or "manner." See *Mannerism*. (632, 682)

maniera greca—Italian, "Greek manner." The Italo-*Byzantine* painting *style* of the 13th century. (404, 14-7A)

Mannerism—A *style* of later *Renaissance* art that emphasized "artifice," often involving contrived imagery not derived directly from nature. Such artworks showed a self-conscious stylization involving complexity, caprice, fantasy, and polish. Mannerist architecture tended to flout the *classical* rules of order, stability, and symmetry, sometimes to the point of parody. (632)

manor—In *feudalism*, the estate of a *liege lord*. (334)

mantra—Sanskrit term for the ritual words or syllables recited in *Shingon* Buddhism. (483)

manulua—Triangular patterns based on the form of two birds, common in Tongan *tapa* designs. (1054)

maqsura—In some *mosques*, a screened area in front of the *mihrab* reserved for a ruler. (283, 288)

martyr—A person who chooses to die rather than deny his or her religious belief. See also *saint*. (237)

martyrium—A shrine to a Christian *martyr*. (274, 619)

Masonry Style—See *First Style mural*. (191)

mass—The bulk, density, and weight of matter in *space*. (8)

Mass—The Catholic and Orthodox ritual in which believers understand that Christ's redeeming sacrifice on the cross is repeated when the priest consecrates the bread and wine in the *Eucharist*. (241)

mastaba—Arabic, "bench." An ancient Egyptian rectangular brick or stone structure with sloping sides erected over a subterranean tomb chamber connected with the outside by a shaft. (58)

matins—In Christianity, early morning prayers. (550, 13-36A)

matte—In painting, pottery, and photography, a dull finish. (538)

maulstick—A stick used to steady the hand while painting. (661)

mausoleum—A monumental tomb. The name derives from the mid-fourth-century BCE tomb of Mausolos at Halikarnassos, one of the Seven Wonders of the ancient world. (225, 537, 980)

mbari—A ceremonial Igbo (Nigeria) house built about every 50 years in honor of the earth goddess Ala. (1070, 1077)

mbulu ngulu—The wood-and-metal *reliquary* guardian figures of the Kota of Gabon. (1064)

meander—An ornament, usually in bands but also covering broad surfaces, consisting of interlocking geometric motifs. An ornamental pattern of contiguous straight lines joined usually at right angles. (108)

medium (pl. **media**)—The material (for example, marble, bronze, clay, *fresco*) in which an artist works; also, in painting, the vehicle (usually liquid) that carries the pigment. (7)

megalith (adj. **megalithic**)—Greek, "great stone." A large, roughly hewn stone used in the construction of monumental prehistoric structures. (27)

megaron—The large reception hall and throne room in a *Mycenaean* palace, fronted by an open, two-*columned* porch. (97)

meiping—A Chinese vase of a high-shouldered shape; the *sgraffito technique* was used in decorating such vases. (467, 472)

mela medica—Italian, "medicinal apples" (oranges). The emblem of the Medici family of *Renaissance* Florence. (580)

memento mori—Latin, "reminder of death." In painting, a reminder of human mortality, usually represented by a skull. (695, 26-7A, 30-25B)

mendicants—In medieval Europe, friars belonging to the Franciscan and Dominican orders, who renounced all worldly goods, lived by contributions of laypersons (the word *mendicant* means "beggar"), and devoted themselves to preaching, teaching, and doing good works. (385, 404)

menorah—In antiquity, the Jewish sacred seven-branched candelabrum. (207)

merlon—See *crenellation*. (382)

Mesoamerica—The region that comprises Mexico, Guatemala, Belize, Honduras, and the Pacific coast of El Salvador. (492, 1023)

Mesolithic—The "middle" Stone Age, between the *Paleolithic* and the *Neolithic* ages. (16)

Messiah—The savior of the Jews prophesied in Hebrew scripture. Christians believe that Jesus of Nazareth was the Messiah. (240)

metamatics—The name Swiss artist Jean Tinguely gave to the motor-driven devices he constructed to produce instant abstract paintings. (935)

metope—The square panel between the *triglyphs* in a *Doric frieze*, often sculpted in *relief*. (116)

mihrab—A semicircular niche set into the *qibla* wall of a *mosque*. (287, 288)

minaret—A distinctive feature of *mosque* architecture, a tower from which the faithful are called to worship. (134, 261, 287, 288, 977)

minbar—In a *mosque*, the *pulpit* on which the *imam* stands. (287, 288)

mingei—A type of modern Japanese folk pottery. (1019)

miniatures—Small individual Indian paintings intended to be held in the hand and viewed by one or two individuals at one time. (978, 979, 28-24A)

Minimalism—A predominantly sculptural American trend of the 1960s characterized by works featuring a severe reduction of *form*, often to single, homogeneous units. (910)

Minoan—The prehistoric art of Crete, named after the legendary King Minos of Knossos. (87)

Minotaur—The mythical beast, half man and half bull, that inhabited the *labyrinth* of the *Minoan* palace at Knossos. (86)

Miraj—The ascension of the Prophet Muhammad to Heaven. (286)

mithuna—In South Asian art, a male-female couple embracing or engaged in sexual intercourse. (431)

moai—Large, blocky figural stone sculptures found on Rapa Nui (Easter Island) in Polynesia. (1052)

mobile—A kind of sculpture, invented by Alexander Calder, combining nonobjective organic forms and motion in balanced structures hanging from rods, wires, and colored, organically shaped plates. (895)

modeling—The shaping or fashioning of three-dimensional forms in a soft material, such as clay; also, the gradations of light and shade reflected from the surfaces of matter in space, or the illusion of such gradations produced by alterations of value in a drawing, painting, or print. (113, 145, 146)

modernism—A movement in Western art that developed in the second half of the 19th century and sought to capture the images and sensibilities of the age. Modernist art goes beyond simply dealing with the present and involves the artist's critical examination of the premises of art itself. (801, 998)

Modernismo—See *Art Nouveau*. (828)

module (adj. **modular**)—A basic unit of which the dimensions of the major parts of a work are multiples. The principle is used in sculpture and other art forms, but it is most often employed in architecture, where the module may be the dimensions of an important part of a building, such as the diameter of a *column*. (10, 323, 457, 582)

moko—The form of tattooing practiced by the Maori of New Zealand. (1055)

moksha—See *nirvana*. (427, 435)

mold—A hollow form for *casting*. (11)

molding—In architecture, a continuous, narrow surface (projecting or recessed, plain or ornamented) designed to break up a surface, to accent, or to decorate. (82)

monastery—A group of buildings in which monks live together, set apart from the secular community of a town. (267, 537)

monastic—Relating to life in a *monastery*. (267, 404, 537)

monastic order—An organization of monks living according to the same rules, for example, the Benedictine, Franciscan, and Dominican orders. (404)

monochrome (adj. **monochromatic**)—One color. (194, 705)

monolith (adj. **monolithic**)—A stone *column shaft* that is all in one piece (not composed of *drums*); a large, single block or piece of stone used in *megalithic* structures. Also, a colossal statue carved from a single piece of stone. (116, 428)

monotheism—The worship of one all-powerful god. (233)

moralized Bible—A heavily illustrated Bible, each page pairing paintings of Old and New Testament episodes with explanations of their moral significance. (385)

mortise-and-tenon system—See *tenon*. (480)

mortuary temple—In Egyptian architecture, a temple erected for the worship of a deceased *pharaoh*. (62)

mosaic—Patterns or pictures made by embedding small pieces (*tesserae*) of stone or glass in cement on surfaces such as walls and floors; also, the *technique* of making such works. (245, 1024, 28-24A)

mosaic tilework—An Islamic decorative *technique* in which large ceramic panels are fired, cut into smaller pieces, and set in plaster. (299)

moschophoros—Greek, "calf bearer." (112)

mosque—The Islamic building for collective worship. From the Arabic word *masjid*, meaning a "place for bowing down." (261, 288)

Mozarabic—Referring to the Christian culture of northern Spain during the time Islamic *caliphs* ruled southern Spain. (316)

mudra—In Buddhist and Hindu iconography, a stylized and symbolic hand gesture. The dhyana (meditation) mudra consists of the right hand over the left, palms upward, in the lap. In the bhumisparsha (earth-touching) mudra, the right hand reaches down to the ground, calling the earth to witness the Buddha's enlightenment. The dharmachakra (Wheel of the Law, or teaching) mudra is a two-handed gesture with right thumb and index finger forming a circle. The abhaya (do not fear) mudra, with the right hand up, palm outward, is a gesture of protection or blessing. (427)

Mughal—"Descended from the Mongols." The Muslim rulers of India, 1526–1857. (975)

Muhaqqaq—A cursive style of Islamic *calligraphy*. (300)

mullion—A vertical member that divides a window or that separates one window from another. (381, 930)

mummification—A *technique* used by ancient Egyptians to preserve human bodies so that they may serve as the eternal home of the immortal *ka*. (61)

muqarnas—Stucco decorations of Islamic buildings in which stalactite-like forms break a structure's solidity. (274, 296, 9-27A)

mural—A wall painting. (22, 407, 408, 409)

Muslim—A believer in Islam. (976)

Mycenaean—The prehistoric art of the Late *Helladic* period in Greece, named after the citadel of Mycenae. (87)

mystery play—A dramatic enactment of the holy mysteries of the Christian faith performed at church portals and in city squares. (409, 538, 12-35A)

mystic marriage—A spiritual marriage of a woman with Christ. (549)

Nabis—Hebrew, "prophet." A group of *Symbolist* painters influenced by Paul Gauguin. (819)

naos—See *cella*. (33, 115, 618)

narthex—A porch or vestibule of a church, generally *colonnaded* or *arcaded* and preceding the *nave*. (243)

natatio—The swimming pool in a Roman bathing establishment. (220)

naturalism—The style of painted or sculptured representation based on close observation of the natural world that was at the core of the *classical* tradition. (401)

Naturalistic Surrealism—See *Surrealism*. (875)

nave—The central area of an ancient Roman *basilica* or of a church, demarcated from *aisles* by *piers* or *columns*. (189, 243, 413, 20-4A)

nave arcade—In *basilica* architecture, the series of *arches* supported by *piers* or *columns* separating the *nave* from the *aisles*. (373)

nduen fobara—A Kalabari Ijaw (Nigeria) ancestral screen in honor of a deceased chief of a trading house. (1060, 1061)

necropolis—Greek, "city of the dead." A large burial area or cemetery. (58, 171)

nembutsu—The six-syllable Japanese prayer professing faith in the compassion of Amida Buddha. (488)

nemes—In ancient Egypt, the linen headdress worn by the *pharaoh*, with the *uraeus* cobra of kingship on the front. (64)

Neoclassicism—A *style* of art and architecture that emerged in the late 18th century as part of a general revival of interest in *classical* cultures. Neoclassical artists adopted themes and styles from ancient Greece and Rome. (745)

Neo-Expressionism—An art movement that emerged in the 1970s and that reflects artists' interest in the expressive capability of art, seen earlier in *German Expressionism* and *Abstract Expressionism*. (905, 30-8D)

Neo-Gothic—The revival of the *Gothic style* in architecture, especially in the 19th century. (788)

Neolithic—The "new" Stone Age. (16)

Neoplasticism—The Dutch artist Piet Mondrian's theory of "pure plastic art," an ideal balance between the universal and the individual using an abstract formal vocabulary. (881)

Neue Sachlichkeit—German, "new objectivity." An art movement that grew directly out of the World War I experiences of a group of German artists who sought to show the horrors of the war and its effects. (872)

ngatu—Decorated *tapa* made by women in Tonga. (1053, 1054)

niello—A black metallic alloy. (100)

nihonga—A 19th-century Japanese painting style that incorporated some Western techniques in Japanese-style painting, as opposed to *yoga* (Western painting). (1019)

nimbus—A halo or aureole appearing around the head of a holy figure to signify divinity. (248, 441)

nio—A Japanese guardian figure. (17-17A)

nipote—Italian, "nephew." (21-41A)

nirvana—In Buddhism and Hinduism, a blissful state brought about by absorption of the individual soul or consciousness into the supreme spirit. Also called moksha. (423, 427)

nishiki-e—Japanese, "brocade pictures." Japanese polychrome *woodcut prints* valued for their sumptuous colors. (1015)

nkisi n'kondi—A power figure carved by the Kongo people of the Democratic Republic of Congo. Such images embodied spirits believed to heal and give life or to be capable of inflicting harm or death. (1066)

nomarch—Egyptian, "great/overlord." A regional governor during the Middle Kingdom. (3-16A)

Nun—In ancient Egypt, the primeval waters from which the creator god emerged. (57)

nymphs—In *classical* mythology, female divinities of springs, caves, and woods. (107)

oba—An African sacred king. (521, 19-13A)

oculus (pl. **oculi**)—Latin, "eye." The round central opening of a *dome*. Also, a small round window in a *Gothic cathedral*. (184, 202, 373, 14-6A, 21-31A)

odalisque—A woman in a Turkish harem. (761)

ogee arch—An *arch* composed of two double-curving lines meeting at a point. (420, 13-42A)

ogive (adj. **ogival**)—The diagonal *rib* of a *Gothic vault*; a pointed, or Gothic, *arch*. (369, 402, 927, 21-31A)

Ogoga—A Yoruba king. (1072)

oil painting—A painting *technique* using oil-based pigments that rose to prominence in northern Europe in the 15th century and is now the standard medium for painting on canvas. (538)

oni—An African ruler. (527)

Op Art—An artistic movement of the 1960s in which painters sought to produce optical illusions of motion and depth using only geometric forms on two-dimensional surfaces. (908)

opere francigeno—See *opus francigenum*. (366, 389)

opisthodomos—In ancient Greek architecture, a porch at the rear of a temple, set against the blank back wall of the *cella*. (115)

optical mixture—The visual effect of juxtaposed *complementary colors*. (813)

optical representation—The representation of people and objects seen from a fixed viewpoint. (35)

opus francigenum—Latin, "French work." Architecture in the *style* of *Gothic* France; *opere francigeno* (adj.), "in the French manner." (366, 389)

opus modernum—Latin, "modern work." The late medieval term for *Gothic* art and architecture. Also called *opus francigenum*. (365, 373, 389)

opus reticulatum—An ancient Roman method of facing *concrete* walls with lozenge-shaped bricks or stones to achieve a netlike ornamental surface pattern. (11-19A)

oracle—A prophetic message. (5-17A)

orant—In Early Christian art, a figure with both arms raised in the ancient gesture of prayer. (238)

oratory—The church of a Christian *monastery*. (267)

orbiculum—A disklike opening. (930)

orchestra—Greek, "dancing place." In ancient Greek theaters, the circular piece of earth with a hard and level surface on which the performance took place. (151)

order—In *classical* architecture, a *style* represented by a characteristic design of the *columns* and *entablature*. See also *superimposed orders*. (116)

Orientalizing—The early phase of *Archaic* Greek art (seventh century BCE), so named because of the adoption of forms and motifs from the ancient Near East and Egypt. See also *Daedalic*. (109)

Orphism—A form of *Cubism* developed by the French painter Robert Delaunay in which color plays an important role. (848)

orrery—A mechanical model of the solar system demonstrating how the planets revolve around the sun. (727)

orthogonal—A line imagined to be behind and perpendicular to the picture *plane*; the orthogonals in a painting appear to recede toward a *vanishing point* on the horizon. (547, 567)

orthogonal plan—The imposition of a strict grid *plan* on a site, regardless of the terrain, so that all streets meet at right angles. See also *Hippodamian plan*. (154)

Ottonian (adj.)—Pertaining to the empire of Otto I and his successors. (324)

overglaze—In *porcelain* decoration, the technique of applying mineral colors over the *glaze* after the work has been fired. The overglaze colors, or *enamels*, fuse to the glazed surface in a second firing at a much lower temperature than the main firing. See also *underglaze*. (992)

oxidizing—The first phase of the ancient Greek ceramic firing process, which turned both the pot and the clay *slip* red. During the second (reducing) phase, the oxygen supply into the kiln was shut off, and both pot and slip turned black. In the final (reoxidizing) phase, the pot's coarser material reabsorbed oxygen and became red again, whereas the smoother slip did not and remained black. (110)

pagoda—An East Asian tower, usually associated with a Buddhist temple, having a multiplicity of winged *eaves*; thought to be derived from the Indian *stupa*. (467, 986)

pala—A panel placed behind and over the altar in a church. (9-26A)

palaestra—An ancient Greek and Roman exercise area, usually framed by a *colonnade*. In Greece, the palaestra was an independent building; in Rome, palaestras were also frequently incorporated into a bathing complex. (133, 220)

Paleolithic—The "old" Stone Age, during which humankind produced the first sculptures and paintings. (16, 522)

palette—A thin board with a thumb hole at one end on which an artist lays and mixes *colors*; any surface so used. Also, the colors or kinds of colors characteristically used by an artist. In ancient Egypt, a slate slab used for preparing makeup. (20, 55)

palette knife—A flat tool used to scrape paint off the *palette*. Artists sometimes also use the palette knife in place of a brush to apply paint directly to the canvas. (777)

Pantokrator—Greek, "ruler of all." Christ as ruler and judge. (272)

papier collé—French, "stuck paper." See *collage*. (850)

papyrus—A plant native to Egypt and adjacent lands used to make paperlike writing material; also, the material or any writing on it. (56, 249)

parade helmet—A masklike helmet worn by Roman soldiers on special ceremonial occasions. (336)

parallel hatching—See *hatching*. (555)

parapet—A low, protective wall along the edge of a balcony, roof, or bastion. (416)

parchment—Lambskin prepared as a surface for painting or writing. (249, 604)

parekklesion—The side chapel in a Byzantine church. (279)

parinirvana—Image of the reclining Buddha, a position often interpreted as representing his death. (427)

parthenos—Greek, "virgin." The epithet of Athena, the virgin goddess. (107)

passage grave—A prehistoric tomb with a long stone corridor leading to a burial chamber covered by a great *tumulus*. (27)

Passional—A Christian book containing the lives of *saints*. (312)

Passover—The annual feast celebrating the release of the Jews from bondage to the *pharaohs* of Egypt. (240)

pastel—A powdery paste of pigment and gum used for making crayons; also, the pastel crayons themselves. (809)

paten—A large shallow bowl or plate for the bread used in the *Eucharist*. (264)

patrician—A Roman freeborn landowner. (181)

patron—The person or entity that pays an artist to produce individual artworks or employs an artist on a continuing basis. (6)

pebble mosaic—A *mosaic* made of irregularly shaped stones of various *colors*. (149, 245)

pectoral—An ornament on the chest. (167)

pediment—In *classical* architecture, the triangular space (gable) at the end of a building, formed by the ends of the sloping roof above the *colonnade*; also, an ornamental feature having this shape. (105, 116, 582)

pendant—The large hanging terminal element of a *Gothic* fan *vault*. (391)

pendentive—A concave, triangular section of a hemisphere, four of which provide the transition from a square area to the circular base of a covering *dome*. Although pendentives appear to be hanging (pendant) from the dome, they in fact support it. (262, 585, 614)

Pentateuch—The first five books of the Old Testament. (235, 312)

peplos (pl. **peploi**)—A simple, long belted garment of wool worn by women in ancient Greece. (114)

Performance Art—An American *avant-garde* art trend of the 1960s that made time an integral element of art. It produced works in which movements, gestures, and sounds of persons communicating with an audience replace physical objects. Documentary photographs are generally the only evidence remaining after these events. See also *Happenings*. (993, 1019)

period style—See *style*. (3)

peripteral—See *peristyle*. (115)

peristyle—In *classical* architecture, a *colonnade* all around the *cella* and its porch(es). A peripteral colonnade consists of a single row of *columns* on all sides; a dipteral colonnade has a double row all around. (115, 190)

Perpendicular—A Late English *Gothic style* of architecture distinguished by the pronounced verticality of its decorative details. (391)

personal style—See *style*. (4)

personification—An *abstract* idea represented in bodily form. (5)

perspective—A method of presenting an illusion of the three-dimensional world on a two-dimensional surface. In linear perspective, the most common type, all parallel lines or surface edges converge on one, two, or three vanishing points located with reference to the eye level of the viewer (the horizon line of the picture), and associated objects are rendered smaller the farther from the viewer they are intended to seem. Atmospheric, or aerial, perspective creates the illusion of distance by the greater diminution of color intensity, the shift in color toward an almost neutral blue, and the blurring of contours as the intended distance between eye and object increases. (8, 409, 547, 565, 567)

pfemba—A Yombe (Democratic Republic of Congo) mother-and-child group. (1066)

pharaoh (adj. **pharaonic**)—An ancient Egyptian king. (55)

phersu—A masked man who appears in scenes of Etruscan funerary games. (165)

philosophe—French, "thinker, philosopher." The term applied to French intellectuals of the *Enlightenment*. (736)

Phoibos—Greek, "radiant." The epithet of the Greek god Apollo. (107)

photomontage—A *composition* made by pasting together pictures or parts of pictures, especially photographs. See also *collage*. (835)

Photorealism—See *Superrealism*. (917)

physical evidence—In art history, the examination of the materials used to produce an artwork in order to determine its date. (2)

piano nobile—Italian, "noble floor." The main (second) floor of a building. (21-37A)

piazza—Italian, "plaza." (672)

pictograph—A picture, usually stylized, that represents an idea; also, writing using such means; also, painting on rock. See also *hieroglyphic*. (32)

Picturesque garden—An "unordered" garden designed in accord with the *Enlightenment* taste for the natural. (750)

pier—A vertical, freestanding masonry support. (12, 72, 184)

Pietà—A painted or sculpted representation of the Virgin Mary mourning over the body of the dead Christ. (241, 396, 544, 842)

pilaster—A flat, rectangular, vertical member projecting from a wall of which it forms a part. It usually has a *base* and a *capital* and is often *fluted*. (175, 575)

pillar—Usually a weight-carrying member, such as a *pier* or a *column*; sometimes an isolated, freestanding structure used for commemorative purposes. (71, 72)

pinakotheke—Greek, "picture gallery." An ancient Greek building for the display of paintings on wood panels. (139)

pinnacle—In *Gothic* churches, a sharply pointed ornament capping the *piers* or flying *buttresses*; also used on church *facades*. (373, 411, 413, 27-43A)

Pittura Metafisica—Italian, "metaphysical painting." An early 20th century Italian art movement led by Giorgio de Chirico, whose work conveys an eerie mood and visionary quality. (875)

pixels—Shortened form of "picture elements." The tiny boxes that make up digital images displayed on a computer monitor. (938)

plan—The horizontal arrangement of the parts of a building or of the buildings and streets of a city or town, or a drawing or diagram showing such an arrangement. In an axial plan, the parts of a building are organized longitudinally, or along a given axis; in a central plan, the parts of the structure are of equal or almost equal dimensions around the center. (12)

plane—A flat surface. (7)

plate tracery—See *tracery*. (375)

Plateresque—A style of Spanish architecture characterized by elaborate decoration based on *Gothic,* Italian *Renaissance,* and Islamic sources; derived from the Spanish word *platero,* meaning "silversmith." (664)

platero—See *Plateresque*. (664)

plebeian—The Roman social class that included small farmers, merchants, and freed slaves. (181)

plein air—An approach to painting very popular among the *Impressionists,* in which an artist sketches outdoors to achieve a quick impression of light, air, and color. The artist then takes the sketches to the studio for reworking into more finished works of art. (798, 799, 801, 805, 806, 28-2A, 28-7A)

poesia—A term describing "poetic" art, notably Venetian *Renaissance* painting, which emphasizes the lyrical and sensual. (626)

pointed arch—A narrow *arch* of pointed profile, in contrast to a semicircular arch. (3, 368, 402, 420, 977, 12-10A, 21-31A)

pointillism—A system of painting devised by the 19th-century French painter Georges Seurat. The artist separates *color* into its component parts and then applies the component colors to the canvas in tiny dots (points). The image becomes comprehensible only from a distance, when the viewer's eyes optically blend the pigment dots. Sometimes referred to as divisionism. (812)

polis (pl. **poleis**)—An independent *city-state* in ancient Greece. (106)

polyptych—An *altarpiece* composed of more than three sections. (538)

polytheism—The belief in multiple gods. (233)

pontifex maximus—Latin, "chief priest." The high priest of the Roman state religion, often the emperor himself. (197)

Pop Art—A term coined by British art critic Lawrence Alloway to refer to art, first appearing in the 1950s, that incorporated elements from consumer culture, the mass media, and popular culture, such as images from motion pictures and advertising. (899)

porcelain—Extremely fine, hard, white ceramic. Unlike *stoneware*, porcelain is made from a fine white clay called kaolin mixed with ground petuntse, a type of feldspar. True porcelain is translucent and rings when struck. (451, 992)

portico—A roofed *colonnade*; also an entrance porch. (154, 576)

positivism—A Western philosophical model that promoted science as the mind's highest achievement. (775)

post-and-lintel system—A system of construction in which two posts support a *lintel*. (28)

Post-Impressionism—The term used to describe the stylistically heterogeneous work of the group of late-19th-century painters in France, including van Gogh, Gauguin, Seurat, and Cézanne, who more systematically examined the properties and expressive qualities of *line,* pattern, *form,* and *color* than the *Impressionists* did. (811)

postmodernism—A reaction against *modernist formalism,* seen as elitist. Far more encompassing and accepting than the more rigid confines of modernist practice, postmodernism offers something for everyone by accommodating a wide range of *styles,* subjects, and formats, from traditional easel painting to *installation* and from *abstraction* to *illusionistic* scenes. Postmodern art often includes irony or reveals a self-conscious awareness on the part of the artist of art-making processes or the workings of the art world. (929)

Post-Painterly Abstraction—An American art movement that emerged in the 1960s and was characterized by a cool, detached rationality emphasizing tighter pictorial control. See also *color-field painting* and *hard-edge painting*. (907)

pou tokomanawa—A sculpture of an ancestor that supports a *ridgepole* of a Maori (New Zealand) meetinghouse. (1043)

pouncing—The method of transferring a sketch onto paper or a wall by tracing, using thin paper or transparent gazelle skin placed on top of the sketch, pricking the contours of the design into the skin or paper with a pin, placing the skin or paper on the surface to be painted, and forcing black pigment through the holes. (482, 979, 32-5A)

poupou—A decorated wall panel in a Maori (New Zealand) meetinghouse. (1043, 1055)

Poussiniste—A member of the French Royal Academy of Painting and Sculpture during the early 18th century who followed Nicolas Poussin in insisting that *form* was the most important element of painting. See also *Rubéniste*. (733)

powwow—A traditional Native American ceremony featuring dancing in quilled, beaded, and painted costumes. (1040)

prasada—In Hindu worship, food that becomes sacred by first being given to a god. (441)

Precisionism—An American art movement of the 1920s and 1930s. The Precisionists concentrated on portraying man-made environments in a clear and concise manner to express the beauty of perfect and precise machine forms. (867)

pre-Columbian (adj.)—The cultures that flourished in the Western Hemisphere before the arrival of Christopher Columbus and the beginning of European contact and conquest. (492)

predella—The narrow ledge on which an *altarpiece* rests on an altar. (411)

prefiguration—In Early Christian art, the depiction of Old Testament persons and events as prophetic forerunners of Christ and New Testament events. (238, 547, 561)

primary colors—Red, yellow, and blue—the *colors* from which all other colors may be derived. (7, 813)

primitivism—The incorporation in early-20th-century Western art of stylistic elements from the artifacts of Africa, Oceania, and the native peoples of the Americas. (845, 846)

princeps—Latin, "first citizen." The title Augustus and his successors as Roman emperor used to distinguish themselves from Hellenistic monarchs. (197)

print—An artwork on paper, usually produced in multiple impressions. (556)

Productivism—An art movement that emerged in the Soviet Union after the Russian Revolution; its members believed that artists must direct art toward creating products for the new society. (860)

pronaos—The space, or porch, in front of the *cella*, or naos, of an ancient Greek temple. (115)

proportion—The relationship in size of the parts of persons, buildings, or objects, often based on a *module*. (10)

proscenium—The part of a theatrical stage in front of the curtain. (675)

prostyle—A *classical* temple *plan* in which the *columns* are only in front of the *cella* and not on the sides or back. (115)

protome—The head, forelegs, and part of the body of an animal. (51)

provenance—Origin or source; *findspot*. (3)

psalter—A book containing the Psalms. (312, 550)

pseudoperipteral—In Roman architecture, a pseudoperipteral temple has a series of engaged *columns* all around the sides and back of the *cella* to give the appearance of a *peripteral colonnade*. (182)

pueblo—A communal multistoried dwelling made of stone or *adobe* brick by the Native Americans of the Southwest. Uppercase *Pueblo* refers to various groups that occupied such dwellings. (518, 1032)

pukao—A small red scoria cylinder serving as a topknot or hat on Easter Island *moai*. (1052)

pulpit—A raised platform in a church or *mosque* on which a priest or *imam* stands while leading the religious service. (402)

pulque—An intoxicating drink, similar to tequila, consumed during *Mesoamerican* religious rituals. (18-7A)

punchwork—Tooled decorative work in *gold leaf*. (412)

Purism—An early-20th-century art movement that embraced the "machine aesthetic" and sought purity of *form* in the clean functional lines of industrial machinery. (853)

purlins—Horizontal *beams* in a roof structure, parallel to the *ridgepoles*, resting on the main *rafters* and giving support to the secondary rafters. (457)

putto (pl. putti)—A cherubic young boy. (570)

pylon—The wide entrance gateway of an Egyptian temple, characterized by its sloping walls. (72)

pyxis (pl. pyxides)—A cylindrical container with a hemispherical lid. (293)

qibla—The direction (toward Mecca) Muslims face when praying. (288, 289, 529)

quadrant arch—An *arch* whose curve extends for one-quarter of a circle's circumference. (359)

quadrifrons—Latin, "four-fronted." An *arch* with four equal *facades* and four *arcuated bays*. (23-14A)

quadro riportato—A ceiling design in which painted scenes are arranged in panels that re-

semble framed pictures transferred to the surface of a shallow, curved *vault*. (680)

quatrefoil—A shape or plan in which the parts assume the form of a cloverleaf. (419)

Quattrocento—Italian, "400," that is, the 1400s or 15th century. (559)

quoins—The large, sometimes *rusticated*, usually slightly projecting stones that often form the corners of the exterior walls of masonry buildings. (621)

radiating chapels—In medieval churches, chapels for the display of *relics* that opened directly onto the *ambulatory* and the *transept*. (337)

radiocarbon dating—A method of measuring the decay rate of carbon isotopes in organic matter to determine the age of organic materials such as wood and fiber. (22, 523)

rafters—The sloping supporting timber planks that run from the *ridgepole* of a roof to its edge. (457)

raking cornice—The *cornice* on the sloping sides of a *pediment*. (116)

ramparts—Defensive wall circuits. (382)

ratha—Small, freestanding Hindu temple *carved* from a huge boulder. (437)

Rayograph—A photograph produced without a camera by placing objects on photographic paper and then exposing the paper to light; named for the American artist Man Ray. (864)

Rayonnant—The "radiant" style of *Gothic* architecture, dominant in the second half of the 13th century and associated with the French royal court of Louis IX at Paris. (381)

Realism—A movement that emerged in mid-19th-century France. Realist artists represented the subject matter of everyday life (especially subjects that previously had been considered inappropriate for depiction) in a relatively *naturalistic* mode. (775)

red-figure painting—In later Greek pottery, the silhouetting of red figures against a black background, with painted linear details; the reverse of *black-figure painting*. (121)

reducing—See *oxidizing*. (110)

refectory—The dining hall of a Christian *monastery*. (267, 576)

regional style—See *style*. (3)

Regionalism—A 20th-century American art movement that portrayed American rural life in a clearly readable, *Realist* style. Major Regionalists include Grant Wood and Thomas Hart Benton. (889)

register—One of a series of superimposed bands or *friezes* in a pictorial narrative, or the particular levels on which motifs are placed. (31)

relics—The body parts, clothing, or objects associated with a holy figure, such as the Buddha or Christ or a Christian *saint*. (243, 336, 984, 1064)

relief—In sculpture, figures projecting from a background of which they are part. The degree of relief is designated high, low (bas), or sunken. In the last, the artist cuts the design into the surface so that the highest projecting parts of the image are no higher than the surface itself. See also *repoussé*. (556)

relief sculpture—See *relief*. (12, 18)

relieving triangle—In *Mycenaean* architecture, the triangular opening above the *lintel* that serves to lighten the weight to be carried by the lintel itself. (99)

reliquary—A container for holding *relics*. (328, 334, 336, 430, 1064)

ren—Chinese, "human-heartedness." The quality that the ideal Confucian *junzi* possesses. (463)

Renaissance—French, "rebirth." The term used to describe the history, culture, and art of 14th- through 16th-century western Europe during which artists consciously revived the *classical* style. (401, 406)

renovatio—Latin, "renewal." During the *Carolingian* period, Charlemagne sought to revive the culture of ancient Rome (renovatio imperi Romani). (317, 318, 402)

reoxidizing—See *oxidizing*. (110)

repoussé—Formed in *relief* by beating a metal plate from the back, leaving the impression on the face. The metal sheet is hammered into a hollow *mold* of wood or some other pliable material and finished with a *graver*. See also *relief*. (100, 248, 320, 354, 2-26A)

respond—An engaged *column*, *pilaster,* or similar element that either projects from a *compound pier* or some other supporting device or is bonded to a wall and carries one end of an *arch*. (373)

retable—An architectural screen or wall above and behind an altar, usually containing painting, sculpture, or other decorations. See also *altarpiece*. (538)

revetment—In architecture, a wall covering or facing. (184, 418)

rhyton—A pouring vessel. (51)

rib—A relatively slender, molded masonry *arch* that projects from a surface. In *Gothic* architecture, the ribs form the framework of the *vaulting*. A diagonal rib is one of the ribs that form the X of a *groin vault*. A transverse rib crosses the *nave* or aisle at a 90° angle. (12, 351, 21-31A)

rib vault—A *vault* in which the diagonal and transverse *ribs* compose a structural skeleton that partially supports the masonry *web* between them. (351, 368, 14-5A)

ridgepole—The *beam* running the length of a building below the peak of the gabled roof.

rocaille—See *Rococo*. (117, 480, 1043)

Rococo—A style, primarily of interior design, that appeared in France around 1700. Rococo interiors featured lavish decoration, including small sculptures, ornamental mirrors, easel paintings, *tapestries, reliefs,* wall paintings, and elegant furniture. The term Rococo derived from the French word *rocaille* (pebble) and referred to the small stones and shells used to decorate grotto interiors. (728)

Romanesque—"Roman-like." A term used to describe the history, culture, and art of medieval western Europe from ca. 1050 to ca. 1200. (333, 413, 588)

Romanticism—A Western cultural phenomenon, beginning around 1750 and ending about 1850, that gave precedence to feeling and imagination over reason and thought. More narrowly, the art movement that flourished from about 1800 to 1840. (762)

roof comb—The elaborately sculpted vertical projection surmounting a Maya temple-pyramid. (500)

rose window—A circular *stained-glass* window. (412, 13-3A)

rostrum—Speaker's platform. (929)

rotulus—The manuscript scroll used by Egyptians, Greeks, Etruscans, and Romans; predecessor of the *codex*. (249, 1023)

rotunda—The circular area under a *dome;* also a domed round building. (472, 538)

roundel—See *tondo.* (219, 585, 10-15A)

rubbing—An impression of a relief made by placing paper over the surface and rubbing with a pencil or crayon. (456)

Rubéniste—A member of the French Royal Academy of Painting and Sculpture during the early 18th century who followed Peter Paul Rubens in insisting that *color* was the most important element of painting. See also *Poussiniste.* (733)

rusticate (n. rustication)—To give a rustic appearance by roughening the surfaces and beveling the edges of stone blocks to emphasize the joints between them. Rustication is a technique employed in ancient Roman architecture, and was also popular during the *Renaissance,* especially for stone *courses* at the ground-floor level. (201, 586)

sabi—Japanese; the value found in the old and weathered, suggesting the tranquility reached in old age. (1012)

sacra conversazione—Italian, "holy conversation." A style of *altarpiece* painting popular after the middle of the 15th century, in which *saints* from different epochs are joined in a unified space and seem to be conversing either with one another or with the audience. (624)

sacra rappresentazione (pl. sacre rappresentazioni)—Italian, "holy representation." A more elaborate version of a *mystery play* performed for a lay audience by a *confraternity.* (409)

sacramentary—A Christian religious book incorporating the prayers priests recite during *Mass.* (312)

saint—From the Latin word *sanctus,* meaning "made holy by God." Applied to persons who suffered and died for their Christian faith or who merited reverence for their Christian devotion while alive. In the Roman Catholic Church, a worthy deceased Catholic who is canonized by the pope. (237, 402)

Saint-Simonianism—An early-19th-century utopian movement that emphasized the education and enfranchisement of women. (779)

sakkos—The tunic worn by a Byzantine priest. (9-35A)

saltimbanque—An itinerant circus performer. (29-11A)

Samarqand ware—A type of Islamic pottery produced in Samarqand and Nishapur in which the ceramists formed the shape of the vessel from dark pink clay and then immersed it in a tub of white slip, over which they painted ornamental or *calligraphic* decoration and which they sealed with a transparent glaze before firing. (294)

samsara—In Hindu belief, the rebirth of the soul into a succession of lives. (427, 435)

samurai—Medieval Japanese warriors. (1006)

sand painting—A temporary painting *technique* using sand, varicolored powdered stones, corn pollen, and charcoal. Sand paintings, also called dry paintings, are integral parts of sacred Navajo rituals. (1032)

sangha—The Buddhist *monastic* order. (15-8A)

sarcophagus (pl. sarcophagi)—Greek, "consumer of flesh." A coffin, usually of stone. (402, 449)

Satimbe—"Sister on the head." A Dogon (Mali) mask representing all women. (1074)

saturation—See *color.* (7, 813)

satyr—A Greek mythological follower of Dionysos having a man's upper body, a goat's hindquarters and horns, and a horse's ears and tail. (159, 27-33A)

saz—Ottoman design of sinuous curved leaves and complex blossoms, a Turkish term recalling an enchanted forest. (10-27A)

scarab—An Egyptian gem in the shape of a beetle. (61)

scarification—Decorative markings on the human body made by cutting or piercing the flesh to create scars. (525)

Scholasticism—The *Gothic* school of philosophy in which scholars applied Aristotle's system of rational inquiry to the interpretation of religious belief. (372)

school—A chronological and stylistic classification of works of art with a stipulation of place. (6)

screen facade—A *facade* that does not correspond to the structure of the building behind it. (12-11A)

scriptorium (pl. scriptoria)—The writing studio of a *monastery.* (311)

scudi—Italian, "shields." A coin denomination in 17th-century Italy. (684)

sculpture in the round—Freestanding figures, *carved* or *modeled* in three dimensions. (12, 18)

seal—In Asian painting, a stamp affixed to a painting to identify the artist, the *calligrapher,* or the owner. See also *cylinder seals.* (997)

secco—Italian, "dry." See also *fresco.* (408, 603)

Second Style mural—The style of Roman *mural* painting in which the aim was to dissolve the confining walls of a room and replace them with the illusion of a three-dimensional world constructed in the artist's imagination. (192)

secondary colors—Orange, green, and purple, obtained by mixing pairs of *primary colors* (red, yellow, blue). (7, 813)

section—In architecture, a diagram or representation of a part of a structure or building along an imaginary *plane* that passes through it vertically. Drawings showing a theoretical slice across a structure's width are lateral sections. Those cutting through a building's length are longitudinal sections. See also *elevation* and *cutaway.* (12)

sedes sapientiae—Latin, "throne of wisdom." A Romanesque sculptural type depicting the Virgin Mary with the Christ Child in her lap. (349)

segmental pediment—A *pediment* with a curved instead of a triangular *cornice.* (621)

senate—Latin senatus, "council of elders." The Senate was the main legislative body in Roman constitutional government. (181)

serdab—A small concealed chamber in an Egyptian *mastaba* for the *statue* of the deceased. (58)

Severe Style—The Early *Classical* style of Greek sculpture, ca. 480–450 BCE. (128)

sexpartite vault—See *vault.* (358)

sfumato—Italian, "smoky." A smokelike haziness that subtly softens outlines in painting; particularly applied to the paintings of Leonardo da Vinci and Correggio. (539, 604)

sgrafitto—A Chinese ceramic technique in which the design is *incised* through a colored *slip.* (467)

shaft—The tall, cylindrical part of a *column* between the *capital* and the *base.* (51, 116, 373)

shakti—In Hinduism, the female power of the deity Devi (or Goddess), which animates the matter of the cosmos. (435)

shaykh—An Islamic mystic *saint.* (975)

sherd—A fragmentary piece of a broken ceramic vessel. (476)

shikara—The beehive-shaped tower of a northern-style Hindu temple. (439)

Shingon—The primary form of Buddhism in Japan through the mid-10th century. Lowercase *shingon* is the Japanese term for the words or syllables recited in Buddhist rituals. (483)

Shino—Japanese ceramic wares produced during the late 16th and early 17th centuries in kilns in Mino. (1012)

shogun—In 12th- through 19th-century Japan, a military governor who managed the country on behalf of a figurehead emperor. (486, 1006)

shogunate—The Japanese military government of the 12th through 19th centuries. (486, 1006)

sibyl—A Greco-Roman mythological prophetess. (540)

signoria—The governing body in the Republic of Florence. (563)

silentiary—An usher responsible for maintaining silence in the *Byzantine* imperial palace in Constantinople. (261)

silk-screen printing—An industrial printing *technique* that creates a sharp-edged image by pressing ink through a design on silk or a similar tightly woven porous fabric stretched tight on a frame. (915)

silverpoint—A *stylus* made of silver, used in drawing in the 14th and 15th centuries because of the fine *line* it produced and the sharp point it maintained. (545, 604)

Simultanéisme—Robert Delaunay's version of *Cubism* in which he created spatial effects and kaleidoscopic movement solely through color contrasts; also known as *Orphism.* (848)

simultaneous contrasts—The phenomenon of juxtaposed *colors* affecting the eye's reception of each, as when a painter places dark green next to light green, making the former appear even darker and the latter even lighter. See also *successive contrasts.* (813)

sinopia—A burnt-orange pigment used in *fresco* painting to transfer a *cartoon* to the *arriccio* before the artist paints the plaster. (408)

siren—In ancient Greek mythology, a creature that was part bird and part woman. (110)

sistrum—An Egyptian percussion instrument or rattle. (95)

site-specific art—Art created for a specific location. See also *Environmental Art*. (932)

skene—Greek, "stage." The stage of a *classical* theater. (151)

skenographia—Greek, "scene painting"; the Greek term for *perspective* painting. (193)

skiagraphia—Greek, "shadow painting." The Greek term for shading, said to have been invented by Apollodoros, an Athenian painter of the fifth century BCE. (149)

slip—A mixture of fine clay and water used in ceramic decoration. (110, 451)

solidus (pl. **solidi**)—A Byzantine gold coin. (263)

space—In art history, both the actual area an object occupies or a building encloses, and the *illusionistic* representation of space in painting and sculpture. (8)

spandrel—The roughly triangular space enclosed by the curves of adjacent *arches* and a horizontal member connecting their vertexes; also, the space enclosed by the curve of an *arch* and an enclosing right angle. The area between the arch proper and the framing *columns* and *entablature*. (206)

spectrum—The range or band of visible colors in natural light. (7)

sphinx—A mythical Egyptian beast with the body of a lion and the head of a human. (63)

splashed-ink painting—See *haboku*. (1008)

springing—The lowest stone of an *arch*, resting on the *impost block*. In *Gothic* vaulting, the lowest stone of a diagonal or transverse *rib*. (340, 373)

squinch—An architectural device used as a transition from a square to a polygonal or circular base for a *dome*. It may be composed of *lintels*, *corbels*, or *arches*. (262)

stained glass—In *Gothic* architecture, the colored glass used for windows. (12, 373, 375, 982)

stamp seal—See *cylinder seal*. (39)

stanza (pl. **stanze**)—Italian, "room." (606)

statue—A three-dimensional sculpture. (12)

stave—A wedge-shaped timber; vertically placed staves embellish the architectural features of a building. (311)

stele (pl. **stelae**)—A *carved* stone slab used to mark graves or to commemorate historical events. (36, 499)

stem stitching—See *embroidery*. (362)

stigmata—In Christian art, the wounds Christ received at his crucifixion that miraculously appear on the body of a *saint*. (405)

still life—A picture depicting an arrangement of inanimate objects. (5, 196, 687)

stoa—In ancient Greek architecture, an open building with a roof supported by a row of *columns* parallel to the back wall. A covered *colonnade* or *portico*. (154)

Stoic—A philosophical school of ancient Greece, named after the *stoas* in which the philosophers met. (154)

stoneware—Pottery fired at high temperatures to produce a stonelike hardness and density. (451, 992)

strategos—Greek, "general." (133)

stretcher bar—One of a set of wooden bars used to stretch canvas to provide a taut surface for painting. (543)

strigil—A tool ancient Greek athletes used to scrape oil from their bodies after exercising. (147)

stringcourse—A raised horizontal *molding*, or band, in masonry. Its principal use is ornamental but it usually reflects interior structure. (586, 11-19A)

strut—A timber plank or other structural member used as a support in a building. Also a short section of marble used to support an arm or leg in a *statue*. (457)

stucco—A type of plaster used as a coating on exterior and interior walls. Also used as a sculptural *medium*. (182)

stupa—A large, mound-shaped Buddhist shrine. (429, 430, 984, 986)

style—A distinctive artistic manner. Period style is the characteristic style of a specific time. Regional style is the style of a particular geographical area. Personal style is an individual artist's unique manner. (3)

stylistic evidence—In art history, the examination of the *style* of an artwork in order to determine its date or the identity of the artist. (3)

stylobate—The uppermost course of the platform of a *classical* Greek temple, which supports the *columns*. (116, 618)

stylus—A needlelike tool used in *engraving* and *incising*; also, an ancient writing instrument used to inscribe clay or wax tablets. (33, 196, 545, 556, 604)

sub gracia—Latin, "under grace." In Christian thought, the period after the coming of Christ. (392)

sub lege—Latin, "under the law." In Christian thought, the period after Moses received the Ten Commandments and before the coming of Christ. See also *sub gracia*. (392)

subtractive light—The painter's light in art; the light reflected from pigments and objects. See also *additive light*. (7)

subtractive sculpture—A kind of sculpture technique in which materials are taken away from the original mass; *carving*. (11, 64)

successive contrasts—The phenomenon of colored afterimages. When a person looks intently at a *color* (green, for example) and then shifts to a white area, the fatigued eye momentarily perceives the *complementary color* (red). See also *simultaneous contrasts*. (813)

sultan—A *Muslim* ruler. (292, 977)

sunken relief—See *relief*. (73)

Sunnah—The collection of the Prophet Muhammad's moral sayings and descriptions of his deeds. (285)

superimposed orders—*Orders* of architecture that are placed one above another in an *arcaded* or *colonnaded* building, usually in the following sequence: Doric (the first story), Ionic, and Corinthian. Superimposed orders are found in later Greek architecture and were used widely by Roman and *Renaissance* builders. (204)

superimposition—In *Mesoamerican* architecture, the erection of a new structure on top of, and incorporating, an earlier structure; the nesting of a series of buildings inside each other. (1026)

Superrealism—A *school* of painting and sculpture of the 1960s and 1970s that emphasized producing artworks based on scrupulous fidelity to optical fact. The Superrealist painters were also called Photorealists because many used photographs as sources for their imagery. (917)

Suprematism—A type of art formulated by Kazimir Malevich to convey his belief that the supreme reality in the world is pure feeling, which attaches to no object and thus calls for new, nonobjective forms in art—shapes not related to objects in the visible world. (859)

surah—A chapter of the *Koran*, divided into verses. (285)

Surrealism—A successor to *Dada*, Surrealism incorporated the improvisational nature of its predecessor into its exploration of the ways to express in art the world of dreams and the unconscious. Biomorphic Surrealists, such as Joan Miró, produced largely *abstract compositions*. *Naturalistic* Surrealists, notably Salvador Dalí, presented recognizable scenes transformed into a dream or nightmare image. (875)

sutra—In Buddhism, an account of a sermon by or a dialogue involving the Buddha. A scriptural account of the Buddha. See also *jataka*. (480)

symbol—An image that stands for another image or encapsulates an idea. (5)

Symbolism—A late-19th-century movement based on the idea that the artist was not an imitator of nature but a creator who transformed the facts of nature into a *symbol* of the inner experience of that fact. (819)

symmetria—Greek, "commensurability of parts." Polykleitos's treatise on his *canon* of proportions incorporated the principle of symmetria. (135)

symposium—An ancient Greek banquet attended solely by men (and female servants and prostitutes). (108)

Synthetic Cubism—A later phase of *Cubism*, in which paintings and drawings were constructed from objects and shapes cut from paper or other materials to represent parts of a subject, in order to engage the viewer with pictorial issues, such as figuration, realism, and abstraction. (848)

taberna—In Roman architecture, a single-room shop usually covered by a barrel *vault*. (209)

tablero—See *talud-tablero construction*. (496)

tablinum—The study or office in a Roman house. (190)

taj—Arabic and Persian, "crown." (980)

talud-tablero construction—The alternation of sloping (talud) and vertical (tablero) rubble layers, characteristic of Teotihuacan architecture in Mesoamerica. (496)

tapa—Barkcloth made particularly in Polynesia. Tapa is often dyed, painted, stenciled, and sometimes perfumed. (1053)

tapestry—A weaving *technique* in which the *weft* threads are packed densely over the *warp* threads so that the designs are woven directly into the fabric. (362, 513, 730)

tatami—The traditional woven straw mat used for floor covering in Japanese architecture. (1011)

tatanua—In New Ireland (Papua New Guinea), the spirits of the dead. (1049)

tatau—*See tattoo.* (1054)

tattoo—A permanent design on the skin produced using indelible dyes. The term derives from the Tahitian, Samoan, and Tongan word *tatau* or *tatu*. (1054)

tatu—See *tattoo.* (1054)

technique—The processes artists employ to create *form*, as well as the distinctive, personal ways in which they handle their materials and tools. (7)

tempera—A *technique* of painting using pigment mixed with egg yolk, glue, or casein; also, the *medium* itself. (219, 404, 502, 538, 539)

templon—The columnar screen separating the sanctuary from the main body of a *Byzantine* church. (277)

tenebrism—Painting in the "shadowy manner," using violent contrasts of light and dark, as in the work of Caravaggio. The term derives from *tenebroso*. (683)

tenebroso—Italian, "shadowy." See *tenebrism*. (683)

tenon—A projection on the end of a piece of wood that is inserted into a corresponding hole (mortise) in another piece of wood to form a joint. (480)

tephra—The volcanic ash produced by the eruption on the *Cycladic* island of Thera. (92)

tepidarium—The warm-bath section of a Roman bathing establishment. (220)

terminus ante quem—Latin, "point [date] before which." (2)

terminus post quem—Latin, "point [date] after which." (2)

terracotta—Hard-baked clay, used for sculpture and as a building material. It may be *glazed* or painted. (90, 414)

tessera (pl. **tesserae**)—Greek, "cube." A tiny stone or piece of glass cut to the desired shape and size for use in forming a *mosaic*. (150, 245, 291, 299)

tetrarch—One of four corulers. (224)

tetrarchy—Greek, "rule by four." A type of Roman government established in the late third century CE by Diocletian in an attempt to foster order by sharing power with potential rivals. (224)

texture—The quality of a surface (rough, smooth, hard, soft, shiny, dull) as revealed by light. In represented texture, a painter depicts an object as having a certain texture even though the pigment is the real texture. (8)

theatron—Greek, "place for seeing." In ancient Greek theaters, the slope overlooking the *orchestra* on which the spectators sat. (151)

Theotokos—Greek, "she who bore God." The Virgin Mary, the mother of Jesus. (245, 267)

thermoluminescence—A method of dating by measuring amounts of radiation found within the clay of ceramic or sculptural forms, as well as in the clay cores from metal castings. (523)

Third Style mural—In Roman *mural* painting, the style in which delicate linear fantasies were sketched on predominantly *monochromatic* backgrounds. (194)

tholos (pl. **tholoi**)—A temple with a circular plan. Also, the burial chamber of a *tholos tomb*. (99, 151, 618)

tholos tomb—In *Mycenaean* architecture, a beehive-shaped tomb with a circular plan. (99)

thrust—The outward force exerted by an *arch* or a *vault* that must be counterbalanced by a *buttress*. (184, 21-31A)

tiki—A Marquesas Islands (Polynesia) three-dimensional carving of an exalted, deified ancestor figure. (1054)

toga—The garment worn by an ancient Roman male citizen. (176)

togu na—"House of words." A Dogon (Mali) men's house, where deliberations vital to community welfare take place. (1078)

tokonoma—A shallow alcove in a Japanese room, which is used for decoration, such as a painting or stylized flower arrangement. (1011)

tonality—See *color.* (7)

tondo (pl. **tondi**)—A circular painting or *relief* sculpture. (219, 585, 10-15A)

Torah—The Hebrew religious scroll containing the *Pentateuch*. (235)

torana—Gateway in the stone fence around a *stupa*, located at the cardinal points of the compass. (430, 15-8A)

torque—The distinctive necklace worn by the Gauls. (156)

tracery—Ornamental stonework for holding *stained glass* in place, characteristic of *Gothic cathedrals*. In plate tracery, the glass fills only the "punched holes" in the heavy ornamental stonework. In bar tracery, the stained-glass windows fill almost the entire opening, and the stonework is unobtrusive. (373, 414)

tramezzo—A screen placed across the *nave* of a church to separate the clergy from the lay audience. (14-6A)

transept—The part of a church with an axis that crosses the *nave* at a right angle. (243, 564, 14-5A)

transubstantiation—The transformation of the Eucharistic bread and wine into the body and blood of Christ. (24-18A)

transverse arch—An *arch* separating one *vaulted bay* from the next. (340)

transverse barrel vault—In medieval architecture, a semicylindrical *vault* oriented at a 90° angle to the *nave* of a church. (12-10A)

transverse rib—See *rib.* (373)

treasury—In ancient Greece, a small building set up for the safe storage of *votive offerings*. (119)

trefoil—A cloverlike ornament or symbol with stylized leaves in groups of three. (425)

trefoil arch—A triple-lobed arch. (402)

tribune—In church architecture, a gallery over the inner *aisle* flanking the *nave*. (337)

triclinium—The dining room of a Roman house. (190, 6-9A)

trident—The three-pronged pitchfork associated with the ancient Greek sea god Poseidon (Roman, Neptune). (107, 435)

triforium—In a *Gothic cathedral*, the blind arcaded gallery below the *clerestory*; occasionally, the *arcades* are filled with *stained glass*. (370, 373, 20-4A)

triglyph—A triple projecting, grooved member of a *Doric frieze* that alternates with *metopes*. (116, 640)

trilithon—A pair of *monoliths* topped with a *lintel*; found in *megalithic* structures. (28)

Trinity—In Christianity, God the Father, his son Jesus Christ, and the Holy Spirit. (240)

tripod—An ancient Greek deep bowl on a tall three-legged stand. (5-17A)

triptych—A three-paneled painting, ivory plaque, or *altarpiece*. Also, a small, portable shrine with hinged wings used for private devotion. (275, 392, 415)

triratna—A tripartite symbol of the three jewels of Buddhism—the Buddha himself, his *dharma*, and the *sangha*. (15-8A)

triumphal arch—In Roman architecture, a freestanding *arch* commemorating an important event, such as a military victory or the opening of a new road. (205, 575)

trompe l'oeil—French, "fools the eye." A form of *illusionistic* painting that aims to deceive viewers into believing they are seeing real objects rather than a representation of those objects. (595, 24-14A)

true fresco—See *fresco.* (408, 409, 502)

trumeau—In church architecture, the *pillar* or center post supporting the *lintel* in the middle of the doorway. (344, 20-2A)

tubicen—Latin, "trumpet player." (157)

tughra—The official signature of an Ottoman emperor. (10-23A)

tukutuku—A stitched lattice panel found in a Maori (New Zealand) meetinghouse. (1043)

tumulus (pl. **tumuli**)—Latin, "burial mound." In Etruscan architecture, tumuli cover one or more subterranean multichambered tombs cut out of the local tufa (limestone). Also characteristic of the Japanese Kofun period of the third and fourth centuries. (27, 170, 309, 478)

tunnel vault—See *vault.* (12, 52, 184, 338, 585, 981)

turris—See *westwork.* (323)

Tuscan column—The standard type of Etruscan *column*. It resembles ancient Greek *Doric* columns but is made of wood, is unfluted, and has a *base*. Also a popular motif in *Renaissance* and *Baroque* architecture. (168, 587, 618)

twisted perspective—See *composite view.* (23, 523)

tympanum (pl. **tympana**)—The space enclosed by a *lintel* and an *arch* over a doorway. (344, 538, 590, 14-12A)

typology—In Christian theology, the recognition of concordances between events, especially between episodes in the Old and New Testaments. (238)

ukiyo-e—Japanese, "pictures of the floating world." During the Edo period, *woodcut prints* depicting brothels, popular entertainment, and beautiful women. (1015, 28-16B)

underglaze—In *porcelain* decoration, the *technique* of applying mineral colors to the surface before the main firing, followed by an application of clear *glaze*. See also *overglaze*. (986, 992)

Upanishads—South Asian religious texts of ca. 800–500 BCE that introduced the concepts of *samsara, karma,* and *moksha*. (427)

uraeus—An Egyptian cobra; one of the emblems of *pharaonic* kingship. (63)

urna—A whorl of hair, represented as a dot, between the brows; one of the *lakshanas* of the Buddha. (427)

ushabti—In ancient Egypt, a figurine placed in a tomb to act as a servant to the deceased in the afterlife. (61)

ushnisha—A knot of hair on the top of the head; one of the *lakshanas* of the Buddha. (427)

Usonian—Frank Lloyd Wright's term for the inexpensive houses he designed for ordinary people. *Usonian* derives from "United States of North America." (896)

valley temple—The temple closest to the Nile River associated with each of the Great Pyramids at Gizeh in ancient Egypt. (62)

value—See *color.* (7, 813)

vanishing point—See *perspective.* (547, 567)

vanitas—Latin, "vanity." A term describing paintings (particularly 17th-century Dutch *still lifes*) that include references to death. (695, 23-3A, 26-7A)

vanth—An Etruscan female winged demon of death. (176)

vassal—In *feudalism,* a person who swears allegiance to a *liege lord* and renders him military service in return for tenure of a portion of the lord's land. (334)

vault (adj. **vaulted**)—A masonry roof or ceiling constructed on the *arch* principle, or a concrete roof of the same shape. A barrel (or tunnel) vault, semicylindrical in cross-*section,* is in effect a deep arch or an uninterrupted series of arches, one behind the other, over an oblong space. A quadrant vault is a half-barrel vault. A groin (or cross) vault is formed at the point at which two barrel vaults intersect at right angles. In a ribbed vault, there is a framework of *ribs* or arches under the intersections of the vaulting sections. A sexpartite vault is one whose ribs divide the vault into six compartments. A fan vault is a vault characteristic of English *Perpendicular Gothic* architecture, in which radiating ribs form a fanlike pattern. (12, 52)

vaulting web—See *web.* (373)

Veda—Sanskrit, "knowledge." One of four second-millennium BCE South Asian compilations of religious learning. (427)

veduta (pl. **vedute**)—Italian, "scenic view." (744)

velarium—In a Roman *amphitheater,* the cloth awning that could be rolled down from the top of the *cavea* to shield spectators from sun or rain. (190)

vellum—Calfskin prepared as a surface for writing or painting. (249, 604)

venationes—Ancient Roman wild animal hunts staged in an *amphitheater.* (203)

veristic—True to natural appearance; superrealistic. (185)

vihara—A Buddhist *monastery,* often cut into a hill. (429)

vimana—A pyramidal tower over the *garbha griha* of a Hindu temple of the southern style. (438, 439, 977)

vita—Italian, "life." Also, the title of a biography. (682)

vita contemplativa—Latin, "contemplative life." The secluded spiritual life of monks and nuns. (342)

vizier—An Egyptian pharaoh's chief administrator. (3-11B)

volume—The *space* that *mass* organizes, divides, or encloses. (8)

volute—A spiral, scroll-like form characteristic of the ancient Greek *Ionic* and the Roman *Composite capital.* (51, 116)

votive offering—A gift of gratitude to a deity. (35)

voussoir—A wedge-shaped stone block used in the construction of a true *arch.* The central voussoir, which sets the arch, is called the keystone. (175, 344, 640)

wabi—A 16th-century Japanese art style characterized by refined rusticity and an appreciation of simplicity and austerity. (1012)

wainscoting—Paneling on the lower part of interior walls. (827)

waka sran—"People of wood." Baule (Côte d'Ivoire) wooden figural sculptures. (1069)

warp—The vertical threads of a loom or cloth. (510)

wat—A Buddhist *monastery* in Cambodia. (443)

web—The masonry blocks that fill the area between the *ribs* of a *groin vault.* Also called vaulting web. (368)

wedjat—The eye of the Egyptian falcon-god Horus, a powerful *amulet.* (57, 61)

weft—The horizontal threads of a loom or cloth. (510)

weld—To join metal parts by heating, as in assembling the separate parts of a *statue* made by *casting.* (11)

were-jaguar—A composite human-jaguar; a common motif in Olmec art. (494)

westwork—German, "western entrance structure." The *facade* and towers at the western end of a medieval church, principally in Germany. In contemporaneous documents the westwork is called a castellum (Latin, "castle" or "fortress") or turris ("tower"). (323)

wet-plate photography—An early photographic process in which the photographic plate is exposed, developed, and fixed while wet. (792)

white-ground painting—An ancient Greek vase-painting *technique* in which the pot was first covered with a *slip* of very fine white clay, over which black *glaze* was used to outline figures, and diluted brown, purple, red, and white were used to color them. (142)

woodcut—A wooden block on the surface of which those parts not intended to *print* are cut away to a slight depth, leaving the design raised; also, the printed impression made with such a block. (554, 556)

yaksha (m.), **yakshi** (f.)—Lesser local male and female Buddhist and Hindu divinities. Yakshis are goddesses associated with fertility and vegetation. Yakshas, the male equivalent of yakshis, are often represented as fleshy but powerful males. (430, 432, 15-6B)

yamato-e—Also known as native-style painting, a purely Japanese style that often involved colorful, decorative representations of Japanese narratives or *landscapes.* (485)

yang—In Chinese cosmology, the principle of active masculine energy, which permeates the universe in varying proportions with yin, the principle of passive feminine energy. (463)

yasti—In Buddhist architecture, the mast or pole that arises from the dome of the *stupa* and its *harmika* and symbolizes the axis of the universe; it is adorned with a series of chatras (stone disks). (430)

yin—See *yang.* (463)

yoga—A method for controlling the body and relaxing the mind used in later Indian religions to yoke, or unite, the practitioner to the divine. (426)

yosegi—Japanese *joined-wood technique.* (17-13A)

Zen—A Japanese Buddhist sect and its doctrine, emphasizing enlightenment through intuition and introspection rather than the study of scripture. In Chinese, Chan. (470, 1007)

ziggurat—In ancient Mesopotamian architecture, a monumental platform for a temple. (33, 289)

zoopraxiscope—A device invented by Eadweard Muybridge in the 19th century to project sequences of still photographic images; a predecessor of the modern motion-picture projector. (796)

BIBLIOGRAPHY

This list of books is very selective but comprehensive enough to satisfy the reading interests of the beginning art history student and general reader. Significantly expanded from the previous edition, the 14th edition bibliography can also serve as the basis for undergraduate research papers. The resources listed range from works that are valuable primarily for their reproductions to those that are scholarly surveys of schools and periods or monographs on individual artists. The emphasis is on recent in-print books and on books likely to be found in college and municipal libraries. No entries for periodical articles appear, but the bibliography begins with a list of some of the major journals that publish art historical scholarship in English.

Selected Periodicals

African Arts
American Art
American Indian Art
American Journal of Archaeology
Antiquity
Archaeology
Archives of American Art
Archives of Asian Art
Ars Orientalis
Art Bulletin
Art History
Art in America
Art Journal
Artforum International
Artnews
Burlington Magazine
Gesta
History of Photography
Journal of Egyptian Archaeology
Journal of Roman Archaeology
Journal of the Society of Architectural Historians
Journal of the Warburg and Courtauld Institutes
Latin American Antiquity
October
Oxford Art Journal
Women's Art Journal

General Studies

Baxandall, Michael. *Patterns of Intention: On the Historical Explanation of Pictures.* New Haven, Conn.: Yale University Press, 1985.

Bindman, David, ed. *The Thames & Hudson Encyclopedia of British Art.* London: Thames & Hudson, 1988.

Boström, Antonia. *The Encyclopedia of Sculpture.* 3 vols. London: Routledge, 2003.

Broude, Norma, and Mary D. Garrard, eds. *The Expanding Discourse: Feminism and Art History.* New York: Harper Collins, 1992.

Bryson, Norman. *Vision and Painting: The Logic of the Gaze.* New Haven, Conn.: Yale University Press, 1983.

Bryson, Norman, Michael Ann Holly, and Keith Moxey. *Visual Theory: Painting and Interpretation.* New York: Cambridge University Press, 1991.

Burden, Ernest. *Illustrated Dictionary of Architecture.* 2d ed. New York: McGraw-Hill, 2002.

Büttner, Nils. *Landscape Painting: A History.* New York: Abbeville, 2006.

Carrier, David. *A World Art History and Its Objects.* University Park: Pennsylvania State University Press, 2009.

Chadwick, Whitney. *Women, Art, and Society.* 4th ed. New York: Thames & Hudson, 2007.

Cheetham, Mark A., Michael Ann Holly, and Keith Moxey, eds. *The Subjects of Art History: Historical Objects in Contemporary Perspective.* New York: Cambridge University Press, 1998.

Chilvers, Ian, and Harold Osborne, eds. *The Oxford Dictionary of Art.* 3d ed. New York: Oxford University Press, 2004.

Corbin, George A. *Native Arts of North America, Africa, and the South Pacific: An Introduction.* New York: Harper Collins, 1988.

Crouch, Dora P., and June G. Johnson. *Traditions in Architecture: Africa, America, Asia, and Oceania.* New York: Oxford University Press, 2000.

Curl, James Stevens. *Oxford Dictionary of Architecture and Landscape Architecture.* 2d ed. New York: Oxford University Press, 2006.

Duby, Georges, ed. *Sculpture: From Antiquity to the Present.* 2 vols. Cologne: Taschen, 1999.

Encyclopedia of World Art. 17 vols. New York: McGraw-Hill, 1959–1987.

Fielding, Mantle. *Dictionary of American Painters, Sculptors, and Engravers.* 2d ed. Poughkeepsie, N.Y.: Apollo, 1986.

Fine, Sylvia Honig. *Women and Art: A History of Women Painters and Sculptors from the Renaissance to the 20th Century.* Rev. ed. Montclair, N.J.: Alanheld & Schram, 1978.

Fleming, John, Hugh Honour, and Nikolaus Pevsner. *The Penguin Dictionary of Architecture and Landscape Architecture.* 5th ed. New York: Penguin, 2000.

Frazier, Nancy. *The Penguin Concise Dictionary of Art History.* New York: Penguin, 2000.

Freedberg, David. *The Power of Images: Studies in the History and Theory of Response.* Chicago: University of Chicago Press, 1989.

Gaze, Delia, ed. *Dictionary of Women Artists.* 2 vols. London: Routledge, 1997.

Hall, James. *Dictionary of Subjects and Symbols in Art.* 2d ed. Boulder, Colo.: Westview, 2008.

Harris, Anne Sutherland, and Linda Nochlin. *Women Artists: 1550–1950.* Los Angeles: Los Angeles County Museum of Art; New York: Knopf, 1977.

Hauser, Arnold. *The Sociology of Art.* Chicago: University of Chicago Press, 1982.

Hults, Linda C. *The Print in the Western World: An Introductory History.* Madison: University of Wisconsin Press, 1996.

Kemp, Martin. *The Science of Art: Optical Themes in Western Art from Brunelleschi to Seurat.* New Haven, Conn.: Yale University Press, 1990.

Kostof, Spiro, and Gregory Castillo. *A History of Architecture: Settings and Rituals.* 2d ed. Oxford: Oxford University Press, 1995.

Kultermann, Udo. *The History of Art History.* New York: Abaris, 1993.

Lucie-Smith, Edward. *The Thames & Hudson Dictionary of Art Terms.* 2d ed. New York: Thames & Hudson, 2004.

Moffett, Marian, Michael Fazio, and Lawrence Wadehouse. *A World History of Architecture.* Boston: McGraw-Hill, 2004.

Morgan, Anne Lee. *Oxford Dictionary of American Art and Artists.* New York: Oxford University Press, 2008.

Murray, Peter, and Linda Murray. *A Dictionary of Art and Artists.* 7th ed. New York: Penguin, 1998.

Nelson, Robert S., and Richard Shiff, eds. *Critical Terms for Art History.* Chicago: University of Chicago Press, 1996.

Pazanelli, Roberta, ed. *The Color of Life: Polychromy in Sculpture from Antiquity to the Present.* Los Angeles: J. Paul Getty Museum, 2008.

Penny, Nicholas. *The Materials of Sculpture.* New Haven, Conn.: Yale University Press, 1993.

Pevsner, Nikolaus. *A History of Building Types.* London: Thames & Hudson, 1987. Reprint of 1979 ed.

———. *An Outline of European Architecture.* 8th ed. Baltimore: Penguin, 1974.

Pierce, James Smith. *From Abacus to Zeus: A Handbook of Art History.* 7th ed. Upper Saddle River, N.J.: Pearson Prentice Hall, 1998.

Placzek, Adolf K., ed. *Macmillan Encyclopedia of Architects.* 4 vols. New York: Macmillan, 1982.

Podro, Michael. *The Critical Historians of Art.* New Haven, Conn.: Yale University Press, 1982.

Pollock, Griselda. *Vision and Difference: Femininity, Feminism, and Histories of Art.* London: Routledge, 1988.

Pregill, Philip, and Nancy Volkman. *Landscapes in History: Design and Planning in the Eastern and Western Traditions.* 2d ed. Hoboken, N.J.: Wiley, 1999.

Preziosi, Donald, ed. *The Art of Art History: A Critical Anthology.* New York: Oxford University Press, 1998.

Read, Herbert. *The Thames & Hudson Dictionary of Art and Artists.* Rev. ed. New York: Thames & Hudson, 1994.

Reid, Jane D. *The Oxford Guide to Classical Mythology in the Arts 1300–1990s.* 2 vols. New York: Oxford University Press, 1993.

Rogers, Elizabeth Barlow. *Landscape Design: A Cultural and Architectural History.* New York: Abrams, 2001.

Roth, Leland M. *Understanding Architecture: Its Elements, History, and Meaning.* 2d ed. Boulder, Colo.: Westview, 2006.

Schama, Simon. *The Power of Art.* New York: Ecco, 2006.

Slatkin, Wendy. *Women Artists in History: From Antiquity to the 20th Century.* 4th ed. Upper Saddle River, N.J.: Prentice Hall, 2000.

Steer, John, and Antony White. *Atlas of Western Art History: Artists, Sites, and Monuments from Ancient Greece to the Modern Age.* New York: Facts on File, 1994.

Stratton, Arthur. *The Orders of Architecture: Greek, Roman, and Renaissance.* London: Studio, 1986.

Summers, David. *Real Spaces: World Art History and the Rise of Western Modernism.* London: Phaidon, 2003.

Sutton, Ian. *Western Architecture: From Ancient Greece to the Present.* New York: Thames & Hudson, 1999.

Trachtenberg, Marvin, and Isabelle Hyman. *Architecture, from Prehistory to Post-Modernism.* 2d ed. Upper Saddle River, N.J.: Prentice Hall, 2003.

Turner, Jane, ed. *The Dictionary of Art.* 34 vols. New ed. New York: Oxford University Press, 2003.

Watkin, David. *A History of Western Architecture.* 4th ed. London: Laurence King, 2010.

West, Shearer. *Portraiture.* New York: Oxford University Press, 2004.

Wittkower, Rudolf. *Sculpture Processes and Principles.* New York: Harper & Row, 1977.

Wren, Linnea H., and Janine M. Carter, eds. *Perspectives on Western Art: Source Documents and Readings from the Ancient Near East through the Middle Ages.* New York: Harper & Row, 1987.

Zijlmans, Kitty, and Wilfried van Damme, eds. *World Art Studies: Exploring Concepts and Approaches.* Amsterdam: Valiz, 2008.

Ancient Art, General

Aruz, Joan, and Ronald Wallenfels, eds. *Art of the First Cities: The Third Millennium BC from the Mediterranean to the Indus.* New York: Metropolitan Museum of Art, 2003.

Beard, Mary, and John Henderson. *Classical Art: From Greece to Rome.* New York: Oxford University Press, 2001.

Boardman, John. *The World of Ancient Art.* London: Thames & Hudson, 2006.

———, ed. *The Oxford History of Classical Art.* New York: Oxford University Press, 1997.

Chitham, Robert. *The Classical Orders of Architecture.* 2d ed. Boston: Architectural Press, 2005.

Clayton, Peter A., and Martin J. Price, eds. *The Seven Wonders of the Ancient World.* New York: Routledge, 1988.

Connolly, Peter, and Hazel Dodge. *The Ancient City: Life in Classical Athens and Rome.* New York: Oxford University Press, 1998.

De Grummond, Nancy Thomson, ed. *An Encyclopedia of the History of Classical Archaeology.* 2 vols. Westport, Conn.: Greenwood, 1996.

Dunbabin, Katherine. *Mosaics of the Greek and Roman World.* New York: Cambridge University Press, 1999.

Gates, Charles. *Ancient Cities: The Archaeology of Urban Life in the Ancient Near East and Egypt, Greece, and Rome.* London: Routledge, 2003.

Grossman, Janet Burnett. *Looking at Greek and Roman Sculpture in Stone: A Guide to Terms, Styles, and Techniques.* Los Angeles: J. Paul Getty Museum, 2003.

Kampen, Natalie B., ed. *Sexuality in Ancient Art.* New York: Cambridge University Press, 1996.

Lexicon Iconographicum Mythologiae Classicae. 10 vols. Zurich: Artemis, 1981–1999.

Ling, Roger. *Ancient Mosaics.* Princeton, N.J.: Princeton University Press, 1998.

Lloyd, Seton, and Hans Wolfgang Muller. *Ancient Architecture: Mesopotamia, Egypt, Crete.* New York: Electa/Rizzoli, 1980.

Oliphant, Margaret. *The Atlas of the Ancient World: Charting the Great Civilizations of the Past.* New York: Simon & Schuster, 1992.

Onians, John. *Classical Art and the Cultures of Greece and Rome.* New Haven, Conn.: Yale University Press, 1999.

Renfrew, Colin, and Paul G. Bahn. *Archaeology: Theories, Methods, and Practices.* London: Thames & Hudson, 1991.

Stillwell, Richard, William L. MacDonald, and Marian H. McAllister, eds. *The Princeton Encyclopedia of Classical Sites.* Princeton, N.J.: Princeton University Press, 1976.

Trigger, Bruce. *Understanding Early Civilizations: A Comparative Study.* New York: Cambridge University Press, 2003.

Ward-Perkins, John B. *Cities of Ancient Greece and Italy: Planning in Classical Antiquity.* Rev. ed. New York: Braziller, 1987.

Wolf, Walther. *The Origins of Western Art: Egypt, Mesopotamia, the Aegean.* New York: Universe, 1989.

Chapter 1: Art before History

Aujoulat, Norbert. *Lascaux: Movement, Space, and Time.* New York: Abrams, 2005.

Bahn, Paul G. *The Cambridge Illustrated History of Prehistoric Art.* New York: Cambridge University Press, 1998.

———. *Cave Art: A Guide to the Decorated Ice Age Caves of Europe.* London: Frances Lincoln, 2007.

Bahn, Paul G., and Jean Vertut. *Journey through the Ice Age.* Berkeley: University of California Press, 1997.

Beltrán, Antonio, ed. *The Cave of Altamira.* New York: Abrams, 1999.

Berghaus, Guner. *New Perspectives on Prehistoric Art.* Westport, Conn.: Praeger, 2004.

Burl, Aubrey. *Great Stone Circles.* New Haven, Conn.: Yale University Press, 1999.

Chauvet, Jean-Marie, Eliette Brunel Deschamps, and Christian Hillaire. *Dawn of Art: The Chauvet Cave.* New York: Abrams, 1996.

Chippindale, Christopher. *Stonehenge Complete.* 3d ed. New York: Thames & Hudson, 2004.

Clottes, Jean. *Cave Art.* London: Phaidon, 2008.

———. *Chauvet Cave: The Art of Earliest Times.* Salt Lake City: University of Utah Press, 2003.

Cunliffe, Barry, ed. *The Oxford Illustrated Prehistory of Europe.* New York: Oxford University Press, 2001.

Guthrie, R. Dale. *The Nature of Paleolithic Art.* Chicago: University of Chicago Press, 2005.

Hodder, Ian. *The Leopard's Tale: Revealing the Mysteries of Çatalhöyük.* London: Thames & Hudson, 2006.

Kenyon, Kathleen M. *Digging up Jericho.* New York: Praeger, 1974.

Leroi-Gourhan, André. *The Dawn of European Art: An Introduction to Paleolithic Cave Painting.* Cambridge: Cambridge University Press, 1982.

Marshack, Alexander. *The Roots of Civilization: The Cognitive Beginnings of Man's First Art, Symbol and Notation.* 2d ed. Wakefield, R.I.: Moyer Bell, 1991.

Pfeiffer, John E. *The Creative Explosion: An Inquiry into the Origins of Art and Religion.* New York: Harper & Row, 1982.

Renfrew, Colin, ed. *British Prehistory: A New Outline.* London: Noyes, 1975.

Ruspoli, Mario. *The Cave of Lascaux: The Final Photographs.* New York: Abrams, 1987.

Scarre, Chris. *Exploring Prehistoric Europe.* New York: Oxford University Press, 1998.

Wainwright, Geoffrey. *The Henge Monuments: Ceremony and Society in Prehistoric Britain.* London: Thames & Hudson, 1990.

White, Randall. *Prehistoric Art: The Symbolic Journey of Humankind.* New York: Abrams, 2003.

Chapter 2: Mesopotamia and Persia

Akurgal, Ekrem. *Art of the Hittites.* New York: Abrams, 1962.

Allen, Lindsay. *The Persian Empire.* Chicago: University of Chicago Press, 2005.

Amiet, Pierre. *Art of the Ancient Near East.* New York: Abrams, 1980.

Ascalone, Enrico. *Mesopotamia: Assyrians, Sumerians, Babylonians.* Berkeley and Los Angeles: University of California Press, 2007.

Bahrani, Zainab. *The Graven Image: Representation in Babylonia and Assyria.* Philadelphia: University of Pennsylvania Press, 2003.

Bienkowski, Piotr, and Alan Millard, eds. *Dictionary of the Ancient Near East.* Philadelphia: University of Pennsylvania Press, 2000.

Collins, Paul. *Assyrian Palace Sculptures.* Austin: University of Texas Press, 2008.

Collon, Dominique. *Ancient Near Eastern Art.* Berkeley: University of California Press, 1995.

———. *First Impressions: Cylinder Seals in the Ancient Near East.* 2d ed. London: British Museum, 1993.

———. *Near Eastern Seals.* Berkeley: University of California Press, 1990.

Crawford, Harriet. *Sumer and the Sumerians.* 2d ed. New York: Cambridge University Press, 2004.

Curatola, Giovanni, ed. *The Art and Architecture of Mesopotamia.* New York: Abbeville, 2007.

Curtis, John E. *Ancient Persia.* Cambridge, Mass.: Harvard University Press, 1990.

Curtis, John E., and Julian E. Reade. *Art and Empire: Treasures from Assyria in the British Museum.* New York: Metropolitan Museum of Art, 1995.

Curtis, John E., and Nigel Tallis, eds. *Forgotten Empire: The World of Ancient Persia.* Berkeley: University of California Press, 2005.

Finkel, Irving L., and Michael J. Seymour, eds. *Babylon.* New York: Oxford University Press, 2008.

Foster, Benjamin R., and Karen Polinger Foster. *Civilizations of Ancient Iraq.* Princeton, N.J.: Princeton University Press, 2009.

Frankfort, Henri. *The Art and Architecture of the Ancient Orient.* 5th ed. New Haven, Conn.: Yale University Press, 1996.

Ghirshman, Roman. *The Arts of Ancient Iran: From Its Origins to the Time of Alexander the Great.* New York: Golden, 1964.

———. *Persian Art: The Parthian and Sassanian Dynasties, 249 BC–AD 651.* New York: Golden, 1962.

Gunter, Ann C., ed. *Investigating Artistic Environments in the Ancient Near East.* Washington, D.C.: Arthur M. Sackler Gallery, 1990.

Harper, Prudence O., Joan Aruz, and Françoise Tallon, eds. *The Royal City of Susa: Ancient Near Eastern Treasures in the Louvre.* New York: Metropolitan Museum of Art, 1992.

Leick, Gwendolyn. *Mesopotamia: The Invention of the City.* New York: Penguin, 2003.

Lloyd, Seton. *The Archaeology of Mesopotamia: From the Old Stone Age to the Persian Conquest.* London: Thames & Hudson, 1984.

Macqueen, James G. *The Hittites and Their Contemporaries in Asia Minor.* Rev. ed. New York: Thames & Hudson, 1986.

Meyers, Eric M., ed. *The Oxford Encyclopedia of Archaeology in the Near East.* 5 vols. New York: Oxford University Press, 1997.

Moortgat, Anton. *The Art of Ancient Mesopotamia.* New York: Phaidon, 1969.

Oates, Joan. *Babylon.* Rev. ed. London: Thames & Hudson, 1986.

Parrot, André. *The Arts of Assyria.* New York: Golden, 1961.

———. *Sumer: The Dawn of Art.* New York: Golden, 1961.

Porada, Edith. *Man and Images in the Ancient Near East.* Wakefield, R.I.: Moyer Bell, 1995.

Porada, Edith, and Robert H. Dyson. *The Art of Ancient Iran: Pre-Islamic Cultures.* Rev. ed. New York: Greystone, 1969.

Postgate, J. Nicholas. *Early Mesopotamia: Society and Economy at the Dawn of History.* London: Routledge, 1992.

Potts, Daniel T. *The Archaeology of Elam: Formation and Transformation of an Ancient Iranian State.* New York: Cambridge University Press, 1999.

Reade, Julian E. *Assyrian Sculpture.* Cambridge, Mass.: Harvard University Press, 1999.

———. *Mesopotamia.* Cambridge, Mass.: Harvard University Press, 1991.

Roaf, Michael. *Cultural Atlas of Mesopotamia and the Ancient Near East.* New York: Facts on File, 1990.

Russell, John M. *Sennacherib's Palace without Rival at Nineveh.* Chicago: University of Chicago Press, 1991.

Saggs, H.W.F. *Babylonians.* London: British Museum, 1995.

Sasson, Jack M., ed. *Civilizations of the Ancient Near East.* 4 vols. New York: Scribner, 1995.

Snell, Daniel C. *Life in the Ancient Near East: 3100–332 BC.* New Haven, Conn.: Yale University Press, 1997.

Strommenger, Eva, and Max Hirmer. *5,000 Years of the Art of Mesopotamia.* New York: Abrams, 1964.

Van de Mieroop, Marc. *The Ancient Mesopotamian City.* New York: Oxford University Press, 1997.

Zettler, Richard L., and Lee Horne. *Treasures from the Royal Tombs of Ur.* Philadelphia: University of Pennsylvania Museum of Archaeology and Anthropology, 1998.

Chapter 3: Egypt under the Pharaohs

Allen, James P., ed., *Egyptian Art in the Age of the Pyramids.* New York: Abrams, 1999.

Arnold, Dieter. *Building in Egypt: Pharaonic Stone Masonry.* New York: Oxford University Press, 1991.

Arnold, Dorothea. *The Royal Women of Amarna.* New York: Metropolitan Museum of Art, 1996.

———. *When the Pyramids Were Built: Egyptian Art of the Old Kingdom.* New York: Rizzoli, 1999.

Baines, John, and Jaromír Málek. *Atlas of Ancient Egypt.* New York: Facts on File, 1980.

Bard, Kathryn A. *An Introduction to the Archaeology of Ancient Egypt.* Oxford: Blackwell, 2007.

———, ed. *Encyclopedia of the Archaeology of Ancient Egypt.* London: Routledge, 1999.

Bianchi, Robert S. *Cleopatra's Egypt: Age of the Ptolemies.* Brooklyn: Brooklyn Museum, 1988.

———. *Splendors of Ancient Egypt from the Egyptian Museum, Cairo.* London: Booth-Clibborn, 1996.

Capel, Anne K., and Glenn E. Markoe, eds. *Mistress of the House, Mistress of Heaven: Women in Ancient Egypt.* New York: Hudson Hills, 1996.

D'Auria, Sue, Peter Lacovara, and Catharine H. Roehrig. *Mummies and Magic: The Funerary Arts of Ancient Egypt.* Boston: Museum of Fine Arts, 1988.

Davis, Whitney. *The Canonical Tradition in Ancient Egyptian Art.* New York: Cambridge University Press, 1989.

Dodson, Aidam, and Salima Ikram. *The Tomb in Ancient Egypt.* New York: Thames & Hudson, 2008.

Hawass, Zahi. *Valley of the Golden Mummies.* New York: Abrams, 2000.

Ikram, Salima, and Aidan Dodson. *The Mummy in Ancient Egypt: Equipping the Dead for Eternity.* New York: Thames & Hudson, 1998.

Kemp, Barry J. *Ancient Egypt: Anatomy of a Civilization.* 2d ed. New York: Routledge, 2006.

Kozloff, Arielle P., and Betsy M. Bryan. *Egypt's Dazzling Sun: Amenhotep III and His World.* Cleveland: Cleveland Museum of Art, 1992.

Lange, Kurt, and Max Hirmer. *Egypt: Architecture, Sculpture, and Painting in Three Thousand Years.* 4th ed. London: Phaidon, 1968.

Lehner, Mark. *The Complete Pyramids: Solving the Ancient Mysteries.* New York: Thames & Hudson, 1997.

Mahdy, Christine, ed. *The World of the Pharaohs: A Complete Guide to Ancient Egypt.* London: Thames & Hudson, 1990.

O'Neill, John P., ed. *Egyptian Art in the Age of the Pyramids.* New York: Abrams, 1999.

Málek, Jaromír. *Egypt: 4,000 Years of Art.* New York: Phaidon, 2003.

———. *Egyptian Art.* London: Phaidon, 1999.

———, ed. *Egypt: Ancient Culture, Modern Land.* Norman: University of Oklahoma Press, 1993.

Redford, Donald B. *Akhenaton, the Heretic King.* Princeton, N.J.: Princeton University Press, 1984.

———, ed. *The Oxford Encyclopedia of Ancient Egypt.* 3 vols. New York: Oxford University Press, 2001.

Reeves, C. Nicholas. *The Complete Tutankhamun: The King, the Tomb, the Royal Treasure.* London: Thames & Hudson, 1990.

Robins, Gay. *The Art of Ancient Egypt.* Rev. ed. Cambridge, Mass.: Harvard University Press, 2008.

———. *Egyptian Painting and Relief.* Aylesbury: Shire, 1986.

———. *Proportion and Style in Ancient Egyptian Art.* Austin: University of Texas Press, 1994.

———. *Women in Ancient Egypt.* London: British Museum, 1993.

Romer, John. *Valley of the Kings: Exploring the Tombs of the Pharaohs.* New York: Holt, 1994.

Russmann, Edna R. *Egyptian Sculpture: Cairo and Luxor.* Austin: University of Texas Press, 1989.

Schäfer, Heinrich. *Principles of Egyptian Art.* Rev. ed. Oxford: Clarendon, 1986.

Schulz, Regina, and Matthias Seidel, eds. *Egypt: The World of the Pharaohs.* Cologne: Könemann, 1999.

Shafer, Byron E., ed. *Temples of Ancient Egypt.* Ithaca, N.Y.: Cornell University Press, 1997.

Shaw, Ian, and Paul Nicholson. *The Dictionary of Ancient Egypt.* London: British Museum, 1995.

Silverman, David P., ed. *Ancient Egypt.* New York: Oxford University Press, 1997.

Smith, William Stevenson, and William Kelly Simpson. *The Art and Architecture of Ancient Egypt.* Rev. ed. New Haven, Conn.: Yale University Press, 1998.

Tiradritti, Francesco. *Egyptian Wall Paintings.* New York: Abbeville, 2008.

Weeks, Kent R. *The Treasures of Luxor and the Valley of the Kings.* Vercelli: White Star, 2005.

———, ed. *Valley of the Kings.* Vercelli: White Star, 2001.

Wildung, Dietrich. *Egypt: From Prehistory to the Romans.* Cologne: Taschen, 1997.

Chapter 4: The Prehistoric Aegean

Andreadaki-Vlazaki, Maria, ed. *From the Land of the Labyrinth: Minoan Crete 3000–1100 B.C.* New York: Alexander S. Onassis Public Benefit Foundation, 2008.

Barber, R.L.N. *The Cyclades in the Bronze Age.* Iowa City: University of Iowa Press, 1987.

Betancourt, Philip P. *A History of Minoan Pottery.* Princeton, N.J.: Princeton University Press, 1965.

———. *Introduction to Aegean Art.* New York: Institute for Aegean Prehistory, 2007.

Cadogan, Gerald. *Palaces of Minoan Crete.* London: Methuen, 1980.

Castleden, Rodney. *Mycenaeans.* London: Routledge, 2005.

Chadwick, John. *The Mycenaean World.* New York: Cambridge University Press, 1976.

Cullen, Tracey, ed. *Aegean Prehistory: A Review.* Boston: Archaeological Institute of America, 2001.

Demargne, Pierre *The Birth of Greek Art.* New York: Golden, 1964.

Dickinson, Oliver P.T.K. *The Aegean Bronze Age.* New York: Cambridge University Press, 1994.

Doumas, Christos. *Thera, Pompeii of the Ancient Aegean: Excavations at Akrotiri, 1967–1979.* New York: Thames & Hudson, 1983.

———. *The Wall-Paintings of Thera.* Athens: Thera Foundation, 1992.

Fitton, J. Lesley. *Cycladic Art.* 2d ed. Cambridge, Mass.: Harvard University Press, 1999.

———. *The Discovery of the Greek Bronze Age.* London: British Museum, 1995.

Forsyth, Phyllis Young. *Thera in the Bronze Age.* New York: Peter Lang, 1997.

Getz-Preziosi, Patricia. *Sculptors of the Cyclades: Individual and Tradition in the Third Millennium BC.* Ann Arbor: University of Michigan Press, 1987.

Graham, James W. *The Palaces of Crete.* Princeton, N.J.: Princeton University Press, 1987.

Hampe, Roland, and Erika Simon. *The Birth of Greek Art: From the Mycenaean to the Archaic Period.* New York: Oxford University Press, 1981.

Higgins, Reynold. *Minoan and Mycenaean Art.* Rev. ed. New York: Thames & Hudson, 1997.

Hood, Sinclair. *The Arts in Prehistoric Greece.* New Haven, Conn.: Yale University Press, 1992.

Immerwahr, Sarah A. *Aegean Painting in the Bronze Age.* University Park: Pennsylvania State University Press, 1990.

MacGillivray, J. A. *Minotaur: Sir Arthur Evans and the Archaeology of the Minoan Myth.* New York: Hill and Wang, 2000.

Marinatos, Nanno. *Art and Religion in Thera: Reconstructing a Bronze Age Society.* Athens: Mathioulakis, 1984.

Marinatos, Spyridon, and Max Hirmer. *Crete and Mycenae.* London: Thames & Hudson, 1960.

McDonald, William A., and Carol G. Thomas. *Progress into the Past: The Rediscovery of Mycenaean Civilization.* 2d ed. Bloomington: Indiana University Press, 1990.

Preziosi, Donald, and Louise A. Hitchcock. *Aegean Art and Architecture.* New York: Oxford University Press, 1999.

Schofield, Louise. *The Mycenaeans.* London: British Museum, 2007.

Shelmerdine, Cynthia W., ed. *The Cambridge Companion to the Aegean Bronze Age.* New York: Cambridge University Press, 2008.

Taylour, Lord William. *The Mycenaeans.* London: Thames & Hudson, 1990.

Vermeule, Emily. *Greece in the Bronze Age.* Chicago: University of Chicago Press, 1972.

Warren, Peter. *The Aegean Civilisations from Ancient Crete to Mycenae*. 2d ed. Oxford: Elsevier-Phaidon, 1989.

Chapter 5: Ancient Greece

Arias, Paolo. *A History of One Thousand Years of Greek Vase Painting*. New York: Abrams, 1962.

Ashmole, Bernard. *Architect and Sculptor in Classical Greece*. New York: New York University Press, 1972.

Barletta, Barbara A. *The Origins of the Greek Architectural Orders*. New York: Cambridge University Press, 2001.

Berve, Helmut, Gottfried Gruben, and Max Hirmer. *Greek Temples, Theatres, and Shrines*. New York: Abrams, 1963.

Biers, William. *The Archaeology of Greece: An Introduction*. 2d ed. Ithaca, N.Y.: Cornell University Press, 1996.

Boardman, John. *Athenian Black Figure Vases*. Rev. ed. New York: Thames & Hudson, 1991.

———. *Athenian Red Figure Vases: The Archaic Period*. New York: Thames & Hudson, 1988.

———. *Athenian Red Figure Vases: The Classical Period*. New York: Thames & Hudson, 1989.

———. *Early Greek Vase Painting, 11th–6th Centuries BC*. New York: Thames & Hudson, 1998.

———. *Greek Sculpture: The Archaic Period*. Rev. ed. New York: Thames & Hudson, 1985.

———. *Greek Sculpture: The Classical Period*. New York: Thames & Hudson, 1987.

———. *Greek Sculpture: The Late Classical Period and Sculpture in Colonies and Overseas*. New York: Thames & Hudson, 1995.

———. *The Parthenon and Its Sculpture*. Austin: University of Texas Press, 1985.

Camp, John M. *The Archaeology of Athens*. New Haven, Conn.: Yale University Press, 2001.

Carpenter, Thomas H. *Art and Myth in Ancient Greece*. New York: Thames & Hudson, 1991.

Charbonneaux, Jean, Roland Martin, and François Villard. *Archaic Greek Art*. New York: Braziller, 1971.

———. *Classical Greek Art*. New York: Braziller, 1972.

———. *Hellenistic Art*. New York: Braziller, 1973.

Clark, Andrew J., Maya Elston, and Mary Louise Hart. *Understanding Greek Vases: A Guide to Terms, Styles, and Techniques*. Los Angeles: J. Paul Getty Museum, 2002.

Cohen, Beth, ed. *The Colors of Clay: Special Techniques in Athenian Vases*. Los Angeles: J. Paul Getty Museum, 2006.

Coldstream, J. Nicholas. *Geometric Greece*. New York: St. Martin's, 1977.

Coulton, J. J. *Ancient Greek Architects at Work*. Ithaca, N.Y.: Cornell University Press, 1982.

Donohue, A. A. *Greek Sculpture and the Problem of Description*. New York: Cambridge University Press, 2005.

Fullerton, Mark D. *Greek Art*. New York: Cambridge University Press, 2000.

Haynes, Denys E. L. *The Technique of Greek Bronze Statuary*. Mainz: von Zabern, 1992.

Houser, Caroline. *Greek Monumental Bronze Sculpture*. New York: Vendome, 1983.

Hurwit, Jeffrey M. *The Acropolis in the Age of Pericles*. New York: Cambridge University Press, 2004.

———. *The Art and Culture of Early Greece, 1100–480 BC*. Ithaca, N.Y.: Cornell University Press, 1985.

———. *The Athenian Acropolis: History, Mythology, and Archaeology from the Neolithic Era to the Present*. New York: Cambridge University Press, 1999.

Jenkins, Ian. *Greek Architecture and Its Sculpture*. Cambridge, Mass.: Harvard University Press, 2006.

———. *The Parthenon Frieze*. Austin: University of Texas Press, 1994.

Lawrence, Arnold W., and R. A. Tomlinson. *Greek Architecture*. Rev. ed. New Haven, Conn.: Yale University Press, 1996.

Martin, Roland. *Greek Architecture: Architecture of Crete, Greece, and the Greek World*. New York: Electa/Rizzoli, 1988.

Mattusch, Carol C. *Classical Bronzes: The Art and Craft of Greek and Roman Statuary*. Ithaca, N.Y.: Cornell University Press, 1996.

———. *Greek Bronze Statuary from the Beginnings through the Fifth Century BC*. Ithaca, N.Y.: Cornell University Press, 1988.

Mee, Christopher. *Greek Archaeology*. Hoboken, N.J.: Wiley-Blackwell, 2011.

Mee, Christopher, and Tony Spawforth. *Greece: An Oxford Archaeological Guide*. New York: Oxford University Press, 2001.

Morris, Sarah P. *Daidalos and the Origins of Greek Art*. Princeton, N.J.: Princeton University Press, 1992.

Neer, Richard T. *The Emergence of the Classical Style in Greek Sculpture*. Chicago: University of Chicago Press, 2010.

Osborne, Robin. *Archaic and Classical Greek Art*. New York: Oxford University Press, 1998.

Palagia, Olga. *The Pediments of the Parthenon*. Leiden: E. J. Brill, 1993.

———, ed. *Greek Sculpture: Functions, Materials, and Techniques in the Archaic and Classical Periods*. New York: Cambridge University Press, 2006.

Palagia, Olga, and Jerome J. Pollitt. *Personal Styles in Greek Sculpture*. New York: Cambridge University Press, 1996.

Pedley, John Griffiths. *Greek Art and Archaeology*. 4th ed. Upper Saddle River, N.J.: Prentice Hall, 2007.

———. *Sanctuaries and the Sacred in the Ancient Greek World*. New York: Cambridge University Press, 2005.

Petrakos, Vasileios. *Great Moments in Greek Archaeology*. Los Angeles: J. Paul Getty Museum, 2007.

Pollitt, Jerome J. *Art and Experience in Classical Greece*. New York: Cambridge University Press, 1972.

———. *Art in the Hellenistic Age*. New York: Cambridge University Press, 1986.

———. *The Art of Ancient Greece: Sources and Documents*. 2d ed. New York: Cambridge University Press, 1990.

Pugliese Carratelli, G. *The Greek World: Art and Civilization in Magna Graecia and Sicily*. New York: Rizzoli, 1996.

Reeder, Ellen D., ed. *Pandora: Women in Classical Greece*. Baltimore: Walters Art Gallery, 1995.

Rhodes, Robin F. *Architecture and Meaning on the Athenian Acropolis*. New York: Cambridge University Press, 1995.

Richter, Gisela M. *The Portraits of the Greeks*. Rev. ed. by R.R.R. Smith. Ithaca, N.Y.: Cornell University Press, 1984.

Ridgway, Brunilde S. *The Archaic Style in Greek Sculpture*. 2d ed. Chicago: Ares, 1993.

———. *Fifth-Century Styles in Greek Sculpture*. Princeton, N.J.: Princeton University Press, 1981.

———. *Fourth-Century Styles in Greek Sculpture*. Madison: University of Wisconsin Press, 1997.

———. *Hellenistic Sculpture I: The Styles of ca. 331–200 BC*. Madison: University of Wisconsin Press, 1990.

———. *Hellenistic Sculpture II: The Styles of ca. 200–100 BC*. Madison: University of Wisconsin Press, 2000.

———. *Prayers in Stone: Greek Architectural Sculpture*. Berkeley: University of California Press, 1999.

———. *Roman Copies of Greek Sculpture: The Problem of the Originals*. Ann Arbor: University of Michigan Press, 1984.

———. *The Severe Style in Greek Sculpture*. Princeton, N.J.: Princeton University Press, 1970.

Robertson, Martin. *The Art of Vase-Painting in Classical Athens*. New York: Cambridge University Press, 1992.

———. *A History of Greek Art*. Rev. ed. 2 vols. New York: Cambridge University Press, 1986.

———. *A Shorter History of Greek Art*. New York: Cambridge University Press, 1981.

Shapiro, H. Alan. *Art and Cult in Athens under the Tyrants*. Mainz: von Zabern, 1989.

———. *Myth into Art: Poet and Painter in Classical Greece*. New York: Routledge, 1994.

Smith, R.R.R. *Hellenistic Sculpture*. New York: Thames & Hudson, 1991.

Spawforth, Tony. *The Complete Greek Temples*. London, Thames & Hudson, 2006.

Spivey, Nigel. *Greek Art*. London: Phaidon, 1997.

Stansbury-O'Donnell, Mark D. *Pictorial Narrative in Ancient Greek Art*. New York: Cambridge University Press, 1999.

Stewart, Andrew. *Art, Desire, and the Body in Ancient Greece*. New York: Cambridge University Press, 1997.

———. *Classical Greece and the Birth of Western Art*. New York: Cambridge University Press, 2008.

———. *Greek Sculpture: An Exploration*. 2 vols. New Haven, Conn.: Yale University Press, 1990.

Whitley, James. *The Archaeology of Ancient Greece*. New York: Cambridge University Press, 2001.

Wycherley, Richard E. *How the Greeks Built Cities*. New York: Norton, 1976.

Chapter 6: The Etruscans

Banti, Luisa. *The Etruscan Cities and Their Culture*. Berkeley: University of California Press, 1973.

Barker, Graeme, and Tom Rasmussen. *The Etruscans*. Oxford: Blackwell, 1998.

Boethius, Axel. *Etruscan and Early Roman Architecture*. 2d ed. New Haven, Conn.: Yale University Press, 1978.

Bonfante, Larissa, ed. *Etruscan Life and Afterlife: A Handbook of Etruscan Studies*. Detroit: Wayne State University Press, 1986.

Brendel, Otto J. *Etruscan Art*. 2d ed. New Haven, Conn.: Yale University Press, 1995.

Cristofani, Mauro. *The Etruscans: A New Investigation*. London: Orbis, 1979.

De Grummond, Nancy Thomson. *Etruscan Myth, Sacred History, and Legend*. Philadelphia: University of Pennsylvania Museum, 2006.

Haynes, Sybille. *Etruscan Civilization: A Cultural History*. Los Angeles: J. Paul Getty Museum, 2000.

Heurgon, Jacques. *Daily Life of the Etruscans*. London: Weidenfeld & Nicolson, 1964.

Pallottino, Massimo. *The Etruscans*. Harmondsworth: Penguin, 1978.

Richardson, Emeline. *The Etruscans: Their Art and Civilization*. Rev. ed. Chicago: University of Chicago Press, 1976.

Ridgway, David, and Francesca Ridgway, eds. *Italy before the Romans*. New York: Academic, 1979.

Spivey, Nigel. *Etruscan Art*. New York: Thames & Hudson, 1997.

Spivey, Nigel, and Simon Stoddart. *Etruscan Italy: An Archaeological History*. London: Batsford, 1990.

Sprenger, Maja, Gilda Bartoloni, and Max Hirmer. *The Etruscans: Their History, Art, and Architecture*. New York: Abrams, 1983.

Steingräber, Stephan. *Abundance of Life: Etruscan Wall Painting*. Los Angeles: J. Paul Getty Museum, 2006.

Torelli, Mario, ed. *The Etruscans*. New York: Rizzoli, 2001.

Chapter 7: The Roman Empire

Aldrete, Gregory S. *Daily Life in the Roman City: Rome, Pompeii, and Ostia*. Westport, Conn.: Greenwood, 2004.

Anderson, James C., Jr. *Roman Architecture and Society*. Baltimore: Johns Hopkins University Press, 1997.

Andreae, Bernard. *The Art of Rome*. New York: Abrams, 1977.

Barton, Ian M., ed. *Roman Domestic Buildings*. Exeter: University of Exeter Press, 1996.

———. *Roman Public Buildings*. 2d ed. Exeter: University of Exeter Press, 1995.

Bianchi Bandinelli, Ranuccio. *Rome: The Center of Power: Roman Art to AD 200*. New York: Braziller, 1970.

———. *Rome: The Late Empire: Roman Art AD 200–400*. New York: Braziller, 1971.

Brendel, Otto J. *Prolegomena to the Study of Roman Art*. New Haven, Conn.: Yale University Press, 1979.

Claridge, Amanda. *Rome: An Oxford Archaeological Guide*. 2d ed. New York: Oxford University Press, 2010.

Clarke, John R. *The Houses of Roman Italy, 100 BC–AD 250*. Berkeley: University of California Press, 1991.

Coarelli, Filippo. *Rome and Environs: An Archaeological Guide*. Berkeley and Los Angeles: University of California Press, 2007.

Cornell, Tim, and John Matthews. *Atlas of the Roman World*. New York: Facts on File, 1982.

D'Ambra, Eve. *Roman Art*. New York: Cambridge University Press, 1998.

———, ed. *Roman Art in Context*. Upper Saddle River, N.J.: Prentice Hall, 1994.

Dobbins, John J., and Pedar W. Foss, eds. *The World of Pompeii*. London: Routledge, 2007.

Dyson, Stephen L. *Rome: A Living Portrait of an Ancient City*. Baltimore: Johns Hopkins University Press, 2010.

Gazda, Elaine K., ed. *Roman Art in the Private Sphere*. Ann Arbor: University of Michigan Press, 1991.

Grant, Michael. *Cities of Vesuvius: Pompeii and Herculaneum*. Harmondsworth: Penguin, 1976.

Hannestad, Niels. *Roman Art and Imperial Policy*. Aarhus: Aarhus University Press, 1986.

Henig, Martin, ed. *A Handbook of Roman Art*. Ithaca, N.Y.: Cornell University Press, 1983.

Kent, John P. C., and Max Hirmer. *Roman Coins*. New York: Abrams, 1978.

Kleiner, Diana E. E. *Roman Sculpture*. New Haven, Conn.: Yale University Press, 1992.

Kleiner, Diana E. E., and Susan B. Matheson, eds. *I Claudia: Women in Ancient Rome*. New Haven, Conn.: Yale University Art Gallery, 1996.

Kleiner, Fred S. *A History of Roman Art*. Enhanced ed. Belmont, Calif.: Wadsworth, 2010.

Kraus, Theodor. *Pompeii and Herculaneum: The Living Cities of the Dead*. New York: Abrams, 1975.

Lancaster, Lynne. *Concrete Vaulted Construction in Imperial Rome*. New York: Cambridge University Press, 2006.

Ling, Roger. *Roman Painting*. New York: Cambridge University Press, 1991.

L'Orange, Hans Peter. *The Roman Empire: Art Forms and Civic Life*. New York: Rizzoli, 1985.

MacCormack, Sabine G. *Art and Ceremony in Late Antiquity*. Berkeley: University of California Press, 1981.

MacDonald, William L. *The Architecture of the Roman Empire I: An Introductory Study*. Rev. ed. New Haven, Conn.: Yale University Press, 1982.

———. *The Architecture of the Roman Empire II: An Urban Appraisal*. New Haven, Conn.: Yale University Press, 1986.

———. *The Pantheon: Design, Meaning, and Progeny*. Cambridge, Mass.: Harvard University Press, 1976.

Mattusch, Carol C., ed. *Pompeii and the Roman Villa: Art and Culture around the Bay of Naples*. New York: Thames & Hudson, 2008.

Mazzoleni, Donatella. *Domus: Wall Painting in the Roman House*. Los Angeles: J. Paul Getty Museum, 2004.

McKay, Alexander G. *Houses, Villas, and Palaces in the Roman World*. Ithaca, N.Y.: Cornell University Press, 1975.

Nash, Ernest. *Pictorial Dictionary of Ancient Rome*. 2d ed. 2 vols. New York: Praeger, 1962.

Pollitt, Jerome J. *The Art of Rome, 753 BC–AD 337: Sources and Documents*. Rev. ed. New York: Cambridge University Press, 1983.

Richardson, Lawrence, Jr. *A New Topographical Dictionary of Ancient Rome*. Baltimore: Johns Hopkins University Press, 1992.

———. *Pompeii: An Architectural History*. Baltimore: Johns Hopkins University Press, 1988.

Sear, Frank. *Roman Architecture*. Rev. ed. Ithaca, N.Y.: Cornell University Press, 1989.

Stambaugh, John E. *The Ancient Roman City*. Baltimore: Johns Hopkins University Press, 1988.

Stamper, John W. *The Architecture of Roman Temples: The Republic to the Middle Empire*. New York: Cambridge University Press, 2005.

Stewart, Peter. *The Social History of Roman Art*. New York: Cambridge University Press, 2008.

Taylor, Rabun. *Roman Builders*. New York: Cambridge University Press, 2003.

Toynbee, Jocelyn M. C. *Death and Burial in the Roman World*. London: Thames & Hudson, 1971.

Wallace-Hadrill, Andrew. *Herculaneum: Past and Future*. London: Frances Lincoln, 2011.

———. *Houses and Society in Pompeii and Herculaneum*. Princeton, N.J.: Princeton University Press, 1994.

Ward-Perkins, John B. *Roman Architecture*. New York: Electa/Rizzoli, 1988.

———. *Roman Imperial Architecture*. 2d ed. New Haven, Conn.: Yale University Press, 1981.

Wilson-Jones, Mark. *Principles of Roman Architecture*. New Haven, Conn.: Yale University Press, 2000.

Wood, Susan. *Roman Portrait Sculpture AD 217–260*. Leiden: E. J. Brill, 1986.

Yegül, Fikret. *Baths and Bathing in Classical Antiquity*. Cambridge, Mass.: MIT Press, 1992.

Zanker, Paul. *Pompeii: Public and Private Life*. Cambridge, Mass.: Harvard University Press, 1998.

———. *The Power of Images in the Age of Augustus*. Ann Arbor: University of Michigan Press, 1988.

———. *Roman Art*. Los Angeles: J. Paul Getty Museum, 2010.

Chapter 8: Late Antiquity

Bowersock, G. W., Peter Brown, and Oleg Grabar, eds. *Late Antiquity: A Guide to the Postclassical World*. Cambridge, Mass.: Harvard University Press, 1998.

Brody, Lisa R., and Gail L. Hoffman, eds. *Dura Europos: Crossroads of Antiquity*. Chestnut Hill, Mass.: McMullen Museum of Art, Boston College, 2010.

Cioffarelli, Ada. *Guide to the Catacombs of Rome and Its Surroundings*. Rome: Bonsignori, 2000.

Elsner, Jas´. *Art and the Roman Viewer: The Transformation of Art from the Pagan World to Christianity*. New York: Cambridge University Press, 1995.

———. *Imperial Rome and Christian Triumph*. New York: Oxford University Press, 1998.

Fine, Steven. *Art and Judaism in the Greco-Roman World: Toward a New Jewish Archaeology*. New York: Cambridge University Press, 2005.

Finney, Paul Corby. *The Invisible God: The Earliest Christians on Art*. New York: Oxford University Press, 1994.

Grabar, André. *The Beginnings of Christian Art, 200–395*. London: Thames & Hudson, 1967.

———. *Christian Iconography*. Princeton, N.J.: Princeton University Press, 1980.

Gutmann, Joseph. *Sacred Images: Studies in Jewish Art from Antiquity to the Middle Ages*. Northampton, Mass.: Variorum, 1989.

Janes, Dominic. *God and Gold in Late Antiquity*. New York: Cambridge University Press, 1998.

Jensen, Robin Margaret. *Understanding Early Christian Art*. New York: Routledge, 2000.

Koch, Guntram. *Early Christian Art and Architecture*. London: SCM, 1996.

Krautheimer, Richard. *Rome, Profile of a City: 312–1308*. Princeton, N.J.: Princeton University Press, 1980.

Krautheimer, Richard, and Slobodan Ćurčić. *Early Christian and Byzantine Architecture*. 4th ed. New Haven, Conn.: Yale University Press, 1986.

Lowden, John. *Early Christian and Byzantine Art*. London: Phaidon, 1997.

Mathews, Thomas P. *The Clash of Gods: A Reinterpretation of Early Christian Art*. Rev. ed. Princeton, N.J.: Princeton University Press, 1999.

Milburn, Robert. *Early Christian Art and Architecture*. Berkeley: University of California Press, 1988.

Nicolai, Vincenzo Fiocchi, Fabrizio Bisconti, and Danilo Mazzoleni. *The Christian Catacombs of Rome: History, Decoration, Inscriptions*. Regensburg: Schnell & Steiner, 2006.

Perkins, Ann Louise. *The Art of Dura-Europos*. Oxford: Clarendon, 1973.

Poeschke, Joachim. *Italian Mosaics, 300–1300*. New York: Abbeville, 2010.

Rutgers, Leonard V. *Subterranean Rome: In Search of the Roots of Christianity in the Catacombs of the Eternal City*. Leuven: Peeters, 2000.

Spier, Jeffrey, ed. *Picturing the Bible: The Earliest Christian Art*. New Haven, Conn.: Yale University Press, 2007.

Volbach, Wolfgang, and Max Hirmer. *Early Christian Art*. New York: Abrams, 1962.

Webb, Matilda. *The Churches and Catacombs of Early Christian Rome: A Comprehensive Guide*. Brighton: Sussex Academic Press, 2001.

Webster, Leslie, and Michelle Brown, eds. *The Transformation of the Roman World, AD 400–900*. Berkeley: University of California Press, 1997.

Weitzmann, Kurt. *Late Antique and Early Christian Book Illumination*. New York: Braziller, 1977.

———, ed. *Age of Spirituality: Late Antique and Early Christian Art, Third to Seventh Century*. New York: Metropolitan Museum of Art, 1979.

Chapter 9: Byzantium

Barber, Charles. *Figure and Likeness: On the Limits of Representation in Byzantine Iconoclasm*. Princeton, N.J.: Princeton University Press, 2002.

Borsook, Eve. *Messages in Mosaic: The Royal Programmes of Norman Sicily*. Oxford: Clarendon, 1990.

Cormack, Robin. *Byzantine Art*. New York: Oxford University Press, 2000.

———. *Icons*. Cambridge, Mass.: Harvard University Press, 2007.

———. *Painting the Soul: Icons, Death Masks, and Shrouds*. London: Reaktion, 1997.

———. *Writing in Gold: Byzantine Society and Its Icons*. New York: Oxford University Press, 1985.

Cormack, Robin, and Maria Vassiliki. *Byzantium, 330–1453*. London: Royal Academy of Arts, 2008.

Cutler, Anthony. *The Hand of the Master: Craftsmanship, Ivory, and Society in Byzantium, 9th-11th Centuries*. Princeton, N.J.: Princeton University Press, 1994.

Deliyannis, Deborah Mauskopf. *Ravenna in Late Antiquity*. New York: Cambridge University Press, 2010.

Demus, Otto. *The Mosaic Decoration of San Marco, Venice*. Chicago: University of Chicago Press, 1990.

Evans, Helen C. *Byzantium: Faith and Power (1261-1557)*. New York: Metropolitan Museum of Art, 2004.

Evans, Helen C., and William D. Wixom, eds. *The Glory of Byzantium: Art and Culture of the Middle Byzantine Era AD 843-1261*. New York: Metropolitan Museum of Art, 1997.

Freely, John. *Byzantine Monuments of Istanbul*. New York: Cambridge University Press, 2004.

Grabar, André. *The Golden Age of Justinian: From the Death of Theodosius to the Rise of Islam*. New York: Odyssey, 1967.

Grabar, André, and Manolis Chatzidakis. *Greek Mosaics of the Byzantine Period*. New York: New American Library, 1964.

Kleinbauer, W. Eugene. *Hagia Sophia*. London: Scala, 2004.

Lowden, John. *Early Christian and Byzantine Art*. London: Phaidon, 1997.

Maguire, Eunice Dauterman, and Henry Maguire. *Other Icons: Art and Power in Byzantine Secular Culture*. Princeton, N.J.: Princeton University Press, 2007.

Maguire, Henry. *Art and Eloquence in Byzantium*. Princeton, N.J.: Princeton University Press, 1981.

———. *The Icons of Their Bodies: Saints and Their Images in Byzantium*. Princeton, N.J.: Princeton University Press, 1996.

Mainstone, Rowland J. *Hagia Sophia: Architecture, Structure, and Liturgy of Justinian's Great Church*. 2d ed. New York: Thames & Hudson, 2001.

Mango, Cyril. *Art of the Byzantine Empire, 312-1453: Sources and Documents*. Toronto: University of Toronto Press, 1986. Reprint of 1972 ed.

———. *Byzantine Architecture*. New York: Electa/Rizzoli, 1985.

Mark, Robert, and Ahmet S. Cakmak, eds. *Hagia Sophia from the Age of Justinian to the Present*. New York: Cambridge University Press, 1992.

Mathews, Thomas F. *Byzantium: From Antiquity to the Renaissance*. New York: Abrams, 1998.

McClanan, Anne. *Representations of Early Byzantine Empresses: Image and Empire*. New York: Palgrave Macmillan, 2002.

Ousterhout, Robert. *Master Builders of Byzantium*. Princeton, N.J.: Princeton University Press, 2000.

Pelikan, Jaroslav. *Imago Dei: The Byzantine Apologia for Icons*. Princeton, N.J.: Princeton University Press, 1990.

Poeschke, Joachim. *Italian Mosaics, 300-1300*. New York: Abbeville, 2010.

Rodley, Lyn. *Byzantine Art and Architecture: An Introduction*. New York: Cambridge University Press, 1994.

Von Simson, Otto G. *Sacred Fortress: Byzantine Art and Statecraft in Ravenna*. Princeton, N.J.: Princeton University Press, 1986.

Weitzmann, Kurt. *The Icon*. New York: Dorset, 1987.

———. *Illustrations in Roll and Codex*. Princeton, N.J.: Princeton University Press, 1970.

Chapter 10: The Islamic World

Allan, James, and Sheila R. Canby. *Hunt for Paradise: Court Arts of Safavid Iran 1501-76*. Geneva: Skira, 2004.

Atil, Esin. *The Age of Sultan Suleyman the Magnificent*. Washington, D.C.: National Gallery of Art, 1987.

Baker, Patricia L. *Islam and the Religious Arts*. London: Continuum, 2004.

———. *Islamic Textiles*. London: British Museum, 1995.

Blair, Sheila S., and Jonathan Bloom. *The Art and Architecture of Islam 1250-1800*. New Haven, Conn.: Yale University Press, 1994.

Bloom, Jonathan M., and Sheila S. Blair. *The Grove Encyclopedia of Islamic Art and Architecture*. New York: Oxford University Press, 2009.

———. *Islamic Arts*. London: Phaidon, 1997.

Brend, Barbara. *Islamic Art*. Cambridge, Mass.: Harvard University Press, 1991.

Canby, Sheila R. *Persian Painting*. London: British Museum, 1993.

Dodds, Jerrilynn D., ed. *Al-Andalus: The Art of Islamic Spain*. New York: Metropolitan Museum of Art, 1992.

Ettinghausen, Richard, Oleg Grabar, and Marilyn Jenkins-Madina. *The Art and Architecture of Islam, 650-1250*. Rev. ed. New Haven, Conn.: Yale University Press, 2001.

Ferrier, Ronald W., ed. *The Arts of Persia*. New Haven, Conn.: Yale University Press, 1989.

Frishman, Martin, and Hasan-Uddin Khan. *The Mosque: History, Architectural Development, and Regional Diversity*. New York: Thames & Hudson, 1994.

Goodwin, Godfrey. *A History of Ottoman Architecture*. 2d ed. New York: Thames & Hudson, 1987.

Grabar, Oleg. *The Alhambra*. Cambridge, Mass.: Harvard University Press, 1978.

———. *The Formation of Islamic Art*. Rev. ed. New Haven, Conn.: Yale University Press, 1987.

———. *Islamic Visual Culture, 1100-1800*. New York: Ashgate, 2006.

Grube, Ernst J. *Architecture of the Islamic World: Its History and Social Meaning*. 2d ed. New York: Thames & Hudson, 1984.

Hattstein, Markus, and Peter Delius, eds. *Islam: Art and Architecture*. Cologne: Könemann, 2000.

Hillenbrand, Robert. *Islamic Architecture: Form, Function, Meaning*. Edinburgh: Edinburgh University Press, 1994.

———. *Islamic Art and Architecture*. New York: Thames & Hudson, 1999.

Irwin, Robert. *The Alhambra*. Cambridge, Mass.: Harvard University Press, 2004.

———. *Islamic Art in Context: Art, Architecture, and the Literary World*. New York: Abrams, 1997.

Michell, George, ed. *Architecture of the Islamic World*. New York: Thames & Hudson, 1978.

Necipoglu, Gulru. *The Age of Sinan: Architectural Culture in the Ottoman Empire*. Princeton, N.J.: Princeton University Press, 2005.

Petruccioli, Attilio, and Khalil K. Pirani, eds. *Understanding Islamic Architecture*. London: Routledge, 2002.

Porter, Venetia. *Islamic Tiles*. London: British Museum, 1995.

Robinson, Frank. *Atlas of the Islamic World*. Oxford: Equinox, 1982.

Schimmel, Annemarie. *Calligraphy and Islamic Culture*. New York: New York University Press, 1984.

Stierlin, Henri. *Islam I: Early Architecture from Baghdad to Cordoba*. Cologne: Taschen, 1996.

———. *Islamic Art and Architecture from Isfahan to the Taj Mahal*. New York: Thames & Hudson, 2002.

Tadgell, Christopher. *Four Caliphates: The Formation and Development of the Islamic Tradition*. London: Ellipsis, 1998.

Ward, Rachel M. *Islamic Metalwork*. New York: Thames & Hudson, 1993.

Welch, Anthony. *Calligraphy in the Arts of the Islamic World*. Austin: University of Texas Press, 1979.

Medieval Art, General

Alexander, Jonathan J. G. *Medieval Illuminators and Their Methods of Work*. New Haven, Conn.: Yale University Press, 1992.

The Art of Medieval Spain, AD 500-1200. New York: Metropolitan Museum of Art, 1993.

Benton, Janetta Rebold. *Art of the Middle Ages*. New York: Thames & Hudson, 2002.

Binski, Paul. *Painters (Medieval Craftsmen)*. Toronto: University of Toronto Press, 1991.

Calkins, Robert G. *Illuminated Books of the Middle Ages*. Ithaca, N.Y.: Cornell University Press, 1983.

———. *Medieval Architecture in Western Europe: From AD 300 to 1500*. New York: Oxford University Press, 1998.

Coldstream, Nicola. *Masons and Sculptors (Medieval Craftsmen)*. Toronto: University of Toronto Press, 1991.

———. *Medieval Architecture*. New York: Oxford University Press, 2002.

Cross, Frank L., and Livingstone, Elizabeth A., eds. *The Oxford Dictionary of the Christian Church*. 3d ed. New York: Oxford University Press, 1997.

De Hamel, Christopher. *A History of Illuminated Manuscripts*. Oxford: Phaidon, 1986.

———. *Scribes and Illuminators (Medieval Craftsmen)*. Toronto: University of Toronto Press, 1992.

Doig, Allan. *Liturgy and Architecture: From the Early Church to the Middle Ages*. New York: Ashgate, 2008.

Holcomb, Melanie, ed. *Pen and Parchment: Drawing in the Middle Ages*. New York: Metropolitan Museum of Art, 2009.

Kessler, Herbert L. *Seeing Medieval Art*. Toronto: Broadview, 2004.

———. *Spiritual Seeing: Picturing God's Invisibility in Medieval Art*. Philadelphia: University of Pennsylvania Press, 2000.

Lasko, Peter. *Ars Sacra, 800-1200*. 2d ed. New Haven, Conn.: Yale University Press, 1994.

Murray, Peter, and Linda Murray. *The Oxford Companion to Christian Art and Architecture*. New York: Oxford University Press, 1996.

Pelikan, Jaroslav. *Mary through the Centuries: Her Place in the History of Culture*. New Haven, Conn.: Yale University Press, 1996.

Prache, Anne. *Cathedrals of Europe*. Ithaca, N.Y.: Cornell University Press, 1999.

Raguin, Virginia Chieffo. *Stained Glass from Its Origins to the Present*. New York: Abrams, 2003.

Ross, Leslie. *Medieval Art: A Topical Dictionary*. Westport, Conn.: Greenwood, 1996.

Schütz, Bernard. *Great Cathedrals*. New York: Abrams, 2002.

Sekules, Veronica. *Medieval Art*. New York: Oxford University Press, 2001.

Snyder, James, Henry Luttikhuizen, and Dorothy Verkerk. *Art of the Middle Ages*. 2d ed. Upper Saddle River, N.J.: Prentice Hall, 2006.

Stokstad, Marilyn. *Medieval Art*. 2d ed. Boulder, Colo.: Westview, 2004.

Tasker, Edward G. *Encyclopedia of Medieval Church Art*. London: Batsford, 1993.

Chapter 11: Early Medieval Europe

Alexander, Jonathan J. G. *Insular Manuscripts, Sixth to the Ninth Century*. London: Miller, 1978.

The Art of Medieval Spain, AD 500-1200. New York: Metropolitan Museum of Art, 1993.

Backhouse, Janet, D. H. Turner, and Leslie Webster, eds. *The Golden Age of Anglo-Saxon Art, 966-1066*. Bloomington: Indiana University Press, 1984.

Bandmann, Günter. *Early Medieval Architecture as Bearer of Meaning*. New York: Columbia University Press, 2005.

Barral i Altet, Xavier. *The Early Middle Ages: From Late Antiquity to AD 1000.* Cologne: Taschen, 1997.

Brown, Katharine Reynolds, Dafydd Kidd, and Charles T. Little, eds. *From Attila to Charlemagne.* New York: Metropolitan Museum of Art, 2000.

Brown, Michelle P. *The Lindisfarne Gospels: Society, Spirituality, and the Scribe.* Toronto: University of Toronto Press, 2003.

Carver, Martin. *Sutton Hoo: A Seventh-Century Princely Burial Ground and Its Context.* London: British Museum, 2005.

Collins, Roger. *Early Medieval Europe, 300–1000.* New York: St. Martin's, 1991.

Conant, Kenneth J. *Carolingian and Romanesque Architecture, 800–1200.* 4th ed. New Haven, Conn.: Yale University Press, 1992.

Davis-Weyer, Caecilia. *Early Medieval Art, 300–1150: Sources and Documents.* Toronto: University of Toronto Press, 1986. Reprint of 1971 ed.

Diebold, William J. *Word and Image: An Introduction to Early Medieval Art.* Boulder, Colo.: Westview Press, 2000.

Dodwell, Charles R. *Anglo-Saxon Art: A New Perspective.* Ithaca, N.Y.: Cornell University Press, 1982.

———. *The Pictorial Arts of the West, 800–1200.* New Haven, Conn.: Yale University Press, 1993.

Farr, Carol. *The Book of Kells: Its Function and Audience.* London: British Library, 1997.

Harbison, Peter. *The Golden Age of Irish Art: The Medieval Achievement 600–1200.* New York: Thames & Hudson, 1999.

Henderson, George. *From Durrow to Kells: The Insular Gospel-Books, 650–800.* London: Thames & Hudson, 1987.

Hubert, Jean, Jean Porcher, and Wolfgang Fritz Volbach. *The Carolingian Renaissance.* New York: Braziller, 1970.

———. *Europe of the Invasions.* New York: Braziller, 1969.

Mayr-Harting, Henry. *Ottonian Book Illumination: An Historical Study.* 2 vols. London: Miller, 1991–1993.

McClendon, Charles. *The Origins of Medieval Architecture: Building in Europe, AD 600–900.* New Haven, Conn.: Yale University Press, 2005.

Megaw, Ruth, and John Vincent Megaw. *Celtic Art: From Its Beginning to the Book of Kells.* New York: Thames & Hudson, 1989.

Mütherich, Florentine, and Joachim E. Gaehde. *Carolingian Painting.* New York: Braziller, 1976.

Nees, Lawrence J. *Early Medieval Art.* New York: Oxford University Press, 2002.

Nordenfalk, Carl. *Celtic and Anglo-Saxon Painting: Book Illumination in the British Isles, 600–800.* New York: Braziller, 1977.

O'Brien, Jacqueline, and Peter Harbison. *Ancient Ireland: From Prehistory to the Middle Ages.* New York: Oxford University Press, 2000.

Richardson, Hilary, and John Scarry. *An Introduction to Irish High Crosses.* Dublin: Mercier, 1990.

Stalley, Roger. *Early Medieval Architecture.* New York: Oxford University Press, 1999.

Wilson, David M. *From Viking to Crusader: Scandinavia and Europe 800–1200.* New York: Rizzoli, 1992.

Wilson, David M., and Ole Klindt-Jensen. *Viking Art.* 2d ed. Minneapolis: University of Minnesota Press, 1980.

Chapter 12: Romanesque Europe

Armi, C. Edson. *Masons and Sculptors in Romanesque Burgundy: The New Aesthetics of Cluny III.* 2 vols. University Park: Pennsylvania State University Press, 1983.

Ashley, Kathleen, and Marilyn Deegan. *Being a Pilgrim: Art and Ritual on the Medieval Routes to Santiago.* Burlington, Vt.: Lund Humphries, 2009.

Bagnoli, Martina, Holger A. Kleiner, C. Griffith Mann, and James Robinson, eds. *Treasures of Heaven: Saints, Relics, and Devotion in Medieval Europe.* New Haven, Conn.: Yale University Press: 2010.

Barral i Altet, Xavier. *The Romanesque: Towns, Cathedrals, and Monasteries.* Cologne: Taschen, 1998.

Burnett, Charles, and Peter Dronke. *Hildegard of Bingen: The Context of Her Thought and Art.* London: Warburg Institute, 1998.

Cahn, Walter. *Romanesque Bible Illumination.* Ithaca, N.Y.: Cornell University Press, 1982.

———. *Romanesque Manuscripts: The Twelfth Century.* 2 vols. London: Miller, 1998.

Conant, Kenneth J. *Carolingian and Romanesque Architecture, 800–1200.* 4th ed. New Haven, Conn.: Yale University Press, 1992.

Demus, Otto. *Romanesque Mural Painting.* New York: Thames & Hudson, 1968.

Dodwell, Charles R. *The Pictorial Arts of the West, 800–1200.* New Haven, Conn.: Yale University Press, 1993.

Fergusson, Peter. *Architecture of Solitude: Cistercian Abbeys in Twelfth-Century Europe.* Princeton, N.J.: Princeton University Press, 1984.

Grape, Wolfgang. *The Bayeux Tapestry: Monument to a Norman Triumph.* New York: Prestel, 1994.

Hearn, Millard F. *Romanesque Sculpture: The Revival of Monumental Stone Sculpture in the Eleventh and Twelfth Centuries.* Ithaca, N.Y.: Cornell University Press, 1981.

Hourihane, Colum, ed. *Romanesque Art and Thought in the Twelfth Century.* Princeton, N.J.: Index of Christian Art, 2008.

Kahn, Deborah, ed. *The Romanesque Frieze and Its Spectator.* London: Miller, 1992.

Kubach, Hans E. *Romanesque Architecture.* New York: Electa, 1988.

Male, Émile. *Religious Art in France: The Twelfth Century.* Rev. ed. Princeton, N.J.: Princeton University Press, 1978.

Minne-Sève, Viviane, and Hervé Kergall. *Romanesque and Gothic France: Architecture and Sculpture.* New York: Abrams, 2000.

Nichols, Stephen G. *Romanesque Signs: Early Medieval Narrative and Iconography.* New Haven, Conn.: Yale University Press, 1983.

Nordenfalk, Carl. *Early Medieval Book Illumination.* New York: Rizzoli, 1988.

Petzold, Andreas. *Romanesque Art.* New York: Abrams, 1995.

Schapiro, Meyer. *The Sculpture of Moissac.* New York: Thames & Hudson, 1985.

Seidel, Linda. *Legends in Limestone: Lazarus, Gislebertus, and the Cathedral of Autun.* Chicago: University of Chicago Press, 1999.

Stalley, Roger. *Early Medieval Architecture.* New York: Oxford University Press, 1999.

Tate, Robert B., and Marcus Tate. *The Pilgrim Route to Santiago.* Oxford: Phaidon, 1987.

Toman, Rolf, ed. *Romanesque: Architecture, Sculpture, Painting.* Cologne: Könemann, 1997.

Wilson, David M. *The Bayeux Tapestry: The Complete Tapestry in Color.* New York: Thames & Hudson, 2004.

Zarnecki, George, Janet Holt, and Tristram Holland, eds. *English Romanesque Art, 1066–1200.* London: Weidenfeld & Nicolson, 1984.

Chapter 13: Gothic Europe

Barnes, Carl F. *The Portfolio of Villard de Honnecourt.* New York: Ashgate, 2009.

Binski, Paul. *Becket's Crown: Art and Imagination in Gothic England, 1170–1300.* New Haven, Conn.: Yale University Press, 2004.

Bony, Jean. *The English Decorated Style: Gothic Architecture Transformed, 1250–1350.* Ithaca, N.Y.: Cornell University Press, 1979.

———. *French Gothic Architecture of the Twelfth and Thirteenth Centuries.* Berkeley: University of California Press, 1983.

Branner, Robert. *Manuscript Painting in Paris during the Reign of St. Louis.* Berkeley: University of California Press, 1977.

———. *St. Louis and the Court Style in Gothic Architecture.* London: Zwemmer, 1965.

———, ed. *Chartres Cathedral.* New York: Norton, 1969.

Brown, Sarah, and David O'Connor. *Glass-Painters (Medieval Craftsmen).* Toronto: University of Toronto Press, 1991.

Camille, Michael. *Gothic Art: Glorious Visions.* New York: Abrams, 1996.

———. *The Gothic Idol: Ideology and Image-Making in Medieval Art.* New York: Cambridge University Press, 1989.

Courtenay, Lynn T., ed. *The Engineering of Medieval Cathedrals.* Aldershot: Scolar, 1997.

Crosby, Sumner McKnight. *The Royal Abbey of Saint-Denis from Its Beginnings to the Death of Suger, 475–1151.* New Haven, Conn.: Yale University Press, 1987.

Erlande-Brandenburg, Alain. *The Cathedral: The Social and Architectural Dynamics of Construction.* New York: Cambridge University Press, 1994.

———. *Gothic Art.* New York: Abrams, 1989.

Favier, Jean. *The World of Chartres.* New York: Abrams, 1990.

Fitchen, John. *The Construction of Gothic Cathedrals: A Study of Medieval Vault Erection.* Chicago: University of Chicago Press, 1981.

Frankl, Paul. *The Gothic: Literary Sources and Interpretations through Eight Centuries.* Princeton, N.J.: Princeton University Press, 1960.

Frankl, Paul, and Paul Crossley. *Gothic Architecture.* New Haven, Conn.: Yale University Press, 2000.

Frisch, Teresa G. *Gothic Art 1140–c. 1450: Sources and Documents.* Toronto: University of Toronto Press, 1987. Reprint of 1971 ed.

Gerson, Paula, ed. *Abbot Suger and Saint-Denis.* New York: Metropolitan Museum of Art, 1986.

Givens, Jean A. *Observation and Image-Making in Gothic Art.* New York: Cambridge University Press, 2004.

Grodecki, Louis. *Gothic Architecture.* New York: Electa/Rizzoli, 1985.

Grodecki, Louis, and Catherine Brisac. *Gothic Stained Glass, 1200–1300.* Ithaca, N.Y.: Cornell University Press, 1985.

Jantzen, Hans. *High Gothic: The Classic Cathedrals of Chartres, Reims, Amiens.* Princeton, N.J.: Princeton University Press, 1984.

Male, Émile. *Religious Art in France: The Thirteenth Century.* Rev. ed. Princeton, N.J.: Princeton University Press, 1984.

Minne-Sève, Viviane, and Hervé Kergall. *Romanesque and Gothic France: Architecture and Sculpture.* New York: Abrams, 2000.

Nussbaum, Norbert. *German Gothic Church Architecture.* New Haven, Conn.: Yale University Press, 2000.

Panofsky, Erwin. *Abbot Suger on the Abbey Church of St. Denis and Its Art Treasures.* 2d ed. Princeton, N.J.: Princeton University Press, 1979.

Radding, Charles M., and William W. Clark. *Medieval Architecture, Medieval Learning.* New Haven, Conn.: Yale University Press, 1992.

Recht, Roland. *Believing and Seeing: The Art of Gothic Cathedrals.* Chicago: University of Chicago Press, 1999.

Rudolph, Conrad. *Artistic Change at St-Denis: Abbot Suger's Program and the Early Twelfth-Century Controversy over Art*. Princeton, N.J.: Princeton University Press, 1990.

Sauerländer, Willibald, and Max Hirmer. *Gothic Sculpture in France, 1140–1270*. New York: Abrams, 1973.

Scott, Robert A. *The Gothic Enterprise: A Guide to Understanding the Medieval Cathedral*. Berkeley and Los Angeles: University of California Press, 2003.

Simson, Otto G. von. *The Gothic Cathedral: Origins of Gothic Architecture and the Medieval Concept of Order*. 3d ed. Princeton, N.J.: Princeton University Press, 1988.

Toman, Rolf, ed. *The Art of Gothic: Architecture, Sculpture, Painting*. Cologne: Könemann, 1999.

Williamson, Paul. *Gothic Sculpture, 1140–1300*. New Haven, Conn.: Yale University Press, 1995.

Wilson, Christopher. *The Gothic Cathedral: The Architecture of the Great Church, 1130–1530*. London: Thames & Hudson, 1990.

Chapter 14: Late Medieval Italy

Bomford, David. *Art in the Making: Italian Painting before 1400*. London: National Gallery, 1989.

Borsook, Eve, and Fiorelli Superbi Gioffredi. *Italian Altarpieces 1250–1550: Function and Design*. Oxford: Clarendon, 1994.

Bourdua, Louise. *The Franciscans and Art Patronage in Late Medieval Italy*. New York: Cambridge University Press, 2004.

Cole, Bruce. *Sienese Painting: From Its Origins to the Fifteenth Century*. New York: Harper Collins, 1987.

Derbes, Anne. *Picturing the Passion in Late Medieval Italy: Narrative Painting, Franciscan Ideologies, and the Levant*. New York: Cambridge University Press, 1996.

Derbes, Anne, and Mark Sandona, eds. *The Cambridge Companion to Giotto*. New York: Cambridge University Press, 2004.

Hills, Paul. *The Light of Early Italian Painting*. New Haven, Conn.: Yale University Press, 1987.

Maginnis, Hayden B. J. *Painting in the Age of Giotto: A Historical Reevaluation*. University Park: Pennsylvania State University Press, 1997.

———. *The World of the Early Sienese Painter*. University Park: Pennsylvania State University Press, 2001.

Meiss, Millard. *Painting in Florence and Siena after the Black Death*. Princeton, N.J.: Princeton University Press, 1976.

Moskowitz, Anita Fiderer. *Italian Gothic Sculpture, c. 1250–c. 1400*. Cambridge: Cambridge University Press, 2001.

———. *Nicola & Giovanni Pisano: The Pulpits: Pious Devotion, Pious Diversion*. London: Harvey Miller, 3005.

Norman, Diana, ed. *Siena, Florence, and Padua: Art, Society, and Religion 1280–1400*. New Haven, Conn.: Yale University Press, 1995.

Poeschke, Joachim. *Italian Frescoes: The Age of Giotto, 1280–1400*. New York: Abbeville, 2005.

Pope-Hennessy, John. *Italian Gothic Sculpture*. 3d ed. Oxford: Phaidon, 1986.

Stubblebine, James H. *Duccio di Buoninsegna and His School*. Princeton, N.J.: Princeton University Press, 1979.

White, John. *Art and Architecture in Italy: 1250–1400*. 3d ed. New Haven, Conn.: Yale University Press, 1993.

———. *Duccio: Tuscan Art and the Medieval Workshop*. London: Thames & Hudson, 1979.

Asian Art, General

Béguin, Giles. *Buddhist Art. An Historical and Cultural Journey*. Bangkok: River Books, 2009.

Brown, Rebecca M., and Deborah S. Hutton. *Asian Art (Blackwell Anthologies in Art History)*. Malden, Mass.: Blackwell, 2006.

Leidy, Denise Patry. *The Art of Buddhism: An Introduction to Its History and Meaning*. Boston: Shambhala, 2008.

McArthur, Meher. *The Arts of Asia: Materials, Techniques, Styles*. New York: Thames & Hudson, 2005.

Chapter 15: South and Southeast Asia before 1200

Asher, Frederick M. *The Art of Eastern India, 300–800*. Minneapolis: University of Minnesota Press, 1980.

Behl, Benoy K. *The Ajanta Caves: Ancient Paintings of Buddhist India*. New York: Thames & Hudson, 2005.

Blurton, T. Richard. *Hindu Art*. Cambridge, Mass.: Harvard University Press, 1993.

Chaturachinda, Gwyneth, Sunanda Krishnamurty, and Pauline W. Tabtiang. *Dictionary of South and Southeast Asian Art*. Chiang Mai, Thailand: Silkworm Books, 2000.

Chihara, Daigoro. *Hindu-Buddhist Architecture in Southeast Asia*. Leiden: E. J. Brill, 1996.

Craven, Roy C. *Indian Art: A Concise History*. Rev. ed. London: Thames & Hudson, 1997.

Dehejia, Vidya. *The Body Adorned: Dissolving Boundaries between Sacred and Profane in India's Art*. New York: Columbia University Press, 2009.

———. *Early Buddhist Rock Temples*. Ithaca, N.Y.: Cornell University Press, 1972.

———. *Indian Art*. London: Phaidon, 1997.

Desai, Vishakha N., and Darielle Mason. *Gods, Guardians, and Lovers: Temple Sculptures from North India AD 700–1200*. New York: Asia Society Galleries, 1993.

Dhavalikar, Madhukar Keshav. *Ellora*. New York: Oxford University Press, 2003.

Encyclopedia of Indian Temple Architecture. 8 vols. New Delhi: American Institute of Indian Studies; Philadelphia: University of Pennsylvania Press, 1983–1996.

Fisher, Robert E. *Buddhist Art and Architecture*. New York: Thames & Hudson, 1993.

Frederic, Louis. *Borobudur*. New York: Abbeville, 1996.

Gopinatha Rao, T. A. *Elements of Hindu Iconography*. 2d ed. 4 vols. New York: Paragon, 1968.

Hardy, Adam. *The Temple Architecture of India*. Chichester: Wiley, 2007.

Harle, James C. *The Art and Architecture of the Indian Subcontinent*. 2d ed. New Haven, Conn.: Yale University Press, 1994.

Huntington, Susan L., and John C. Huntington. *The Art of Ancient India: Buddhist, Hindu, Jain*. New York: Weatherhill, 1985.

Jacques, Claude. *The Khmer Empire: Cities and Sanctuaries from the 5th to the 13th Century*. Bangkok: River Books, 2007.

Jacques, Claude, and Michael Freeman. *Angkor: Cities and Temples*. Bangkok: River Books, 1997.

Jessup, Helen Ibbitson. *Art & Architecture of Cambodia*. New York: Thames & Hudson, 2004.

Jessup, Helen Ibbitson, and Thierry Zephir, eds. *Sculpture of Angkor and Ancient Cambodia: Millennium of Glory*. Washington, D.C.: National Gallery of Art, 1997.

Kerlogue, Fiona. *Arts of Southeast Asia*. New York: Thames & Hudson, 2004.

McIntosh, Jane R. *A Peaceful Realm: The Rise and Fall of the Indus Civilization*. Boulder, Colo.: Westview, 2002.

Michell, George. *Elephanta*. Mumbai: India Book House, 2002.

———. *Hindu Art and Architecture*. New York: Thames & Hudson, 2000.

———. *The Hindu Temple: An Introduction to Its Meaning and Forms*. Chicago: University of Chicago Press, 1988.

Mitter, Partha. *Indian Art*. New York: Oxford University Press, 2001.

Possehl, Gregory L. *The Indus Civilization: A Contemporary Perspective*. Lanham, Md.: AltaMira, 2002.

Rawson, Phillip. *The Art of Southeast Asia*. New York: Thames & Hudson, 1990.

Seth, Mira. *Indian Painting: The Great Mural Tradition*. New York: Harry N. Abrams, 2006.

Srinivasan, Doris Meth. *Many Heads, Arms, and Eyes: Origin, Meaning, and Form of Multiplicity in Indian Art*. Leiden: E. J. Brill, 1997.

Stierlin, Henri. *Hindu India from Khajuraho to the Temple City of Madurai*. Cologne: Taschen, 1998.

Williams, Joanna G. *The Art of Gupta India: Empire and Province*. Princeton, N.J.: Princeton University Press, 1982.

Chapter 16: China and Korea to 1279

Bush, Susan, and Shio-yen Shih. *Early Chinese Texts on Painting*. Cambridge, Mass.: Harvard University Press, 1985.

Cahill, James. *The Painter's Practice: How Artists Lived and Worked in Traditional China*. New York: Columbia University Press, 1994.

Clunas, Craig. *Art in China*. New York: Oxford University Press, 1997.

Fahr-Becker, Gabriele, ed. *The Art of East Asia*. Cologne: Könemann, 1999.

Fisher, Robert E. *Buddhist Art and Architecture*. New York: Thames & Hudson, 1993.

Fong, Wen C. *Beyond Representation: Chinese Painting and Calligraphy, 8th–14th Century*. New Haven, Conn.: Yale University Press, 1992.

———. *The Great Bronze Age of China: An Exhibition from the People's Republic of China*. New York: Metropolitan Museum of Art, 1980.

Fong, Wen C., and James C. Y. Watt. *Preserving the Past: Treasures from the National Palace Museum, Taipei*. New York: Metropolitan Museum of Art, 1996.

Fraser, Sarah Elizabeth. *Performing the Visual: The Practice of Buddhist Wall Painting in China and Central Asia, 618–960*. Palo Alto: Stanford University Press, 2004.

Howard, Angela Falco, Li Song, Wu Hong, and Yang Hong. *Chinese Sculpture*. New Haven, Conn.: Yale University Press, 2006.

Kim, Kumja Paik. *Goryeo Dynasty: Korea's Age of Enlightenment, 918–1392*. San Francisco: Asian Art Museum, 2003.

Kim, Lena. *Buddhist Sculpture of Korea*. Elizabeth, N.J.: Hollym, 2007.

Lee, Hui-Shu. *Empresses, Art, and Agency in Song Dynasty China*. Seattle: University of Washington Press, 2010.

Li, Chu-tsing, ed. *Artists and Patrons: Some Social and Economic Aspects of Chinese Painting*. Lawrence, Kans.: Kress Department of Art History, in cooperation with Indiana University Press, 1989.

Little, Stephen, and Shawn Eichman. *Taoism and the Arts of China*. Chicago: Art Institute of Chicago, 2000.

Murck, Alfreda. *Poetry and Painting in Song China: The Subtle Art of Dissent*. Cambridge, Mass.: Harvard University Press, 2000.

Nelson, Sarah Milledge. *The Archaeology of Korea*. New York: Cambridge University Press, 1993.

Pak, Youngsook, and Roderick Whitfield. *Earthenware and Celadon (Handbook of Korean Art)*. London: Laurence King, 2003.

———. *Buddhist Sculpture (Handbook of Korean Art)*. London: Laurence King, 2003.

Portal, Jane. *Korea: Art and Archaeology*. New York: Thames & Hudson, 2000.

Powers, Martin J. *Art and Political Expression in Early China*. New Haven, Conn.: Yale University Press, 1991.

Rawson, Jessica. *Ancient China: Art and Archaeology*. New York: Harper & Row, 1980.

———, ed. *The British Museum Book of Chinese Art*. New York: Thames & Hudson, 1992.

Sickman, Laurence, and Alexander C. Soper. *The Art and Architecture of China*. 3d ed. New Haven, Conn.: Yale University Press, 1992.

Silbergeld, Jerome. *Chinese Painting Style: Media, Methods, and Principles of Form*. Seattle and London: University of Washington Press, 1982.

Steinhardt, Nancy S., ed. *Chinese Architecture*. New Haven, Conn.: Yale University Press, 2002.

Sullivan, Michael. *The Arts of China*. 5th ed. Berkeley: University of California Press, 2009.

———. *The Birth of Landscape Painting*. Berkeley: University of California Press, 1962.

Thorp, Robert L., and Richard Ellis Vinograd. *Chinese Art and Culture*. New York: Abrams, 2001.

Vainker, S. J. *Chinese Pottery and Porcelain: From Prehistory to the Present*. New York: Braziller, 1991.

Watson, William. *The Arts of China to AD 900*. New Haven, Conn.: Yale University Press, 1995.

———. *The Arts of China 900–1620*. New Haven, Conn.: Yale University Press, 2000.

Weidner, Marsha, ed. *Flowering in the Shadows: Women in the History of Chinese and Japanese Painting*. Honolulu: University of Hawaii Press, 1990.

Whitfield, Roderick. *Dictionary of Korean Art and Archaeology*. Elizabeth, N.J.: Hollym, 2004.

Whitfield, Roger, and Anne Farrer. *Caves of the Thousand Buddhas: Chinese Art of the Silk Route*. New York: Braziller, 1990.

Whitfield, Roderick, Susan Whitfield, and Neville Agnew. *Cave Temples of Dunhuang: Art and History on the Silk Road*. Los Angeles: J. Paul Getty Museum, 2000.

———. *Cave Temples of Mogao: Art and History on the Silk Road*. Los Angeles: J. Paul Getty Museum, 2000.

Wu, Hung. *Monumentality in Early Chinese Art*. Palo Alto, Calif.: Stanford University Press, 1996.

———. *The Wu Liang Shrine: The Ideology of Early Chinese Pictorial Art*. Palo Alto, Calif.: Stanford University Press, 1989.

Xin, Yang, Nie Chongzheng, Lang Shaojun, Richard M. Barnhart, James Cahill, and Hung Wu. *Three Thousand Years of Chinese Painting*. New Haven, Conn.: Yale University Press, 1997.

Zhiyan, Li, Virginia L. Bower, and He Li. *Chinese Ceramics: From the Paleolithic Period through the Qing Dyansty*. New Haven, Conn.: Yale University Press, 2010.

Chapter 17: Japan before 1333

Aikens, C. Melvin, and Takayama Higuchi. *Prehistory of Japan*. New York: Academic, 1982.

Coaldrake, William H. *Architecture and Authority in Japan*. London: Routledge, 1996.

Elisseeff, Danielle, and Vadime Elisseeff. *Art of Japan*. Translated by I. Mark Paris. New York: Abrams, 1985.

Kidder, J. Edward, Jr. *The Art of Japan*. New York: Park Lane, 1985.

Kurata, Bunsaku. *Horyu-ji: Temple of the Exalted Law*. Translated by W. Chie Ishibashi. New York: Japan Society, 1981.

Mason, Penelope. *History of Japanese Art*. 2d ed. New York: Abrams, 2004.

Mizoguchi, Koji. *An Archaeological History of Japan: 30,000 B.C. to A.D. 700*. Philadelphia, University of Pennsylvania Press, 2002.

Murase, Miyeko. *The Tale of Genji: Legends and Paintings*. New York: Braziller, 2001.

Nishi, Kazuo, and Kazuo Hozumi. *What Is Japanese Architecture?* Translated by H. Mack Horton. New York: Kodansha International, 1985.

Nishikawa, Kyotaro, and Emily Sano. *The Great Age of Japanese Buddhist Sculpture AD 600–1300*. Fort Worth, Tex.: Kimbell Art Museum, 1982.

Noma, Seiroku. *The Arts of Japan: Ancient and Medieval*. New York: Kodansha, 1966.

Okudaira, Hideo. *Narrative Picture Scrolls*. Adapted by Elizabeth ten Grotenhuis. New York: Weatherhill, 1973.

Pearson, Richard J. *Ancient Japan*. New York: Braziller, 1992.

Pearson, Richard J., Gina Lee Barnes, and Karl L. Hutterer, eds. *Windows on the Japanese Past*. Ann Arbor: Center for Japanese Studies, University of Michigan, 1986.

Rosenfield, John M. *Japanese Art of the Heian Period, 794–1185*. New York: Asia Society, 1967.

Shimizu, Yoshiaki, ed. *The Shaping of Daimyo Culture 1185–1868*. Washington, D.C.: National Gallery of Art, 1988.

Stanley-Baker, Joan. *Japanese Art*. Rev. ed. New York: Thames & Hudson, 2000.

Suzuki, Kakichi. *Early Buddhist Architecture in Japan*. Translated and adapted by Mary Neighbor Parent and Nancy Shatzman Steinhardt. New York: Kodansha International, 1980.

Ten Grotenhuis, Elizabeth. *Japanese Mandalas: Representations of Sacred Geography*. Honolulu: University of Hawaii Press, 1999.

Weidner, Marsha, ed. *Flowering in the Shadows: Women in the History of Chinese and Japanese Painting*. Honolulu: University of Hawaii Press, 1990.

Chapter 18: Native Arts of the Americas before 1300

Alva, Walter, and Christopher Donnan. *Royal Tombs of Sipán*. Los Angeles: Fowler Museum of Cultural History, 1993.

Andrews, E. Wyllys, and William L. Fash, eds. *Copán: The History of an Ancient Maya Kingdom*. Santa Fe, N.M.: School of American Research, 2005.

Benson, Elizabeth P., and Beatriz de la Fuente, eds. *Olmec Art of Ancient Mexico*. Washington, D.C.: National Gallery of Art, 1996.

Berlo, Janet Catherine, ed. *Art, Ideology, and the City of Teotihuacan*. Washington, D.C.: Dumbarton Oaks, 1992.

Berlo, Janet Catherine, and Ruth B. Phillips. *Native North American Art*. New York: Oxford University Press, 1998.

Berrin, Kathleen, and Virginia M. Fields. *Olmec: Colossal Masterworks of Ancient Mexico*. New Haven, Conn.: Yale University Press, 2010.

Berrin, Kathleen, ed. *The Spirit of Ancient Peru: Treasures from the Museo Arqueologico Rafael Larco Herrera*. San Francisco: Fine Arts Museums of San Francisco, 1997.

Bourget, Steve, and Kimberly L. Jones, eds. *The Art and Archaeology of the Moche: An Ancient Andean Society of the Peruvian North Coast*. Austin: University of Texas Press, 2008.

Brody, J. J., and Rina Swentzell. *To Touch the Past: The Painted Pottery of the Mimbres People*. New York: Hudson Hills, 1996.

Brose, David. *Ancient Art of the American Woodland Indians*. New York: Abrams, 1985.

Bruhns, Karen O. *Ancient South America*. New York: Cambridge University Press, 1994.

Burger, Richard. *Chavín and the Origins of Andean Civilization*. New York: Thames & Hudson, 1992.

Carrasco, David. *The Oxford Encyclopedia of Mesoamerican Cultures: The Civilizations of Mexico and Central America*. New York: Oxford University Press, 2001.

Clark, John E., and Mary E. Pye, eds. *Olmec Art and Archaeology in Mesoamerica*. Washington, D.C.: National Gallery of Art, 2000.

Coe, Michael D. *The Maya*. 8th ed. New York: Thames & Hudson, 2011.

———. *Mexico: From the Olmecs to the Aztecs*. 6th ed. New York: Thames & Hudson, 2008.

Conklin, William J., and Jeffrey Quilter, eds. *Chavín: Art, Architecture, and Culture*. Los Angeles: Cotsen Institute of Archaeology, 2008.

Cordell, Linda S. *Ancient Pueblo Peoples*. Washington, D.C.: Smithsonian Institution, 1994.

Donnan, Christopher. *Moche Portraits from Ancient Peru*. Austin: University of Texas Press, 2003.

Fagan, Brian. *Ancient North America: The Archaeology of a Continent*. 4th ed. New York: Thames & Hudson, 2005.

———. *The First North Americans*. New York: Thames & Hudson, 2011.

Fash, William. *Scribes, Warriors, and Kings: The City of Copan and the Ancient Maya*. New York: Thames & Hudson, 1991.

Feest, Christian F. *Native Arts of North America*. 2d ed. New York: Thames & Hudson, 1992.

Foster, Michael S., and Shirley Gorenstein, eds. *Greater Mesoamerica: The Archaeology of West and Northwest Mexico*. Salt Lake City: University of Utah Press, 2000.

Grube, Nikolai, ed. *Maya: Divine Kings of the Rain Forest*. Cologne: Könemann, 2000.

Janusek, John Wayne. *Ancient Tiwanaku*. New York: Cambridge University Press, 2008.

Kolata, Alan. *The Tiwanaku: Portrait of an Andean Civilization*. Cambridge: Blackwell, 1993.

Kubler, George. *The Art and Architecture of Ancient America: The Mexican, Maya, and Andean Peoples*. 3d ed. New Haven, Conn.: Yale University Press, 1992.

Marken, Damien B., ed. *Palenque: Recent Investigations at the Classic Maya Center*. Lanham, Md.: Altamira, 2007.

Miller, Mary Ellen. *The Art of Mesoamerica, from Olmec to Aztec*. 4th ed. New York: Thames & Hudson, 2006.

———. *Maya Art and Architecture*. New York: Thames & Hudson, 1999.

Miller, Mary Ellen, and Karl Taube. *The Gods and Symbols of Ancient Mexico and the Maya: An Illustrated Dictionary of Mesoamerican Religion*. New York: Thames & Hudson, 1993.

Milner, George R. *The Moundbuilders: Ancient Peoples of Eastern North America*. New York: Thames & Hudson, 2004.

Morris, Craig, and Adriana von Hagen. *The Inka Empire and Its Andean Origins*. New York: Abbeville, 1993.

Nabokov, Peter, and Robert Easton. *Native American Architecture*. New York: Oxford University Press, 1989.

Pasztory, Esther. *Pre-Columbian Art*. New York: Cambridge University Press, 1998.

———. *Teotihuacan: An Experiment in Living*. Norman: University of Oklahoma Press, 1997.

Paul, Anne. *Paracas Ritual Attire: Symbols of Authority in Ancient Peru*. Norman: University of Oklahoma Press, 1990.

Penney, David, and George C. Longfish. *Native American Art*. Hong Kong: Hugh Lauter Levin and Associates, 1994.

Pillsbury, Joanne, ed. *Moche Art and Archaeology in Ancient Peru*. Washington, D.C.: National Gallery of Art, 2005.

Pool, Christopher A. *Olmec Archaeology and Early Mesoamerica*. New York: Cambridge University Press, 2007.

Rohm, Arthur H., and William M. Ferguson. *Puebloan Ruins of the Southwest*. Albuquerque: University of New Mexico Press, 2006.

Schele, Linda, and Peter Mathews. *The Code of Kings: The Language of Seven Sacred Maya Temples and Tombs*. New York: Scribner, 1998.

Schele, Linda, and Mary E. Miller. *The Blood of Kings: Dynasty and Ritual in Maya Art*. Fort Worth, Tex.: Kimbell Art Museum, 1986.

Schmidt, Peter, Mercedes de la Garza, and Enrique Nalda, eds. *Maya*. New York: Rizzoli, 1998.

Sharer, Robert J., and Loa P. Traxler. *The Ancient Maya*. 6th ed. Palo Alto: Stanford University Press, 2006.

Silverman, Helaine, and William H. Isbell, eds. *Handbook of South American Archaeology*. New York: Springer, 2008.

Stone-Miller, Rebecca. *Art of the Andes from Chavín to Inca*. 2d ed. New York: Thames & Hudson, 2002.

———. *To Weave for the Sun: Ancient Andean Textiles*. New York: Thames & Hudson, 1994.

Townsend, Richard F., ed. *Ancient West Mexico*. Chicago: Art Institute of Chicago, 1998.

Von Hagen, Adriana, and Craig Morris. *The Cities of the Ancient Andes*. New York: Thames & Hudson, 1998.

Wardwell, Allen. *Ancient Eskimo Ivories of the Bering Strait*. New York: Rizzoli, 1986.

Whiteford, Andrew H., Stewart Peckham, and Kate Peck Kent. *I Am Here: Two Thousand Years of Southwest Indian Arts and Crafts*. Santa Fe: Museum of New Mexico Press, 1989.

Chapter 19: Africa before 1800

Bacquart, Jean-Baptiste. *The Tribal Arts of Africa*. New York: Thames & Hudson, 2002.

Bassani, Ezio. *Arts of Africa: 7,000 Years of African Art*. Milan: Skira, 2005.

Ben-Amos, Paula. *The Art of Benin*. New York: Thames & Hudson, 1980.

Berzock, Kathleen Bickford. *Benin: Royal Arts of a West African Kingdom*. Chicago: Art Institute of Chicago, 2008.

Blier, Suzanne P. *Royal Arts of Africa: The Majesty of Form*. New York: Abrams, 1998.

Campbell, Alec, and David Coulson. *African Rock Art: Paintings and Engravings on Stone*. New York: Abrams, 2001.

Connah, Graham. *African Civilizations*. 2d ed. Cambridge: Cambridge University Press, 2001.

Coulson, David, and Alec Campbell. *African Rock Art: Painting and Engravings on Stone*. New York: Abrams, 2001.

Dewey, William J. *Legacies of Stone: Zimbabwe Past and Present*. Tervuren: Royal Museum for Central Africa, 1997.

Drewal, Henry J., John Pemberton, and Rowland Abiodun. *Yoruba: Nine Centuries of African Art and Thought*. New York: Center for African Art, in association with Abrams, 1989.

Drewal, Henry John, and Enid Schildkrout. *Dynasty and Divinity: Ife Art in Ancient Nigeria*. Seattle: University of Washington Press, 2010.

Eyo, Ekpo, and Frank Willett. *Treasures of Ancient Nigeria*. New York: Knopf, 1980.

Fagg, Bernard. *Nok Terracottas*. Lagos: Ethnographica, 1977.

Garlake, Peter. *Early Art and Architecture of Africa*. Oxford: Oxford University Press, 2002.

———. *Great Zimbabwe*. London: Thames & Hudson, 1973.

Grunne, Bernard de. *The Birth of Art in Africa: Nok Statuary in Nigeria*. Paris: Biro, 1998.

Huffman, Thomas N. *Snakes and Crocodiles: Power and Symbolism in Ancient Zimbabwe*. Johannesburg: Witwatersrand University Press, 1996.

Lajoux, Jean-Dominique. *The Rock Paintings of Tassili*. Cleveland: World Publishing, 1963.

Le Quellec, Jean-Loïc. *Rock Art in Africa: Mythology and Legend*. Paris: Flammarion, 2004.

Perani, Judith, and Fred T. Smith. *The Visual Arts of Africa: Gender, Power, and Life Cycle Rituals*. Englewood Cliffs, N.J.: Prentice Hall, 1998.

Phillips, Tom, ed. *Africa, the Art of a Continent*. New York: Prestel, 1995.

Phillipson, D. W. *African Archaeology*. 3d ed. New York: Cambridge University Press, 2005.

———. *Ancient Ethiopia: Aksum, Its Antecedents and Successors*. London: British Museum Press, 1998.

Schädler, Karl-Ferdinand. *Earth and Ore: 2,500 Years of African Art in Terra-Cotta and Metal*. Munich: Panterra Verlag, 1997.

Shaw, Thurstan. *Nigeria: Its Archaeology and Early History*. London: Thames & Hudson, 1978.

———. *Unearthing Igbo-Ukwu: Archaeological Discoveries in Eastern Nigeria*. New York: Oxford University Press, 1977.

Visonà, Monica B., ed. *A History of Art in Africa*. 2d ed. Englewood Cliffs, N.J.: Prentice Hall, 2007.

Willett, Frank. *Ife in the History of West African Sculpture*. New York: McGraw-Hill, 1967.

Renaissance Art, General

Adams, Laurie Schneider. *Italian Renaissance Art*. Boulder, Colo.: Westview, 2001.

Andrés, Glenn M., John M. Hunisak, and Richard Turner. *The Art of Florence*. 2 vols. New York: Abbeville, 1988.

Campbell, Gordon. *The Grove Encyclopedia of Northern Renaissance Art*. New York: Oxford University Press, 2009.

———. *Renaissance Art and Architecture*. New York: Oxford University Press, 2005.

Campbell, Lorne. *Renaissance Portraits: European Portrait-Painting in the Fourteenth, Fifteenth, and Sixteenth Centuries*. New Haven, Conn.: Yale University Press, 1990.

Christian, Kathleen, and David J. Drogin, eds. *Patronage and Italian Renaissance Sculpture*. Burlington, Vt.: Ashgate, 2010.

Cole, Bruce. *Italian Art, 1250–1550: The Relation of Renaissance Art to Life and Society*. New York: Harper & Row, 1987.

———. *The Renaissance Artist at Work: From Pisano to Titian*. New York: Harper Collins, 1983.

Cranston, Jodi. *The Poetics of Portraiture in the Italian Renaissance*. New York: Cambridge University Press, 2000.

Frommel, Christoph Luitpold. *The Architecture of the Italian Renaissance*. London: Thames & Hudson, 2007.

Furlotti, Barbara, and Guido Rebecchini. *The Art of Mantua: Power and Patronage in the Renaissance*. Los Angeles: J. Paul Getty Museum, 2008.

Hall, Marcia B. *Color and Meaning: Practice and Theory in Renaissance Painting*. Cambridge: Cambridge University Press, 1992.

Hartt, Frederick, and David G. Wilkins. *History of Italian Renaissance Art*. 7th ed. Upper Saddle River, N.J.: Prentice Hall, 2010.

Haskell, Francis, and Nicholas Penny. *Taste and the Antique: The Lure of Classical Sculpture 1500–1900*. New Haven, Conn.: Yale University Press, 1981.

Kent, F. W., and Patricia Simons, eds. *Patronage, Art, and Society in Renaissance Italy*. Canberra: Humanities Research Centre and Clarendon Press, 1987.

King, Catherine E. *Renaissance Women Patrons: Wives and Widows in Italy, c. 1300–1550*. Manchester: Manchester University Press, 1998.

Levey, Michael. *Florence: A Portrait*. Cambridge, Mass.: Harvard University Press, 1998.

Lubbock, Jules. *Storytelling in Christian Art from Giotto to Donatello*. New Haven, Conn.: Yale University Press, 2006.

Paoletti, John T., and Gary M. Radke. *Art, Power, and Patronage in Renaissance Italy*. Upper Saddle River, N.J.: Prentice Hall, 2005.

Partridge, Loren. *Art of Renaissance Florence, 1400–1600*. Berkeley and Los Angeles: University of California Press, 2009.

Pope-Hennessy, John. *Introduction to Italian Sculpture*. 3d ed. 3 vols. New York: Phaidon, 1986.

Richardson, Carol M., Kim W. Woods, and Michael W. Franklin, eds. *Renaissance Art Reconsidered: An Anthology of Primary Sources*. Malden, Mass.: Blackwell, 2007.

Smith, Jeffrey Chipps. *The Northern Renaissance*. New York: Phaidon, 2004.

Snyder, James, Larry Silver, and Henry Luttikhuizen. *Northern Renaissance Art: Painting, Sculpture, the Graphic Arts from 1350 to 1575*. Upper Saddle River, N.J.: Prentice Hall, 2005.

Strinati, Claudio, and Pomeroy, Jordana. *Italian Women Artists from Renaissance to Baroque*. Milan: Skira, 2007.

Thomson, David. *Renaissance Architecture: Critics, Patrons, and Luxury*. Manchester: Manchester University Press, 1993.

Tinagli, Paola. *Women in Italian Renaissance Art: Gender, Representation, Identity*. Manchester: Manchester University Press, 1997.

Wittkower, Rudolf. *Architectural Principles in the Age of Humanism*. 4th ed. London: Academy, 1988.

Woods, Kim W. *Making Renaissance Art*. New Haven, Conn.: Yale University Press, 2007.

———. *Viewing Renaissance Art*. New Haven, Conn.: Yale University Press, 2007.

Woods-Marsden, Joanna. *Renaissance Self-Portraiture: The Visual Construction of Identity and the Social Status of the Artist*. New Haven, Conn.: Yale University Press, 1998.

Chapter 20: Late Medieval and Early Renaissance Art in Northern Europe

Ainsworth, Maryan W., and Maximiliaan P. J. Martens. *Petrus Christus, Renaissance Master of Bruges*. New York: Metropolitan Museum of Art, 1994.

Art from the Court of Burgundy: The Patronage of Philip the Bold and John the Fearless 1364–1419. Cleveland: Cleveland Museum of Art, 2004.

Baxandall, Michael. *The Limewood Sculptors of Renaissance Germany*. New Haven, Conn.: Yale University Press, 1980.

Borchert, Till-Holger. *Age of Van Eyck: The Mediterranean World and Early Netherlandish Painting, 1430–1530*. New York: Thames & Hudson, 2002.

Brinkmann, Bodo. *Konrad Witz*. Ostfildern: Hatje Cantz, 2011.

Campbell, Lorne. *The Fifteenth-Century Netherlandish Schools*. London: National Gallery Publications, 1998.

———. *Van der Weyden*. London: Chaucer, 2004.

Châtelet, Albert. *Early Dutch Painting*. New York: Konecky, 1988.

Friedlander, Max J. *Early Netherlandish Painting*. 14 vols. New York: Praeger/Phaidon, 1967–1976.

———. *From Van Eyck to Bruegel*. 3d ed. Ithaca, N.Y.: Cornell University Press, 1981.

Harbison, Craig. *The Mirror of the Artist: Northern Renaissance Art in Its Historical Context*. New York: Abrams, 1995.

Jacobs, Lynn F. *Early Netherlandish Carved Altarpieces, 1380–1550: Medieval Tastes and Mass Marketing*. Cambridge: Cambridge University Press, 1998.

Kemperdick, Stephan. *Rogier van der Weyden.* Cologne: H. F. Ullmann, 2007.

Kemperdick, Stephan, and Jocen Sander, eds. *The Master of Flémalle and Rogier van der Weyden.* Ostfildern: Hatje Cantz, 2009.

Lane, Barbara G. *The Altar and the Altarpiece: Sacramental Themes in Early Netherlandish Painting.* New York: Harper & Row, 1984.

Meiss, Millard. *French Painting in the Time of Jean de Berry: The Limbourgs and Their Contemporaries.* New York: Braziller, 1974.

Michiels, Alfred. *Hans Memling.* London: Parkstone, 2008.

Müller, Theodor. *Sculpture in the Netherlands, Germany, France, and Spain: 1400-1500.* New Haven, Conn.: Yale University Press, 1986.

Nash, Susie. *Northern Renaissance Art.* New York: Oxford University Press, 2008.

Pächt, Otto. *Early Netherlandish Painting from Rogier van der Wayden to Gerard David.* New York: Harvey Miller, 1997.

Panofsky, Erwin. *Early Netherlandish Painting: Its Origins and Character.* 2 vols. Cambridge, Mass.: Harvard University Press, 1966.

Parshall, Peter, ed. *The Woodcut in Fifteenth-Century Europe.* New Haven, Conn.: Yale University Press, 2009.

Parshall, Peter, and Rainer Schoch. *Origins of European Printmaking: Fifteenth-Century Woodcuts and Their Public.* New Haven, Conn.: Yale University Press, 2005.

Prevenier, Walter, and Wim Blockmans. *The Burgundian Netherlands.* Cambridge: Cambridge University Press, 1986.

Tomlinson, Amanda. *Van Eyck.* London: Chaucer, 2007.

Wolfthal, Diane. *The Beginnings of Netherlandish Canvas Painting, 1400-1530.* New York: Cambridge University Press, 1989.

Chapter 21: The Renaissance in Quattrocento Italy

Ahl, Diane Cole. *Fra Angelico.* New York: Phaidon, 2008.

———, ed. *The Cambridge Companion to Masaccio.* New York: Cambridge University Press, 2002.

Ames-Lewis, Francis. *Drawing in Early Renaissance Italy.* 2d ed. New Haven, Conn.: Yale University Press, 2000.

———. *The Intellectual Life of the Early Renaissance Artist.* New Haven, Conn.: Yale University Press, 2000.

Baxandall, Michael. *Painting and Experience in Fifteenth-Century Italy: A Primer in the Social History of Pictorial Style.* 2d ed. New York: Oxford University Press, 1988.

Bober, Phyllis Pray, and Ruth Rubinstein. *Renaissance Artists and Antique Sculpture: A Handbook of Sources.* Oxford: Oxford University Press, 1986.

Borsook, Eve. *The Mural Painters of Tuscany.* New York: Oxford University Press, 1981.

Cole, Alison. *Virtue and Magnificence: Art of the Italian Renaissance Courts.* New York: Abrams, 1995.

Cole, Bruce. *Masaccio and the Art of Early Renaissance Florence.* Bloomington: Indiana University Press, 1980.

Dempsey, Charles. *The Portrayal of Love: Botticelli's* Primavera *and Humanist Culture at the Time of Lorenzo the Magnificent.* Princeton, N.J.: Princeton University Press, 1992.

Edgerton, Samuel Y., Jr. *The Heritage of Giotto's Geometry: Art and Science on the Eve of the Scientific Revolution.* Ithaca, N.Y.: Cornell University Press, 1991.

———. *The Renaissance Rediscovery of Linear Perspective.* New York: Harper & Row, 1976.

Gilbert, Creighton, ed. *Italian Art 1400-1500: Sources and Documents.* Evanston, Ill.: Northwestern University Press, 1992.

Goldthwaite, Richard A. *The Building of Renaissance Florence: An Economic and Social History.* Baltimore: Johns Hopkins University Press, 1980.

Goy, Richard J. *Building Renaissance Venice: Patrons, Architects, and Builders c. 1430-1500.* New Haven, Conn.: Yale University Press, 2006.

Heydenreich, Ludwig H. *Architecture in Italy, 1400-1500.* 2d ed. New Haven, Conn.: Yale University Press, 1996.

Hollingsworth, Mary. *Patronage in Renaissance Italy: From 1400 to the Early Sixteenth Century.* Baltimore: Johns Hopkins University Press, 1994.

Holmes, Megan. *Fra Filippo Lippi: The Carmelite Painter.* New Haven, Conn.: Yale University Press, 1999.

Kemp, Martin. *Behind the Picture: Art and Evidence in the Italian Renaissance.* New Haven, Conn.: Yale University Press, 1997.

Kempers, Bram. *Painting, Power, and Patronage: The Rise of the Professional Artist in the Italian Renaissance.* London: Penguin, 1992.

Kent, Dale. *Cosimo de' Medici and the Florentine Renaissance: The Patron's Oeuvre.* New Haven, Conn.: Yale University Press, 2000.

Lieberman, Ralph. *Renaissance Architecture in Venice.* New York: Abbeville, 1982.

Lindow, James R. *The Renaissance Palace in Florence: Magnificence and Splendour in Fifteenth-Century Italy.* Burlington Vt.: Ashgate, 2007.

Manca, Joseph. *Andrea Mantegna and the Italian Renaissance.* New York: Parkstone, 2006.

McAndrew, John. *Venetian Architecture of the Early Renaissance.* Cambridge, Mass.: MIT Press, 1980.

Murray, Peter. *Renaissance Architecture.* New York: Electa/Rizzoli, 1985.

Olson, Roberta J. M. *Italian Renaissance Sculpture.* London: Thames & Hudson, 1992.

Osborne, June. *Urbino: The Story of a Renaissance City.* Chicago: University of Chicago Press, 2003.

Poeschke, Joachim. *Donatello and His World: Sculpture of the Italian Renaissance.* New York: Abrams, 1993.

Radke, Gary M., ed. *The Gates of Paradise: Lorenzo Ghiberti's Renaissance Masterpiece.* New Haven, Conn.: Yale University Press, 2007.

Seymour, Charles. *Sculpture in Italy: 1400-1500.* New Haven, Conn.: Yale University Press, 1992.

Turner, A. Richard. *Renaissance Florence: The Invention of a New Art.* New York: Abrams, 1997.

Wackernagel, Martin. *The World of the Florentine Renaissance Artist: Projects and Patrons, Workshops and Art Market.* Princeton, N.J.: Princeton University Press, 1981.

Welch, Evelyn. *Art and Society in Italy 1350-1500.* Oxford: Oxford University Press, 1997.

White, John. *The Birth and Rebirth of Pictorial Space.* 3d ed. Boston: Faber & Faber, 1987.

Wright, Alison. *The Pollaiuolo Brothers: The Arts of Florence and Rome.* New Haven, Conn.: Yale University Press, 2005.

Zöllner, Frank. *Sandro Botticelli.* New ed. New York: Prestel, 2009.

Chapter 22: Renaissance and Mannerism in Cinquecento Italy

Beltramini, Guido, and Howard Burns. *Palladio.* London: Royal Academy, 2008.

Blunt, Anthony. *Artistic Theory in Italy, 1450-1600.* London: Oxford University Press, 1975.

Brambilla Barcilon, Pinnin. *Leonardo: The Last Supper.* Chicago: University of Chicago Press, 2001.

Brock, Maurice. *Bronzino.* Paris: Flammarion, 2002.

Brown, David Alan, and Sylvia Ferino-Pagden, eds. *Bellini, Giorgione, Titian, and the Renaissance of Venetian Painting.* New Haven, Conn.: Yale University Press, 2006.

Brown, Patricia Fortini. *Art and Life in Renaissance Venice.* New York: Abrams, 1997.

Cole, Bruce. *Titian and Venetian Painting, 1450-1590.* Boulder, Colo.: Westview, 2000.

Cooper, Tracy E. *Palladio's Venice: Architecture and Society in a Renaissance Republic.* New Haven, Conn.: Yale University Press, 2005.

Cranston, Jodi. *The Muddled Mirror: Materiality and Figuration in Titian's Later Paintings.* University Park, Pa.: Pennsylvania State University Press, 2010.

Dal Pozzolo, Enrico. *Giorgione.* Milan: Motta, 2010.

De Vecchi, Pierluigi. *Raphael.* New York: Abbeville, 2002.

Ekserdjian, David. *Correggio.* New Haven, Conn.: Yale University Press, 1997.

———. *Parmigianino.* New Haven, Conn.: Yale University Press, 2006.

Falomir, Miguel, ed. *Tintoretto.* Madrid: Museo Nacional del Prado, 2007.

Ferino-Pagden, Sylvia, and Giovanna Nepi Scirè. *Giorgione: Myth and Enigma.* Milan: Skira, 2004.

Franklin, David. *Painting in Renaissance Florence, 1500-1550.* New Haven, Conn.: Yale University Press, 2001.

Freedberg, Sydney J. *Painting in Italy: 1500-1600.* 3d ed. New Haven, Conn.: Yale University Press, 1993.

Goffen, Rona. *Piety and Patronage in Renaissance Venice: Bellini, Titian, and the Franciscans.* New Haven, Conn.: Yale University Press, 1986.

———. *Renaissance Rivals: Michelangelo, Leonardo, Raphael, Titian.* New Haven, Conn.: Yale University Press, 2002.

Hall, Marcia B. *After Raphael: Painting in Central Italy in the Sixteenth Century.* Cambridge: Cambridge University Press, 1999.

———. *Rome.* Artistic Centers of the Italian Renaissance. New York: Cambridge University Press, 2005.

———. *The Sacred Image in the Age of Art: Titian, Tintoretto, Barocci, El Greco, Caravaggio.* New Haven, Conn.: Yale University Press, 2011.

———, ed. *The Cambridge Companion to Raphael.* New York: Cambridge University Press, 2005.

Hollingsworth, Mary. *Patronage in Sixteenth Century Italy.* London: John Murray, 1996.

Holt, Elizabeth Gilmore, ed. *A Documentary History of Art. Vol. 2, Michelangelo and the Mannerists.* Rev. ed. Princeton, N.J.: Princeton University Press, 1982.

Humfrey, Peter. *Painting in Renaissance Venice.* New Haven, Conn.: Yale University Press, 1995.

———. *Titian.* London: Phaidon, 2007.

Huse, Norbert, and Wolfgang Wolters. *The Art of Renaissance Venice: Architecture, Sculpture, and Painting.* Chicago: University of Chicago Press, 1990.

Ilchman, Frederick, ed. *Titian, Tintoretto, Veronese: Rivals in Renaissance Venice.* Boston: Museum of Fine Arts, 2009.

Kliemann, Julian-Matthias, and Michael Rohlmann. *Italian Frescoes: High Renaissance and Mannerism, 1510-1600.* New York: Abbeville, 2004.

Levey, Michael. *High Renaissance.* New York: Viking Penguin, 1978.

Lotz, Wolfgang. *Architecture in Italy, 1500-1600.* 2d ed. New Haven, Conn.: Yale University Press, 1995.

Meilman, Patricia, ed. *The Cambridge Companion to Titian.* New York: Cambridge University Press, 2004.

Nichols, Tom. *Tintoretto: Tradition and Identity.* London: Reaktion, 2004.

Partridge, Loren. *The Art of Renaissance Rome.* New York: Abrams, 1996.

Pietrangeli, Carlo, André Chastel, John Shearman, John O'Malley, S.J., Pierluigi de Vecchi, Michael Hirst, Fabrizio Mancinelli, Gianluigi Colalucci, and Franco Bernbei. *The Sistine Chapel: The Art, the History, and the Restoration*. New York: Harmony, 1986.

Pilliod, Elizabeth. *Pontormo, Bronzino, Allori: A Genealogy of Florentine Art*. New Haven, Conn.: Yale University Press, 2001.

Pope-Hennessy, John. *Italian High Renaissance and Baroque Sculpture*. 3d ed. 3 vols. Oxford: Phaidon, 1986.

Rosand, David. *Painting in Cinquecento Venice: Titian, Veronese, Tintoretto*. New Haven, Conn.: Yale University Press, 1982.

Rowe, Colin, and Leon Satkowski. *Italian Architecture of the 16th Century*. New York: Princeton Architectural Press, 2002.

Shearman, John K. G. *Mannerism*. Baltimore: Penguin, 1978.

———. *Only Connect . . . Art and the Spectator in the Italian Renaissance*. Princeton, N.J.: Princeton University Press, 1990.

Summers, David. *Michelangelo and the Language of Art*. Princeton, N.J.: Princeton University Press, 1981.

Talvacchia, Bette. *Raphael*. London: Phaidon, 2007.

Tronzo, William, ed. *St. Peter's in the Vatican*. New York: Cambridge University Press, 2005.

Wilde, Johannes. *Venetian Art from Bellini to Titian*. Oxford: Clarendon, 1981.

Williams, Robert. *Art, Theory, and Culture in Sixteenth-Century Italy: From Techne to Metatechne*. New York: Cambridge University Press, 1997.

Zöllner, Frank. *Leonardo da Vinci: The Complete Paintings and Drawings*. Cologne: Taschen, 2007.

Chapter 23: High Renaissance and Mannerism in Northern Europe and Spain

Ainsworth, Maryan W. *Man, Myth, and Sensual Pleasures: Jan Gossart's Renaissance. The Complete Works*. New York: Metropolitan Museum of Art, 2010.

Bartrum, Giulia, ed. *Albrecht Dürer and His Legacy: The Graphic Work of a Renaissance Artist*. Princeton, N. J.: Princeton University Press, 2003.

Bätschmann, Oskar, and Pascal Griener. *Hans Holbein*. Princeton, N. J.: Princeton University Press, 1997.

Blunt, Anthony. *Art and Architecture in France, 1500–1700*. Rev. ed. New Haven, Conn.: Yale University Press, 1999.

Brinkmann, Bodo, ed. *Cranach*. London: Royal Academy of Arts, 2008.

Buck, Stephanie, and Jochen Sander. *Hans Holbein the Younger: Painter at the Court of Henry VIII*. New York: Thames & Hudson, 2004.

Chapius, Julien. *Tilman Riemenschneider: Master Sculptor of the Late Middle Ages*. Washington, D.C.: National Gallery of Art, 1999.

Chastel, André. *French Art: The Renaissance, 1430–1620*. Paris: Flammarion, 1995.

Davies, David, and John H. Elliott. *El Greco*. London: National Gallery, 2003.

Dixon, Laurinda. *Bosch*. New York: Phaidon, 2003.

Farago, Claire, ed. *Reframing the Renaissance: Visual Culture in Europe and Latin America, 1450–1650*. New Haven, Conn.: Yale University Press, 1995.

Foister, Susan. *Holbein and England*. New Haven, Conn.: Paul Mellon Centre for British Art, 2005.

Gibson, W. S. *"Mirror of the Earth": The World Landscape in Sixteenth-Century Flemish Painting*. Princeton, N.J.: Princeton University Press, 1989.

Harbison, Craig. *The Mirror of the Artist: Northern Renaissance Art in Its Historical Context*. New York: Abrams, 1995.

Koerner, Joseph Leo. *The Reformation of the Image*. Chicago: University of Chicago Press, 2004.

Landau, David, and Peter Parshall. *The Renaissance Print: 1470–1550*. New Haven, Conn.: Yale University Press, 1994.

Price, David Hotchkiss. *Albrecht Dürer's Renaissance: Humanism, Reformation, and the Art of Faith*. Ann Arbor: University of Michigan Press, 2003.

Roberts-Jones, Philippe, and Françoise Roberts-Jones. *Pieter Bruegel*. New York: Abrams, 2002.

Silver, Larry. *Hieronymous Bosch*. New York: Abbeville, 2006.

Smith, Jeffrey C. *German Sculpture of the Later Renaissance, c. 1520–1580: Art in an Age of Uncertainty*. Princeton, N.J.: Princeton University Press, 1993.

Stechow, Wolfgang. *Northern Renaissance Art, 1400–1600: Sources and Documents*. Evanston, Ill.: Northwestern University Press, 1989.

Zerner, Henri. *Renaissance Art in France: The Invention of Classicism*. Paris: Flammarion, 2003.

Baroque Art, General

Blunt, Anthony, ed. *Baroque and Rococo: Architecture and Decoration*. Cambridge: Harper & Row, 1982.

Harris, Ann Sutherland. *Seventeenth-Century Art & Architecture*. Upper Saddle River, N.J.: Prentice Hall, 2005.

Harrison, Charles, Paul Wood, and Jason Gaiger, eds. *Art in Theory, 1648–1815: An Anthology of Changing Ideas*. Oxford: Blackwell, 2000.

Held, Julius, and Donald Posner. *17th- and 18th-Century Art: Baroque Painting, Sculpture, Architecture*. New York: Abrams, 1971.

Lagerlöf, Margaretha R. *Ideal Landscape: Annibale Carracci, Nicolas Poussin, and Claude Lorrain*. New Haven, Conn.: Yale University Press, 1990.

Lawrence, Cynthia, ed. *Women and Art in Early Modern Europe: Patrons, Collectors, and Connoisseurs*. University Park: Pennsylvania State University Press, 1997.

Lemerle, Frédérique, and Yves Pauwels. *Baroque Architecture, 1600–1750*. Paris: Flammarion, 2008.

Minor, Vernon Hyde. *Baroque & Rococo: Art & Culture*. New York, Abrams, 1999.

Norberg-Schulz, Christian. *Baroque Architecture*. New York: Rizzoli, 1986.

———. *Late Baroque and Rococo Architecture*. New York: Electa/Rizzoli, 1985.

Toman, Rolf. *Baroque: Architecture, Sculpture, Painting*. Cologne: Könemann, 1998.

Chapter 24: The Baroque in Italy and Spain

Bissel, R. Ward. *Artemisia Gentileschi and the Authority of Art*. University Park: Pennsylvania State University Press, 1999.

Brown, Jonathan. *The Golden Age of Painting in Spain*. New Haven, Conn.: Yale University Press, 1991.

———. *Velázquez: Painter and Courtier*. New Haven, Conn.: Yale University Press, 1988.

Christiansen, Keith, and Judith W. Mann. *Orazio and Artemisia Gentileschi*. New York: Metropolitan Museum of Art, 2001.

Enggass, Robert, and Jonathan Brown. *Italy and Spain, 1600–1750: Sources and Documents*. Upper Saddle River, N.J.: Prentice Hall, 1970.

Freedberg, Sydney J. *Circa 1600: A Revolution of Style in Italian Painting*. Cambridge, Mass.: Harvard University Press, 1983.

Fried, Michael. *The Moment of Caravaggio*. Princeton, N.J.: Princeton University Press, 2010.

Haskell, Francis. *Patrons and Painters: A Study in the Relations between Italian Art and Society in the Age of the Baroque*. Rev. ed. New Haven, Conn.: Yale University Press, 1980.

Krautheimer, Richard. *The Rome of Alexander VII, 1655–1677*. Princeton, N.J.: Princeton University Press, 1985.

Montagu, Jennifer. *Roman Baroque Sculpture: The Industry of Art*. New Haven, Conn.: Yale University Press, 1989.

Puglisi, Catherine. *Caravaggio*. London: Phaidon, 2000.

Schroth, Sarah, and Ronni Baer. *El Greco to Velazquez: Art during the Reign of Philip III*. Boston: Museum of Fine Arts, 2008.

Strinati, Claudio, and Pomeroy, Jordana. *Italian Women Artists from Renaissance to Baroque*. Milan: Skira, 2007.

Tomlinson, Janis. *From El Greco to Goya: Painting in Spain 1561–1828*. Upper Saddle Ridge, N.J.: Prentice Hall, 1997.

Tronzo, William, ed. *St. Peter's in the Vatican*. New York: Cambridge University Press, 2005.

Varriano, John. *Caravaggio: The Art of Realism*. University Park: Pennsylvania University Press, 2006.

———. *Italian Baroque and Rococo Architecture*. New York: Oxford University Press, 1986.

Wittkower, Rudolf. *Art and Architecture in Italy 1600–1750*. 6th ed. 3 vols. Revised by Joseph Connors and Jennifer Montagu. New Haven, Conn.: Yale University Press, 1999.

Chapter 25: The Baroque in Northern Europe

Alpers, Svetlana. *The Art of Describing: Dutch Art in the Seventeenth Century*. Chicago: University of Chicago Press, 1984.

———. *The Making of Rubens*. New Haven, Conn.: Yale University Press, 1995.

———. *Rembrandt's Enterprise: The Studio and the Market*. Chicago: University of Chicago Press, 1988.

Belkin, Kristin Lohse. *Rubens*. London: Phaidon, 1998.

Biesboer, Pieter, Martina Brunner-Bulst, Henry D. Gregory, and Christian Klemm. *Pieter Claesz: Master of Haarlem Still Life*. Zwolle: Waanders, 2005.

Blunt, Anthony. *Art and Architecture in France, 1500–1700*. Rev. ed. New Haven, Conn.: Yale University Press, 1999.

Brown, Christopher. *Scenes of Everyday Life: Dutch Genre Painting of the Seventeenth Century*. London: Faber & Faber, 1984.

Bryson, Norman. *Word and Image: French Painting of the Ancien Régime*. Cambridge: Cambridge University Press, 1981.

Carr, Dawson W., ed. *Velázquez*. London: National Gallery, 2006.

Chapman, Perry. *Rembrandt's Self-Portraits: A Study in 17th-Century Identity*. Princeton, N.J.: Princeton University Press, 1990.

Chastel, André. *French Art: The Ancien Régime, 1620–1775*. New York: Flammarion, 1996.

Chong, Alan, and Wouter Kloek. *Still-Life Paintings from the Netherlands, 1550–1720*. Zwolle: Waanders, 1999.

Franits, Wayne. *Dutch Seventeenth-Century Genre Painting: Its Stylistic and Thematic Evolution*. New Haven, Conn.: Yale University Press, 2008.

———. *Looking at Seventeenth-Century Dutch Art: Realism Reconsidered*. Cambridge: Cambridge University Press, 1997.

———, ed. *The Cambridge Companion to Vermeer*. New York: Cambridge University Press, 2001.

Haak, Bob. *The Golden Age: Dutch Painters of the Seventeenth Century*. New York: Abrams, 1984.

Hochstrasser, Julie Berger. *Still Life and Trade in the Dutch Golden Age*. New Haven, Conn.: Yale University Press, 2007.

Keazor, Henry. *Nicholas Poussin, 1594–1665*. Cologne: Taschen, 2007.

Kiers, Judikje, and Fieke Tissink. *Golden Age of Dutch Art: Painting, Sculpture, Decorative Art.* New York: Thames & Hudson, 2000.

Liedtke, Walter. *Vermeer: The Complete Paintings.* Antwerp: Ludion, 2008.

———. *A View of Delft: Vermeer and His Contemporaries.* Zwolle: Wanders, 2000.

Mérot, Alain. *French Painting in the Seventeenth Century.* New Haven, Conn.: Yale University Press, 1995.

Muller, Sheila D., ed. *Dutch Art: An Encyclopedia.* New York: Garland, 1997.

North, Michael. *Art and Commerce in the Dutch Golden Age.* New Haven, Conn.: Yale University Press, 1997.

Olson, Todd P. *Poussin and France.* New Haven, Conn.: Yale University Press, 2000.

Rosenberg, Jakob, Seymour Slive, and E. H. ter Kuile. *Dutch Art and Architecture, 1600–1800.* New Haven, Conn.: Yale University Press, 1979.

Schama, Simon. *The Embarrassment of Riches: An Interpretation of Dutch Culture in the Golden Age.* Berkeley: University of California Press, 1988.

Schroth, Sarah, and Ronni Baer, eds. *El Greco to Velázquez: Art during the Reign of Philip III.* Boston: Museum of Fine Arts, 2008.

Slatkes, Leonard J., and Wayne Franits. *The Paintings of Hendrick ter Brugghen 1588–1629: Catalogue Raisonné.* Philadelphia: John Benjamins, 2007.

Stechow, Wolfgang. *Dutch Landscape Painting of the 17th Century.* 3d ed. Oxford: Phaidon, 1981.

Summerson, John. *Inigo Jones.* New Haven, Conn.: Yale University Press, 2000.

Vlieghe, Hans. *Flemish Art and Architecture, 1585–1700.* New Haven, Conn.: Yale University Press, 1998.

Westermann, Mariët. *Rembrandt.* London: Phaidon, 2000.

———. *A Worldly Art: The Dutch Republic 1585–1718.* New Haven, Conn.: Yale University Press, 1996.

Zega, Andres, and Bernd H. Dams. *Palaces of the Sun King: Versailles, Trianon, Marly: The Châteaux of Louis XIV.* New York: Rizzoli, 2002.

Zell, Michael. *Reframing Rembrandt: Jews and the Christian Image in Seventeenth-Century Amsterdam.* Berkeley: University of California Press, 2002.

Chapter 26: Rococo to Neoclassicism: The 18th Century in Europe and America

Beddington, Charles. *Venice: Canaletto and His Rivals.* London: National Gallery, 2010.

Bermingham, Ann. *Landscape and Ideology: The English Rustic Tradition, 1740–1850.* Berkeley: University of California Press, 1986.

Boime, Albert. *Art in the Age of Revolution, 1750–1800.* Chicago: University of Chicago Press, 1987.

Bowron, Edgar Peters, and Joseph J. Rishel, eds. *Art in Rome in the Eighteenth Century.* Philadelphia: Philadelphia Museum of Art, 2000

Braham, Allan. *The Architecture of the French Enlightenment.* Berkeley: University of California Press, 1980.

Brion, Marcel. *Art of the Romantic Era: Romanticism, Classicism, Realism.* New York: Praeger, 1966.

Conisbee, Philip. *Painting in Eighteenth-Century France.* Ithaca, N.Y.: Phaidon/Cornell University Press, 1981.

Craske, Matthew. *Art in Europe, 1700–1830: A History of the Visual Arts in an Era of Unprecedented Urban Economic Growth.* Oxford: Oxford University Press, 1997.

Crow, Thomas E. *Painters and Public Life in Eighteenth-Century Paris.* New Haven, Conn.: Yale University Press, 1985.

Gaunt, W. *The Great Century of British Painting: Hogarth to Turner.* New York: Phaidon, 1971.

Goodman, Elise, ed. *Art and Culture in the Eighteenth Century: New Dimensions and Multiple Perspectives.* Newark: University of Delaware Press, 2001.

Harrison, Charles, Paul Wood, and Jason Gaiger, eds. *Art in Theory, 1648–1815: An Anthology of Changing Ideas.* Oxford: Blackwell, 2000.

Hedley, Jo. *François Boucher: Seductive Visions.* London: Wallace Collection, 2004.

Herrmann, Luke. *British Landscape Painting of the Eighteenth Century.* New York: Oxford University Press, 1974.

Honour, Hugh. *Neo-Classicism.* Harmondsworth: Penguin, 1968.

Irwin, David. *Neoclassicism.* London: Phaidon, 1997.

Jarrassé, Dominique. *18th-Century French Painting.* Paris: Terrail, 1999.

Kalnein, Wend Graf, and Michael Levey. *Art and Architecture of the Eighteenth Century in France.* New York: Viking/Pelican, 1973.

Lee, Simon. *David.* London: Phaidon, 1999.

Levey, Michael. *Rococo to Revolution: Major Trends in Eighteenth-Century Painting.* London: Thames & Hudson, 1966.

Rosenblum, Robert. *Transformations in Late Eighteenth-Century Art.* Princeton, N.J.: Princeton University Press, 1970.

Roston, Murray. *Changing Perspectives in Literature and the Visual Arts, 1650–1820.* Princeton, N.J.: Princeton University Press, 1990.

Rykwert, Joseph. *The First Moderns: Architects of the Eighteenth Century.* Cambridge, Mass.: MIT Press, 1983.

Stillman, Damie. *English Neo-Classical Architecture.* 2 vols. London: Zwemmer, 1988.

Waterhouse, Ellis Kirkham. *Painting in Britain: 1530–1790.* 4th ed. New Haven, Conn.: Yale University Press, 1979.

Wilton, Andrew. *The Swagger Portrait: Grand Manner Portraiture in Britain from Van Dyck to Augustus John, 1630–1930.* London: Tate Gallery, 1992.

19th and 20th Centuries, General

Arnason, H. H., and Peter Kalb. *History of Modern Art: Painting, Sculpture, Architecture, Photography.* 6th ed. Upper Saddle River, N.J.: Prentice Hall, 2009.

Ashton, Dore. *Twentieth-Century Artists on Art.* New York: Pantheon Books, 1985.

Barnitz, Jacueline. *Twentieth-Century Art of Latin America.* Austin: University of Texas Press, 2001.

Brettell, Richard R. *Modern Art, 1851–1929: Capitalism and Representation.* New York: Oxford University Press, 1999.

Brown, Milton, Sam Hunter, and John Jacobus. *American Art: Painting, Sculpture, Architecture, Decorative Arts, Photography.* New York: Abrams, 1979.

Burnham, Jack. *Beyond Modern Sculpture: The Effects of Science and Technology on the Sculpture of This Century.* New York: Braziller, 1968.

Butler, Cornelia, and Alexandra Schwartz, eds. *Modern Women: Women Artists at the Museum of Modern Art.* New York: Museum of Modern Art, 2010.

Chipp, Herschel B. *Theories of Modern Art.* Berkeley: University of California Press, 1968.

Chu, Petra ten-Doesschate. *Nineteenth-Century European Art.* 2d ed. Upper Saddle River, N.J.: Prentice Hall, 2006.

Coke, Van Deren. *The Painter and the Photograph from Delacroix to Warhol.* Rev. ed. Albuquerque: University of New Mexico Press, 1972.

Colquhoun, Alan. *Modern Architecture.* New York: Oxford University Press, 2002.

Craven, Wayne. *American Art: History and Culture.* Rev. ed. New York: McGraw-Hill, 2002.

Dennis, Rafael Cardoso, and Colin Trodd, eds. *Art and the Academy in the Nineteenth Century.* New Brunswick, N.J.: Rutgers University Press, 2000.

Doordan, Dennis P. *Twentieth-Century Architecture.* New York: Abrams, 2002.

Doss, Erika. *Twentieth-Century American Art.* New York: Oxford University Press, 2002.

Driskell, David C. *Two Centuries of Black American Art.* Los Angeles: Los Angeles County Museum of Art; New York: Knopf, 1976.

Eisenmann, Stephen F., ed. *Nineteenth-Century Art: A Critical History.* 4th ed. New York: Thames & Hudson, 2011.

Elsen, Albert. *Origins of Modern Sculpture.* New York: Braziller, 1974.

Facos, Michelle. *An Introduction to Nineteenth-Century Art.* New York: Routledge, 2011.

Foster, Hal, Rosalind Krauss, Yve-Alain Bois, and Benjamin H. D. Buchloh. *Art since 1900: Modernism, Antimodernism, Postmodernism.* New York: Thames & Hudson, 2004.

Frampton, Kenneth. *Modern Architecture: A Critical History.* 4th ed. New York: Thames & Hudson, 2007.

Frascina, Francis, and Charles Harrison, eds. *Modern Art and Modernism: A Critical Anthology.* New York: Harper & Row, 1982.

Giedion, Siegfried. *Space, Time, and Architecture: The Growth of a New Tradition.* 4th ed. Cambridge, Mass.: Harvard University Press, 1965.

Goldwater, Robert, and Marco Treves, eds. *Artists on Art.* 3d ed. New York: Pantheon, 1958.

Greenough, Sarah, Joel Snyder, David Travis, and Colin Westerbeck. *On the Art of Fixing a Shadow: One Hundred and Fifty Years of Photography.* Washington, D.C.: National Gallery of Art; Chicago: Art Institute of Chicago, 1989.

Hamilton, George H. *Painting and Sculpture in Europe, 1880–1940.* 6th ed. New Haven, Conn.: Yale University Press, 1993.

Harrison, Charles, and Paul Wood. *Art in Theory, 1900–2000: An Anthology of Changing Ideas.* Oxford: Blackwell, 2003.

Herbert, Robert L., ed. *Modern Artists on Art.* Upper Saddle River, N.J.: Prentice Hall, 1971.

Hertz, Richard, and Norman M. Klein, eds. *Twentieth-Century Art Theory: Urbanism, Politics, and Mass Culture.* Englewood Cliffs, N.J.: Prentice Hall, 1990.

Heyer, Paul. *Architects on Architecture: New Directions in America.* New York: Van Nostrand Reinhold, 1993.

Hills, Patricia. *Modern Art in the USA: Issues and Controversies of the 20th Century.* Upper Saddle River, N.J.: Prentice Hall, 2000.

Hitchcock, Henry-Russell. *Architecture: Nineteenth and Twentieth Centuries.* 4th ed. New Haven, Conn.: Yale University Press, 1977.

Hunter, Sam, John Jacobus, and Daniel Wheeler. *Modern Art: Painting, Sculpture, Architecture, Photography.* Rev. 3d ed. Upper Saddle River, N.J.: Prentice Hall, 2004.

Janson, Horst W. *19th-Century Sculpture.* New York: Abrams, 1985.

Jencks, Charles. *Modern Movements in Architecture.* Garden City, N.Y.: Anchor; Doubleday, 1973.

Kaufmann, Edgar, Jr., ed. *The Rise of an American Architecture.* New York: Metropolitan Museum of Art; Praeger, 1970.

Krauss, Rosalind E. *The Originality of the Avant-Garde and Other Modernist Myths.* Cambridge, Mass.: MIT Press, 1985.

———. *Passages in Modern Sculpture.* Cambridge, Mass.: MIT Press, 1981.

Lewis, Samella S. *African American Art and Artists.* Rev. ed. Berkeley: University of California Press, 1994.

Licht, Fred. *Sculpture, Nineteenth and Twentieth Centuries.* Greenwich, Conn.: New York Graphic Society, 1967.

Marien, Mary Warner. *Photography: A Cultural History.* 3d ed. Upper Saddle River, N.J.: Prentice Hall, 2011.

Mason, Jerry, ed. *International Center of Photography Encyclopedia of Photography.* New York: Crown, 1984.

McCoubrey, John W. *American Art, 1700–1960: Sources and Documents.* Englewood Cliffs, N.J.: Prentice Hall, 1965.

Newhall, Beaumont. *The History of Photography.* New York: Museum of Modern Art, 1982.

Osborne, Harold. *The Oxford Companion to Twentieth-Century Art.* New York: Oxford University Press, 1981.

Pohl, Frances K. *Framing America: A Social History of American Art.* 2d ed. New York: Thames & Hudson, 2008.

Rose, Barbara. *American Art since 1900.* Rev. ed. New York: Praeger, 1975.

Rosenblum, Naomi. *A World History of Photography.* 4th ed. New York: Abbeville, 2007.

Rosenblum, Robert. *Modern Painting and the Northern Romantic Tradition: Friedrich to Rothko.* New York: Harper & Row, 1975.

Rosenblum, Robert, and Horst W. Janson. *19th-Century Art.* Rev. ed. Upper Saddle River, N.J.: Prentice Hall, 2005.

Ross, Stephen David, ed. *Art and Its Significance: An Anthology of Aesthetic Theory.* Albany: State University of New York Press, 1987.

Russell, John. *The Meanings of Modern Art.* New York: Museum of Modern Art; Thames & Hudson, 1981.

Scully, Vincent. *Modern Architecture.* Rev. ed. New York: Braziller, 1974.

Spalding, Francis. *British Art since 1900.* London: Thames & Hudson, 1986.

Spencer, Harold. *American Art: Readings from the Colonial Era to the Present.* New York: Scribner, 1980.

Steinberg, Leo. *Other Criteria: Confrontations with 20th-Century Art.* New York: Oxford University Press, 1972.

Szarkowski, John. *Photography until Now.* New York: Museum of Modern Art, 1989.

Upton, Dell. *Architecture in the United States.* Oxford: Oxford University Press, 1998.

Weaver, Mike. *The Art of Photography: 1839–1989.* New Haven, Conn.: Yale University Press, 1989.

Whiffen, Marcus, and Frederick Koeper. *American Architecture, 1607–1976.* Cambridge, Mass.: MIT Press, 1983.

Wilmerding, John. *American Art.* Harmondsworth: Penguin, 1976.

Wilson, Simon. *Holbein to Hockney: A History of British Art.* London: Tate Gallery & Bodley Head, 1979.

Chapter 27: Romanticism, Realism, Photography: Europe and America, 1800 to 1870

Amic, Sylvain, et al. *Gustave Courbet.* Ostfildern: Hatje Cantz, 2008.

Bartoli, Damien, and Frederick C. Ross. *William Bouguereau.* 2 vols. New York: Antique Collectors' Club, 2010.

Bellenger, Sylvain. *Girodet, 1767–1824.* Paris: Gallimard, 2005.

Bergdoll, Barry. *European Architecture 1750–1890.* New York: Oxford University Press, 2000.

Boime, Albert. *The Academy and French Painting in the 19th Century.* London: Phaidon, 1971.

———. *Art in the Age of Bonapartism, 1800–1815.* Chicago: University of Chicago Press, 1990.

Bordes, Philippe. *Jacques-Louis David: Empire to Exile.* New Haven, Conn.: Yale University Press, 2007.

Brown, David Blayney. *Romanticism.* New York: Phaidon, 2001.

Bryson, Norman. *Tradition and Desire: From David to Delacroix.* New York: Cambridge University Press, 1984.

Burns, Sarah, and John Davis. *American Art to 1900: A Documentary History.* Berkeley and Los Angeles: University of California Press, 2009.

Clark, T. J. *The Absolute Bourgeois: Artists and Politics in France, 1848–1851.* London: Thames & Hudson, 1973.

———. *Image of the People: Gustave Courbet and the 1848 Revolution.* London: Thames & Hudson, 1973.

———. *The Painting of Modern Life: Paris in the Art of Manet and His Followers.* Princeton, N.J.: Princeton University Press, 1984.

Clay, Jean. *Romanticism.* New York: Phaidon, 1981.

Eitner, Lorenz. *Neoclassicism and Romanticism, 1750–1850: An Anthology of Sources and Documents.* New York: Harper & Row, 1989.

Fried, Michael. *Courbet's Realism.* Chicago: University of Chicago Press, 1982.

———. *Manet's Modernism, or, The Face of Painting in the 1860s.* Chicago: University of Chicago Press, 1996.

Hilton, Timothy. *The Pre-Raphaelites.* New York: Oxford University Press, 1970.

Hofmann, Werner. *Caspar David Friedrich.* New York: Thames & Hudson, 2001.

———. *Goya.* New York: Thames & Hudson, 2003.

Holt, Elizabeth Gilmore, ed. *From the Classicists to the Impressionists: A Documentary History of Art and Architecture in the Nineteenth Century.* Garden City, N.J.: Anchor Books; Doubleday, 1966.

Honour, Hugh. *Romanticism.* New York: Harper & Row, 1979.

Koerner, Joseph Leo. *Caspar David Friedrich and the Subject of Landscape.* 2d ed. London: Reaktion, 2009.

Krell, Alain. *Manet and the Painters of Contemporary Life.* London: Thames & Hudson, 1996.

Kroeber, Karl. *British Romantic Art.* Berkeley: University of California Press, 1986.

Le Men, Ségolène. *Courbet.* New York: Abbeville, 2008.

Lewis, Michael J. *The Gothic Revival.* New York: Thames & Hudson, 2002.

Licht, Fred. *Goya.* New York: Abbeville, 2001.

Mainardi, Patricia. *Art and Politics of the Second Empire: The Universal Expositions of 1855 and 1867.* New Haven, Conn.: Yale University Press, 1987.

———. *The End of the Salon: Art and the State in the Early Third Republic.* Cambridge: Cambridge University Press, 1993.

Middleton, Robin. *Architecture of the Nineteenth Century.* London: Phaidon, 2003.

Middleton, Robin, and David Watkin. *Neoclassical and 19th-Century Architecture.* 2 vols. New York: Electa/Rizzoli, 1987.

Needham, Gerald. *19th-Century Realist Art.* New York: Harper & Row, 1988.

Nochlin, Linda. *Realism and Tradition in Art, 1848–1900: Sources and Documents.* Upper Saddle River, N.J.: Prentice Hall, 1966.

Novak, Barbara. *American Painting of the Nineteenth Century: Realism and the American Experience.* New York: Harper & Row, 1979.

Novak, Barbara. *Nature and Culture: American Landscape and Painting, 1825–1875.* 3d ed. New York: Oxford University Press, 2007.

Nature and Culture: American Landscape and Painting, 1825–1875. 3d ed. New York: Oxford University Press, 2007.

Novotny, Fritz. *Painting and Sculpture in Europe, 1780–1880.* 3d ed. New Haven, Conn.: Yale University Press, 1988.

Porterfield, Todd. *The Allure of Empire: Art in the Service of French Imperialism 1798–1836.* Princeton, N.J.: Princeton University Press, 1998.

Rosen, Charles, and Henri Zerner. *Romanticism and Realism: The Mythology of Nineteenth-Century Art.* New York: Viking, 1984.

Rubin, James Henry. *Courbet.* London: Phaidon, 1997.

———. *Manet: Initial M, Hand and Eye.* Paris: Flammarion, 2010.

Shelton, Andrew Carrington. *Ingres.* London: Phaidon, 2008.

Sloane, Joseph C. *French Painting between the Past and the Present: Artists, Critics, and Traditions from 1848 to 1870.* Princeton, N.J.: Princeton University Press, 1973.

Symmons, Sarah. *Goya.* London: Phaidon, 1998.

Taylor, Joshua, ed. *Nineteenth-Century Theories of Art.* Berkeley: University of California Press, 1987.

Tillier, Betrand, et al. *Gustave Courbet.* New York: Metropolitan Museum of Art, 2008.

Toman, Rolf, ed. *Neoclassicism and Romanticism: Architecture, Sculpture, Painting, Drawings, 1750–1848.* Cologne: Könemann, 2006.

Vaughn, William. *German Romantic Painting.* New Haven, Conn.: Yale University Press, 1980.

Wolf, Bryan Jay. *Romantic Revision: Culture and Consciousness in Nineteenth-Century American Painting and Literature.* Chicago: University of Chicago Press, 1986.

Wood, Christopher. *The Pre-Raphaelites.* New York: Viking, 1981.

Chapter 28: Impressionism, Post-Impressionism, Symbolism: Europe and America, 1870 to 1900

Baal-Teshuva, Jacob. *Louis Comfort Tiffany.* Cologne: Taschen, 2008.

Bergdoll, Barry. *European Architecture 1750–1890.* New York: Oxford University Press, 2000.

Bryson, Norman. *Tradition and Desire: From David to Delacroix.* New York: Cambridge University Press, 1984.

Calloway, Stephen. *Aubrey Beardsley.* New York: Harry N. Abrams, 1998.

Clark, T. J. *The Painting of Modern Life: Paris in the Art of Manet and His Followers.* Princeton, N.J.: Princeton University Press, 1984.

Cogeval, Guy, ed. *Claude Monet, 1840–1926.* Paris: Réunion des Musées Nationaux, 2010.

Distel, Anne. *Renoir.* New York: Abbeville, 2010.

Eitner, Lorenz. *Neoclassicism and Romanticism, 1750–1850: An Anthology of Sources and Documents.* New York: Harper & Row, 1989.

Facos, Michelle. *Symbolism in Context.* Berkeley: University of California Press, 2009.

Hauptmann, Jodi. *Beyond the Visible: The Art of Odilon Redon.* New York: Museum of Modern Art, 2005.

Loyrette, Henri, Sebastien Allard, and Laurence Des Cars. *Nineteenth Century French Art: From Romanticism to Impressionism, Post-Impressionism, and Art Nouveau.* Paris: Flammarion, 2007.

Masson, Raphaël, and Véronique Mattiussi. *Rodin.* Paris: Flammarion, 2004.

McShine, Kynaston, ed. *Edvard Munch: The Modern Life of the Soul.* New York: Museum of Modern Art, 2006.

Middleton, Robin. *Architecture of the Nineteenth Century.* London: Phaidon, 2003.

Middleton, Robin, and David Watkin. *Neoclassical and 19th-Century Architecture.* 2 vols. New York: Electa/Rizzoli, 1987.

Pfeiffer, Ingrid, et al. *Women Impressionists.* Ostfildern: Hatje Cantz, 2008.

Swinbourne, Anna. *James Ensor.* New York: Museum of Modern Art, 2009.

Thomson, Belinda, ed. *Gauguin: Maker of Myth*. London: Tate, 2010.

Zerbst, Rainer. *Gaudí: The Complete Buildings*. Cologne: Taschen, 2005.

Chapter 29: Modernism in Europe and America, 1900 to 1945

Antliff, Mark. *Cultural Politics and the Parisian Avant-Garde*. Princeton, N.J.: Princeton University Press, 1993.

Antliff, Mark, and Patricia Leighten. *Cubism and Culture*. New York: Thames & Hudson, 2001.

Arnaldo, Javier, and Max Hollein. *Kirchner*. Ostfildern: Hatje Cantz, 2010.

Baigell, Matthew. *The American Scene: American Painting of the 1930s*. New York: Praeger, 1974.

Barr, Alfred H., Jr. *Cubism and Abstract Art: Painting, Sculpture, Constructions, Photography, Architecture, Industrial Arts, Theatre, Films, Posters, Typography*. Cambridge, Mass.: Belknap, 1986.

Barron, Stephanie. *Exiles and Emigrés: The Flight of European Artists from Hitler*. Los Angeles: Los Angeles County Museum of Art, 1997.

———, ed. *Degenerate Art: The Fate of the Avant-Garde in Nazi Germany*. Los Angeles: Los Angeles County Museum of Art, 1991.

Bayer, Herbert, Walter Gropius, and Ise Gropius. *Bauhaus, 1919–1928*. New York: Museum of Modern Art, 1975.

Bearden, Romare, and Harry Henderson. *A History of African-American Artists from 1792 to the Present*. New York: Pantheon, 1993.

Bergdoll, Barry. *Bauhaus 1919–1933*. New York: Museum of Modern Art, 2009.

Bouvet, Vincent, and Gérard Durozoi. *Paris between the Wars 1919–1939: Art, Life & Culture*. New York: Vendome, 2010.

Breton, André. *Surrealism and Painting*. New York: Harper & Row, 1972.

Brown, Milton. *Story of the Armory Show: The 1913 Exhibition That Changed American Art*. 2d ed. New York: Abbeville, 1988.

Campbell, Mary Schmidt, David C. Driskell, David Lewis Levering, and Deborah Willis Ryan. *Harlem Renaissance: Art of Black America*. New York: Studio Museum in Harlem; Abrams, 1987.

Cowling, Elizabeth, ed. *Picasso: Challenging the Past*. London: National Gallery, 2011.

Cox, Neil. *Cubism*. London: Phaidon, 2000.

Curtis, Penelope. *Sculpture 1900–1945*. New York: Oxford University Press, 1999.

Curtis, William J. R. *Modern Architecture since 1900*. Upper Saddle River, N.J.: Prentice Hall, 1996.

Davidson, Abraham A. *Early American Modernist Painting, 1910–1935*. New York: Harper & Row, 1981.

Dietrich, Dorothea, ed. *Dada: Zurich, Berlin, Hannover, Cologne, New York, Paris*. Washington, D.C.: National Gallery, 2008.

Du Pont, Diana C. *Tamayo: A Modern Icon Reinterpreted*. Santa Barbara, Calif.: Santa Barbara Museum of Art, 2007.

Eberle, Matthias. *World War I and the Weimar Artists: Dix, Grosz, Beckmann, Schlemmer*. New Haven, Conn.: Yale University Press, 1985.

Edwards, Steve, and Paul Wood, eds. *Art of the Avant-Gardes*. New Haven, Conn.: Yale University Press, 2004.

Elderfield, John. *The "Wild Beasts": Fauvism and Its Affinities*. New York: Museum of Modern Art, 1976.

Fer, Briony, David Batchelor, and Paul Wood. *Realism, Rationalism, Surrealism: Art between the Wars*. New Haven, Conn.: Yale University Press, 1993.

Friedman, Mildred, ed. *De Stijl, 1917–1931: Visions of Utopia*. Minneapolis: Walker Art Center; New York: Abbeville, 1982.

Gale, Matthew. *Dada and Surrealism*. London: Phaidon, 1997.

Goldberg, Rose Lee. *Performance: Live Art 1909 to the Present*. New York: Abrams, 1979.

Golding, John. *Cubism: A History and an Analysis, 1907–1914*. Cambridge, Mass.: Belknap, 1988.

Gordon, Donald E. *Expressionism: Art and Idea*. New Haven, Conn.: Yale University Press, 1987.

Harrison, Charles, Francis Frascina, and Gil Perry. *Primitivism, Cubism, Abstraction: The Early Twentieth Century*. New Haven, Conn.: Yale University Press, 1993.

Herbert, James D. *Fauve Painting: The Making of Cultural Politics*. New Haven, Conn.: Yale University Press, 1992.

Herrera, Hayden, ed. *Frida Kahlo*. Minneapolis: Walker Art Center, 2007.

Hills, Patricia. *Painting Harlem Modern: The Art of Jacob Lawrence*. Berkeley and Los Angeles: University of California Press, 2009.

Hitchcock, Henry-Russell, and Philip Johnson. *The International Style*. New York: Norton, 1995.

Hurlburt, Laurance P. *The Mexican Muralists in the United States*. Albuquerque: University of New Mexico Press, 1989.

Jaffé, Hans L. C. *De Stijl, 1917–1931: The Dutch Contribution to Modern Art*. Cambridge, Mass.: Belknap, 1986.

Krauss, Rosalind. *The Originality of the Avant-Garde and Other Modernist Myths*. Cambridge, Mass.: MIT Press, 1986.

Kuspit, Donald. *The Cult of the Avant-Garde Artist*. Cambridge: Cambridge University Press, 1993.

Lloyd, Jill. *German Expressionism: Primitivism and Modernity*. New Haven, Conn.: Yale University Press, 1991.

Lodder, Christina. *Russian Constructivism*. New Haven, Conn.: Yale University Press, 1983.

Lozano, Luis Martin, and Juan Coronel Rivera. *Diego Rivera: The Complete Murals*. Cologne: Taschen, 2008.

Martin, Marianne W. *Futurist Art and Theory*. Oxford: Clarendon, 1968.

Motherwell, Robert, ed. *The Dada Painters and Poets: An Anthology*. 2d ed. Boston: Hall, 1981.

Mundy, Jennifer. *Duchamp, Man Ray, Picabia*. London: Tate, 2008.

Orvell, Miles. *American Photography*. New York: Oxford University Press, 2003.

Peters, Olaf. *Otto Dix*. New York: Prestel, 2010.

Rhodes, Colin. *Primitivism and Modern Art*. New York: Thames & Hudson, 1994.

Richter, Hans. *Dada: Art and Anti-Art*. London: Thames & Hudson, 1961.

Rochfort, Desmond. *Mexican Muralists: Orozco, Rivera, Siqueiros*. San Francisco: Chronicle, 1998.

Rosenblum, Robert. *Cubism and Twentieth-Century Art*. Rev. ed. New York: Abrams, 1984.

Rubin, William S. *Dada and Surrealist Art*. New York: Abrams, 1968.

———, ed. *Pablo Picasso: A Retrospective*. New York: Museum of Modern Art; Boston: New York Graphic Society, 1980.

———. *"Primitivism" in 20th-Century Art: Affinity of the Tribal and the Modern*. 2 vols. New York: Museum of Modern Art, 1984.

Selz, Peter. *German Expressionist Painting*. Berkeley: University of California Press, 1974. Reprint of 1957 edition.

Silver, Kenneth E. *Esprit de Corps: The Art of the Parisian Avant-Garde and the First World War, 1914–1925*. Princeton, N.J.: Princeton University Press, 1989.

Smith, Terry. *Making the Modern: Industry, Art, and Design in America*. Chicago: University of Chicago Press, 1993.

Stott, William. *Documentary Expression and Thirties America*. New York: Oxford University Press, 1973.

Taylor, Joshua C. *Futurism*. New York: Museum of Modern Art, 1961.

Taylor, Michael R., ed. *Arshile Gorky: A Retrospective*. New Haven, Conn.: Yale University Press, 2009.

Terraroli, Valerio, ed. *Art of the Twentieth Century, 1900–1919: The Avant-Garde Movements*. Milan: Skira, 2006.

———. *Art of the Twentieth Century, 1920–1945: The Artistic Culture between the Wars*. Milan: Skira, 2006.

Tisdall, Caroline, and Angelo Bozzolla. *Futurism*. New York: Oxford University Press, 1978.

Trachtenberg, Alan. *Reading American Photographs: Images as History—Mathew Brady to Walker Evans*. New York: Hill and Wang, 1989.

Troyen, Carol, ed. *Edward Hopper*. Boston: Museum of Fine Arts, 2007.

Tsujimoto, Karen. *Images of America: Precisionist Painting and Modern Photography*. Seattle: University of Washington Press, 1982.

Tucker, William. *Early Modern Sculpture*. New York: Oxford University Press, 1974.

Vogt, Paul. *Expressionism: German Painting, 1905–1920*. New York: Abrams, 1980.

Weiss, Jeffrey S. *The Popular Culture of Modern Art: Picasso, Duchamp, and Avant-Gardism*. New Haven, Conn.: Yale University Press, 1994.

Whitford, Frank. *Bauhaus*. New York: Thames & Hudson, 1984.

Chapter 30: Modernism and Postmodernism in Europe and America, 1945 to 1980

Alloway, Lawrence. *American Pop Art*. New York: Whitney Museum of American Art; Macmillan, 1974.

———. *Topics in American Art since 1945*. New York: Norton, 1975.

Altshuler, Bruce. *Isamu Noguchi*. New York: Abbeville, 1994.

Anfam, David. *Abstract Expressionism*. New York: Thames & Hudson, 1990.

Archer, Michael. *Art since 1960*. New ed. New York: Thames & Hudson, 2002.

Ashton, Dore. *American Art since 1945*. New York: Oxford University Press, 1983.

———. *The New York School: A Cultural Reckoning*. Harmondsworth: Penguin, 1979.

Ballantyne, Andrew, ed. *Architectures: Modernism and After*. Malden, Mass: Blackwell, 2004.

Battcock, Gregory, ed. *Idea Art: A Critical Anthology*. New York: Dutton, 1973.

———. *Minimal Art: A Critical Anthology*. New York: Studio Vista, 1969.

———. *The New Art: A Critical Anthology*. New York: Dutton, 1973.

———. *New Artists Video: A Critical Anthology*. New York: Dutton, 1978.

Battcock, Gregory, and Robert Nickas, eds. *The Art of Performance: A Critical Anthology*. New York: Dutton, 1984.

Beardsley, John, and Jane Livingston. *Hispanic Art in the United States: Thirty Contemporary Painters and Sculptors*. Houston: Museum of Fine Arts; New York: Abbeville, 1987.

Beardsley, Richard. *Earthworks and Beyond: Contemporary Art in the Landscape*. New York: Abbeville, 1984.

Broude, Norma, and Mary D. Garrard. *The Power of Feminist Art: The American Movement of the 1970s, History and Impact*. New York: Abrams, 1994.

Bürger, Peter. *Theory of the Avant-Garde*. Minneapolis: University of Minnesota Press, 1984.

Butler, Cornelia H., ed. *WACK! Art and the Feminist Revolution*. Cambridge, Mass.: MIT Press, 2007.

Causey, Andrew. *Sculpture since 1945.* New York: Oxford University Press, 1998.

Caws, Mary Ann. *Robert Motherwell.* New York: Columbia University Press, 1996.

Cockcroft, Eva, John Weber, and James Cockcroft. *Toward a People's Art.* New York: Dutton, 1977.

Cohn, Marjorie, and Eliza Rathbone. *Mark Rothko.* Ostfildern: Hatje Cantz, 2001.

Crow, Thomas. *The Rise of the Sixties: American and European Art in the Era of Dissent.* New Haven, Conn.: Yale University Press, 2005.

Finch, Christopher. *Chuck Close: Work.* New York: Prestel, 2010.

Frascina, Francis, ed. *Pollock and After: The Critical Debate.* New York: Harper & Row, 1985.

Gale, Matthew, ed. *Francis Bacon.* New York: Rizzoli, 2009.

Gaugh, Harry F. *Franz Kline.* New York: Abbeville, 1994.

Geldzahler, Henry. *New York Painting and Sculpture, 1940–1970.* New York: Dutton, 1969.

Godfrey, Tony. *Conceptual Art.* London: Phaidon, 1998.

Goldberg, Rose Lee. *Performance Art: From Futurism to the Present.* Rev. ed. New York: Abrams, 1988.

Goldhagen, Sarah Williams, and Réjean Legault. *Anxious Modernisms: Experimentation in Postwar Architectural Culture.* Cambridge, Mass.: MIT Press, 2002.

Goodman, Cynthia. *Digital Visions: Computers and Art.* New York: Abrams, 1987.

Goodyear, Frank H., Jr. *Contemporary American Realism since 1960.* Boston: New York Graphic Society, 1981.

Gouma-Peterson, Thalia. *Miriam Schapiro: Shaping the Fragments of Art and Life.* New York: Abrams, 2000.

Green, Jonathan. *American Photography: A Critical History 1945 to the Present.* New York: Abrams, 1984.

Greenberg, Clement. *Clement Greenberg: The Collected Essays and Criticism.* Edited by J. O'Brien. 4 vols. Chicago: University of Chicago Press, 1986–1993.

Grundberg, Andy. *Photography and Art: Interactions since 1945.* New York: Abbeville, 1987.

Guilbaut, Serge. *How New York Stole the Idea of Modern Art.* Chicago: University of Chicago Press, 1983.

Hays, K. Michael, and Carol Burns, eds. *Thinking the Present: Recent American Architecture.* New York: Princeton Architectural, 1990.

Henri, Adrian. *Total Art: Environments, Happenings, and Performance.* New York: Oxford University Press, 1974.

Hobbs, Robert. *Lee Krasner.* New York: Abbeville, 1993.

Hoffman, Katherine. *Explorations: The Visual Arts since 1945.* New York: Harper Collins, 1991.

Hopkins, David. *After Modern Art, 1945–2000.* New York: Oxford University Press, 2000.

Hughes, Robert. *The Shock of the New.* New York: Knopf, 1981.

Hunter, Sam. *An American Renaissance: Painting and Sculpture since 1940.* New York: Abbeville, 1986.

Jacobs, Jane. *The Death and Life of Great American Cities.* New York: Random House, 1961.

Jacobus, John. *Twentieth-Century Architecture: The Middle Years, 1940–1964.* New York: Praeger, 1966.

Jencks, Charles. *The Language of Post-Modern Architecture.* 6th ed. New York: Rizzoli, 1991.

———. *What Is Post-Modernism?* 3d ed. London: Academy Editions, 1989.

Johnson, Ellen H., ed. *American Artists on Art from 1940 to 1980.* Boulder, Colo.: Westview, 1982.

Joselit, David. *American Art since 1945.* New York: Thames & Hudson, 2003.

Kaprow, Allan. *Assemblage, Environments, and Happenings.* New York: Abrams, 1966.

Kirby, Michael. *Happenings.* New York: Dutton, 1966.

Kotz, Mary Lynn. *Rauschenberg: Art and Life.* New York: Abrams, 2004.

Kramer, Hilton. *The Age of the Avant-Garde: An Art Chronicle of 1956–1972.* New York: Farrar, Straus & Giroux, 1973.

Leja, Michael. *Reframing Abstract Expressionism: Subjectivity and Painting in the 1940s.* New Haven, Conn.: Yale University Press, 1993.

Lippard, Lucy R. *Mixed Blessings: New Art in a Multicultural America.* New York: Pantheon, 1990.

———. *Pop Art.* New York: Praeger, 1966.

———, ed. *From the Center: Feminist Essays on Women's Art.* New York: Dutton, 1976.

———. *Six Years: The Dematerialization of the Art Object from 1966 to 1972.* New York: Praeger, 1973.

Livingston, Jane, ed. *The Paintings of Joan Mitchell.* New York: Whitney Museum of American Art, 2002.

Lovejoy, Margot. *Postmodern Currents: Art and Artists in the Age of the Electronic Media.* Ann Arbor, Mich.: UMI Research Press, 1989.

Lucie-Smith, Edward. *Art Now.* Edison, N.J.: Wellfleet, 1989.

———. *Movements in Art since 1945.* New ed. New York: Thames & Hudson, 2001.

Mamiya, Christin J. *Pop Art and Consumer Culture: American Super Market.* Austin: University of Texas Press, 1992.

Marder, Tod A. *The Critical Edge: Controversy in Recent American Architecture.* New Brunswick, N.J.: Rutgers University Press, 1980.

———. *An International Survey of Recent Painting and Sculpture.* New York: Museum of Modern Art, 1984.

Mercurio, Gianni. *Lichtenstein: Meditations on Art.* Milan: Skira, 2010.

Meyer, Ursula. *Conceptual Art.* New York: Dutton, 1972.

Mitchell, William J. *The Reconfigured Eye: Visual Truth in the Post-Photographic Era.* Cambridge, Mass.: MIT Press, 1992.

Morris, Francis, ed. *Louise Bourgeois.* New York: Rizzoli, 2008.

Polcari, Stephen. *Abstract Expressionism and the Modern Experience.* Cambridge: Cambridge University Press, 1991.

Popper, Frank. *Origins and Development of Kinetic Art.* Translated by Stephen Bann. Greenwich, Conn.: New York Graphic Society, 1968.

Price, Jonathan. *Video Visions: A Medium Discovers Itself.* New York: New American Library, 1977.

Reichardt, Jasia, ed. *Cybernetics, Art, and Ideas.* Greenwich, Conn.: New York Graphics Society, 1971.

Robbins, Corinne. *The Pluralist Era: American Art, 1968–1981.* New York: Harper & Row, 1984.

Rorimer, Anne. *New Art in the 60s and 70s: Redefining Reality.* New York: Thames & Hudson, 2001.

Rosen, Randy, and Catherine C. Brawer, eds. *Making Their Mark: Women Artists Move into the Mainstream, 1970–1985.* New York: Abbeville, 1989.

Rosenberg, Harold. *The Tradition of the New.* New York: Horizon, 1959.

Rush, Michael. *New Media in Art.* 2d ed. New York: Thames & Hudson, 2005.

Russell, John, and Suzi Gablik. *Pop Art Redefined.* New York: Praeger, 1969.

Sandford, Mariellen R., ed. *Happenings and Other Acts.* New York: Routledge, 1995.

Sandler, Irving. *Art of the Postmodern Era.* New York: Harper Collins, 1996.

———. *The Triumph of American Painting: A History of Abstract Expressionism.* New York: Praeger, 1970.

Sayre, Henry M. *The Object of Performance: The American Avant-Garde since 1970.* Chicago: University of Chicago Press, 1989.

Schneider, Ira, and Beryl Korot. *Video Art: An Anthology.* New York: Harcourt Brace Jovanovich, 1976.

Shapiro, David, and Cecile Shapiro. *Abstract Expressionism: A Critical Record.* New York: Cambridge University Press, 1990.

Shiff, Richard. *Barnett Newman: A Catalogue Raisonné.* New Haven, Conn.: Yale University Press, 2004.

Sims, Lowery Stokes. *Wifredo Lam and the International Avant-Garde, 1923–1982.* Austin, Tex.: University of Texas Press, 2002.

Smagula, Howard. *Currents: Contemporary Directions in the Visual Arts.* 2d ed. Upper Saddle River, N.J.: Prentice Hall, 1989.

Smee, Sebastian. *Lucian Freud: Beholding the Animal.* Cologne: Taschen, 2009.

Sonfist, Alan, ed. *Art in the Landscape: A Critical Anthology of Environmental Art.* New York: Dutton, 1983.

Sontag, Susan. *On Photography.* New York: Farrar, Straus & Giroux, 1973.

Stiles, Kristine, and Peter Selz. *Theories and Documents of Contemporary Art: A Sourcebook of Artists' Writings.* Berkeley and Los Angeles: University of California Press, 1996.

Taylor, Brendon. *Contemporary Art: Art since 1970.* Upper Saddle River, N.J.: Prentice Hall, 2005.

Terraroli, Valerio, ed. *Art of the Twentieth Century, 1946–1968: The Birth of Contemporary Art.* Milan: Skira, 2007.

Tuchman, Maurice. *American Sculpture of the Sixties.* Los Angeles: Los Angeles County Museum of Art, 1967.

Varnedoe, Kirk. *Pictures of Nothing: Abstract Art since Pollock.* Princeton: Princeton University Press, 2006.

Venturi, Robert. *Complexity and Contradiction in Architecture.* New York: Museum of Modern Art, 1966.

Venturi, Robert, Denise Scott-Brown, and Steven Isehour. *Learning from Las Vegas.* Cambridge, Mass.: MIT Press, 1972.

Waldman, Diane. *Collage, Assemblage, and the Found Object.* New York: Abrams, 1992.

Wallis, Brian, ed. *Art after Modernism: Rethinking Representation.* New York: New Museum of Contemporary Art in association with David R. Godine, 1984.

Wheeler, Daniel. *Art since Mid-Century: 1945 to the Present.* Upper Saddle River, N.J.: Prentice Hall, 1991.

Wood, Paul. *Modernism in Dispute: Art since the Forties.* New Haven, Conn.: Yale University Press, 1993.

Chapter 31: Contemporary Art Worldwide

Buchhart, Dieter, et al., *Jean-Michel Basquiat.* Ostfildern: Hatje Cantz, 2010.

Butler, Cornelia H., and Lisa Gabrielle Mark. *WACK!: Art and the Feminist Revolution.* Cambridge, Mass.: MIT Press, 2007.

Celent, Germano. *Anselm Kiefer.* Milan: Skira, 2007.

Chilvers, Ian, and John Glaves-Smith. *Oxford Dictionary of Modern and Contemporary Art.* 2d ed. New York: Oxford University Press, 2009.

Cook, Peter. *New Spirit in Architecture.* New York: Rizzoli, 1990.

Cummings, P. *Dictionary of Contemporary American Artists.* 6th ed. New York: St. Martin's, 1994.

Deepwell, K., ed. *New Feminist Art.* Manchester: Manchester University Press, 1994.

Enwezor, Okwui, and Chika Okeke-Agulu. *Contemporary African Art since 1980.* Bologna: Damiani, 2009.

Ferguson, Russell, ed. *Discourses: Conversations in Postmodern Art and Culture.* Cambridge, Mass.: MIT Press, 1990.

Fineberg, Jonathan. *Art since 1940: Strategies of Being.* 2d ed. Upper Saddle River, N.J.: Prentice Hall, 2000.

Galassi, Peter. *Andreas Gursky*. New York: Museum of Modern Art, 2001.

Ghirardo, Diane. *Architecture after Modernism*. New York: Thames & Hudson, 1996.

Goldsworthy, Andy. *Andy Goldsworthy: A Collaboration with Nature*. New York: Abrams, 1990.

Heartney, Eleanor, Helaine Posner, Nancy Princenthal, and Sue Scott. *After the Revolution: Women Who Transformed Contemporary Art*. New York: Prestel, 2007.

Hertz, Richard, ed. *Theories of Contemporary Art*. 2d ed. Upper Saddle River, N.J.: Prentice Hall, 1993.

Hopkins, David. *After Modern Art, 1945–2000*. New York: Oxford University Press, 2000.

Jencks, Charles. *The New Paradigm in Architecture: The Language of Post-Modernism*. New Haven, Conn.: Yale University Press, 2002.

Jodidio, Philip. *100 Contemporary Architects*. Cologne: Taschen, 2008.

Kasfir, Sidney Littlefield. *Contemporary African Art*. New York: Thames & Hudson, 1999.

Kolossa, Alexandra. *Keith Haring 1958–1990: A Life for Art*. Cologne: Taschen, 2009.

Kotz, Mary Lunn. *Rauschenberg: Art and Life*. New York: Abrams, 2004.

Lippard, Lucy R. *Mixed Blessings: New Art in a Multicultural America*. New York: Pantheon, 1990.

Mullins, Charlotte. *Painting People: Figure Painting Today*. New York: Thames & Hudson, 2008.

Nesbitt, Judith, ed. *Chris Ofili*. London: Tate, 2010.

Norris, Christopher, and Andrew Benjamin. *What Is Deconstruction?* New York: St. Martin's, 1988.

Paul, Christiane. *Digital Art*. 2d ed. New York: Thames & Hudson, 2008.

Pauli, Lori, ed. *Manufactured Landscapes: The Photographs of Edward Burtynsky*. New Haven, Conn.: Yale University Press, 2003.

Perry, Gill, and Paul Wood. *Themes in Contemporary Art*. New Haven, Conn.: Yale University Press, 2004.

Raskin, David. *Donald Judd*. New Haven, Conn.: Yale University Press, 2010.

Risatti, Howard, ed. *Postmodern Perspectives: Issues in Contemporary Art*. Upper Saddle River, N.J.: Prentice Hall, 1990.

Sandler, Irving. *Art of the Postmodern Era*. New York: Harper Collins, 1996.

Smith, Terry. *What Is Contemporary Art?* Chicago: University of Chicago Press, 2009.

Sollins, Susan, ed. *Art: 21 (Art in the Twenty-first Century)*. 5 vols. New York: Abrams, 2001–2009.

Stiles, Kristine, and Peter Selz. *Theories and Documents of Contemporary Art: A Sourcebook of Artists' Writings*. Berkeley and Los Angeles: University of California Press, 1996.

Taylor, Brendon. *Contemporary Art: Art since 1970*. Upper Saddle River, N.J.: Prentice Hall, 2005.

Terraroli, Valerio, ed. *Art of the Twentieth Century, 1969–1999: Neo-avant-gardes, Postmodern and Global Art*. Milan: Skira, 2009.

Wands, Bruce. *Art of the Digital Age*. New York: Thames & Hudson, 2007.

Warren, Lynne. *Jeff Koons*. New Haven, Conn.: Yale University Press, 2008.

Wines, James. *Green Architecture*. Cologne: Taschen, 2008.

Asian Art, General

Brown, Rebecca M., and Deborah S. Hutton. *Asian Art (Blackwell Anthologies in Art History)*. Malden, Mass.: Blackwell, 2006.

Clark, John. *Modern Asian Art*. Honolulu: University of Hawaii Press, 1998.

McArthur, Meher. *The Arts of Asia: Materials, Techniques, Styles*. New York: Thames & Hudson, 2005.

Chapter 32: South and Southeast Asia, 1200 to 1980

Asher, Catherine B. *Architecture of Mughal India*. New York: Cambridge University Press, 1992.

Beach, Milo Cleveland. *Mughal and Rajput Painting*. Cambridge: Cambridge University Press, 1992.

Blurton, T. Richard. *Hindu Art*. Cambridge, Mass.: Harvard University Press, 1993.

Chaturachinda, Gwyneth, Sunanda Krishnamurty, and Pauline W. Tabtiang. *Dictionary of South and Southeast Asian Art*. Chiang Mai, Thailand: Silkworm Books, 2000.

Craven, Roy C. *Indian Art: A Concise History*. Rev. ed. London: Thames & Hudson, 1997.

Dallapiccola, Anna Libera, ed. *Vijayanagara: City and Empire*. 2 vols. Stuttgart: Steiner, 1985.

Dehejia, Vidya. *Indian Art*. London: Phaidon, 1997.

Encyclopedia of Indian Temple Architecture. 8 vols. New Delhi: American Institute of Indian Studies; Philadelphia: University of Pennsylvania Press, 1983–1996.

Girard-Geslan, Maud, ed. *Art of Southeast Asia*. New York: Abrams, 1998.

Harle, James C. *The Art and Architecture of the Indian Subcontinent*. 2d ed. New Haven, Conn.: Yale University Press, 1994.

Huntington, Susan L., and John C. Huntington. *The Art of Ancient India: Buddhist, Hindu, Jain*. New York: Weatherhill, 1985.

Lambah, Abha Narian, and Alka Patel, eds. *The Architecture of the Indian Sultanates*. Mumbai: Marg, 2006.

Michell, George. *Architecture and Art of Southern India: Vijayanagara and the Successor States, 1350–1750*. Cambridge: Cambridge University Press, 1995.

———. *Hindu Art and Architecture*. New York: Thames & Hudson, 2000.

———. *The Hindu Temple: An Introduction to Its Meaning and Forms*. Chicago: University of Chicago Press, 1988.

Mitter, Partha. *Indian Art*. New York: Oxford University Press, 2001.

Pal, Pratapaditya, ed. *Master Artists of the Imperial Mughal Court*. Mumbai: Marg, 1991.

Rawson, Phillip. *The Art of Southeast Asia*. New York: Thames & Hudson, 1990.

Schimmel, Annemarie. *The Empire of the Great Mughals: History, Art, and Culture*. London: Reaktion, 2006.

Stadtner, Donald M. *The Art of Burma: New Studies*. Mumbai: Marg, 1999.

Stevenson, John, and John Guy, eds. *Vietnamese Ceramics: A Separate Tradition*. Chicago: Art Media Resources, 1997.

Stierlin, Henri. *Hindu India from Khajuraho to the Temple City of Madurai*. Cologne: Taschen, 1998.

Stronge, Susan. *Painting for the Mughal Emperor: The Art of the Book, 1560–1660*. London: Victoria & Albert Museum, 2002.

Tingley, Nancy, ed. *Arts of Ancient Viet Nam: From River Plain to Open Sea*. Houston: Museum of Fine Arts, 2009.

Verna, Som Prakash. *Painting the Mughal Experience*. New York: Oxford University Press, 2005.

Welch, Stuart Cary. *Imperial Mughal Painting*. New York: Braziller, 1978.

———. *India: Art and Culture 1300–1900*. New York: Metropolitan Museum of Art, 1985.

Chapter 33: China and Korea, 1279 to 1980

Andrews, Julia Frances, and Kuiyi Shen. *A Century in Crisis: Modernity and Tradition in the Art of Twentieth-Century China*. New York: Guggenheim Museum, 1998.

Barnhart, Richard M. *Painters of the Great Ming: The Imperial Court and the Zhe School*. Dallas: Dallas Museum of Art, 1993.

Cahill, James. *The Painter's Practice: How Artists Lived and Worked in Traditional China*. New York: Columbia University Press, 1994.

Clunas, Craig. *Art in China*. New York: Oxford University Press, 1997.

———. *Pictures and Visuality in Early Modern China*. Princeton: Princeton University Press, 1997.

Fahr-Becker, Gabriele, ed. *The Art of East Asia*. Cologne: Könemann, 1999.

Fisher, Robert E. *Buddhist Art and Architecture*. New York: Thames & Hudson, 1993.

Fong, Wen C., and James C. Y. Watt. *Preserving the Past: Treasures from the National Palace Museum, Taipei*. New York: Metropolitan Museum of Art, 1996.

Hearn, Maxwell K. *How to Read Chinese Paintings*. New York: Metropolitan Museum of Art, 2008.

Howard, Angela Falco, Li Song, Wu Hong, and Yang Hong. *Chinese Sculpture*. New Haven, Conn.: Yale University Press, 2006.

Laing, Ellen Johnston. *The Winking Owl: Art in the People's Republic of China*. Berkeley: University of California Press, 1989.

Li, Chu-tsing, ed. *Artists and Patrons: Some Social and Economic Aspects of Chinese Painting*. Lawrence, Kans.: Kress Department of Art History in cooperation with Indiana University Press, 1989.

Li, He, and Michael Knight. *Power and Glory: Court Arts of China's Ming Dynasty*. San Francisco: Asian Art Museum, 2008.

Marks, Andreas. *Japanese Woodblock Prints: Artists, Publishers, and Masterworks: 1680–1900*. North Clarendon, Vt.: Tuttle, 2010.

Nakata, Yujiro, ed. *Chinese Calligraphy*. New York: Weatherhill, 1983.

Portal, Jane. *Korea: Art and Archaeology*. New York: Thames & Hudson, 2000.

Rawson, Jessica, ed. *The British Museum Book of Chinese Art*. New York: Thames & Hudson, 1992.

Sickman, Laurence, and Alexander C. Soper. *The Art and Architecture of China*. 3d ed. New Haven, Conn.: Yale University Press, 1992.

Silbergeld, Jerome. *Chinese Painting Style: Media, Methods, and Principles of Form*. Seattle: University of Washington Press, 1982.

Steinhardt, Nancy S., ed. *Chinese Architecture*. New Haven, Conn.: Yale University Press, 2002.

Sullivan, Michael. *Art and Artists of Twentieth-Century China*. Berkeley: University of California Press, 1996.

———. *The Arts of China*. 5th ed. Berkeley: University of California Press, 2009.

Thorp, Robert L. *Son of Heaven: Imperial Arts of China*. Seattle: Son of Heaven, 1988.

Thorp, Robert L., and Richard Ellis Vinograd. *Chinese Art and Culture*. New York: Abrams, 2001.

Vainker, S. J. *Chinese Pottery and Porcelain: From Prehistory to the Present*. London: Braziller, 1991.

Watson, William. *The Arts of China 900–1260*. New Haven, Conn.: Yale University Press, 2000.

———. *The Arts of China after 1260*. New Haven, Conn.: Yale University Press, 2007.

Watt, James C. Y., ed. *The World of Khubilai Khan: Chinese Art in the Yuan Dynasty*. New York: Metropolitan Museum of Art, 2010.

Weidner, Marsha, ed. *Flowering in the Shadows: Women in the History of Chinese and Japanese Painting*. Honolulu: University of Hawaii Press, 1990.

———. *Views from Jade Terrace: Chinese Women Artists 1300–1912*. Indianapolis: Indianapolis Museum of Art, 1988.

Xin, Yang, Nie Chongzheng, Lang Shaojun, Richard M. Barnhart, James Cahill, and Wu Hung. *Three Thousand Years of Chinese Painting*. New Haven, Conn.: Yale University Press, 1997.

Zhiyan, Li, Virginia L. Bower, and He Li. *Chinese Ceramics: From the Paleolithic Period through the Qing Dyansty*. New Haven, Conn.: Yale University Press, 2010.

Zhongshi, Ouyang, Wen C. Fong, et al. *Chinese Calligraphy*. New Haven, Conn.: Yale University Press, 2008.

Chapter 34: Japan, 1336 to 1980

Addiss, Stephen. *The Art of Zen*. New York: Abrams, 1989.

Baekeland, Frederick. *Imperial Japan: The Art of the Meiji Era (1868–1912)*. Ithaca, N.Y.: Herbert F. Johnson Museum of Art, 1980.

Brown, Kendall. *The Politics of Reclusion: Painting and Power in Muromachi Japan*. Honolulu: University of Hawaii Press, 1997.

Cahill, James. *Scholar Painters of Japan*. New York: Asia Society, 1972.

Calza, Gian Carlo. *Ukiyo-e*. New York: Phaidon, 2005.

Coaldrake, William H. *Architecture and Authority in Japan*. London: Routledge, 1996.

Fontein, Jan, and Money L. Hickman. *Zen Painting and Calligraphy*. Greenwich, Conn.: New York Graphic Society, 1970.

Guth, Christine. *Art of Edo Japan: The Artist and the City, 1615–1868*. New York: Abrams, 1996.

Hickman, Money L., John T. Carpenter, Bruce A. Coats, Christine Guth, Andrew J. Pekarik, John M. Rosenfield, and Nicole C. Rousmaniere. *Japan's Golden Age: Momoyama*. New Haven, Conn.: Yale University Press, 1996.

Kawakita, Michiaki. *Modern Currents in Japanese Art*. Translated by Charles E. Terry. New York: Weatherhill, 1974.

Kidder, J. Edward, Jr. *The Art of Japan*. New York: Park Lane, 1985.

Lane, Richard. *Images from the Floating World: The Japanese Print*. New York: Dorset, 1978.

Mason, Penelope. *History of Japanese Art*. 2d ed. New York: Abrams, 2004.

Meech, Julia, and Jane Oliver. *Designed for Pleasure: The World of Edo Japan in Prints and Drawings, 1680–1860*. Seattle: University of Washington Press, 2008.

Munroe, Alexandra. *Japanese Art after 1945: Scream against the Sky*. New York: Abrams, 1994.

Nishi, Kazuo, and Kazuo Hozumi. *What Is Japanese Architecture?* Translated by H. Mack Horton. New York: Kodansha International, 1985.

Ohki, Sadak. *Tea Culture of Japan*. New Haven, Conn.: Yale University Press, 2009.

Sanford, James H., William R. LaFleur, and Masatoshi Nagatomi. *Flowing Traces: Buddhism in the Literary and Visual Arts of Japan*. Princeton, N.J.: Princeton University Press, 1992.

Shimizu, Yoshiaki, ed. *Japan: The Shaping of Daimyo Culture, 1185–1868*. Washington, D.C.: National Gallery of Art, 1988.

Singer, Robert T. *Edo: Art in Japan 1615–1868*. Washington, D.C.: National Gallery of Art, 1998.

Stanley-Baker, Joan. *Japanese Art*. Rev. ed. New York: Thames & Hudson, 2000.

Stewart, David B. *The Making of a Modern Japanese Architecture, 1868 to the Present*. New York: Kodansha International, 1988.

Tiampo, Ming. *Gutai: Decentering Modernism*. Chicago: University of Chicago Press, 2011.

Chapter 35: Native Arts of the Americas, 1300 to 1980

Bawden, Garth. *Moche*. Oxford: Blackwell, 1999.

Berlo, Janet Catherine, ed. *Plains Indian Drawings 1865–1935*. New York: Abrams, 1996.

Berlo, Janet Catherine, and Ruth B. Phillips. *Native North American Art*. New York: Oxford University Press, 1998.

Boone, Elizabeth. *The Aztec World*. Washington, D.C.: Smithsonian Institution Press, 1994.

Bruhns, Karen O. *Ancient South America*. New York: Cambridge University Press, 1994.

Burger, Richard L., and Lucy C. Salaza, eds. *Machu Picchu: Unveiling the Mystery of the Incas*. New Haven, Conn.: Yale University Press, 2004.

Coe, Michael D. *The Maya*. 7th ed. New York: Thames & Hudson, 2005.

———. *Mexico: From the Olmecs to the Aztecs*. 5th ed. New York: Thames & Hudson, 2002.

D'Altroy, Terence N. *The Incas*. New ed. Oxford: Blackwell, 2003.

Davies, Nigel. *The Ancient Kingdoms of Peru*. New York: Penguin, 1997.

Feest, Christian F. *Native Arts of North America*. 2d ed. New York: Thames & Hudson, 1992.

Fienup-Riordan, Ann. *The Living Tradition of Yup'ik Masks*. Seattle: University of Washington Press, 1996.

Fitzhugh, William W., and Aron Crowell, eds. *Crossroads of Continents: Cultures of Siberia and Alaska*. Washington, D.C.: Smithsonian Institution Press, 1988.

Gasparini, Graziano, and Luise Margolies. *Inca Architecture*. Bloomington: Indiana University Press, 1980.

Hill, Tom, and Richard W. Hill, Sr., eds. *Creation's Journey: Native American Identity and Belief*. Washington, D.C.: Smithsonian Institution Press, 1994.

Jonaitis, Aldona. *Art of the Northwest Coast*. Seattle: University of Washington Press, 2006.

Kubler, George. *The Art and Architecture of Ancient America: The Mexican, Maya, and Andean Peoples*. 3d ed. New Haven, Conn.: Yale University Press, 1992.

Malpass, Michael A. *Daily Life in the Inca Empire*. Westport, Conn.: Greenwood, 1996.

Mathews, Zena, and Aldona Jonaitis, eds. *Native North American Art History*. Palo Alto, Calif.: Peek, 1982.

Matos, Eduardo M. *The Great Temple of the Aztecs: Treasures of Tenochtitlan*. New York: Thames & Hudson, 1988.

Maurer, Evan M. *Visions of the People: A Pictorial History of Plains Indian Life*. Seattle: University of Washington Press, 1992.

McEwan, Gordon F. *The Incas: New Perspectives*. Santa Barbara, Calif.: ABC-CLIO, 2006.

Miller, Mary Ellen. *The Art of Mesoamerica, from Olmec to Aztec*. 4th ed. New York: Thames & Hudson, 2006.

Miller, Mary, and Karl Taube. *An Illustrated Dictionary of the Gods and Symbols of Ancient Mexico and the Maya*. New York: Thames & Hudson, 1993.

Minelli, Laura Laurencich. *The Inca World*. Norman: University of Oklahoma Press, 2000.

Morris, Craig, and Adriana von Hagen. *The Incas*. New York: Thames & Hudson, 2011.

———. *The Inka Empire and Its Andean Origins*. New York: Abbeville, 1993.

Moseley, Michael E. *The Incas and Their Ancestors: The Archaeology of Peru*. Rev. ed. New York: Thames & Hudson, 2001.

Nabokov, Peter, and Robert Easton. *Native American Architecture*. New York: Oxford University Press, 1989.

Pasztory, Esther. *Aztec Art*. New York: Abrams, 1983.

———. *Pre-Columbian Art*. New York: Cambridge University Press, 1998.

Penney, David W. *North American Indian Art*. New York: Thames & Hudson, 2004.

Phillips, Ruth B. *Trading Identities: The Souvenir in Native North American Art*. Seattle: University of Washington Press, 1998.

Samuel, Cheryl. *The Chilkat Dancing Blanket*. Norman: University of Oklahoma Press, 1982.

Schaafsma, Polly, ed. *Kachinas in the Pueblo World*. Albuquerque: University of New Mexico Press, 1994.

Silverman, Helaine. *The Nasca*. Oxford: Blackwell, 2002.

———, ed. *Andean Archaeology*. Oxford: Blackwell, 2004.

Smith, Michael Ernest. *The Aztecs*. 2d ed. Oxford: Blackwell, 2003.

Stewart, Hilary. *Looking at Totem Poles*. Seattle: University of Washington Press, 1993.

Townsend, Richard F. *The Aztecs*. 2d ed. New York: Thames & Hudson, 2000.

Von Hagen, Adriana, and Craig Morris. *The Cities of the Ancient Andes*. New York: Thames & Hudson, 1998.

Wardwell, Allen. *Tangible Visions: Northwest Coast Indian Shamanism and Its Art*. New York: Monacelli, 1996.

Washburn, Dorothy. *Living in Balance: The Universe of the Hopi, Zuni, Navajo, and Apache*. Philadelphia: University Museum, 1995.

Weaver, Muriel Porter. *The Aztecs, Mayas, and Their Predecessors*. 3d ed. San Diego: Academic, 1993.

Wright, Robin K. *Northern Haida Master Carvers*. Seattle: University of Washington Press, 2001.

Wyman, Leland C. *Southwest Indian Drypainting*. Albuquerque: University of New Mexico Press, 1983.

Chapter 36: Oceania before 1980

Caruana, Wally. *Aboriginal Art*. 2d ed. New York: Thames & Hudson, 2003.

Cox, J. Halley, and William H. Davenport. *Hawaiian Sculpture*. Rev. ed. Honolulu: University of Hawaii Press, 1988.

D'Alleva, Anne. *Arts of the Pacific Islands*. New York: Abrams, 1998.

Ellis, Juniper. *Tattooing the World. Pacific Designs in Print & Skin*. New York: Columbia University Press, 2008.

Feldman, Jerome, and Donald H. Rubinstein. *The Art of Micronesia*. Honolulu: University of Hawaii Art Gallery, 1986.

Greub, Suzanne, ed. *Authority and Ornament: Art of the Sepik River, Papua New Guinea*. Basel: Tribal Art Centre, 1985.

Hanson, Allan, and Louise Hanson, eds. *Art and Identity in Oceania*. Honolulu: University of Hawaii Press, 1990.

Kaeppler, Adrienne L., Christian Kaufmann, and Douglas Newton. *Oceanic Art*. New York: Abrams, 1997.

Kjellgren, Eric. *Oceania: Art of the Pacific Islands in the Metropolitan Museum of Art*. New York: Metropolitan Museum of Art, 2007.

Kjellgren, Eric, and Carol Ivory. *Adorning the World: Art of the Marquesas Islands*. New York: Metropolitan Museum of Art, 2005.

Kooijman, Simon. *Tapa in Polynesia*. Honolulu: Bishop Museum Press, 1972.

Lilley, Ian, ed. *Archaeology of Oceania: Australia and the Pacific Islands*. Malden, Mass: Blackwell, 2006.

Mead, Sidney Moko, ed. *Te Maori: Maori Art from New Zealand Collections*. New York: Abrams in association with the American Federation of Arts, 1984.

Morphy, Howard. *Aboriginal Art*. London: Phaidon, 1998.

Rainbird, Paul. *The Archaeology of Micronesia*. New York: Cambridge University Press, 2004.

Sayers, Andrew. *Australian Art*. New York: Oxford University Press, 2001.

Schneebaum, Tobias. *Embodied Spirits: Ritual Carvings of the Asmat*. Salem, Mass.: Peabody Museum of Salem, 1990.

Smidt, Dirk, ed. *Asmat Art: Woodcarvings of Southwest New Guinea*. New York: Braziller in association with Rijksmuseum voor Volkenkunde, Leiden, 1993.

Starzecka, Dorota, ed. *Maori Art and Culture*. Chicago: Art Media Resources, 1996.

Sutton, Peter, ed. *Dreamings: The Art of Aboriginal Australia*. New York: Braziller in association with the Asia Society Galleries, 1988.

Thomas, Nicholas. *Oceanic Art*. London: Thames & Hudson, 1995.

Chapter 37: Africa, 1800 to 1980

Abiodun, Roland, Henry J. Drewal, and John Pemberton III, eds. *The Yoruba Artist: New Theoretical Perspectives on African Arts*. Washington, D.C.: Smithsonian Institution Press, 1994.

Bassani, Ezio. *Arts of Africa: 7,000 Years of African Art*. Milan: Skira, 2005.

Binkley, David A., and Patricia Darish. *Kuba*. Milan: 5 Continents, 2009.

Blier, Suzanne P. *The Royal Arts of Africa*. New York: Abrams, 1998.

Boyer, Alain-Michel. *Baule*. Milan: 5 Continents, 2007.

Cole, Herbert M. *Icons: Ideals and Power in the Art of Africa*. Washington, D.C.: National Museum of African Art, Smithsonian Institution, 1989.

————, ed. *I Am Not Myself: The Art of African Masquerade*. Los Angeles: UCLA Fowler Museum of Cultural History, 1985.

Cole, Herbert M., and Chike C. Aniakor. *Igbo Art: Community and Cosmos*. Los Angeles: UCLA Fowler Museum of Cultural History, 1984.

Fraser, Douglas F., and Herbert M. Cole, eds. *African Art and Leadership*. Madison: University of Wisconsin Press, 1972.

Geary, Christraud M. *Bamum*. Milan: 5 Continents, 2011.

————. *Things of the Palace: A Catalogue of the Bamum Palace Museum in Foumban (Cameroon)*. Weisbaden: Franz Steiner Verlag, 1983.

Glaze, Anita J. *Art and Death in a Senufo Village*. Bloomington: Indiana University Press, 1981.

Kasfir, Sidney L. *Contemporary African Art*. London: Thames & Hudson, 1999.

————. *West African Masks and Cultural Systems*. Tervuren: Musée Royal de l'Afrique Centrale, 1988.

Magnin, Andre, with Jacques Soulillou. *Contemporary Art of Africa*. New York: Abrams, 1996.

Nooter, Mary H. *Secrecy: African Art That Conceals and Reveals*. New York: Museum for African Art, 1993.

Oguibe, Olu, and Okwui Enwezor, eds. *Reading the Contemporary: African Art from Theory to the Marketplace*. London: Institute of International Visual Arts, 1999.

Perani, Judith, and Fred T. Smith. *The Visual Arts of Africa: Gender, Power, and Life Cycle Rituals*. Upper Saddle River, N.J.: Prentice Hall, 1998.

Perrois, Louis. *Fang*. Milan: 5 Continents, 2008.

Phillips, Ruth B. *Representing Women: Sande Masquerades of the Mende of Sierra Leone*. Los Angeles: UCLA Fowler Museum of Cultural History, 1995.

Plankensteiner, Barbara. *Benin*. Milan: 5 Continents, 2010.

Sieber, Roy, and Roslyn A. Walker. *African Art in the Cycle of Life*. Washington, D.C.: Smithsonian Institution Press, 1987.

Stepan, Peter. *Spirits Speak: A Celebration of African Masks*. Munich: Prestel, 2005.

Thompson, Robert F., and Joseph Cornet. *The Four Moments of the Sun: Kongo Art in Two Worlds*. Washington, D.C.: National Gallery of Art, 1981.

Vinnicombe, Patricia. *People of the Eland: Rock Paintings of the Drakensberg Bushmen as a Reflection of Their Life and Thought*. Pietermaritzburg: University of Natal Press, 1976.

Visonà, Monica B., ed. *A History of Art in Africa*. 2d ed. Englewood Cliffs, N.J.: Prentice Hall, 2007.

Vogel, Susan M. *Baule: African Art, Western Eyes*. New Haven, Conn.: Yale University Press, 1997.

————, ed. *Africa Explores: Twentieth-Century African Art*. New York: Te Neues, 1990.

Walker, Roslyn A. *Olowe of Ise: A Yoruba Sculptor to Kings*. Washington, D.C.: National Museum of African Art, 1998.

Wastiau, Boris. *Chokwe*. Milan: 5 Continents, 2008.

CREDITS

16-7: Far Eastern Seminar Collection, Princeton University Art Museum.; **16-8:** The Nelson-Atkins Museum of Art, Kansas City, Missouri. Purchase, Nelson Trust, 33-521. Photo: Robert Newcombe.; **16-9:** The Nelson-Atkins Museum of Art, Kansas City, Missouri. Purchase, Nelson Trust; **16-11:** © Asian Art Museum of San Francisco, The Avery Brundage Collectio; **16-12:** © The Trustees of the British Museum/Art Resource, NY; **16-13:** © Réunion des Musées Nationaux/Art Resource, NY; **16-13A:** © Wolfgang Kaehler/Corbis; **16-13B:** Photograph @ 2011 Museum of Fine Arts, Boston. 22.47; **16-14:** © TAO Images Limited/PhotoLibrary; **16-14A:** © Trustees of the British Museum; **16-15:** Cultural Relics Publishing House, Beijing.; **16-16:** Photograph © 2011 Museum of Fine Arts, Boston; **16-17:** © Inmagine; **16-18:** © Victoria & Albert Museum, London/Art Resource, NY; **16-19:** The Art Archive/National Palace Museum Taiwan/Picture Desk; **16-20:** Cultural Relics Publishing House, Beijing.; **16-21:** Asian Art Museum of San Francisco, The Avery Brundage Collection; **16-21A:** Nelson-Atkins Museum of Art; **16-22a:** © Bruno Barbier/PhotoLibrary; **16-23:** Collection of the National Palace Museum; **16-23A:** Xia Gui, Chinese, act. 1180-1224. Also known as: Hsia Kuei, Chinese, act. 1180-1224. Twelve Views of Landscape (Shan-shui shih-erh-ching), Southern Song Dynasty (1127-1279). Handscroll, ink on silk. 11 inches x 7 feet 6 3/4 inches (27.94 x 230.51 cm). Purchase: William Rockhill Nelson Trust, 32-159/2; **16-24:** Photograph © 2011 Museum of Fine Arts, Boston; **16-25:** Toyko National Museum. Image ©TNM Image Archives. Source: http://TnmArchives.jp; **16-26:** © DeA Picture Library/Art Resource, NY; **16-27:** National Museum of Korea; **16-28:** © Archivo Iconografico, S.A./Corbis; **16-29:** © Philadelphia Museum of Art/Corbis; **UNF 16-2:** © Chu Yong/PhotoLibrary; **UNF 16-3:** © Réunion des Musées Nationaux/Art Resource, NY; **UNF 16-4:** Photograph © 2011 Museum of Fine Arts, Boston; **UNF 16-5:** © Bruno Barbier/PhotoLibrary; **UNF 16-1:** Asian Art Museum of San Francisco, The Avery Brundage Collection.

Chapter 17—Opener: © Fotosearch/Photolibrary; **(detail 1):** © Robert Harding Picture Library/SuperStock; **(detail 2):** Iberfoto/The Image Works; **(detail 3):** Iberfoto/The Image Works; **(detail 4):** Horyuji, Nara. Photo: Benrido; **timeline:** Iberfoto/The Image Works; **17-2:** Toyko National Museum. Image ©TNM Image Archives.; **17-3:** Toyko National Museum. Image ©TNM Image Archives.; **17-4:** Georg Gerster/Photo Researchers, Inc.; **17-5:** Toyko National Museum. Image ©TNM Image Archives.; **17-6:** Jingu-Shicho, Mie; **17-7:** Iberfoto/The Image Works; **17-8:** Yakushiji Temple, Nara.; **17-9:** Iberfoto/The Image Works; **17-10:** Horyuji, Nara. Photo:Benrido; **17-11:** © Sakamoto Photo Research Laboratory/Corbis; **17-12:** Kyoogokokuji (Toji), Kyoto; **17-13:** © All Creation/PhotoLibrary; **17-13A:** © Francesco Venturi/Corbis; **17-13B:** Freer Gallery of Art, Smithsonian Institution, Washington, D.C.; **17-14:** The Gotoh Art Museum, Tokyo.; **17-15:** Chogosonshiji Temple, Nara, Japan; **17-16:** Todaiji, Nara; **17-17:** Asanuma Photo Studio Co.,Ltd, with permission from the Rokuharamitsuji-Temple, Kyoto; **17-17A:** Todaiji Temple; **17-18:** Photograph © 2011 Museum of Fine Arts, Boston; **17-19:** Zenrin-ji Temple.; **UNF 17-01:** Toyko National Museum. Image ©TNM Image Archives.; **UNF 17-2:** Georg Gerster/Photo Researchers, Inc.; **UNF 17-3:** Iberfoto/The Image Works; **UNF 17-4:** The Gotoh Art Museum, Tokyo.; **UNF 17-5:** Todaiji, Nara.

Chapter 18—Opener: © Yann Arthus-Bertrand/Corbis; **(detail 1):** © Yann Arthus-Bertrand/Corbis; **(detail 2):** © Yann Arthus-Bertrand/Corbis; **(detail 3):** © DeA Picture Library/Art Resource, NY; **(detail 4):** © Scala/Art Resource, NY; **timeline:** © Yann Arthus-Bertrand/Corbis; **18-2:** © JTB Photo/PhotoLibrary; **18-3:** © Erich Lessing/Art Resource, NY; **18-4:** © Museum Associates/LACMA/Art Resource, NY; **18-5:** © Georg Gerster/Photo Researchers, Inc.; **18-6:** © Gianni Dagli Orti/Corbis; **18-7:** © Richard Maschmeyer/age fotostock; **18-7A:** Image © The Cleveland Museum of Art (1963.252); **18-8:** Sean Sprague/The Image Works; **18-9:** © Stuart Westmorland/PhotoLibrary; **18-10:** © Yoshio Tomii Photo Studio/PhotoLibrary; **18-10A:** © Mel Longhurst/PhotoLibrary; **18-11:** akg-images/François Guénet; **18-12:** 207 Peabody Museum of Archaeology and Ethnology , Harvard University; **18-13:** © Dumbarton Oaks Pre-Columbian Collection, Washington, D.C.; **18-14:** The British Museum/HIP/The Image Works; **18-15:** © Danny Lehman/Corbis; **18-16:** © Yann Arthus-Bertrand/Corbis; **18-17:** © Scala/Art Resource, NY; **18-18:** © DeA Picture Library/Art Resource, NY; **18-19:** © Jonathan Blair/Corbis; **18-20:** Image copyright © The Metropolitan Museum of Art/Art Resource, NY; **18-21:** © Bildarchiv Steffens Henri Stierlin/The Bridgeman Art Library; **18-22:** Photograph © 2011 Museum of Fine Arts, Boston; **18-23:** Photography © The Art Institute of Chicago.; **18-24:** © SGM SGM/PhotoLibrary; **18-25:** © Nathan Benn/Corbis; **18-26:** Copyright © 2011 by Robert Frerck and Odyssey Productions, Inc.; **18-27:** © Hubert Stadler/Corbis; **18-28:** © National Museum of Archaeology, Anthropology, and History of Peru; **18-29:** © Werner Forman/Corbis; **18-30:** Ohio Historical Society; **18-30A:** © Michael S. Lewis/Encyclopedia/Corbis; **18-31:** © Tony Linck/SuperStock; **18-32:** © Werner Forman/Art Resource, NY; **18-33:** Photography © The Art Institute of Chicago; **18-33A:** © Richard A. Cooke/Encyclopedia/Corbis; **18-34:** © Mark Newman/PhotoLibrary; **UNF 18-01:** © JTB Photo/PhotoLibrary; **UNF 18-2:** © Yoshio Tomii Photo Studio/PhotoLibrary; **UNF 18-3:** © SGM SGM/PhotoLibrary; **UNF 18-4:** © National Museum of Archaeology, Anthropology, and History of Peru; **UNF 18-5:** © Mark Newman/PhotoLibrary.

Chapter 19—Opener: © The Trustees of the British Museum/Art Resource, NY; **timeline:** © The Trustees of the British Museum/Art Resource, NY; **19-2:** Jean-Dominique Lajoux; **Map 19-1:** © Cengage Learning; **19-3:** Photograph ©1980 Dirk Bakker; **19-4:** Artwork in the Social History Collection ofthe Izlko Museums. Image courtesy of Izlko Museums; **19-4A:** © Dirk Bakker; **19-5:** Photograph ©1980 Dirk Bakker; **19-6:** Photograph ©1980 Dirk Bakker; **19-6A:** Ancient Art and Architecture Collection Ltd./The Bridgeman Art Library International; **19-7:** © Scala/Art Resource, NY; **19-8:** Photograph by Franko Khoury, National Museum of African Art, Smithsonian Institution, Museum purchase, 86-12-1; **19-9:** © Yann Arthus-Bertrand/Corbis; **19-10:** © Gavin Hellier/PhotoLibrary; **19-11:** © Vanderharst/Robert Harding World Imagery/Getty Images; **19-12:** © Colin Hoskins/Alamy; **19-13:** Image copyright © The Metropolitan Museum of Art/Art Resource, NY; **19-13A:** © Werner Forman/Art Resource, NY; **19-14:** Museo Nazionale Preistorico e Etnografico Luigi Pigorini, Rome.; **UNF 19-01:** Jean-Dominique Lajoux; **UNF 19-2:** Photograph ©1980 Dirk Bakker; **UNF 19-3:** Photograph ©1980 Dirk Bakker; **UNF 19-4:** Yann Arthus-Bertrand/Corbis; **UNF 19-5:** © The Trustees of the British Museum/Art Resource, NY.

Chapter 20—Opener: Image copyright © The Metropolitan Museum of Art/Art Resource, NY; **Map 20-1:** © Cengage Learning; **timeline:** Image copyright © The Metropolitan Museum of Art/Art Resource, NY; **timeline:** Image copyright © The Metropolitan Museum of Art/Art Resource, NY; **20-2:** © Erich Lessing/Art Resource, NY; **20-2A:** © Jonathan Poore/Cengage Learning; **20-3a:** © Erich Lessing/Art Resource, NY; **20-3b:** © Erich Lessing/Art Resource, NY; **20-4:** © Scala/Art Resource, NY; **20-5A:** © Bildarchiv Preussischer Kulturbesitz/Art Resource, NY; **20-5:** © Erich Lessing/Art Resource, NY; **20-6:** © Erich Lessing/Art Resource, NY; **20-7:** Copyright © National Gallery, London; **20-8:** © Erich Lessing/Art Resource, NY; **20-8A:** © Jonathan Poore/Cengage Learning; **20-9:** Photograph © 208 Museum of Fine Arts, Boston; **20-9A:** Copyright © 1999 Board of Trustees, National Gallery of Art, Washington, D.C.; **20-10:** Image copyright © The Metropolitan Museum of Art/Art Resource, NY; **20-11A_a** © Giraudon/Art Resource, NY; **20-11:** The Art Archive/St Peters Church Louvain/Picture Desk; **20-11A_b** © Scala/Art Resource, NY.; **20-12:** © Scala/Art Resource, NY; **20-13:** © Erich Lessing/Art Resource, NY; **20-14:** © Erich Lessing/Art Resource, NY; **20-14A:** Image copyright © The Metropolitan Museum of Art/Art Resource, NY; **20-14B:** Image copyright © The Metropolitan Museum of Art/Art Resource, NY; **20-15:** © Réunion des Musées Nationaux/Art Resource, NY; **20-16:** © Réunion des Musées Nationaux/Art Resource, NY; **20-16A:** The Art Archive/Osterreichisches National Bibliothek Vienna/Eileen Tweedy/Picture Desk; **20-17a:** © Bildarchiv Preussischer Kulturbesitz/Art Resource, NY; **20-17b:** © Scala/Art Resource, NY; **20-18:** Musee d'Art et d'Histoire, Geneva; **20-18A:** Photo Credit: © Erich Lessing/Art Resource, NY; **20-19:** © Erich Lessing/Art Resource, NY; **20-20A:** John Rylands University Library, University of Manchester, Manchester.; **20-20:** © Erich Lessing/Art Resource, NY; **20-21:** © Historical Picture Archive/Corbis; **20-22:** © Scala/Art Resource, NY; **UNF 20-01:** © Erich Lessing/Art Resource, NY; **UNF 20-2:** Image copyright © The Metropolitan Museum of Art/Art Resource, NY; **UNF 20-3:** © Erich Lessing/Art Resource, NY; **UNF 20-4:** © Réunion des Musées Nationaux/Art Resource, NY; **UNF 20-5:** Historical Picture Archive/CORBIS.

Chapter 21—Opener: © Scala/Art Resource, NY; **timeline:** © Scala/Art Resource, NY; **Map 21-1:** © Cengage Learning; **21-2:** © Erich Lessing/Art Resource, NY; **21-3:** © Erich Lessing/Art Resource, NY; **21-4, 21-5, 21-6, 21-7, 21-8:** © Jonathan Poore/Cengage Learning; **21-9:** © Scala/Art Resource, NY; **21-10:** © Jonathan Poore/Cengage Learning; **21-12:** © Scala/Art Resource, NY; **21-12A:** akg-images/Rabatti - Domingie; **21-13:** © Scala/Art Resource, NY; **21-14:** © Scala/Art Resource, NY; **21-15:** © Jonathan Poore/Cengage Learning; **21-16:** Elio Ciol/Corbis; **21-17:** © 2010 Fred Kleiner; **21-18:** © Erich Lessing/Art Resource, NY; **21-19:** © Scala/Art Resource, NY; **21-20:** Canali Photobank, Italy; **21-21:** © Erich Lessing/Art Resource, NY; **21-22:** Canali Photobank, Italy; **21-23:** © Scala/Art Resource, NY; **21-24:** Canali Photobank, Italy; **21-25:** © Scala/Art Resource, NY; **21-25A:** © Nicolo Orsi Battaglini/Art Resource, NY; **21-26:** © Scala/Art Resource; **21-27:** © The Bridgeman Art Library; **21-28:** © National Gallery, London/Art Resource, NY; **21-29:** Summerfield Press Ltd.; **21-29A:** akg-images/Rabatti - Domingie; **21-30:** Image copyright © The Metropolitan Museum of Art/Art Resource, NY; **21-30A, 21-31:** © Jonathan Poore/Cengage Learning; **21-32:** © Alinari/Art Resource, NY; **21-32A:** © The Bridgeman Art Library; **21-33:** © Cengage Learning; **21-35:** © Cengage Learning; **21-34, 21-36, 21-36A, 21-37, 21-38, 21-39, 21-40:** © Jonathan Poore/Cengage Learning; **21-37A:** © 2010 Fred Kleiner; **21-41:** © Scala/Art Resource, Inc.; **21-41A:** © Scala/Art Resource, NY; **21-42:** © Scala/Art Resource, NY; **21-43A:** © Scala/Art Resource, NY; **21-43:** © Scala/Ministero per i Beni e le Attività culturali/Art Resource, NY; **21-44:** © Scala/Art Resource, NY; **21-45:** © Alinari/Art Resource, NY; **21-46:** © Cengage Learning; **21-47:** Canali Photobank, Italy; **21-48:** © Scala/Art Resource, NY; **21-49:** © Scala/Art Resource, NY; **21-49A:** © Alinari/The Bridgeman Art Library; **21-50:** © Erich Lessing/Art Resource, NY; **UNF 21-01:** © Scala/Art Resource, NY; **UNF 21-2:** © Erich Lessing/Art Resource, NY; **UNF 21-3:** © Jonathan Poore/Cengage Learning; **UNF 21-4:** © Scala/Ministero per i Beni e le Attività culturali/Art Resource, NY; **UNF 21-5:** © Alinari/Art Resource, NY.

Chapter 22—Opener: Canali Photobank; **(detail 1):** Photo Vatican Museums; **(detail 2):** © Bracchietti-Zigrosi/Vatican Museums; **(detail 3):** Vatican Museums and Galleries, Vatican City, Italy/The Bridgeman Art Library International; **(detail 4):** akg-images/Electa; **timeline:** akg-images/Electa; **22-2:** © Erich Lessing/Art Resource, NY; **22-3:** The Art Archive/National Gallery London/Eileen Tweedy/Picture Desk; **22-4:** © Alinari/Art Resource, NY; **22-3A:** © Scala/Art Resource, NY; **22-5:** © Réunion des Musées Nationaux/Art Resource, NY; **22-6:** Collection @ 2011 Her Majesty Queen Elizabeth II; **22-6A:** Bibliothèque de l'Institut de France/© Réunion des Musées Nationaux/Art Resource, NY; **22-7:** © Erich Lessing/Art Resource, NY; **22-8:** © Erich Lessing/Art Resource, NY; **22-8A:** © Scala/Art Resource, NY; **22-9:** © M. Sarri 1983/Photo Vatican Museums; **22-10:** © Scala/Ministero per i Beni e le Attività culturali/Art Resource, NY; **22-10A:** © Erich Lessing/Art Resource, NY; **22-11:** © Scala/Art Resource, NY; **22-12:** © Araldo de Luca/CORBIS; **22-13:** © Arte & Immagini srl/Corbis; **22-14:** © Scala/Art Resource, NY; **22-15:** © Scala/Art Resource, NY; **22-16:** © Scala/Art Resource, NY; **22-17:** Photo Vatican Museums; **22-18:** © Bracchietti-Zigrosi/Vatican Museums; **22-18A:** Vatican Museums and Galleries, Vatican City, Italy/The Bridgeman Art Library International; **22-18B_1:** Vatican Museums and Galleries, Vatican City, Italy/The Bridgeman Art Library International; **22-19:** akg-images/Electa; **22-20:** © Erich Lessing/Art Resource, NY; **22-21:** © Scala/Art Resource, NY; **22-22:** © Cengage Learning; **22-23:** © The Trustees of the British Museum/Art Resource, NY; **22-24:** © Cengage Learning; **22-25:** © Guido Alberto Rossi/Photolibrary; **22-26:** © Alinari Archives/Corbis; **22-26A:** © Guido Alberto Rossi/Photolibrary; **22-27:** © Alinari Archives/Corbis; **22-28:** © Mark Edward Smith/Photolibrary; **22-29:** © Cengage Learning; **22-30:** © 2010 Fred Kleiner; **22-30A:** © Scala/Art Resource, NY; **22-31:** © John Heseltine/Corbis; **22-31A:** © The Frick Collection, NY. 1915.1.3; **22-32:** © Scala/Art Resource, NY; **22-33:** © 1999 Board of Trustees, National Gallery of Art,

Washington, D.C.; **22-34:** © Cameraphoto Arte, Venice/Art Resource, NY; **22-35:** © Erich Lessing/Art Resource, NY; **22-36:** © Scala/Art Resource, NY; **22-37:** © Scala/Art Resource, NY; **22-38:** © Erich Lessing/Art Resource, NY; **22-39:** © Scala/Ministero per i Beni e le Attività culturali/Art Resource, NY; **22-40:** © Erich Lessing/Art Resource, NY; **22-40A:** Photograph © 2011 National Museum of Women in the Arts; **22-41:** © Scala/Art Resource, NY; **22-42:** © Scala/Art Resource, NY; **22-42A:** The Art Archive/Pinacoteca Nazionale di Siena/Alfredo Dagli Orti/Picture Desk; **22-43:** © Erich Lessing/Art Resource, NY; **22-44:** © Scala/Art Resource, NY; **22-45:** © National Gallery, London; **22-46A:** Image copyright © The Metropolitan Museum of Art/Art Resource, NY; **22-46:** © The Bridgeman Art Library International; **22-47:** © The Bridgeman Art Library International; **22-48:** © Scala/Art Resource, NY; **22-49:** © Scala/Art Resource, NY; **22-50:** Canali Photobank, Italy; **22-51:** © Alinari/Art Resource, NY; **22-52:** © Erich Lessing/Art Resource, NY; **22-52A:** © Lauros/Giraudon/The Bridgeman Art Library; **22-53:** © 206 Fred S. Kleiner; **22-54:** Superstock/Photolibrary; **22-54A:** © Scala/Art Resource, NY; **22-55:** © Jonathan Poore/Cengage Learning; **22-56:** The Art Archive/Gianni Dagli Orti/Picture Desk; **22-57:** © Cengage Learning; **UNF 22-01:** © Arte & Immagini srl/Corbis; **UNF 22-2:** © Scala/Art Resource, NY; **UNF 22-3:** © Erich Lessing/Art Resource, NY; **UNF 22-4:** © Scala/Art Resource, NY; **UNF 22-5:** © Erich Lessing/Art Resource, NY.

Chapter 23—Opener: © Institut Amatller D'art Hispànic; (all details) akg-images/Electa; **timeline:** © Institut Amatller D'art Hispànic; **23-2:** © Musée Unterlinden, Colmar Musée Unterlinden, Colmar Inv. 88.RP.139; **23-3:** © The Trustees of the British Museum/Art Resource, NY; **23-3A:** © Erich Lessing/Art Resource, NY; **23-4:** akg-images; **23-4A:** © Graphische Sammlung Albertina, Vienna, Austria/The Bridgeman Art Library; **23-5:** Photograph © 2011 Museum of Fine Arts, Boston; **23-5A:** © The Trustees of The British Museum/Art Resource, NY; **23-6:** © Victoria & Albert Museum, London/Art Resource, NY; **23-7a:** © Bildarchiv Preussischer Kulturbesitz/Art Resource, NY; **23-7b:** © Bildarchiv Preussischer Kulturbesitz/Art Resource, NY; **23-8:** © The Trustees of The British Museum; **23-9:** Staatliche Kunsthalle, Karlsruhe.; **23-10:** © Bildarchiv Preussischer Kulturbesitz/Art Resource, NY; **23-11:** © National Gallery, London/Art Resource, NY; **23-11A:** © Scala/Art Resource, NY; **23-12:** © Réunion des Musées Nationaux/Art Resource, NY; **23-13:** © Jonathan Poore/Cengage Learning; **23-14:** © Jonathan Poore/Cengage Learning; **23-14A:** © 209 Fred. S. Kleiner; **23-15:** © Bildarchiv Preussischer Kulturbesitz/Art Resource, NY; **23-15A:** © Erich Lessing/Art Resource, NY; **23-16:** © Réunion des Musées Nationaux/Art Resource, NY; **23-17:** Uppsala University Art Collection; **23-18:** Oeffentliche Kunstsammlung Basel, photo Martin Bühler; **23-19:** The Royal Collection © 2011 Her Majesty Queen Elizabeth II; **23-20:** © Erich Lessing/Art Resource, NY; **23-21:** © Bildarchiv Preussischer Kulturbesitz/Art Resource, NY; **23-22:** Kunsthistorisches Museum, Vienna; **23-22A:** © Scala/Art Resource, NY; **23-23:** © Institut Amatller D'art Hispànic; **23-23A:** © John Elk III; **23-24:** © Adam Woolfitt/Photolibrary; **23-25:** © Scala/Art Resource, NY; **23-26:** © The Metropolitan Museum of Art/Art Resource, NY; **UNF 23-01:** Photograph © 2011 Museum of Fine Arts, Boston; **UNF 23-2:** © National Gallery, London/Art Resource, Ny; **UNF 23-3:** © Réunion des Musées Nationaux/Art Resource, NY; **UNF 23-4:** Kunsthistorisches Museum, Vienna; **UNF 23-5:** © Institut Amatller D'art Hispànic.

Chapter 24—Opener: The Art Archive/Gianni Dagli Orti/Picture Desk; **(detail 1):** © Massimo Listri/Corbis; **(detail 2):** © 2011 Fred Kleiner; **(detail 3):** © Vanni/Art Resource, NY; **(detail 4):** akg-images/Gerard Degeorge; timeline © Vanni/Art Resource, NY; **24-2:** akg-images/Pirozzi; **24-3:** © Andrea Jemolo/Corbis; **24-4:** © Cubo-images/Photolibrary; **24-4A:** Canali Photobank, Italy; **24-5:** akg-images/Joseph Martin; **Map 24-1:** © Cengage Learning; **24-6:** © Scala/Art Resource, NY; **24-6A:** © Araldo de Luca/Corbis; **24-7:** © Araldo de Luca; **24-8:** akg-images/Pirozzi; **24-9:** © Scala/Art Resource, NY; **24-9A:** © Scala/Art Resource, NY; **24-11:** © Bednorz-Images; **24-12:** © Raimund Kutter/Photolibrary; **24-13:** © Cengage Learning; **24-14A:** © Alinari/The Bridgeman Art Library; **24-14:** © Scala/Ministero per i Beni e le Attività culturali/Art Resource, NY; **24-15:** © Alinari/Art Resource, NY; **24-16:** © Scala/Art Resource, NY; **24-17:** © Scala/Art Resource, NY; **24-17A:** Image copyright © The Metropolitan Museum of Art/Art Resource, NY; **24-18A:** © Scala/Art Resource, NY; **24-18:** © Scala/Art Resource, NY; **24-19:** © Alinari/Art Resource, NY; **24-20:** The Royal Collection © 2011 Her Majesty Queen Elizabeth II; **24-21:** © Nimatallah/Art Resource, NY; **24-22:** © The Bridgeman Art Library International; **24-23:** © Scala/Art Resource, NY; **24-24:** Summerfield Press Ltd.; **24-25:** © Erich Lessing/Art Resource, NY; **24-25A:** © Erich Lessing/Art Resource, NY; **24-26:** © Erich Lessing/Art Resource, NY; **24-27:** © Wadsworth Atheneum Museum of Art/Art Resource, NY; **24-28:** © Victoria & Albert Museum, London/Art Resource, NY; **24-28A:** © Scala/Art Resource, NY; **24-28B:** © 2011 The Frick Collection, NY; **24-29:** © Scala/Art Resource, NY; **24-30:** © Erich Lessing/Art Resource, NY; **UNF 24-01:** © Bednorz-Images; **UNF 24-2:** © Araldo de Luca; **UNF 24-3:** © Jonathan Poore/Cengage Learning; **UNF 24-4:** Summerfield Press Ltd.; **UNF 24-5:** © Erich Lessing/Art Resource, NY.

Chapter 25—Opener: akg-images; **timeline:** akg-images; **25-01A:** © Erich Lessing/Art Resource, NY; **25-2:** IRPA-KIK, Brussels, www.kikirpa.be; **25-2A:** © Erich Lessing/Art Resource, NY; **25-3:** © Erich Lessing/Art Resource, NY; **25-4:** © Scala/Art Resource, NY; **25-5:** © Réunion des Musées Nationaux/Art Resource, NY; **25-6:** © Scala/Art Resource, NY; **25-7:** Centraal Museum, Utrecht, photo Ernst Moritz, The Hague; **25-8:** © Alinari/The Bridgeman Art Library; **25-9:** Frans Halsmuseum, Haarlem; **25-10:** Frans Halsmuseum, Haarlem; **25-11:** National Gallery of Art; **25-12:** © Erich Lessing/Art Resource, NY; **25-13:** © The Bridgeman Art Library; **25-13A:** akg-images; **25-14:** © The Bridgeman Art Library; **25-15:** © English Heritage Photo Library/The Bridgeman Art Library International; **25-15A:** © 2011 The Frick Collection, NY. 196.1.97; **25-16:** © The Pierpont Morgan Library/Art Resource, NY; **25-17:** © National Gallery, London/Art Resource, NY; **25-18:** Mauritshuis, The Hague; **25-18A:** © Erich Lessing/Art Resource, NY; **25-18B:** © Giraudon/The Bridgeman Art Library; **25-19:** National Gallery of Art; **25-20:** © Erich Lessing/Art Resource, NY; **25-20A:** akg-images; **25-21:** Rijksmuseum, Amsterdam; **25-22:** The Bridgeman Art Library International; **25-23:** The Toledo Museum of Art, OH. Purchased with funds from the Libbey Endowment, Gift of Edward Drummond Libbey, 1956.57; **25-24:** © Réunion des Musées Nationaux/Art Resource, NY; **25-25:** © Jonathan Poore/Cengage Learning; **25-26:** © Yann Arthus-Bertrand/Altitude; **25-27:** © Massimo Listri/Corbis; **25-28:** g Bernard Annebicque/CORBIS SYGMA; **25-29:** akg-images/Paul M. R. Maeyaert; **25-30:** © Jonathan Poore/Cengage Learning; **25-31:** © Erich Lessing/Art Resource, NY; **25-32:** Photograph: The Art Institute of Chicago.; **25-32A:** © Scala/Art Resource, NY; **25-33:** Photo copyright © Philadelphia Museum of Art, E1950-2-1; **25-34:** © Réunion des Musées Nationaux/Art Resource, NY; **25-35:** © Erich Lessing/Art Resource, NY; **25-36:** © Erich Lessing/Art Resource, NY; **25-37:** © Angelo Hornak/CORBIS; **25-38:** © Angelo Hornak/CORBIS; **UNF 25-01:** © Scala/Art Resource, NY; **UNF 25-2:** © The Pierpont Morgan Library/Art Resource, NY; **UNF 25-3:** National Gallery of Art; **UNF 25-4:** © Erich Lessing/Art Resource, NY; **UNF 25-5:** © Angelo Hornak/CORBIS.

Chapter 26—Opener: © Bridgeman-Giraudon/Art Resource, NY; **26-01A:** © Jason Hawkes/Terra/Corbis; **Map 26-1:** © Cengage Learning; **timeline:** © Bridgeman-Giraudon/Art Resource, NY; **26-2:** akg-images/Bildarchiv Monheim; **26-3:** © Erich Lessing/Art Resource, NY; **26-3A:** Hervé Champollion/akg-images; **26-4:** © Erich Lessing/Art Resource, NY; **26-5A:** ~~akg-images/Bildarchiv Monheim;~~ **26-5B:** © Erich Lessing/Art Resource, NY; **26-6:** The Art Archive/Musée du Louvre Paris/Gianni Dagli Orti; **26-7:** © Scala/Art Resource, NY; **26-7A:** © Bildarchiv Preussischer Kulturbesitz/Art Resource, NY; **26-8:** By kind permission of the Trustees of the Wallace Collection, London.; **26-9:** © Wallace Collection, London, UK/The Bridgeman Art Library; **26-10:** © Scala/Ministero per i Beni e le Attività culturali/Art Resource, NY; **26-11:** Image copyright © The Metropolitan Museum of Art/Art Resource, NY; **26-11A:** © National Gallery, London/Art Resource, NY; **26-12:** The Art Archive/John Meek/Picture Desk; **26-13:** © Réunion des Musées Nationaux/Art Resource, NY; **26-14:** The Art Archive/Musée du Louvre Paris/Gianni Dagli Orti; **26-15:** Summerfield Press, Ltd; **26-15A:** © Erich Lessing/Art Resource, NY; **26-16:** Image copyright © The Metropolitan Museum of Art/Art Resource, NY; **26-17:** National Gallery, London; **26-18:** The National Gallery of Art; **26-19:** © National Gallery, London, UK/The Bridgeman Art Library; **26-20:** National Gallery of Canada; **26-21:** Photograph © 2011 Museum of Fine Arts, Boston, 30.781; **26-22:** © Scala/Art Resource, NY; **26-23:** © Peter Aprahamian/CORBIS; **26-23A:** Electa/akg-images; **26-24:** Photo: Katherine Wetzel © Virginia Museum of Fine Arts; **26-25:** © Réunion des Musées Nationaux/Art Resource, NY; **26-26:** © Scala/Art Resource, NY; **26-27:** © Jonathan Poore/Cengage Learning; **26-27A:** akg-images/Bildarchiv Monheim; **26-28:** © Eric Crichton/Encyclopedia/Corbis; **26-28A:** akg/Bildarchiv Monheim; **26-29:** © ART on FILE/Corbis Art/Corbis; **26-30:** Thomas Jefferson Foundation; **26-31:** © Michael Freeman/Value Art/Corbis; **26-32:** Photo © The Library of Virginia; **26-33:** © Smithsonian American Art Museum, Washington, DC/Art Resource, NY; **UNF 26-01:** akg-images/Bildarchiv Monheim; **UNF 26-2:** © Bridgeman-Giraudon/Art Resource, NY; **UNF 26-3:** © Scala/Art Resource, NY; **UNF 26-4:** Photo: Katherine Wetzel © Virginia Museum of Fine Arts; **UNF 26-5:** © Jonathan Poore/Cengage Learning; **UNF 26-5:** © Jonathan Poore/Cengage Learning.

Chapter 27—Opener: © Réunion des Musées Nationaux/Art Resource, NY; **timeline:** © Réunion des Musées Nationaux/Art Resource, NY; **27-01A:** © Erich Lessing/Art Resource, NY; **27-2:** © Réunion des Musées Nationaux/Art Resource, NY; **27-2A:** © Erich Lessing/Art Resource, NY; **27-3:** © Jonathan Poore/Cengage Learning; **27-4:** © Scala/Ministero per i Beni e le Attività culturali/Art Resource, NY; **27-4A:** © Réunion des Musées Nationaux/Art Resource, NY; **27-5:** © Réunion des Musées Nationaux/Art Resource, NY; **27-5A:** © Réunion des Musées Nationaux/Art Resource, NY; **27-6:** © Réunion des Musées Nationaux/Art Resource, NY; **27-7:** © Réunion des Musées Nationaux/Art Resource, NY; **27-8:** © The Bridgeman Art Library International; **27-9:** © The Pierpont Morgan Library/Art Resource, NY; **27-10:** Image copyright © The Metropolitan Museum of Art/Art Resource, NY; **27-10A:** © Erich Lessing/Art Resource, NY; **27-11:** The Art Archive/Museo del Prado Madrid/Gianni Dagli Orti/Picture Desk; **27-12:** © Erich Lessing/Art Resource, NY; **27-13:** © Erich Lessing/Art Resource, NY; **27-13A:** © Réunion des Musées Nationaux/Art Resource, NY; **27-14:** © Giraudon/Art Resource, NY; **27-15:** © Réunion des Musées Nationaux/Art Resource, NY; **27-15A:** © Erich Lessing/Art Resource, NY; **27-16:** © Réunion des Musées Nationaux/Art Resource, NY; **27-17A:** © Erich Lessing/Art Resource, NY; **27-17:** The Art Archive/Musée d'Orsay Paris/Gianni Dagli Orti/Picture Desk; **27-18:** © Jonathan Poore/Cengage Learning; **27-19:** © Bildarchiv Preussischer Kulturbesitz/Art Resource, NY; **27-20:** © Bildarchiv Preussischer Kulturbesitz/Art Resource, NY; **27-21:** © National Gallery, London/Art Resource, NY; **27-22:** Photograph © 2011 Museum of Fine Arts, Boston, 99.22; **27-23:** Image copyright © The Metropolitan Museum of Art/Art Resource, NY; **27-24:** © Smithsonian American Art Museum, Washington, DC/Art Resource, NY; **27-25:** Photo copyright © The Cleveland Museum of Art; **27-26:** © Staatliche Kunstsammlungen Dresden/The Bridgeman Art Library; **27-27:** © Erich Lessing/Art Resource, NY; **27-28:** © Réunion des Musées Nationaux/Art Resource, NY; **27-29:** © Erich Lessing/Art Resource, NY; **27-30:** Image copyright © The Metropolitan Museum of Art/Art Resource, NY; **27-31:** Image copyright © The Metropolitan Museum of Art/Art Resource, NY; **27-32:** © Erich Lessing/Art Resource, NY; **27-33:** © Scala/Art Resource, NY; **27-33A:** © The Bridgeman Art Library International; **27-34:** © Bildarchiv Preussischer Kulturbesitz/Art Resource, NY; **27-35:** Image copyright © The Metropolitan Museum of Art/Art Resource, NY; **27-36:** Photo copyright © Philadelphia Museum of Art, 207-1-1; **27-37:** Photograph © 2011 Museum of Fine Arts, Boston, 19.124; **27-38:** © Art Resource, NY; **27-39:** Howard University Gallery of Art, Washington, D.C; **27-40:** © Tate, London/Art Resource, NY; **27-41:** © Tate, London/Art Resource, NY; **27-42:** akg-images/Bildarchiv Monheim; **27-43:** © Travel Pix/Robert Harding; **27-43A:** © Leo Sorel; **27-44:** © Roger Antrobus/CORBIS; **27-45:** © Jonathan Poore/Cengage Learning; **27-46:** © Collection Artedia/Leemage; **27-47:** Private Collection/The Stapleton Collection/The Bridgeman Art Library International; **27-46A:** © Bettmann/Corbis; **27-48:** © Louis Daguerre/Time & Life Pictures/Getty

MUSEUM INDEX

Note: *Figure numbers in blue indicate bonus images.*

1131

Pietà (unfinished) (Michelangelo
Buonarroti), 617
Museo Nazionale del Bargello
David (Donatello), 568
David (Verrocchio), 569
Hercules and Antaeus (Pollaiuolo), 569
Sacrifice of Isaac (Brunelleschi), 562
Sacrifice of Isaac (Ghiberti), 562
Saint George (Donatello), 564
Saint George and the Dragon, Or San
Michele (Donatello), 565
Or San Michele
Four Crowned Saints (Nanni di Banco),
563
Madonna and Child (della Robbia),
21-36A
Saint Mark (Donatello), 564
tabernacle (Orcagna), 14-19A
Palazzo Pitti: *Consequences of War*
(Rubens), 700
San Lorenzo: tomb of Giuliano de' Medici
(Michelangelo Buonarroti), 613
San Marco: *Annunciation* (Fra Angelico),
576
Sant'Apollonia: *Last Supper* (Andrea del
Castagno), 577
Santa Croce: tomb of Leonardo Bruni
(Rossellino), 570
Santa Felicità: *Entombment of Christ*
(Pontormo), 632
Santa Maria del Carmine
Expulsion of Adam and Eve from Eden
(Masaccio), 575
Tribute Money (Masaccio), 574
Santa Maria Gloriosa dei Frari: *Madonna
of the Pesaro Family* (Titian), 628
Santa Maria Novella
Birth of the Virgin (Ghirlandaio), 579
Holy Trinity (Masaccio), 575
Fort Worth, Texas (U.S.A.)
Amon Carter Museum: *The Steerage*
(Stieglitz), 869
Kimbell Art Museum
Bodhisattva Maitreya, Prakhon Chai
(sculpture), 15-29A
Chibinda Ilunga, Chokwe (sculpture),
1068
Frankfurt (Germany): Städelsches
Kunstinstitut: *Blinding of Samson*
(Rembrandt), 25-13A

G

Geneva (Switzerland)
Bibliotheca Bodmeriana: Initial R, recto
of a passional, 12-23A
Musée Barbier-Mueller
Abelam yam mask, Maprik district, 1048
"Beautiful Lady" dance mask, Senufo,
1074
reliquary guardian figure (mbulu
ngulu), Kota, 1064
Prince Sadruddin Aga Khan Collection:
Shahnama (Book of Kings) (Sultan-
Muhammad), 303
Ghent (Belgium): Saint Bavo Cathedral:
Ghent Altarpiece (van Eyck and van
Eyck), 540, 541
Glasgow (Scotland)
Glasgow Art Galleries and Museum, 807
Ingram Street Tea Room
(reconstruction), 828
Gloucester (England): Gloucester Cathedral:
Tomb of Edward II, 570, 13-42A
Great Zimbabwe (Zimbabwe): Great
Zimbabwe Site Museum: monolith
with bird and crocodile (sculpture),
531
Güstrow (Germany): Güstrow Cathedral:
War Monument (Barlach)
(destroyed), 875
Gyeongju (Korea): Gyeongju National
Museum: crown, Cheonmachong
tomb, Hwangnam-dong, 470

H

Haarlem (Netherlands)
Frans Halsmuseum
Archers of Saint Hadrian (Hals), 704

*The Women Regents of the Old Men's
Home at Haarlem* (Hals), 705
The Hague (Netherlands)
Mauritshuis
Anatomy Lesson of Dr. Tulp
(Rembrandt), 706
View of Delft (Vermeer), 25-18B
*View of Haarlem from the Dunes at
Overveen* (Ruisdael), 710
Hamburg (Germany)
Hamburger Kunsthalle
Saint Mary of Egypt among Sinners
(Nolde), 840
Three Women in a Village Church
(Leibl), 782
Wanderer above a Sea of Mist
(Friedrich), 700
Hartford, Connecticut (U.S.A.): Wadsworth
Athaneum Museum of Art: *Saint
Serapion* (Zurbarán), 689
Herakleion (Greece)
Archaeological Museum
bull-leaping, palace, Knossos (fresco),
91
Harvesters Vase, Hagia Triada, 95
Kamares Ware jar, Phaistos, 93
lintel of Temple A, Prinias, 5-6B
Marine Style octopus flask, Palaikastro,
93
Minoan woman or goddess (*La
Parisienne*), Knossos (fresco), 90
sarcophagus, Hagia Triada, 84
Herculaneum (Italy)
House of Neptune and Amphitrite: Neptune
and Amphitrite (mosaic), 196
Samnite House: First Style wall painting,
191
Hereford (England): Hereford Cathedral:
Mappamundi of Henry III (Richard
de Bello), 13-38B
Hildesheim (Germany)
Dom-Museum: doors with relief panels,
Saint Michael's, Hildesheim, 326, 327
Römer-and Pelizaeus-Museum: Hemiunu
seated statue, Gizeh, 3-13B
Honolulu, Hawaii (U.S.A.)
Bishop Pauahi Museum: feather cloak,
Hawaii, 1058
Honolulu Academy of Arts: *Carnations
and Garden Rock* (Wen Shu), 999
Huntington, New York (U.S.A.): Hekscher
Museum of Art: *The Eclipse of the
Sun* (Grosz), 872

I

Ife (Nigeria)
Museum of Ife Antiquities
head of an Ife king, Wunmonije
compound, Ile-Ife (sculpture), 19-6A
king, Ita Yemoo, Ife (sculpture), 527
Indianapolis, Indiana (U.S.A.): Indianapolis
Museum of Art: *Still Life with a Late
Ming Ginger Jar* (Kalf), 713

J

Jerusalem: Israel Museum: *Allegiance and
Wakefulness* (Neshat), 952
Jiaxiang (China): Wu family shrines: The
archer Yi(?) and a reception in a
mansion (rubbing of relief
sculpture), 456

K

Kansas City, Missouri (U.S.A.)
Nelson-Atkins Museum of Art
Bather (Lipchitz), 29-20A
bi disk with dragons, Jincun(?), 454
Bodhisattva Guanyin seated on
Potalaka, Shanxi (sculpture), 16-21A
Masks (Nolde), 29-6A
model of a house, Han dynasty, 457
Poet on a Mountaintop (Shen Zhou),
33-12A
Twelve Views from a Thatched Hut (Xia
Gui), 16-23A
Karachi (Pakistan): National Museum of
Pakistan: robed male figure,
Mohenjo-daro, 425

Karlsruhe (Germany): Staatliche Kunsthalle:
Judgment of Paris (Cranach), 654
Khajuraho (India): Vishvanatha Temple:
mithuna reliefs, 440
Klosterneuberg (Austria): Stiftsmuseum:
Klosterneuburg Altar (Nicholas of
Verdun), 392, 13-44A
Kolkata (India): Rabindra Bharati Society:
Bharat Mata (Mother India) (Tagore),
32-10A
Kyoto (Japan)
Kyoogokukuji (Toji): Taizokai (Womb
World) mandara (hanging scroll),
483
National Museum of Modern Art: large
bowl, Showa period (Hamada), 1019
Zenrinji: *Amida Descending over the
Mountains* (hanging scroll), 488
Kyoto(Japan): Rokuharamitsuji: portrait
statue of the priest Kuya preaching
(Kosho), 487
Kyunggi-Do (Korea): Hoam Art Museum:
Geumgangsan Mountains (Jeong
Seon), 1002

L

L'Aquila (Italy): Museo Nazionale d'Abruzzo:
relief with funerary procession,
Amiternum, 7-11A
Lagos (Nigeria)
National Museum
equestrian figure on fly-whisk hilt, Igbo
Ukwu (sculpture), 526
Nok head, Rafin Kura (sculpture), 525
roped water basin on a stand, Igbo
Ukwu, 19-4A
seated man, Tada (sculpture), 528
Lambayeque (Peru): Bruning Archaeological
Museum: ear ornament, Moche,
Sipán, 512
Lanzhou (China): Gansu Provincial
Museum: flying horse, tomb of
Governor-General Zhang, Wuwei
(sculpture), 466
Liège (France): Saint-Barthélemy: *Baptism of
Christ* (Rainer of Huy), 353
Lima (Peru)
Instituto Nacional de Cultura: *Raimondi
Stele*, Chavín de Huántar, 508
Museo Arqueológico Rafael Larco
Herrera: vessel in the shape of a
portrait head, Moche, 511
Museo Nacional de Antropologia
Arqueología e História del Perú:
Lima Tapestry, Wari, 513
Lincoln (Nebraska): Sheldon Memorial Art
Gallery: *New York, Night* (O'Keeffe),
868
London (England)
British Library: *Lindisfarne Gospels*, 313,
314
British Museum
A'a, Rurutu (sculpture), 1056
Achilles killing Penthesilea (Exekias),
Vulci (vase painting), 5-20A
*Admonitions of the Instructress to the
Court Ladies* (Gu Kaizhi), 459
Altar to the Hand, Benin (cast bronze),
520
ancestral screen (nduen fobara),
Kalabari Ijaw, 1060
Ashurbanipal hunting lions, palace of
Ashurbanipal, Nineveh (relief
sculpture), 48
Ashurnasirpal II with attendants and
soldier, Kalhu (mural), 47
Assyrian archers pursuing enemies,
Kalhu (relief sculpture), 47
banquet scene cylinder seal, tomb of
Pu-abi, Ur, 39
belt buckle, Sutton Hoo ship burial,
11-3A
*Bodhisattva Guanyin as the Guide of
Souls*, Dunhuang Grottoes (wall
painting), 16-14A
bull-headed harp with inlaid sound
box, tomb of Pu-abi, Ur, 38
canoe prow ornament, Chuuk, 1050

centauromachy, Parthenon metope,
Athens (relief sculpture), 136
ceremonial ax in the form of a were-
jaguar, Olmec, La Venta (sculpture),
494
Corinthian black-figure amphora with
animal friezes, Rhodes, 110
Crucifixion (ivory carving), 251
head of a queen mother, Benin
(sculpture), 19-13A
head of Lono, Hawaii, 1057
Helios and his horses, and Dionysos
(Herakles?), Parthenon east
pediment, Athens (sculpture), 137
Kuka'ilimoku, Hawaii (sculpture), 1056
last judgment of Hunefer, Thebes
(scroll), 80
Law and Gospel (Lucas Cranach the
Elder), 653
medal showing Bramante's design for
Saint Peter's (Caradosso), 619
Mildenhall Treasure, 250
mosque lamp of Sayf al-Din
Tuquztimur, 301
mummy portrait of a priest of Serapis,
Hawara (encaustic painting), 218
mummy portrait of Artemidorus,
Hawara (encaustic painting), 7-62A
musicians and dancers, tomb of
Nebamun, Thebes (mural), 75
Nebamun hunting fowl, tomb of
Nebamun, Thebes (mural), 75
Ohisa of the Takashima Tea Shop
(Utamaro), 34-12A
Panathenaic Festival procession frieze,
Parthenon, Athens, 138
purse cover, Sutton Hoo ship burial, 309
Saint Michael the Archangel (ivory
panel), 257
Shield Jaguar and Lady Xoc, Yaxchilán
(relief sculpture), 503
shrine of the king's head, royal palace,
Ikere (Olowe of Ise), 1072
The Standard of Ur, 36, 37
Suicide of Judas (ivory carving), 251
Summer Trees (Song), 31-22A
Taharqo as a sphinx, Kawa (sculpture),
81
Three goddesses (Hestia, Dione, and
Aphrodite?), Parthenon east
pediment, Athens (sculpture), 137
Winchester Psalter, 12-35A
Witches' Sabbath (Baldung Grien), 649
Woman with Dead Child (Kollwitz), 843
Cortauld Institute of Art Gallery: *A Bar at
the Folies-Bergère* (Manet), 807
Fridart Foundation: *The Dance* (Derain),
839
Kenwood House: *Self-Portrait*, ca. 1659-
1660 (Rembrandt), 708
National Gallery
Battle of San Romano (Uccello), 580
Breakfast Scene, Marriage à la Mode
(Hogarth), 741
*Distant View of Dordrecht, with a
Milkmaid and Four Cows, and Other
Figures (The "Large Dort")* (Cuyp), 710
Embarkation of the Queen of Sheba
(Claude Lorrain), 9
*An Experiment on a Bird in the Air-
Pump* (Wright of Derby), 26-11A
The French Ambassadors (Holbein the
Younger), 656
Giovanni Arnolfini and His Wife (van
Eyck), 542
The Haywain (Constable), 772
Landscape with Aeneas at Delos (Claude
Lorrain), 750
Lord Heathfield (Reynolds), 742
*Madonna and Child with Saint Anne
and the Infant Saint John*, cartoon for
(Leonardo da Vinci), 602
Man in a Red Turban (van Eyck), 543
Meeting of Bacchus and Ariadne
(Titian), 629
Summer's Day (Morisot), 28-7A
Venus, Cupid, Folly, and Time
(Bronzino), 634

SUBJECT INDEX

Notes:
- *Page numbers in italics indicate illustrations.*
- *Page numbers in italics followed by b indicate bonus images in the text.*
- *Page numbers in italics followed by map indicate maps.*
- *Figure numbers in blue indicate bonus images.*

Caravaggio (Michelangelo Merisi) (continued)
Conversion of Saint Paul, 682–683, *683*
Entombment, 682, *682b*, 24-18A
and La Tour, 722
Musicians, 681, *681b*, 24-17A
and Rembrandt, 706, 25-13A
and Ribera, 688
and Rubens, 697, 698
and ter Brugghen, 702
and van Honthorst, 702
and Velázquez, 689, 692
Carcassonne (France), 382–383, *382*
Saint-Nazaire Cathedral, 383
cardo, 189
Cardona (Spain): Sant Vicenç, 337, *337b*, 339, 12-4A
Caricature (journal), 779
Carlo Emanuele II (duke of Savoy), 24-9A, 24-14A
Carlsmelite order, 404
Carnations and Garden Rock (Wen Shu), 998–999, *999*
Caroline Islands art, 1050, 1052
Caroline minuscule, 317
Carolingian, 317
Carolingian art, *308map*, 317–324
architecture, 320–324, 11-19A
books, 5, 317, 318–320, 11-13A, 11-15A
sculpture, 317–318
Carolingian Empire, 270, *308map*
See also Carolingian art
Carpeaux, Jean-Baptiste
The Dance, Paris Opéra, 825, *825b*, 28-31A
Ugolino and His Children, 824–825, *824*, 826
carpet from the funerary mosque of Safi al-Din (Maqsud of Kashan), 300–301, *301*
carpet pages, 311, 312, 313
carpets, 300–301
Carrà, Carlo, 854
Carracci, Agostino, 679
Carracci, Annibale
and Claude Lorrain, 720
Flight into Egypt, 679–680, *679*
Loves of the Gods, Palazzo Farnese, Rome, 680–681, *680*
and Mengs, 26-23A
and Poussin, 25-32A
and Reni, 684
and Rubens, 697
Carracci, Ludovico, 679
Carrying of the Cross, 241
Carson, Pirie, Scott Building, Chicago (Sullivan), 832, *832*
Carter, Howard, 78
Carthaginians, 181
Carthusian order, 537–538
cartography, 13-38B
cartoons (preliminary drawings), 408, 602–603
carving, 11
caryatids, 72, 117, 119, 140, 141, 200, 212, 370, 5-17A
caryatids, Erechtheion, Athens, *140*, 141, 200, 212
Casa de Montejo, Mérida, *664b*, 23-23A
Casa Milá, Barcelona (Gaudí), 829, *829*
Casino Rospigliosi, Rome, 684–685, *685*
Cassatt, Mary, 862
The Bath, 809, *809*
Japonisme and, 808
and the Steins, 844
cassone/cassoni, 628, 631
cast iron, 737, 789, 790–791, 830, 832
caste system, 427
castellum. *See* westwork
Castiglione, Baldassare, 22-10A
Castiglione, Giuseppe (Lang Shining): *Auspicious Objects*, 1000, *1000*
Castillo, Chichén Itzá, 505, *505*
casting, 11
See also bronze casting
Castle of Love (jewelry box lid), 388–389, *389*
The Castle of Otranto: A Gothic Story (Walpole), 26-27A
Castor and Pollux, 175
castrum, 207

Catacomb of Commodilla, Rome, 239, *239b*, 8-6A
Catacomb of Saints Peter and Marcellinus, Rome, 237–239, *237*
catacombs, 236, 237–239, 7-54A, 8-5A, 8-6A
Çatal Höyük (Anatolia), 24, 26–28
deer hunt (cave painting), 26, *26*, 3-1A
landscape with volcanic eruption (?), 27, *27*
restored view of, *26b*, 1-16A
cathedra, 350
Cathedral of Saint Peter, Geneva, 552–553
Cathedral of Santa María, León, 389, *389b*, 13-38A
cathedrals, 350, 412
See also specific cathedrals
Catherine of Alexandria, Saint, 549, 624
Catherine the Great (empress of Russia), 729
Catullus, 628
Causai et curae (Causes and Cures) (Hildegard of Bingen), 352
Cavallini, Pietro, 407, 14-5B
Last Judgment, Santa Cecilia, Trastevere, *407b*, 409, 14-7A
cave paintings
Ajanta, 433–434
Altamira, 20–21, 22, 58, 829
Apollo 11 Cave, Namibia, 16–17
Çatal Höyük, 26, 3-1A
Chauvet Cave, 22, 23
Lascaux, 14, 15, 20, 22–23, 26
La Magdeleine, *18b*, 22, 1-6A
painting techniques, 20, 22
Pech-Merle, France, 21–22
cave sculptures
Elephanta, 435–436, *436*
Longmen Caves, Luoyang, 461
Mahishasuramardini cave temple, 438
Paleolithic, 18, 19, 1-6A
Udayagiri, 434–435
Yungang Grottoes, 461, 16-13A
cavea, 151, 189, 190
celadon, 472
Celer: Domus Aurea (Golden House), 194, *195*, 201–202, *202*, 203–204
Celestine (Pope), 8-10A
cella, 33, 115, 117, 124, 136, 168, 183, 224, 618
Cellini, Benvenuto
autobiography, 638–639
and Clodion, 735
Genius of Fontainebleau, 639, *639b*, 22-52A
and Northern European High Renaissance/Mannerist art, 657, 23-14A
Saltcellar of Francis I, *638*, 639, 22-52A
Celts, 308, 311, 494
cemen, 1046
cement, 184
Cenni di Pepo. *See* Cimabue
Cennini, Cennino, 414, 539, 573
centauromachy, 104, 105, 120, 136–137, 5-32A
centauromachy, Parthenon metope, Athens (relief sculpture), 105, 136–137, *136*
centauromachy, Temple of Zeus west pediment, Olympia (sculpture), 126, 128, *128b*, 5-32A
centaurs, 105, 109
See also centauromachy
central plans
in Byzantine architecture, 244, 263
in Early Christian architecture, 244, 246, 247, 8-19A
in Islamic architecture, 286, 288, 297
in Italian Baroque architecture, 678
in Italian Cinquecento Renaissance architecture, 605, 620, 623, 22-6A
in Italian Quattrocento Renaissance architecture, 583, 585, 586
in Italian Romanesque architecture, 356
Centre Georges Pompidou (Beaubourg), Paris (Rogers and Piano), 932, *932*, 964
Centula (France): Abbey of Saint-Riquier, 323, *323b*, 11-19B
Centzon Huitznahua (Aztec deities), 1027
ceramics
Andean South American, 510–511
Chinese, 451, 464, 466, 467, 992, 993, 1000

contemporary, 31-27A
Early Islamic, 294, *295*
Elamite, 45, 2-19A
Greek, 110
Intermediate Area Native American, 507
Japanese, 476–477, 1012, 1019
Korean, 472
Mesoamerican, 495, 500–501, 503
Minoan, 93
Native North American, 517, 1034, 1035
Southeast Asian, 986
tilework, 299–300
See also sculpture; terracotta; vase painting
Cerberus, 171
ceremonial ax in the form of a were-jaguar, Olmec, La Venta (sculpture), 494, *494*
Ceres. *See* Demeter
Cerveteri (Italy)
Banditaccia necropolis, 169, *169*, 170–171, *170*, *171*, 6-7A
fibula, Regolini-Galssi Tomb, *166*, 167
Herakles wrestling Antaios (Euphronios) (vase painting), 122–123, *122*, 570
sarcophagus with reclining couple, 169, *169*
Tomb of the Reliefs, 171, *171*
Tomb of the Shields and Chairs, 170, 171, *171b*, 6-7A
cestrum, 218
Cézanne, Paul
Basket of Apples, 818–819, *818*
The Large Bathers, 819, *819b*, 28-22A, 29-2A
and Modersohn-Becker, 29-9A
Mont Sainte-Victoire, 817–818, *817*
and Picasso, 845
and the Steins, 844
chacmool, Platform of the Eagles, Chichén Itzá (sculpture), 505–506, *505*
chacmools, 491, 505–506, 883
Chaco Canyon, New Mexico (U.S.A.): Pueblo Bonito, 518, *518b*, 1032, 18-33A
Chaeronea, battle of (338 BCE), 144–145, 161
chaitya hall, Ajanta, 434, *434*
chaitya hall, Karle, 430–431, *431*, 434
chaitya halls, 429, 430–431, 434
chakras, 423, 429
chakravartin, 429, 985
Chalchas examining a liver, Vulci (engraved mirror), *175b*, 6-13A
Chalgrin, Jean François Thérèse: Arc de Triomphe, Paris, 770, *770*
Chalukya dynasty (South Asia), 435–436
Chamberlain, Neville, 902
Chambord (France): Château de Chambord, 657–658, *657*
Champfleury, Jules-François-Félix Husson, 777
Champollion, Jean-François, 56
Champs de Mars (The Red Tower) (Delaunay), 848, *848b*, 29-15A
Chan Buddhism, 468–469, 470, 999, 1006, 1007
chancel arches, 228, 243, 413, 12-4A
Chandella dynasty (South Asia), 437, 438–439
Chandigarh (India): urban planning (Le Corbusier), 887
Chandragupta II (Gupta king), 433, 435
Chandragupta Maurya (Mauryan emperor), 428
chantries, 13-42A
chapel of Henry VII (Vertue and Vertue), Westminster Abbey, 391, *391*, 13-42A, 26-27A
Chapel of Saint Ivo, Rome (Borromini), 678, *678*, 679
Chapel of the Holy Shroud (Cappella della Santissima Sindone), Turin (Guarini), 678, *678b*, 24-14A
chaplets, 130
chapter houses, 585
characters, Chinese, 450, 997
Chardin, Jean-Baptiste-Siméon
Diderot on, 738, 739
Saying Grace, 738–739, *738*
Charging Chasseur (Géricault), 765, *765b*, 27-13A

chariot procession of Septimius Severus, Arch of Septimius Severus, Lepcis Magna (relief sculpture), 220, *220*, 235
chariot race of Pelops and Oinomaos, Temple of Zeus east pediment, Olympia (sculpture), 126, *126*
charioteer (dedicated by Polyzalos of Gela), Delphi (sculpture), 130–131, *130*
Charlemagne (Holy Roman Emperor), 317–318, *317*, 320, 322, 324, 402, 11-13A, 11-19B
Charles I (king of England), 697, 701, 723
Charles I Dismounted (Van Dyck), 701, *701*
Charles II (king of England), 724
Charles IV (king of Spain), 764, 27-10A
Charles V (Holy Roman Emperor), 656, 664
Charles VI (emperor of Austria), 26-3A
Charles VII (king of France), 383
Charles X (king of France), 768
Charles Martel (Frankish ruler), 284
Charles the Bald (Holy Roman Emperor), 317
Charles the Bold (duke of Burgundy), 555
Charlottesville, Virginia (U.S.A.)
Monticello (Jefferson), 750, *751*
University of Virginia (Jefferson), 751, *751*
Chartres Cathedral
and Amiens Cathedral, 378
nave height diagram, *371*
Porch of the Confessors, *377b*, 13-18A
post-1194 rebuilding, 364, 365, 374, *374*
and Reims Cathedral, 380, 13-23A
Royal Portal, 369–370, *369*, *370*, 13-3A
South transept sculpture, 377, *377b*, *377*, 564, 13-18A
stained-glass windows, 365, 374, 375, *375*, 376–377, *376*, *377*, 386
chartreuse, 537
Chartreuse de Champmol, Dijon (Drouet de Dammartin), 537–538, *537*, 20-2A
charuns, 176
chasing, 673
chasseur, 27-13A
Chatar Muni: *Akbar and the Elephant Hawai, Akbarnama*, 978, *978*
Château de Chambord, 657–658, *657*
Chateaubriand, François René de, 760, 788
châteaux, 657
chatras, 430
Chauvet Cave, Vallon-Pont-d'Arc: aurochs, horses, and rhinoceroses (cave painting), 22, *22*, 23
Chavín art, 508–509
Chavín de Huántar (Peru)
Old Temple, 508
Raimondi Stele, 508–509, *508*
Cheonmachong tomb, Hwangnam-dong, *470*, 471
cherubs, 552
Chevalier, Étienne, 552
Chevreul, Michel Eugène, 768, 813
Cheyenne art, 1035
Chhatrapati Shivaji Terminus (Victoria Terminus), Mumbai (Stevens), 982, *982*
chi-rho-iota (Christogram), 230, 264, 306, 307
chi-rho-iota (XPI) page, *Book of Kells*, 306, 307
chiaroscuro
in Cubist art, 847
in Italian 14th century art, 409
in Italian Baroque art, 681, 682
in Italian Cinquecento Renaissance art, 601, 604, 606, 22-8A
in Italian Mannerist art, 637
chiaroscuro woodcuts, 649
Chibinda Ilunga, 1067–1068
Chibinda Ilunga, Chokwe (sculpture), 1068, *1068*
Chicago (Illinois)
Marshall Field wholesale store (Richardson), 831, *831*
Robie House (Wright), 870, *871*, 896
Chicago, Illinois (U.S.A.)
Carson, Pirie, Scott Building (Sullivan), 832, *832*
Willis Tower (Sears Tower) (Skidmore, Owings, and Merrill), 928–929, *928*, 961

Chicago, Judy: *The Dinner Party*, 921–922, *921*

Chicago Board of Trade II (Gursky), 970, *970*

Chichén Itzá (Mexico), *490*, 491, 501, 504–506, *505*, *506*, 1024

Chiesa degli Eremitani, Padua, *596b*, 21-49A

chigi, 480

Chigi, Agostino, 608–609

Child with Toy Hand Grenade in Central Park (Arbus), 920, *920*

children: in Roman Early Empire art, 200

Chilkat blanket with stylized animal motifs, Tlingit, 1038, *1038*

chimera, 174

Chimera of Arezzo (sculpture), 174, *174*

China: and Myanmar, 15-28A

Chinese architecture
    Han dynasty, 456, 457
    Liao dynasty, 467–468
    Ming dynasty, 988, 989, 993–994, 996
    Neolithic, 450–451
    Qin dynasty, 454
    Tang dynasty, 16-15A

Chinese art, 450–470, *450map*, 988–1002, *993map*
    contemporary, 953, 956, 1001
    Han dynasty, 448, 449, 455–456, 457, 473, 16-6A
    Liao dynasty, 467–468, 473, 16-21A
    Ming dynasty, 988, 989, 993–999, 1003, 33-12A
    Neolithic, 450–451, 454, 473
    People's Republic, 1001, 1003
    Period of Disunity, 458–461, 473, 16-13A
    Qin dynasty, 454–455, 473
    Qing dynasty, 999–1000, 1003
    Sanxingdui, 453
    Shang dynasty, 452, 473
    societal contexts, 452, 454, 455, 458, 461, 465
    Song dynasty, 465–467, 468–470, 473, 16-23A
    Sui dynasty, 461, 16-13B
    Tang dynasty, 461–462, 464, 472, 473, 16-14A, 16-15A
    timelines, 450, 990
    Yuan dynasty, 990–993, 1003, 33-1A, 33-4A
    Zhao dynasty, 458–459
    Zhou dynasty, 453, 457, 473
    See also Chinese Buddhist art; Chinese painting; Chinese sculpture

Chinese Buddhist art
    Liao dynasty, 467–468, 16-21A
    Period of Disunity, 458–459, 460–461, 16-13A
    Song dynasty, 468–470
    Sui dynasty, 16-13B
    Tang dynasty, 461–462, 472, 16-14A
    "Chinese horse," Lascaux (cave painting), 23, *23b*, 1-12A

Chinese Lions (Eitoku), 1010, *1010*

Chinese painting
    formats, 459
    Ming dynasty, 994, 995, 996–999, 33-12A
    Qing dynasty, 999, 1000
    Song dynasty, 465–466, 468–470
    Tang dynasty, 462–463, 464, 16-14A
    Xie He's canons of, 460
    Yuan dynasty, 990–993, 33-1A, 33-4A

Chinese sculpture
    Han dynasty, 455–456
    Liao dynasty, 16-21A
    Period of Disunity, 458–459, 460–461, 16-13A
    Qin dynasty Chinese, 454–455
    Sanxingdui Chinese, 453
    Sui dynasty Chinese, 16-13B
    Tang dynasty Chinese, 461, 464, 472
    Zhao dynasty Chinese, 458–459
    Zhou dynasty Chinese, 453, 454

Chios (Greece): head of a woman (sculpture), 145, *145b*, 5-62A

chisels, 18

Chiswick House, near London (Boyle and Kent), 749, *749*, 750

chiton, 115

Chiusi (Italy): girl preparing to bathe (Onesimos) (vase painting), 123, *123b*, 145, 5-23A

chivalry, 370, 385, 414

choir, 12, 264

Chokwe art, 1067–1068

Chola dynasty (South Asia), 438, 441

Chopin, Frédéric, 767

Choragic Monument (Lysikrates), 152–153, 153

Chosroes II (Sasanian king), 21-24A

Chrétien de Troyes, 388

Christ, 240
    as alpha and omega, 251, 8-6A, 12-8A
    in Carolingian art, 320, 11-13A
    in Dutch Baroque art, 709
    in Early Byzantine art, 259, 267–268, 9-18A
    in Early Christian art, 232, 238–239, 247, 248, 250, 252, 266, 8-6A, 8-8A, 8-13A
    in French/Spanish Romanesque art, 340, 345, 346, 12-8B
    in Gothic art, 379
    in Italian Romanesque art, 356
    in Late Byzantine art, 279
    in Middle Byzantine art, 272–273, 275, 277, 9-25A, 9-27A
    in Ottonian art, 327, 328–329
    in Symbolist art, 822
    See also Anastasis; Christ as ruler; Jesus, life of; Passion of Christ; Pietàs; Resurrection of Christ; Second Coming

Christ (*Beau Dieu*), Amiens Cathedral (sculpture), 379, *379*

Christ, Doubting Thomas, and apostles, Santo Domingo (relief sculpture), 12-8B

Christ as Good Shepherd, 238–239, 247, 248, 266

Christ as the Good Shepherd (sculpture), 239, *239*

Christ as Good Shepherd, Mausoleum of Galla Placidia, Ravenna (mosaic), 247, *247*, 248, 266, 8-17A

Christ as Pantokrator, Church of the Dormition, Daphni (mosaic), 272–273, *272*

Christ as ruler
    in Carolingian art, 11-13A
    in Early Byzantine art, 254, 255
    in Early Christian art, 232, 233, 239, 8-13A
    in French/Spanish Romanesque art, 12-8A
    in Middle Byzantine art, 273, 275, 9-27A
    Christ as Savior of Souls, Saint Clement, Ohrid (icon), 279, *279*

Christ as Sol Invictus, 8-13A

Christ as Sol Invictus, Mausoleum of the Julii, Rome (mosaic), 245, *245b*, 8-13A

Christ before Pilate, Rossano Gospels, 250, *250*, 251

Christ between Constantine IX Monomachus and the empress Zoe, Hagia Sophia (mosaic), 273–274, *273*, 275

Christ blessing, monastery of Saint Catherine, Mount Sinai (icon), *268b*, 277, 9-18A

Christ blessing Otto II and Theophanu (ivory plaque), 328, *328*

Christ Delivering the Keys of the Kingdom to Saint Peter, Sistine Chapel (Perugino), 567, 589–590, *589*, 22-18B

Christ enthroned with saints (*Harbaville Triptych*) (ivory carving), 275–276, *275*, 277

Christ in Majesty (Bernardus Gelduinus), Saint-Sernin, 340, *340*, 356

Christ in Majesty (Maiestas Domini), Saint-Genis-des-Fontaines (relief sculpture), *340b*, 12-8A, 12-14A

Christ in Majesty, Santa María de Mur (fresco), 348, *349*

Christ in the House of Levi (Veronese), *636*, 637

Christ on the Cross (Velázquez), 689, *689b*, 24-28A

Christ seated, Civita Latina (sculpture), *239b*, 8-8A

Christ with the Sick around Him, Receiving the Children (Hundred-Guilder Print) (Rembrandt), 709, *709*, 755

Christ's Entry into Brussels in 1889 (Ensor), 822, *822*

Christian community house, Dura-Europos, 236, *236*

Christianity
    in Andean South America, 1031
    and Byzantine Empire, 258
    in China, 1000
    Counter-Reformation, 616, 617, 637, 641, 646, 670, 672, 675, 686, 24-18A
    early medieval period, 307, 311
    in Ethiopia, 529–530
    Great Schism, 404, 536, 21-41A
    and medieval books, 312
    in Mesoamerica, 1024, 1028–1029
    monasticism, 267
    Monophysite heresy, 258, 270
    in Oceania, 1054, 36-14A
    Purgatory, 584
    and the Roman Empire, 225–226, 230, 236, 239, 242
    on salvation, 653
    Scholasticism, 372
    and Second Commandment, 239, 269, 348, 8-8A
    See also Byzantine art; early Christian art; four evangelists; medieval art; monasticism; Protestant Reformation; Renaissance

Christo: *Surrounded Islands, Biscayne Bay, Miami, Florida, 1980–1983*, 968, *968*

Christogram (chi-rho-iota), 230, 264, 306, 307

Christopher, Saint, 20-21A

chromatic abstraction, 903, 905–907

Chronica (Gervase of Canterbury), 339

Chronik der Brücke (Kirchner), 839

chronology, 2–3, 22

Chrysaor, 118

chryselephantine sculpture, 94–95, *105*, 136

Chrysler Building, New York (van Alen), 871–872, *871*, 894

Church, Frederic Edwin: *Twilight in the Wilderness*, 774, 775

church furniture, 392, 9-14A, 13-44A

Church of Christ in Chora, Constantinople, 278, 279

Church of Jesus (Il Gesù), Rome (della Porta and Vignola), 641–642, *642*, 671, 686, *686*

Church of Ognissanti, Florence, 407–408, *407*, 14-19A

Church of Saint Charles Borromaeus (Karlskirche), Vienna (Fischer von Erlach), 731, *731b*, 26-3A

Church of Saints Sergius and Bacchus, Constantinople, 263

Church of the Dormition, Daphni, 272–273, *272*, *272*, 9-25A

Church of the Holy Apostles, Constantinople, 274

Church of the Holy Sepulcher, Jerusalem, 286

Church of the Invalides (Église du Dôme), Paris (Hardouin-Mansart), 718, *718*

Church of the Theotokos, Hosios Loukas, 271, *271*, 9-25A

Church of the Virgin, monastery of Saint Catherine, Mount Sinai, 267–268, *267*, 279

Church of the Virgin Peribleptos, Ohrid, 279–280, *280*

Churchill, John (duke of Marlborough), 26-1A

Chuuk (Caroline Islands), 1050

Cicero, 407

Cimabue, 410, 14-5B
    and Giotto, 407
    Madonna Enthroned with Angels and Prophets, Santa Trinità, Florence, 406, *406*

Cincinnatus, 752, 782

cinema. *See* motion pictures

Cinquecento, 599
    See also Italian Cinquecento Renaissance art; Italian Mannerism

circles of confusion, 711

circumambulation, 429, 430, 15-28A

Circus Maximus, Rome, 208, 7-44A

cire perdue. *See* lost-wax process

cista/cistae, 175, 6-13A

Cistercian order, 322, 342, 343, 347, 12-10A

Citadel, Teotihuacán, *495*, 496, 497

citadel of Sargon II, Dur Sharrukin (Khorsabad), 46, *46b*, 2-20A

citadel of Tiryns, 96–97, *96*, 97

The City (Léger), 853, *853*

city planning. *See* urban planning

city-states, 31, 32, 36, 406

Civil War (U.S.A.), 775, 782–783, 794–795

Claesz, Pieter
    and Daguerre, 793
    and Peeters, 701
    Vanitas Still Life, 694, 695, 713

Claesz van Ruijven, Pieter, 25-18B

Clarkson, Thomas, 772

Classic period Maya art, 498–503, 18-10A

Classic Veracruz art, 504

classical art, 124, 402
    See also classical influences on later art; Greek art; Roman art

classical influences on Italian Cinquecento Renaissance art
    architecture, 618, 623, 22-30A
    Bellini, 625
    Giorgione, 626
    Leonardo da Vinci, 602–603
    Michelangelo Buonarroti, 611, 615
    Raphael, 606–607, 608–609
    Titian, 628

classical influences on Italian Quattrocento Renaissance art
    architecture, 584, 586, 587–588, 594, 21-31A
    Botticelli, 558, 559, 581
    Donatello, 568, 571
    Ghiberti, 562
    Ghirlandaio, 580
    humanism and, 560
    Mantegna, 21-49A
    Nanni, 563
    Piero della Francesca, 592, 21-24A
    Pollaiuolo, 569, 570

classical influences on later art
    18th century European and American architecture, 26-1A
    Burgundian/Flemish late medieval/early Renaissance art, 543
    Carolingian art, 317–318, 319, 320, 11-19A
    early 19th century European and American architecture, 27-46A
    Early Byzantine art, 257, 258, 258–259, 9-3A, 9-14A, 9-18A
    Early Christian art, 239, 244, 246, 248, 250, 8-5A, 8-8A, 8-13A, 8-17A, 8-19A
    Fauve art, 29-2A
    Flemish Baroque art, 698
    French academic art, 27-33A
    French Baroque art, 717, 718, 720
    French/Spanish Romanesque art, 12-8A, 12-14A
    Gothic art, 377, 380
    Hiberno-Saxon art, 314
    Holy Roman Empire Romanesque art, 354
    Islamic world as transmitter of, 284, 289
    Italian 14th century art, 402, 409, 415
    Italian Baroque art, 680–681, 684–685, 24-6A
    Italian Cinquecento Renaissance art. *See* classical influences on Italian Cinquecento Renaissance art
    Italian late medieval art, 401, 402, 403
    Italian Quattrocento Renaissance art. *See* classical influences on Italian Quattrocento Renaissance art
    Italian Romanesque art, 356, 357, 12-27B
    late 19th century art European and American art, 825, 28-31A, 28-33A, 28-40B
    Late Antique art, 233, 237, 250–251, 252, 8-5A

death of Sarpedon, Greppe Sant'Angelo (vase painting), *122b*, 5-22A
    Herakles wrestling Antaios, Cerveteri (vase painting), 122–123, *122*, 570
Euripides, 107, 125, 151
Europe: A Prophecy (Blake), 763
European interwar Modernism, 872–887, 897
    architecture, 884–887
    and Bauhaus, 884, 885, 29-66A, 29-66B
    De Stijl, 880–881, 884
    Neue Sachlichkeit, 872–874, 29-48A
    sculpture, 874, 875, 879, 881–884, 29-61A
    Surrealism. *See* Surrealism
European prewar Modernism, 836–861, 897
    architecture, 860–861
    Constructivism, 860
    Cubism. *See* Cubism
    Dada. *See* Dada
    Fauvism, 813, 836–839, 840, 29-2A, 29-4A
    Futurism, 853–855, 856, 863, 29-15A, 29-36A
    German Expressionism. *See* German Expressionism
    Picasso, 844–845, 846, 847, 29-11A, 2 9-19A
    and the Steins, 844, 858, 29-11A
    Suprematism, 858–860, 29-30A
Eusebius of Caesarea, 269
Euthymides, 582, 5-22A, 5-23A
    three revelers, Vulci (vase painting), 123, *123*
Euxitheos: death of Sarpedon, Greppe Sant'Angelo (vase painting), *122b*, 5-22A
evangelists, 314
    See also four evangelists
Evans, Arthur, 86, 87, 90
Eve. *See* Adam and Eve
Eve (Gislebertus), Saint-Lazare, 12-13B
Evening Bell at the Clock, Eight Views of the Parlor series (Harunobu), *1016*, 1017
Events, 935
Events of the Heiji Period (handscroll), 488, *488*
ewer in the form of a bird (Sulayman), 293, *293*
exedrae, 196, 263–264, 929
Exekias
    Achilles and Ajax playing a dice game, Vulci (vase painting), 120–121, *121*
    Achilles killing Penthesilea, Vulci (vase painting), *120b*, 5-20A
    exemplum virtutis, 746
existentialism, 901
exoticism
    in Napoleonic era art, 754, 755, 759, 760, 761, 27-5A
    in Romantic art, 767, 769, 27-17A
    in Symbolist art, 28-24A
    An Experiment on a Bird in the Air-Pump (Wright of Derby), *737b*, 26-11A
Expressionism, 839, 901–902, 30-3A
    See also Abstract Expressionism; German Expressionism
Expulsion of Adam and Eve from Eden, Santa Maria del Carmine, Florence (Masaccio), 574, *575*, 22-18A

F

facades
    in Egyptian architecture, 60, 71, 72, 73, 82
    in French/Spanish Romanesque architecture, 12-11A
    in Greek architecture, 117, 123, 124, 135, 136, 139, 141
    in Hellenistic period Greek architecture, 154, 155
    in Italian 14th century architecture, 412
    in Italian Quattrocento Renaissance architecture, 594
    in Mycenaean architecture, 97
    in Persian architecture, 52
    See also specific buildings
face. *See* human face
faience, 94
Fall of Icarus (Bruegel the Elder), 662–663, *663b*, 23-22A

Fall of Man (Adam and Eve) (Dürer), 650–651, *650*, 659, 23-3A
Fall of Man, Sistine Chapel ceiling (Michelangelo Buonarroti), *598*, 615, *615b*, 22-18A
Fall of the Giants from Mount Olympus, Palazzo del Tè, Mantua (Giulio Romano), *640b*, 22-54A
Fall of the Rebel Angels (Beccafumi), 632, *632b*, 22-42A
Fall of the Rebel Angels (later version) (Beccafumi), 22-42A
The Falling Rocket (Nocturne in Black and Gold) (Whistler), 810, *810*
The False Mirror (Magritte), 878, *878b*, 29-56A
family chapels, 574, 575, 584, 585
Family of Charles IV (Goya), 764, *764b*, 27-10A
Family of Country People (Le Nain), 721–722, *721*
Family of Saltimbanques (Picasso), 844, *844b*, 29-11A
Fan Kuan, 998
    Travelers among Mountains and Streams, 465, *465*, 468, 16-23A
    fan paintings, 998–999
fan vaults, 391
Fang art, 1061, 1064
fans, 459
fantasia, 604
Farnese, Odoardo, 680
Farnese Hercules (weary Herakles) (Lysippos of Sikyon), 148, *148*
fasces, 752
Fasti (Ovid), 625
Fate of the Animals (Marc), 842, *842*
fauces, 190
Faustina the Younger (Roman empress), 198, 7-59A
Fauvism, 813, 836–839, 840, 29-2A, 29-4A
Favrile, 28-36B
Feast of Herod, Siena Cathedral (Donatello), 565, *565*
Feast of Saint Nicholas (Steen), 712–713, *712*
Feast of the Gods (Bellini and Titian), 625, *625*, 626, 628
feather cloak, Hawaii, 1058, *1058*
feather heads, 1057
Federal Arts Project (U.S.A.), 887, 30-40A
Federico da Montefeltro, 590, 592, 605, 21-43A
Felix, Saint, 8-6A
female head (Inanna?), Uruk (sculpture), 34–35, *34*
female head, Mycenae (sculpture), 101, *101*
female mask, Mende, 1075, *1075*
female personification (Tellus?), Ara Pacis Augustae, Rome (relief sculpture), 99, *199*
feminist art
    contemporary, 942–943, 957, 973, 31-2A, 31-6A
    late 20th century European and American, 921–925, 935, 30-26A
    and race, 945–946, 31-6A
    Saint-Phalle, 30-26A
Feminist Art Program, 921
femmages, 922
femme fatale, 820
femmes savants, 729
Fénelon, François de Salignac de la Mothe, 760
fenestra coeli, 688
fenestration, 184, 228
Fenollosa, Ernest, 1018–1019
Fenton, Roger, 794
Ferdinand II (king of Aragon), 284, 618
Ferdinand VII (king of Spain), 764
Ferrara (Italy): Camerino d'Alabastro, Palazzo Ducale, 625, 628, 629
fête galante, 732, 733
The Fetus and Lining of the Uterus (Leonardo da Vinci), *604*, 605
feudalism, 334, 536
fiber arts. *See* textiles

fibula, Regolini-Galssi Tomb, Cerveteri, *166*, 167
fibulae, 166, 167, 309
Ficino, Marsilio, 581, 651
Ficoroni Cista (Novios Plautios) (bronze container), *174*, 175, 6-13A
Fidenza Cathedral, 356–357, *357*, 12-14A
Fielding, Henry, 740
Fifty-three Stations of the Tokaido Highway (Hokusai), 1005
Figure with Meat (Bacon), *902b*, 30-3A
figurine of a woman, Syros, 87, *87*
film. *See* motion pictures
fin-de-siècle, 823
Finding and Proving of the True Cross, Legend of the True Cross, Cappella Maggiore (Piero della Francesca), 578, *578b*, 21-24A
findspot, 18
finials, 294, 541, 977
Finley, Karen, 944
Fiorentino, Rosso, 657
fire and architecture, 184, 201, 339, 373, 724, 830
First Style (Masonry Style), 191
First Surrealist Manifesto, 874–875
Fischer von Erlach, Johann Bernhard
    Entwurf einer historischen Architektur (Outline for a History of Architecture), 26-3A
    Karlskirche (Church of Saint Charles Borromaeus), Vienna, 731, *731b*, 26-3A
Fission (Riley), 909, *909*
Fit for Active Service (Grosz), *872b*, 29-48A
Fitzgerald, F. Scott, 844
Five Dynasties period Chinese art, 465
Flack, Audrey: *Marilyn*, 917–918, *917*
Flagellation (Piero della Francesca), 592–593, *592*, 21-24A
Flagellation of Jesus, 241, 592–593, 21-24A
Flamboyant style, 381, 381–382, 384, 391, 398
Flamininus (Roman general), 161
flashing, 375
Flaubert, Gustave, 777
Flavian Amphitheater. *See* Colosseum, Rome
Flavian period, 203–207
    See also Roman Early Empire art
Flaxman, John, 745
Fleck, John, 944
Flemish Baroque art, 10, 696–701, *696map*, 725, 25-1A, 25-2A
Flemish late medieval/early Renaissance art. *See* Burgundian/Flemish late medieval/early Renaissance art
fleurs-de-lis, 376, 388, 698
Flight into Egypt, 240, 538, 539, 548, 661, 679–680
Flight into Egypt (Carracci), 679–680, *679*
Flitcroft, Henry: Stourhead park, 750, *750*
Floreale. *See* Art Nouveau
Florence (Italy)
    14th century art, 417–419, 14-18A, 14-18B, 14-19A
    Church of Ognissanti, 407–408, *407*, 14-19A
    Or San Michele, 419, *419b*, 562–565, *563*, *564*, *565*, 14-19A, 21-36A
    Ospedale degli Innocenti (Foundling Hospital) (Brunelleschi), 410, 582–583, *583*, 21-36A
    Palazzo della Signoria (Palazzo Vecchio) (Arnolfo di Cambio), 417, *417b*, 14-18B, 21-37A
    Palazzo di Parte Guelfa, 585
    Palazzo Medici-Riccardi (Michelozzo di Bartolommeo), 585–586, *586*, *587*, 621, 21-37A
    Palazzo Rucellai (Alberti and Rossellino), 587–588, *587*
    San Lorenzo, *583b*, 594, 613–614, *613*, 21-37A, 31-32A
    San Marco, 576, *576*
    San Miniato al Monte, 356, *356b*, 588, 12-27A
    Sant'Apollonia, 576, *577*
    Sant'Egidio, 548

    Santa Maria del Carmine, 574, *574*, *575*, 584
    Santa Maria Gloriosa dei Frari, 627, *627*, 628, *628*
    Santa Trinità, 406, *406*, 572, 573
    Santo Spirito (Brunelleschi), 583–584, *583*, *583*, 586, 594, 21-31A
    See also Baptistery of San Giovanni; Florence Cathedral; Florentine 14th century art; Florentine Quattrocento Renaissance painting; Florentine Quattrocento Renaissance sculpture; Santa Croce; Santa Maria Novella
Florence Cathedral (Santa Maria del Fiore) (Arnolfo di Cambio), Florence, 410, 417–418, 560, 584
    campanile (Giotto di Bondone), *417*, 418
    dome (Brunelleschi), 582, *582b*, 620, 21-31A
Florentine 14th century art, 417–419, 14-18A, 14-18B, 14-19A
Florentine Quattrocento Renaissance painting, 572–581
    Andrea del Castagno, 576, 577
    Botticelli, 558, 559, 581, 21-29A
    Fra Angelico, 576
    Gentile da Fabriano, 572, 573
    Ghirlandaio, 579–580
    Lippi, 577–578
    Masaccio, 573–576
    Piero della Francesca, 578–579, 21-24A
    Uccello, 580–581
Florentine Quattrocento Renaissance sculpture, 560–572
    Baptistery of San Giovanni competition, 560–562, 582
    David (Verrocchio), 569
    David, Medici palace, Florence (Donatello), 568, 611, 674, 675
    della Robbia, 585, 21-36A
    equestrian statues, 571–572
    Gates of Paradise (Ghiberti), 566–568
    Or San Michele, 562–565, *563*, *564*, *565*, 21-36A
    Penitent Mary Magdalene (Donatello), 568, 21-12A, 21-24A
    perspective in, 566–568
    Pollaiuolo, 569–570
    tomb of Leonardo Bruni (Rossellino), 570–571
florins, 417
Flower Still Life (Ruysch), 713, *713*
Flowers on Body, Silueta series (Mendieta), 923, *923*
fluted columns, 51, 68, 116, 175, 3-5A
Fluxus, 935
flying buttresses, 12
    in Gothic architecture, 359, 364, 365, 372, 372–373, 373, 374, 376, 383, 390, 20-4A
flying horse, tomb of Governor-General Zhang, Wuwei (sculpture), 456, *456*
The Flying Storehouse, Legends of Mount Shigi (handscroll), 485–486, *486*
Foguang Si (Buddha Radiance Temple), Mount Wutai, 462, *462b*, 16-15A
Foguang Si Pagoda, Yingxian, 467–468, *467*
folios, 248, 249
Fon art, 1066
Fontaine, Pierre-François-Léonard, 757
Fontana, Carlo, 26-3A
Fontana, Lavinia, 630
    Portrait of a Noblewoman, *630b*, 22-40A
Fontana, Prospero, 630, 22-40A
Fontenay (France): Notre-Dame, 343, *343b*, 349–350, 12-10A
Forbidden City, Beijing, *988*, 989, 993–994, *994*, 1002
Force, Juliana, 865
Foreshortened Christ (Lamentation over the Dead Christ) (Mantegna), 596, *596*, 21-49A
foreshortening, 10
    in Babylonian art, 44
    in Baroque art, 10, 697, 706
    in contemporary art, 957
    in Greek art, 123, 143, 149–150, 5-22A, 5-23A, 5-58A

Ile-Ife (Nigeria), 533
    head of an Ife king, Wunmonije compound
        (sculpture), 528, *528b*, 19-6A
    king, Ita Yemoo (sculpture), 527–528, *527*
Ile-Ife art, 527–529, 533, 19-6A
Iliad (Homer), 85, 86, 96cap, 107, 120, 148,
    654, 4-18A, 6-13A
    See also Homer
Illisos stele (grave stele of a young hunter),
    Athens, 146–147, *147*, 5-64A
illuminated manuscripts, 405
    Byzantine, 258, 268, 276–277, 405, 9-3A,
        9-17A
    Carolingian, 317, 318–320, 11-13A, 11-15A
    French Gothic, 384–388, 13-36A
    French late medieval/early Renaissance,
        550–551, 20-15A
    French/Spanish Romanesque, 347–348,
        12-15A
    Hiberno-Saxon, 306, 307, 311–315
    Holy Roman Empire Romanesque,
        352–353, 12-23A
    Late Antique, 248–250
    Mesoamerican, 1022, 1023, 1024–1025
    Norman Romanesque, 359–361, 12-35A
    Ottonian, 329–330, 11-29A
    South Asian, 978, 32-5A
    See also books
illuminated tughra of Suleyman the
    Magnificent, *297b*, 10-23A
illusionism, 8
    in Burgundian/Flemish late medieval/
        early Renaissance art, 538, 543, 546,
        550
    in Byzantine art, 270, 279
    in Carolingian art, 318, 319
    in European interwar Modernist art, 876
    in French academic art, 27-33A
    in Italian 14th century art, 408, 409, 415
    in Italian Baroque art, 681, 686, 24-14A
    in Italian Mannerist art, 637, 638
    in Italian Quattrocento Renaissance art,
        562, 565, 575–576, 595–596, 21-41A,
        21-43A, 21-49A
    in Op Art, 909
    in Pompeian/Vesuvius area art, 192–193,
        196, 595
    Realism and, 777, 780–781
    in Rococo art, 735
    See also perspective
illustrated books. *See* books; illuminated
    manuscripts
Iltutmish (sultan of Delhi), 976
imagines, 185, 196, 200
imago hominis, 315
imam, 288
Imam (Shah) Mosque, Isfahan, 299–300, *299*
Imhotep
    mortuary precinct of Djoser, 58, *58b*, *59*,
        60, *60*, 3-5A
    stepped pyramid of Djoser, 58, *59*, 496
imitation, 573
Immaculate Conception of the Escoria
    (Murillo), 688, *688b*, 24-25A
impasto, 632, 902
imperator, 197
imperialism, 788, 846
    See also colonialism
impluvium, 190, *191*
impost blocks, 21-31A
Impression: Sunrise (Monet), 801, *802*
Impressionism, 798, 799, 801–810, 833
    Caillebotte, 804
    Cassatt, 809
    and Courbet, 777
    Degas, 807–809
    and Delacroix, 768
    and Fauvism, 836, 29-4A
    Manet, 780, 798, 799
    Monet, 801–804, 28-2A
    Morisot, 804–805, 28-7A
    and photography, 793, 804, 809
    Pissarro, 804
    Renoir, 806
    and Rodin, 825
    societal contexts, 804–805
    Whistler, 810
Improvisation 28 (Kandinsky), 841–842, *841*

in antis (columns), 115, 117
In Praise of Folly (Erasmus), 647
In Praise of Scribes (Johannes Trithemius),
    386
Inanna (Ishtar) (Mesopotamian deity), 34, 35
incense burner (boshan) from the tomb of
    Prince Liu Sheng, Mancheng, 455, *455b*,
    16-6A
incised gorget with running warrior,
    Sumner County, Tennessee, 517, *517*
incising, 556
incrustation, 202, 355, 12-27A
incubus, 762
Independent Group, 899, 913
India. *See* South Asian art
L'Indifférent (Watteau), 732–733, *732*
Indra (Aryan deity), 427
Indravarman (Khmer king), 444
indulgences, 374, 616, 652
Indus Civilization art, 424–426, 447
Industrial Revolution, 728
    and Art Nouveau, 28-36A
    and Arts and Crafts movement, 827
    and the Enlightenment, 727, 736–737
    and German Expressionism, 839
    and Impressionist art, 799, 806
    and late 19th century art European and
        American art, 799, 800, 806, 827
    and Napoleonic era art, 757
    and Neo-Gothic architecture, 788
    and Pre-Raphaelite art, 786
    and Realism, 779
    and Romanticism, 771–772
    and social Darwinism, 801
Inferno (Dante), 824
ingegno, 604
Inghelbrecht, Peter, 534, 535
Ingram Street Tea Room, Glasgow, 828, *828*
Ingres, Jean-Auguste-Dominique
    Apotheosis of Homer, 760, *761*
    Grande Odalisque, 761, *761*
    and Léger, 29-22A
    and Matisse, 29-2A
    Napoleon on His Imperial Throne, 758,
        758b, 27-2A
    and photography, 791
    and Romanticism, 766
    and Rousseau, 28-26A
    Inka art, 510, 1029–1031, 35-8A
inlaid dagger blade with lion hunt, Grave
    Circle A, Mycenae, 100, *100*, 4-23A
Innocent III (Pope), 584
Innocent X (Pope), 669, 670
Insane Woman (Géricault), 766, *766*
installations, 950–951, 953, 956–957,
    970–971, 972, 30-25B
Insula of the Painted Vaults, Ostia, 214,
    214b, 7-54A
insulae, 213–214, *213*
Insular art. *See* Hiberno-Saxon art
intaglio, 556
intensity, 7
interaxial (intercolumniation), 135, 152
intercolumniation (interaxial), 135, 152
interlace
    in Carolingian art, 11-13A
    in French/Spanish Romanesque art, 347
    in Hiberno-Saxon art, 312, 313, 315, 11-9A
    in Viking art, 311, 11-4A
    Intermediate Area Native American art,
        507
internal evidence, 3
International Style (medieval Europe),
    413–414, 572, 573, 581
International style (Modernist architecture),
    886–887
The Interpretation of Dreams (Freud), 819,
    856
intonaco, 408
Introduction to the Three Arts of Design
    (Vasari), 365
Inuit art, 1038
invenzione, 604
investiture of Zimri-Lim, palace, Mari
    (mural), 43, *43b*, 44, 45, 46, 2-18A
investment (in lost-wax process), 130
Ionic order, 116, *116*
    and Composite capitals, 206, 587

in Greek architecture, 117, 119, 136, 141,
    152, 5-17A
in Italian Cinquecento Renaissance
    architecture, 22-30A
in Roman Republic architecture, 182
iota. *See* chi-rho-iota (Christogram)
Ipiutak, Alaska (U.S.A.): burial mask,
    Eskimo, 514, *515*
iron. *See* cast iron; wrought iron
iron bridge, Coalbrookdale (Darby and
    Pritchard), 737, *737*
iron-wire lines, 459, 482
Isaac, 246
    See also Abraham and Isaac
Isaac and His Sons, Gates of Paradise,
    Baptistery of San Giovanni, Florence
    (Ghiberti), 566–567, *567*
Isabella (queen of Castile), 284, 618
Isabella d'Este (Titian), 630, *630*, 631,
    22-40A
Isabella Stewart Gardner Museum, Boston,
    865
Ise (Japan): Ise Jingu, 478–480, *479*
Ise Jingu, Ise, 478–480, *479*
Isenheim (Germany): Hospital of Saint
    Anthony, 647, *648*
Isenheim Altarpiece (Grünewald), 647, *648*,
    874
Isfahan (Iran)
    Friday Mosque, 291–292, *292*, 299
    Imam (Shah) Mosque, 299–300, *299*
    Madrasa Imami, 300, *300*
Ishiyama-gire (Fujiwara no Sadanobu), *484b*,
    17-13B
Ishtar (Inanna) (Mesopotamia deity), 34, 35,
    48, 2-18A
Ishtar Gate, Babylon, 34, 48, *49*
Ishtar temple, Mari, 36, *36b*, 2-6A
Isidorus of Miletus. *See* Hagia Sophia
Isis (Egyptian deity), 57, 80, 7-62A
Islam, 284, 285
    in Africa, 529
    in South Asia, 441, 976
    in Southeast Asia, 984
    See also Crusades; Islamic art; Ottoman
        Empire
Islamic art, 282–305, *284map*
    19th century English architecture and,
        789
    Art Nouveau architecture and, 829
    Byzantine art and, 274–275, 287, 9-27A
    Christian patronage of, 304
    and Romanesque art, 345
    societal contexts, 284, 285, 294–295
    South Asian, 977, 980
    Spanish High Renaissance/Mannerist
        architecture and, 664
    timeline, 284
    See also early Islamic art; later Islamic art
Isola Sacra, Ostia, 214–215
Issus, battle of, 150
Istanbul. *See* Constantinople
Ita Yemoo (Nigeria): king, Ife (sculpture),
    527–528, *527*
Italian 13th century art, 3–4, 402–406, 421,
    14-6A
Italian 14th century art, 406–420, 421
    Cavallini, 407, 409, 14-7A
    Florence (Florentine), 417–419, 14-18A,
        14-18B, 14-19A
    Giotto di Bondone, 400, 401, 407–409,
        14-7A, 14-8A, 14-8B
    Pisa, 419–420
    Siena, 409, 411–416, 417, 14-10A, 14-12A,
        14-16A
    societal contexts, 406–407, 409, 410,
        14-16A
    Venice, 420
Italian Baroque art, 670–686, *673map*, 693
    architecture, 668, 669, 670–673, 676–678,
        24-4A, 24-9A, 24-14A
    and late 19th century art European and
        American sculpture, 28-31A
    painting. *See* Italian Baroque painting
    Rembrandt and, 25-13A
    sculpture, 673, 674–675, 24-6A
    timeline, 670

Italian Baroque painting
    Caravaggio, 681–683, 24-17A, 24-18A
    Carracci, 679–681, 682
    Gaulli, 686
    Gentileschi, 683–684
    Pietro da Cortona, 685–686
    Pozzo, 686, 687
    Reni, 684–685
Italian Cinquecento Renaissance art,
    600–632, *600map*, 643
    Andrea del Sarto, 22-8A
    architecture, 605, 618–624, 22-6A, 22-26A,
        22-30A
    and David, 747
    and Dürer, 649, 23-5A
    and Flemish Baroque art, 698
    Leonardo da Vinci, 601–605, 22-3A, 22-6A
    Michelangelo Buonarroti, 11, 598, 599,
        609–618, 619–621, 22-18A, 22-18B,
        22-26A
    painting. *See* Italian Cinquecento
        Renaissance painting
    Raphael, 605–609, 22-10A
    and Rococo architecture, 26-1A
    societal contexts, 600, 622
    timeline, 600
Italian Cinquecento Renaissance painting
    Andrea del Sarto, 22-8A
    Bellini, 624–625, 22-32A
    Giorgione, 626–627
    Leonardo da Vinci, 601–602, 603–604
    Michelangelo Buonarroti, 598, 599,
        614–616, 22-18A, 22-18B
    Raphael, 605–609, 22-10A
    Titian, 627–629, 630, 631–632
Italian late medieval art, 400–421, *405map*
    13th century, 402–406, 421, 14-6A
    14th century. *See* Italian 14th century art
    societal contexts, 404, 406–407
    timeline, 402
    See also Renaissance
Italian Mannerism, *600map*, 632–642, 643
    architecture, 640–642
    and El Greco, 665
    and Francis I, 657
    and Goujon, 23-14A
    and Napoleonic era art, 761
    painting, 632–638, 22-42A, 22-46A,
        22-54A
    sculpture, 638–639, 22-52A
    timeline, 600
Italian Quattrocento Renaissance art,
    558–597
    Florence, 560–588, *561map*, 597
        architecture, 582–588, 593–594,
            21-31A, 21-32A, 21-37A
        engraving, 581–582
        painting. *See* Florentine Quattrocento
            Renaissance painting
        sculpture. *See* Florentine
            Quattrocento Renaissance sculpture
    princely courts, 589–596, 597, 21-41A,
        21-43A, 21-49A
    societal contextss, 560, 561, 563, 584,
        588
    timeline, 560
    Venice, 21-37A
Italian Romanesque art, 354, 355–357,
    363, 12-27A, 12-27B
Itzamna B'ahlam II (Maya ruler), 503
ivi p'o, 1054
ivory carvings
    African, 531–532
    Early Byzantine, 257, 258–259, 264,
        9-14A
    Early Christian, 251–252, 12-13A
    Early Islamic, 292–293
    Gothic, 388–389
    Middle Byzantine, 275–276, 277
    Minoan, 94–95
    Mycenaean, 100–101
    Ottonian, 327, 328
    Paleolithic, 17, 19, 1-5A
    ivory figurine, Hohle Fels, 18
iwans, 52, *52*, 288, 292, 296
Ixion Room: House of the Vettii, Pompeii,
    194–195, *195*, 7-16A
iy'oba, 532, 19-13A

Monet, Claude (continued)
Sailboats on the Seine, Argenteuil, 799
Saint-Lazare Train Station, 803–804, *803*
and salons, 802
Money-Changer and His Wife (Massys), 659–660, *660*
Mongols, 295, 472, 990
Monk's Mound, Cahokia, 515, *515b*, 18-30A
monochrome
in Dutch Baroque art, 705
in late 20th century European and American art, 912
in Pompeian/Vesuvius area art, 194
in Roman art, 194
monolith with bird and crocodile, Great Zimbabwe (sculpture), 531, *531*
monolithic columns, 116, 428–429
monoliths, 531, 1053
See also monolithic columns
Monophysite heresy, 258, 270
monotheism, 233, 235, 285
Monreale cathedral, 275, *275*, 348, 9-26A
Monroe, Marilyn, 916, 917–918, 30-25A
Mont Sainte-Victoire (Cézanne), 817–818, *817*
Monte Albán (Mexico), 504, 1024
Montejo the Younger, Francisco, 23-23A
Monterozzi necropolis, Tarquinia, 164, *164*, 165, 171–172, *172*, *173*, 6-9A
Monticello, near Charlottesville (Jefferson), 750, *751*
Monument to the Third International (Tatlin), 860–861, *861*
Moore, Charles: Piazza d'Italia, New Orleans, 929–930, *929*
Moore, Henry
on abstract sculpture, 882
Reclining Figure, 883, *883*
Moorish art. *See* Islamic art
Moralia in Job (Saint Gregory), 347–348, *347*
moralized Bibles, 384–386
More, Thomas, 647, 23-11A
Moreau, Gustave, 28-26A
The Apparition, 820, *820*
Jupiter and Semele, *820b*, 28-24A
Morgan Madonna, 349, *349*
Morisot, Berthe
Summer's Day, 805, *805b*, 28-7A
Villa at the Seaside, 805, *805*
Morozov, Ivan, 844, 858
Morris, William, 808, 840
Green Dining Room, South Kensington Museum, 827, *827*
mortise-and-tenon system, 480
mortuary precinct of Djoser, Saqqara, 58, *58b*, 59, 60, 60, 68, 3-5A
mortuary temples, 62
Djoser mortuary precinct, Saqqara, 58, 60, 68, 3-5A
Great Pyramid complex, 62
Hatshepsut mortuary temple, Deir el-Bahri, 69–71, 73
mosaic tilework, 299–300
mosaics, 28-24A
Early Byzantine, 254, 255, 264–268
Early Christian, 244–245, 245, 247–248, 8-13A, 8-17A, 8-19A
Greek Late Classical period, 149, 150–151, 196, 214, 654
Islamic, 287, 291, 299–300
Mesoamerican, 504, 1024
Middle Byzantine, 270–271, 272–274, 275, 9-25A, 9-27A
Roman, 196, 214
moschophoros, 112
Moses, 33, 360, 8-10A, 22-32A, 23-15A
Moses, tomb of Julius II (Michelangelo Buonarroti), 360, 612–613, *612*
Moses Expounding the Law, Bury Bible (Master Hugo), 360, *360*
mosque lamp of Sayf al-Din Tuquztimur, 301, *301*
mosque lamps, 301
Mosque of Selim II, Edirne (Sinan the Great), 298, *298*, 299
mosques, 261, 287, 288, 290–292, 297, 10-5A
See also great mosques; specific mosques
Mother India (Bharat Mata) (Tagore), *983b*, 32-10A

Mother of God, 245, 267, 280, 380
modern mother as, 824
See also Theotokos; Virgin Mary
Mother of the Gracchi (Cornelia Presenting Her Children as Her Treasures) (Kauffmann), 746–747, *746*
Motherwell, Robert, 905
Elegy to the Spanish Republic, Spanish Elegies series, *905b*, 30-8B
motion pictures, 796, 855, 30-3A
Motonobu: *Zen Patriarch Xiangyen Zhixian Sweeping with a Broom*, 1007, 1008–1009, *1009*
Le Moulin de la Galette (Renoir), 806, *806*
Mount Sinai (Egypt): monastery of Saint Catherine, 267–268, *267*, 269, *269*, 270, 277, 279, 9-18A
Mount Vesuvius, eruption of, 188, 745
See also Pompeian/Vesuvius area art
Mount Wutai (China): Foguang Si (Buddha Radiance Temple), 462, *462b*, 16-15A
Mountains at Collioure (Derain), *839b*, 29-4A
Mouth of Hell, Winchester Psalter, 12-35A
Mozarabic art, 316
Mrs. Richard Brinsley Sheridan (Gainsborough), 741–742, *741*
Mshatta (Jordan): Umayyad palace, 287, *287b*, 10-5A, 10-5B
mudras, 427
abhaya mudra, 427, 432–433, 480, 984, 15-11A, 16-13B
bhumisparsha mudra, 427
dharmachakra mudra, 427, 443
dhyana mudra, 427, 431, 458–459, 16-13A
in Shingon, 483
Mughal Empire art, 294–295, 302, 945, 974, 975, 978–980, 981, 987, 32-5A
Muhammad, 284, 285, 289–290
Muhammad V (sultan of Granada), 295
Muhammad ibn al-Zayn: basin (*Baptistère de Saint Louis*), 303–304, *303*
Muhammad of Ghor, 294, 976
Muhaqqaq, 300
Mukherjee, Meera, 983–984
Ashoka at Kalinga, 984, *984*
Mukhina, Vera: *The Worker and the Collective Farmworker*, 883–884, *883*
mullions, 381, 930
Mumbai (India): Victoria Terminus (Chhatrapati Shivaji Terminus) (Stevens), 982, *982*
mummification, 61, 78, 218, 7-62A
mummy portrait of a priest of Serapis, Hawara (encaustic painting), *218*
mummy portrait of a young woman, Hawara (encaustic painting), *218b*, 7-62B
mummy portrait of Artemidorus, Hawara (encaustic painting), 218, *218b*, *218*, 7-62A
mummy portraits, 218, 7-62A, 7-62B
Munch, Edvard
and Schiele, 843
The Scream, 822, *823*, 840, 30-3A
Mundy, Peter, 695
Munich (Germany)
Amalienburg, 730, *730*
Olympic Park (Behnisch), 962
muqarnas, 274, 296, 297, 9-27A
mural painting
Byzantine, 9-25A
Chinese, 462, 16-14A
contemporary, 969
Early Christian, 237–239, 8-5A, 8-6A
Egyptian, 56–57, *57b*, 58, 74–75, 3-1A, 3-11B
Greek, 144, 149–150, 191
Italian 13th century, 407, 14-5A, 14-5B
Italian 14th century, 400, 401, 408, 409, 416–417, 419–420, 14-8A, 14-8B
Italian Quattrocento Renaissance, 574–576, 578–579, 589–590, 594–596, 21-24A, 21-41A, 21-49A
Italian Romanesque, 12-27B
Japanese, 482, 17-13A
Late Antique Jewish, 235–236
Mesoamerican, 497–498, 18-7A
Mesopotamian, 46, 47, 2-18A
Mexican interwar Modernist, 890–891

Minoan, 90–93
Native North American, 1032, 1033
Ottonian, 11-23A
Pompeian/Vesuvius area, 189–190, 191–195, 196, 197, 248, 7-25A, 7-25B
prehistoric, 22, 26–27
Roman High Empire, 7-54A
Romanesque, 348
See also cave paintings
Murasaki Shikubu: *Tale of Genji*, 484–485, *485*, 486, 487
Murillo, Bartolomé Esteban: *Immaculate Conception of the Escoria*, 688, *688b*, 24-25A
Muromachi period Japanese art, 1006, 1008–1009, 1021
Musée Africain, Marseilles, 846
Musée d'Ethnographie du Trocadéro, Paris, 846
Musée Permanent des Colonies, Paris, 846
Museum für Völkerkunde, Berlin, 846
Museum of Modern Art (MoMA), New York, 865, 895, 909, 930
museums: Greek forerunner of, 139
music
and American Modernism, 867
and contemporary art, 937, 947
and new media, 937
and Performance Art, 933–934
and Rococo architecture, 731
and Romanticism, 767
and Symbolist art, 28-24A
See also musical instruments
musical instruments, 38–39, 88
Musicians (Caravaggio), 681, *681b*, 24-17A
musicians and dancers, tomb of Nebamun, Thebes (mural), 75
Muslims, 976
See also Islam; Islamic art
Mut (Egyptian deity), 57, 3-24A
Muybridge, Eadweard, 784
Horse Galloping, 796, *796*, 825
Mwashamboy masks, 1076
My Egypt (Demuth), 868, *868*
Myanmar art (Burmese art), 443, 986, 15-28A
Mycenae (Greece)
female head (sculpture), 101, *101*
funerary mask, Grave Circle A, 100, *100*
Grave Circle A, 99–100, *99b*, 100, 4-22A, 4-23A
inlaid dagger blade with lion hunt, 100, *100*, 4-23A
Lion Gate, *98*, 99, 101, 4-18A
Treasury of Atreus, 98, *99*, 99, 170, 184
two goddesses(?) and a child (sculpture), 100–101, *101*
Warrior Vase, 102, *102*
See also Mycenaean art
Mycenaean art, 95–102
and archaeology, 85, 86, 87
architecture, 96–99, 115, 170, 184, 244, 4-18A, 4-22A, 5-6A
ivory carvings, 100–101
metalwork, 99–100, 4-23A
sculpture, 98, 99, 101–102
societal contexts, 95
vase painting, 102
Myokian temple, Kyoto (Sen no Rikyu), 1011, *1011*
Myron: *Diskobolos (Discus Thrower)*, 131–132, *131*, 617–618, 674
mystery plays, 409, 538, 548, 12-35A
mystic marriage, 549
mythology. *See* religion and mythology

N

the Nabis, 819
Nabu (Mesopotamian deity), 34, 48
Nadar (Gaspar-Félix Tournachon), 792, 793–794
Eugène Delacroix, 794, *794*
Nadar Raising Photography to the Height of Art (Daumier), 794, *794*
nail figure (nkisi n'kondi), Kongo (sculpture), 1066–1067, *1067*
Naked Portrait (Freud), 919, *919*
Namdaemun, Seoul, 1002, *1002*

Namuth, Hans: Jackson Pollock painting in his studio in Springs, Long Island, New York, 904
Nanas series (Saint-Phalle), 917, *917b*, 30-26A
Nandi (bull), 435, 436, 15-22B
Nanna (Mesopotamian deity), 34, 41
Nanni di Banco: *Four Crowned Saints*, Or San Michele, 563, *563*
naos. *See* cella
Napir-Asu (queen of Elam), 45
Napoleon III (emperor of France), 802, 804
Napoleon at the Plague House at Jaffa (Gros), 754, 755, 760, 766, 27-1A, 27-4A, 27-5A
Napoleon Bonaparte, 56, 755, 757, 764, 27-1A, 27-4A, 27-5A
See also Napoleonic era art
Napoleon Crossing the Saint-Bernard Pass (David), 757, *757b*, 948, 27-1A, 27-13A
Napoleon Leading the Army over the Alps (Wiley), 948, *948*
Napoleon on His Imperial Throne (Ingres), 758, *758b*, 27-2A
Napoleonic era art, 754, 756–761, *756map*, 797, 27-2A
and Romanticism, 755, 759, 27-1A, 27-5A
societal contexts, 756–757
timeline, 756
Nara (Japan): Todaiji, 482–483, *482*, 486
Nara period Japanese art, 474, 475, 481–483, 489
Nara Prefecture (Japan)
Horyuji temple, *474*, 475, 480, *480*, 481–482, *481*, *482*
Yakushi triad, Yakushiji, 481, *481*
Naram-Sin (king of Akkad), 40, 41
Naram-Sin victory stele, Susa, 40, 41, 44, 47
Narmer (pharaoh of Egypt), 54, 55, 57
narrative art
18th century European and American, 739, 740–741, 747–748
African, 1073
Akkadian, 40, 41
Baroque, 692
Burgundian/Flemish late medieval/early Renaissance, 20-11A
contemporary art, 946
early Christian, 249–250, 251–252, 8-21A
early medieval, 319, 326–327, 11-15A
Egyptian, 55, 58, 66, 78
Gothic, 369–370, 377, 13-3A
Greek Archaic period, 118, 119, 120, 122–123
Greek Early/High Classical period, 104, 105, 126, 128, 143
Greek Geometric period, 109, 128
Greek late Classical period, 150–151
Hellenistic period Greek, 156
Italian 14th century, 409, 412, 14-8A
Italian Cinquecento Renaissance art, 614–615
Italian late medieval, 405
Italian Quattrocento Renaissance, 565, 568, 21-24A
Japanese, 488
Late Antique Jewish, 235
Mycenaean, 102, 4-23A
Native North American, 35-16A
Neolithic, 27
Paleolithic, 22, 23
Pompeian/Vesuvius area, 192
Roman, 179, 187, 206–207, 208, 7-44A
Romanesque, 356, 361–362, 12-8B, 12-11A
Romantic, 764, 765–767
South Asian, 422, 423, 426, 432, 436, 438, 978, 15-22A
Sumerian, 30, 31, 35, 36, 37, 38
narthex, 243, 264, 350, 8-19A
Nasca art, 510–511
Nasca Plain (Peru): hummingbird, 511, *511*
Nash, John: Royal Pavilion, Brighton, 788–789, *789*
al-Nasir Muhammad, 301
Nasrid dynasty, 295
natatio, 220
National Endowment for the Arts (NEA) (U.S.A.), 944, 945
national identity in contemporary art, 945, 948–949, 973, 31-10A

Northern European art. *See* Burgundian/
Flemish late medieval/early
Renaissance art; Dutch . . . art; Flemish
Baroque art; French . . . art; German
art; Holy Roman Empire . . . art;
Northern European . . . art

Northern European High Renaissance/
Mannerist art, 644–663, *646map*, 667
Dutch, 658–663, 667
French, 656–658, 667, 23-14A
societal contexts, 646–647, 652–653,
656–657, 658–659
timeline, 646

Northern European late medieval/early
Renaissance art, 534–557, *536map*
Burgundian/Flemish. *See* Burgundian/
Flemish late medieval/early
Renaissance art
French, 550–552, 557, 20-15A
Holy Roman Empire, 552–556, 557,
20-18A, 20-21A
societal contexts, 536–537, 550, 555–556
timeline, 536

northern Hindu temple style, 439
Northern Wei dynasty Chinese art,
460–461
Northwest Coast Native American art, 514,
1034, 1036–1038, 35-14A
Notre Dame Cathedral, Chartres. *See*
Chartres Cathedral
Notre Dame de la Belle Verrière, Chartres
Cathedral (stained-glass window),
376–377, *376*, *377*, 386
Notre-Dame, Fontenay, 343, *343b*, 349–350,
12-10A
Notre-Dame Cathedral, Paris, *371*, 372–373,
372, 378, 381, *381*, 388, 788
Notre-Dame-du-Haut, Ronchamp (Le
Corbusier), 887, 926, *926*
Notre-Dame-la-Grande, Poitiers, 344, *344b*,
12-11A
Noumea (New Caledonia): Tjibaou Cultural
Centre (Piano), *961*
Novios Plautios, 168
Ficoroni Cista (bronze container), *174*,
175, 6-13A
Nsangu (Bamum king), 1065
Nubia, 81, 3-16A
Nude (Weston), 870, *870b*, 29-44A
Nude Descending a Staircase, No. 2
(Duchamp), 858, 863, *863*
nude male torso, Harappa, 426, *426*
Nude Self-Portrait, Grimacing (Schiele), 843,
843
nude woman *(Venus of Willendorf)*, 18, *18*,
25, 30-26A
nudity
in 18th century European and American
art, 752
in American modernist art, 870, 29-44A
in Conceptual Art, 30-55A
in contemporary art, 944, 945, 957, 958
in Cubist art, 29-22A
in Early Christian art, 252
in Fauve art, 29-2A
in French/Spanish Romanesque art,
12-13A, 12-13B
in German Expressionist art, 843, 29-9A
in Greek culture, 109, 112, 145, 158–159,
5-23A
in Italian Baroque art, 680–681, 24-17A
in Italian Cinquecento Renaissance art,
628, 631
in Italian Mannerist art, 639, 22-52A
in Italian Quattrocento Renaissance art,
568, 579, 582
in late 19th century art European and
American sculpture, 28-31A
in Mexican interwar Modernist art,
29-74A
in Napoleonic era art, 759, 761
in Northern European High Renaissance/
Mannerist art, 645, 649, 654, 659,
23-3A
in Performance Art, 935
in Post-Impressionist art, 28-22A
in Realist art, 780–781, 781–782
in Rococo art, 735

in Roman art, 187
in Romantic art, 770
in South Asian art, 440, 980, 981, 15-6B
in Symbolist art, 28-26A
Number 1, 1950 (Lavender Mist)
(Pollock), 903–904, *903*
nummus with portrait of Constantine, 230,
230
Nun (Egyptian deity), 57
Nuñez de Balboa, Vasco, 664
Nuremberg Chronicle (Koberger) (ill. by
Wolgemut and shop), 554–555, *555*, 556
Nut (Egyptian deity), 57
Nymph and Satyr Carousing (Clodion), 735,
735
nymphs, 107
Nymphs, Fountain of the Innocents, Paris
(Goujon), 658, *658b*, 23-14A
Nymphs and a Satyr (Bouguereau), 782,
782b, 27-33A
Nyx (Greek deity), 137

O

O'Keeffe, Georgia
Chicago (Judy) and, 921
Jack in the Pulpit No. 4, 4, *4*, 869, 870
New York, Night, 868, 869
and Stieglitz, 868–869
O'Sullivan, John L., 774
O'Sullivan, Timothy: *A Harvest of Death,
Gettysburg, Pennsylvania, July 1863*,
795, *795*
Oath of the Horatii (David), 728, 747–748,
747, 755, 757–758, 760
oba, 521, 19-13A
Object (Le Déjeuner en Fourrure)
(Oppenheim), 879, *879*
Oceanic art, 1042–1059, *1044map*
Australian, 1045–1046, 1059, 31-22B
contemporary, 949, 1058, 31-22B
Micronesia, 1050, 1052, 1059
New Guinean, 1045, 1046–1048, 1051,
36-1A
New Ireland, 1049
New Zealand, 13, 949, 1042, 1043, 1058
Polynesian, 1052–1058, 1059, 36-14A
societal contexts, 1042, 1044–1045, 1046,
1047, 1050, 1052, 1054, 1055
tattoo, 13, 525, 861, 1043, 1054, 1055
timeline, 1044
Trobriand Islands, 1049–1050, 1051
Western fascination with. *See* primitivism
Oceanic sculpture
New Guinean, 1045, 1046, 1047, 36-1A
New Zealand, 1042, 1043
Polynesian, 1052–1053, 1054, 1056, 1057,
36-14A
Trobriand Islands, 1049–1050
Oceanus and Nereids, and drinking contest
between Bacchus and Hercules, "Great
Dish", Mildenhall Treasure, 250–251,
250
Octavian (Roman emperor). *See* Augustus
oculus/oculi, 184, *184*, 202, 210, 372, 373,
383, 14-6A, 21-31A
Oda Nobunaga (shogun), 1009, 34-5A
odalisques, 761, 27-17A
Odo (bishop of Bayeux), 361
Odoacer, Flavius (king of Italy), 246
Odysseus, 162
Odyssey (Homer), 85, 107, 162
See also Homer
Ofili, Chris: *The Holy Virgin Mary*, 934,
948–949, *949*
Ogata Korin. *See* Korin
ogee arches, 420, 13-42A
ogival arches. *See* pointed arches
ogoga, 1072
Ohisa of the Takashima Tea Shop (Utamaro),
1017b, 34-12A
Ohrid (Macedonia)
Church of the Virgin Peribleptos,
279–280
Saint Clement, 279
oil painting
Italian Cinquecento Renaissance, 601,
624, 631
in Japan, 1018

Northern European late medieval/early
Renaissance, 538
vs. tempera painting, 538, 539
See also painting
Oinomaos (king of Pisa), 126
Oiran (Grand Courtesan) (Takahashi), 1018,
1018
Okakura Kakuzo, 1019
Okeanos (Oceanus) (Greek/Roman deity),
107
Old Farmer of Corycus, Vatican Vergil, 248,
249
Old Kingdom period Egyptian art, 49,
60–67, 83, 3-11A, 3-11B, 3-12A, 3-13A,
3-13B
old market woman (sculpture), 160, *161*
Old Saint Peter's, Rome, 242–243, *242*, 317,
607
Old Stone Age. *See* Paleolithic art
Old Temple, Chavín de Huántar, 508
Old Testament prophet (Jeremiah or
Isaiah?), Saint-Pierre, Moissac (relief
sculpture), *344*, 345, 12-8B
Old Testament themes
in Baroque art, 683, 25-13A
in Burgundian/Flemish late medieval/
early Renaissance art, 537–538, 540,
547
in Byzantine art, 264, 9-14A
in Early Christian art, 232, 233, 237–238,
245–246, 8-5A, 8-10A, 8-13A
in Gothic art, 370, 376, 386–387, 392,
13-23A, 13-44A
in Italian 13th century art, 14-5B
in Italian Cinquecento Renaissance art,
612–613, 614, 615, 22-18A
in Italian Quattrocento Renaissance art,
561–562, 566
in Ottonian art, 326
in Romanesque art, 344, 348, 353, 356,
12-11A
Oldenburg, Claes, 962
*Lipstick (Ascending) on Caterpillar
Tracks*, 916–917, *917*
Olmec art, 493–494, 501
Olokun (Benin deity), 532
Olowe of Ise, 1071
doors, shrine of the king's head, royal
palace, Ikere (relief sculpture),
1072–1073, *1072*
veranda post, Akure (sculpture), *1072b*,
37-16A
Olympia (Greece)
Athena, Herakles, and Atlas with the
apples of the Hesperides, Temple of
Zeus metope, Olympia (sculpture),
128, *128*, 148
chariot race of Pelops and Oinomaos,
Temple of Zeus east pediment
(sculpture), 126, *126*
hero and centaur (Herakles and Nessos?)
(sculpture), 109, *109*
seer, Temple of Zeus east pediment
(sculpture), 126, *127*, 146–147
Temple of Hera, 115, 146
Temple of Zeus (Libon of Elis), 125–126,
126, *127*, 128, 146–147, 5-32A
Zeus (Phidias) (sculpture), 49, 752, 27-2A
Olympia (Manet), 781–782, *781*, 27-33A
Olympic Games, 108, 109, 128, 246
Olympic Park, Munich (Behnisch), 962
Olympic stadiums, Tokyo (Tange), 1020,
1020
On a Mountain Path in Spring (Ma Yuan),
468, *468*
On Architecture (Vitruvius), 167, 603, 622,
22-3A
See also Vitruvius
On Love (Ficino), 581
On Painting (Alberti), 566
On the Art of Building (Alberti), 568, 586,
588
On the Bank of the Seine, Bennecourt
(Monet), *801b*, 28-2A, 28-7A
On the Dignity and Excellence of Man
(Manetti), 588
*On the Origin of Species by Means of Natural
Selection* (Darwin), 800

Northern European late medieval/early
Renaissance, 538
One and Three Chairs (Kosuth), 936–937, *936*
One Hundred Famous Views of Edo series
(Hiroshige), *1004*, 1005, 28-16B
Onesimos: girl preparing to bathe, Chiusi
(vase painting), 123, *123b*, 145, 5-23A
oni, 527
Op Art, 8, 908–909
open-air art, 18, 910
See also specific works of art
opere francigeno (opus francigenum), 366,
389, 13-38A
Opet Festival (Egypt), 3-24A
Ophelia (Millais), 786, 795
Ophelia, Study no. 2 (Cameron), 794, *795*
opisthodomos, 115
Oppenheim, Meret: *Object (Le Déjeuner en
Fourrure)*, 879, *879*
optical effects, 135, 138, 909
optical mixture, 813
optical representation, 23, 35
opus francigenum (opere francigeno), 366,
389, 13-38A
opus modernum, 365, 366, 373, 389
opus reticulatum, 11-19A
Or San Michele, Florence, 419, *419b*, 562–565,
563, *564*, *565*, 14-19A, 21-36A
oracles, 5-17A
orants, 238, 266, 8-10A, 9-25A
oratory, 267
orbiculum, 930
Orcagna, Andrea: tabernacle, Or San
Michele, Florence, 419, *419b*, 14-19A
Orchard Factory: table with drawers, Ming
dynasty, 994, 995, *995*
orchestra, 151
Ordelafo Falier (doge of Venice), 9-26A
Order of Mercy, 688–689
orders (of Greek temple architecture), 116,
116, 751
See also Doric order; Ionic order
orders, monastic. *See* monastic orders
Oresteia (Aeschylus), 125, 126
Orestes, 217
Orestes sarcophagus, 216–217, *217*
Orientalizing period Etruscan art, 167, 177
Orientalizing period Greek art, 109, 109–111,
163, 169, 5-6A, 5-6B
Ornament and Crime (Loos), 861
Ornament in Architecture (Sullivan), 861
Orozco, José Clemente: *Epic of American
Civilization: Hispano-America*, Baker
Memorial Library, Dartmouth College,
Hanover, 890–891, *891*
Orpheus, 276
Orphism, 848
orrery, 726, 727
Orthodox Baptistery (Sant'Apollinare
Nuovo), Ravenna, 247–248, *247*, *248*,
250, 266, 8-17A, 8-19A, 12-27B
Orthodox Christianity, 258
See also Byzantine art
orthogonal plans, 154
orthogonals, 547, 567, 574, 581
Orvieto (Italy)
Achilles and Ajax playing a dice game
(Andokides Painter) (vase painting),
121–122, *121*
Artemis and Apollo slaying the children
of Niobe (Niobid Painter) (vase
painting), 143, *143*
Orvieto Cathedral (Maitani), 412–413,
413, 418, 590, *590*, 14-12A
Orvieto Cathedral (Maitani), 412–413,
413, 418, 590, *590*, 14-12A
Oseberg ship burial, 310–311, *310*, 11-4A
Osiris (Egyptian deity), 57, 71, 80, 7-62A
Osman I (Ottoman emperor), 297
Ospedale degli Innocenti (Foundling
Hospital), Florence (Brunelleschi), 410,
582–583, *583*, 585, 21-36A
Ostia (Italy), 213–215, *213*
Baths of Neptune, 214, *214*
Insula of the Painted Vaults, 214, *214b*,
7-54A
insulae, 213–214, *213*, 7-54A
Isola Sacra, 214–215
Ostrogoths, 246, 247, 255, 258, 263, 308
Otto I (Holy Roman Emperor), 324, 327, 328

Greek Archaic period, 112
Greek Early/High Classical period, 129–130
Japan, 17-13A
lost-wax process, 130, 452, 507, 526, 673, 983–984, 19-4A, 22-52A, 35-8A
Neo-Sumerian, 40–41
Neoclassical, 27-4A
Neolithic, 25
Paleolithic, 17, 18, 19, 1-5A, 1-6A
Roman Early Empire art, 205
Roman High Empire art, 179
Roman Late Empire art, 7-64A, 7-68A
South Asia, 983–984
Seagram Building, New York (Mies van der Rohe and Johnson), 928, 928, 930, 961
seal with seated figure in yogic posture, Mohenjo-daro, 426, 426
seals
    Chinese, 997
    Mesopotamian, 39
    South Asian, 426
Sears Tower (Willis Tower), Chicago (Skidmore, Owings, and Merrill), 928–929, 928, 961
The Seasons (Krasner), 904b, 30-7A
seated Amida, Phoenix Hall, Byodoin, Uji (Jocho) (sculpture), 484, 484b, 17-13A
seated boxer, Rome (sculpture), 160, 160
seated buddha and standing bodhisattva, Yungang Grottoes, Datong (cave sculpture), 16-13A
seated Buddha preaching first sermon, Sarnath (sculpture), 432, 433, 472
seated couple, Dogon, 1068–1069, 1068
seated figure with drinking cup, Colima (sculpture), 495, 495, 29-74A
seated man, Tada (sculpture), 528, 528
seated portrait of the Greek poet Menander, House of the Menander, Pompeii (mural), 196b, 318, 7-25B
seated scribe, Saqqara (sculpture), 65–66, 65
seated statue of Lady Sennuwy, Kerma, 67b, 3-16A
seated statues of Rahotep and Nofret, Maidum, 64b, 65, 3-11A, 3-13B
seated statuette of Urnanshe, Mari, 36, 36b, 43, 45, 2-6A
Seated Youth (Lehmbruck), 843, 843b, 29-10A
Sebastian, Saint, 647
Second Coming
    in Early Byzantine art, 254, 255, 264
    in French Gothic art, 369, 369–370
    in French/Spanish Romanesque art, 343, 344, 345–346
    See also Last Judgment
Second Coming of Christ, Saint-Pierre, Moissac (relief sculpture), 343, 344, 346, 369–370, 12-11A
Second Commandment, 235, 239, 269, 348, 8-8A
Second Style, 192–194, 213, 595
Second Style wall paintings, Villa of Publius Fannius Synistor, Boscoreale, 192–193, 193, 213
secondary colors, 7, 813
Secrets of Landscape Painting (Huang Gongwang), 992–993
sections (architectural), 12
sedes sapientiae, 349
Seduction of Yusuf, Bustan (Sadi) (ill. by Bihzad), 978
seer, Temple of Zeus east pediment, Olympia (sculpture), 126, 127, 146–147
Segal, George: *The Gas Station*, 916, 916b, 30-25B
segmental pediments, 621
Selene (Luna) (Greek/Roman deity), 107, 137
Seleucus I Nicator, 52, 428
Self-Portrait (Dürer), 649–650, 650, 23-11A
Self-Portrait (Leyster), 705, 705
Self-Portrait (Mapplethorpe), 944, 945
Self-Portrait (Te Pehi Kupe), 13, 13, 1055
Self-Portrait (van Hemessen), 661, 661
Self-Portrait (Vigée-Lebrun), 739–740, 739, 26-15A

Self-Portrait, 1658 (Rembrandt), 708, 708b, 25-15A
Self-Portrait, ca. 1659-1660 (Rembrandt), 705, 708, 708
Self-Portrait as a Fountain (Nauman), 937b, 30-55A
Self-Portrait as the Allegory of Painting (La Pittura) (Gentileschi), 683–684, 684
Self-Portrait in a Convex Mirror (Parmigianino), 633, 633
Self-Portrait Looking at the Last Supper (Marisol), 959, 959
Self-Portrait with Amber Necklace (Modersohn-Becker), 842, 842b, 29-9A
Self-Portrait with Two Pupils (Labille-Guiard), 740, 740
self-portraits
    18th century European and American, 739–740
    Burgundian/Flemish late medieval/early Renaissance, 543, 545cap, 546
    Conceptual Art, 30-55A
    contemporary, 944, 945, 957, 31-27A
    and cultural differences, 13
    Dadaist, 835
    Dutch Baroque, 695, 705, 708, 25-15A
    El Greco, 665
    German Expressionist, 843
    Italian Baroque, 683–684, 24-17A
    Italian Cinquecento Renaissance, 607, 618, 633
    Italian Mannerist, 633
    Italian Quattrocento Renaissance, 578
    Northern European High Renaissance/Mannerist, 649–650
    Photorealist, 918
    Post-Impressionist, 811
    in Romantic art, 27-10A
    in South Asian art, 974, 975
Selim II (Ottoman sultan), 302
Seljuks, 292, 297
Sen no Rikyu, 1012
    Taian teahouse, Myokian temple, Kyoto, 1011, 1011, 1013
Senefelder, Alois, 778
senate, 181
Senmut (chancellor of Egypt), 69–70, 74
Senmut with Princess Nefrura, Thebes (sculpture), 74, 74
Senufo art, 1073–1074, 37-17A
Senusret I (pharaoh of Egypt), 3-16A
Senusret III (pharaoh of Egypt), 67–68
Seokguram cave temple, 471–472, 471
Seoul (South Korea): Namdaemun, 1002, 1002
Septimus Severus (Roman emperor), 219
Serapion, Saint, 688–689
Serapis (Egyptian deity), 218
serdab, 58
Serpent Mound, 516, 516, 517
Serra, Richard: *Tilted Arc*, New York, 944, 966–967, 967
Serrano, Andres: *Piss Christ*, 944
Servite order, 404
Sesshu Toyo: splashed-ink (haboku) landscape (hanging scroll), 1008, 1008
Seth (Egyptian deity), 57, 75
Seti I (pharaoh of Egypt), 80
Seurat, Georges, 802, 909
    A Sunday on La Grande Jatte, 802, 812, 812, 813, 819–820, 822
Seven Wonders of the ancient world, 48, 49, 60, 5-64B
Severan period, 219–221, 7-64A
    See also Roman Late Empire art
Severe Style (Greek art), 128
    See also Greek Early/High Classical period art
Severini, Gino, 854
    Armored Train, 855, 855
Severus: Domus Aurea (Golden House), 194, 195, 201–202, 202, 203–204
Severus Alexander (Roman emperor), 221
sexpartite vaults, 358
sexuality. *See* eroticism
Sforza, Battista, 590, 591, 592
Sforza, Caterina, 630
Sforza, Francesco, 605

Sforza, Ludovico, 601
sfumato, 539, 604
sgrafitto, 451, 467
shafts (of columns), 51, 116, 373
Shah Tahmasp Meditating (Banu), 978–979, 979
Shahn, Ben: *The Passion of Sacco and Vanzetti*, 4, 4, 6, 888
Shahnama (Book of Kings) (Sultan-Muhammad), 302–303, 303
Shaka, 480
Shaka triad, Horyuji temple (Tori Busshi) (sculpture), 474, 475, 480, 481
shakti, 435
Shakespeare, William, 760, 786
Shakyamuni and Prabhutaratna, Hebei Province, Northern Wei dynasty (sculpture), 460–461, 460, 471
Shakyamuni Buddha
    attributes of, 427, 458, 15-11A
    in Chinese art, 458–459, 460–461
    in Gupta period South Asian art, 432, 433–434
    in Japanese art, 474, 475
    in Korean art, 471, 472
    life of, 422, 423, 427, 432, 15-8A
    in Shunga/Andhra/Kushan period art, 422, 423, 431–433, 15-11A
Shakyamuni Buddha, Hebei Province, Later Zhao dynasty (sculpture), 458–459, 458
Shakyamuni Buddha, Seokguram (sculpture), 471, 472
Shamash (Utu) (Mesopotamian deity), 34, 44
Shang dynasty Chinese art, 452, 473
Shang Xi: *Guan Yu Captures General Pang De*, 994, 995
Shanxi (China): Bodhisattva Guanyin seated on Potalaka (sculpture), 467, 467b, 16-21A
Shapur I (Sasanian king), 52, 2-28A
Shapur I, palace of, Ctesiphon, 52, 52, 296
shaykhs, 975
Shchukin, Sergei, 844, 858
Sheeler, Charles, 868
Sheep and Goat (Zhao), 990b, 33-1A
Shelley, Mary Wollstonecraft, 767, 26-27A
Shelley, Percy Bysshe, 767
Shen Zhou
    Lofty Mount Lu, 996, 997, 997, 998, 33-12A
    Poet on a Mountaintop, 998, 998b, 33-12A
sherds, 476
Sherman, Cindy, 942, 31-6A
    Untitled Film Stills series, 922–923, 923
Shi Huangdi (Chinese emperor), 454–455
Shield Jaguar and Lady Xoc, Yaxchilán (relief sculpture), 503, 503
shikhara, 439, 440, 15-28A
Shingon, 483
shingon (mantras), 483
Shino, 1012
Shinto, 478–480, 956, 957, 1005
Shiraga, Kazuo: *Making a Work with His Own Body*, 1020, 1020
Shirasagi (White Heron Castle), Himeji, 1010, 1010b, 34-5A
Shitao (Daoji)
    Man in a House beneath a Cliff, 999, 999
    Sayings on Painting from Monk Bitter Gourd, 999
Shiva (Hindu deity), 435–436, 438, 440–441, 443–444, 15-22A, 15-22B
Shiva as Mahadeva, Elephanta (cave sculpture), 436, 436
Shiva as Nataraja, 440–441, 441
Shodo Shima Stone Study (Noguchi), 913, 913b, 30-21A
shogunate, 486, 1006
shoguns, 486, 1006
Shomu (Japanese emperor), 482
Shop Block, Bauhaus, Dessau (Gropius), 884, 885
A Short History of Modernist Painting (Tansey), 959B, 31-28A
Shotuku Taishi (Japanese prince), 480
Showa period Japanese art, 1019–1020, 1021
shrine of the king's head, royal palace, Ikere (Olowe of Ise), 1072–1073, 1072

Shrine of the Three Kings (Nicholas of Verdun), 393, 393
Shu (Egyptian deity), 57
Shunga dynasty (South Asia), 429, 447
Shunjobo Chogen, 486, 17-17A
sibyls, 540
Siddal, Elizabeth, 787–788
Siena (Italy)
    Campo, 415, 415
    Palazzo Pubblico, 415–416, 415, 416, 417, 14-16A, 14-18B
    San Niccolò del Carmine, 22-42A
    See also Siena Cathedral; Sienese 14th century art
Siena Cathedral, 14-12A
    Annunciation altarpiece (Martini and Memmi), 413–415, 413
    Birth of the Virgin (Lorenzetti), 415, 415
    Feast of Herod (Donatello), 565, 565
    Maestà altarpiece (Duccio), 410, 411–412, 411, 412b, 412, 13-36A, 14-8B, 14-10A
    and Santa Maria del Fiore, 417
Sienese 14th century art, 411–416
    architecture, 412–413, 415–416, 14-12A
    painting, 411–412, 413–415, 416, 417, 14-7A, 14-10A, 14-16A
    societal contexts, 409, 14-16A
Sigismund (Holy Roman Emperor), 404
Signboard of Gersaint (Watteau), 733, 733b, 26-7A
Signorelli, Luca: *The Damned Cast into Hell*, Orvieto Cathedral (Signorelli), 590, 590, 616
Signoria, 563
Sikander, Shahzia, 32-10A
    Perilous Order, 945, 945
silentiaries, 261
silk
    in Chinese art, 458, 16-14A, 16-23A
    in early Islamic art, 10-15A
    in Han dynasty Chinese art, 448, 449
    in Japanese art, 483
Silk Road, 412, 449, 455, 458
silk textile, Zandana, 292b, 10-15A
silk-screen printing, 915
Silla kingdom (Korea), 470, 471–472, 473
Silos (Spain): Santo Domingo, 340b, 12-8B
Silueta series (Mendieta), 923, 923
silver. *See* metalwork
silverpoint, 545, 604
Sima Qian, 455
Simmons Architects: Sony Building (AT&T building), New York, 930–931, 930
Simpson, Lorna, 954
    Stereo Styles, 946b, 31-6A
Simultanéisme, 848
simultaneous contrasts, 813
Sin (Nanna) (Mesopotamian deity), 34, 41
Sinan the Great, 297, 10-23A
    Mosque of Selim II, Edirne, 298, 298, 299
Singh, Jaswant (ruler of Jodhpur), 983
sinopia, 408
Sipán (Peru)
    ear ornament, Moche, 512, 512
    tombs, 512
Siphnian Treasury, Delphi, 119, 119, 119, 141, 156
sirens, 110–111
Sistine Chapel, Vatican, Rome
    ceiling (Michelangelo Buonarroti), 598, 599, 605, 614–615, 614, 615, 681, 698, 22-18A, 22-18B
    Christ Delivering the Keys of the Kingdom to Saint Peter, Sistine Chapel (Perugino), 567, 589–590, 589, 22-18B
    Last Judgment (Michelangelo Buonarroti), 598, 616, 616, 22-18B, 22-54A
    restoration, 408, 615, 22-18B
    sistrum, 95
Sitani, Mele: ngatu with manulua designs, 1053, 1054
site-specific art, 932–933, 964–969, 973
six canons of painting (Xie He), 460
Sixth Avenue and Thirtieth Street, New York City (Sloan), 862, 862

Tegea (Greece): Temple of Athena Alea (Skopas of Paros), 5-64A
tempera painting
  in Italian 13th century art, 404–405
  in Italian 14th century art, 407–408, 411–412, 413–415, 14-10A
  in Italian Cinquecento Renaissance art, 602, 22-32A
  in Italian Quattrocento Renaissance art, 572, 573, 577–578, 579–580, 581, 591, 592, 21-29A
  in Late Antique Jewish art, 235
  in Mesoamerican art, 502
  vs. oil painting, 538, 539
  in Roman art, 219
  See also mural painting; painting
The Tempest (Giorgione da Castelfranco), 626–627, 626, 666
Tempietto, Rome (Bramante), 618–619, 618, 623, 22-6A
Temple A, Prinias, 111, 111b, 115, 5-6A, 5-6B
Temple of Aphaia, Aegina, 123–124, 123, 124, 125, 126
Temple of Apollo, Didyma (Paionios of Ephesos and Daphnis of Miletos), 153–154, 153
Temple of Artemis, Corfu, 118, 118, 124
Temple of Artemis, Ephesos, 49
Temple of Athena Alea (Skopas of Paros), Tegea, 5-64A
Temple of Athena Nike (Kallikrates), Athens, 134, 141, 141, 152
Temple of Fortuna Virilis (Temple of Portunus), Rome, 182, 182
Temple of Geshtinanna, Girsu, 43
Temple of Hera, Olympia, 115, 146
Temple of Hera I ("Basilica"), Paestum, 117–118, 117, 123, 135
Temple of Hera II or Apollo, Paestum, 125–126, 126
Temple of Horus, Edfu, 82, 82, 3-1A
Temple of Jupiter Optimus Maximus, Capitoline Hill, Rome (Vulca of Veii), 168, 181
Temple of Portunus (Temple of Fortuna Virilis), Rome, 182, 182
Temple of Quetzalcoatl, Teotihuacán, 496, 497
Temple of Ramses II, Abu Simbel, 71–72, 71
Temple of the Giant Jaguar, Tikal, 500, 500
Temple of the Inscriptions, Palenque, 500, 500b, 18-10A
Temple of the Sun, Cuzco, 1031, 1031
Temple of Venus, Baalbek, 224, 224, 225, 748, 750
Temple of Vesta(?), Tivoli, 183, 183
Temple of Zeus, Olympia (Libon of Elis), 125–126, 126, 127, 128, 146–147, 148, 5-32A
Templo Mayor (Great Temple), Tenochtitlán, 1022, 1023, 1026–1028, 1026, 1027, 1028
templon, 277
Temptation of Saint Anthony (Grünewald), 647, 648
Tendai Buddhism, 483
tenebrism, 682–683, 683, 698
tenebroso. See tenebrism
Tenochtitlán (Mexico), 1022, 1024, 1025
  Coatlicue (sculpture), 1028, 1029
  Coyolxauhqui (relief sculpture), 1026–1028, 1027
  Templo Mayor (Great Temple), 1022, 1023, 1026–1028, 1026, 1027, 1028
  Tlaltecuhtli (relief sculpture), 1028, 1028
tenons. See mortise-and-tenon system
Teotihuacán (Mexico), 491
  architecture, 495–497, 495, 496
  Aztecs and, 496, 1026
  and ball games, 501
  destruction of, 504, 1024
  and Modernist art, 29-74A
  murals, 497–498, 18-7A
  Tetitla apartment complex, 497, 498
tephra, 92
tepidarium, 220
ter Brugghen, Hendrick, 723
  Calling of Saint Matthew, 702, 702
Teresa of Avila, Saint, 675, 688

Terminal 5, John F. Kennedy International Airport, New York (Saarinen), 926, 927
terminus ante quem, 2
terminus post quem, 2
terracotta
  in African art, 524, 525, 528, 529
  in Chinese art, 451, 454–455
  in Etruscan art, 168, 169, 181
  in Intermediate Area Native American art, 507
  in Italian 14th century art, 414
  in Italian Quattrocento Renaissance art, 583, 585, 21-36A
  in Minoan architecture, 90
  in Roman art, 214–215
terribilità, 599
tesserae, 150, 245, 291, 299
tetrarchs, 224
  See also tetrarchy
tetrarchy, 224–225
textiles
  African, 1070, 1071, 37-13A
  Andean South American, 509, 510, 513, 1029–1030
  Bauhaus, 29-66B
  Chinese, 448, 449, 458, 10-15A, 16-14A
  contemporary, 945–946
  early Islamic, 10-15A
  in feminist art, 922, 924–925
  and Italian 14th century art, 412
  Japanese, 483
  Late Byzantine, 9-35A
  later Islamic, 300–301, 10-27A
  Native North American, 1033
  Norman Romanesque, 361–362
  Oceanic, 1042, 1043, 1047, 1051, 1053–1054, 1058
texture, 8
Thai art, 443, 984–985, 15-29A
Thangmar of Heidelberg, 324–325
Thanjavur (India): Rajarajeshvara Temple, 438, 439, 15-22B
The Thankful Poor (Tanner), 784–785, 785
The Eight (artist group), 862
theater of Epidauros (Polykleitos the Younger), 151, 151
theatron, 151
Thebes (Egypt), 69
  first millenium BCE, 80–81
  funerary chapel of Rekhmire, 64b, 3-11B
  Senmut with Princess Nefrura (sculpture), 74, 74
  tomb of Hunefer, 80, 80
  tomb of Nebamun, 74–75, 75
  tomb of Tutankhamen, 78, 78, 79, 100
  Valley of the Kings, 72
  See also Luxor
Thebes (Greece): Mantiklos Apollo (sculpture), 109–110, 109, 112
Theodora (Byzantine empress, wife of Justinian), 254, 255, 264, 265, 266, 275, 309
Theodora (Byzantine empress, wife of Theophilos), 270, 273
Theodora and attendants, San Vitale, Ravenna (mosaic), 254, 255, 264, 265, 266, 275, 309
Theodore, Saint, 268, 269, 377
Theodoric (king of the Ostrogoths), 246, 247, 263, 308, 317
Theodoros of Phokaia: tholos, Delphi, 151–152, 151
Theodosius I (Roman emperor), 246, 256
Theodulf of Orléans, 265, 317
Theogony (Genealogy of the Gods) (Hesiod), 107
Theophanu, 328
Theopompus, 169
theosophy, 841, 880
Theotokos
  in Early Byzantine art, 267, 268–270, 269
  in Early Christian art, 245
  in Gothic art, 370, 396
  in Middle Byzantine art, 270–271, 271, 275, 275, 276, 277
  western European version, 349
  See also Virgin and Child; Virgin Mary
Thera (Cyclades), 87, 91–92, 194

Theravada Buddhism, 427, 446, 984, 15-28A
thermoluminescence, 523
Theseion, Athens, 26-28A
Theseus (king of Athens), 89–90, 120, 137, 5-17A
Thessaloniki (Greece)
  Hagios Georgios (Church of Saint George), 248, 248b, 257, 8-17A, 8-19A
  Saint Catherine, 278, 278b, 9-32A
Thierry of Chartres, 369
The Thinker, Gates of Hell (Rodin), 826, 826
Third Dynasty of Ur, 42, 43
Third of May (Goya), 764, 764, 779, 855
Third Style, 194
Third Style wall painting, Villa of Agrippa Postumus, Boscotrecase, 194, 194
Third-Class Carriage (Daumier), 779, 779
The Thirteen Emperors (Yan Liben), 462, 463
Thirty Years' War (1618–1648), 687, 696, 700, 722
Thirty-six Views of Mount Fuji series (Hokusai), 1016, 1017, 1017
tholos, Delphi (Theodoros of Phokaia), 151–152, 151
tholos tombs, 98, 99, 170, 244
tholos/tholoi, 99, 151, 183, 184, 618
Thomas, Saint, 241, 12-8B
Thomas Aquinas, Saint, 372
Thomas de Cormont: Amiens Cathedral, 371, 375, 377–379, 377, 377, 379, 396, 418, 13-38A
Thoth (Egyptian deity), 57, 61
Three Angels (Rublyev), 280, 280
Three Flags (Johns), 914, 914
Three goddesses (Hestia, Dione, and Aphrodite?), Parthenon east pediment, Athens (sculpture), 137, 137, 602–603
Three Kingdoms period (Korea), 470–471
Three Marys at the Tomb, 241
The Three Musicians (Picasso), 851, 851b, 29-19A
three revelers (Euthymides), Vulci (vase painting), 123, 123
The Three Shades, Gates of Hell (Rodin), 826, 826
Three Women (Le Grand Déjeuner) (Léger), 853b, 29-22A
Three Women in a Village Church (Leibl), 782, 782
throne and footstool of King Nsangu, Bamum, 1065, 1065
Throne of Maximianus (ivory furniture), 264, 264b, 9-14A
thrust, 184, 21-31A
Thutmose (sculptor): Nefertiti, 76–77, 77, 78
Thutmose I (pharaoh of Egypt), 70, 72
Thutmose II (pharaoh of Egypt), 69
Thutmose III (pharaoh of Egypt), 69, 70, 73, 3-11B
Ti, mastaba of, Saqqara, 66, 66, 67, 74
Ti watching a hippopotamus hunt, mastaba of Ti, Saqqara (relief sculpture), 66, 66
Tiberius (Roman emperor), 162
Tiepolo, Giambattista
  Apotheosis of the Pisani Family, Villa Pisani, Stra, 735, 735
  Kaisersaal (Imperial Hall), Residenz (Episcopal Palace), Würzburg, 731, 731b, 26-5A
Tiffany, Louis Comfort: water lily table lamp, 829, 829b, 28-36B
Tiger Hunt (Delacroix), 768, 769, 769
Tikal (Guatemala)
  Temple of the Giant Jaguar, 500, 500
  urban planning, 500
tiki, 1054
tilework, 299–300, 34-5A
Tilted Arc, New York (Serra), 944, 966–967, 967
timelines
  18th century European and American art, 728
  Aegean art, 86
  African art, 522, 1062
  Byzantine Empire, 256
  Chinese/Korean art, 450, 990
  contemporary art, 942
  early 19th century European and American art, 756

early medieval European art, 308
Egyptian art, 56
Etruscan art, 166
Gothic art, 366
Greece, 106
Islamic art, 284
Italian Baroque art, 670
Italian Cinquecento Renaissance/ Mannerism art, 600
Italian late medieval art, 402
Italian Quattrocento Renaissance art, 560
Japanese art, 476, 1006
late 19th century art European and American art, 800
late 20th century European and American art, 900
Late Antique art, 234
Mesopotamian art, 32
Modernism, 836
Native American art, 492, 1024
Northern European Baroque art, 696
Northern European High Renaissance/ Mannerist art, 646
Northern European late medieval/early Renaissance art, 536
Oceanic art, 1044
Persian art, 32
prehistoric art, 16
Roman art, 180
Romanesque art, 334
South Asian art, 424, 976
Timgad, Algeria, 207, 207
Timur (Tamerlane), 302, 975
Timurid dynasty, 302, 305
Tinguely, Jean: Homage to New York, 935–936, 936
Tinia (Etruscan deity), 167, 168
Tintoretto (Jacopo Robusti), 665, 666
  Last Supper, 636–637, 636
Tiryns (Greece): citadel, 96–97, 96, 97
Titans, 107
Titian (Tiziano Vecelli)
  Assumption of the Virgin, 627, 627
  and Carracci, 681
  and El Greco, 665
  Feast of the Gods, 625, 625, 626, 628
  Isabella d'Este, 630, 630, 631, 22-40A
  Madonna of the Pesaro Family, 628, 628
  and Matisse, 29-3A
  Meeting of Bacchus and Ariadne, 628, 629
  Palma il Giovane on, 631
  Pastoral Symphony, 626, 627, 780
  Pietà, 631–632, 631
  and Poussin, 718
  and Rousseau, 28-26A
  and Rubens, 697
  and Tintoretto, 636
  Venus of Urbino, 628, 629, 631
Titus (Roman emperor), 203, 204, 205, 236, 286
Tivoli (Italy)
  Hadrian's Villa, 212–213, 212
  Temple of Vesta(?), 183, 183
Tiwanaku (Bolivia): Gateway of the Sun, 512–513, 512
Tiwanaku art, 512–513
Tiye (queen of Egypt), 77
Tiye, Ghurab (sculpture), 77, 77
Tjibaou Cultural Centre, Noumea (Piano), 961, 961
Tlaloc (Aztec deity), 1026, 1027
Tlaltecuhtli (Aztec deity), 1027, 1028
Tlaltecuhtli, Great Temple of Tenochtitlán (relief sculpture), 1028, 1028
Tlingit art, 1036, 1037, 1038
Todaiji, Nara, 482–483, 482, 486, 17-17A
togas, 176
togu na, 1078
Tohaku: Pine Forest, 1010, 1011
tokonoma, 1011
Tokugawa Ieyasu (shogun), 1009, 1012, 34-5A
Tokugawa shogunate. See Edo period Japanese art
Tokyo (Japan): Olympic stadiums (Tange), 1020, 1020
Toltecs, 506, 1024, 1025
Tom Jones (Fielding), 740

Tomb 100 wall paintings, Hierakonpolis, 56–57, *57b*, 3-1A
Tomb of Edward II, Gloucester Cathedral, *391b*, 570, 13-42A
tomb of Emperor Nintoku, Sakai, 478, *478*
tomb of Giuliano de' Medici, San Lorenzo, Florence (Michelangelo Buonarroti), 613–614, *613*, 22-52A
Tomb of Hunting and Fishing, Monterozzi necropolis, Tarquinia, 172, *173*
tomb of Julius II (Michelangelo Buonarroti), 360, 611–613, *612*, 614
tomb of Leonardo Bruni (Rossellino), 570–571, *570*
tomb of Lorenzo, San Lorenzo, Florence (Michelangelo Buonarroti), 613, 614
tomb of Mausolos (Mausoleum): Halikarnassos, 49, *146b*, 5-64A, 5-64B
tomb of Nebamun, Thebes, 74–75, *75*
Tomb of the Augurs (Tarquinia), *164*, 165, 171
Tomb of the Diver, Paestum, 144, *144*, 172
Tomb of the Leopards, Monterozzi necropolis, Tarquinia, 172, *172*
tomb of the marquise of Dai, Mawangdui, *448*, 449
Tomb of the Reliefs, Banditaccia necropolis, Cerveteri, 171, *171*
Tomb of the Shields and Chairs, Banditaccia necropolis, Cerveteri, *170*, 171, *171b*, 6-7A
Tomb of the Triclinium, Monterozzi necropolis, Tarquinia, *172b*, 6-9A
tomb of Ti, Saqqara, 66, *66*, 67
tomb of Tutankhamen, Thebes, 78, *78*, *79*, 100
Tomb of Yongtai, Qianxian, 462, 464, *464*
tombs. *See* funerary customs
Tommaso Portinari and Maria Baroncelli (Memling), 549, *549b*, 20-14A
tonality, 7
tondo/tondi, 219, 583, 585, 7-48A, 10-15A
Tongan art, 1053–1054
Torah, 235
toranas, 430, 15-8A
Torhalle, Lorsch, 232, *323b*, 11-19A
Tori Busshi: Shaka triad, Horyuji temple (sculpture), 474, 475, 480, *480*, 481
Tornabuoni, Giovanna, 580
Tornabuoni, Giovanni, 579
Tornabuoni, Lucrezia, 630
torques, 156
totem poles, 136–137
Toulouse (France). *See* Saint-Sernin
Toulouse-Lautrec, Henri de, 808, 29-11A
At the Moulin Rouge, 811, *811*
Jane Avril, *811b*, 28-15A
tourism
Grand Tour, 743–744, 745, 750, 26-11A, 26-23A, 26-28A
and landscape painting, 770
Tournachon, Gaspar-Félix. *See* Nadar
Tournus (France): Saint-Philibert, 337, *337b*, 339, 12-4B
Tours (France): Saint Martin's, 335, 338
Tower of Babel (Babylon ziggurat), 34, 48, 49, 289
Toyotomi Hideyoshi (shogun), 1009, 34-5A
tracery, 373, 375, 414, 664, 13-23A
Trade (Gifts for Trading Land with White People) (Smith), *940*, 941
Traini, Francesco: *Triumph of Death*, 419–420, *419*
Trajan (Roman emperor), 178, 179, 207–209, 216, 234–235, 7-44A, 7-44B
Trajan Decius (Roman emperor), 221–222, 236
Trajan's Arch, Benevento, 208, *208b*, 7-44A, 7-44B
Trajan's Column. *See* Column of Trajan
tramezzo, 14-6A
transepts
in Early Christian architecture, 243
in early medieval architecture, 323, 324, 325
in French/Spanish Romanesque architecture, 12-4A, 12-7B
in Gothic architecture, 390
in Italian 13th century architecture, 14-5A

in Italian Quattrocento Renaissance architecture, 564
Transfiguration of Christ, 240, 267–268, 412
Transfiguration of Jesus, Church of the Virgin, Mount Sinai, 267–268, *267*, 279
transubstantiation, 24-18A
transverse arches
in French/Spanish Romanesque architecture, 339, 340, 12-4A, 12-4B, 12-7B
in Gothic architecture, 368
in Holy Roman Empire Romanesque architecture, 350
in Norman Romanesque architecture, 358, 359
transverse barrel vaults, 12-10A
transverse ribs, 373
Trastavere (Italy)
Santa Cecilia, *407b*, 409, 14-7A
Santa Maria, 14-7A
Travelers among Mountains and Streams (Fan Kuan), 465, *465*, 468, 16-23A
The Treachery (or Perfidy) of Images (Magritte), 878, *878*, 29-56A
treasuries, 119
Treasury of Atreus, Mycenae, *98*, 99, *99*, 170, 184
Treasury Relief Art Project (U.S.A.), 887
Treatise on Painting (Leonardo da Vinci), 609
Treaty of Westphalia (1648), 670, 696–697
Trebonianus Gallus (Roman emperor), 222
tree of Jesse, 376
trefoil arches, 402, 14-18B
trefoils, 425
Les Très Riches Heures du Duc de Berry (Limbourg brothers (Pol, Herman, Jean)), 550–551, *550*, *551*
Trials of Jesus, 233, 241, 250
tribunes, 337, 338, 340, 12-7A
See also galleries
Tribute Money, Santa Maria del Carmine, Florence (Masaccio) (fresco), 574, *574*
triclinium, 190, 6-9A
trident, 107, 435
triforium, 364, 370, 373, 374, 390, 13-38A, 20-4A
triglyphs, 116, 152, 640
trilithons, 28
Trinity, 240
and Byzantine Christianity, 258, 264, 280cap
in Gothic art, 385, 386
in Italian Baroque architecture, 24-14A
in Italian Quattrocento Renaissance art, 574–576
Trinity Church, Boston (Richardson), 831
Trinity Church, New York (Upjohn), 788, *788b*, 27-43A
tripods, 5-17A
Triptolemos, 101
triptychs, 275–276, 392, 415
triratnas, 15-8A
Triumph of Death (Traini or Buffalmacco), 419–420, *419*
Triumph of Shapur I over Valerian, Bishapur (relief sculpture), 52, *52b*, 2-28A
Triumph of the Barberini, Palazzo Barberini, Rome (Pietro da Cortona), 685–686, *685*
Triumph of the Name of Jesus, Il Gesù (Gaulli), 686, *686*
Triumph of Titus, relief panel, Arch of Titus, *206*, 207, 220
Triumph of Venice (Veronese), 637, *637*
triumphal arches, 175, 205–207, 226–227, 575, 594
Trobriand Islands art, 1049–1050, 1051
Trojan War, 86, 118, 124, 162, 5-20A
trompe l'oeil, 595, 24-14A
Tropical Garden II (Nevelson), 912, *912*
The True Artist Helps the World by Revealing Mystic Truths (Nauman), 937, *937*
True Principles of Pointed or Christian Architecture (Pugin), 788, 27-43A
true view painting, 1002
trumeaus, 344, 20-2A
Tsuchiya, Kimio, 1020

Symptom, 956–957, *956*
Tsutaya Juzaboro, 34-12A
The Tub (Degas), 808, *808*, 809
tubicen, 157
tughras, 10-23A
tukutuku, 1043
Tula (Mexico), 1024, 1025
colossal atlantids (sculpture), 506, *506*
Tullia, 169
tumulus/tumuli, 27, 170, 309, 478
tunnel vaults. *See* barrel vaults
Tupou IV (king of Tonga), 1054
Tuquztimur, Sayf al-Din, 301
Turin (Italy)
Cappella della Santissima Sindone (Chapel of the Holy Shroud) (Guarini), 678, *678b*, 24-14A
Palazzo Carignano (Guarini), 676, *676b*, 24-9A
Turner, Joseph Mallord William
and Grand Tour, 744
The Slave Ship (Slavers Throwing Overboard the Dead and Dying, Typhoon Coming On), 772–773, *773*
turris. *See* westwork
Tuscan columns, 168, 587, 618, 640, 22-30A
Tutankhamen (pharaoh of Egypt), 78, 79, 80, 100
Tutankhamen, tomb of, Thebes, 78, *78*, *79*, 100
Tuttomondo, Sant'Antonio, Pisa (Haring), 969, *969*
Tuzuk-i Jahangiri (Memoirs of Jahangir), *979b*, 32-5A
Twelve Views from a Thatched Hut (Xia Gui), *468b*, 16-23A
twentieth century art. *See* 20th century art
Twickenham (England): Strawberry Hill (Walpole and others), 749, *749b*, 26-27A
Twilight in the Wilderness (Church), 774, 775
twisted perspective. *See* composite view
Twittering Machine (Klee), 880, *880*, 936
two Asante noblemen wearing kente cloth robes, Kumasi (photograph), *1071b*, 37-13A
two bison cave reliefs, Le Tuc D'Audoubert, 19, *19*
Two Children Are Threatened by a Nightingale (Ernst), 876–877, *876*
The Two Fridas (Kahlo), 893, *893*
two goddesses(?) and a child, Mycenae (sculpture), 100–101, *101*
two men sitting at a table of food (linguist's staff) (Bonsu), 1072, *1072*
two saints, Hagios Georgios (Church of Saint George), Thessaloniki (mosaic), 8-19A
Two Women at the Bath (Kiyonaga), 808, *808*
tympanum/tympana, 332, 344, 345–346, 538, 590, 13-3A, 13-23A, 13-38A, 14-12A
typology, 238

U

Uccello, Paolo: *Battle of San Romano*, 580–581, *580*
Udayagiri (India): cave sculptures, 434–435
Ugolino and His Children (Carpeaux), 824–825, *824*, 826
Uji (Japan): Phoenix Hall, Byodoin, 483–484, *484*, 17-13A
ukiyo-e, 1015, 1016, 1017, 1018, 28-16B, 34-12A
Uma (Parvati) (Hindu deity), 435, 436
Umayyad dynasty, 285, 287, 289, 290, 305, 10-5A, 10-5B
Umayyad palace, Mshatta, 287, *287b*, 10-5A, 10-5B
Umugote Orishaeze (Nigeria): mbari house, 1078, *1078*
Unas (pharaoh of Egypt), 61
underglazes, 986, 992
unfinished statues (Michelangelo Buonarroti), 11, 617–618, 632
Uni (Etruscan deity), 167, 168
unicorn legend, 389
Unified Silla Kingdom (Korea), 471–472, 473
Unique Forms of Continuity in Space (Boccioni), 854–855, *855*

Unité d'Habitation, Marseilles (Le Corbusier), 887
University of Virginia, Charlottesville (Jefferson), 751, *751*
Unkei, 487
Agyo, Todaiji (sculpture), *487b*, 17-17A
Untash-Napirisha (king of Elam), 45
Untitled (Donovan), 957, *957*
Untitled (Holzer), 970–971, *970*
Untitled (Judd), 911, *911*
Untitled (Kngwarreye), *956b*, 31-22B
Untitled (Man Smoking/Malcolm X), Kitchen Table series (Weems), *946b*, 31-6B
Untitled (Mitchell), *905b*, 30-8C
Untitled (Smith), 958, *958*
Untitled (Your Gaze Hits the Side of My Face) (Kruger), 942–943, *943*
Untitled Film Stills series (Sherman), 922–923, *923*
Upanishads, 427
Upjohn, Richard: Trinity Church, New York, 788, *788b*, 27-43A
Ur (Tell Muqayyar) (Iraq)
banquet scene cylinder seal, tomb of Pu-abi, 39, *39*
bull-headed harp, tomb 789 ("King's Grave"), 38–39, *38*, 88
bull-headed harp with inlaid sound box, tomb of Pu-abi, 38, *38*, 88
Royal Cemetery, 32, 58, 60
The Standard of Ur, 30, 31, 37–38, *37*, 39, 2-6A
votive disk of Enheduanna, 41, *41*
ziggurat, 42, *42*
uraeus, 63, 64, 79, 81
Urban II (Pope), 346
Urban VI (Pope), 404
Urban VIII (Pope), 669, 670, 673, 685, 686
urban planning
China, 461, 989
early 19th century European and American, 804
early Islamic, 287
European interwar Modernist, 887
Gothic era, 382–383
Greek Early/High Classical period, 154, 207
Japan, 480
Mesoamerica, 496, 500, 1026
Roman Empire, 207, 14-18B
urbanization, 800, 804, 1015
Urbino (Italy), 590, 592–593
urna, 427, 15-11A
Urnanshe statuette, Mari, 36, *36b*, 43, 45, 2-6A
Urnes (Norway): stave church, 311, *311*
Ursus (bishop of Ravenna), 8-17A
Uruk (Iraq)
female head (Inanna?) (sculpture), 34–35, *34*
Warka Vase (presentation of offerings to Inanna), 35, *35*
White Temple and ziggurat, 33, *33*, 34
U.S. art. *See* American art
U.S. Capitol, Washington, D.C. (Latrobe), 750–751
ushabtis, 61
ushnisha, 427, 458, 15-11A, 16-13A
Usonian houses, 896
Uta (abbess of Niedermünster), 330
Uta Codex, 330, *330*
Utamaro, 1017
Ohisa of the Takashima Tea Shop, *1017b*, 34-12A
Utrecht (Netherlands): Schröder House (Rietveld), 884, *884*
Utrecht Psalter, 319, *319*, 326, 361, 11-15A
Utu (Shamash) (Mesopotamian deity), 34, 44
Utzon, Joern: Sydney Opera House, 926–927, *927*, 1020

V

Vairocana Buddha, 461, 482
Vairocana Buddha, disciples, and bodhisattvas, Longmen Caves, Luoyang (sculpture), *461*
Valerian (Roman emperor), 52, 2-28A
Valley of the Golden Mummies, 61